World Sustainable Development Outlook 2018

Edited by

Allam Ahmed

PUBLIC PRIVATE PARTNERSHIPS FOR THE IMPLEMENTATION OF THE 2030 AGENDA FOR SUSTAINABLE DEVELOPMENT

World Association for Sustainable Development (WASD)

16th International Annual Conference
and
5th Diaspora International Conference

 Joint Inspection Unit of the United Nations System

Independent system-wide oversight for efficiency, effectiveness and coordination

co-organised and hosted by the
United Nations Joint Inspection Unit (JIU)
Palais de Nations, Geneva, Switzerland
10–13 April 2018

WORLD SUSTAINABLE DEVELOPMENT OUTLOOK 2018 can be ordered from WASD:

World Association for Sustainable Development (WASD)
Room US2.33
University Square Stratford (USS)
1 Salawy Road
London E15 1NF
United Kingdom

Website: www.wasd.org.uk
E-mail: admin@wasd.org.uk

ISBN: 978-1-907106-46-0

Printed and bound by CPI Group (UK) Ltd, Croydon, CR0 4YY

TABLE OF CONTENTS

Table of Contents

ACKNOWLEDGEMENTS

The 2018 WASD Conference was made possible because of the invaluable input of many people and their institutions. On behalf of WASD, we wish to extend our deepest thanks to the following individuals and institutions for their generosity and unwavering support. Also, for their continuous and endless assistance and support to the conference. We are particularly grateful for the Joint Inspection Unit (JIU) of the United Nations for their generosity and hosting the conference and most sincerely Dr. Petru Dumitriu, co-chair of the conference and Inspector JIU and his team. We are also very grateful for our distinguished International Advisory Board (IAB) which includes distinguished international academic and professional experts in issues relating to Public Private Partnerships (PPPs), public policy and management. We are also very grateful for all our international partners who helped us in organising the various regional international networks events in London, Morocco, Sudan and Bahrain.

WASD Team

- Allam Ahmed: Conference Chair and President WASD
- Siraj Sait: Director for Research, University of East London
- Janet Snow: International Coordinator and Editor
- Salma Hassan: Marketing and Communication
- Ahmed Abdeldaim: Project Coordinator
- Sara Altigani: Social Media
- N. Joseph Navinraj: Publishing
- Mhdi Safe Aldeen Ibrahim: Webmaster
- Sheema Hassan: Network Coordinator
- Siham Ismail: Network Coordinator
- Joseph Adamson: Video Production
- Moniem Ibrahim: Video Production
- Vicky Trainer: Graphic Designer

JIU Team

- Dr. Petru Dumitriu: Conference Chair and author of the JIU report on the partnership between the United Nations and the private sector
- Hervé Baudat: Research Assistant
- Lucie Pelfort: Intern
- Pierre Alan Seya: Intern

International Advisory Board (IAB)

- Prof. John Adams, British University in Egypt, Egypt
- Dr. Hend Al Muftah, Doha Institute for Graduate Studies, Qatar
- Prof. Amer Al-Roubaie, Ahlia University, Kingdom of Bahrain
- Prof. Beverlee Anderson, California State University San Marcos, USA
- Dr. Jason J Blackstock, University College London, UK
- Prof. Michael Busler, Stockton University, USA
- Dr Adil Dafa'Alla, Airbus Group UK Ltd., UK
- Prof. Pranav N. Desai, Jawaharlal Nehru University, India
- Prof. Abdelkader Djeflat, University of Lille, France
- Prof. Rick Edgeman, Utah State University, USA
- Prof. Douglas A. Hensler, University of Wisconsin-Green Bay, USA
- Prof. Hunud Abia Kadouf, International Islamic University Malaysia, Malaysia
- Prof. Lynette Louw, Rhodes University in Grahamstown, South Africa
- Prof. Ronald W McQuaid, University of Stirling, UK
- Hon. Dr. Gale T. C. Rigobert, Government of Saint Lucia, St Lucia
- Prof. Siraj Sait, University of East London, London – United Kingdom
- Prof. Danilo de Oliveira Sampaio, Federal University of Juiz de For a, Brazil

International Partners and Network

- United Nations Joint Inspection Unit of the United Nations system (JIU)
- United Nations International Children Fund (UNICEF), UK
- United Nations Global Compact Network UK
- UNESCO Cousteau Eco-technie Chair
- Central Regional Investment Marrakesh, Morocco
- United Nations Major Group for Children and Youth (UN MGCY)
- AngloAmerican, UK
- Bait Altijjar, Bahrain Chamber of Commerce and Industry (BCCI), Kingdom of Bahrain

Acknowledgements

- Ahlia University, Kingdom of Bahrain
- Centre for Islamic Finance Law and Communities (CIFLAC), University of East London, UK
- Future University, Sudan
- Environment and Natural Resources and Desertification Research Institute (ENDRI), National Centre for Research (NCR), Sudan
- Impact Hub Khartoum, Sudan
- Salih Hamed Training and Capacity Building Center, Sudan
- Science Policy Research Unit (SPRU), University of Sussex, UK
- Middle Eastern Knowledge Economy Institute (MEKEI), UK
- Emerald Group Publishing, UK
- Greenleaf Publishing, UK
- Palgrave Macmillan, UK
- Sudan Knowledge, UK

CONFERENCE RESEARCH TRACKS

- Accounting, banking and finance
- Agenda 2030
- Agricultural research and technology
- Animal research and veterinary medicine

- Beyond incubators: entrepreneurship and innovation
- Book review
- Business and agribusiness management

- Change management
- Changing demography of the world
- Climate change and environmental sustainability
- Culture and development

- Diasporic tourism, investment and brain circulation

- Economics and monetary policies
- Ecotourism and sustainable tourism development
- Employment, leadership and HRM
- Engineering applications and management
- Environment and development
- Environment, energy and water

- Food nutrition and public health
- Food security and indigenous development
- Future directions of communities and voluntary organisations in the Diaspora

- Global crisis: death or resurgence of neoliberalism?
- Global crisis: potentialities, tendencies in modes of accumulation, consumption and global configuration

- Heritage and historical contexts

- ICTs applications, knowledge management, human capital and development
- Impact of financial crises and risks of innovation sustainability on SMEs
- International business and trade
- International development

- Marketing
- Mathematical sciences and quantitative methods
- Medical and health sciences
- Millennium Development Goals (MDGs)
- MIS and E-Commerce

- New regionalisms and the changing context of global politics

- Oil, gas and coal technologies

- Performance management
- Performative, visual and creative arts
- Political and economic governance structures: towards reform
- Political science
- Public Private Partnerships (PPPs)
- Public policy and higher education

- Real estate for economic development
- Renewable energy technologies
- Rethinking human progress: towards a balance of diversity and efficiency
- Risk management
- Role of multilateral institutions in sustainable development

- Science, technology and innovation
- Security
- Services research
- Sustainable cities and communities
- Sustainable development goals (SDGs)
- Sustainable infrastructure systems and environmentally-conscious design

- The Emergence of BRICSAM as power brokers in the GPE
- Traditional, alternative and complementary medicine
- Traditions, commerce and cultural transmissions
- Transportation studies

- Wildlife research

- Youth advocacy and sustainable development
- Youth and gender issues

CONTRIBUTORS

Abu-Lebdeh, Ghassan
Agullo, Blanca Juan
Ahmad, Naveed
Ahmed, Allam
Ahmed, Elsadig Musa
Al Dallal, Shawqi
Alaafia, Mahmood Habib
Alam, Mohammed Nurul
Alhaj, Rasha
Alrawi, Khalid
Alrawi, Waleed
Al-Roubaie, Amer
Anderson, Beverlee B.
Arraj, Hala Abou

Bedoya Bahamon, Vilma Dahiana
Bekele, Dawit

Dafa'alla, Adil A.
de Oliveira Sampaio, Danilo
Djeflat, Abdelkader
Dumitriu, Petru

Eldoma, Ahmed M.A.
El-Kafafi, Siham

Gadzama, Njidda M.
Ganguli, Subhadra
Gebreslase, Mikiale

Hoque, M. Samsul
Hossain, Moazzem
Hussein, Elmouiz S.

Joseph-Aluko, Olivia

Kabura, Bukar H.
Kachora, Rengi
Kaldapa, Jummai T.
Khalfalla, Limiaa Abdelghafar
Khalifa, Nahlaa A.

Lalinde, Irene Vivas

Matti, Cristian
McQuaid, Ronald W.

Nayak, Bhabani Shankar
Noor, Nurulayn Binte

Ogamba, Ikedinachi
Olugbemi, Lade
Osman, Sufyan.A.M.

Panny, Julia
Purohit, Alan

Ratiu, Catalin
Rehn, Rebecca

Saad, Sarra A.M.
Sathe, Shraddha S.
Seedahmed, Adil M.A.

Tarfa, Martha

Zhu, Yuming

PREFACE

Allam Ahmed

World Sustainable Development Outlook series is developed to provide an overview of sustainable development and why it is important and to provoke forward thinking on the development of a more coherent approach in solving global problems related to sustainability. In doing so, a holistic approach is used to critically examine the inter-relationship between the natural, the governmental, the economic and the social dimensions of our world and how science and technology can contribute to solutions.

Outlook 2018 is a truly global source book reflected in the varied national and cultural origins of the contributors as well as the topics and case studies covered. This volume includes selection of the best full papers presented during WASD 16th International Annual Conference and 5th Diaspora International Conference, both co-organised and hosted by the United Nations Joint Inspection Unit in the UN Palais de Nations, Geneve, Switzerland, 10–13 April 2018.

The four-day conferences entitled aimed at exploring ways and means to improve the contribution of the private sector to the implementation of the 2030 Agenda and stimulate its interest to engage in partnership with the UN system organisations as well as to improve efficiency in the use of resources.

The conferences brought together the experiences and lessons learned from across the world focusing on various initiatives and case studies in the vital role of Public Private Partnerships in the implementation of Agenda 2030. The structure of the conference's myriad knowledge and learning events were designed to foster maximum peer-learning and experience sharing. The format allowed for panelists to present their views on specific topical issues followed by a question and answer session. This provided opportunities for delegates to effectively engage in dialogue and share their individual experiences and perspectives on the given issue or topic.

The thematic focus of the two conferences is **"Public Private Partnerships for the Implementation of the 2030 Agenda for Sustainable Development"**. Both JIU and WASD are inspired by the conviction that the 2030 Agenda and its 17 goals provides momentum for a renewed UN engagement with the private sector.

Paragraph 67 of United Nations General Assembly resolution 70/1 recognises the role of the private sector in development and calls upon its contribution:

> *"Private business activity, investment and innovation are major drivers of productivity, inclusive economic growth and job creation. We acknowledge the diversity of the private sector, ranging from micro-enterprises to cooperatives to multinationals. We call upon all businesses to apply their creativity and innovation to solving sustainable development challenges. We will foster a dynamic and well-functioning business sector, while protecting labour rights and environmental and health standards in accordance with relevant international standards and agreements and other ongoing initiatives in this regard [...]".*

The need for partnerships is recognised in Sustainable Development **Goal 17**: *Strengthen the means of implementation and revitalise the Global Partnership for Sustainable Development.* This implies more qualitative and quantitative engagement of the private sector in the implementation of the 2030 Agenda, an enhanced impact of the United Nations values and objectives, in particular related to sustainability, on the business models of private companies, advances in the engagement of businesses from corporate social responsibility to direct contributions to the realisation of the Sustainable Development Goals, or expansion of for-profit actors' activities in areas which were usually addressed by public entities.

From that perspective, the initial idea of the conference was proposed by Dr. Petru Dumitriu, conference co-chair and author of the JIU report on the partnership between the United Nations and the private sector (JIU/REP/2017/8). JIU undertakes in 2017 a review of **"United Nations – private sector partnership in the context of the 2030 Agenda for Sustainable Development"** aiming to explore ways and means to improve the contribution of the private sector to the implementation of the Agenda, and stimulate its interest to engage in partnership with the United Nations system organisations as well as to improve efficiency in the use of resources.

The expected results of the conferences include:

- a better understanding of the evolving nature of existing and emerging partnerships and provide the United Nations system and its Member States with valuable information regarding good practices innovative approaches, lessons learned in engaging private sector;
- an assessment of the fitness for purpose of existing models of multi-stakeholders partnerships arrangements involving the private sector, as means to leverage resources and concerted efforts towards the implementation of the Sustainable Development Goals;

- a critical examination of current policies, administrative set ups, frameworks and structures and of their potential to stimulate and valorise the partnerships with the private sector;
- the identification of good practices and opportunities to enhance coherence, synergies and coordination in building United Nations/ public partnerships with the private sector and to build bridges of common interest, values and mutual understanding;
- an exploration of new ways to enhance the inter-operability between the United Nations organisations and the enterprises and to improve conceptual, operational and administrative elements of the partnership framework, based on knowledge common platform;
- the stimulation of new forms of interaction dialogue and partnership between the UN system, the private companies and the academia in service of the Sustainable Development Goals.

Similar to previous conferences organised by WASD, the response to our call-for-papers has been so high with more than 250 abstracts and papers submitted covering a wide range of focus and scope of the theme of the conference. We have selected 30 papers after the review process (not refereed) with an interesting profile for this volume covering a wide geographical spectrum from across the world.

The main parts of the book are:

- GOAL 17 (5 chapters) Partnerships for the Goals
- GOAL 16 (1 chapter) Peace, Justice and Strong Institutions
- GOALS 6/7/13/14/15 (4 chapters) Clean Water and Sanitation/Affordable and Clean Energy/Climate Action/Life Below Water/Life on Land
- GOAL 11 (2 chapters) Sustainable Cities and Communities
- GOAL 9 (4 chapters) Industry, Innovation and Infrastructure
- GOAL 8 (4 chapters) Decent Work and Economic Growth
- GOALS 5/10 (2 chapters) Gender Equality/Reduced Inequality
- GOAL 4 (2 chapters) Quality Education
- GOALS 3/12 (3 chapters) Good Health and Well-being/Responsible Consumption and Production
- GOALS 1/2 (3 chapters) No Poverty/Zero Hunger

We hope that the ensemble of papers presented in this volume will help to stimulate debate amongst scholars, researchers and policymakers and you find this volume interesting and thought-provoking.

We would like to congratulate the authors for their valuable contribution and we are grateful to our track chairs and many reviewers for graciously offering their invaluable comments that have enriched the quality of the papers in this volume and also for making available to us their valuable time and efforts. Our most sincere thanks go to all of the keynote speakers and panelists who shared with us their expertise and knowledge.

The 2018 WASD Conferences were made possible because of the invaluable input of many people and their institutions. On behalf of WASD, we wish to extend our deepest thanks to all individuals and institutions for their generosity and unwavering support. Also, for their continuous and endless assistance and support to the conference. We are particularly grateful for the Joint Inspection Unit (JIU) of the United Nations for their generosity and hosting the conferences and most sincerely Dr. Petru Dumitriu, co-chair of the conferences and author of the JIU report on the partnership between the UN and the private sector (JIU/REP/2017/8) and his team. We also very grateful for our distinguished International Advisory Board (IAB) which includes distinguished international academic and professional experts in issues relating to Public Private Partnerships, public policy and management. We also very grateful for all our international partners who helped us in organising the various regional international networks events in London, Morocco, Sudan and Bahrain.

Finally, we would like also to thank all the members of WASD organizing committee including Janet Snow (International Coordinator and Editor), Salma Hassan (Marketing and Communication), Sara Altigani (Social Media), N. Joseph Navinraj and Karthikeyan (Publishing), Sheema Hassan and Siham Ismail (Network Coordinators), Joseph Adamson and Moniem Ibrahim (Audio/Visual Production), Ahmed Abdeldaim (Project Coordinator), Mhdi Safe Aldeen Ibrahim (Webmaster) and Vicky Trainer (Graphic Designer) for their continuous and endless assistance and support to the conference

Allam Ahmed
London, United Kingdom
March 2018

PUBLIC PRIVATE PARTNERSHIPS FOR THE IMPLEMENTATION OF THE 2030 AGENDA FOR SUSTAINABLE DEVELOPMENT

Petru Dumitriu[1]
Allam Ahmed[*2]

[1]Inspector
Joint Inspection Unit
Palais des Nations, Room D-509
1211 Geneva 10
Switzerland
[2]Founding President
World Association for Sustainable Development (WASD)
Science Policy Research Unit (SPRU)
School of Business, Management & Economics
Room 364, Jubilee Building
University of Sussex
Brighton BN1 9SL
United Kingdom
allam@sussex.ac.uk

ABSTRACT

Until the late 1960s, the state has been the major sector responsible for promoting economic and social development. In 2015, the United Nations adopted the 2030 Agenda for Sustainable Development and its 17 sustainable development goals (SDGs), which provides momentum for

*Corresponding Author

a renewed UN engagement with the private sector. How have governments across the world, if at all, incorporated the private sector in their development strategies, and how inclusive has this process been? This paper will attempt to answer these key questions by examining the experiences and lessons learned from across the UN system, including some aspects of the cooperation of the UN system with the private sector. In doing so, the paper will provide a summary of the key recommendations from the recent UN Joint Inspection Unit report entitled *United Nations – Private sector partnership in the context of the 2030 Agenda for Sustainable Development*. Central to discussions was the need to create an enabling environment that encourages the contribution of the private sector to the implementation of the 2030 Agenda and stimulate its interest to engage in partnership with the UN system organisations as well as to improve efficiency in the use of resources. More importantly the paper will outline the challenges that can be observed and what opportunities for improving the UN system are available. Finally, the paper concludes with a discussion of strategic and policy implications of these findings and provides recommendations.

Keywords: Public-Private-Partnerships; Sustainable Development; Sustainable Development Goals; Agenda 2030; United Nations; Strategy and Policy

INTRODUCTION

Until the late 1960s, the state was the major sector responsible for promoting economic and social development in most developed and emerging countries. In 2015, the United Nations (UN) General Assembly adopted the 2030 Agenda for Sustainable Development[1] and its 17 sustainable development goals (SDGs). This agenda has provided the momentum for a renewed UN engagement with the private sector. Paragraph 67 recognises the role of the private sector in development and calls on their contribution:

> *Private business activity, investment and innovation are major drivers of productivity, inclusive economic growth and job creation ..... We call upon all businesses to apply their creativity and innovation to solving sustainable development challenges. We will foster a dynamic and well-functioning business sector, while protecting labour rights and environmental and health standards [...]".*

As part of its mandate, and the only independent external oversight body entrusted by the UN General Assembly to conduct system-wide evaluations, the Joint Inspection Unit (JIU) organised a major conference at the Palais de Nations, Geneva, Switzerland

---

[1]http://www.un.org/sustainabledevelopment/development-agenda/

(10-13 April 2018). This was held jointly with the World Association for Sustainable Development (WASD) and used to present its report from the recent Public Private Partnerships (PPPs) review entitled *United Nations - Private sector partnership in the context of the 2030 Agenda for Sustainable Development* (JIU/REP/2017/8). However, this is not the first time that JIU has examined some aspects of the cooperation of the UN system with the private sector. In the past, JIU looked into the basic elements necessary for the undertaking of successful partnerships and for protecting the UN image, reputation and values[2]. Special attention was paid to self-protecting measures to mitigate reputational risk and misuse of the UN symbols.

The four-day conference, entitled *Public private partnerships for the implementation of the 2030 Agenda for Sustainable Development*, aimed to explore ways and means of improving the contribution of the private sector to the implementation of the 2030 Agenda, and stimulate its interest of engaging in partnership with the UN system organisations, as well as improving efficiency in the use of resources. The conference brought together the experiences and lessons learned from across the world, focusing on initiatives and case studies in the vital role of PPPs in the implementation of Agenda 2030.

The JIU report that is summarised in this paper is more comprehensive in scope and more ambitious in intention than previous reports. It proposes a coherent and bold set of recommendations that encompass all the rules, regulations and practices that affect the way the UN works with the private sector. Despite the inherent differences between the norms that operate in distinct organisations, so diverse in mandates and governance configurations, all recommendations were inspired by reflections and ideas coming from experienced practitioners; they aspire to be a common denominator at the highest possible level.

PARTNERSHIPS FOR SUSTAINABLE DEVELOPMENT

Central to discussions in this paper is the need, as recognised in SDG17, for partnerships to: *Strengthen the means of implementation and revitalize the Global Partnership for Sustainable Development* (UN, 2015). This implies more qualitative and quantitative engagement of the private sector in the implementation of the 2030 Agenda, an enhanced impact of UN values and objectives, in particular related to sustainability, on the business models of private companies, advances in the engagement of businesses from corporate social responsibility to direct contributions to the realisation of the

---

[2]*United Nations corporate partnerships: The role and functioning of the Global Compact (JIU/REP/2010/9); Corporate sponsoring in the United Nations system: Principles and Guidelines (JIU/NOTE/2009/1), and Private sector involvement and cooperation with the United Nations system (JIU/REP/1999/6).*

SDGs, or expansion of for-profit actors' activities in areas that were usually addressed by public entities.

According to the UN, SDG 17 aims to create an umbrella under which various forms of collaboration can occur. Partnerships between governments and the private sector can happen on a bilateral basis, but they can also happen as part of a larger set-up in a multi-stakeholder, multi-level (*local, national, supra-national*) and multi-dimensional framework, involving different relevant actors with their respective roles in fostering sustainable development (SD) in a country.

The concept of partnerships as a vehicle for the UN facilitating actions in achieving SDGs has evolved over decades. Since the adoption of the Millennium Development Goals (MDGs) and the launching of the Global Compact, partnerships with the private sector, as a means of the implementation of UN objectives, has been increasingly recognised by Member States. The multiple commitments taken through the adoption of the 2030 Agenda for SD[3] include the Global Partnership, SDG 17, as an essential instrument to capture expertise and knowledge, and to mobilise financial as well as in-kind resources from multiple sources, including the private sector.

Partnerships between public, private and NGO sectors, have been the subject of numerous UN sessions and resolutions and the UN system agenda, as confirmed by the UN Chief Executives Board for Coordination (CEB) of the High-level Committee on Management of the UN System (HLCM) strategic plan for 2017-2020; this includes six priorities, one of which is to *Increase the capacity of the UN System to work effectively with multi- stakeholder and multi-sectorial partnerships.*

SO WHAT DO THE TERMS 'PARTNERSHIP' AND 'PRIVATE SECTOR' REALLY MEAN?

Over recent years, PPPs have been suggested as a way of providing public infrastructure and services by many international and national bodies (e.g. European Commission; OECD; World Bank; ADB/IADB; UN). The UN encourages the use of PPPs, acknowledging the importance of collaboration among a multitude of stakeholders, and the complexity and far reach of their goals; however, PPPs should not be accepted uncritically. In this paper, the concepts of 'partnership' and 'business sector' are defined according to the *Guidelines on a principle-based approach to the cooperation between the UN & the business sector*[4].

---

[3]United Nations, General Assembly, *Transforming our world: the 2030 Agenda for Sustainable Development*, 25 September 2015, A/RES/70/1.
[4]See para. 8a in "Guidelines on a principle-based approach to the Cooperation between the United Nations and the business sector" at https://business.un.org/en/documents/5292.

Partnership: "voluntary and collaborative agreement or arrangement between one or more parts of the UN system and the business sector, in which all participants agree to work together to achieve a common purpose or undertake a specific task and to coordinate their respective responsibilities, resources, and benefits. Neither party has power to bind the other party to any specific course of action without that party's consent, or to contract in the name of the other party, or to create a liability against the other in any manner whatsoever";

Business sector (private sector): "either for-profit, and commercial enterprises or businesses; or business associations and coalitions (cross-industry, multi-issue groups; cross industry, issue-specific initiatives; industry-focused initiative); including but not limited to corporate philanthropic foundations".

METHODOLOGY

The JIU review used different mixed methods, combining qualitative and quantitative approaches for data collection and analysis. The evaluation begins with the preparation of the review of preliminary objectives to be further updated with the output of brainstorming sessions with representatives of participating organisations, followed by a desk review of any documentation available.

Moreover, an additional data collection phase, including questionnaires and interviews with selected participating organisations and private sector firms, was undertaken.

- **Questionnaires** were developed to seek the formal views of public sector organisations, as well as to collect data and information on their respective involvement in partnerships with the private sector. An online survey of key actors (*based on identified organisations with an interest in partnership with the private sector and civil society*) was used to facilitate data collection, compilation and quick data analysis.
- **Interview** guidelines were also be prepared, submitted to concerned organisations and analysed before missions were undertaken. The following **evaluation criteria and questions** have been identified.

Relevance

- To what degree is the engagement in private sector partnerships relevant and responsive (fit for purpose) to the implementation of the 2030 Agenda? Are organisations 'fit-for-Partnerships'?
- Do participating organisations use the *Guidelines for the Cooperation between the Governments and the business sector* in a consistent manner? Are these guidelines still considered relevant, comprehensive and up-to-date?

Effectiveness

- What are the enabling factors for the successful and effective engagement in partnerships with the private sector? What are the main obstacles in this regard?
- Are participating organisations effective partners from the perspective of the private sector?
- Do governments provide incentives and a relevant policy-frame to favour partnerships with the private sector?
- How are media involvement and information campaigns conducted to promote partnership with private sector firms?

Efficiency

- What resources/structures are allocated by organisations to deal with the private sector, including partnerships with the private sector?
- How is the partnership's efficiency determined?
- How is the partnership with the private sector being implemented and monitored at a regional level to gain efficiency and effective proximity?

Coherence

- Are any frameworks for cooperation with the private sector shared by all organisations in the country, and are they coherent with the values upheld by the system?
- What measures have been introduced to ensure a coherent application of the *Guidelines on a Principle-based Approach* to the cooperation between the government and the business sector?
- Is the process of selection of private sector partners consistently applied across organisations? Is there a system-wide central information hub to facilitate partner selection?
- How is partnership information, including lessons learned and best practices, shared across the system?

Impact

- What is the sustainability and impact of major partnership initiatives for development?
- What are the main mechanisms for the monitoring and reporting of partnership progress?
- How are government values and principles internalised and applied by private sector partners?

- What is the impact of the private sector contribution on major global partnership initiatives? What are the main areas/modalities for cooperation with the private sector (i.e. capacity development, finance, knowledge sharing, policy dialogue, philanthropy, etc.)?

The data collection phase is followed by an in-depth analysis of data.

PUBLIC-PRIVATE-PARTNERSHIPS (PPPs)

The existing literature on the concepts and history of PPPs locate its relevance for budgeting and development planning in developed as well as developing countries. Such literature often draws out the advantages and disadvantages of these concepts with a strong focus on the financial implications to the shareholders (McQuaid, 2016, 2010). Important PPP issues in the literature include innovation, efficiency, budget enlargement, governance, transparency and a growing emphasis on services rather than infrastructure. However, there appears to be less emphasis on the effects of these concepts and gaps between theory and practice of PPPs.

Many models of PPPs have emerged, depending on the object of the partnerships. These types of alliances can be used to generate value (Austin, 2000), build infrastructure (Rocca, 2017), or reduce the effects of natural disasters (Auzzir et al., 2014). The most important models of infrastructure and service PPPs are Design-Build-Finance (DBF), Build-Operate-Transfer (BOT), Design-Build-Finance-Operate-Maintenance (DBFOM) and many others (Zhao, 2011). The Triple Helix concept of university-industry-government relationships is another form of PPP that was introduced by Etzkowitz (1993), and refined later by Etzkowitz and Leydesdorff (1995). The Triple Helix forms the basis of a triadic relationship between university-industry-government and for the Knowledge Society. The Triple Helix advocated in the early 1990s is a 'derived' form of PPP. It has been considered as a neo-institutional perspective that promotes a growing prominence of universities, research centres, and other R&D institutions to favour and develop public (government) and private (business) partnerships. As an evolutionary form, the Triple Helix aims to make effective and quick benefits of innovation, R&D and knowledge for society, by gathering in an efficient and relevant partnership between university-industry-government.

The definitions of PPPs, whether formulated by researchers or practitioners, vary with regard to the scope of what can be considered as a PPP, its content, and applicable services (Gardiner et al., 2016; Grimseu and Lewis, 2016). The term PPP is often defined broadly and ambiguously as a joint venture between a government and a private entity to undertake a traditional public activity together in capital intensive infrastructure development projects (Savas, 2000). Today, PPPs are becoming central to infrastructural development projects all over the world. *Efficiency, performance standard and value for money (VfM)* are the three strategic objectives of PPPs in infrastructural development projects (Akintoye et al., 2003; Zhang, 2006). Savas (1982) reinforces the reduction of the role of the state in the provision of public services through private companies, which results in greater public efficiency.

The World Bank defines PPPs as a *long-term contract between a private party and a government agency, for providing a public asset or service, in which the private party bears significant risk and management responsibility* (World Bank, 2014, p.17).

The literature review also helped draw lessons learned from various reports published by other international organisations such as the Organisation for Economic Co-operation and Development (OECD)[5]; World Bank Group[6]; Global Environmental Facility (GEF)[7]; European Union (EU)[8]; UN System Staff College (UNSSC)[9]; UN Institute for Training and Research (UNITAR)[10]; UN Research Institute for Social Development (UNRISD)[11],[12]; CEB and the UN-Business Action Hub website[12].

Regarding the links between PPPs and SD, many scholars have observed that there are many concepts associated with SD. Making the world a better place is an assumption of SD; for this research, however, Sachs's (2004, pp.15-16) definition of SD, which outlines five pillars necessary for SD, is more relevant. Sachs (2004) warns that without the active participation of individuals in the five pillars, SD is compromised. The factors that underpin SD are the avoidance of wasting education for conscious and ecological consumption, promoting population growth in a balanced manner, avoiding conflicts and violence, reducing poverty and miserable conditions, and environmental degradation and precarious education.

Sachs's (2004) **Five Pillars** for SD include: *Social*: fundamental for both intrinsic and instrumental reasons, since social differences exist in a threatening way in many problematic places on the planet, including in Africa; *Environmental*: life sustaining system as a provider of resources and as a 'container' for the disposal of waste (often unnecessarily produced); *Territorial*: related to the spatial distribution of

---

[5]See http://www.oecd-ilibrary.org/docserver/download/4316031e.pdf?expires=1477573353&id=id&accn ame=guest&checksum=624F2B7818054B0144BDECB3E01E98B9.
[6]See https://ppp.worldbank.org/public-private-partnership/library/public-private-partnerships-reference-guide-version-20.
[7]See https://www.thegef.org/topics/private-sector.
[8]See COM (2014) 263.
[9]Recently, UNSSC has opened the Knowledge Centre for Sustainable Development in Bonn to equip the United Nations and its partners with a vehicle to deliver on the learning agenda pertaining to Agenda 2030.
[10]https://www.unitar.org/partnerships/home
[11]See Ann Zammit (2003) Development at Risk: Rethinking UN-Business Partnerships, UNRISD.
[12]See Moira V. Faul (2016) Multi-sectoral Partnerships and Power, UNRISD.
[12]Global hand is a matching service: a non-profit brokerage facilitating public/private partnership designed to bring together people from all parts of the spectrum.

resources, populations and activities; *Economic*: economic viability is indispensable for a country; and *Politics*: democracy is a fundamental value and a necessary tool to make things happen.

ANALYSIS AND DISCUSSION

The JIU report is based on the widely shared conviction that the 2030 Agenda for SD provides unique momentum for a renewed engagement of the private sector in the service of the SDGs. Such a need is not only dictated by the authority of the 2030 Agenda: it is also an expression of the changes in the conditions for global collective action and the rise of non-governmental emerging powers, whose dynamics surpass the pace of multilateral intergovernmental processes. While acknowledging and reviewing the existing safeguards in due diligence and risk management, the JIU report places emphasis on making the UN system more effective in its cooperation with the private sector to support the 2030 Agenda and to implement sustainability in their business models.

The Imperative for Change

The JIU report intends to find ways of improving the existing arrangements of cooperation with the private sector to reflect the new context, namely the holistic, integrative and universal approach of the 2030 Agenda. The changes needed are not easy to carry out. However, **the UN system could not "transform our world" unless it transforms itself.** High-level political commitments contained in the 2030 Agenda still represent an aspiration: they do not describe the existing reality. They rather imply a process that would need to be supported by concrete and effective changes in the current normative, administrative and operational arrangements.

It is against this reality that, on the one hand, the JIU report suggests possible lines of action by the UN system to indicate its own readiness to adapt itself to the imperatives of its current responsibilities, and, on the other hand, to convey this vision and these goals to the private sector and to motivate the latter to internalise and put them into practice.

An overwhelming majority of UN organisations have adapted, or are in the process of adapting, their respective strategies and/or policies to reflect the 2030 Agenda. The review ascertains the existence of advanced and comprehensive practices of dealing with the private sector. The review does not attempt to focus on individual UN system organisations. A valuable collection of mature frameworks and formal agreements for partnerships with the private sector is available. What is needed is more system-wide coordination and efficiency.

A Focus on System-wide Action

Indeed, one could witness, once again, a new wave of creating silos, based on the same good intentions for the future, but following the same individualistic ways as in the past. While many organisations consider the 2030 Agenda as an overall framework to guide their work, most of them indicated that there was a need for a coherent and coordinated approach to the engagement with the private sector, from a UN system-wide perspective.

The 2030 Agenda also calls imperatively on all stakeholders to "enhance policy coherence for sustainable development". While contributing to the global goals, the UN should provide such policy coherence in its own courtyard, namely at the system-wide level. This explains the main emphasis placed by the JIU report on recommendations for joint action.

The JIU report looks into the supporting framework provided by the UN system to facilitate the contribution of the private sector to the implementation of the 2030 Agenda under several aspects: legal, financial, administrative, operational, and motivational. The report favours system-wide solutions that will fuel permanent and reliable forms of inter-agency interaction, resource pooling, and knowledge sharing. The recommendations are intended to be realistic and do not necessarily require additional financial resources. Instead, they call for additional willingness to fight individual resistance to change and institutional inertia.

The JIU report was also inspired by the increased need for a gradual shift in emphasis from *ad hoc*, short-term partnerships, focused primarily on resource mobilisation, towards multiple, long-term, more strategic and stable collaboration with the private sector. While aware of the pre-existence of counter-arguments, the report also took the opportunity to recommend a system-wide coordination on innovation partnerships. The implementation of this recommendation may prove that the system can indeed "deliver as one", at least on a newly emerged priority and in an environment conducive to change inspired by the 2030 Agenda.

Converging Wills

The author of the JIU report[13]; was pleased to note that the spirit of some recommendations made had also been underpinned by the Secretary-General's report *Repositioning the United Nations development system to deliver on the 2030 Agenda – Ensuring a Better Future for All*[14]. As several recommendations are addressed

---

[13]Dr Petru Dumitriu.
[14]United Nations, Report of the Secretary-General: *Repositioning the United Nations development system to deliver on the 2030 Agenda – Ensuring a better Future for All*; June 2017. A/72124 – E/2018/3.

directly to the Secretary-General, the Inspector hoped that the potential synergies and complementarity would be valued in implementation.

Although the global engagement of the private sector regarding the SDGs is still at an early stage and much remains to be done, the Inspector found that there is progress, at least at the level of perception and awareness among diverse players in the private sector itself. Some companies have already included sustainability as part of their business models. Small and medium-sized enterprises represent an immense potential owner of support for the SDGs. This category of companies is largely uncharted and non-utilised. While the Global Compact is already a good promoter of private sector energies, the local Global Compact networks wait for new guidance and inputs to facilitate the activation of latent energies.

A majority of the private sector entities, irrespective of their size and specificity, still need information and understanding of the nature and scope of the SDGs, and of the modalities to engage. Certainly, these educational efforts are a major responsibility of the United Nations system, as the orchestrator and facilitator of partnerships at regional, national and global levels.

RECOMMENDATIONS AND POLICY IMPLICATIONS

The analysis of the challenges currently faced by many UN operational staff in charge of partnerships with the private sector, is complemented by a set of 12 formal recommendations clustered in 7 lines of action. They are addressed to either the General Assembly or to the Secretary-General of the UN, to the Executive Heads of all other organisations or to a group of the latter. Some of the recommendations, especially 4 and 5, may be less understandable for the readers who are not very familiar with the internal organisational complexity of the UN Secretariat. Nevertheless, they are reproduced because they represent significant actions to be taken at the working level, in a coherent and synergetic whole. After all, while JIU's report is addressed to its own 28 UN participating organisations, it is also a presentation of its working credentials to the immense multitude of businesses that are invited to respond to the call to work in partnerships for the implementation of the United Nations agenda.

Action line I: Revision of the Guidelines

1. Based on a report by the Secretary-General of the United Nations to be submitted during the 73rd session of the General Assembly, the General Assembly of the United Nations should consider a review of the "Guidelines on a principle based approach to the cooperation between the United Nations to the private

sector"[15]. This is with a view to reflect the changes needed for the increased contribution expected from the private sector in the implementation of the 2030 Agenda for Sustainable Development and their system-wide implications. The review should take into account an updated common interpretation of the stipulations of the General Assembly Resolution 92 (I) entitled the "Official Seal and Emblem of the United Nations", shared by the network of legal advisers from all United Nations organisations that are members of the United Nations System Chief Executives Board for Coordination. Particular attention should be paid to the scope of the "authorisation by the Secretary-General", the meaning of "prohibition", and the definition of "commercial purposes". This common interpretation will be reflected in the revision of the "Guidelines". The use of individually conceived and adapted logos for specific activities, projects and campaigns, limited in scope and time, should also be considered in this context; adequate safeguards for their protection should be stipulated in the partnership agreements. All things considered, the revision process should aim at an outcome that remains pragmatic, agile in scope and implementation and, at the same time, rigorous.

Action line II: Towards a system-wide coordinated operational framework

2. **A set of rules and operational guidelines for partnerships with the private sector:** The Secretary-General of the United Nations should propose, after prior consultation with all participating organisations, a set of rules and operational guidelines, designed to match the specific needs of partnerships with private sector entities, allowing more flexibility, simplification of procedures and speed in reaction. The proposals of the Secretary-General should be submitted to the General Assembly, at the latest during its 74th session (2019-2020).

The set may include, *inter alia*:

- more flexible financial rules governing the transfer of funds in relation to businesses, in the specific context of partnerships;
- a methodology for the valuation of in-kind contributions;
- allowing space for innovative financial tools to facilitate the co-creation and co-development of projects;
- the introduction of selection criteria related to the promotion and use of sustainable development practices in the rules on procurement, where applicable, and in an adequate form;

---

[15]https://business.un.org/en/documents/5292

- the re-evaluation of the red-lines between partnership and procurement;
- the simplification of the internal operational processes and workflow;
- granting more delegation of authority to lower managerial and operational levels where appropriate, while taking additional measures aimed at building capacity and increasing accountability and transparency;
- an outline of soft system-wide monitoring, assessing, and reporting guidelines for partnership engagement with the private sector.

Such a minimum set of rules and operational guidelines should be considered, having in mind the need to simplify, as opposed to adding layers to, existing processes and workflow. The common frameworks, when feasible, should not necessarily entail joint operational procedures if they cannot reflect the specificity of individual mandates.

3. **Partnerships' brokering and advice facilitation:** The Secretary-General of the United Nations and the heads of United Nations system organisations, assisted by the United Nations Global Compact, should coordinate and streamline a unique, system-wide package of information about the opportunities for partnerships offered to the private sector by the Sustainable Development Goals, for the benefit of interested organisations. The package should contain the description of the specific needs and exigencies of the United Nations system, an indication of the potential partners, existing good practices, etc., and is to be used by all interested private companies, as one entry point, in a coherent, uniform and comprehensive way. It may be built around a central existing platform or by associating all the existing initiatives in a single platform with multiple entries. The system-wide package is not supposed to preclude or prevent individual organisations from using existing information and communications modalities that are strictly specific to their own mandates.

4. **Streamlining responsibilities within the United Nations Secretariat:** Within his current reform initiatives, the Secretary-General of the United Nations should review, streamline, clarify and strengthen the division of labour, and the specific lines of responsibility and accountability within various departments of the Secretariat, in particular the mandate of the United Nations Office for Partnerships, to provide advice on, guide and facilitate partnership events and initiatives in support of the Sustainable Development Goals.

5. **An enhanced role for the Private Sector Focal Points Network:** The heads of United Nations organisations should enhance the role and responsibilities of the Private Sector Focal Points network to share knowledge, promote good practices, and find innovative solutions to problems related to partnerships with the private sector, including entrusting them with specific tasks and agenda items on which to report.

Action line III: Towards a common vetting system

6. **A system-wide database:** All heads of the United Nations system organisations, assisted by the United Nations Global Compact, should jointly create a common database on the profile and performance of the businesses involved with, or potentially interested in, partnerships with the United Nations, based on the information inputs voluntarily submitted by the participating organisations. With inputs and feedback coming from, and accessed by, all organisations, the database should serve as a minimal resource in any vetting and due diligence processes, without prejudice to the final decision of each participating organisation. A special chapter of the database should include shadow reports from civil society organisations.

7. **Common standard procedures and safeguards for due diligence:** The Secretary-General of the United Nations, and all the Executive Heads of participating organisations, should identify and agree on a minimum set of common standard procedures and safeguards for an efficient and flexible due diligence procedure, to be applied system-wide in a transparent way by the United Nations operational staff engaged in the initiation and implementation of partnerships with the private sector. The Inspector is aware of the existing advanced due diligence systems that have been developed in organisations, which may not see added value in a common vetting system. However, many other organisations, as well as entities under the authority of the United Nations Secretariat, claimed the need for a common approach. Recommendations 6 and 7 do not propose a 'common' system in the sense of 'centralised' and 'compulsory'. It proposes only a common resource for voluntary use by interested organisations, in a more efficient and transparent way than in the current situation.

Action line IV: Winning the Global Compact's new battles

8. **Revised mandate for the Global Compact:** The General Assembly, based on a report by the Secretary-General, should initiate a revision in the current mandate of the Global Compact, which should include, *inter alia*:

- a clearer role of the Global Compact, at global and national levels, in effectively engaging business to support the implementation of the 2030 Agenda;
- an enhanced role of Member States in its governance structure;
- an updated definition of the relationship between the Global Compact Office and the Global Compact Foundation, with an emphasis on the transparency of the Foundation's fundraising activities;
- a clear definition of the relationship between the Global Compact Headquarters and the Local Global Compact Networks.

Action line V: Enhancing ownership and partnership at regional and country level

9. The Economic and Social Council should invite the Executive Secretaries of the regional economic commissions, if they have not done so already, to initiate and institutionalise a systematic and regular consultative dialogue with high-level representatives of private sector companies that contribute to, or have expressed interest in, contributing to the implementation of the 2030 Agenda for Sustainable Development.

10. The Secretary-General of the United Nations should, in concertation with the Executive Heads of UNAIDS[16], UNDP[17], UNESCO[18], UNFPA[19], UNHCR[20], UNICEF[21], UNIDO[22], UNOPS[23], WFP[24] and other Executive Heads of any interested United Nations organisations with a presence in the field, encourage a multi-stakeholder mechanism of consultations and solution-seeking at the country level, steered by the Resident Coordinator, in which businesses can be involved from the beginning in the design of partnerships in support of the 2030 Agenda for Sustainable Development. Where such mechanisms initiated by the governments exist, the United Nations country teams should encourage multi-stakeholder participation.

Action line VI: towards a system-wide innovation coordination service

11. **Coordination of innovation partnerships:** The Secretary-General, in his capacity as Chair of the United Nations Chief Executives Board for Coordination, and the Executive Heads of interested organisations, should build on existing and on-going efforts and continue to empower the United Nations Innovation Network or other existing United Nations joint innovation initiatives to identify and discuss issues that are relevant for the coordination of the existing innovation initiatives, funds, labs, accelerators and incubators, and their interface with the private sector, with a view to facilitating and stimulating innovation in the implementation of the 2030 Agenda.

---

[16]Joint United Nations Programme on HIV/AIDS (UNAIDS)
[17]United Nations Development Programme (UNDP)
[18]United Nations Educational, Scientific and Cultural Organization (UNESCO)
[19]United Nations Population Fund (UNFPA)
[20]UN High Commissioner for Refugees (UNHCR)
[21]United Nations International Children's Emergency Fund (UNICEF)
[22]Industrial Development Organization (UNIDO)
[23]Office for Project Services (UNOPS)
[24]World Food Programme (WFP)

Action line VII: A platform for SMEs

12. **Support for SMEs' engagement:** The Secretary-General should request that the United Nations System Staff College Knowledge Centre for Sustainable Development, in cooperation with the International Trade Centre, host a system-wide online platform to facilitate communication with micro-, small- and medium sized enterprises on the 2030 Agenda, interaction among enterprises, information on access to funding, promotion of good practices, and opportunities to engage in United Nations operations.

In addition to the 12 formal recommendations described above, the JIU report also included some soft actions **aimed at building a United Nations-private sector *esprit de corps* around SDGs, based on engagement, trust and accountability.** These recommendations include:

a. that the Executive Heads of the United Nations organisations, where appropriate, encourage human resources exchanges with businesses (internships, joint training programmes, sabbatical years, etc.) on a reciprocal or unilateral basis, in order to bridge the cultural and operational differences and incompatibilities, as well as create a pool of experts capable of understanding and guiding partnerships both ways;

b. that the Executive Heads of the United Nations organisations consider using a system of symbolic Sustainable Development Goals related awards, when appropriate, individually or system-wide, aimed at publicly recognising and rewarding companies that introduced the sustainability elements as contained in the 2030 Agenda for Sustainable Development in their business models, based on clear and transparent criteria, and supported by verifiable evidence.

c. that the Global Compact identify and encourage among existing external professional services, those who could provide an impartial and objective certification or ratings of companies according to their adherence to the Sustainable Development Goals and their implementation, based on a strict and transparent methodology, which would include inputs from the United Nations system organisations and civil society organisations.

CONCLUSIONS

The overarching objective of the 2030 Agenda for Sustainable Development is the transformation of the world. It is no longer enough – to echo the words of the United Nations Charter – "to save succeeding generations from the scourge of war". Wars are still part of our human landscape, but humankind is conscious that current and future generations must face other forms of self-destruction, such as the exhaustion of the planet's natural resources, climate change, the extinction of living species, increased polarisation and inequalities, etc. The private sector is called on by the United Nations to change policies, mentalities and practices, and to engage in the implementation of the 2030 Agenda. Even more importantly, the private sector is asked to make sustainability a key component of their business models. The JIU report is an attempt to bridge the operational and conceptual gaps between the business world and the United Nations mechanisms, based primarily on values and public service. The private sector is expected to understand and to act. The essential tacit assumption of the author of these lines is a very bold and risky bet: maybe profit-making and providing global public goods can sometimes be compatible, after all.

REFERENCES

Akintoye, A., Hardcastle, C., Beck, M., Chinyio, E. and Asenova, D. (2003), Achieving best value in private finance initiative project procurement, *Construction Management and Economics*, Vol. 21, No. 5, pp. 461-70.

Austin, J.E. (2000), *The collaboration challenge: How nonprofits and businesses succeed through strategic alliances*. San Francisco, Wiley.

Auzzir, Z.A., Haigh, R.P. and Amaratunga, D. (2014), Public-private partnerships (PPP) in disaster management in developing countries: A conceptual framework. *Procedia Economics and Finance*, Vol. 18, pp.807-814. https://doi.org/10.1016/S2212-5671(14)01006-5

Etzkowitz, H. (1993), Technology transfer: The second academic revolution. *Technology Access Report*, Vol. 6, Nos. 7-9.

Etzkowitz, H. and Leydesdorff, L. (1995), The Triple Helix: University-Industry-Government Relations: A Laboratory for Knowledge-Based Economic Development. *EASST Review*, Vol. 14, pp. 14-19.

Gardiner, A., Bardout, M., Grossi, F. and Dixson-Declève, S. (2016), *Public-Private Partnerships for Climate Finance*, Available at: http://norden.diva-portal.org/smash/record.jsf?pid=diva2%3A915864&dswid=5183#sthash.It5bz3Fy.dpbs (accessed 04 October 2017).

Grimseu, D. and Lewis, M.K. (2016), *Public Private Partnerships Research Roadmap*, International Council for Research and Innovation in Building and Construction.

McQuaid, R. (2010), Theory of Organisational Partnerships – partnership advantages, disadvantages and success factors, in Osborne, S.P. (Ed.): *The New Public Governance: Emerging perspectives on the theory and practice of public governance* (Routledge, London, New York), pp. 125-46.

McQuaid, R. (2016), *Public-Private Partnerships (PPPs) in China*, ADBI Working Paper for the Asian Development Bank Institute.

Rocca, M.D. (2017), *The rising advantage of public-private partnerships*. McKinsey & Company, July 2017.

Sachs, I. (2004), *Development: inclusive, sustainable, sustained*. Rio de Janeiro: Garamond.

Savas, E.S. (1982), *Privatizing the Public Sector: How to Shrink Government*, Chatham House Publishers, Chatham.

Savas, E.S. (2000), *Privatization and public-private partnerships*. London: Chatham House Publishers.

United Nations (UN) (2015), *Sustainable Development Goals*. Retrieved from https://sustainabledevelopment.un.org/?menu=1300, on 29 August 2017.

World Bank (2017), *Report on private participation in infrastructure.* Retrieved from: http://ppi.worldbank.org/~/media/GIAWB/PPI/Documents/Global-Notes/PPI2017_HalfYear_Update.pdf., on 16 October 2017.

World Bank Group (2014), *Public Private Partnerships: Reference Guide,* available at: http://api.ning.com/files/IumatxxOjz3owSB05xZDkmWIE7GTVYA3cXwt4K4s3UyONtPPRgPWYO1lLrWaTUqybQe TXIeuSYUxbPFWlysuyNI5rL6b2Ms/PPPReferenceGuidev02Web.pdf (accessed 19 October 2017)

Zhang, X.Q. (2006), Public clients' best value perspectives of public private partnerships in infrastructure development, *Journal of Construction Engineering and Management,* Vol. 132, No. 2, pp. 107-14.

Zhao, Z. (2011), Advancing public interest in public-private partnership of state highway development, Public Affairs, Minnesota Department of Transportation, Research Services Section, St Paul, Minnesota 55155-1899. http://www.pwfinance.net/document/research_reports/Research%20Misc%20Advancing.pdf (accessed on 30/10/2017)

BIOGRAPHY

Petru Dumitriu has been a member of the Joint Inspection Unit of the United Nations system since 1 January 2016. Previously, he was Ambassador and Permanent Observer of the Council of Europe to the United Nations Office and other International Organisations in Geneva (2011-2014), Representative of Romania in the Executive Board of UNESCO (2010-2011), National Coordinator of the United Nations Alliance of Civilizations (2008-2011), and Director General for Multilateral Affairs and Director General for Global Affairs in the Ministry of Foreign Affairs of Romania (2006-2010). Prior to this appointment he served in the Permanent Mission of Romania to the United Nations in Geneva (2001-2005) and New York (1994-1998). He has also been a member of the International Advisory Board of New or Restored Democracies (2006 to 2009), an elected member of the UN Committee on Contributions (2001-2009), rapporteur of the Geneva phase of the World Summit on the Information Society (2002), and Secretary-General of the Third International Conference of New and Restored Democracies (1997). He was also vice-president of the UNICEF Executive Board (1995), the UN Commission on Disarmament (1997), and the Special Political and Decolonisation Committee (1997). His flagship books are *The United Nations System in the Context of Globalization: The Reform as Will and Representation* (in Romanian) and *Diversité dans l'unité: La capacité de négociation de l'Union Européenne au sein de la Commission des droits de l'homme des Nations unies.*

Allam Ahmed (www.allamahmed.org) obtained his MSc/MBA from the Royal Agricultural University, UK, and was awarded the RAU Scholarship and Prestigious Book Prize for Best MSc/MBA Dissertation. He completed his PhD in Economics (*Technology and Knowledge Transfer for Development*) in two years at Edinburgh Napier University, UK. He is a Fellow and Chartered Marketer of the Chartered

Institute of Marketing, UK. Allam is based at the Science Policy Research Unit – SPRU (*world leader in research, consultancy and teaching in the field of Science and Technology Policy*) University of Sussex, where he established and led the postgraduate programme MSc International Management. He is a visiting Professor at the Royal Dock School of Business and Law, University of East London, UK (2016-now) and Visiting Professor at Brighton Business School, University of Brighton, UK (2012-2015). Allam has an extensive background in academia, public and private sectors, specialising in KM, technology transfer, SD, business process re-engineering, change management and organisational transformation. He is the Founding President of the World Association for Sustainable Development (WASD) and all its journals; Founding Director of Middle Eastern Knowledge Economy Institute; and Founder of Sudan Knowledge. In 2009, Allam led the Government of Abu Dhabi major and first of its kind in the Middle East Knowledge Management Framework (Musharaka). His work featured and archived by major international institutions and top universities such as World Bank; UN; EU; DFID; Government of St Lucia; WFP; Imperial College; Cambridge; Oxford; Princeton; Yale; Harvard; MIT; Stanford; Toronto; etc. Expert Advisor to the European Commission on International Scientific Cooperation (2006-2008); International Co-ordinator UNESCO Chair on Transfer of Technology (2008-now); and Advisor African Capacity Building Foundation (2011-2013). He is listed in Who's Who in the World 2009-2017.

GOAL 17

PARTNERSHIPS FOR THE GOALS

PUBLIC PRIVATE PARTNERSHIPS (PPPS) IN HISTORY, THEORY AND PRACTICE

Bhabani Shankar Nayak*

Senior Lecturer in Business Strategy
Coventry Business School
Coventry University, UK
ac6767@coventry.ac.uk

ABSTRACT

Purpose: The purpose of this paper is to reject the essentialist and neoliberal approach to PPPs by critically evaluating both normative and empirical arguments within existing literature.

Design Methodology/Appproach: The paper draws its methodological lineages to nonlinear historical narrative around the concept and construction of the idea and language of 'PPPs'. The paper follows discourse analysis (Fairclough, 2003) to locate the way in which PPPs were incorporated within the language of global public policy.

Findings: The paper finds that most of the existing literature looks at managerial, operational, functional and essentialist aspects of PPPs. Therefore, the paper argues that critical success of PPPs depends on its social value for the common good with an emancipatory outlook.

Originality/value: The study encourages future researchers to move beyond functional aspects of PPPs and locate emancipatory possibilities within the praxis of PPPs from an holistic perspective of global public policy.

Keywords: Public Private Partnership; theory; practice; history; global public policy

*Corresponding Author

INTRODUCTION

The existing literature on the concepts and history of Public Private Partnerships (PPPs) locates its relevance for budgeting and development planning in developed as well as developing countries. Such literature often draws out the advantages and disadvantages of these concepts with a strong focus on financial implications to shareholders. However, there appears to be less emphasis on the effects of these concepts and gaps between theory and practice of PPPs. This paper rejects essentialist and functional aspects of PPPs. It explores different dynamics of PPPs in theory and practice within global public policy.

The growth of Public Private Partnerships (PPPs) and their role in different development projects is not a new concept; however, there is renewed interest in the study of PPPs as a tool of economic development planning. Public debt is putting pressure on the state and governments around the world to engage with private capital or corporations for different social and economic development activities (Grimsey and Lewis, 2002; Pongsiri, 2002; Yong, 2010). It is considered as a panacea for the crisis ridden world economy, and its sustainable recovery depends on investment through PPPs. PPPs are legally binding contracts of working arrangements based on mutual commitment between public sector organisations with any organisation outside of the public sector (Bovaird, 2004: 200). In this way, PPPs are central to the political economy of global public policy and social welfare (Boardman and Vining, 2012).

The existing literature locates PPPs as cooperative and contractual partnerships between state, government and private organisations to share resources, risks and costs to perform certain responsibilities and tasks to achieve a common goal (Panda, 2016; Chinyere, 2013). Therefore, the success of PPPs is central to the success of public policy. The term "public private partnership" (PPP) is often defined broadly and ambiguously as a joint venture between a government and a private entity to undertake a traditional public activity together in capital intensive infrastructure development projects (Savas, 2000). Today, PPPs are becoming central to infrastructural development projects all over the world.

Efficiency, performance standards and value for money (VfM) are the three strategic objectives of PPPs in infrastructural development projects (Akintoye et al., 2003; Zhang, 2006). These strategic objectives and visions depend on the "public client's overall strategic plan and mission objectives, private sector's long-term development and payoff strategy, the general public's requirements of quality public facilities and services" (Yuan et al., 2009:257). However, VfM is central to the strategic objective of PPPs (Akintoye et al., 2003; Henjewele et al., 2011). These strategic objectives are said to be achieved by the contractual agreements between the private and public sectors. Such partnerships play a major role in designing, constructing, financing, operating, maintaining, renovating and operating different public delivery systems (Bovaird, 2004). The most important models of

PPPs are *Design-Build-Finance* (DBF), *Build-Operate-Transfer* (BOT), and *Design-Build-Finance-Operate-Maintenance* (DBFOM); there are many others (Zhao, 2011).

These contractual arrangements between private and public sectors were fashionable in economic development planning around 60 years ago, but the concept of PPPs has become a contested concept. They are considered to be a method of diluting political control over decision-making from the 'traditional public administration' perspective, and 'new public management' theories consider PPPs as a process of undermining competition between potential providers (*ibid*). They also create a culture of 'vendorism' (Salamon, 1995:103), which is dangerous for the state-citizenship relationship as it minimises the role of the state in the management of everyday life of the state and its citizens.

The language of PPP is 'a loose term' (Stern and Harding, 2002:127), designed to hide strategies of the privatisation of public services by weakening the state and its capacity. Savas (2000) argues that "PPPs invite more people and organisations to join the debate". However, PPP is 'just a fashionable word' (Gibelman and Demone, 1983; Bovaird, 1986; Kettner and Martin, 1989). Thus, Teisman and Klijn (2002), Stern and Harding (2002), Linder (1999), and Savas (2000), although writing from different perspectives agree on the broad conceptualisation of PPPs. Bennet and Krebs (1994) define PPPs as a form of cooperation between private and public agencies that work together with an objective of local economic development. Recent literature argues that good governance and social commitments are central to the success of PPPs (Ismail, 2013; Cheung et al., 2012).

In this way, PPPs are "just another catchy piece of terminology that governments would like to promote to keep off the attention of the more mundane contracting for public services arrangements" (Greve, 2003:60). Therefore, there is a call for the establishment of a United Nations PPP Centre to address challenges to PPPs, ensuring a long term flow of finance for investment in sustainable infrastructural development projects. The successes and failures of such international engagement for the expansion of PPP-led investment depends on understanding the history of PPPs and their conceptual linages in economic development planning.

HISTORY OF PUBLIC PRIVATE PARTNERSHIPS (PPPS) IN ECONOMIC DEVELOPMENT PLANNING

The history of PPPs can be traced back to the Roman Empire. The postal networks and highway systems were developed in the Roman Empire 2,000 years ago in Europe by following the principles of PPPs. The construction of fortified towns and villages in the south-western region of France during the 12th and 13th centuries was another example of the use of PPPs. The further expansion of public works concession programmes in canal construction, roads, public distribution, and transportation systems was developed with the help of PPPs in France during the 16th and 17th centuries. The industrialisation and urbanisation of Europe during the 19th century witnessed the growth of PPPs in the expansion of expansion of public networks in transport (railways, tramways, metropolitan), water supply and sewerage and energy. PPPs were used as a mechanism of expanding colonial business enterprises during the European colonialism in Asia, Africa and the Americas (Link, 2006). There was a reversal of the PPP trend with the growth of the welfare state in 20th century post-war Europe and in post-colonial countries in Asia and Africa, whereas PPPs were growing in the USA during and after the wars. Salamon (1987) described PPPs as the "Third Party Welfare State", where governmental agencies form partnerships and fund private organisations to deliver public services (Oakley, 2006). The origin of 'welfare' in the USA is rooted in a combination of government and private action (Kramer, 1981).

PPPs have developed worldwide with the growth of liberalisation and privatisation of infrastructural development (World Bank, 2009:34−35). Therefore, the universal character of PPPs as experienced today is a product of neoliberal political economy of development planning. The neoliberal policies were promoted to dismantle the welfare state and expand market opportunities for private capital to accumulate profit (Brenner and Theodore, 2002; Kirk, 1980). The 'Washington Consensus' of the 1990s led to the dominance of neoliberalism as the universal ideology of economic policy making and development planning (Srinivasen, 2000; Williamson, 2000). As a result of this, states became an agent of the neoliberal market, promoting the maximum involvement of the private sector in the provision of public services and infrastructure (Allen, 2007; George, 2004; Harvey, 2005; Whitfield, 2006).

The OECD (2008) brings together different states and governments for a market-led democracy. Another report (2005) outlines the practical application of neoliberal theory (OECD, 2005); in the name of efficiency PPPs were reintroduced and received universal character within the neo-liberalisation processes (IPPR, 2001; Osborne, 2000; Payne, 1999; Whitfield, 2001). PPP mechanisms are used by governments all over the world to intensify the neoliberal transformation of society and marketisation of state-led public services (Hodkinson, 2011; Monbiot, 2003).

However, the PPPs also play a major role in policy formulation, planning, design, coordination, implementation, monitoring and policy evaluation to resource mobilisation and management in contemporary development planning (Bovaird, 2004:202). Therefore, the advocates of PPPs argued that PPPs are central to address public infrastructure deficits and gaps within service delivery (European Commission, 2003; Payne, 1999). It was also argued that PPPs would help to expand innovation, increase efficiency, improve public services and promote value for money by higher productivity of labour, capital and other resources (Sparks, 1998; Hall and Pfeiffer, 2000; Osborne, 2000; Price Waterhouse Cooper, 2005; Williamson, 2000).

However, the functioning and outcomes of PPPs reveal a worrying trend in terms of their failures, inefficiency in delivery of public services, lack of democratic accountability and poor value for money (Grubnic and Hodges, 2003; Murray, 2006; Pollock et al., 2002). It is also argued that PPPs are responsible for the growth of poverty and inequality. Therefore, there is huge opposition to the introduction and expansion of PPPs (Callinicos, 2003; George, 2004; Monbiot, 2000). Profit before people by commercialising public service delivery has become the central motto of PPP programmes. The practices of PPPs reveal that their primary objective is to ensure profit maximisation for adequate returns to private investors at the cost of public services. Operational and other risks of PPPs were also transferred to the state and government to manage (Hearne, 2006; 2009). The origin, growth and historical experiences of PPPs give insights into the theoretical and philosophical lineages of PPPs as a tool of economic development policy and planning.

THEORETICAL TRENDS OF PUBLIC PRIVATE PARTNERSHIPS (PPPS)

The Smithian philosophy of new public management provides a theoretical and conceptual foundation to PPPs around the 'principal-agent theory' and 'transactions cost analysis' (Halachmi and Boorsma, 1998). The twin approach of 'principal' (state and government) and the 'agent' (private organisations/capital) is a reductionist duality to understand the way PPPs work in different environments. Similarly, the 'transaction cost analysis' of PPPs locate the PPP framework within hierarchies of the market and its networks (Williamson, 1975; Walsh, 1995; Ouchi, 1980 and Powell, 1990). It is very difficult to calculate the cost of PPP projects as costs incurred at both the design and operation stages of the projects are non-verifiable (Laffont, 2005; Estache and Wren-Lewis, 2009; Iossa and Martimort, 2012). These two theoretical strands and their economic reasoning is based on efficiency and cost effectiveness of public service delivery. These two theories did not include social, economic, cultural, religious, legal, and political conditions under which contractual obligations of PPPs are carried out within a specific sector or context.

However, the functional and essentialist theorists of PPPs locate the collaboration as a 'cost dumping' and 'benefits raiding' mechanism (Lorange and Roos, 1992; Doz and Hamel, 1998). Such approaches to PPPs create an environment of trust deficit and a culture of accountability loss where PPPs fail to achieve their desired objectives. Therefore, governance theorists argue that PPPs need to conform to the norms of democratic accountability, and decision-making must be shared within partnerships and networks based on transparency (Bovaird et al., 2002; Bovaird, 2004; Newman, 2001). The success of PPPs depends on their theoretical approach to 'holistic governance', where partnerships between "organisations will help each other in the recognition of long-term reciprocity or status in the organisational community rather than immediate return" (Goss, 2001:114).

The strategic management literature locates PPPs as a risk reduction strategy of investment with long term returns (Dussauge and Garrette, 1999). Therefore, the Department of Transport (DOT), Government of USA, argued that private sectors should participate more in taking risk and sharing responsibilities (USDOT, 2004:193). The risk of any PPP projects "should be assigned to the partners who can best handle it" (Savas, 2000). In reality, however, the strategies of private corporations always focus on the 'socialisation of risk' and 'privatisation of profit'. It is the state that takes responsibility to socialise risk; it also ensures the privatisation of profit with the help of its contractual and legal obligations. In this way, contemporary PPPs promote the idea of good governance (transparency, accountability, and rule of law) at a theoretical level; however, at the operational level, strategies and legal contracts are hidden under official secrecy laws and not available for scrutiny under a Freedom of Information Act. These challenges are inherent within the neoliberal theories of PPPs all over the world. This is because neoliberal theories promote PPPs as a risk reduction mechanism to maximise profit on a secure and long-term basis, where public service delivery becomes a secondary objective within public policy.

However, debates on the success and failure of PPPs (Hodge, 2004; Duffield, 2005; Bult-Spiering and Dewulf, 2008; Regan et al., 2011a, b) are reductionist by nature as they have failed to document the ideological foundations of PPPs as a concept. They have also failed to locate whether PPPs can be structured to achieve the goals of public policy (Yong, 2010). The praxis of PPPs has failed to achieve this goal (Liu et al., 2014).

CONCLUSIONS

The direction of global public policy within the context of PPPs is moving in a direction with two specific objectives. The first objective of PPPs is to privatise, maximise and consolidate profit; the second objective is to socialise risk by developing legal partnerships with the state. Such essentialist trends and functional aspects dominate even the normative literature on PPPs. As a result of this, the effectiveness is measured in terms of performance of PPPs and market logic. Therefore, it is important to have a fresh look at PPPs beyond the cost benefit analysis within the institutionalist framework of state and market. It is necessary to evaluate PPPs by looking at the history of their origin and growth. Its emancipatory contributions in terms of human development and social welfare remain elusive within the literature on PPPs.

Human development and welfare is critical to the success and effectiveness of PPPs. The future and sustainability of PPPs and their performance depend on achieving public policy objectives. Therefore, PPPs need to move away from the strategies of profit maximisation by socialising risk.

REFERENCES

Akintoye, A., Hardcastle, C., Beck, M., Chinyio, E. and Asenova, D. (2003), Achieving best value in private finance initiative project procurement, *Construction Management and Economics*, Vol. 21, No. 5, pp. 461–70.

Allen, K. (2007), *The Corporate Takeover of Ireland*, Dublin: Irish Academic Press Ltd.

Bennet, R.J. and Krebs, G. (1994), Local Economic Development Partnerships: An analysis of Policy Networks in EC-LEDA Local Employment Development Strategies, *Regional Studies*, Vol. 28, No. 2, pp. 119–40.

Boardman, A.E. and Vining, A.R. (2012), The political economy of public private partnerships and analysis of their social values, *Annals of Public and Cooperative Economics*, Vol. 83, No. 2, pp. 117–41.

Bovaird, A.G., Löffler, E. and Parrado-Diez, S. (Eds) (2002), *Developing Local Governance Networks in Europe* (Vol. 1). Baden-Baden: Nomos.

Bovaird, T. (1986), Public and Private Partnerships for Financing Urban Programme, in Rose, E.A. (Ed.) *New Roles for Old Cities*, Gower Press: Aldershot.

Bovaird, T. (2004), Public-private partnerships: from contested concepts to prevalent practice, *International Review of Administrative Sciences*, Vol. 70, No. 2, pp. 199–14.

Brenner, N. and Theodore, N. (2002), Cities and the geographies of actually existing neo-liberalism, *Antipode*, Vol. 34, No. 3, pp. 349–79.

Bult-Spiering, M. and Dewulf, G. (2008), *Strategic Issues in Public-Private Partnerships: An International Perspective*, John Wiley & Sons.

Callinicos, A. (2003), *An Anti-Capitalist Manifesto*, London: Polity.

Cheung, E., Chan, A.P. and Kajewski, S. (2012), Factors contributing to successful public private partnership projects: Comparing Hong Kong with Australia and the United Kingdom, *Journal of Facilities Management*, Vol. 10, No. 1, pp. 45–58.

Chinyere, I.I. (2013), Comprehensive objectives for PPP projects: case of Beijing Olympic stadium, *International Journal of Business and Management*, Vol. 8, No. 9, p. 88.

Doz, Y.L. and Hamel, G. (1998), *Alliance Advantage: the art of creating value through partnering*. Cambridge, MA: Harvard Business School Press.

Duffield, C.F. (2005), PPPs in Australia, in Ng, T.S. (Ed.): *Public Private Partnership: Opportunities and Challenges*, Centre for Infrastructure and Construction Industry Development, The University of Hong Kong, Pokfulam, pp. 5–14.

Dussauge, P. and Garrette, B. (1999), *Cooperative Strategy: Competing Successfully through Strategic Alliances*. Chichester: John Wiley.

Estache, A. and Wren-Lewis, B. (2009), Toward a Theory of Regulation for Developing Countries: Following Jean-Jacques Laffont's Lead. *Journal of Economic Literature*, Vol. 47, No. 3, pp. 730–71.

European Commission (2003), *Guidelines for Successful Public Private Partnerships*, http://ec.europa.eu/regional_policy/sources/docgener/guides/ppp_en.pdf (accessed on 11/06/2017).

Fairclough, N. (2003), *Analysing Discourse: Textual Analysis for Social Research*, Routledge, London.

George, S. (2004), *Another World is Possible If--*, London: Verso.

Gibelman, M. and Demone, H. (1983), Purchase of Service Forging Public-Private Partnerships in the Human Services, *Urban and Social Change Review*, Vol. 16, No. 1, pp. 21–60.

Goss, S. (2001), *Making Local Governance Work: Networks, Relationships and the Management of Change*. Houndmills, UK: Palgrave.

Greve, C. (2003), Public-Private Partnerships in Scandinavia, *International Public Management Review*, Vol. 4, No. 2, pp. 59–69.

Grimsey, D. and Lewis, M.K. (2002), Evaluating the risks of public private partnerships for infrastructure projects, *International Journal of Project Management*, Vol. 20, No. 2, pp. 107–118.

Grubnic, S. and Hodges, R. (2003), Information, Trust and the Private Finance Initiative in Social Housing, *Public Money and Management*, Vol. 23, No. 3, pp. 177–84.

Halachmi, A. and Boorsma, P. (Eds) (1998), *Inter and Intra Government Arrangements for Productivity: A Principal–Agent Approach*. Dordrecht: Kluwer.

Hall, P. and Pfeiffer, U. (2000), *Urban Future 21- A Global Agenda for 21st Century Cities*, The Federal Ministry of Transport; Building and Housing of the Republic of Germany.

Harvey, D. (2005), *A Brief History of Neo-liberalism*, London: Oxford.

Hearne, R. (2006), Neo-liberalism, Public Services and PPPs in Ireland, *Progress in Irish Urban Studies*, Vol. 2, pp. 1–14.

Hearne, R. (2009), *Origins, Development and Outcomes of Public Private Partnerships in Ireland: The Case of PPPs in Social Housing Regeneration*, Poverty Research Initiative, Working Paper Series 09/07, Combat Poverty Agency, Dublin.

Henjewele, C., Sun, M. and Fewings, P. (2011), Critical parameters influencing value for money variations in PFI projects in the healthcare and transport sectors, *Construction Management and Economics*, Vol. 29, No. 8, pp. 825–39.

Hodge, G.A. (2004), The risky business of public-private partnerships, *Australian Journal of Public Administration*, Vol. 63, No. 4, pp. 37–49.

Hodkinson, S. (2011), Regenerating council estates within a neoliberal straitjacket: the Private Finance Initiative in Little London, Leeds (UK). *Antipode*, Vol. 43, No. 2, pp. 358–83.

Iossa, E. and Martimort, D. (2012), Risk allocation and the costs and benefits of public-private partnerships, *RAND Journal of Economics*, Vol. 43, No. 3, pp. 442–74.

IPPR (2001), *Building Better Partnerships: The Final Report of the Commission on Public Private Partnerships*, London: IPPR.

Ismail, S. (2013), Critical success factors in public private partnership (PPP) implementation in Malaysia, *Asia-Pacific Journal of Business Administration*, Vol. 5, No. 1, pp. 6–19.

Kettner, P. and Martin, L. (1989), Making Decisions about Purchase of Service Contracting, in Demone, H. and Gibelone, M. (Eds): *Services for Sale: Purchasing Health and Human Services*, Rutgers University Press: Newark, NJ.

Kirk, G. (1980), *Urban Planning in a Capitalist Society*, London: Croom Helm.

Kramer, R.M. (1981), *Voluntary Agencies in the Welfare State*. Berkeley, CA: University of California Press.

Laffont, J.J. (2005), *Regulation and Development*. Cambridge: Cambridge University Press.

Linder, S.H. (1999), Coming to Terms with the Public-Private Partnership: A Grammar of Multiple Meanings, *The American Behavioral Scientist*, Vol. 43, No. 1, pp. 35–51.

Link, A.N. (2006), *Public/Private Partnerships; Innovation, Strategies and Policy Alternatives*, Springer, USA.

Liu, J., Love, P.E.D, Smith, J., Regan, M. and Sutrisna, M. (2014), Public-Private Partnerships: a review of theory and practice of performance measurement, *International Journal of Productivity and Performance Management*, Vol. 63, No. 4, pp. 499–12.

Lorange, P. and Roos, J. (1992), *Strategic Alliances: Formation, Implementation and Evolution*. Oxford: Blackwell.

Monbiot, G. (2000), *Captive State: The Corporate Takeover of Britain*, London: MacMillan.

Monbiot, G. (2003), *The Age of Consent: A Manifesto for a New World Order*, London: Flamingo.

Murray, S. (2006), *Value for Money? Cautionary Lessons About P3s From British Columbia*, Ontario: Canadian Centre for Policy Alternatives.

Newman, J. (2001), *Modernising Governance: New Labour, Policy and Society*. London: Sage.

Oakley, D. (2006), The American Welfare State Decoded: Uncovering the Neglected History of Public-Private Partnerships; A Case Study of Homeless and Relief Services in New York City: 1920s and 1990s, *City & Community*, Vol. 5, No. 3, pp. 243–67. September, American Sociological Association, Washington.

OECD (2005), *Growth in Services*, London: OECD.

OECD (2008), *Towards an Integrated Public Service*, Ireland; OECD.

Osborne, S.P. (Ed.) (2000), *Public-Private Partnerships*, London: Routledge.

Ouchi, W.G. (1980), Markets, Bureaucracies and Clans, *Administrative Science Quarterly*, Vol. 25, pp. 129–41.

Panda, D.K. (2016), Public private partnerships and value creation: the role of relationship dynamics, *International Journal of Organizational Analysis*, Vol. 24, No. 1, pp. 162–83.

Payne, G. (Ed.) (1999), *Making Common Ground: Public Private Partnerships in Land for Housing*, London: Intermediate Technology Publications.

Pollock, A., Shaoul, J. and Vickers, N. (2002), Private Finance and Value for Money in NHS Hospitals: a Policy in Search of a Rationale? *British Medical Journal*, Vol. 324, No. 7347, pp. 1205–09.

Pongsiri, N. (2002), Regulations and public-private partnerships, *International Journal of Public Sector Management*, Vol. 15, No. 6, pp. 487–95.

Powell, W.W. (1990), Neither Market Nor Hierarchy: Network Forms of Organization, *Research in Organizational Behaviour*, Vol. 12, pp. 295–36.

Price Waterhouse Cooper (2005), *Delivering the PPP Promise: A Review of PPP Issues and Activity*, London: Price Waterhouse Cooper.

Regan, M., Smith, J. and Love, P.E. (2011a), Impact of the capital market collapse on public-private partnership infrastructure projects, *Journal of Construction Engineering and Management*, Vol. 137, No. 6, pp. 6–16.

Regan, M., Smith, J. and Love, P.E. (2011b), Infrastructure procurement: learning from private-public experiences down under, *Environment and Planning C: Government and Policy*, Vol. 29, No. 2, pp. 363–78.

Salamon, L.M. (1987), Of Market Failure, Voluntary Failure, and Third-Party Government: Toward a Theory of Government-Nonprofit Relations in the Modern Welfare State, *Journal of Voluntary Action Research*, Vol. 16, Nos 1–2, pp. 29–49.

Salamon, L.M. (1995), *Partners in Public Service: Government-Non-profit Relations in the Modern Welfare State*, Baltimore, MD: Johns Hopkins University Press.

Savas, E.S. (2000), *Privatization and public-private partnerships*. London: Chatham House Publishers.

Sparks, F.G. (1998), *A Report Submitted to the Inter Departmental Group in Relation to Public Private Partnerships*, Dublin.

Srinivasen, T.N. (2000), The Washington Consensus a Decade Later: Ideology and the Art and Science of Policy Advice, *The World Bank Research Observer*, Vol. 15, No. 2, pp. 265–70.

Stern, S. and Harding, D. (2002), Profits and Perils of Public Private Partnerships, Euromoney, in Hodge, G.A. and Greve, C. (Eds): *The Challenges of Public Private Partnerships- Learning from International Experience*, Edward Elgar Publishing Limited: UK, pp. 95–116.

Teisman, G. and Klijn, E.H. (2002), Partnership Agreements: Governmental Rhetoric or Governance Scheme?, *Public Administration Review*, Vol. 62, No. 2, pp. 197–05.

US Department of Transportation (USDOT) (2004), *Report to congress on public private partnerships*, Washington, D.C.

Walsh, K. (1995), *Public Services and Market Mechanisms: Competition, Contracting and the New Public Management*. Houndmills, UK: Macmillan.

Whitfield, D. (2001), *Public Services or Corporate Welfare*, London: Pluto Press.

Whitfield, D. (2006), *New Labour's Attack on Public Services*, London: Russell Press.

Williamson, J. (2000), What Should the World Bank Think About The Washington Consensus? *The World Bank Research Observer*, Vol. 15, No. 2, pp. 251–64.

Williamson, O. (1975), *Markets and Hierarchies: Analysis and Antitrust Implications*. New York: Free Press.

World Bank (2009), *Toolkit for Public-Private Partnerships in Roads and Highways*, World Bank and Public-Private Infrastructure Advisory Facility (PPIAF), PPIRC, Washington.

Yong, H.K. (2010), *Public-Private Partnerships Policy and Practice*, Commonwealth Secretariat, London.

Yuan, J., Zeng, A.Y., Skibniewski, M.J. and Li, Q. (2009), Selection of performance objectives and key performance indicators in public-private partnership projects to achieve value for money, *Construction Management and Economics*, Vol. 27, No. 3, pp. 253–70.

Zhang, X.Q. (2006), Public clients' best value perspectives of public private partnerships in infrastructure development, *Journal of Construction Engineering and Management*, Vol. 132, No. 2, pp. 107–14.

Zhao, Z. (2011), *Advancing public interest in public-private partnership of state highway development*, Public Affairs, Minnesota Department of Transportation, Research Services Section, St Paul, Minnesota 55155-1899. http://www.pwfinance.net/document/research_reports/Research%20Misc%20Advancing.pdf (accessed on 30/10/2017).

BIOGRAPHY

Dr Bhabani Shankar Nayak is a political economist working as a Senior Lecturer in Business Strategy at the Coventry Business School. Before moving to Coventry University, he worked at the universities in Sussex, Glasgow, Manchester and York for last 14 years. Dr Nayak's research interests consist of four closely inter-related and mutually guiding programmes: i) political economy of sustainable development, gender and environment in South Asia, ii) market, microfinance, religion and social business, iii) faith, freedom, globalisation and governance, and iv) Hindu religion and capitalism. The regional focus of his research is on the impacts of neoliberalism on social, cultural and economic transition of indigenous and rural communities in South Asia.

CONTRACT-TYPE PUBLIC PRIVATE PARTNERSHIPS IN SERVICES

RONALD W. MCQUAID[*]

Stirling Management School
University of Stirling
Stirling FK9 4LA, Scotland, UK
ronald.mcquaid@stir.ac.uk

ABSTRACT

Purpose: Public Private Partnerships (PPPs) have been used in attempts to improve efficiency, effectiveness and innovation in infrastructure and services, and to enlarge public budgets in the short-term. There appears to be large potential scope for the greater use of PPPs in many countries, but it is crucial that the mistakes made elsewhere are avoided and that there is a transparent and robust system of regulation and support. This paper critically assesses some of the micro- and macro-economic reasons for using Public Private Partnerships (PPPs) for infrastructure and services.

Design/methodology/approach: This paper reviews some selected evidence related to policy arguments in favour of PPPs, and some potential shortcomings of PPPs in practice.

Findings: There are a number of reasons why PPPs can provide improved infrastructure and services, however, in practice these may often not be fully realised due to in-built incentives, biases and implementation shortcomings. A transparent and on-going evaluation for deciding on PPPs needs to be set up, and PPPs need to be used effectively compared to alternative funding sources. If not, there is scope for inefficiencies and misuse of PPPs. Necessary support for PPPs includes strong, robust

[*]Corresponding Author

and transparent regulatory and governance systems and the dissemination of good practice to all partners, as well as good quality advice and training.

Originality/value: The paper sets out a number of reasons for using PPPs, but also assesses potential drawbacks associated with them.

Keywords: Public Private Partnerships; PPP; budget enlargement; motivations

INTRODUCTION

In many countries, Public-Private Partnerships (PPPs) have become a relatively popular way of providing public infrastructure and services, and their use is supported by many international and national bodies (e.g. European Commission, 2012; OECD, 2012a, b; UN, 2011; World Bank, 2015; Bull, 2010). The main reasons cited for using PPPs include: introducing greater innovation, efficiency and effectiveness (mainly through introducing private sector techniques and inputs and greater competition); plus budget enlargement by bringing in private financing. Other broad reasons for the greater use of PPPs are grounded in: changing perceptions of the role of the public sector from being a provider of infrastructure and services to being an enabler and, usually, funder of them; moves to measures of public service provision success rather than output or input measures; and a shift of some public budgets towards the private sector.

Although PPPs have been used for millennia, in recent decades the UK has been an early adopter of PFI type PPPs. This is where the private sector funds upfront costs in return for a long-term payment, accounting for around 10% of public infrastructure (OECD, 2014, p.14). The use of PPPs has declined in the UK in recent years, arguably due to improved transparency, questions about value for money, inflexibility, austerity and changing accounting standards removing an accounting advantage of PPPs in terms of them counting as part of the national debt. This means that the high payments for existing PPPs will gradually decline until around 2028−9, and afterwards decline more rapidly until around 2050 (HM Treasury, 2016a, b).

Based on a variety of sources (including The Public-Private Infrastructure Advisory Facility (PPIAF) and Dealogic), Inderst (2016) estimate that total global volumes of PPPs have been around US$60–$100 billion in recent years (around 0.1% of GDP). Unlike Europe (EPEC, 2016), Asia is well below the global average: there appears to be considerable interest in PPPs, not only in infrastructure provision but also services[1].

---

[1]Less contractually based PPPs are more concerned with a partnership between stakeholders such as the ILO (2008, p.1, building on UN, 2001): *'voluntary and collaborative relationships among various actors in both public (State) and private (non-State) sectors, in which all participants agree to work together to achieve a common goal or undertake specific tasks. Partnerships may serve various purposes, including advancing a cause, to implement normative standards or codes of conduct, or to share and coordinate resources and expertise'.* However, while important (McQuaid, 2010), these are not the focus of the current paper focus.

There is no universal definition of PPPs (examples include: Hodge and Greve, 2013; OECD, 2008, pp.15–17; UN, 2011). The OECD (2014) states that:

'Public-Private Partnerships (PPPs) are long term contractual arrangements between the government and a private partner whereby the latter delivers and funds public services using a capital asset, sharing the associated risks.'

Services are explicitly included in the World Bank's (2014) definition of a PPP as a:

'long-term contract between a private party and a government agency, for providing a public asset or service, in which the private party bears significant risk and management responsibility' (World Bank, 2014, p.17),

and the European Commission's (2004) Green paper on PPPs:

'forms of cooperation between public authorities and the world of business which aim to ensure the funding, construction, renovation, management or maintenance of an infrastructure or the provision of a service'.

'Contractual PPPs' involve: private provision of infrastructure and/or services that are usually provided by the public sector for the *common good*, therefore involving some continued public sector involvement; mainly *private sector investment*, but usually funded over the long term by the public sector; the sharing of substantial *risks* (financial, technological and operation) related to the project's design, build, operation or financing; *long-term projects and contracts*; and are *output* rather than input focused (for example, Malone, 2005).

The remainder of the paper assesses the various reasons for PPPs, and how and why some of these may not be realised. These broad overlapping factors are now discussed in terms of: budget enlargement; efficiency and value for money; certainty of expenditure and delivery; flexibility; financing costs; risk sharing; procurement process and transaction costs; legacy and public assets; and the wider impacts of PPP on the local economy.

REASONS FOR PPPS

Major reasons for using PPPs, rather than usual public financing mechanisms, are often based on micro-economic arguments that they can: increase innovation, effectiveness and efficiency when providing public infrastructure and services; meet increased choice and quality of public services; and improve the equality of social services between different geographical areas (such as urban-rural) (for example, Thieriot and Dominguez, 2015; NHS Executive, 2004).

In addition to these motivations, PPPs can present more macro-economic opportunities for governments to access greater private finance and to 'spend today and pay tomorrow' (so-called 'budget enlargement'). They can also provide opportunities for private and NGO bodies to access major new income streams and markets, formerly reserved for public sector providers (McQuaid and Scherrer, 2010). For instance, the European Commission (2004) identified four main private sector roles in PPPs, the first about access to finance, and the others generally about improving delivery: providing additional capital; providing alternative skills in management and implementation; adding value to both the consumer and the general public; and identifying needs and the optimal use of resources.

Budget Enlargement

PPPs have often been presented as a means of enlarging the effective public sector budget over the short-term (e.g. UNECE, 2008, 2012), through keeping much of the capital costs of PPPs 'off' the balance sheet. The OECD (2011) found that this was more important than value for money in some countries, while IOB[2] (2013) found that most PPPs were based on budget enlargement (additional financial mobilisation) reasons rather than on improved effectiveness.

International accounting standards have changed so more expenditure is shown 'on balance sheet', particularly where there is only a limited transfer of risk (McQuaid and Scherrer, 2010; House of Lords, 2010). The effects of these standards (e.g. Financial Reporting Advisory Board (FRAB), 2007) are sometimes unclear as they may depend on their exact interpretation by national and international bodies. If their rules are fully applied then this should lead to PPPs being compared more accurately to other procurement methods. Interestingly, a potential change from the former UK PFI to the PFI2 system is that now the public sector no longer pays for the project's capital costs over the construction period, but rather over the life of the project (HM Treasury, 2016b). This may mean that costs are spread out over a longer period, which may mean that costs are spread out longer than under previous regulations requiring them to be included when paid.

Budget enlargement is especially attractive when there are major infrastructure needs. PPPs can allow official public debt to be kept lower than under 'traditional' procurement, and so improve the government's position in international financial markets, or to meet debt limits on public borrowing. In addition, overall tax burdens in the medium term might be reduced if PPPs are more cost-effective than traditional public procurement. The evidence on the effects of PPPs on public finances is mixed (Hodge and Greve, 2007). If previously sheltered sectors undergo deregulation and economic structural change, then PPPs may raise efficiency (McQuaid and Scherrer, 2010, p.30). However, the efficiency gains from PPPs need to at least compensate for the extra financial and transaction costs that they incur, otherwise, the budget

---

[2] Policy and Operations Evaluation Department (IOB), Ministry of Foreign Affairs, The Netherlands

financing leads to a 'fiscal illusion' where the financial burden of PPPs is spread out over many years and is not seen immediately in public budgets. Therefore, it is essential that PPPs are adequately monitored and the true levels of risk, capital and revenue liabilities are shown, in a way consistent with international accounting standards. Without clear and transparent public accounts for PPPs, it is difficult to determine if PPPs increase or decrease the long-term tax and debt burden.

Efficiency and value for money

Micro-economic factors focus on the potential for improving the efficiency, effectiveness and value for money of projects. It does this through the introduction of new (largely private sector) skills and practices, incentives and innovation, together with potential economies of scale and scope, and more efficient utilisation of assets and 'cradle-to-grave' or whole life asset management (European Commission, 2004; NHS Executive, 2004; HM Treasury, 2000, 2006; World Bank, 2009).

This is based to some degree on bringing concepts from New Public Management (NPM) into public sector management (McQuaid, 2010, 2016), although NPM may be in decline (Dunleavy et al., 2006). It remains to be seen if new forms of public and network governance influence future PPPs. Under PPPs, the public sector still has democratic accountability and responsibility for defining the service (or infrastructure characteristics) and choosing between the objectives, therefore seeking to ensure that the wider public interest is taken fully into account (McQuaid and Scherrer, 2010, p.29). It also decides on monitoring performance measures and standards of delivery, with performance measures including effectiveness measured in terms of outputs, service quality measures, efficiency, financial performance and process and activity measures (OECD, 2008).

A further reason for improved efficiency is the introduction of greater competition for, and the contestability of, the PPP. However, experience suggests that sometimes competition in PPPs can been limited, partly as economies of scale may limit competition to larger firms, technical and financial resources may restrict the numbers of firms able to bid, and PPPs are usually put forward by consortia (hence several potential competitors may be working together, reducing competition overall). PPPs generally have low numbers of bidders, therefore reducing the real level of competition and its potential benefits. In addition, under 'traditional' procurement there is often considerable competition (e.g. when tenders are requested to build, or design and build, infrastructure). In this way, the specific benefits of PPPs are in the way competition is introduced. However, compared to a purely public sector delivered project, rather than traditional procurement using outside (non-public sector) contractors, there is likely to be greater competition.

Hoppe et al. (2010) suggest that while PPP type contracts should have greater incentives for cost reductions than using a single contractor, quality might go up or down. Current public operations may include additional services that are not explicitly set out in the contract – and so these will no longer be provided by the PPP. It is useful if such extra services (e.g. special treatment for those with disabilities) are made explicit and so are properly funded; in practice, however, this may not be the case.

Factors that may negatively affect PPP development and implementation include differing value and ethical systems of the public and private sector actors (OECD, 2008), poor design of contracts and inappropriate risk sharing, and a lack of accountability (Pollock et al., 2007; Pollock and Price, 2013). In terms of value for money, Barlow et al. (2013) argue that results for healthcare PPPs in the European Union, across different forms of financing and PPPs, have been mixed, and accommodation only PPPs (e.g. building and maintaining hospitals) have not seen the expected cost savings. Meanwhile, Torchia et al. (2015) found that while PPPs have been used to address internationally emerging public health issues, their effectiveness, efficiency and convenience are unclear.

A UK House of Commons (2011, p.3) Committee review argued that PFIs (Private Finance Initiative types of PPP) had been a better deal for private investors than the taxpayer. Similarly, there was a UK review of PFI in 2012 with changes made to the PFI model so as to improve transparency, value for money and partnership working (now called PF2) (HM Treasury, 2012; National Audit Office, 2009; Reynaers and Grimmelikhuijsen, 2015). IOB (2013) found that evaluations tended to focus on resource sharing, and the issues of risk-sharing and revenue distribution in PPPs received little attention in half of the selected studies. Most goals were quite general (e.g. improved co-ordination) and few were output specific. Although most of the small number of PPPs reviewed had positive outputs, it was usually unclear if these were attributable to the PPP, and most evaluations were not particularly robust scientifically (e.g. scoring lowly on the Maryland Scale of Scientific Methods). Therefore, the conclusion is clear – few of PPP evaluations were based on rigorous and robust impact analysis.

Certainty of expenditure and delivery

In general, public sector expenditure flows have greater certainty under PPPs. This is partly due to fixed costs (with an added inflation element) generally being agreed over the entire life of the project, with the developer usually taking the risk of cost overruns or increased costs above some agreed level, or of lower income than expected.

However, there may be greater difficulties in changing a PPP contract after it is signed (e.g. specification or design features are difficult to change). Other types of procurement may include greater temptation and scope for the project's public sector commissioner to change specifications at a late stage or during its development: this can incur large additional costs. PPPs usually therefore introduce greater discipline to the public sector, although this could be achieved through better project planning, procurement and discipline among commissioners after signing the initial contract.

PPPs may restrict the decision makers' ability to alter or merge infrastructure as these are set out for decades in the contract. An example is if a group of social service facilities (e.g. schools) are to be amalgamated. The PPP funded ones are likely to be kept open even if circumstances have changed, while the other non-PPP facilities are preferred to be kept open. This can lead to the potential inefficient location of services in the long-term.

There are normally strong incentives for the private partner to complete PPP projects on time, as added costs or delay penalties can be incorporated into the contract. In some cases payments may not start until after completion, giving incentives especially where the developer has financing costs. The agreement of the design and build PPP may include streamlined land assembly, planning and other agreements, so reducing potential delays. Overall this can lead to shorter and more certain construction times, but other forms of procurement could also achieve them.

In terms of the certainty of maintenance, in the 1980s and 1990s in the UK, and elsewhere at other times, the maintenance of the public infrastructure (e.g. school buildings, roads, etc.) has been poor. This was because reduced maintenance was perceived as short-term 'savings' but with higher long-term costs due to the need for major, costly reconstruction later. PPPs can help reduce the risk of poor maintenance due to short-term public sector decisions as they normally include maintaining the infrastructure at a specified level over its life, even if budgets come under pressure elsewhere: the public sector commissioner has a legal obligation to pay the PPP contract, so they cannot cut maintenance.

Flexibility

Circumstances and partnerships are likely to change over time, so PPPs need to adapt over time and this may require continued trust building and adaptation to changing local or wider circumstances (Bloomfield, 2006).

The lack of flexibility after a contract starts is a major problem with PPPs. For instance, if a hospital is built then it may not be easy to add in changes to, for example, information technology (including Internet provision, new processes for delivering services, etc.), opportunities or requirements for changing infrastructure standards (e.g. the need for greater energy efficiency or the addition of alternative energy sources such as solar panels), or changing the way of organising work (which may require changes to the physical structure of the building), etc. Therefore, the project may suffer from being 'locked-in' to a particular technological and organisational approach for many years, or the PPP contract may need to be renegotiated.

External changes may also affect the PPP. In the case of the Skye Bridge PPP, changes to European Union legislation on tax (VAT) for toll bridges forced the renegotiation of the original contract. An increase in tax affected the demand for the facility and therefore the income of the project.

Financing costs

In general the capital and financing costs of PPPs are likely to be higher than public sector borrowings. So even with efficiency savings, PPPs may cost more than 'traditional' procurement. The rate of return expected on different types of PPP projects varies (e.g. schools versus toll roads) (OECD, 2014). When estimating the rate of return expected by private sector capital, financial indicators of PPP performance, particularly Internal Rate of Returns (IRR), are often used. However, these may be misleading (HM Treasury, 2013), except where related payment streams are flat, like an annuity. Cuthbertson and Cuthbertson (2012) found this assumption was rarely met, based on data on actual PFI-type PPPs, so the opportunity cost to the public sector and the potential scope for profit by the private sector were both understated. They suggested that outstanding debt may be a more reliable indicator of how much the annuity type payment assumptions are bent.

Overall, PPPs lack transparent monitoring (often due to the 'hidden' or non-transparent and non-public nature of the contracts). Monitoring often includes physical monitoring (e.g. the meeting of building codes or standards); but should also include the financial monitoring at project, public body (such as local authority) and national levels. It is important that full information on project contracts, and the financial models used by the public sector, be publicly available (and developers told of this requirement before bids are called for).

Risk sharing

A key aspect of PPPs is the transfer and sharing of endogenous (controlled by the partners) or exogenous (beyond control of the partners) risk between the public and private sectors, so the party that is best able to is the one to bear the risk. These may include construction, operation, inflation, technological and demand risks. Exogenous risks are usually assumed by the public sector or shared (with the private sector partner getting a premium related to their share of the risk) (see OECD, 2008).

However, there will be pressure on the public sector to stop the private partners or the project from going bankrupt, or failing where projects are politically or economically 'sensitive', so the real risk is likely to rest more with them. The public sector may have to take back control of the operation at short notice, or find another provider or renegotiate the contact, all possibly at high cost. An example is the UK government having to be involved when a large firm, Carillion, went into liquidation early in

2018, with contracts covering many sensitive public service areas, including hospitals, maintaining Ministry of Defence housing, and school dinners (House of Commons, 2018; House of Commons Library, 2018; National Audit Office, 2018).

A further technological risk is that as PPPs are long-term contracts, these can tie the project to a specific type of technology, therefore reducing flexibility. It can also make it more difficult in future to introduce more modern technologies, leading to potentially costly re-negotiations, unless the contracts are carefully constructed and build in necessary flexibility.

Procurement process and transaction costs

While some of the procurement costs are transferred to the PPP in terms of the private sector bidders developing their own solutions to meet the requirements of the PPPs, the complexity of projects over their life cycles may lead to poor protection of the public interest (Da Cruz and Marques, 2012). PPPs may lead to a reduction in protection of public resources through rigorous procurement procedures (Verhoest et al., 2016). Establishing dedicated PPP units in government (OECD, 2010) and the standardisation of PPP contracts (Van den Hurk and Verhoest, 2016) can help alleviate these problems. However, in a study of 19 European countries, Van den Hurk et al. (2016) found that support agencies for PPPs varied considerably, distinguishing four categories from sceptical systems of zero support to fully organised PPP systems.

The costs of developing PPP contracts are likely to be greater than under traditional procurement; this is due to their complexity and long-term nature leading to higher transaction costs. These transaction costs are mostly fixed; they therefore increase the minimum efficient sizes of PPPs and favour large organisations with their economies of scale or scope. There may be information asymmetries between the public partners (especially small local public bodies) and the private sector (particularly large experienced private firms), which can be exploited by the private partners in the contract or in negotiations on PPP projects. Over time, the public sector may also lose their expertise in the delivery of services going to PPPs and therefore suffer from further expertise and information gaps, especially in services where outputs are difficult to measure.

The procurement of PPPs can include systematic cognitive and social biases amongst the public sector actors commissioning PPPs and their partners, which may lead to non-rational decisions. Examples of behavioural biases include:

- hyperbolic discounting results in the preference for immediate payoffs to more 'rational' longer-term pay-offs, which is a fundamental aspect of budget enlargement PPP activity (Laibson, 1997);
- optimism bias may be present in many PPPs where the positives are given greater weight than potential negatives (Sharot et al., 2007);

- anchoring biases, where one characteristic of the project (e.g. the published open-ing date) is overly focused upon (Tversky and Kahneman, 1974);
- 'availability cascade', where a collective belief (such as the perceived efficiency of the private sector) is self-reinforced by repetition in public discourse (Kuran and Sunstein, 1999);
- framing effects, where different decisions are made depending on whether the ef-fects are presented as a positive rather than a cost (e.g. focusing on "the project would be opened next year and the cost per year is small" rather than "the total cost over the lifetime is high") (Tversky and Kahneman, 1981);
- and many other biases.

This is an area that would benefit from further research.

One way of widening perspectives on thinking about PPPs before they are commis-sioned is to have greater involvement of the public and future users of the services. Boyer et al. (2016) argue that, empirically, public involvement can improve the wider support for PPPs and the adaptation of project design to local conditions. However, the processes do not have much influence on the delivery of the project or imbalances of power between public and private sectors.

Legacy and public assets

The legacy, both after the PPP starts and after it ends, needs consideration. As pub-lic sector officials are usually not directly involved in providing a service, PPPs may reduce the public sector's ability to learn the lessons from providing service and so affect the development of future policy, and 'learn' from past experience, therefore repeating mistakes of the past, leading them to repeat policy mistakes due to a lack of corporate 'memory'. Local public and SME knowledge may be lost if large external firms deliver most of the PPP. Therefore, mechanisms are needed to ensure that such knowledge continues to be accessible to the relevant public sector bodies.

The state of handing over a service or building after the end of the PPP needs care-ful consideration. If a contract states that the infrastructure is handed back to the public sector at the same standard after 30 years, it is important to explicitly state if this handing over is to be at the original building standards (e.g. in terms of energy efficiency, structural standards, IT etc.) or at the standards current at the date when handed over. If the former then what is being handed over may be a totally out of date structure.

PPPs have sometimes been used to realise value of land or other assets and so raise public expenditure. Some UK local authorities have generated land value by building schools on Greenbelt land and houses on former school sites (so allowing high housing land values to be realised). Planning permission might not have been given to building houses directly on the Greenbelt, so this might mean that local planning regulations have been influenced by the PPP (McQuaid and Scherrer, 2010).

Wider impacts of PPP on the local economy

PPPs may assist in developing the capabilities of SMEs and larger firms in the local private sector, as they learn from joint ventures with larger national or international firms, as well as promote regional innovation (Kristensen et al., 2014). Potential also exists for gaining sub-contracts (e.g. services provision or facilities management). However, most PPPs are large, especially when projects are 'bundled' together in a package. Therefore, only lower level contracts or service provision may available and they may have to deal with PPP main contractors who maintain considerable market power, limiting technology transfer and restricting development.

A negative impact on the public good can be a consequence of reducing the risks for a PPP. For instance, where the public sector agrees not to build or improve potentially competing roads near a PPP toll road (Plewik, 2000), can lead to a degree of monopoly power for the PPP and hinder future economic development of the region.

CONCLUSIONS

It is important to create a clear and transparent policy and processes for the use of PPPs in various sectors, and to also identify and monitor the effects across the economy as a whole. It is essential that there is expertise to support this both nationally and at regional and local levels and in specific industrial sectors.

A clear and transparent *a priori* and on-going evaluation process for deciding on PPPs needs to be set up and compared to alternatives so as to identify the one offering best value for money over the entire lifespan of the infrastructure or service. Alternatives may be to use significantly improved 'traditional' procurement processes. Linked to this, a clear process for approving projects and recognising all their costs and benefits is needed, which includes developing criteria and instruments to measure each phase of a PPP and its overall value added to the economy and society over its lifetime.

All PPPs and their evaluation processes must be transparently and rigorously monitored – at project, regional, public agency and national level. This should be public and transparent, otherwise we cannot determine the benefits or otherwise of the PPPs: there is large scope for excessive profits or corruption.

In summary, there appears to be large potential scope for the greater use of PPPs, but it is crucial that the mistakes made elsewhere are avoided and that a transparent and robust system of support is set up.

REFERENCES

Barlow, J., Roehrich, J. and Wright, S. (2013), Managing Health Care Facilities and Services Europe sees Mixed Results from Public-Private Partnerships for Building and Services, *Health Affairs*, Vol. 32, No. 1, pp. 146–54.

Bloomfield, P. (2006), The challenging business of long-term public-private partnerships: reflections on local, *Public Administrative Review*, Vol. 66, No. 3, pp. 400211.

Boyer, E.J., Van Slyke, D.M. and Rogers, J.D. (2016), An Empirical Examination of Public Involvement in Public-Private Partnerships: Qualifying the Benefits of Public Involvement in PPPs, *Journal of Public Administration Research and Theory*, Vol. 26, No. 1, pp. 45261.

Bull, B. (2010), Public-Private Partnerships: the United Nations Experience, in Hodge, G. Greve, C. and Boardman, A. (Eds): *International Handbook on Public-Private Partnerships*, Cheltenham: Edward Elgar, pp. 479298.

Cuthbertson, J.R. and Cuthbertson, M. (2012), Why IRR is an inadequate indicator of costs and returns in relation to PFI schemes, *Critical Perspectives on Accounting*, Vol 23, No. 6, pp. 420233. Available at: http://www.sciencedirect.com/science/article/pii/S1045235412000652

Da Cruz, N.F. and Marques, R.C. (2012), Mixed companies and local governance: no man can serve two masters, *Public Administration*, Vol. 90, No. 3, pp. 737258.

Dunleavy, P., Margetts, H., Bastow, S. and Tinkler, J. (2006), *Digital era governance: IT corporations, the state and e-government*, Oxford University Press, Oxford.

EPEC (The European PPP Expertise Centre) (2016), Market Update: Review of the European PPP Market in 2015. Brussels: EPEC.

European Commission (2004), *Green Paper on public-private partnerships and Community law on public contracts and concessions* [COM2004. 327 final]. Brussels: CEC.

European Commission (2012), *New public-private partnerships for research in the manufacturing, construction and automotive sectors: European PPP research supports economic recovery; Progress Report*, Directorate-General for Research and Innovation, Unit G2 "New Forms of Production". Luxembourg: Publication Office of the European Union, July.

Financial Reporting Advisory Board (FRAB) (2007), *Accounting for PPP Arrangements including PFI Contracts*, 10 December 2007. London: TSO.

Hodge, G.A. and Greve, C. (2007), Public-Private Partnerships: an international performance review, *Public Administration Review*, Vol. 67, No. 3, pp. 545258.

HM Treasury (2000), *Public Private Partnerships: the Government's Approach*. London: GSO.

HM Treasury (2006), *PFI: strengthening long-term partnerships*. London: HM Treasury.

HM Treasury (2008), *Infrastructure Procurement: Delivering Long-Term Value*, March. London: HM Treasury.

HM Treasury (2012), *A new approach to public private partnerships*. London: HM Treasury. Available at: https://www.gov.uk/government/uploads/system/uploads/attachment_data/file/205112/pf2_infrastructure_new_approach_to_public_private_parnerships_051212.pdf

HM Treasury (2013), *Guidance Note: the use of internal rates of return in PFI projects*. London: HM Treasury. Available at: https://www.gov.uk/government/uploads/system/uploads/attachment_data/file/225363/02_pfi_internalratesguidance1_210307.pdf

HM Treasury (2016a), *National Infrastructure Delivery Plan 201622021*. London: HM Treasury. Available at: https://www.gov.uk/government/uploads/system/uploads/attachment_data/file/520086/2904569_nidp_deliveryplan.pdf

HM Treasury (2016b), *Private Finance Initiative and Private Finance 2 projects: 2015 summary data*. London: HM. Treasury.

Hodge, G. and Greve, C. (2013), Public-private partnerships in turbulent times, in Greve, C. and Hodge, G. (Eds): *Rethinking Public-Private Partnerships*. London and New York: Routledge, pp.1232.

Hoppe, E.I., Kunsterer, D.J. and Schmitz, P.W. (2010), *Public-private partnerships versus traditional procurement: Innovation incentives and information gathering*. CEPR Discussion Paper 7681. London: CEPR.

House of Commons, Committee of Public Accounts (2011), *Lessons from PFI and other projects*, Forty-fourth Report of Session 2010212, HC1201. London: Stationery Office. Available at: http://www.publications.parliament.uk/pa/cm201012/cmselect/cmpubacc/1201/120102.htm

House of Commons (2018), *Carillion former directors questioned on collapse*, The Work and Pensions and Business, Energy and Industrial Strategy Committees, https://www.parliament.uk/business/committees/committees-a-z/commons-select/work-and-pensions-committee/news-parliament-2017/carillion-directors-17–19/

House of Commons Library (2018), *The collapse of Carillion*, Briefing Paper No. 08206. London: House of Commons. Available at: http://researchbriefings.files.parliament.uk/documents/CBP-8206/CBP-8206.pdf

House of Lords (2010), *Private Finance Projects and off balance sheet debt*, HL Paper 632I. London: The Stationery Office.

Inderst, G. (2016), *Infrastructure Investment, Private Finance, and Institutional Investors: Asia from a Global Perspective*. ADBI Working Paper 555. Tokyo: Asian Development Bank Institute. Available at: http://www.adb.org/publications/infrastructure-investment-private-finance-and-institutional-investors-asia-global/

ILO (International Labour Organisation) (2008), *Private Public Partnerships*. GB.301/TC/1. Geneva: ILO.

IOB (2013), *Public-Private Partnerships in developing countries 2 A systematic literature review*, Ministry of Foreign Affairs, The Netherlands, Amsterdam.

Kristensen, I., McQuaid, R. and Scherrer, W. (2014), Regional Innovation Policy and Public-Private Partnerships, in Hilpert, U. (Ed.): *Handbook on Politics and Technology*. London: Routledge.

Kuran, T. and Sunstein, C.R. (1999), Availability cascades and risk regulation. *Stanford Law Review*, pp. 6832768.

Laibson, D. (1997), Golden eggs and hyperbolic discounting, *The Quarterly Journal of Economics*, Vol. 112, No. 2, pp. 443278.

Malone, N. (2005), The Evolution of Private Financing of Government Infrastructure in Australia—2005 and Beyond, *Australian Economic Review*, Vol. 38, No. 4, pp. 420230.

McQuaid, R. (2010), Theory of Organisational Partnerships 2 partnership advantages, disadvantages and success factors, in Osborne, S.P. (Ed.): *The New Public Governance: Emerging perspectives on the theory and practice of public governance*. London: Routledge, pp.125246.

McQuaid, R. (2016), *Public-Private Partnerships in China*, draft working paper for ADBI.

McQuaid, R.W. and Scherrer, W. (2010), Changing reasons for public private partnerships (PPPs), *Public Money and Management*, Vol. 30, No. 1, pp. 27234.

National Audit Office (2009), *Private Finance Projects, Paper for the Lords Economic Affairs Committee*. London: House of Lords.

National Audit Office (2018), *PFI and PF2*, HC 718 SESSION 201722019, 18 January 2018. London: NAO. Available at: https://www.nao.org.uk/wp-content/uploads/2018/01/PFI-and-PF2.pdf

NHS (National Health Service Executive) (2004), *Public Private Partnerships in the National Health Service: The Private Finance Initiative Good Practice*, Treasury Taskforce, London.

OECD (Organisation for Economic Development and Co-operation) (2008), *Public-Private Partnerships: In Pursuit of Risk Sharing and Value for Money*. OECD: Paris.

OECD (2011), *Regions and Innovation Policy, OECD Reviews of Regional Innovation*. OECD: Paris.

OECD (2012a), *OECD Principles for the Public Governance of Public-Private Partnerships*. OECD: Paris.

OECD (2012b), *Policy Framework for Investment*. OECD: Paris.

OECD (2014), *Pooling of Institutional Investors Capital. Selected Case Studies in Unlisted Equity Infrastructure*. OECD: Paris

Plewik, M. (2000), Public-Private Partnership: Toll Motorways Construction in Poland, in Montanheiro, L. and Linehan, M. (Eds): *Public and Private Sector Partnerships: The Enabling mix*. Sheffield, Sheffield Hallam University Press, pp. 4992506.

Pollock, A.M., Price, D. and Player, S. (2007), An examination of the UK Treasury's evidence base for cost and time overrun data in UK value-for-money policy and appraisal, *Public Money and Management*, Vol. 27, No. 8, pp. 127234.

Pollock, A.M. and Price, D. (2013), *PFI and the National Health Service in England*. Available at: http://www.allysonpollock.com/wp-content/uploads/2013/09/AP_2013_Pollock_PFILewisham.pdf

Reynaers, A.-M. and Grimmelikhuijsen, S. (2015), Transparency in Public2Private Partnerships: Not So Bad After All? *Public Administration*, Vol. 93, No. 3, pp. 609226.

Sharot, T., Riccardi, A.M., Raio, C.M. and Phelps, E.A. (2007), Neural mechanisms mediating optimism bias. *Nature*, Vol. 450, No. 7166, pp. 102205.

Thieriot, H. and Dominguez, C.C. (2015), *Public-Private Partnerships in China, On 2014 as a landmark year, with past and future challenges*, Discussion Paper, IISD, April 2015. Available at: https://www.iisd.org/sites/default/files/publications/public-private-partnerships-china.pdf

Torchia, M., Calabrò, A. and Morner, M. (2015), Public2Private Partnerships in the Health Care Sector: A systematic review of the literature, *Public Management Review*, Vol. 17, No. 2, pp. 236261.

Tversky, A. and Kahneman, D. (1974), Judgment under uncertainty: Heuristics and biases, *Science*, Vol. 185, No. 4157, pp. 11242131.

Tversky, A. and Kahneman, D. (1981), The framing of decisions and the psychology of choice, *Science*, Vol. 211, No. 4481, pp. 453258.

UN (United Nations) (2001), *Cooperation between the United Nations and all relevant partners, in particular the private sector*, UN, New York http://www.un.org/partnerships/Docs/partnershipreport_a-56-323.pdf

UN (2011), *A Guidebook on public-private partnership in Infrastructure*. Bangkok: Economic and Social Commission for Asia and the Pacific.

United Nations UN PPPKnowledgelab (No date), Available at: https://pppknowledgelab.org/countries/china

UNECE (United Nations Economic Commission for Europe) (2008), *Guidebook on Promoting Good Governance in Public-Private Partnerships*, UNECE, Geneva. Available at: http://www.unece.org/fileadmin/DAM/ceci/publications/ppp.pdf

UNECE (2012), *Report of the Team of Specialists on Public-Private Partnerships*. Geneva: The Committee. Available at: http://www.unece.org/fileadmin/DAM/ceci/Latest_Documents/ECE_CECI_PPP_2012_2.pdf

Van den Hurk, M. and Verhoest, K. (2016), The challenge of using standard contracts in public2private partnerships, *Public Management Review*, Vol. 18, No. 2, pp. 278299.

Van den Hurk, M., Brogaard, L., Lember, V., Petersen, O.H. and Witz, P. (2016), National varieties of Public2Private Partnerships (PPPs): A comparative analysis of PPP-supporting units in 19 European countries, *Journal of Comparative Policy Analysis*, Vol. 18, No. 1, pp. 1220.

Verhoest, K., Van Garsse, S., Van den Hurk, M. and Willems, T. (2016), Developments of public private partnership in Belgium, *Public-private partnerships: A global review,* pp. 45258.

World Bank (2009), *About Public-private partnership in infrastructure*. Washington: World Bank.

World Bank (2014), *World Bank private participation in infrastructure database*. Available at: http://ppi.worldbank.org/

World Bank (2015), *PPP Arrangements / Types of Public-Private Partnership Agreements*. Washington: World Bank. Available at: http://ppp.worldbank.org/public-private-partnership/agreements

BIOGRAPHY

Ronald W. McQuaid is Professor of Work and Employment at the University of Stirling. He has a Bachelor's degree from Lancaster University, an MSc(Econ) from London School of Economics, and a doctorate from Harvard University. He was formerly the Director of the Employment Research Institute. His research interests include employment and employability, the effects of ageing populations on labour markets, entrepreneurship, partnership-working and economic development. He has written over 100 academic papers on these issues. He has carried out research and policy studies for many regional, national and supra-national bodies such as the European Commission, UK, Scottish and Northern Ireland governments, UK Commission for Employment and Skills, the British Council, Asia Development Bank, Joseph Rowntree Foundation, and various other agencies and employers. Professor McQuaid is a Fellow of the Academy of Social Sciences, Fellow of the Higher Education and a Fellow of the Royal Society for the encouragement of Arts, Manufactures & Commerce.

WASD

PUBLIC-PRIVATE PARTNERSHIPS AND THEIR RELATIONSHIP WITH SUSTAINABLE DEVELOPMENT IN BRAZIL

Danilo de Oliveira Sampaio*

Faculty of Business Administration and Accounting (FACC)
DESCOR, research group
Federal University of Juiz de Fora (UFJF)
Minas Gerais, Brazil
danilo.sampaio@ufjf.edu.br

ABSTRACT

Objective: Public-private partnerships in Brazil started in 2004 through a federal law, but the number of these partnerships is still small. There is a need for the country to involve more private organisations in projects that have different types of risks. Given this scenario, the objective of this research was to verify the model of private public partnerships in Brazil and their relationship with sustainable development, to point out cases and present critiques evaluating the positive aspects and pointing out possibilities for improvements.

Design/methodology/approach: The research was of a bibliographic and documentary type, with scientific papers and Brazilian federal laws as sources of data. A case study of public-private partnerships in Brazil was also carried out to verify whether there is a direct relationship with the promotion of sustainable development.

Results: The results show that, despite being innovative, the Brazilian model of public-private partnerships needs to be improved. Just removing

*Corresponding Author

the financial burden from the state and passing it on to private organisations does not solve the final situation of a partnership. There was more use of administrative concessions than partnerships, with the financial sustainability of the partnership being highlighted more than sustainable development as the basis or relation of the signed cases.

Originality: The research carried out is original because it relates the Brazilian model of private public partnership with the promotion of sustainable development, mainly when suggesting proposals and public policies to be implemented by the Brazilian government. In this sense, it is hoped to strengthen policy and legislation to implement and revitalise mainly the global partnership for sustainable development.

Keywords: Brazil; Public-Private Partnerships (PPP); 2030 agenda for sustainable development.

INTRODUCTION

The behaviour of individuals when they are in the role of citizens as well as mere consumers, assumes a more critical view of society. In this case, it is observed that the citizen has been passing through a moment in which the quality of life is highlighted and value in the aspects that the citizen considers as fundamental. In this context, questions are raised by individuals about concerns regarding the environment, social inequalities and economic differences.

The scenario for the search for a better quality of life is observed in both developed and emerging countries, since a life in peace and with better conditions of citizenship is the responsibility of the people, companies, social organisations and, mainly, the governments. Citizens are better informed and aware regarding the acquisition of products of companies that have ethical policies regarding respect for nature and the working relationship. This awareness, combined with the agility of the traditional media and social networks, results in a migration of decision-making powers of purchase, which had previously belonged to the companies and happened to be in the hands of the consumers.

In a world where there is a distribution of income that is always favourable to a richer minority of the population, initiatives to implement programmes and strategies for a more sustainable world by companies are far from ideal, even if governments and companies invest in programmes of environmental, economic and social sustainability.

Organisations and consumer associations and entities that bring together hundreds of leaders from governments and companies are holding meetings and discussions to propose actions and studies for a better world in which to live. Developing and growing in economic, social and environmental terms is considered a challenge for governments, because uniting these three pillars is an exhaustive management exercise. This is because, in many cases, economic growth may involve social inequality.

The challenge in managing sustainable development with capitalism is necessary, but must be based on respect for the human being, especially those who have less available money and lower quality of life. There is no point in economic development without there being a global consumer market with possibilities of buying and using the products offered. Unemployment and lack of education caused by distorted economic growth only exacerbates the planet's social and environmental conditions.

An initiative in 2015 in New York City at the United Nations Headquarters (UN, 2015) shows that there is a path possible towards a fairer world. In this opportunity the 17 goals of sustainable development, involving researchers, companies and governments, were launched in the search for a better quality of life, with favourable environmental and social conditions.

This joint effort is to be welcomed when seeking sustainable development for the planet. The rapprochement between state and business can solve problems of financial management of governments and share responsibilities in society. With this in mind, in this research it was decided to highlight the 17th UN objective as a study proposal. This objective is to strengthen the means of implementation and revitalise global partnerships for sustainable development. By aligning the UN proposal with this work, the objective was to verify the model of Public-Private Partnership (PPP) in Brazil and its relationship with sustainable development, to point out cases and present critiques evaluating the positive aspects and signalling possibilities for improvements.

The support of the planet today is in line with the sustainability of the business – there is no way one does not depend on the other. Organisational leaders have realised that in order to achieve economic growth and consequently higher transaction volume, it is critical to work on the concept and practice of sustainable development (Fujihara and Lopes, 2009). Public-Private Partnerships (PPPs or 3Ps) bring together organisations, companies and government in favour of sustainable development, and therefore can together promote and make projects and programmes to generate economic, social and environmental growth feasible.

Until the late 1960s, in most developed and emerging countries, the state has been the major sector responsible for promoting economic and social development. With the economic crises that originated in different countries in the 1970s, we began to rethink the management model for development and growth. One of the ways, known as more liberal, was to reduce the size of the state and reduce spending by passing on part of this responsibility to companies, which, on the other hand, could have deals with sectors previously only managed by governments. In the more liberal view of capitalism, by reducing the size of the state, corporations have an active role in economic development and disown government obligations.

In addition to this introductory section, this paper has a literature review chapter on sustainable development and PPPs, followed by methodology, data analysis, final considerations and finally references.

LITERATURE REVIEW

Public-Private Partnerships (PPPs)

What is a Public-Private Partnership? In the bibliography we can answer this question according to two main aspects: the legal aspect, involving the specific legislation of each country, and management aspect, involving the results, either related to the state or companies and organisations. In the true meaning of the word, a partnership leads to an idea of mutual gain, in which the parties involved win without prejudicing each other; in the case of the PPP, in the end, the final beneficiary is the citizen.

PPPs were created from the Roman Empire, passing through Medieval Europe, America and then the Asian continent, always based on infrastructure works such as road construction, railways and exchange markets (Sundaram et al., 2016). The authors studied different countries and concluded that there is a need for a common definition of PPPs and international guidelines that can be accepted. Other researchers report the same from Sundaram et al. (2016), and add that the laws of each country make a common conceptual adjustment of PPP difficult (Whitfield, 2010).

A long-term partnership between business and government as an alternative to a division of responsibilities and resources is found in Public-Private Partnerships (PPPs). Financially relieving the state and giving new business opportunities to partner companies is the focal point of a PPP. Savas (1982) reinforces the reduction of the role of the state in the provision of public services through private companies, which results in greater public efficiency.

Two studies should be properly addressed in the implementation and analysis of PPPs with a focus on sustainable development: (a) legal study and (b) management study. Legal study is complex and depends on laws governed by each country. The management study is the responsibility of the state agency that will regulate the PPP. Some examples of sectors that use PPPs are those linked to infrastructure, such as the execution of works and services.

PPPs emerged as a public management option in the 1980s in the UK, more specifically under the Margaret Thatcher government. However, the partnership system was in fact only effectively used in the 1990s. Like any novelty that brings change, there was resistance, both from politicians and businessmen, to instituting and initiating PPPs, mainly motivated by cultural issues and even by simple mistrust.

What most interested neoliberal ideas was the fact that it reduced the weight of the state in terms of financing and infrastructure spending. On disbanding obligations before only the state, the British model of 1992 was a precursor in supporting the private initiative, which started to finance projects that previously only fell to the Government. The so-called Project Finance Initiative (PFI) eventually influenced many countries from different continents to establish their own models of Public-Private Partnerships. Brazil was one of these countries influenced; however, the partnerships in the country began late.

Since the British initiative, several countries from different continents have taken advantage of PPPs to defray state spending, and reduce the risks of infrastructure projects through the partnership relationship with companies. This discourse allowed the government to resume investments in the areas of construction of railroads, highways, hydroelectric, among other works, which promote the economic multiplier effect of generating employment, income and domestic consumption.

Grimsey and Lewis (2002) point out a total of nine types of risk factors, which, according to the authors, should be inserted and managed in PPP contracts and notices:

(1) technical risk (engineering and design);
(2) construction risk (materials and construction);
(3) operational risk (maintenance and operation);
(4) revenue risk (demand);
(5) financial risk (flow errors);
(6) risk of force majeure (calamities and war);
(7) regulatory/political risk (change of government);
(8) environmental risk (environment); and
(9) default risk (overall project failure).

Despite knowing the possible risks of any business involving PPPs, many cases of partnerships in Brazil were cancelled or presented delays and fines; this ended up making many projects unfeasible. The Brazilian case is best explained in the next chapter.

PUBLIC-PRIVATE PARTNERSHIPS (PPPs) IN BRAZIL

The Brazilian PPP model formally began with Law No. 11.079 of 2004[1], known as the Public-Private Partnerships Law, which directs the types of partnerships and contracting guidelines. However, the origin of PPPs occurred years earlier, mainly due to the financial crisis of the 1980s. During this crisis, the State, previously centralised in terms of financing, was forced to carry out risk assignments in the area of public infrastructure for the private sector. This fact culminated in the creation of the National Privatisation Plan (PND) during the Collor government. By Law No. 8.987/1995, this established rules of concessions and permissions of public services for private companies.

Brazil's experience in public concessions to the private sector has shown both positive and negative results; these can be discussed and defended by different interests. One fact was that in some PPPs the state showed signs of inefficiency, mainly due to the lack of regulation control, because in many cases, the companies turned to the

---

[1]Law No. 11.079/2004: this Law establishes general rules for the bidding and contracting of Public-Private Partnerships within the scope of the Powers of the Union, the States, the Federal District and the Municipalities.

state banks to finance the infrastructure of the partners. The risks of PPP projects were also cases that undermined some ventures. According to Campos Lima and Coelho (2015), who surveyed 15 PPP contracts in Brazil between 2004 and 2010, the risks were more overlapping in companies than in government. However, the latter also took risks, especially in relation to public financing of PPPs.

It is necessary to point out some differences and specificities that occur involving the public sector in Brazil and partnerships involving public money. There are basically three options that allowed private initiative to engage with public partnerships and thus reduce expenses and the weight of the Brazilian state: concessions, privatisations, and PPPs.

Concessions in Brazil mainly involve the provision of services such as the maintenance of highways and railways, without the transfer of public property to companies. However, for a fixed period, the concessionaire has the right to offer and explore the public service or good. The payment of the concessions is carried out by the users using tariffs. Privatisation in Brazil configures the sale of the public good to the private initiative through an auction, and the buyers assume all expenses and losses where they occur.

In Brazil, PPP is considered as an administrative concession contract, in the sponsored or administrative modality (Law No. 11.079/2004). In the 30 articles of this law, the meaning of the contract between the public and private sector is detailed. Some of these details are:

- the provision of the service varies from 5 to 35 years;
- the amounts cannot be less than 20 million Brazilian reais (equivalent to US$6.2 million on 31 October 2017) without a maximum ceiling; and,
- no contracts can be entered into for the sole purpose of providing labour, supplying and installing equipment, or carrying out public works.

In Brazil, both the federal government and state and municipal government can create their policies and encourage PPPs. There are two types of PPPs in Brazil: administrative and sponsored. In the administrative PPP the payment to the private sector comes only from the public sector. On the other hand, in the sponsored PPP, a certain part of the payment comes from users in addition to a part coming from the public sector.

The reduction in the size of the state was delayed and gradual, with the preparation of laws after a period of military dictatorship. Infrastructure obligations that were previously only public were gradually being reduced, and the participation of companies became part of investments for society. Starting in 1995, the state initiated a series of direct and indirect concessions, which culminated in the PPP Law.

In this paper, there is information in the data analysis about the number of PPPs in Brazil and particularities can be seen.

SUSTAINABLE DEVELOPMENT (SD) AND
THE LINK WITH PPPs

What is the definition of SD? Is there a single concept that can express SD? Checking the literature, it is observed that there are different areas of knowledge that study SD, and shows that there is not a single concept about it.

There are many concepts that lead to SD. Making the world a better place is an assumption of SD, that is, promoting a world with peace and with just employment relationships, income distribution, care for the natural environment, and respect for diversity generates a long-term structured social development.

Regardless of entering the field of discussion about the best SD definition, this research chose to establish a common point among researchers and organisations, namely, it is fundamental to attempt an harmonious interaction between social, economic developments and environmental preservation.

If there is a definition to be better dealt with in this study, one can mention that from Sachs (2004), a French-born Polish economist, who brings with him five pillars necessary to have SD:

(1) **Social:** fundamental for both intrinsic and instrumental reasons, since social differences exist in a threatening way on many problematic places on the planet, including in Brazil;
(2) **Environmental:** life sustaining system as a provider of resources and as a "container" for the disposal of waste (often unnecessarily produced);
(3) **Territorial:** related to the spatial distribution of resources, populations and activities;
(4) **Economic:** economic viability is indispensable for a country;
(5) **Politics:** democracy is a fundamental value and a necessary tool to make things happen (Sachs, 2004, pp. 15–16).

Sachs (2004) warns that without the active participation of individuals in the five pillars, SD is compromised. The avoidance of wasting educating for conscious and ecological consumption, promoting population growth in a balanced manner, avoiding conflicts and violence, reducing poverty and miserable conditions, environmental degradation and precarious education, these are the factors that underpin SD.

Sustainable Development (SD) has been measured in different ways by researchers and governments. In Brazil, the Brazilian Institute of Geography and Statistics (IBGE) periodically carries out a report on sustainable development indicators, which has 63 indicators in four areas: environmental, social, economic and institutional. The most recent report with data up to 2015 points to both positive and disturbing statistics.

In Brazil, in social terms, the statistics show more progress than setbacks. Adult literacy and life expectancy at birth have achieved substantial improvements. The literacy rate in Brazil, which was 91.5% in 2013, was 94% in 2015; the target for 2024 is to have 100% of the Brazilian population being literate. Another good result was between 2008 and 2009, the number of health care places per thousand inhabitants increased from 0.37 to 0.49. Malnutrition in children under five years of age declined from 18.4% between 1974 and 1975 to 2.8% between 2008 and 2009 (IBGE, 2017). Between 2000 and 2012, the Brazilian earned a further 4.7 years of life expectancy, which made the Brazilian life expectancy rise from 69.8 years of age to 74.5 years of age.

With regard to the environment, Brazil improved some indices. According to the Project for Monitoring Deforestation in the Legal Amazon by Satellite (PRODES, 2017), within the Brazilian Amazon, a region that involves nine states, only one was recorded as being high in deforestation. Between August 2016 and July 2017, the amount of deforested area corresponded to less than 1% of the total of the region.

Regarding pollution, in Brazil the most affected is air pollution, responsible for most deaths in Brazil. According to The Lancet (2017), a respected scientific journal, out of a total of 188 countries analysed, Brazil ranked 148th, which means that 7.49% of the country's deaths in 2015 derived from pollution.

Sustainable development is still very confused with sustainability; developing means more than economic growth. Sustainable development is a constant concern with the quality of life of the planet, the whole being bigger than some parts. All countries must meet the 17 goals in the United Nations for a better world, because the initiative of some does not ensure the success of all.

The importance of Sustainable Development and its significance has come from the creation of the Club of Rome in 1968, which aimed at the integrated debate of economic, natural; social and political aspects. The UNESCO conference on the rational use of biosphere resources took place in 1972. In that same year, the United Nations organised a conference on the human environment, creating the programme on the environment, called UNEP (United Nations Environment Programme). All these events prove the importance of SD and its necessary dissemination to society.

The moment to raise the awareness of governments and companies is over. Now is the time to charge the authorities and encourage the use of SD in practical terms, i.e., thoughts on economic growth, as well as thinking about social and environmental growth. In this sense, consumerism gives space to sustainable consumption and capitalism can finally show signs of deeper adjustment for the very continuity of this system.

In addition to a concept, SD is a philosophy that can be translated by a process of social knowledge, in which individuals, organisations, companies and government must guide public policies towards envisaging a structured and possible development of the relationship between people and the natural environment. SD is a process that aims to give a better quality of life to Man and to the planet.

The next section explains the methodological design of this research.

METHODOLOGY

This research had a documentary and bibliographical purpose, to meet the objective of the work. According to Creswell (2003), the collection of secondary data can be done through papers, books, laws and reports in order to gain better knowledge of the facts. In this paper, different sources were consulted, which are linked to the theme of PPPs and SD. In this way, documents and research in the area of management, SD, environmental law and PPPs supported the theoretical foundation.

The data collection allowed the verification of how PPPs in Brazil are managed by the state. With the data collected in this research, other studies can be initiated and continued in order to discover solutions and improvements in PPP policies in Brazil, and even for other countries.

DATA ANALYSIS

In this research secondary data were collected through different sources of information and knowledge, such as state and federal data, and international institutions such as the World Bank. Data were also collected from the Ministry of Planning, Development and Management of the federal government.

According to the World Bank database released in 2017, based on 150 low- and middle-income developing countries, it has been reported that Brazil and India account for 55% of private participation in infrastructure investments. Also according to

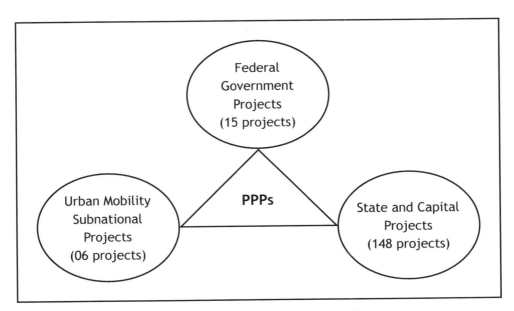

Figure 1   Types of PPP Projects in Brazil
Source: Adapted from the Ministry of Planning, Development and Management (2017)

the World Bank report, Brazil owns 87% of total investments in the Latin American and Caribbean region (World Bank, 2017).

Campos Lima and Coelho (2015) point out that between 2004 and 2010, PPPs in Brazil obtained a greater presence of international companies (60% of cases) than the domestic companies (40% of cases). For the authors, it was evident that the concession period was long, that is, it was found that 47% of PPPs in Brazil by 2010 were between 26 and 35 years, 13% between 21 and 25 years and 40 below 20 years.

PPPs in Brazil are mostly for construction and infrastructure works, especially roads, ports, football stadia, schools, water and sewage treatment plants, construction of subway stations, construction of prisons, airports and others.

In Brazil, data on PPPs performed are segmented in the Ministry of Planning, Development and Management (2017). These data refer to three types of projects, being federal projects of PPPs, state projects and subnational projects (see Figure 1).

According to the Ministry of Planning, Development and Management (2017), there have been 15 federal projects carried out in Brazil (see Figure 2).

1. Datacentre Complex
2. Military College of Manaus. Construction and maintenance of a new Military College in Manaus - AM
3. Physical Education Centre Almirante Adalberto Nunes (CEFAN)
4. National Parks of Jericoacoara, Serra das Confusões, Sete Cidades and Ubajara
5. Vila Naval de Itaguaí - Module I
6. Supply and Fleet Management (AGEFROT)
7. National Parks of Brasilia, Chapada dos Veadeiros and Emas
8. Arsenal of the Navy
9. Fuzil-Imbel
10. Irrigation Point
11. Sustainable Esplanade
12. Brazilian Geostationary Satellite
13. Digital Public TV Network (RTVDB)
14. BR 116-324
15. North-South Railroad

Figure 2   Federal PPP Projects in Brazil

Source: Adapted from the Ministry of Planning, Development and Management (2017)

On the other hand, state projects are greater in number, totalling 148 in the different sectors, such as highways, schools, hospitals, football stadia and sports complexes, hotels, among others.

There were six subnational projects for urban mobility; these were the subways of São Paulo, Salvador, Curitiba, Porto Alegre, Rio de Janeiro, and Light Rail Vehicle (VLT) in Rio de Janeiro. There are three projects in operation, and the other three projects are currently in the public query or study phase.

One of the main problems of PPP projects in Brazil is the slowness and bureaucracy of the processes, as well as an efficient control of regulation. For these reasons, the Public Ministry has audited and found management problems, which further delay the execution of works.

FINAL THOUGHTS AND RECOMMENDATIONS

The objective of this study was to verify the model of Private-Public Partnerships in Brazil and its relation with Sustainable Development, to point out cases and present critiques, evaluating the positive aspects and pointing out possibilities for improvements.

Given the context of the Brazilian model of PPPs, there are indications that the SD concept is not contemplated, since the focus on the results of the partnership projects focuses on the economic aspect above any other environmental and social aspect. The British neoliberal model that influenced Brazil and several countries in the policy of creation and implementation of PPPs, contemplates regulation and privatisation, through the principle of economy and a heavy and over-spending state. In the case of Brazil, PPPs in those projects that actually met the desired result, reached the finalisation of infrastructure works, and generated a tax exemption for the State. However, from an environmental and social point of view, the legacy left until then was minimal.

In Brazil, several PPP projects were interrupted by the Public Prosecutor's Office, due to the slow execution of the works, and the financing and irregularities found throughout the project. In addition, it is observed that there is a need for legal improvements to be avoided over the course of contracts, for companies to withdraw due to lack of, for example, financing for infrastructure works.

Despite the necessary and fundamental improvements to the PPPs, the Brazilian model is in the process of adjustment. They have already achieved, with many problems, some improvements and have implemented some important PPPs, such as federal highways, works for the Football World Cup in 2014 and for the Olympic Games in 2016, mobility systems such as subway stations in the main Brazilian metropolises, and many others.

PPPs have a less overburdened state in terms of building infrastructure works, and in most cases, they also favour greater agility to rely on the initiative of the private sector. In these cases, the citizen wins a service that will be implemented even faster. In the Brazilian model, PPPs do not have good control by the Government of the whole partnership. This can lead to a decrease in the quality of the works carried out, as well as a corrupt system that may favour some contractors, who have recently been accused by the Public Prosecutor's Office of corrupting public managers. These cases of corruption are being exemplarily treated by the Ministry of Justice with the support of the Federal Police of Brazil, and especially the opinion power of the Brazilian citizen, who is harmed by the inefficiency and control of PPPs.

As suggestions for recommendations for improvements in the planning of PPPs for the Brazilian case, this research points out that:

(1) in developing PPP policies, the Brazilian government must be rigorous in placing items in projects that include the tripod of the SD, or the triple bottom line, profit, people and planet, during and after the project ends. It should become a formal requirement to enforce the obligations of the executing companies on the economic benefits to the local population where the work will be carried out, with respect to environmental laws and social development;

(2) a monitoring of each stage of the project by a designated team should be carried out, which should check whether the company is complying with both the correct execution of the schedule and applies the tripod of the SD;

(3) in the project, make the management of risks arising from the PPP in order to safeguard public money clear;

(4) to take account of the State for a dependence on private companies in the execution of public works without the criteria of control and regulation, which may provoke inefficiency and disregard the sovereignty of the Federal Constitution, a law is required that regulates the democratic state of law in Brazil; and finally,

(5) it is recommended to train and instruct the new generation of public and private managers by training them in the concept of SD application, as well as to demand transparency and administrative and ethical efficiency of public agents involved in PPPs.

Finally, for future study possibilities, it is expected that the work will continue through field research, collecting primary and non-secondary data. In this way, it is planned to link SD to the context of PPPs by conducting interviews with managers of private companies, public managers, and the Public Prosecutor's Office. This is in order to verify with each of these agents, positive and negative aspects of the PPP model in Brazil and its link with SD in the search for more equality, social justice and environmental development.

Support and thanks:

✓ *This research was supported by the Research Support Foundation of the State of Minas Gerais, Brazil (FAPEMIG).*

✓ *The DESCOR research group supported this work.*

REFERENCES

Brazilian Institute of Geography and Statistics (IBGE) (2017), *Indicators of sustainable development, Brazil 2015*. Retrieved from: https://biblioteca.ibge.gov.br/visualizacao/livros/liv94254.pdf., on 19 October 2017.

Campos Lima, C.M.and Coelho, A.C. (2015), Alocação e mitigação dos riscos em parcerias público-privadas no Brasil. Revista de Administração Pública - RAP, v. 49, n. 2, mar–apr., p. 267–91.

Creswell, J.W. (2003), *Research design: Qualitative, quantitative, and mixed method approaches* (2nd edn). Thousand Oaks, CA: Sage.

Fujihara, M.A. and Lopes, F.G. (2009), *Sustentabilidade e mudanças climáticas: guia para o amanhã*. São Paulo: Senac.

Grimsey, D. and Lewis, M.K. (2002), Evaluating the risks of public-private partnerships for infra-structure projects. *International Journal of Project Management*, Vol. 20, No. 2, pp.107–18.

Ministry of Planning, Development and Management of Brazil (2017), *Projects of PPPs*. Retrieved from: http://www.planejamento.gov.br/assuntos/desenvolvimento/parcerias-publico-privadas/projetos, on 13 September 2017.

PRODES (2017), *Project for Monitoring Deforestation in the Legal Amazon by Satellite*. Retrieved from http://www.obt.inpe.br/OBT/assuntos/programas/amazonia/prodes, on 11th August 2017.

Sachs, I. (2004), *Development: inclusive, sustainable, sustained*. Rio de Janeiro: Garamond.

Savas, E.S. (1982), *Privatizing the Public Sector: How to Shrink Government*, Chatham House Publishers, Chatham.

Sundaram, J.K., Chowdhury, A., Sharma, K. and Platz, D. (2016), Public-Private Partnerships and the 2030 agenda for sustainable development: fit for purpose? DESA working paper n. 148ST/ESA/2016/DWP/148, Department of Economic & Social Affairs, United Nations, New York, N.Y. from: http://www.un.org/esa/desa/papers/2016/wp148_2016.pdf, on 25 August 2017.

The Lancet (2017), *The Lancet Commission on pollution and health*. Retrieved from: http://www.thelancet.com/commissions/pollution-and-health, on 25 January 2017.

United Nations, UN (2015), *Sustainable Development Goals*. Retrieved from https://sustainabledevelopment.un.org/?menu=1300, on 29 August 2017.

Whitfield, D. (2010), *Global Auction of Public Assets: Public sector alternatives to the infrastructure market and Public-Private Partnerships*, Spokesman Books, Nottingham.

World Bank (2017), *Report on private participation in infrastructure*. Retrieved from: http://ppi.worldbank.org/~/media/GIAWB/PPI/Documents/Global-Notes/PPI2017_HalfYear_Update.pdf., on 16 October 2017.

BIOGRAPHY

Dr Danilo de Oliveira Sampaio is professor of Marketing and Consumer behaviour at the Faculty of Business Administration and Accounting (FACC), at the Federal University of Juiz de Fora (UFJF), Juiz de Fora, Minas Gerais, Brazil. He has a Doctor of Business Administration from the School of Economics (FACE), Centre for Graduate and Research Administration (CEPEAD), Federal University of Minas Gerais (UFMG), Minas Gerais, Brazil. He is a researcher in marketing and consumer behaviour in the area of sustainable development in terms of public administration and business management, and author of articles in journals and at national and international conferences. Dr Sampaio is coordinator of the Master's Degree in Business Administration and the research group Descor.

PUBLIC-PRIVATE PARTNERSHIPS FOR SUSTAINABLE DEVELOPMENT: HOW CUSTOMERS, EMPLOYEES AND INVESTORS CAN INFORM THE SELECTION PROCESS

Beverlee B. Anderson* and Catalin Ratiu

College of Business Administration
California State University San Marcos
San Marcos, CA 92096-0001
banderso@csusm.edu
cratiu@csusm.edu

ABSTRACT

Purpose: The purpose of this paper is to explore how an understanding of the alignment of goals of customers, employees and investors can aid in the partner selection process.

Approach: The design uses secondary data focused on customers, employees and investors' goals and their alignment with Sustainable Development Goals (SDGs). Consumer behaviour data on issues related to SDGs, research on employee's work motivation, and the goals of investors, both institutional and individual, are investigated.

Findings: To develop effective Public-private Partnerships (PPP), the goals and behaviours of both parties must be recognised, considered and addressed. The goals and priorities of these entities are not always well

*Corresponding Author

aligned with SDGs. In selecting partners, Non-government Organisations (NGOs) will benefit from recognising the differing goals of stakeholders and common ground for actions.

Originality/value: The paper addresses some issues seldom addressed in SDG public-private partnership writing.

Practical and Social Implications: While PPPs have the potential be successful, to achieve significant gains in advancing the SDG agenda, there must be "buy-in" from relevant stakeholders associated with the partnerships.

Keywords: Sustainable Development Goals; Public-private partnerships; Consumer priorities; Employee goals; Investor desires

INTRODUCTION

To achieve the very ambitious and necessary 17 Sustainable Development Goals (SDG) formulated by the United Nation (UN), the use of public-private partnerships has been encouraged. This is an acknowledgment not only of the importance of collaboration among a multitude of stakeholders, but also of the complexity and far reach of these goals. Among the 17 goals, many of which are very specific, it is the last one that broadly aims to create an umbrella under which various forms of collaboration can occur:

> SDG 17: Strengthen the means of implementation and revitalise the global partnership for sustainable development (United Nations, 2015).

Scholarly, technical, and trade literature on Public-private partnerships (PPP) is vast and dates back decades. Many models of PPPs have emerged, depending on the object of the partnerships. These types of alliances can be used to generate value (Austin, 2000), build infrastructure (Rocca, 2017), or reduce the effects of natural disasters (Auzzir et al., 2014). With regards to the SDGs, there is precedent for developing PPPs in connection with firms' corporate social responsibility (Twigg, 2001). Dahan et al. (2010) suggest that complementary social and economic value can be created. For example, corporations may wish to obtain social legitimacy in markets where foreign multinationals are often viewed with suspicion and scepticism.

Despite these important advances in our understanding of the role of PPPs, we know far less about how these collaborations are to be selected and executed for maximum impact (Austin, 2000). This space presents us with an important opportunity to ask, how can NGOs improve the execution of PPPs by improving the selection process of partners? We answer this question by proposing a model that assists NGOs working on fulfilling the SDG agenda in improving the likelihood of success by selecting partners that are more likely to align with the SDGs.

Public-Private Partnerships – The Domain

At a time when no organisation can succeed on its own, when businesses are expected to act in more socially responsible ways, and when NGOs are expected to behave more like businesses, partnerships across divides have gained in importance and attention from business and non-profit leaders. These divides are defined in terms of dominant logics that drive the values, missions, and strategies of very distinct organisations. Companies in most industries have benefited from partnerships with NGOs, who bring expertise in social or environmental causes. Whether it is well publicised efforts by the TOMS[1] company and their *one for one* work in South America, or Gap's P.A.C.E.[2] programme, these initiatives benefit greatly from their NGO partners who carry out the social work. Currently, few Fortune 500 companies lack an NGO partnership that advances some socio-environmental cause.

One of the areas where public-private partnerships are found to be beneficial is in infrastructure work. While a Syracuse University study found significant benefits of PPPs for infrastructure projects, a McKinsey & Company article (Rocca, 2017) described the reluctance of US elected officials to engage with private investors, citing eight areas of concern. The areas of concern were:

- unclear responsibilities;
- poor alignment with strategy;
- inefficient optimisation of project features;
- lack of discipline in execution;
- lack of an ownership mind-set in the delivery team;
- poor project controls;
- low initial cost mind-set;
- poor resource optimisation.

It will be noted that while all eight areas of concern in infrastructure PPPs involve strategy and/or execution, none relate to the influence of consumers, employees or investors, the major stakeholders of private organisations.

The McKinsey study recognises that PPPs are not appropriate for every project; in many cases the challenges can be solved, as has been found in a growing number of successful public-private ventures from around the world. For example the McKinsey report found that published studies from Europe and the UK suggest that life cycle costs can be reduced by up to 20% compared to traditional approaches. Other studies from Australia and Canada also indicate successful track records for PPPs. The successful PPPs mentioned are not directly related to the SDGs.

---

[1]TOMS – http://www.toms.com.
[2]Personal Advancement and Career Enhancement, a programme aimed at girls in various countries around the world – https://www.bewhatspossible.com/pace.

When Multinational Enterprises (MNEs) desire to enter developing countries, many turn to NGOs to help them overcome a variety of challenges, from culture and economics to regulations and distribution channels. Dahan et al. (2010) cite many ways in which NGOs can help MNEs complete business models. They identify four strategic imperatives for the success of these PPPs:

- innovative combinations of firm and NGO resources and skills;
- the importance of trust building;
- the fit between the two organisations' goals;
- supporting and understanding of the local business infrastructure and environment.

Rocca (2017) cites a major PPP success in the USA with the George Dukmejian Courthouse building in Long Beach, California. This infrastructure project was the largest availability payment-based social infrastructure project in US history. The building, which opened in 2014, was completed on time and within budget. Other success stories in the US are the I-595 reversible managed lanes in Broward County Florida and the I-495 lanes in Virginia.

The joint effort of Cemex, Mexico's largest integrated building solutions company, and Patrimonio Hoy, a self-financing non-profit programme, developed a new offering for Mexico's self-construction housing market. This PPP reduced self-construction time by 60% and costs by 35%. By 2008, more than 200,000 Mexican families had benefited from their efforts (Dahan et al., 2010).

These stories show that PPPs can be successful, especially for accomplishing projects related to the SDGs. However, NGOs need to recognise the role and impact of stakeholders in approaching and selecting private partners to accomplish SDGs.

Stakeholder Potential to Influence Firm Commitment to SDGs

Customers

The importance of customers cannot be underestimated. Unless customers respond positively to firms' offerings, there will be no revenue – the lifeblood of business firms. The benefits of the goods and service must be communicated to the right customers and at the right price. How customers think and feel about the firm itself, and the social causes it may support, will influence their purchase behaviour. The customers whose views are consistent with the causes supported by the firm will likely be pleased to do business with the firm, and may even use social media to advocate for the firm's support. On the other hand, if consumers do not support – or are even strongly opposed to a cause – they may go to the extreme of boycotting the firm. This has happened in the US to firms that supported controversial causes (for recent examples, see the #grabyourwallet campaigns).

Firms that have substantial numbers of socially conscious consumers, those who care about the issues associated with environmental, social and economic goals, would likely be more open to engaging in PPPs that focused on these issues. A Nielsen survey (2012) found that approximately two-thirds of consumers around the world said they would prefer to buy products from firms that give back to society. From a list of 18 causes, environmental sustainability was the most frequently cited as a cause companies should support. Other causes, many of which are related to the UN's SDGs, were also seen as worthy of company support, but by fewer respondents (Steinberg, 2012).

Not all consumers are concerned about social or environmental issues. A Harris survey conducted in 2012 found that only about 34% of US adults said they are concerned about the planet we are leaving behind for future generations. This was a decrease of almost 10% from when the question was asked 2009. The survey also found declines in some "green" behaviours, such as purchasing all natural products or purchasing organic products. There was even a decline in the percentage of respondents who said they make an effort to use less water. In contrast, a Harris poll conducted in 2016 found most Americans care at least somewhat about the environment: only 7% said they did not care at all. While encouraging, the poll found a disconnect between what respondents said and what they did. Just 35% of the respondents supported environmental efforts by donating, advocating, participating in an event or volunteering (Salomon, 2016).

Just as consumers may have different levels of support for various causes, the "green consumers" also differ in their level of commitment. Banikarim's (2010) research identified five different green segments, from the most deeply committed Alpha Ecos to the most cost conscious, Economically Ecos. The largest segment, Eco-Chics buy a few green products – but may buy conspicuous green products. Two of the segments, Alpha Ecos and Eco-Centrics, are willing to pay more for eco-friendly products. Identifying their customers' priorities is a key issue for many firms in their willingness to support and partner with NGOs in the advancement of SDG goals. A challenge for NGOs is to identify organisations whose customers' priorities include the causes they desire to pursue.

Investors

Firms engaging in Sustainable, Responsible and Impact investing (SRI) take into account Environmental, Social, and Corporate Governance (ESG) issues as they seek to create positive sustainable development outcomes together with above average financial returns. At the end of 2015, more than one out of every five dollars invested through professionally managed funds in the US was invested using SRI fundamentals, amounting to nearly US$9 trillion (US SIF, 2016).

The rising interest of investors in sustainability can be looked at from two primary perspectives: risk mitigation and return on investment. While not mutually exclusive, these two represent distinct logics and perspectives on business opportunities or threats. While the former logic focuses on risk profiling based on the potential for environmental and reputation hazards, the latter seeks to build a "green" investment portfolio with the expectation of superior financial performance. A growing body of scholarly research suggests a predictable link between ESG criteria and financial performance, as firms embed a long-term view in their strategies for growth. In a review of over 2,000 empirical studies dating back to the 1970s, Friede et al. (2015) show strong support for the relationship between ESG strategies and positive financial performance.

Asset management firms, such as UBS, now sell sustainable investment products that advertise 'doing well by doing good', and showcase the UN's SDGs as the foundational principles for investments in addition to financial fundamentals. In addition, they also claim that PPPs are the working mechanism for implementing these goals, while at the same time achieving strong shareholder returns. A recent clipping from UBS' informational materials reads:

> *"The United Nations has 17 sustainable development goals that aim to end poverty, protect the planet, and bring prosperity to all by 2030. These can only be achieved using private capital as well as public investments. So, at the 2017 World Economic Forum, we pledged to direct $5bn of our clients' investments over the next five years to sustainable or impact investments. In fact, all of our businesses are engaged in initiatives to help meet the UN's goals, and our clients' investment needs. This year, for the third year running, we were confirmed as the industry group leader for diversified financials in the Dow Jones Sustainability Index."*

> *"We've partnered with visionaries who've developed innovative ways to meet the UN's SDGs, while also generating financial returns for their investors."* (UBS, 2017)

The anecdotal evidence presented above suggests that investments connected with SDGs are moving into the mainstream and provide avenues for growth. Sandberg et al. (2009) note that the mainstreaming of SRI is more heterogeneous than conventional investments, due to cultural and ideological variation among regions, stakeholder values, and financial markets. This would indicate a lower institutionalisation of the SRI markets, and would suggest that these types of investment instruments linked with SDGs can benefit from consistent innovation.

At the same time, Busch et al. (2016) caution that SR investors may have a modest role in facilitating increased sustainable business practices in firms. While they acknowledge that financial market participants have been integrating ESG benchmarks in their financial positions, organisational stakeholders have been slow to shift towards more sustainable practices. The key to improving this relationship is linking investments to a long-term orientation, while at the same time pushing for more transparency in ESG data.

To conclude this section, it should be noted that investors have an important role in influencing the agenda of firms as they move towards more sustainable business practices. As shown, the market for sustainable investments connected with SDGs has grown to a sizeable proportion of the economy. Nevertheless, in certain cases, awareness of ESG criteria does not tightly connect to more sustainable organisations. In other words, where investors hold a significant amount of power over investment targets, there are certain limitations inhibiting their influence on strategy.

Employees

Why employees work?

According to several sources (Heathfield, 2017; Ruyan, 2010; Schwartz, 2015) the most basic reason people work is for money. Whether it be compensation, salary, bonuses, benefits or remuneration, money pays the bills. However, given the choice of where to work, people will consider non-monetary factors. These are the factors that influence their satisfaction level with their jobs.

In the 1920s, Lewin (1935) found that employees want to have a say; they will support what they help create. As explained by Sashkin (1984), participation may take several different forms:

> "First, employees may participate in setting goals. Second, they may participate in making decisions, choosing from among alternative courses of action. Third, employees may participate in solving problems-a process that includes the definition of issues and the generation of alternative courses of action as well as choice among the alternatives. Finally, participation may involve making changes in the organisation (that is, "organisation development" (OD) activities)" (Sashkin, 1984).

Douglas McGregor's (1957) idea was that some employees are self-motivated, while others are not. Theory X assumed employees were not self-motivated, while Theory Y assumed they were self-motivating. He postulated that different types of employees would respond best under different approaches to leadership. The notion that employees want to be respected, and desire to contribute, is consistent with Lewin's (1935) concept of employee participation.

More recently, Schwartz (2015) reports the top five non-monetary reasons people go to work each day:

1. to lose one's self in one's work (engaging);
2. challenges them, forces them to grow;
3. feel they are in charge (autonomy and discretion);

4. social engagement and interaction;
5. finally, what they do is meaningful - their work makes a difference in the world.

The earlier research leads to the conclusion that an organisation's employees are likely to be supportive of the formation of PPPs, if they participate in some aspect of the partnership. This may include goals, as well as more operational decisions.

Generational Effects

Within the US there are shifts in work values among the generations. Twenge et al. (2010) found the largest change in work values to be an increase in the value placed on leisure. The incoming workforce (GenMe) places a higher value on leisure than either Gen X or Boomers. GenMe was also found to place more value on extrinsic rewards - wanting more money and status. Their research also found that there were no significant generational differences in altruistic values. US GenMe is no more likely than older generations to value work that helps others or is worthwhile to society. Younger generations were not found to place a higher value on meaningful work than previous generations.

Twenge et al. (2010) further state that:

> "Generational differences in work values can also affect the perceived fit of employees with the organisation. Organisational climates [and goals] often reflect the values and goals of founding members or organisational leaders. If entering employees hold values that are different from those of the leaders of the company, GenMe employees may experience person-organisation misfit, which could yield more negative attitudes toward work, decreased performance, and greater likelihood of turnover." (Twenge et al., 2010)

Challenges to Organisations

The role of employees in carrying out their organisation's sustainability goals is undeniable. In a recent study, Le Blanc et al. (2017) propose that sustainable innovation can be achieved through job redesign, where employees have the ability to craft their jobs to embed sustainable development roles. The authors show how top-down job redesign interventions can often be ineffective. They offer a model that recognised bottom-up redesign strategies that help achieve the broader organisational goals, while at the same time gaining and maintaining the employees' motivation towards fulfilling these objectives.

Employee perceptions and engagement is emphasised in various studies that explore functional contexts within the organisation, be they information systems (Yang et al., 2017), marketing and branding (Biedenbach and Manzhynski, 2016), or entrepreneurship (Markman et al., 2016). In each of these studies, the role of the employees in implementing ESG strategies is emphasised. The authors also caution that employee buy-in and incentives play an important role towards the development of SDG goals.

Where PPPs can be interpreted as adding to the employees' job role, prior engagement can moderate that perception.

DISCUSSION

The aim of this paper is to move the needle towards strengthening the means of implementation and revitalisation of global partnerships for sustainable development (SDG 17). We focus on the selection process used by NGOs looking to partner with business firms as a mode of improving the likelihood of success of PPPs. The core argument we offer is that NGOs can improve the likelihood of success of these part-nerships if they understand the customers, investors and employees of the target firm, and the dynamics between these stakeholders and the firm. We illustrate this argument in Figure 1, which describes the dynamic relationships between selected stakeholders, the firm, and the NGO.

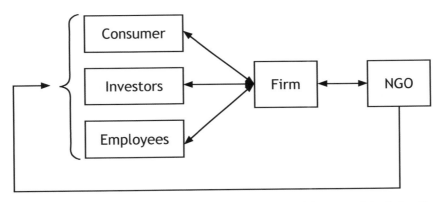

Figure 1   Modelling the Relational Challenges of Partnership Selection
Source: Devised by author

The restrained stakeholder model focuses on the proximity of stakeholders with an ability to influence tactical and strategic decisions on a short- and long-term basis. The model has potential for success because it offers NGO leaders a way of learning about the overlap in values without the common pitfalls that such negotiations entail. Researching these stakeholders can be a more cost and time effective way of learning about the range of shared values between the NGO and the firm. Shared values have been shown to be the primary predictor of alliance success, whether in for-profit or non-profit contexts (Austin, 2000).

    Our overview of the three stakeholder groups indicates that there are both oppor-tunities and challenges in terms of the level of influence any of these stakeholders can have on the company acting alone. For instance, some customers may have interest in social or environmental causes and even engage in advocacy; however, many other customers may continue to patronise the company despite unsustainable behaviour. Similarly, investors may have internalised sustainable development values; however, taking an investment position in a firm does not guarantee their ability to change the strategy of the firm. Finally, employees have been shown to be motivated by more than financial compensation, and many see their role expanding to include activities that improve the sustainability of the organisation. However, many variables can either enhance or reduce the chances that employees can influence their company and engage effectively in these initiatives.

NGOs seeking partnerships with business firms would be well advised to look for a shared sustainability agenda among these three stakeholder groups. Whether tacit or explicit, having more than one stakeholder align along certain sustainability goals is likely to increase the influence on the firm in those areas. For example, customers and employees (who are often also customers) aligning in their interest for transparency and governance are more likely to push the firm to develop strategic initiatives that improve their performance in those regards than if isolated stakeholder groups acted independently. Also, if investors coincided with customers in their push towards stronger pollution prevention practices, the firm would be obligated to take notice and respond. Observing stakeholders interest would allow NGOs to predict the interactive effects of these dynamics as well as firm reactions.

Another dynamic observable at the stakeholder level is the extent to which any of the three core stakeholders are closer and/or louder to the firm. Whether through company statements or corporate responses to various issues, NGOs can sense if customers, investors, or employees receive more importance or have a stronger voice. We argue that the importance of an issue increases the closer the stakeholder group is to the company, at any given moment in time. This would lead the firm to push these issues to the top of its agenda, above other issues. This variable would moderate the relationship expressed previously regarding the potential for multiple stakeholders to explicitly or implicitly coincide on any issue and influence a firm's strategic agenda. Conversely, issues are likely to decrease in overall importance if the firm has the ability to *mute* one or more stakeholder groups.

CONCLUSIONS

This paper contributes to the literature on PPPs for sustainable development by offering a model of partner selection that reduces the typical risks of alliance formation; it does this by improving the likelihood that partnerships will share relevant values towards achieving desired goals. We explain the opportunities and challenges offered by a keen examination of a restrained stakeholder view of the firm. We also explain the relational challenges of partner selection together with the interactive effects of these variables.

Practitioners seeking improved partnerships with business firms should revel in the knowledge that a selection process based on a solid understanding of key stakeholders of these firms can offer the necessary information to target partners that are more likely to succeed in implementing strategies geared towards these goals.

REFERENCES

Austin, J.E. (2000), *The collaboration challenge: How nonprofits and businesses succeed through strategic alliances*. San Francisco, Wiley.

Auzzir, Z.A., Haigh, R.P. and Amaratunga, D. (2014), Public-private partnerships (PPP) in disaster management in developing countries: A conceptual framework. *Procedia Economics and Finance*, Vol. 18, pp. 807–814. https://doi.org/10.1016/S2212-5671(14)01006-5

Banikarim, M. (2010), Seeing Shades in Green Consumers. *Brandweek*, Vol. 51, No. 16, p.18. April 2010, Copyrighted 2013, Prometheus Global Media.

Biedenbach, G. and Manzhynski, S. (2016), Internal branding and sustainability: investigating perceptions of employees. *Journal of Product & Brand Management*, Vol. 25, No. 3, pp. 296–06, https://doi.org/10.1108/JPBM-06-2015-0913

Busch, T., Bauer, R. and Orlitzky, M. (2016), Sustainable development and financial markets: Old paths and new avenues. *Business & Society*, Vol. 55, No. 3, pp. 303–29.

Dahan, N.M., Doh, J.P., Oetzel, J. and Yaziji, M. (2010), Corporate-NGO Collaboration: Co-creating New Business Models for Developing Markets. *Long Range Planning*, Vol. 43, No. 2, pp. 326–42.

Friede, G., Busch, T. and Bassen, A. (2015), ESG and financial performance: aggregated evidence from more than 2000 empirical studies. *Journal of Sustainable Finance & Investment*, Vol. 5, No. 4, pp. 210–33.

Heathfield, S.M. (2017), What People want from work: motivation. The Balance. Downloaded from https://www.thebalance.com/what-people-want-from-work-motivation-1919051

Le Blanc, P.M., Demerouti, E., Bakker, A.B., Fraccaroli, F. and Sverke, M. (2017), How can I shape my job to suit me better? job crafting for sustainable employees and organizations, *An Introduction to Work and Organizational Psychology: An International Perspective*, pp. 48–63. 10.1002/9781119168058.ch3.

Lewin, K. (1935), *A dynamic theory of personality*. New York: McGraw-Hill.

Markman, G.D., Russo, M., Lumpkin, G.T., Jennings, P.D. and Mair, J. (2016), Entrepreneurship as a Platform for Pursuing Multiple Goals: A Special Issue on Sustainability, Ethics, and Entrepreneurship. *Journal of Management Studies*, Vol. 53, No. 5, pp. 673–94. doi:10.1111/joms.12214.

McGregor, D.M. (1957), The Human Side of Enterprise, in *Adventure in Thought and Action*, Proceedings of the Fifth Anniversary Convocation of the School of Industrial Management, Massachusetts Institute of Technology, Cambridge, MA, 9 April 1957.

Nielsen (2012), *The Global, Socially Conscious Consumer*. Downloaded from http://www.nielsen.com/us/en/news/2012/the-global-socially-conscious-consumer.html on 10 August 2017.

Rocca, M.D. (2017), *The rising advantage of public-private partnerships*. McKinsey & Company, July 2017.

Ruyan, A. (2010), 4 Reasons People Really go to work. Classy Career Girl. Downloaded from http://www.classycareergirl.com/2010/05/why-do-people-go-to-work/.

Salomon, M. (2016), This Earth Day it's Time to Put Our Money where our mouth is. *The Harris Poll* (27) April 21, 2016.

Sandberg, J., Juravle, C., Hedesström, T.M. and Hamilton, I. (2009), The heterogeneity of socially responsible investment. *Journal of Business Ethics*, Vol. 87, No. 4, pp. 519–33.

Sashkin, M. (1984), Participative Management Is an Ethical Imperative, *Organizational Dynamics*, Vol. 12, No. 4, pp. 5–22. Periodicals Division, American Management Associations.

Schwartz, B. (2015), *Why We Work*. Simon & Schuster/Ted Book. Downloaded from https://qz.com/498951/why-work-a-psychologist-explains-the-deeper-meaning-fof-your-daily-grind/.

Steinberg, K. (2012), Fewer Americans 'Thinking Green': new poll reveals continued decrease on 'Green' Attitudes and Behavior since 2009. *The Harris Poll* (41) April 22, 2012.

Twenge, J.M., Campbell, S.M., Hoffman, B.J. and Lance, C.E. (2010), Generational Differences in Work Values: Leisure and Extrinsic Values Increasing, Social and Intrinsic Values Decreasing. *Journal of Management*, Vol. 36, No. 5, pp. 1117-142.

Twigg, J. (2001), *Corporate social responsibility and disaster reduction. A global overview.* Benfield Greig Hazard Research Centre, University College of London

UBS (2017), Sustainable investing. Retrieved 23 September 2017. https://content.ubs.com/microsites/together/en/spotlight/sustainable-investing.html?s_kwcid=AL!430!3!221878612030!b!!!!%2Bsustainable%20%2Binvestment&ef_id=VOHDDwAAACBAdXUa:20170924005813:s

United Nations (2015), Sustainable Development Goals. http://www.un.org/sustainabledevelopment/sustainable-development-goals/.

US SIF (2016), Report on US Sustainable, Responsible and Impact Investing Trends. *The Forum for Sustainable and Responsible Investment*.

Yang, Z., Sun, J., Zhang, Y., Wang, Y. and Cao, L. (2017), Employees' collaborative use of green information systems for corporate sustainability: motivation, effort and performance. *Information Technology for Development*, pp. 1–21.

BIOGRAPHY

Beverlee B. Anderson received her PhD from Ohio State University. She currently serves as Professor Emerita at California State University San Marcos. She has held a variety of teaching and administrative positions at the University of Kansas, University of Cincinnati, Wright State University, and University of Wisconsin – Parkside. Her research focuses on cross-cultural and international topics, and has been published in numerous academic journals; she has been an invited speaker in professional venues. She is past president of the Marketing Educators Association, and served as a member of the Board of Directors for San Diego Financial Executives International, the Marketing Management Association, and the Academy of Marketing Science, among others.

Catalin Ratiu received his PhD from Concordia University in Montreal, Canada. He currently serves as Associate Professor of Strategic Management at California State University San Marcos. His research examines corporate strategies in the social, natural, and global environments, with specific focus on the intersection of sustainability and international strategies. Catalin is an award winning scholar, having published over 20 papers in scholarly outlets, including the *Academy of Management Review, Critical Perspectives on International Business,* and *World Journal of Science, Technology and Sustainable Development*.

TOWARDS MODELLING DIASPORA ROLE AS INTERNATIONAL AGENTS FOR DEVELOPMENT

Adil A. Dafa'alla* and Elmouiz S. Hussein

Airbus UK
Filton, Bristol, United Kingdom
adil.dafaalla@airbus.com and elmouiz.hussein@airbus.com

ABSTRACT

Purpose: To conceptually model the economic contribution of the Diaspora as a Public Private Partnership (PPP) to promote business, investment and industry, both in their host countries and countries of origin. As such, the model promotes Diaspora as International Agents for Development.

Design/Methodology/Approach: A qualitative research methodology is used in order to understand the huge potential that Diaspora may have in benefiting the economic growth in their host countries, effecting economic and industrial development in their countries of origin as well as boosting their own personal investment portfolio through utilising the expertise they gained and links they developed. This could conceptually be built as a triangular model of PPP.

Findings: The Diaspora population is rising steadily: over 244 million people live outside their country of birth. Their host countries benefit from their skills and innovation. However, although the role played by Diaspora in the development, poverty reduction and reconstruction of their countries of origin is significant, this role is not fully recognised by their host countries or countries of origin. There is a powerful triangle of

*Corresponding Author

Diaspora, host countries and countries of origin that can potentially be used to promote business, investment and industry, both in the countries of origin and destination. This presents the Diaspora, in partnership with their countries of origin and residence, as a potential tool for achieving sustainable development and fighting poverty. It is therefore a step towards achieving the UN sustainable development goals for 2030.

Originality/Value: The role of Diaspora in "fire-fighting" economic crises in their countries of origin is well covered in the literature. However, very little has been highlighted about the benefits they bring to their host countries, both in economic terms and as a source of innovation. This paper aims to widen the scope to look at the Diaspora as International Agents for Sustainable Development, and model their contribution as PPPs between the Diaspora, host countries and countries of origin.

Keywords: Diaspora; host; homeland; origin; partnership; agent; Sustainable Development; industry; business; investment; model

INTRODUCTION

The present economic situation of Third World countries is in part the result of low levels of development, their backward industries, and outdated agricultural methods. According to UN Documents (1987), most of the global research and development effort is devoted to military purposes or the commercial objectives of large corporations. Little of this is of direct relevance to conditions in developing countries. This is still true today as it was then! Developing countries therefore have to work, individually and together, to build up their technological capabilities. Likewise, to get out of the poverty zone, under-developed countries need to adopt an integrated sustainable development plan, in which collaboration for industry, economic growth and capacity building represents the pivotal point (Dafa'Alla et al., 2016).

According to the Organisation for Economic Co-operation and Development (OECD), poor and struggling countries will need national development strategies that respond to global macroeconomic trends to ensure that they thrive in a global economy (OECD, 2010): this is where the role of Diaspora comes into play. For many countries, the Diaspora are a major source of Foreign Direct Investment (FDI), market development (including outsourcing of production), technology transfer, philanthropy, tourism, political contributions, and more intangible flows of knowledge, new attitudes, and cultural influence. This emphasises the potential role of Diaspora in development, hence poverty reduction, in their own countries of origin, provided their huge resources and impact can be utilised intelligently and effectively.

Whatever the role they may play, the Diaspora are indeed in the interesting position of making a natural link between their countries of origin and residence. Hence they are well suited to play an active and unique role as International Agents for Development in both countries. This paper highlights this role and contributes towards modelling it as a three-way Public Private Partnership (PPP) between the Diaspora, their host countries and countries of origin.

DIASPORA FACTS AND FIGURES

The recent International Migration Report 2015, published in United Nations (2016), offers interesting statistics about migration. As such, unless otherwise explicitly stated, it is used as the main source for the figures quoted herein. According to the report, the number of international migrants (i.e., persons living in a country other than where they were born) reached 244 million in 2015 for the world as a whole, with a median age of 39 years; a prime productive working age. This represents a 41% increase compared to 2000. In 2015, two thirds (67%) of all international migrants were living in just 20 countries. The largest number of international migrants (47 million) resided in the United States of America, equal to about a fifth (19%) of the world's total. With 12 million each, Germany and the Russian Federation host the second and third largest numbers of migrants worldwide, followed by Saudi Arabia that hosts 10 million foreigners (United Nations, 2016).

Interestingly, the majority of the Diaspora population (64%) originated from middle-income countries, and the majority of these settled in a high-income country. Between 2000 and 2015, the number of migrants originating from middle-income countries increased more rapidly than those from countries in any other income group. Indeed, 25% of them originated from countries in Europe and 43% in Asia. Some migrants came from the richest countries of the world as well. For example, migrants from France live in more countries than migrants from any other nation. The poorest countries represent a minority. Indeed, Africa contributes only 14% of migrants, despite the recently increased level of African's migration to Europe extensively covered in the media. This shows that the main driver for migration is not poverty. Note that, despite the lack of accurate statistics, a significant portion of these migrants are well-educated, skilled workers and professionals in their prime productive working age, seeking to fulfil personal or professional ambitions that they could not fulfil in their countries of birth due to developmental, social or political reasons.

On the other hand, the high-income countries, including the G7 countries, have been the main recipients, and hence beneficiaries of the added value that Diaspora contributions bring to their economy. Between 2000 and 2015, positive net migration contributed to 42% of the population growth in Northern America and 32% in Oceania. Indeed, the size of the population in Europe would have fallen between 2000 and 2015 in the absence of positive net migration. Overall, 76 million international migrants were residing in Europe, compared to 75 million in Asia. Northern America hosted the third largest number of international migrants (54 million), followed by Africa (21 million), Latin America and the Caribbean (9 million), and Oceania (8 million) (United

Nations, 2016). It is also interesting to note that 84% of the United Arab Emirates' population is foreign born. This is the highest share of migrants compared to all countries in the world. The next three highest — Qatar (74%), Kuwait (60%) and Bahrain (55%) — are also in the Gulf region; most come from India, Bangladesh and Pakistan. However, by hosting 10 million migrants (31% of the population), Saudi Arabia has the largest group of Diaspora population in the gulf region. These figures reflect the huge reliance of the gulf region on foreign migration.

CONTRIBUTION OF DIASPORA TO GLOBAL ECONOMY

The migration experience benefits the migrants in many ways. They gain new skills, benefit financially and are exposed to new cultures. During this process, they also contribute a great deal to their host countries, as well as to their countries of origin. Over the past few decades, Diaspora groups have increasingly become significant players in the international political, social and economic arenas, thanks to new communication technologies improving abilities to mobilise, and multiculturalism policies in receiving countries that revitalised ethnic pride and assertiveness (Vertovec, 2005). A few examples of politically active Diaspora communities are the Jewish-, Greek-, Cuban- and Armenian-American associations that represent some of the strongest lobbies in Washington, DC. Prime illustrations of Diasporic political payoff occurred in 1990 when Croatians abroad donated US$4 million towards the election campaign of Fanjo Tudjman and were subsequently rewarded with representation in parliament, and in 2003 when Diasporic Iraqi groups and individuals played crucial roles in encouraging American military intervention in Iraq (Vertovec, 2005). Perhaps rich countries, feeling the pinch of economic slowdown and increasing burden of aid and military intervention, were driven to explore and exploit the potential influence of Diaspora on their soil to play politically active roles in their countries of origin or *homelands*, as sometimes referred to in the literature. With regard to their national Diaspora, countries of origin certainly want remittances and may appreciate lobbying, but they may resent too much political involvement. There is a good volume of evidence in the literature regarding the role of Diaspora in political changes, nation and capacity building, peace-making, technology transfer and economic development, both in their host countries and countries of origin, as discussed in (Vertovec, 2005), for example. However, in this paper, we are confining our discussion only to the economic and development role of the Diaspora.

Irrespective of the motive, it seems that the governments of migrant-sending (*homeland* or *origin*) and receiving (*host*) countries, international agencies, and academics are now paying considerable attention to the relationship between Diaspora groups and development. Although economic motivations of migration have long been recognised, the economic development effects of migration on host countries and countries of origin are only recently coming into focus. In this context, the contribution of the international Diaspora to the world economy is estimated by the North American Integration Development Centre of California University to be around US$7.1 trillion, equivalent to the sixth largest economy in the world (Hinojosa-Ojeda, 2017). Indeed, the rise in the number of international migrants reflects the increasing importance of international migration, which has become an integral part of world economies and societies. However, this contribution is largely dispersed among the 20 countries that host two thirds of Diaspora, and hence does not reflect in any specific economic or political agenda of the Diaspora population as such. In fact, to date, there is no pressure group or organisation that represents the international Diaspora's interests, or that has the legitimacy to speak on their behalf. Nevertheless, the United Nations 2030 Agenda for Sustainable Development recognises the positive contribution of migrants for inclusive growth and sustainable development. It further recognises that international migration is a multi-dimensional reality of major relevance for the development of countries of origin, transit and destination (United Nations, 2016).

Contribution of Diaspora to Host Countries

The Economist (2011) commented that migrant networks are a rare bright spark in the world economy: rich countries should welcome them. It added that Diaspora bring benefit to the host countries via the networks they establish as well as the ideas and money they spread. They have the skill and expertise to apply, the ideas to drive innovation and research, and some of them bring in direct and indirect investment to feed the economy in their host countries. To clarify this further, note that while migrants make up an eighth of America's population, they founded a quarter of the country's technology and engineering firms. Also, by linking the West with emerging markets, Diaspora help rich countries to plug into fast-growing economies. Indeed, the US State Department has both acknowledged and recognised their huge contribution to the American economy and society. For example, in 2011 and 2012, the US State Department hosted two 'Secretary's Global Diaspora Forums' in Washington, which attracted hundreds of delegates representing over 70 countries. This was a very public and international recognition and realisation of looking at Diaspora groups in different ways. The key messages of these Forums revolved around a number of themes (Diaspora Matters, 2011; Diaspora Alliance, 2012):

- leveraging the diversity of the United States as an asset;
- Diaspora engagement is key for exploring new markets;
- Diaspora drive innovation in Silicon Valley and beyond;
- Diaspora groups can play active roles in building bridges between the US and their countries of origin;
- Diaspora groups have unique expertise, insights and personal commitment to development in their countries of origin,

- Diaspora groups have local knowledge and contacts that diplomats sometimes don't have;
- Diaspora groups offer an opportunity to reorient ties with developing and emerging economies.

Likewise, European migrants who have arrived in the UK since 2000 have contributed more than £20bn to UK public finances between 2001 and 2011. Moreover, they have endowed the country with productive human capital that would have cost the UK £6.8bn in spending on education (Dustmann and Frattini, 2014). As a result, migration to the UK since 2000 has been of substantial net fiscal benefit, with migrants contributing more than they have received in benefits and transfers. This is true for migrants from Central and Eastern Europe as well as the rest of the EU. Indeed, Diaspora investment in education does not only keep UK universities financially viable, but also benefits from them as a source of innovation and keeping the research wheel revolving. In fact, the benefit to the UK goes beyond the research area to directly feed into the UK economy in many different and interesting ways, as discussed in Dustmann and Frattini (2014).

In this context, if one takes the example of the Sudanese Diaspora in the Gulf region, these Diaspora were born in the Sudan, largely educated and skilled in the UK and USA, and now work in the Gulf region. One can think of them as a natural extension of the Sudanese Diaspora in the UK and USA respectively. Some of them made substantial financial gains in the Gulf. If they cannot invest their wealth in Sudan for political reasons, and have no direct legal avenue to invest in the Gulf countries, they would naturally be inclined to invest in the countries where they were skilled. Hence, for the host countries, investment in Diaspora education is a means of gaining from their future investment, irrespective of whether they stay in the country for the long term or not.

In fact, the benefits that Diaspora bring to local economies are not limited to the USA and the UK, but shared between all rich countries that host a significant Diaspora population; many of them consider the Diaspora as a "national asset" (Diaspora Matters, 2011). The above examples suffice to highlight the contribution of the Diaspora to the economy of their host countries and, consequently, the global impact of their contribution.

Contribution of Diaspora to Countries of Origin

As shown above, rich countries are likely to benefit from looser migration policy, and fears that poor countries will suffer as a result of a "brain drain" are over exaggerated. The prospect of working abroad spurs more people to acquire valuable skills, and not all subsequently migrate. Skilled migrants send money home, and they often return to set up new businesses. One study found that unless they lose more than 20% of their university graduates, the brain drain makes poor countries richer (The Economist, 2011).

Diaspora remittances and financial contributions are well mobilised through various instruments, including, but not limited to, bonds, securitised remittances, and special banking arrangements. The World Bank and other development partners have revealed that remittances by African Diaspora, for example, surged by 3.4% to US$35.2 billion in 2015. However, this amount does not directly translate into development due to many challenges, such as the very high costs involved in money transfer, the technical complexity and alternative innovative platforms, going beyond funds for the day-to-day needs of families. A larger, more consolidated option channelled towards productive investments fostering an entrepreneurial rather than a dependency culture is needed (Madichie, 2016).

Meanwhile, a recent joint report from the World Bank and the African Development Bank argues that African governments should do more to realise the economic benefits of migration. "With about 30 million Africans living outside their home countries, migration is a vital lifeline for the continent", the report says, adding that migrants' remittances have helped to reduce poverty in Africa and have led to increased investments in health, education and housing (Cummins and Provost, 2011). Sinatti and Horst (2015) noted that an increased focus on the role of Diaspora as new agents in the development arena was noticeable in the first decade of the millennium, when enthusiasm about migrants' potential for complementing mainstream development efforts rose among key development actors. This came at a time of increased debate on aid effectiveness and growing interest in "new development actors". This interest was further strengthened by emerging Diaspora investment trends and awareness. The publication of the 2003 Global Financial Report of the World Bank stated that remittances far outweigh official development aid (Raghuram, 2009). However, these efforts have mainly revolved around the pivotal point of aid, poverty reduction and directed towards the countries of origin. This confines the role of Diaspora to "fire-fighting" economic crises in their countries of origin, while ignoring the benefits that the host countries also gain from Diaspora investments. This makes the main objective of the role of Diaspora politically, rather than economically, driven.

International migration is now widely seen to have the potential to contribute to technology transfer and development in the migrants' countries of origin, and many government and development agencies are seeking ways to maximise its benefits. There are different models for how countries of origin have elected to benefit from their respective Diaspora. For example, 26% of the Jordanian GDP (Gross Domestic Product) comes directly from Diaspora remittances. China, India and Taiwan, however, focus less on remittances in favour of pursuing three very different business-oriented models in seeking Diaspora contributions to development. China has long worked to attract direct investment and open trade opportunities through overseas Chinese communities. India has recently launched a Diaspora policy that is multi-pronged, pursing direct investment, portfolio investment, technology transfer, market opening and out-sourcing opportunities. Taiwan, on the other hand, has pursued a "brain trust" model, focused on attracting human capital from the Diaspora (Newland and Patrick, 2004). While the Chinese and Indian models are attractive from business and investment perspectives, the Taiwanese model is of special interest to facilitating technology transfer and building up technological capabilities as part of the national industrial and economic development strategies in the developing and underdeveloped countries of origin of the Diaspora.

MODELLING THE CONTRIBUTION OF DIASPORA AS PUBLIC PRIVATE PARTNERSHIPS

As discussed above, there is a recent growing understanding and recognition of the contribution of Diaspora to the economies of their host countries. The Annual Global Diaspora Forum hosted by the US State Department is one example of such growing interest. However, the examples quoted above also show that the role of Diaspora is uni-directional. This role utilises Diaspora to influence economic, political or social events in their countries of origin, but not in host countries. Literature is full of examples emphasising this role: see DeWind and Holdaway (2005) for a collation of such examples.

Paradoxically, while the Diaspora are important actors in economic development, they are still mainly considered shortcuts to leveraging financing (especially remittances), channelling funds for sustained development albeit in a sub-optimal manner. This attitude underplays alternative platforms of innovative contributions of the Diaspora. A parochial focus of such financial contributions poses risks of failure and ultimately jeopardises the UN 2030 Agenda for Sustainable Development (Madichie, 2016). Madichie went on to advocate that Diaspora should be considered, not just as sources of finance for development, but also as development partners. He added, while the Diaspora may have the capacity and patriotic mind-set to contribute to national development, concerted efforts must be made by all stakeholders to develop policy objectives that could facilitate Diaspora mobilisation: we agree with him. However, this paradigm was recommended in the same traditional uni-directional context of using the Diaspora to help the development path in their countries of origin. Confining the contribution of the Diaspora in this uni-directional role ignores the legitimate interests and ambitions of the Diaspora themselves, and risks exploiting them for the political and economic aims of the countries of origin and/or host countries. This is clearly not a satisfactory situation from their perspective and surely does not exploit the full potential of the Diaspora. With a population of 244 million, an economic value of US$7.1 trillion and ability to donate, for example, US$4 million towards the one cause of supporting a general election campaign in Croatia alone as quoted above, the real weight of the Diaspora should really reflect their true potential as International Agents for Development.

What we are advocating is a new perspective that satisfies the ambitions of the Diaspora, requirements of host countries and needs of countries of origin. This aim can be achieved by considering a three-way Public Private Partnership model (PPP) of equals between the Diaspora, the host countries and the countries of origin, as de-picted diagrammatically in Figure 1. The figure demonstrates how such a partnership model works in practice. The symbol in the middle of the triangle is meant to rep-resent the "integration" between the roles of the three partners in the model. Also, note that the examples of the contribution of each partner towards the others shown in the figure are not exhaustive. The three partners should work collaboratively in an integrated manner to resolve inhibitors and build enablers to economic growth, both in host countries and countries of origin, and allow the Diaspora to fulfil their dreams of investment while contributing to nation and capacity building in their countries of origin as well as residence. It is a PPP Model for formulating industrial and economic strategies, building capacity, driving development and making investment. As such, although general, the model is of particular relevance to developing and under-devel-oped countries, where these issues are of high priority.

This model sees and recognises the Diaspora as International Agents for Develop-ment and can be readily replicated in economic, social and political arenas in com-plementary or isolated terms. It can also be used in a "softer" mode as a vehicle for

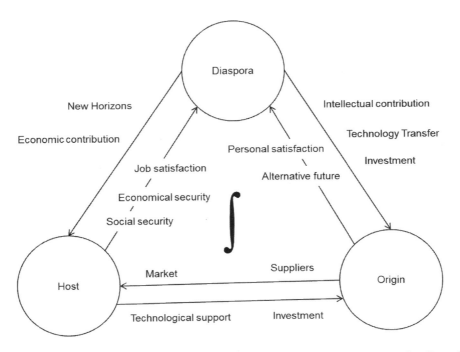

Figure 1   Three-Way PPP Model for the Diaspora as International Agents for Development
Source: Devised by author

knowledge and technology transfer between the partners. This can be delivered in a form of advice or expert support to formulate economic and industrial strategies, for example. The model is not meant to replace the current role of Diaspora, but to complement and enlarge it in a meaningful and more comprehensive and effective manner. However, for it to work as designed, it has to be a partnership between equals where transparency and democratic means of taking decisions is the order of the day. This may require political reform and cultural change in some Third World countries before they can take full advantage of the model. It also requires clarification and agreement on the objectives and targets right at the start of any practical project based on this model. These prerequisites are essential to avoid exploitation of the Diaspora and prevent the partnership from reverting back to the traditional uni-directional context it is aiming to avoid. It also needs official recognition of the role of Diaspora both in the host countries and, more importantly, countries of origin. This is important in order to alleviate fears of Diaspora of risking being associated with the corrupt and undemocratic regimes in many countries of origin. Recognising their role in these countries and legislating for it in the statues of the country will serve to take the partnership outside the political arena and make it less vulnerable to abuse by corrupt officials. This will also give host countries the political leverage or cover to sell their partnership and investment in Third World countries to their own public. This process can be enhanced by the Diaspora being organised in institutions that can articulate their views on these legislations and ensure that they are a fair reflection of their needs and interests. These institutions/organisations/associations can be formed in a way and play a role similar to the trade unions in mature democracies or the Royal Colleges in the UK. These organisations should also set the standard and monitor behaviour of the Diaspora, as well as represent them and defend their rights.

As partners in this model, the Diaspora can contribute as individuals, small groups, or even organisations. The presence of the host country in the partnership may also be seen as safeguarding the Diaspora's rights from being abused by their countries of origin's governments. At the same time, the presence of the countries of origin's governments in the partnership may provide the official monitoring that only governments can provide in order to guard public interest from being exploited by foreign investors; this is highlighted in Dafa'Alla (2016). Note that the involvement of governments can be either directly by committing public funds to nominated projects, or indirectly by creating the right environment for investment and following that up by encouraging their private sector to commit funds and actively engage in the projects. However, the direct involvement of at least one of the two governments is essential for the PPP to work. Irrespective of the format of the government participation, giving the partnership a legal framework will guard against lack of democratisation and rampant corruption, ensure protection, and make investment in countries of origin more appealing and attractive while protecting against exploitation by any party. Furthermore, forming and legalising such a three-way PPP can also encourage and incentivise other countries and sources of investment to come to the country and ask for similar treatment — *a win-win situation for all.*

Hence, the model presents the Diaspora, in partnership with their host countries and countries of origin, as a potential tool for achieving sustainable development and fighting poverty. This is a step towards achieving the UN sustainable development goals for 2030.

CONCLUSIONS

The roles played by Diaspora in the development, poverty reduction, nation building and reconstruction of their countries of origin are significant. These roles had been extensively covered in the literature, but not yet fully and suitably recognised by their host countries or their countries of origin.

However, these roles are uni-directional in the sense that they reflect the contribution of Diaspora towards their countries of origin. They do not recognise or reflect the benefits that host countries gain from hosting Diaspora in terms of the skill and innovation they bring and contribution to the local economy in the country of destination.

More importantly, although these roles give the Diaspora some satisfaction through improving the conditions in their countries of origin, they do not fulfil the legitimate ambitions of the Diaspora of improving their own lives and investing their wealth for their own benefit and the benefit of their families. As such, they fall short of using the full potential of Diaspora and risk their exploitation for the political and economic aims of the countries of origin and residence alike.

To get out of this trap, and in an attempt to give the Diaspora an alternative route for contribution and investment, we advocate a three-way Public Private Partnership Model between the Diaspora, host countries and countries of origin. The model presents the Diaspora as International Agents for Development in a Public Private Partnership between equals with the governments of their host countries and countries of origin. This partnership works collaboratively in an integrated manner to resolve inhibitors and build enablers to economic growth, both in host countries and countries of origin.

The model sees and recognises the Diaspora as International Agents for Development. It can be readily replicated in economic, social and political arenas in complementary or isolated terms. It can also be used as a vehicle for knowledge and technology transfer.

However, for the model to work as designed, it should have clear objectives and targets, needs to be a partnership between equals, operate in a transparent democratic environment, and the role of Diaspora needs to be recognised and legalised in both the countries of origin and host countries.

Although the model is universally applicable, it is of special interest to developing and under-developed countries as it aims to tackle developmental issues, such as making investment while building capacity, driving development, transferring technology and helping to formulate industrial and economic strategies.

The model presents the Diaspora, in partnership with their host countries and countries of origin, as a potential tool for achieving sustainable development and fighting poverty. This is a step towards achieving the UN sustainable development goals for 2030.

REFERENCES

Cummins, J.U. and Provost, C. (2011), Talk point: Development and the diaspora, Article published by the *Guardian* Newspapaer @ https://www.theguardian.com/global-development/2011/apr/12/migration-diaspora-development-impact, Visited on 13/08/2017.

Dafa'Alla, A.A. (2016), Review of the Contribution and Role of the Manufacturing Sector in the Sudanese Economy, Proceedings of the 3rd Sudanese Diaspora International Conference, London, 25–26 July 2016 on *The Critical Role of Diaspora in International Scientific Cooperation with the Country of Origin*, edited by Allam Ahmed, 2016, pp. 239–55.

Dafa'Alla, A.A., Hussein, E.S. and Adam, M.A.A. (2016), Towards an effective industrialisation Policy in the Sudan, *International Journal of Sudan Research (IJSR)*, Vol. 7, No. 2, pp. 85–102.

DeWind, J. and Holdaway, J. (2005), Internal and International Migration in Economic Development, report No. UN/POP/MIG-FCM/2005/11 on the *4th Coordination Meeting on International Migration*, published by the Population Division, Department of Economic and Social Affairs, United Nations Secretariat, New York, 26027 Oct 2005.

Diaspora Alliance (2012), *Moving forward by looking back – Overview of the Global Diaspora Forum 2012*, published by the International Diaspora Engagement Alliance @ http://www.diasporaalliance.org/global-diaspora-forum-2012/, Visited on 21/08/2017.

Diaspora Matters (2011), *Why Diaspora are Important – Invited Public online Discussion*. Organised and published by DiasporaMatters @ http://www.diasporamatters.com/why-diasporas-are-important/, Visited on 21/08/2017.

Dustmann, C. and Frattini, T. (2014), The fiscal effects of immigration to the UK, *The Economic Journal*, published by the *Royal Economic Society*, Vol. 124, No. 580, pp. F593–F643. Also published in summary as Positive economic impact of UK immigration from the European Union: new evidence, in UCL News @ http://www.ucl.ac.uk/news/news-articles/1114/051114-economic-impact-EU-immigration, Visited on 23/08/2017.

Hinojosa-Ojeda, R. (2017), *Creating Virtuous Cycle of Transnational Migration, Remittances and Sustainable Development*, Presentation during Panel Discussion at the 4th Diaspora International Conference, London, 8 July 2017. Also, for video recording, see https://www.youtube.com/channel/UCvqfrbcFD-PFaerZZ2n8GKrQ, Visited on 19/09/2017.

Madichie, C. (2016), Diaspora contribution to achieving the SDGs, *GREAT Insights Magazine*, Vol. 5, No. 5, pp. 23–24, October/November 2016.

Newland, K. and Patrick, E. (2004), Beyond Remittances: The Role of Diaspora in Poverty Reduction in their countries of origin, A scoping study by the Migration Policy Institute for the Department of International Development, http://www.migrationpolicy.org/research/beyond-remittances-role-diaspora-poverty-reduction-their-countries-origin, Visited on 19/08/2017.

OECD (2010), Economy: Developing countries set to account for nearly 60% of world GDP by 2030, according to new estimates, published @ http://www.oecd.org/dev/pgd/economydevelopingcountriesset-toaccountfornearly60ofworldgdpby2030accordingtonewestimates.htm Visited on 19/08/2017.

Raghuram, P. (2009), Which Migration, What Development? Unsettling the edifice of Migration and Development, *Population, Space and Place*, Vol. 15, No. 2, pp. 103–17.

Sinatti, G. and Horst, C. (2015), Migrants as Agents of Development: Diaspora Engagement Discourse and Practice in Europe, *Ethnicities*, Vol. 15, No. 1, pp. 134–52.

The Economist (2011), *The Magic of Diasporas*, an article appeared in the Leaders section of the print edition on 19 November 2011 and @ http://www.economist.com/node/21538742 Visited on 19/08/2017.

UN Documents: Gathering a body of global agreements (1987), On our common Future, Chapter 3: The Role of the International Economy, A/42/427 Annex, Compiled by the NGO committee on Education of the conference of NGOs from the UN websites. June 1987. Also see http://www.un-documents.net/ocf-03.htm Visited on 18/09/2017.

United Nations, Department of Economic and Social Affairs, Population Division (2016), International Migration Report 2015 (ST/ESA/SER.A/384) & International Migration Report 2015 Highlights (ST/ESA/SER.A/375), UN publication @ http://www.un.org/en/development/desa/population/migration/publications/migrationreport/docs/MigrationReport2015.pdf and http://www.un.org/en/development/desa/population/migration/publications/migrationreport/docs/MigrationReport2015_Highlights.pdf Visited on 20/08/2017.

Vertovec, S. (2005), *The Political Importance of Diasporas*, Published by the Migration Policy Institute @ http://www.migrationpolicy.org/article/political-importance-diasporas Visited on 19/08/2017.

BIOGRAPHY

Dr Adil A. Dafa'Alla (PhD; C.Eng.; EurIng) graduated in Mechanical Engineering from the University of Khartoum, Sudan in 1981. He did postgraduate studies at UMIST, England, where he was awarded his PhD in 1988. Dr Dafa'Alla joined Airbus UK Ltd in 1996. He has vast academic and industrial experience. As part of his quest for continuous development, he has become a Chartered Engineer (C.Eng.) followed by EurIng testimony to his high standard of professional experience and conduct. His research interests cover aspects of CFD, aircraft safety as well as airport capacity planning issues. Coming from a Sudanese background, he also has a special interest in topics related to education, industry and sustainable development in Africa. His research activities are reported in a number of international journals and conferences in addition to many technical reports. He is an active member of WASD, and has been Associate Editor of its flagship journal, WRSTSD, since its inception in 2003.

Elmouiz Siddeg Hussein (BSc (Hons), MSc) is a Mechanical Engineering graduate of the University of Khartoum, Sudan (1999). He then gained work experience as a Mechanical Engineer at a private workshop in Khartoum North, Sudan. During this period, he also worked as a part-time Teaching Assistant at the Faculty of Engineering, University of Khartoum. He subsequently moved to the University of Portsmouth, UK, to do his MSc in Advanced Manufacturing Technology (2003–2004). In 2006, he joined Airbus UK as a Manufacturing Engineer. Currently, he develops and integrates industrial systems for the A350XWB Wing, develops and optimises business processes, and manages industrial risk.

GOAL 16

PEACE, JUSTICE AND STRONG INSTITUTIONS

SUSTAINABLE ECONOMIC DEVELOPMENT IN POST-CONFLICT COLOMBIA

Vilma Dahiana Bedoya Bahamón*

International Business Professional
University of Tolima, Colombia
Avenida 3ª N°40N-166 Cali, Colombia
Bedoya.vilma@hotmail.com

ABSTRACT

Purpose: As an independent writer, the author of this paper shares the vision of Colombian citizens about the history that caused the conflict between the Colombian State and extreme illegal left-wing groups, Colombians' efforts to build a better country through peace, and how the different economic actors could contribute to the sustainability of this social project that has a transversal relationship with all the characters and institutions in this South American country.

Approach: The research is focused on the compilation of historical and economic data about the Colombian Conflict, and the recent advances in the consolidation of a sustainable peace in Colombia. The research is based on official information and other journalist sources.

Findings: The paper suggests an analysis of the history of the Colombian conflict, its economic implications for the local people, and the main strategies implemented by the government to promote the inversion of the private sector and their more active participation in the post-conflict scenario.

Practical implications: This publication shares an independent view of past and current Colombian facts, its hard and long process to obtain peace and equitable life conditions for its people, and future perspectives with the international community. Among others, it considers that international support and recognition of the accomplished purposes, in the prospect of a peaceful country for the construction of a sustainable peace, are fundamental for the promotion of enterprise and growth of foreign investment in Colombia.

Originality/value: The paper offers a fresh and easy content, and gives the reader a real perspective of the peace process in Colombia, linking the historical, economic and social facts that contributed to the beginning and end of a conflict that impacted the lives of more than three generations. This paper is dedicated to all who want to learn more about Colombian history, and who want to work in the project of a more equitable Colombia.

Keywords: Colombia; post-Conflict; peace; economic sustainability; proColombia; coffee

INTRODUCTION

The contribution that private enterprises and the government make in the economical dynamisation of the most devastated regions as result of the war between the Colombian State and illegal armed groups, will be translated into the construction of a durable and sustainable peace, in which the agricultural sector will be the main driving force.

It is important to consider the efforts that organisations such as ProColombia are investing in the promotion of exports of Small and Medium Enterprises (SMEs), as a basis of the country's economic growth. That economic strength will ensure the continuity of the recently signed peace agreement with the FARC guerrillas, and the opportunity to establish peace negotiations with other illegal groups.

Contributing to the sustainable construction of the post-conflict economy, with projects such as coffee bean production for exports sales, will be the best way of attracting the community's interest in a peaceful coexistence in the post-conflict scenario.

Colombian people have learnt their lesson. For decades our people have lived in fear, wondering whether the next bomb would explode near their home. Living in a province like Tolima meant living in fear, especially during the years 1994–2012; this chaos caused an innumerable number of problems. Among others, the concentration of displaced people from the mountains and farms to the cities, and the unemployment as a result: insecurity began to increase. However, at the same time, Government efforts were canalised to attack the enemy. That enemy did not come from outside; war is always war from wherever the enemy comes.

When your "enemy" is your own compatriot, things are different. The fight is not because of aims to expand territory, as happens in the majority of wars between one country and another; here the fight was among brothers, born in the same land, blood from the same body.

When the different actors of the conflict realised this, they gave themselves the chance of being close to one another, to stop the sound of guns and begin to hear the "enemy's" arguments. Instead of killing them before they spoke, they turned into a more developed society, still under construction, but with the aim of growing in the values of peace and equity.

This work presents a brief history of the Colombian conflict to the international community, the origins of the actual peace agreement between the Colombian Government and the FARC-EP guerrillas, and finally offers some insights about the importance of the socio-economic strategy development in the agreements as key factors to ensure a stable and durable peace.

THE HISTORY OF THE COLOMBIAN WAR AND THE ORIGIN OF THE FINAL PEACE AGREEMENT WITH THE FARC-EP

Colombia as a country began its history as independent country around 1819 with the victory of the Bridge of Boyacá on 7th August of that year. This was when the liberators General Simón Bolivar and General Francisco de Paula Santander settled the route up to the foundation of a Democratic Republic of the New Colombia, as it was known until then.

As a consequence of its colonial origin, the country carried the scarf of innumerable social problems that involved some of the following actors: African slaves, an indigenous and growing population of mixed native-Spanish people (known as 'criollos'), who were the protagonists in the declaration of independence from the Spanish Crown in the middle of the 19th century (Colombia hoy — Etapas y sentido de la historia de Colombia, 1996)[1].

We could affirm that the origin of the Colombian conflict comes from its foundation itself. To be exact, however, this was around 60 years ago, when a group of farmers, most of them analphabetic and underestimated by the central national government, armed themselves with ideals of an equitable distribution of land, better quality of life, education and access to basic services. At least these were their fundamentals at the beginning of the 1960s, when under the command of Manuel Marulanda Vélez, and with no more than 50 members, the FARC-EP (Colombian Revolutionary Armed Forces — People's Army) was founded in the region of Marquetalia South of Tolima Department[2].

Before and after that moment, the conflict against the State by the extreme left guerrillas and paramilitary groups was always a part of Colombian reality. The conflicts

---

[1]All the historic facts of the colonial period came from this referenced essay.
[2]The above concept came from the lecture of the FARC EP website, sección quiénes somos.

were occasioned by intolerance among right and left political positions that caused suffering among the civilians who were in the middle of the war.

In the last decades of the FARC-EP, its participation in drug trafficking activities increased. This meant that the real purpose of its fight, i.e., its political stance and the repression of the State, was lost. The State was then looking to put an end to the influence of the 'narco-guerrilla' by systematically eliminating the principal war leaders of this group; they were supported by the government of the United States of America with programmes such as Plan Colombia (signed in 2000 under Bill Clinton's presidency).

Until the consolidation of the final peace agreement, peace negotiations were chaotic and often failed. There had been about seven attempts for a peace agreement since 1982, most of them promoted by civilians, victims, the Catholic Church and the Colombian Government itself (Lopez and Cueter, 2016).

One of the most remembered peace negotiations was during President Andrés Pastrana's administration from 1998 to 2002. Under a model of distension areas, the FARC-EP guerrillas had time and space to become strong enough to kidnap a commercial aeroplane and make it land on a rural runway. They released most of the passengers, but kept a Senator called Jorge Eduardo Gechem. That was the end of the peace attempt, but also the beginning of one of the hardest armed campaigns during which the Government consolidated its forces, breaking the guerrilla structure and bringing them to the recent peace dialogues established in 2012. This was carried out with the cooperation of foreign governments such as Cuba and Norway.

The negotiations for signing the present agreement were developed under war conditions; there was a good result, at least for the people who inhabit rural areas. In the cities life continues almost the same; this is because the war was concentrated in the mountains and hard to access territories. Only occasionally were the principal cities such as Bogotá and Cali under attack during the worst periods of the war.

During the post-conflict period, the members of the oldest communist guerrilla unit in the world began their new lives as a political party and as civil citizens. They tried to compensate their victims, perhaps not always in the way society expected, but definitely far from the violent trajectory they followed during their illegal existence.

It is possible that, in the future, other illegal groups will follow the same road to peace negotiations as the EPL (Popular Liberation Army), which closely observed the process with the FARC-EP. With the integration of the FARC into civilian life, its first steps towards the consolidation of a political party, founded under the communist ideologies in a clearly conservative and electorally traditional country as Colombia, are the ingredients of the new political perspective that common Colombians are experiencing for the first time in many years.

The last attempt of such a change was in the 1980s, when the negotiations between President Belisario Betancourt and the FARC-EP guerrillas resulted in the instauration of a political party for this communist group called "Patriotic Union (UP)" in 1984.

Unfortunately, this all turned into chaos, when the government lost its ability to provide accurate protection to the leaders of the party. As a result, about 3,000 militants were illegally executed, including two presidential candidates from this party.

Despite the negativism of past events, Colombians still believe that a peaceful co-existence could be a reality in the country, jointly working for the same purpose – to become a more equitable society with the same opportunities for each individual.

Implications of War on the Rural Economy

As a result of the violent actions, thousands of families had to leave their productive lands travelling principally to the main cities of Bogotá, Cali and Medellín where, day-by-day, the unemployment rates got higher. This is because most of them were there working under informal conditions, earning less than required to feed their families; this still happens in Colombia.

As a result of the forced mobilisation of those families, land productivity decreased and the prices of food and primary raw materials for industrial production were higher than expected.

Entrepreneurs located in areas such as Tolima, Cauca, and Guaviare were forced, against their will, to periodically pay the guerrillas to finance the war. Obviously if they did not pay they would have to suffer the consequences; these consequences included murders and terrorist acts such as bombs in the commercial areas, all under the law of silence.

Even companies located in the cities had problems in providing their products to remote areas of the country, because the guerrillas also forced them to pay for the right to distribute their merchandise in the regions.

The costs of transportation were also a problem in these areas, because of the low presence of the State infrastructure inversions. This was especially true after 2002, when the National Armed Forces fought harder against the illegal groups. Again the people in the middle just had to run away.

Figures for this period are overwhelming. There were 6 million deaths during the approximately 55 year war, millions of displaced civilians were forced to live in cities with no land to work, most of them within the misery belts of cities such as Bogotá, Medellín and Cali.

Private Enterprise and Government Roles in Post-Conflict Colombia

The peace agreement includes specific strategies to facilitate the process of economic reactivation of the demobilised people, securing their integration into the economic system and return to civilian life. In consequence, the inversions in the rural economy are the way by which new economic players can successfully contribute to the sustainable construction of the post-conflict economy and the peaceful coexistence among the protagonists and their victims.

The main participants of this economic project are the groups of reinserted people, now with civilian status, but knowing almost nothing about how they should begin to build their new life. As stated by the Conpes document (National Reintegration Policy 2008), reintegration is defined as the process through which the demobilised people acquire civilian status, gain employment and, as one of the main objectives of the National Social and Economic Reintegration Policy, contribute to the development of skills and abilities that allow their successful insertion to the labour market for the generation of their own incomes, as part of the Colombian National Development. It demonstrates the importance of private enterprises in the post-conflict scenario as generators of employment.

According to the Final Agreement itself (Síntesis de los Acuerdos Alcanzados, 2016) and other legal mechanisms (Decreto 454 Ministerio del Trabajo República de Colombia, 2017) the reintegrated people will have the financial support to begin their new lives, including inversions for entrepreneurial projects and a high attention to rural initiatives with the purpose of incrementing the production of food and the eradication of illegal crops. These new Small and Medium Enterprises (SMEs) are now the opportunity to save lives and strengthen the micro and macroeconomic Colombian future.

Reintegration processes have been developed over the last 14 years for the National Agency for the Reintegration and Normalisation of the Colombian Government, as reported by them (La Reintegración, hechos y estadísticas — Datos a Junio de, 2017). They have reported that 18,129 ex-combatants from different illegal organisations voluntarily entered the programme; 70% of them are employed by 650 local companies. One of the most relevant figures is the comparison between the expense of having a prisoner and that person being reintegrated into society. The cost of maintaining a prisoner is about COP 17,000,000 (approximately US$5,800); the same concept is reduced to COP 5,700,000 by offering minimum conditions of life to reinserted people.

Just with that inversion, an average 76% of the participants in the reintegration process retain lawful behaviour, reducing the proportion of deaths to a third of demobilised people that did not join the reintegration programme. The participants of the reintegration programme also say they feel an increase of 90% in their quality of life. Another important fact to consider is that 90% of the programme's participants arrived with psychosocial diseases, but after finishing the programme, 93% of them had overcome that situation.

One of the regions where coffee has had a long history with people's lives is the South of Tolima, the place where it all began. Today, Tolima is offering an exemplary lesson of perseverance, showing how different associations of coffee bean producers had worked hard in the performance of high quality coffee to export to the rest of the world. Processed or as a raw material, coffee is once again the key to opening Colombia's doors to the rest of the world. With towns such as Planadas, Gaitania and Chaparral, Tolima are pioneers in the region with different brands of their special manufactured coffee.

Meanwhile, organisations such as ProColombia, the Exports and Tourism Investment Country Brand, are promoting the products of Colombian entrepreneurs worldwide. Investments in coffee projects have become signs in the most affected territories of Colombia in overcoming poverty, including vulnerable communities, protagonists and their victims jointly working for the same purposes.

According to this organisation (Análisis de las Exportaciones Colombianas, informe enero – octubre de 2016), during 2016 (January–October), coffee export sales were US$1,779 million, representing 15% of the country's non-mining and energy exports. This was followed by other products such as fresh flowers (9.6%) and bananas US$734 million (6.4%). The United States, with a participation of 27.3%, was the principal commercial destination, followed by Ecuador, Perú and Mexico. These figures show that there is still a lot of work to do in economic terms, but it has to be seen as an opportunity to grow instead of as a weakness.

Some of the activities that ProColombia have developed to contribute to the economic sustainability of exports involve the promotion of Colombian products in foreign countries, support for entrepreneurs participating in issues such as international trade, and offering services such as business meetings and opening spaces for networking between buyers and sellers, and entrepreneurial consultancy.

CONCLUSIONS

Colombia is a country with several times more geographical and environmental advantages than other nations in the region. Even with a prolonged war, Colombia is one of the most solid democracies in the whole of South America, with an economic structure that made it an attractive place to the foreign inversion in diverse industries. This is not just in agriculture but also in medicine and the services industry. The culture of hard work and immense internal force pushes the Colombian people to become a more profitable society.

The signing of the peace agreement was a question of time. Perhaps from a short term view the war probably would not have ended, but analysing the length of the country's history, we can see that the efforts to find common points were stronger than the aim of a long illogical fight.

The problem of Colombia as stated by Francisco de Roux in the article "La paz llama a la equidad" (Peace calls to equity), is not a problem of poverty, but is a problem of lack of consciousness for compatriots' needs, to become closer to the suffering of others and begin to work together to find a collective solution.

Now it is time for private enterprises, civil society and even the international community to turn to see the side where the most vulnerable of us live, to know their problems and to contribute directly or indirectly to the construction of a more equal social web, where all points of view can be heard and respected.

That is the only manner through which a prolonged conflict can be prevented. It is true that there are still many problems, including (among others) the drugs traffic, corruption and slavery, but as a society it is important to understand that every single step in the right direction counts towards reaching the common objectives.

REFERENCES

Análisis de las Exportaciones Colombianas, informe enero — octubre de (2016), Procolombia Exportaciones, Turismo e Inversión, Ministerio de Industria y Comercio, Bogotá, Colombia. pages 6 and 10.

Decreto 454 Ministerio del Trabajo República de Colombia (2017), Gobierno de la República de Colombia, Bogotá.

Francisco de Roux, La paz llama a la equidad (2017), Retrieved from http://www.eltiempo.com/opinion/columnistas/francisco-de-roux/la-paz-llama-a-la-igualdad-101414

La Reintegración, hechos y estadísticas — Datos a Junio de (2017), Retrieved from http://www.reintegracion.gov.co/es/la-reintegracion/Paginas/cifras.aspx

López Montaño Cecilia, Cueter Nicolás. "¿Por qué Santos sí pudo dialogar con las Farc?" Periodico El Tiempo (30.09.2016), Retrieved from http://www.eltiempo.com/politica/proceso-de-paz/procesos-de-paz-en-colombia-44168

Melo González, Jorge Orlando, Jaramillo Uribe Jaime (1996), Colombia hoy - Etapas y sentido de la historia de Colombia (Período Colonial, La Gran Colombia, 1820—1830, La República de la Nueva Granada, 1830—1850, Las reformas liberales de 1850...)

Política Nacional de Reintegración Social y Económica para personas y grupos armados ilegales Documento Conpes 3454 (2008), Consejo Nacional de Política Económica y Social República de Colombia Departamento Nacional de Planeación, Bogotá, Colombia.

Política Nacional de Reintegración Social y Económica para personas y grupos armados ilegales Documento Conpes 3454, 2008.

"¿Por qué Santos sí pudo dialogar con las Farc?" (30.09.2016), Retrieved from http://www.eltiempo.com/politica/proceso-de-paz/procesos-de-paz-en-colombia-44168

"Quiénes somos y por qué luchamos" (29.08.2017), Secretariado Nacional de las FARC-EP Retrieved from http://www.farc-ep.co/nosotros.html

Síntesis-Definitiva Acuerdo de Paz (2016), page 9 Retrieved from http://www.acuerdodepaz.gov.co/sites/all/themes/nexus/files/Sintesis-Definitiva.pdf

BIOGRAPHY

Vilma D. Bedoya is an International Business Professional from the University of Tolima. During her bachelor studies, Vilma was actively involved in projects directed to student welfare, with the objective of decreasing their leaving rate. Activities included cultural events and systems to ensure access to feeding services.

Currently Ms Bedoya is a student of the Specialisation in Project Management of the Open and Distance National University of Colombia, and employee of one of the most relevant industrial producers of edible oils and fats in her country.

Since 2014, she has developed volunteer activities related to export councillorship to agricultural producers in the region of South Tolima Colombia, especially with coffee farmers. As a member of the DAAD Alumni Network, Bedoya has participated in several initiatives such as virtual international projects. She has also attended national and international seminars and conferences related to the entrepreneurial promotion of exports from the agro-industrial sector.

GOALS 6/7/13/14/15

CLEAN WATER AND SANITATION/ AFFORDABLE AND CLEAN ENERGY/ CLIMATE ACTION/LIFE BELOW WATER/ LIFE ON LAND

RENEWABLE ENERGY FOR SUSTAINABLE DEVELOPMENT AND THE IMPACT ON THE GLOBAL ECONOMIC SYSTEM

SHAWQI AL DALLAL[*]

College of Graduate Studies and Research
Ahlia University, PO Box 10878
Manama, Kingdom of Bahrain
shaldallal@gmail.com

ABSTRACT

Purpose: Energy has been always the main driver of human civilisation. This paper highlights the impact of switching from fossil fuel to renewable energy on the global economic system.

Methodology: In this paper, we discuss the unavoidable future reliance on renewable energy sources. This is achieved by investigating the global energy needs map and the future market shaped by the new technological development, and its impact on the global economic system.

Findings: This work investigates the influence of oil companies worldwide on the global economic system, and their struggle for survival when faced with ever rising and developing renewable energy systems. However, even for the foreseeable future, oil companies will not completely vanish; this is because certain oil products are used in applications and uses beyond the reach of renewable energies. In this work we also highlight the efforts deployed to produce environmentally friendly nuclear energy.

[*]Corresponding Author

Value: Energy is a key factor in shaping the development of nations. There is a global consensus on the negative impact of fossil fuel on the environment, and on the importance of developing alternative clean energies.

Keywords: Renewable energy; Sustainable Development; Global economic system; Solar energy; Nuclear energy

INTRODUCTION

Since antiquity, energy has always been the source of advancement of civilisations. It is the driver of humankind to excel in various disciplines related to their daily life. In the first part of this paper we discuss the problem of harnessing energy as a measure for classifying the degree of advancement of cosmic civilisations, and the position of the Planet Earth in this classification.

Wood and coal were the main sources of energy for millennia. However, certain historians claim that the earliest oil wells were drilled in China in 347AD or earlier (Dalvi, 2015). The oil was burned to evaporate brine and produce salt. Ancient records of China and Japan referred to the allusions of using natural gas for lighting and heating. Petroleum was known as *burning water* in Japan in the 7th century (Chisholm, 1911). Fossil fuel today constitutes the main source of energy. Oil, gas, and coal are among the main drivers of the economic system worldwide, and they are also the main threat to the environment. In the second part of this paper we highlight the available gas and oil reserves in various countries, and emphasise their potential impact on the environment and on the stability of the world's economic system. Nuclear ores, such as uranium and thorium, have been attractive to many advanced countries as a source of energy. The impact of using nuclear fission or thorium to produce energy is highlighted and discussed.

In the third part of this paper, we introduce solar energy as a clean everlasting source of energy. The solar energy distribution around the globe and its consequences are discussed.

In the last part of this paper, we discuss how the global oil and gas companies impact the world economy.

ENERGY: A COSMIC PERSPECTIVE

It is interesting to identify the level of Earth's future energy needs. Harnessing available energy resources while safeguarding the environment will be one of the major challenges that humanity needs to seek for survival. Energy consumption is regarded by scientists as a viable element for measuring the degree of advancement of a cosmic civilisation. Recent astronomical observations using different methods to discover extra solar planets reveal the existence of billions of planets in our galaxy alone. Statistically, using the Drake equation (Burchell, 2006), an important number of advanced cosmic civilisations exist that are capable of establishing radio or other means of intergalactic communication and beyond. The Kardashev scale is designed to measure the level of technological advancement of a civilisation based on the amount of energy used for communication. The scale identifies three categories of civilisation (Kardashev, 1964):

- **Type I civilisation**, also called a planetary civilisation, can harness all of the energy received from the parent star. In the case of the Sun, this energy amounts to 7×10^{17} watts; this is five orders of magnitude higher than the amount presently attained on Earth (4×1012 watts) (Kardashev, 1964);
- **Type II civilisation**, also called a stellar civilisation, can harness all the energy produced by its parent star. In the case of the Sun, the energy utilisation would then be comparable to its luminosity, or 4×10^{26} watts (Lemarchand, 1994);
- **Type III civilisation**, also called a galactic civilisation, can harness energy on the scale of its entire host galaxy. For our galaxy, the energy utilisation would then be comparable to the luminosity of the entire Milky Way, or about 4×10^{37} watts (Lemarchand, 1994).

Michio Kaku suggested that humans may attain Type I status in 100–200 years, Type II status in a few thousand years, and Type III status in 100,000 to a million years (Kaku, 2010).

The above energy consumption of the planet Earth traces a viable energy road map for future generations. There are many implications resulting from human civilisation undergoing large-scale transitions. As an example, the transition between Kardashev scale levels could potentially lead to a dramatic period of social upheaval, because it may entail surpassing the ultimate limits of the resources available in a civilisation's existing territory. Scientists speculate that the transition from a Type 0 to a Type I civilisation might carry a strong risk of self-destruction, since, in some scenarios, the room for further expansion on the civilisation's home planet becomes highly restricted (Dyson, 1960).

Figure 1 shows the total world annual primary energy consumption. It increases almost linearly at an annual rate of 133 million tonnes equivalent. The total consumption in 2008 amounted to 11,000 billion barrel equivalent. Extrapolating the data, we obtain a total energy consumption of 12,200 billion barrels for the year 2017.

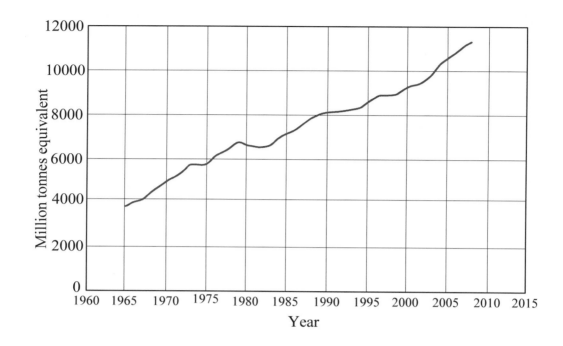

Figure 1 Total World Annual Primary Energy Consumption
Source: http://www.bp.com/assets/bp_internet/globalbp/globalbp_uk_english/reports

The excessive consumption of energy without adequate disposal of heat, for example, could affect the planet Earth when approaching a Type I civilisation, in a way that is unsuitable to the biology of the dominant life-forms and food chains. The rise of sea temperature to 35°C on planet Earth, for example, would jeopardise marine life. As a conclusion, the Kardashev scale is a viable tool for measuring the degree of advancement of a civilisation.

FOSSIL SOURCES OF ENERGY

Oil, gas, coal, uranium, and other nuclear materials are the main sources of energy today. A common feature of these sources is their negative impact on the environment. However, an important number of developed countries depend heavily on fossil fuel resources, and a switch to clean energy for the foreseen future is restricted to certain sectors where a balance between economy and pressure from environmental bodies play a major part. In the following sections, we highlight the reserves and energy production from different types of fossil fuel. We shall also address the contribution and impact of each of these sources of energy.

Oil and Gas

Oil and gas today constitute the main fossil fuels used by different countries to satisfy their energy needs. The market for these energy sources shapes the world economy, and is at the origin of major conflicts after World War II. In 2016, the total world oil reserve was 1,492 billion barrels. The OPEC share amounted to 81% of the total oil world reserve. Among the most oil productive OPEC countries are Venezuela, Saudi Arabia, Iran, Iraq, Kuwait, and United Arab Emirates. Their total oil reserve was 1,073.73 billion barrels, or about 72% of the total world oil reserves. The trend in the change of oil reserves for the top five countries (1980–2013) is shown in Figure 2.

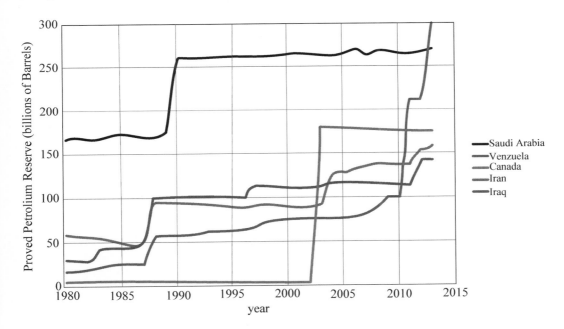

Figure 2   Trends in Proven Petroleum Reserves, Top Five Countries, 1980–2013
Source: Data from US Energy Information Administration

The world natural gas reserves amounted to 200 trillion cubic metres in 2012. They are increasing at a constant rate of about 3.4 trillion cubic meters a year, as shown in Figure 3. Russia, Iran, Qatar, USA, and Saudi Arabia are at the top of the list of natural gas reserves owners.

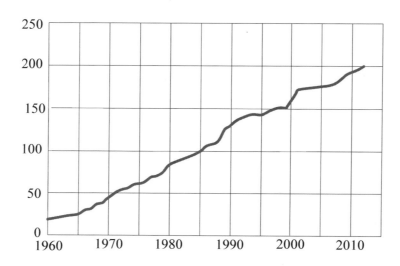

Figure 3   World Natural Proven Gas Reserves (1960−2012)
Source: OPEC

The proven gas reserves in the top five gas producing countries is shown in Figure 4: Russia has by far the greatest proven gas reserves.

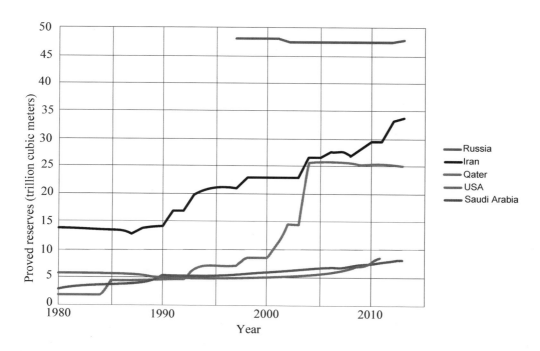

Figure 4   Proven Gas Reserves in the Top Five Countries, 1980−2013
Source: US AIA

Coal Reserves

Planet Earth has an appreciable amount of coal reserves: these reserves are sufficient to meet 153 years of global production. The United States alone possesses 25% of the total world coal reserves. It mined about 900 million tonnes in 2015, and most is destined for domestic electricity generation. The USA, Russia, China, India, Australia, and South Africa are among the leading countries of coal reserves (see Table 1).

Of all the fossil-fuel sources, coal is the least expensive for its energy content, and it constitutes a major factor in the cost of electricity in the United States. However, CO_2 emissions may have a drastic implication on the environment. To reduce the effect of harmful emissions, gases are allowed to pass through scrubbers or other developed technologies that remove pollutants. Even so, the smoke still contains nitrogen oxides and sulphur dioxides that cause smog and acid rain. Fortunately, advanced technologies are being developed to reduce harmful emissions. However, these new technologies are not equally developed among all countries. Pollution has no border and can contaminate the Earth's atmosphere with all known consequences. Coal makes up 42% of US electrical power generation and 65% in China (Morse, 2012).

Table 1   Coal Production in 2007

Rank	Country	Production	Share
	World	6395.6	100
1	China	2536.7	39.7
2	United States	1039.2	16.2
—	European Union	590.5	9.2
3	India	478.2	7.5
4	Australia	393.9	6.2
5	Russia	314.2	4.9
6	South Africa	269.4	4.2
7	Germany	201.9	3.2
8	Indonesia	174.8	2.7
9	Poland	145.8	2.3
10	Kazakhstan	94.4	1.5
11	Turkey	76.6	1.2

Source: Statistical Review of World Energy 2008

ENERGY FROM NUCLEAR FISSION

Nuclear fission was developed during the period from 1895 to 1945, with an accelerated pace during the last six of those years. Much of the efforts during the period 1939–45 were focused on the production of the atomic bomb. From 1945 research was concentrated on harnessing fission energy in a controlled fashion for naval propulsion and for generating electricity. An important number of countries have joined the nuclear fission club since 1945. Today, 16 countries depend on nuclear fission power for at least a quarter of their electricity needs. The United States alone produces 798TWh of nuclear power; France comes next with around 419TWh, representing three quarters of its power from nuclear energy. Other countries, such as the Czech Republic, Sweden, Switzerland, Belgium, Finland, Slovenia, Hungary, Ukraine, and Slovakia produce one third or more of their needs of power from nuclear fission. Figure 5 shows the nuclear generation via fission by country in 2015.

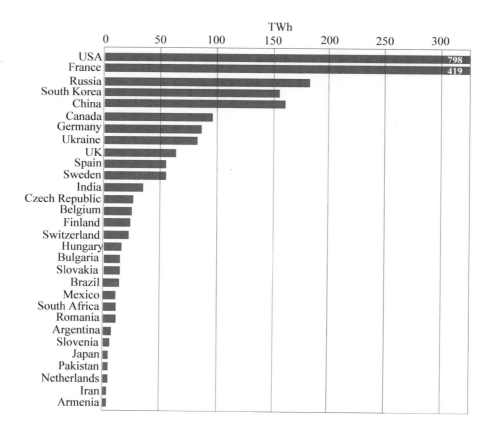

Figure 5   Nuclear Generation by Country (2015)
Source: IAEA PRIS Database

THORIUM-BASED NUCLEAR ENERGY

Thorium is a chemical element high up in the periodic table with atomic number 90. It was discovered in 1829 by Norwegian amateur mineralogist Morten Thrane Esmark, and identified by the Swedish chemist Jöns Jacob Berzelius in 1828. Thorium is slightly radioactive, and is found in small amounts in most rocks and soil. It is three times more abundant than uranium. Like uranium, it exhibits properties allowing it to be used as fuel. Thorium was formerly used as an alloying element in welding electrodes, and as a material in high-end optics and scientific instrumentation; it was also used as a light source in gas mantles. However, these uses become marginal when it was realised that thorium could replace uranium as a nuclear fuel in nuclear reactors.

The renewed interest in thorium has been highlighted in a number of scientific conferences. A nuclear reactor is fed with specific fissile isotopes to generate energy. The three most practical nuclear reactors are fuelled with uranium-235, plutonium-239, and uranium-233, transmuted from thorium-232. The latter is derived from natural mined thorium. It is believed that thorium is a key to developing a new generation of cleaner, safer nuclear power (The Energy From Thorium Foundation Thorium). The advantage of using thorium as a fuel for reactors is that it produces up to two orders of magnitude of nuclear waste)Moir and Teller, 2005(. Chinese scientists claim that hazardous waste will be a thousand times less than with uranium (Evans-Pritchard, 2010). At the same time, the radioactivity of the produced waste drops to a safe level

Table 2   World Thorium Reserves (2007)

Country	Tonnes	%
Australia	489,000	18.7%
USA	400,000	15.3%
Turkey	344,000	13.2%
India	319,000	12.2%
Brazil	302,000	11.6%
Venezuela	300,000	11.5%
Norway	132,000	5.1%
Egypt	100,000	3.8%
Russia	75,000	2.9%
Greenland (Denmark)	54,000	2.1%
Canada	44,000	1.7%
South Africa	18,000	0.7%
Other countries	33,000	1.2%
World Total	2,610,000	100.0%

Source: Data taken from Uranium 2007: Resources, Production and Demand, Nuclear Energy Agency (June 2008), NEA#6345 (ISBN 9789264047662). The 2009 figures are largely unchanged. Australian data from Thorium, in Australian Atlas of Minerals Resources, Mines & Processing Centers, Geoscience Australia

after just one or few hundred years. It is estimated that one tonne of thorium can generate as much energy as 200 tonnes of uranium or 3,500,000 tonnes of coal (Evans-Pritchard, 2013). Thorium is generally more cost efficient than uranium and a less environmentally damaging fuel source. Its mining is also easier than mining uranium, and less dangerous. On the other hand, thorium reactor's by-products are not suitable for making a practical nuclear bomb, and thus do not constitute a threat of nuclear weapon proliferation or the production of radioactive pollution. Table 2 below shows the world thorium reserves in 2007.

The above figures are reserves referring to the amount of thorium inventoried so far and estimated to be extractable at current market prices. The total amount of thorium existing in the Earth's crust amounts to 3×10^{19} tonnes (Ragheb, 2011; American Geophysical Union, 2007). Mining this quantity of thorium is enough to move the planet Earth towards a Type I civilisation.

RENEWABLE ENERGIES

Renewable energy is any type of energy that is naturally replenished on a human timescale. This includes direct sunlight, wind, geothermal heat, waves, tides, and nuclear fusion. We shall discuss in this paper some of these energy sources and highlight their impact on the environment and the well-being of mankind in general.

Solar Energy

The Sun is a main sequence star that fuses hydrogen to produce radiant light and heat. Active solar energy is harnessed using a range of ever-evolving technologies, including photovoltaic systems, concentrated solar radiation, solar water heating, and many other applications. Passive solar techniques include heat insulating systems, orientation of buildings, and using materials with favourable thermal properties.

In 2011, the International Energy Agency declared that, "the development of affordable, inexhaustible and clean solar energy technologies will have huge longer-term benefits. It will increase countries' energy security through reliance on an indigenous, inexhaustible and mostly important-independent resource, enhance sustainability, reduce pollution, lower the mitigating global warming, and keep fossil fuel prices lower than otherwise. These advantages are global. Hence the additional costs of the incentives for early deployment should be considered learning investments; they must be wisely spent and need to be widely shared" (Solar Energy Perspectives). This statement highlights the importance of clean energy sources in establishing a secure and safe world economic system.

The planet Earth receives a huge amount of solar radiation. The energy available makes this a highly attractive source of electricity. In 2000, the United Nations Development Program found that the annual solar energy was 1575−49837 exajoules (EJ = 10^{18} joules). This exceeds world energy consumption several times over; consumption was 559.8 EJ in 2012. The upper atmosphere of Earth receives 174 petawatts (PW) of incoming solar radiation, 30% of which is reflected back to space while the rest is absorbed by the clouds, oceans and land. The solar spectrum at the Earth's surface falls mostly in visible and near infrared regions of the spectrum, with a small amount in the ultraviolet region. Most of the world's population occupies areas with insolation levels of 150−300 watts/m^2, or equivalently 3.5 to 7.0kWh/m^2 per day.

The total annual solar energy absorbed by the Earth's atmosphere, ocean and land masses amounts to approximately 3,850,000 exajoules. In 2002, this amount of energy exceeded the total energy consumed worldwide during one year in one hour. The amount of energy reaching the surface of Earth is so vast that in one year it is about twice as much as will ever be obtained from all of Earth's non-renewable resources of oil, natural gas, coal, and mined uranium combined. Table 3 below shows the annual solar energy potential by region.

Table 3 Annual Solar Energy Potential by Region (Exajoule)

Maximum	Minimum	Region
7410	181.1	North America
3385	112.6	Latin America and Caribbean
914	25.1	Western Europe
154	4.5	Central and Eastern Europe
8655	199.3	Former Soviet Union
11060	412.4	Middle East and North Africa
9528	371.9	Sub-Saharan Africa
994	41.0	Pacific Asia
1339	38.8	South Asia
4135	115.5	Centrally Planned Asia
2263	72.6	Pacific OECD

Source: United Nations Development Programme and World Energy Council, 2000

The above table reveals that the Middle East and North Africa enjoy the highest annual solar energy potential. How do these important data impact the world future economy if renewable energies emerge as the main source of energy in the future? To answer this question we have to investigate the impact of big oil and gas companies on the global economic system.

GLOBAL OIL AND GAS COMPANIES IMPACTING THE WORLD ECONOMY

Oil and gas companies began to shape the world economy soon after World War II. They become the main driver of economic systems and associated political issues. The various regional wars that the planet Earth witnessed after World War II were basically the fruit of everlasting efforts by the world's leading powers to control the sources of energy. There are 48 big gas and oil companies worldwide, with a total revenue in 2015 that amounted to US$6.130 trillion. This constitutes an important share of the world's economic system. Table 4 below shows the revenue of the top 10 oil and gas companies worldwide.

Table 4   Revenue of Oil and Gas Companies as of 2015

Company name	Revenue 2015 (US$ billion)
Saudi Aramco	478.00
Sinopec	454.99
China National Petroleum Corporation	428.62
PetroChina	367.982
Exxon Mobil	268.90
Royal Dutch Shell	265.00
Kuwait Petrolium Corporation	251.94
BP	222.80
Total SA	212.00

Source: Wikipedia and author's own work

Some of these companies shaped the whole economic system of the countries to which they belong. Others have a wider regional or even global influence. It is clear that a sudden switch to renewable energy would cause a collapse of the world's economic system. The transformation to a new global energy source therefore has to follow a gradual trend, whereby countries relying heavily on oil and gas as the main source of their economy can adjust themselves to the promotion of other sources of income. A smooth passage to a new world economic system requires joint global efforts to solve the problems impacting this transformation. Failure to achieve this task may result in the emergence of regional or global conflicts with unforeseen consequences.

On 1 November 2017, the IMF advised energy-rich Gulf economies to speed up their diversification away from oil. The Gulf Cooperation Council has been hit hard by the collapse in crude prices that provided a major part of their finances. Following this slump, GCC members undertook fiscal measures and reforms to cut public spending and boost non-oil revenues. This is just a glimpse of the alarming situation resulting from the collapse of oil prices. Countries around the world have to set a new strategy for their economic systems to cope with the ever growing dependence on renewable energy.

CONCLUSIONS

In this paper we highlighted the various aspects impacting the world's economic system resulting from the emergence of highly competing renewable energy sources. Renewable energies can be obtained with minimum cost from natural resources and have the potential to safeguard the environment. In the first part of this paper we discussed the advancement of the Earth's civilisation according to the Kardashev scale. It was found that the planet Earth needs 100 to 200 years to switch to a Type I cosmic civilisation; this transformation may entail the potential risk of global conflicts.

Fossil fuel is highly consumed today, resulting in an alarming increase in CO_2 gas that has a devastating effect as greenhouse gas. Energy from fission is limited by available uranium ore, and produces dangerous waste that is difficult to dispose of. On the other hand, Thorium is three times more abundant than uranium and produces much lower waste products. Fusion energy produces no nuclear waste, and can be obtained easily from hydrogen available in nature, but the technology to transfer it to a practical source of energy requires decades to come. On the other hand, solar energy and other renewable energies can be harnessed freely or with minimum cost.

The economy of many influential countries today relies on oil, gas and other fossil fuel sources. Oil and gas alone provide a revenue of about US$6 trillion, which constitutes an important portion of the global world economic system. A sudden switch to renewable energy may cause a collapse of the world's economic system with all related consequences.

REFERENCES

American Geophysical Union, Fall Meeting (2007), abstract #V33A-1161. *Mass and Composition of the Continental Crust.*

Burchell, M.J. (2006), W(h)ither the Drake equation?. *International Journal of Astrobiology,* Vol. 5, No. 3, pp. 243–50. Bibcode: 2006IJAsB...5..243B. doi:10.1017/S1473550406003107.

Chisholm, H. (Ed.) (1911), *Petroleum. Encyclopaedia Britannica (11th edn). Cambridge University Press.*

Dalvi, S. (2015), *Fundamentals of Oil & Gas Industry for Beginners.* Notion Press. ISBN 978-9352064199.

Dyson, F.J. (1960), Search for Artificial Stellar Sources of Infrared Radiation. *Science,* Vol. 131, No. 3414, pp. 1667–68. Bibcode: 1960Sci...131.1667D. PMID 17780673.doi:10.1126/science.131.3414.1667. Retrieved 30 January 2008.

Evans-Pritchard, A. (2010), Obama could kill fossil fuels overnight with a nuclear dash for thorium, *The Daily Telegraph,* UK, 29 August 2010.

Evans-Pritchard, A. (2013), Safe nuclear does exist, and China is leading the way with thorium, *The Telegraph*, UK, 20 March 2013.

Kaku, M. (2010), *The Physics of Interstellar Travel: To one day, reach the stars*. Retrieved 29 August 2010.

Kardashev, N.S. (1964), Transmission of Information by Extraterrestrial Civilizations. *Soviet Astronomy*, Vol. 8, p. 217. Bibcode: 1964SvA.....8..217K

Lemarchand, G.A. (1994), Detectability of Extraterrestrial Technological Activities. *SETI*-Quest, Vol. 1, No. 1, pp. 3–13. Coseti.1992.

Moir, R.W. and Teller, E. (2005), Thorium-fuelled Reactor Using Molten Salt Technology, *Journal of Nuclear Technology*, Vol. 151, p. 334.

Morse, R.K. (2012), Cleaning Up Coal, *Foreign Affairs*, Vol. 91, July/August 2012.

Ragheb, M. (12 August 2011), *Thorium Resources in Rare Earth Elements*. scribd.com.

Statistical Review of World Energy (2008), British Petroleum. Archived from the original on 27 July 2008.

The Energy From Thorium Foundation Thorium. *Energyfromthorium.com. 2010-08-30*. Retrieved 6 September 2013.

Energy and the challenge of sustainability *(PDF), United Nations Development Programme and* World Energy Council, *September 2000.*

BIOGRAPHY

Professor **Shawqi Al Dallal,** a Bahraini national, obtained his BSc in Electrical Engineering from Baghdad University, and a DEA, Doctorat d'Ingenière, Doctorat d'Etat from Universty Piere et Marie Curie, Paris, France. He is currently Dean of Graduate Studies and Research, Acting Dean of the College of Medical and Health Sciences, Ahlia University, (2010–present). Professor Al Dallal has organised twelve regional and international conferences, and has participated in more than seventy regional and international conferences. Professor Al Dallal teaches a wide spectrum of courses in Physics and Engineering, and has published over 116 papers in reputed international journals in the fields of Advanced Materials, Energy, Astronomy and Astrophysics, and Nanotechnology. He has authored books such as the *Encyclopedia of Astronomy and Astrophysics and Space Science*, other books on Astronomy, and a textbook on Laser Physics.

STRIVING FOR ENVIRONMENTAL EXCELLENCE BY CONTROLLING FUTURE BROWNFIELDS IN AFRICA SPECIFICALLY FOR ETHIOPIA: A GREY INCIDENCE DECISION-MAKING APPROACH

Mikiale Gebreslase*[1], Yuming Zhu[2]

Naveed Ahmad[3] and Dawit Bekele[4]

[1, 2, 3]School of Management
Northwestern Polytechnical University, Xi'an, China
[4]Faculty of Science and Technology
University of Newcastle, Australia
[1]eyjoshua21@mail.nwpu.edu.cn, [2]zym1886@nwpu.edu.cn
[3]naveedahmad@mail.nwpu.edu.cn and [4]dawit.bekele@newcastle.edu.au

ABSTRACT

Purpose: The increasing African population, and economic growth leading to urbanisation, continues to increase the need to redevelop brownfields as a strategy of encouraging the sustainable development of cities, in particular in Ethiopia. In the 21st century, most African countries have adopted an industry-led economy to support an ever increasing population growth and urbanisation; this involves using large volumes and types of hazardous chemicals. Accidental spills and damping of these chemicals leads to environmental contamination and, subsequently, to brownfields. This research reviewed key dimensions of the definition of brownfields

*Corresponding Author

in developed countries, and recommends a consensus-based pioneer brownfield definition and proposals for brownfield redevelopment guidelines in Ethiopia. In addition, the research highlights the framework based on a grey incidence decision-making approach to manage brownfields in African countries by taking Ethiopia as case example. The grey incidence decision-making model integrates multiple factors such as economic, social, environmental, technical and associated risk, and provides an effective decision-making and management tool for environmental practitioners and government agencies.

Design/methodology/approach: Questionnaires were used to collect data on terms and definitions of brownfields. The questions were prepared on the basis of currently used definitions developed by a number of developed countries. Moreover, this study utilises a grey incidence decision-making approach to help in management and decision-making for the implementation of brownfield redevelopment projects in the remediated sites.

Findings: Standard definitions and essential guidelines for brownfield redevelopment are proposed for the Ethiopian context. The grey incidence decision-making approach is applied for the evaluation of brownfield redevelopment projects in the remediated sites. The research findings were tested and verified using literature data and surveys from major stakeholders. In addition, a framework is proposed to control future brownfields for African countries by taking Ethiopia as case example.

Originality/value: This research stresses the significance of urban structure to address sustainable development, and the need to consider redevelopment of brownfields and identify the potential for a specific government policy framework. In addition, the research recommends brownfield redevelopment support from international development programmes. The new research provides the best opportunity for Ethiopia and Africa at large:

- to devise an urban land policy and create a strategy to contribute social, economic, financial and environmental benefits;
- to provide a foundation to solve environmental issues by involving all major stakeholders, including community citizens, municipalities, environmentalists, government agencies and policy makers; and
- to serve as guidelines to transform brownfields into greenfields.

Focusing on the vision of striving for excellence and developing smart cities, the concrete application of a study framework to manage brownfield problems will help to remove hazardous substances and improve the quality of life. The fair participation of all stakeholders, learning from the lessons of developed countries, and improved urban infrastructure will help Ethiopia and Africa at large.

Keywords: brownfields; environment; contamination; research framework; guidelines; urbanisation; Sustainable Development; grey incidence decisions

INTRODUCTION

Albert Einstein said that "intellectuals solve problems; geniuses prevent them" (Ushakov, 2007). Unlike in the industrialised world, the concept of brownfield is not widely recognised on the African continent as a whole and particularly in Ethiopia. However, with the increasing population growth and economic development in Ethiopia, the significant role of brownfield redevelopment will be investigated as a strategy of encouraging sustainable development in Ethiopian cities. From the developing countries point of view, brownfield sites are the result of waste materials from air pollution control facilities, wastewater treatment plants, community activities, agricultural operations, mining, commercial, industrial and other interrelated problems, such as urban sprawl and residential segregation (Van Rooyen, 2001). These environmental issues are creating hurdles in achieving environmental excellence in Ethiopia. Brownfield redevelopment projects (BRPs) are the practical solution to achieving environmental excellence and sustainable cities in Ethiopia.

In the present circumstances, brownfield problems are capturing a deepening concentration of government policy makers, real estate developers, investors, and researchers. There are a suspected 500,000–600,000 contaminated brownfield sites in the United States (Simons, 1998), with around 362,000 in Germany (National Round Table on the Environment and the Economy, 2003). There is still an ambiguity about the common understanding of brownfields and their basic concept. However, an initial effort has been made by the United States Environmental Protection Agency (USEPA), who defined brownfields as underutilised land where redevelopment or expansion is not an easy task due to real or perceived environmental contamination (van Vliet, 2003). There is different perspective about the definition of brownfield in the UK planning context. In the UK, a brownfield site can be any kind of property that has been previously developed for non-rural purposes (Alker et al., 2000).

It is clear from the above definitions that brownfield land is that having real or perceived contamination problems, affected by previous use, ruined and underused properties in urban areas that require redevelopment for sustainable development. Worldwide, brownfield redevelopment land strategy is taken as sustainable land use strategy due to the focus on the environmental and health protection; they have a major role in the contribution towards economic development and community revitalisation (Brebbia, 2006; De Sousa, 2003, 2005; Dixon, 2007).

In order to achieve the sustainable development goal, the Ethiopian government is collaborating with different international private and governmental agencies in order to create a green economy and save the country from the negative effects of environment and conventional development. Considering all the points, such as greater growth in population, urban growth, and development through the green economy, the Ethiopian government is trying to encourage the city municipalities to adopt brownfield redevelopment as a strategy for sustainable development.

The countless benefits of brownfield redevelopment for sustainable development make brownfields significant in the eyes of developing countries. The major benefits of brownfield redevelopment have been described as including social, environmental, economics, improved quality life around the community, the minimisation of health threats by removing hazardous waste materials, the transformation of brownfields into greenfields in congested urban areas, housing facilities, employment opportunities in the surroundings and neighbourhood, payment of taxes and duties to government (De Sousa, 2006; Greenberg et al., 2001). Currently, BRPs are capturing more attention from policy makers due to the focus on environmental issues. They are also gaining deepening interest from different government agencies, financial institutions, environmental scientists, scientific research scholars, environment legal advisors and community citizens for the betterment of society (Eckerd and Heidelberg, 2015).

Different approaches from the social sciences and management fields have been used to deal with the environmental problems. An approach, named as a rough set approach, was employed by Chen et al. (2009) to solve problems related to brownfield redevelopment in urban areas. Another approach was used by Guo et al. (2010) to evaluate BRPs with multi-hierarchical grey evaluation modelling. For the evaluation of compound and financial benefits provided by BRPs, BenDor et al. (2011) utilised the system dynamic model. Chrysochoou et al. (2012) developed an index for evaluating different alternatives for brownfield sites, and focused on the strategic view of brownfield sites for the allocation of resources.

In a case study, the results of Schädler et al. (2013) show that a spatially explicit algorithm assessment of different indicators of sustainable development can successfully improve its application, comprehensiveness and reliability. Grey cluster methods can also be an effective way of dealing with the environmental issues related to renewable energy resources and climate change (Wang et al., 2014). Zhu et al. (2015) developed a framework for optimising and establishing an evaluation index for BRPs. Structural equation modelling was used in order to verify the effectiveness of the index with the help of a real world example. Furthermore, the further application of this index was recommended for the evaluation of brownfield projects, and the construction of guidelines for other researchers in the area of brownfield redevelopment. Although all these approaches were mainly utilised by developed countries, there is less attention in developing countries. Specifically, BRPs are at the development stage in Africa, and there is no focus by the Ethiopian Government specifically.

METHODOLOGY

A great deal of international literature was reviewed to create a foundation for defining brownfield in the Ethiopian context. However, there is no consensus-based universal definition of brownfield, and every country has its own definition and parameters of brownfield. For example, the US definition focuses on the presence of contaminants, while the UK definition focuses on previously developed sites in urban areas. Due to the unfamiliarity of the term brownfield in the Ethiopian context, this research is dependent on international literature to devise primary guidelines. Moreover, it was also difficult to take the appropriate population and sample due to lack of awareness about the brownfield problem. Therefore, multiple non-probability sampling techniques were used to solve the population and sampling issues.

Three sampling techniques including judgement, convenient and snowball, were utilised to simplify the data collection by following the guidelines of Nachmias and Nachmias (2008), as their research proves the significance of using multiple sampling techniques in research. The judgement sampling technique is useful to propose a sample based on researcher experience; the convenient sampling technique also increases the flexibility in data collection due to the involvement of multiple stakeholders. Data were collected from government employees working in environmental agencies and municipalities, private investors, community citizens, real estate agents, and academicians. A pilot test was conducted before the data collection by asking some basic questions related to brownfields and the transformation of brownfields into greenfields for environmental excellence. If the average score obtained by a respondent was up to mark, that respondent was considered an appropriate participant in the research.

A survey-based questionnaire consisting of two parts was developed to gather information. The first part was about different elements of brownfields that can be a part of the pioneer definition of brownfield in the Ethiopian context. Definitions developed by different countries were considered as a base, and different elements of brownfield (e.g. vacant, derelict, contaminated, underused, etc.) were included in the final questionnaire. A sample question related to the definition of brownfield redevelopment was, for example, is brownfield a location or land vacant for development. The second part includes questions related to the evaluation of brownfields. This study received support from the research of Hou et al. (2014), including social economic and ecological benefits of brownfield redevelopment, and Zhu et al. (2015), including health benefits, brownfield development policy, financial, public welfare policy. Although the reliability and validity of both questionnaires are appropriate, the analysis technique is different. As far as their studies are concerned, the Likert scale was utilised under the rigorous analysis technique of structural equation modelling. However, this study utilised the grey incidence approach to evaluate brownfield redevelopment projects.

Data were collected during the period July–December 2015. It took three months to collect data with 10 key members helping with the data collection. Masters' level students from three key Ehtiopian universities, Addis Ababa University, Mekelle University, and Awassa University, were hired for the collection of data. A nominal remuneration was given to them for keeping the ethical consideration of the research. Questionnaires were sent out to relevant stakeholders as mentioned above. From the 300 questionnaires that were sent out, only 221 completed questionnaires were returned; 79 respondents declined to complete the questionnaire as they were not aware of the term "brownfields" and were not in a position to complete the questionnaire.

This led to the conclusion that the above survey assisted us to extract the elements of brownfield definitions based on Potts and Cloete (2012), and on judgements of different stakeholders in Ethiopia as shown below in Figure 1:

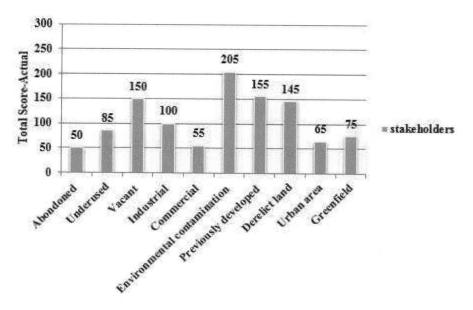

Figure 1   Elements of Brownfield Definitions
Source: Potts and Cloete, 2012

Brownfield Definition: an Overview

Generally, brownfield refers to underused, abandoned, derelict and often contaminated lands and premises, which can vary in terms of size and location. The first official definition of brownfields was proposed by the US Environmental Protection Agency (USEPA) as follows:

> "Abandoned, idled, or under-used industrial and commercial facilities where expansion or redevelopment is complicated by real or perceived environmental contamination" (USEPA, 2002).

Similarly, in Europe, Ferber et al. (2006) defined brownfields as:

> "Currently derelict or underused sites which have been affected by former uses of the site or surrounding land; they are mainly located in fully or

partly developed urban areas and may have real or perceived contamination problems thus require intervention to bring them back to beneficial use" (Ferber et al., 2006).

However, this concept of brownfield does not work in the UK. According to the views of UK brownfield professionals, it is not necessary to have hazardous contaminants on the site. Michael Gwilliam, Director of the Civic Trust, stated that in the UK:

"Brownfield sites are buildings and land either now vacant or that could become vacant or suitable for development, during a relevant [develop-ment] plan period" (Gwilliam, 1997).

In France, it is taken as a different concept. Darmendrail (1999) reports that the French Ministry of Environment interprets brownfield as,

"A space that has been temporarily abandoned following the cessation of activity (agricultural, protoindustrial, service, processing, military defense, storage or transport) and that needs to be reclaimed for a future use." (Darmendrail, 1999)

Karin Freier of the German Environment Agency (Freier, 1998) has defined brown-field land as,

"Abandoned pieces of land, mainly in inner cities, which are often blocked for economic development due to their ecological and economic risks." (Freier, 1998)

An Australian expert web site (Plater-Zyberk, 1998) suggests that:

"A brownfield site is one which has been urbanised or used industrially, sub-sequently vacated and available for re-urbanisation." (Plater-Zyberk, 1998)

This definition implies that the site is urban and vacant, but it does not consider the condition of any buildings that might be on the site, nor does it incorporate any mention of land contamination.

Potts and Cloete (2012) devise a definition for South Africa described as;

"A brownfield site is infill land or premises where remedial action is required prior to redevelopment. It may also be vacant, derelict or contaminated. No specific land use is attributed." (Potts and Cloete, 2012)

Comprehensive literature reviews on the definitions of brownfields are used to pro-pose a definition for the Ethiopian context, as well as draft the direction for prepara-tion of the guidelines.

RESULTS

Proposed Definition of Brownfields for the Ethiopian Context

Potts and Cloete's (2012) definition in the South African context was the base to get a basic concept of brownfields in Africa. When considering the extensive international literature review and the research that was undertaken, one can conclude that it is essential to set out a common definition of the term brownfields. In proposing a definition, it is important that the Ethiopian context is taken into consideration in order to ensure that the proposed definition is broad enough to cover all relevant aspects. Special consideration has also been given to the questions that the respondents were asked in relation to the understanding and development of its definition in the Ethiopian context. It is obvious that there already exist various accepted categories of land use, for instance, vacant, derelict, and statutory contaminated land, which impinge on the definition of brownfield, and that this has the potential to cause confusion. Taking into account the factors related to brownfield in the Ethiopian context, and the internationally accepted definitions of brownfields, the following definition for Ethiopian usage is proposed:

> *"A brownfield site is land located in urban areas where remedial action is required for development or redevelopment. It could be vacant, derelict or contaminated; regardless of the quality of the land use."*

Proposed guidelines for brownfield redevelopment in Ethiopia

The following guidelines are merely based on the international literature, however, as previously mentioned, brownfield redevelopment is at the rising stage in Africa, particularly in the Ethiopian context. Indeed, it is important to only depend on the international literature. The following guidelines are proposed:

- In order to achieve environmental excellence by controlling future brownfields in Africa as a whole and particularly in Ethiopia, it is necessary to propose a common definition for the so called "brownfield". The proposed brownfield definition based on the Ethiopian context should be accepted and assimilated into Ethiopian National Environmental Policy for standard use.
- The Environmental Policy of Ethiopia should update its policy and legislation in order to assimilate a relevant policy on brownfield redevelopment, and the concerned bodies must set out brownfield redevelopment as a priority to achieve environmental excellence.
- The government of the Federal Democratic Republic of Ethiopia should place a high premium on the environmental excellence by controlling future brownfields.

To achieve this, risk assessments should be carried out for brownfield redevelopment; identifying the possible risks that might be associated with brownfield sites could assist in setting out a strategy about how to control future brownfield problems. Risks associated with brownfield sites could be:

o Environmental risks
o Public welfare risks
o Healthy risks, etc.

- Certainly, BRPs contribute a great deal to sustainable development goals. In order to set up excellent brownfield redevelopment planning, it is critical to include the following elements in the brownfield redevelopment planning database:

  o Identifying the site circumstances. For example, site size, location and boundaries.
  o Identifying the circumstance of land from different angles. For instance, previous land use, proposed future redevelopment planning options, and its ownership.
  o Identifying types of contamination. For example, groundwater contamination, soil contamination, air contamination.
  o Evaluating the potential cost of remediation and its geotechnical circumstances.

- In the present circumstances, governments are facing financial deficits; identifying potential stakeholders and supporting Public-Private Partnerships for brownfield restoration projects are the icing on the cake. Above and beyond that, allowing public participation and preparing conferences will add value in the achievement of environmental excellence by controlling brownfields in Ethiopia. Their advantages are infinitely greater than grateful. Such as:

  o satisfying community health concerns;
  o making sites with poor ground conditions economically viable;
  o minimise overall environmental damage;
  o restore the land as a contributing element of the local ecosystem;
  o prevent future contamination.

MANAGEMENT FRAMEWORK FOR BROWNFIELDS IN ETHIOPIA

Progress and Need to Control Brownfield Issues

Ethiopia is growing significantly in Africa; Africa's degree of urbanisation (the percentage of urban population in the total population) by continent in 2017 was 41%. Ethiopia's urban growth rate in 2017 was 20.2%. Although this is not the highest growth rate in the continent, it is greater than the least developed nations in the African continent. All these indicators can be seen in Worldometers (2017).

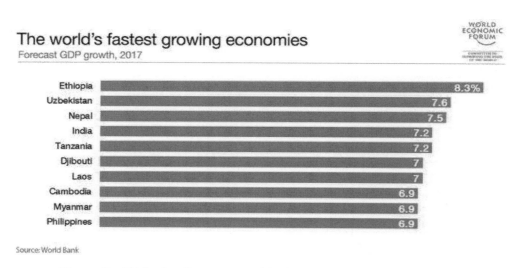

Figure 2   Ethiopian Progress and its Future Brownfield Challenges

The growth of Ethiopia is indicated by the report of the International Monetary Fund (IMF), as shown in Figure 2. The IMF ranked Ethiopia in the list of top five fastest growing economies in the world. The growth can be seen over the last decade, and it is continuously growing by 8.3% (Gray, 2017).

Every sector in the country is part of the country's growth. Ethiopia is also showing responsibility for the betterment of society and climate change. It has a very important role to play in the different environmental changes for a sustainable world. The major aim of Ethiopia at this moment is to gain the status of a middle-income country by adopting green economic strategies; this is also necessary for Ethiopia to progress. Following the conventional methods of development, this progress impacted adversely and caused a rise in GHG emissions (Federal Democratic Republic of Ethiopia, 2011). It also created a hazardous environment by utilising natural resources in an unsustainable way.

Therefore, as Ethiopia's economy and population growth continue to increase, the possible role of brownfield redevelopment will be investigated as a strategy for encouraging sustainable development in Ethiopia. Proposing a framework to control future brownfields could help to achieve the sustainable development goals in Ethiopia.

Proposed research framework to control future brownfields

The research framework has been prepared for African governments in a precise and simple way to understand the core source of brownfield sites and their health, environmental and public welfare risks. It also outlines an opportunity for African countries to encourage and facilitate the forming of legislation for brownfield redevelopment.

A project that is evaluated using a research framework, as shown below in Figure 3, illustrates the stages for controlling future brownfields in African countries by taking Ethiopia as an example. These stages are described below:

Stage 1 Summarises the core sources of brownfield sites. In this phase, it is mentioned that the possible source of brownfield sites is solid waste due to improper land administration. According to the international context, solid waste means any garbage, refuse, sludge from a wastewater treatment plant, water supply treatment plant, or air pollution control facility, and other discarded materials including solid, liquid, semi-solid, or contained gaseous material, resulting from industrial, commercial, mining and agricultural operations, and from community activities (Department of Environmental Conservation, 2017). From this work, African countries can learn and be aware of the possible sources of brownfields sites.

Stage 2 Establishes policy for brownfield redevelopment and includes a relevant policy of brownfield redevelopment on the Ethiopian National Environmental Policy. Ethi-

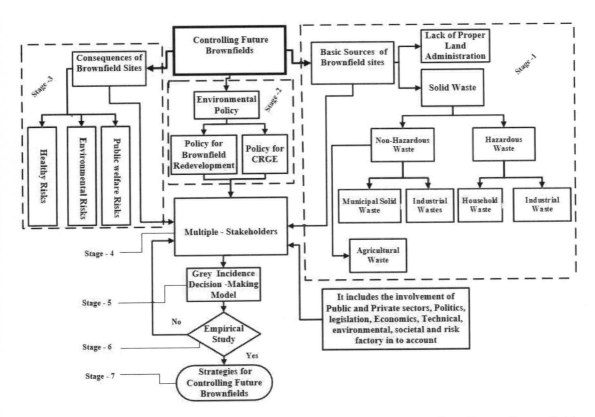

Figure 3   Evaluating Project-using a Research Framework for Controlling Future Brownfield
Source: Devised by authors

opia is experiencing the effects of climate change. In addition to the direct effects, such as an increase in average temperature or a change in rainfall patterns, climate change also presents the necessity and opportunity of switching to a new sustainable development model.

The Government of the Federal Democratic Republic of Ethiopia has therefore initiated the Climate-Resilient Green Economy (CRGE) initiative to protect the country from the adverse effects of climate change, and to build a green economy that will help realise the country's ambition of reaching middle-income status before 2025 (Federal Democratic Republic of Ethiopia, 2011). Therefore, establishing a policy for brownfield development will accelerate Ethiopia's vision of achieving middle-income status by 2025 in a climate-resilient green economy (CRGE).

Stage 3 Summarises and analyses the risks and consequences of brownfield sites. Through this work, African countries can learn and be aware of the risks and consequences of brownfield sites.

Stage 4 Indicates the multiple stakeholder's involvements in the evaluation system. The evaluation system will include criteria from the public and private sectors, political, legislative, economic, technical, environmental, and societal and risk factors, and take the different characteristics of stakeholders into consideration within the context of a project's full life span. While establishing an evaluation criteria system, one has to take every factor into consideration, and must be aware that the factors will change together with the different phases of the full life span of the projects (Zhu and Hipel, 2007).

Stage 5 Establishes a grey incidence decision-making model for brownfield redevelopment. An illustrative example is prepared in the next section to show how the proposed grey incidence decision-making model works. The decision-making process starts from an overview of the situation, from which three alternatives, A) industrial park planning, B) commercial centre planning, and C) real estate planning, are identified for further evaluation. Above and beyond that, the grey incidence decision-making approach is selected because it is a convenient approach to utilise, regardless of the sample size. In addition, the amount of computation assimilated is small and can be succeeded classically, without the difficulty between quantitative and qualitative conclusions (Gebreslase and Zhu, 2016). The process of a grey incidence decision-making model will be explained in detail below in the next section.

Stage 6 Verifies the established grey incident decision-making model through empirical studies.

Stage 7 Recommends strategic opinions for controlling future brownfields to African countries based on the obtained analytical results.

BASIC CONCEPTS OF THE GREY INCIDENCE DECISION-MAKING APPROACH

The grey system theory and application is well studied and applied around the globe in different disciplines. Over the past 30 years, it has been a well-known theory in the area of artificial intelligence; as a result it has attracted a wide range of researchers from the four corners of the world. The grey relation analysis approach is employed by Delcea et al. (2012), in shaping the relationship between a firm's situation, its symptoms, the bankruptcy syndrome and the causes that led to a certain situation. A new structure grey forecasting model, NSGM (1, 1), is proposed by Zeng et al. (2017) to forecast the trend of China's total energy consumption.

Grey incidence analysis was used by Zhan and Liu (2015) to optimise agricultural industrial structure and distribute the ratio of various inputs in agriculture, farming, forestry, animal husbandry and fishery, so as to improve the GPA of Huangshan City.

Above all, grey system theory mainly deals with uncertain systems, mini samples and poor information. Therefore, its application assimilates industry, environment, ecology, agriculture, economy, biological protection, medicine, and management. In addition, remarkable projects have been completed successfully with grey system theory, including; regional economic planning for several provinces in China, analysing the agricultural economy in China, forecasting yields of grain for some provinces in China, and building a diagnosis model available for medicine, to estimate economic effects (Liu et al., 2012). This led to the conclusion that the grey incidence decision-making approach is selected because it is a convenient approach to utilise, regardless of the sample size. In addition, the amount of computation assimilated is small and can be succeeded classically without the difficulty between quantitative and qualitative conclusions (Gebreslase and Zhu, 2016).

Let $X = \{X_{ij} = (a_i, b_j) \mid a_i \in A, b_j \in B\}$ be a set of circumstances, and $Z_{i_0 j_0} = \{Z_{i_0 j_0}^{(1)}, Z_{i_0 j_0}^{(2)}, ..., Z_{i_0 j_0}^{(x)}\}$ the optimum effect vector. If the circumstances corresponding to $Z_{i_0 j_0}$, fulfils $Z_{i_0 j_0} \notin x$, then $Z_{i_0 j_0}$ is called the imagined optimum effect vector, and $x_{i_0 j_0}$ is called the imagined optimum circumstance (Liu and Forrest, 2010).

Definition 1 Let M_i and M_j be two sequences having the same length (Zhang et al., 2012) represented as:

$$x_i = \int_1^n M_i^0 dt \qquad x_j = \int_1^n M_j^0 dt \qquad x_i - x_j = \int_1^n (M_i^0 - M_j^0) dt$$

Then: $\varepsilon_{ij} = \dfrac{1 + |x_i| + |x_j|}{1 + |x_i| + |x_j| + |x_i - x_j|}$ is known as an absolute degree of grey incidence between M_i^0 and M_j^0

Proposition 1 Let X be a set of circumstances and the effect vector of situation X_{ij} is $Z_{ij} = \left\{Z_{ij}^{(1)}, Z_{ij}^{(2)}, ..., Z_{ij}^{(k)}\right\}$ for i = 1, 2, ..., m.

1) When K is a purpose such that the larger its effect vector is the best, and it is defined as:

$$Z_{i_0 j_0}^{(k)} = \max_{1 \leq i \leq n,\, 1 \leq j \leq m}\left\{Z_{ij}^{(k)}\right\};$$

2) When K is a purpose such that the closer to a fixed moderate value Z_0 its effect value is the best, and it is defined as: $Z = Z_0$; and

3) When K is a purpose such that the smaller its effect value is the best, and it is defined as:

$$Z_{i_0 j_0}^{(k)} = \min_{1 \leq i \leq n,\, 1 \leq j \leq m}\left\{Z_{ij}^{(k)}\right\},$$

Then $Z_{i_0 j_0} = \left\{Z_{ij}^{(1)}, Z_{ij}^{(2)}, ..., Z_{ij}^{(k)}\right\}$ is the imagined optimum effect vector.

Proposition 2 Let $Z_{i_0 j_0} = \left\{Z_{i_0 j_0}^{(1)}, Z_{i_0 j_0}^{(2)}, ..., Z_{i_0 j_0}^{(k)}\right\}$ be the imagined optimum effect vector, ε_{ij} the absolute degree of grey incidence between Z_{ij} and $Z_{i_0 j_0}$, for i = 1, 2, ..., n, j = 1, 2, ..., m. if for any $i \in \{1, 2, ..., m\}$ satisfying $i \neq j_1$, $\varepsilon_{i_1 j_1} \geq \varepsilon_{ij}$ always holds true, then $Z_{i_1 j_1}$ is a quasi-optimum effect vector and $X_{i_1 j_1}$ a quasi-optimum situation.

THE APPLICATION OF GREY INCIDENCE DECISION-MAKING TO CONTROL BROWNFIELDS IN ETHIOPIA

Numerical Example

A hypothetical scenario was developed in order to apply grey incidence decision-making approach to control the brownfield issue in Ethiopia. The scenario assumes that government intends to clean up a brownfield site, and after the remediation of the contaminated site the government has to select the best development proposal from three planning options. For example, A) Industrial park planning, B) Commercial centre planning, and C) Real estate planning.

The decision-making process starts from an overview of the situation, from which three alternatives, A, B, and C are identified for further evaluation. Next, the government employs the evaluation index system derived completely from a literature review as shown in Table 1 (Zhu et al., 2015). Relevant stakeholders evaluate each alternative based on their own skills by filling questionnaires. The values from the questionnaires are then used as the input to a grey incidence analysis, which computes the absolute degrees of grey incidence; this example is used to demonstrate the proposed approach.

Let us denote the event of evaluating the proposed option models by a_1.

Then the events set is A = {a_1}.

There are three plans of the development options under consideration:

Plan 1: building an industrial park which is considered as counter-measure A;

Plan 2: building a commercial centre, which is considered as counter-measure B;

Plan 3: building a real estate, which is counter-measure C.

So, the set of counter-measures is:

B = {b1, b2, b3}, and

The set of circumstances is:

$X = \{X_{ij} = (a_i, b_j) \ a_i \in A, b_j \in B\} = \{X_{11}, X_{12}, X_{13}\}$

$\mathcal{J}^{21}$: We used the software so called *"Grey System Theory Modeling Software 6.0 (GTMS6.0)"* to get the following results:

Table 1   Comprehensive Evaluation Index for Brownfield Redevelopment Project

Factor	Purposes	Development planning options		
		A	B	C
Environmental and Health Benefits	Improvement of the quality of groundwater	75	85	77
	Improvement of soil quality	70	82	60
	Improvement of air quality	78	84	65
	Lowering the health risk of local residents	80	89	68
	Increase of green cover percentage	77	87	85
	Improvement of remediation technologies	75	80	90
Financial	Payback period (PP)	5	7	4
	Return on investment (ROI)	21	30	17
	Total cost of brownfield remediation and construction	1500	2700	2100
	Ratio of brownfield remediation cost to total cost	15	27	18
	Net present value (NPV)	2580	3500	2600
Brownfield	Location of brownfield	75	85	80
	Status of infrastructure facilities of brownfield area	85	82	90
	Transportation convenience of brownfield area	80	88	90
	Size of brownfield	55	80	85
Societal Stability	Increase local employment rate	90	92	75
	Increase local tax base	85	90	72
	Improvement of local security status	80	75	88

Table 1 (*continued*)

Factor	Purposes	Development planning options		
		A	*B*	*C*
Policy and Technical	Protecting and recycling the land/soil resource	75	90	75
	Influence from other contamination hazards nearby	60	65	60
	Easing the pressure on green land development	60	90	85
Performance	Matchup with city planning	70	85	80
	Improvement of image of local community & government	70	80	85
	Increase land value of neighbourhood	75	70	85

Source: Devised by authors

Twenty-four (24) purposes were chosen. Following this, we compute situational effect sequences $Z^K(k = 1, 2 \ldots 24)$ with respect to the purposes.

For purpose 1, we have extracted $Z^1 = (Z_{11}^{(1)}, Z_{12}^{(1)}, Z_{13}^{(1)}) = (75, 85, 77)$

For purpose 2, we have extracted $Z^2 = (Z_{11}^{(2)}, Z_{12}^{(2)}, Z_{13}^{(2)}) = (70, 82, 60)$

For purpose 3, we have extracted $Z^3 = (Z_{11}^{(3)}, Z_{12}^{(3)}, Z_{13}^{(3)}) = (78, 84, 65)$

For purpose 4, we have extracted $Z^4 = (Z_{11}^{(4)}, Z_{12}^{(4)}, Z_{13}^{(4)}) = (80, 89, 68)$

For purpose 5, we have extracted $Z^5 = (Z_{11}^{(5)}, Z_{12}^{(5)}, Z_{13}^{(5)}) = (77, 87, 85)$

For purpose 6, we have extracted $Z^6 = (Z_{11}^{(6)}, Z_{12}^{(6)}, Z_{13}^{(6)}) = (75, 80, 90)$

For purpose 7, we have extracted $Z^7 = (Z_{11}^{(7)}, Z_{12}^{(7)}, Z_{13}^{(7)}) = (5, 7, 4)$

For purpose 8, we have extracted $Z^8 = (Z_{11}^{(8)}, Z_{12}^{(8)}, Z_{13}^{(8)}) = (21, 30, 17)$

For purpose 9, we have extracted $Z^9 = (Z_{11}^{(9)}, Z_{12}^{(9)}, Z_{13}^{(9)}) = (1500, 2700, 2100)$

For purpose 10, we have extracted $Z^{10} = (Z_{11}^{(10)}, Z_{12}^{(10)}, Z_{13}^{(10)}) = (15, 27, 18)$

For purpose 11, we have extracted $Z^{11} = (Z_{11}^{(11)}, Z_{12}^{(11)}, Z_{13}^{(11)}) = (2580, 3500, 2600)$

For purpose 12, we have extracted $Z^{12} = (Z_{11}^{(12)}, Z_{12}^{(12)}, Z_{13}^{(12)}) = (75, 85, 80)$

For purpose 13, we have extracted $Z^{13} = (Z_{11}^{(13)}, Z_{12}^{(13)}, Z_{13}^{(13)}) = (85, 82, 90)$

For purpose 14, we have extracted $Z^{14} = (Z_{11}^{(14)}, Z_{12}^{(14)}, Z_{13}^{(14)}) = (80, 85, 85)$

For purpose 15, we have extracted $Z^{15} = (Z_{11}^{(15)}, Z_{12}^{(15)}, Z_{13}^{(15)}) = (55, 80, 85)$

For purpose 16, we have extracted $Z^{16} = (Z_{11}^{(16)}, Z_{12}^{(16)}, Z_{13}^{(16)}) = (90, 92, 75)$

For purpose 17, we have extracted $Z^{17} = (Z_{11}^{(17)}, Z_{12}^{(17)}, Z_{13}^{(17)}) = (85, 90, 72)$

For purpose 18, we have extracted $Z^{18} = (Z_{11}^{(18)}, Z_{12}^{(18)}, Z_{13}^{(18)}) = (80, 90, 88)$

For purpose 19, we have extracted $Z^{19} = (Z_{11}^{(19)}, Z_{12}^{(19)}, Z_{13}^{(19)}) = (75, 90, 75)$

For purpose 20, we have extracted $Z^{20} = (Z_{11}^{(20)}, Z_{12}^{(20)}, Z_{13}^{(20)}) = (60, 65, 60)$

For purpose 21, we have extracted $Z^{21} = (Z_{11}^{(21)}, Z_{12}^{(21)}, Z_{13}^{(21)}) = (60, 90, 85)$

For purpose 22, we have extracted $Z^{22} = (Z_{11}^{(22)}, Z_{12}^{(22)}, Z_{13}^{(22)}) = (70, 85, 80)$

For purpose 23, we have extracted $Z^{23} = (Z_{11}^{(23)}, Z_{12}^{(23)}, Z_{13}^{(23)}) = (70, 80, 85)$

For purpose 24, we have extracted $Z^{24} = (Z_{11}^{(24)}, Z_{12}^{(24)}, Z_{13}^{(24)}) = (75, 70, 85)$

Hereafter we computed the average images of the situational effect sequences for each of the purposes:

$Z^1 = (1, 1.13, 1.03)$ $\quad$ $Z^4 = (1, 1.11, 0.85)$ $\quad$ $Z^7 = (1, 1.40, 0.80)$ $\quad$ $Z^{10} = (1, 1.80, 1.20)$

$Z^2 = (1, 1.17, 0.86)$ $\quad$ $Z^5 = (1, 1.13, 1.10)$ $\quad$ $Z^8 = (1, 1.43, 0.81)$ $\quad$ $Z^{11} = (1, 1.36, 1.01)$

$Z^3 = (1, 1.08, 0.83)$ $\quad$ $Z^6 = (1, 1.07, 1.20)$ $\quad$ $Z^9 = (1, 1.80, 1.40)$ $\quad$ $Z^{12} = (1, 1.13, 1.07)$

$Z^{13} = (1, 0.96, 1.06)$ $\quad$ $Z^{16} = (1, 1.02, 0.83)$ $\quad$ $Z^{19} = (1, 1.20, 1)$ $\quad$ $Z^{22} = (1, 1.21, 1.14)$

$Z^{14} = (1, 1.06, 1.06)$ $\quad$ $Z^{17} = (1, 1.06, 0.85)$ $\quad$ $Z^{20} = (1, 1.08, 1)$ $\quad$ $Z^{23} = (1, 1.14, 1.21)$

$Z^{15} = (1, 1.45, 1.55)$ $\quad$ $Z^{18} = (1, 1.13, 1.10)$ $\quad$ $Z^{21} = (1, 1.50, 1.42)$ $\quad$ $Z^{24} = (1, 0.93, 1.13)$

And then effect vectors Z_{ij} of the situations X_{ij}, $i = 1$, $j = 1, 2, 3$;

$Z_{11} = (Z_{11}^{(1)}, Z_{11}^{(2)}, ..., Z_{11}^{(24)}) = (1, 1, 1, 1, 1, 1, 1, 1, 1, 1, 1, 1, 1, 1, 1, 1, 1, 1, 1, 1, 1, 1, 1, 1)$

$Z_{12} = (Z_{12}^{(1)}, Z_{12}^{(2)}, ..., Z_{12}^{(24)}) = (1.13, 1.17, 1.08, 1.11, 1.13, 1.07, 1.40, 1.43, 1.80, 1.80,$
$1.36, 1.13, 0.96, 1.06, 1.45, 1.02, 1.06, 1.13, 1.20, 1.08, 1.50, 1.21, 1.14, 0.93)$

$U_{13} = (Z_{13}^{(1)}, Z_{13}^{(2)}, ..., Z_{13}^{(24)}) = (1.03, 0.86, 0.83, 0.85, 1.10, 1.20, 0.80, 0.81, 1.40, 1.20,$
$1.01, 1.07, 1.06, 1.06, 1.55, 0.83, 0.85, 1.10, 1, 1, 1.42, 1.14, 1.21, 1.13)$

Finally, we calculated the optimum reference sequences, from the average images of the situational effect sequences of the purposes as follows:

For Purpose 1, the larger effect value is the best, so $Z_{i_0 j_0}^{(1)} = \max_{1 \leq i \leq n, 1 \leq j \leq m} \{Z_{ij}^{(1)}\} = \{Z_{12}^{(1)}\} = 1.13$

For Purpose 2, the larger effect value is the best, so $Z_{i_0 j_0}^{(2)} = \max_{1 \leq i \leq n, 1 \leq j \leq m} \{Z_{ij}^{(2)}\} = \{Z_{12}^{(2)}\} = 1.17$;

For Purpose 3, the larger effect value is the best, so $Z_{i_0 j_0}^{(3)} = \max_{1 \leq i \leq n, 1 \leq j \leq m} \{Z_{ij}^{(3)}\} = \{Z_{12}^{(3)}\} = 1.08$;

For Purpose 4, the larger effect value is the best, so $Z_{i_0 j_0}^{(4)} = \max_{1 \leq i \leq n, 1 \leq j \leq m} \{Z_{ij}^{(4)}\} = \{Z_{12}^{(4)}\} = 1.11$;

For Purpose 5, the larger effect value is the best, so $Z_{i_0 j_0}^{(5)} = \max_{1 \leq i \leq n, 1 \leq j \leq m} \{Z_{ij}^{(5)}\} = \{Z_{12}^{(5)}\} = 1.13$;

For Purpose 6, the larger effect value is the best, so $Z_{i_0 j_0}^{(6)} = \max_{1 \le i \le n, 1 \le j \le m}\{Z_{ij}^{(6)}\} = \{Z_{13}^{(6)}\} = 1.20$;

For Purpose 7, the mini effect value is the best, so $Z_{i_0 j_0}^{(7)} = \min_{1 \le i \le n, 1 \le j \le m}\{Z_{ij}^{(7)}\} = \{Z_{13}^{(7)}\} = 0.80$;

For Purpose 8, the mini effect value is the best, so $Z_{i_0 j_0}^{(8)} = \min_{1 \le i \le n, 1 \le j \le m}\{Z_{ij}^{(8)}\} = \{Z_{13}^{(8)}\} = 0.81$;

For Purpose 9, the mini effect value is the best, so $Z_{i_0 j_0}^{(9)} = \min_{1 \le i \le n, 1 \le j \le m}\{Z_{ij}^{(9)}\} = \{Z_{11}^{(9)}\} = 1$;

For Purpose 10, the mini effect value is the best, so $Z_{i_0 j_0}^{(10)} = \min_{1 \le i \le n, 1 \le j \le m}\{Z_{ij}^{(10)}\} = \{Z_{11}^{(10)}\} = 1$;

For Purpose 11, the mini effect value is the best, so $Z_{i_0 j_0}^{(11)} = \min_{1 \le i \le n, 1 \le j \le m}\{Z_{ij}^{(11)}\} = \{Z_{11}^{(11)}\} = 1$;

For Purpose 12, the mini effect value is the best, so $Z_{i_0 j_0}^{(12)} = \min_{1 \le i \le n, 1 \le j \le m}\{Z_{ij}^{(12)}\} = \{Z_{11}^{(12)}\} = 1$;

For Purpose 13, the mini effect value is the best, so $Z_{i_0 j_0}^{(13)} = \min_{1 \le i \le n, 1 \le j \le m}\{Z_{ij}^{(13)}\} = \{Z_{12}^{(13)}\} = 0.96$;

For Purpose 14, the mini effect value is the best, so $Z_{i_0 j_0}^{(14)} = \min_{1 \le i \le n, 1 \le j \le m}\{Z_{ij}^{(14)}\} = \{Z_{11}^{(14)}\} = 1$;

For Purpose 15, the mini effect value is the best, so $Z_{i_0 j_0}^{(15)} = \min_{1 \le i \le n, 1 \le j \le m}\{Z_{ij}^{(15)}\} = \{Z_{11}^{(15)}\} = 1$;

For Purpose 16, the larger effect value is the best, so $Z_{i_0 j_0}^{(16)} = \max_{1 \le i \le n, 1 \le j \le m}\{Z_{ij}^{(16)}\} = \{Z_{12}^{(16)}\} = 1.02$;

For Purpose 17, the larger effect value is the best, so $Z_{i_0 j_0}^{(17)} = \max_{1 \le i \le n, 1 \le j \le m}\{Z_{ij}^{(17)}\} = \{Z_{12}^{(17)}\} = 1.06$;

For Purpose 18, the larger effect value is the best, so $Z_{i_0 j_0}^{(18)} = \max_{1 \le i \le n, 1 \le j \le m}\{Z_{ij}^{(18)}\} = \{Z_{12}^{(18)}\} = 1.13$;

For Purpose 19, the larger effect value is the best, so $Z_{i_0 j_0}^{(19)} = \max_{1 \le i \le n, 1 \le j \le m}\{Z_{ij}^{(19)}\} = \{Z_{12}^{(19)}\} = 1.20$;

For Purpose 20, the mini effect value is the best, so $Z_{i_0 j_0}^{(20)} = \min_{1 \le i \le n, 1 \le j \le m}\{Z_{ij}^{(20)}\} = \{Z_{13}^{(20)}\} = 1$;

For Purpose 21, the larger effect value is the best, so $Z_{i_0 j_0}^{(21)} = \max_{1 \le i \le n, 1 \le j \le m}\{Z_{ij}^{(21)}\} = \{Z_{12}^{(21)}\} = 1.50$;

For Purpose 22, the larger effect value is the best, so $Z_{i_0 j_0}^{(22)} = \max_{1 \le i \le n, 1 \le j \le m}\{Z_{ij}^{(22)}\} = \{Z_{12}^{(22)}\} = 1.21$;

For Purpose 23, the larger effect value is the best, so $Z_{i_0 j_0}^{(23)} = \max_{1 \le i \le n, 1 \le j \le m}\{Z_{ij}^{(23)}\} = \{Z_{12}^{(23)}\} = 1.14$;

For Purpose 24, the larger effect value is the best, so $Z_{i_0 j_0}^{(24)} = \max_{1 \le i \le n, 1 \le j \le m}\{Z_{ij}^{(24)}\} = \{Z_{13}^{(24)}\} = 1.13$;

We obtain the following optimum reference sequence:

$Z_{i_0 j_0}^{(11)} = (Z_{i_0 j_0}^{(1)}, Z_{i_0 j_0}^{(2)}, ..., Z_{i_0 j_0}^{(24)}) = (1.13, 1.17, 1.08, 1.11, 1.13, 1.20, 0.80, 0.81, 1, 1, 1, 1, 0.96, 1, 1, 1.02, 1.06, 1.13, 1.20, 1, 1.50, 1.21, 1.14, 1.13)$

From Z_{ij} and $Z_{i_0 j_0}$, we computed the absolute degrees of grey incidence:

$\varepsilon_{11} = 0.6359$, $\varepsilon_{12} = 0.8251$, $\varepsilon_{13} = 0.8370$

This led to the conclusion that since Max $\{\varepsilon_{ij}\} = \varepsilon_{13} = 0.8370$, Z_{23} is the quasi-optimum vector and X_{13} the quasi-optimum situation. In terms of building the development planning, the commercial centre is most ideal choice among all the possible plans of the development planning.

CONCLUSIONS, PRACTICAL IMPLICATIONS AND FUTURE RESEARCH

The research indicates that very little understanding of brownfield redevelopment exists with the relevant stakeholders, and no common definitions exist for brownfield development in Ethiopia. The research did, however, propose a suitable definition of brownfield that can be used in the Ethiopian context. Due to health, environmental and public welfare risks associated with brownfield sites, it is convenient to design a framework to guide the theoretical and practical applications in brownfield redevelopment, which constitutes the main purpose of this study.

Under the umbrella of a grey incidence decision-making model, and with the consideration of multiple-stakeholders, tight environmental and economic constraints, the proposed research framework integrates different criteria from economic, social, environmental, technical and risk aspects into a grey incidence decision-making model, and gives useful guidance to control future brownfields on the African continent, particularly in Ethiopia.

Moreover, this research provides a significant opportunity for African governments in the following ways. First, this study will be helpful for African countries to utilise the urban land effectively, long term improvement in environmental quality, public and economic health. It will also be supportive in devising a strategy for employment, housing, taxation and environmental policy. Second, it identifies the potential for specific government policy frameworks for brownfield redevelopment to reduce city carbon emissions. Third, it recommends that government departments consider the coordinated facilitation of brownfield redevelopment. Lastly, it recommends brownfield redevelopment support from international development programmes.

Removing barriers to brownfield redevelopment, risk assessment using project life cycles, building up a comprehensive evaluation index for brownfield redevelopment projects according to Africa's situation, and evaluating brownfield redevelopment projects using grey incidence system theory can be potential work in the future.

ACKNOWLEDGEMENTS

The authors would like to dedicate this contemporary work to the **Blessed Mother Mary** and to **Archangel St Michael**. Last but not least, this project was supported by the provincial Natural Science Foundation in Shaanxi, China through the project "Research on Risk Allocation and Income Distribution Mechanism of Public Private Partnership for Brownfield Regeneration Project" (2017JM7002)

REFERENCES

Alker, S., Joy, V., Roberts, P. and Smith, N. (2000), The Definition of Brownfield. *Journal of Environmental Planning and Management,* Vol. 43, No. 1, pp. 49–69.

BenDor, T.K., Metcalf, S.S. and Paich, M. (2011), The Dynamics of Brownfield Redevelopment. *Sustainability,* Vol. 3, No. 6, pp. 914–36.

Brebbia, C. (2006), *Brownfields III: Prevention, Assessment, Rehabilitation and Development of Brownfield Sites* (Brownfields 2006). Wit Press, Southampton, UK.

Chen, Y., Hipel, K.W., Kilgour, D.M. and Zhu, Y. (2009), A Strategic Classification Support System for Brownfield Redevelopment. *Environmental Modelling & Software,* Vol. 24, No. 5, pp. 647–54.

Chrysochoou, M., Brown, K., Dahal, G., Granda-Carvajal, C., Segerson, K., Garrick, N. and Bagtzoglou, A. (2012), A GIS and Indexing Scheme to Screen Brownfields for Area-Wide Redevelopment Planning. *Landscape and Urban Planning,* Vol. 105, No. 3, pp. 187–98.

Darmendrail, D. (1999), *Personal Communication.*

De Sousa, C. (2005), Policy Performance and Brownfield Redevelopment in Milwaukee, Wisconsin. *The Professional Geographer,* Vol. 57, No. 2, pp. 312–27.

De Sousa, C.A. (2003), Turning Brownfields into Green Space in the City of Toronto. *Landscape and Urban Planning,* Vol. 62, No. 4, pp. 181–98.

De Sousa, C.A. (2006), Unearthing the Benefits of Brownfield to Green Space Projects: An Examination of Project Use and Quality of Life Impacts. *Local Environment,* Vol. 11, No. 5, pp. 577–600.

Delcea, C., Scarlat, E. and Mărăcine, V. (2012), Grey Relational Analysis Between Firm's Current Situation and its Possible Causes: A Bankruptcy Syndrome Approach, *Grey Systems: Theory and Application,* Vol. 2, No. 2, pp. 229–39.

Department of Environmental Conservation (2017): *What is Solid Waste* [online]. Available at: http://www.dec.ny.gov/chemical/8732.html [Accessed 15 August 2017].

Dixon, T. (2007), The Property Development Industry and Sustainable Urban Brownfield Regeneration in England: An Analysis of Case Studies in Thames Gateway and Greater Manchester. *Urban Studies,* Vol. 44, No. 12, pp. 2379–400.

Eckerd, A. and Heidelberg, R.L. (2015), Public Incentives, Market Motivations, and Contaminated Properties: New Public Management and Brownfield Liability Reform. *Public Administration Review,* Vol. 75, No. 2, pp. 252–61.

Economy, C.R.G. (2011), Ethiopia's Climate-Resilient Green Economy, Green Economy Strategy. *Addis Ababa: Fdre.*

Federal Democratic Republic of Ethiopia (2011), Ethiopia's Climate Resilient Green Economy, Green Economy Strategy, pp. 1–3, September 2011.

Ferber, U., Grimski, D., Millar, K. and Nathanail, P. (2006), Sustainable Brownfield Regeneration: CABERNET Network Report. The Concerted Action on Brownfield and Economic Regeneration Network (CABERNET). Nottingham, UK: Cabernet. http://www. Cabernet. Org. UK_2014-12-01.

Freier, K. (1998), Clarinet Working Group 1: Brownfield Redevelopment Workplan (Berlin, German Environmental Agency).

Gebreslase, M. and Zhu, Y. (2016), The Application of Grey-Incidence Decision Making in the Analysis of Brownfield Redevelopment Project. In *Systems, Man and Cybernetics (SMC),* 2016 IEEE International Conference, IEEE, 000773-000778.

Gray, A. (2017), *These are the World's Fastest-Growing Economies in 2017* [Online]. World Economic Forum. Available: Https://Www.Weforum.Org/Agenda/2017/06/These-Are-The-World-S-Fastest-

Growing-Economies-In-2017-2?Utm_Content=Buffer30bc1&Utm_Medium=Social&Utm_Source=Twitter. Com&Utm_Campaign=Buffer [Accessed 15 August 2017].

Greenberg, M., Lowrie, K., Mayer, H., Miller, K.T. and Solitare, L. (2001), Brownfield Redevelopment as a Smart Growth Option in the United States. *Environmentalist*, Vol. 21, No. 2, pp. 129–43.

Guo, P., Liang, Y.-H. and Zhu, Y.-M. (2010), Multi-Hierarchical Grey Evaluation of the Brownfield Redevelopment Project Based on Combinational Weight [J]. *Operations Research and Management Science*, Vol. 5, p. 023.

Gwilliam, M. (1997), Something Old, Something New (Brownfield Sites). *Planning*, Vol. 1233, p. 23.

Hou, D., Al-Tabbaa, A., Chen, H. and Mamic, I. (2014), Factor Analysis and Structural Equation Modelling of Sustainable Behaviour in Contaminated Land Remediation. *Journal of Cleaner Production*, Vol. 84, pp. 439–49.

Liu, S. and Forrest, J.Y.L. (2010), *Grey Systems: Theory and Applications*, Springer.

Liu, S., Forrest, J. and Yang, Y. (2012), A Brief Introduction To Grey Systems Theory. *Grey Systems: Theory and Application*, Vol. 2, No. 2, pp. 89–104.

Nachmias, D. and Nachmias, C. (2008), *Research Methods in the Social Sciences*, New York, Worth Publishers.

National Round Table on the Environment and the Economy (2003), *Cleaning up the Past, Building the Future: A National Brownfield Redevelopment Strategy for Canada*, National Round Table.

Plater-Zyberk, D. (1998), *Architects and Town Planners*: Glossary of Terms.

Potts, L. and Cloete, C.E. (2012), Developing Guidelines for Brownfield Development in South Africa. *WIT Transactions on Ecology and the Environment*, Vol. 162, pp. 389–99.

Schädler, S., Finkel, M., Bleicher, A., Morio, M. and Gross, M. (2013), Spatially Explicit Computation of Sustainability Indicator Values for the Automated Assessment of Land-Use Options. *Landscape and Urban Planning*, Vol. 111, pp. 34–45.

Simons, R.A. (1998), How Many Urban Brownfields Are Out There?: An Economic Base Contraction Analysis of 31 US Cities. *Public Works Management & Policy*, Vol. 2, No. 3, pp. 267–73.

United States Environmental Protection Agency (USEPA) (2002), Brownfields homepage [Online]. Available: http://www.epa.gov/ebtpages/cbrownfields.html 2015.

Ushakov, I.A. (2007), *Histories of Scientific Insights*, Lulu.Com, p. 152.

Van Rooyen, E. (2001), Integrated Development and the Brownfields Phenomena, *Journal of Public Administration*, Vol 36, No. 1, pp. 61–80.

van Vliet, D. (2003), Book review of Brebbia, C.A, Almorza, D. and Klapperich, H. (Eds). Brownfield Sites: Assessment, Rehabilitation & Development. *Canadian Journal of Urban Research*, Vol. 12, No. 1, pp. 147–48.

Wang, B., Ke, R.Y., Yuan, X.C. and Wei, Y.M. (2014), China's Regional Assessment of Renewable Energy Vulnerability to Climate Change. *Renewable and Sustainable Energy Reviews*, Vol. 40, pp. 185–95.

Worldometers (2017), http://www.worldometers.info/world-population/ethiopia-population/

Zeng, B. and Luo, C. (2017), Forecasting the Total Energy Consumption in China Using a New-structure Grey System Model, *Grey Systems: Theory and Application*, Vol. 7, No. 2, pp. 194–217.

Zhan, H. and Liu, S. (2015), An Analysis of Intermediate Inputs Influencing the Gross Products of Agriculture and its Composition Based on Grey Incidence Analysis, *Grey Systems: Theory and Application*, Vol. 5, No. 2, pp. 206–21.

Zhang, K., Ye, W. and Zhao, L. (2012), The Absolute Degree of Grey Incidence for Grey Sequence Base on Standard Grey Interval Number Operation. *Kybernetes*, Vol. 41, Nos 7/8, pp. 934–44.

Zhu, Y. and Hipel, K.W. (2007), Life Span Risk Management in Brownfield Redevelopment. In *Systems, Man and Cybernetics, 2007*. ISIC. IEEE International Conference 2007. IEEE, pp. 4052–56.

Zhu, Y., Hipel, K.W., Ke, G.Y. and Chen, Y. (2015), Establishment and Optimization of an Evaluation Index System for Brownfield Redevelopment Projects: An Empirical Study. *Environmental Modelling & Software*, Vol. 74, pp. 173–82.

BIOGRAPHY

Mikiale Gebreslase is a senior control engineer and researcher on environmental remediation and Life Span Risk Management of Brownfield Redevelopment Projects in China, at Northwestern Polytechnical University. Control engineering became his passion after he received his BSc in Electrical Engineering from Bahir Dar University, Ethiopia in 2010. His continued interests drove him to further improve his education, and in 2014 he gained an MSc in Control Theory and Control Engineering from Northwestern Polytechnical University, China. After he completed his MSc, Northwestern Polytechnical University awarded him a full university scholarship to continue his PhD in System Engineering in 2014. He is also very much concerned about environmental issues such as climate change and pollution, which are affecting the whole world. He has authored several peer-reviewed articles.

Yuming Zhu is an Associate Professor at the School of Management Science and Engineering at Northwestern Polytechnical University. He gained an MBA in 2001 from Northwestern Polytechnical University, and is currently a PhD student at the same University. His research interests are in Managerial System Engineer, Corporate Strategic Management, and Project Management. Zhu has written several articles for peer reviewed journals, and has attended many international conferences. He has several awards, and is a member of the Youth Scientist Commission of NPU.

Naveed Ahmad is a PhD student in the School of Management, Northwestern Polytechnical University, Xi'an, China. He did his Master's of Marketing in 2013 from Mohammad Ali Jinnah University, Pakistan. His areas of interest are sustainable development, marketing, and HRM. His research covers different topics including Internal Marketing, Organisational Performance, Marketing Outcomes, and Brownfield Redevelopment Projects. He has taught in different institutes including Bahaudin Zakaria University, Multan and Government College University, Faisalabad.

Dawit Bekele is Research Fellow and Senior Hydrogeologist at the Global Centre for Environmental Remediation (GCER) at the University of Newcastle, Australia, conducting and directing environmental projects and research in the assessment, remediation and management of contaminated sites. He has qualifications in Civil Engineering (BSc), Water Resource Management (MSc) and Environmental Public Health and Remediation (PhD). With over 10 years' experience in the environmental field, he specialises in providing strategic environmental advice to clients relating to brownfield site assessment and remediation, including the assessment of contaminant fate and transport. His current research focuses on adding new dimensions in vapour intrusion risk assessment and mitigation at volatile hydrocarbon impacted grounds. He is lead contaminant hydrogeologist, soil and groundwater remediation at GCER. His area of research includes risk-based approaches to the clean-up or management of contaminated sites.

COMBATTING DESERTIFICATION IN SUDAN: EXPERIENCES AND LESSONS LEARNED

Sarra A.M. Saad[1]
Adil M.A. Seedahmed[2]
Allam Ahmed[*3]
Sufyan A.M. Ossman[4]
Ahmed M.A. Eldoma[5]

[1]National Centre for Research
Ministry of Higher Education & Scientific Research
PO Box 6096, 11111, Khartoum-Sudan
Email: soilsarra@gmail.com
[2]Ministry of Agriculture, Khartoum-Sudan
[3]Science Policy Research Unit (SPRU)
School of Business, Management & Economics
Jubilee Building, University of Sussex, Brighton BN1 9SL, United Kingdom
Email: allam@sussex.ac.uk
[4]Khartoum Refinery Company
Ministry of Oil, Khartoum-Sudan
[5]Faculty of Forestry & Range Sciences, Sudan University of Science and Technology
Ministry of Higher Education, Khartoum-Sudan

ABSTRACT

Problem statement: Sudan is the largest (2.5 million km^2) country most seriously affected by desertification in Africa. The arid and semi-arid lands

*Corresponding Author

cover an area of 1.78 million km², which represents about 72% of the country's total area[1]. Sudan has collaborated with and contributed to the international efforts to combat desertification. It is one of the first countries that signed the United Nations Convention to Combat Desertification (UNCCD) and assigned the National Drought and Desertification Control Unit (NDDCU) for the coordination of programmes to mitigate the effects of drought and to combat desertification as a focal point. Since the 1930s, programmes to combat desertification and its component projects and interventions have been launched in Sudan through technical and financial assistance (local and international) to improve land resources, production systems, and protection of the environment. Sudan, like other African countries, needs plant cover: an earlier study for the UN Food and Agriculture Organization (FAO) indicated that Sudan has lost between 250,000 and 1,250,000 hectares of the total area of its forests since 2005; this is the main reason for the expansion of the desertification phenomenon. Therefore, unless serious and immediate action is pursued, the gap between the sustainability of resources and the degree of exploitation will widen further[2].

Objectives: The objective of this paper is to review the efforts taken by Sudan in combatting desertification from governmental and private sectors, and to assess the reasons for the failure of past efforts to combat desertification.

Methodology: Previous acts and agreements from national and international sources have been collected. The hazards of desertification and their impacts on economic and social lives have been evaluated.

Findings: Many conclusions and lessons emerged from previous experiences of government, NGOs, civil society and private sectors in implementing desertification programmes in Sudan. The analytical review of Sudan desertification policies showed a lack of an intersectoral approach that integrates forestry activities and land use into the social, economic and developmental process of the country. They also lacked linkages to other sectors that use and actually compete for the available natural resources.

Values: Therefore it was recommended that capacity building, public awareness, and integration of NGOs, governmental sectors including research institutions, ministries and international organisations is urgently needed.

Keywords: Sudan; desertification; conflicts; environment

---

[1]Republic of Sudan. Ministry of Agriculture and Forestry; NDDCU; SNAP; A frame work of combating desertification in Sudan in the context of the UN Convention to combat desertification, Khartoum-Sudan, March 2006.
[2]African News. www.Xinhuanet.com (2016).

INTRODUCTION

Desertification has been defined as land degradation in arid, semi-arid, and dry sub-humid areas resulting from various factors, including climatic variations and human activities (IPCC, 2001). Another definition of desertification is the spread of desert-like conditions of low biological productivity due to human impact under climatic variations (Helldén, 1991; Reynolds, 2001; Reynolds and Stafford Smith, 2002).

It is estimated that three-quarters of dry lands have suffered from some degree of desertification (UNCOD, 1977; FAO, 1984; UNEP, 1992; FAO, 2000). The removal of vegetation cover exacerbates desertification and accelerates soil erosion; this causes reduced soil fertility and eventually renders the land unproductive. This situation has often led to the assumption that it is a human induced process that leads to the depletion of soil nutrients and a reduction of biological productivity. Desertification is one of the central problems that pose very real and severe challenges to the sustainable development of the dry land's ecosystem. Rainfall variability, both in time and space, coupled with the inherent ecological fragility of the dry lands, weakens the resilience of the ecosystem and its ability to return to its original condition (Abdi et al., 2013).

According to Dregne and Rozonov (1991) and Maliva and Missimer (2012), desertification has been with us for thousands of years, but has not received attention for a very long time. It was not until the 20th century that governments and people in general finally realised that land degradation and desertification threatened their future.

There are conflicting propositions regarding the dynamics of the Sahelian desert, which lies in the northern part of the African continent. The absence of a universally agreed definition of drought, and an understanding of its relationship to desertification, makes understanding the Sahelian ecosystem difficult. The definitions of the terms 'desert' and 'desertification' are complex issues in themselves, and open to various interpretations (Richards, 1994; Toulmin, 1995). In a 1975 report, Lamprey stated that it is evident that the desert's southern boundary has shifted south by an average of 90–100km in the previous 17 years, representing a southwards shift of 5–6km per year. This assertion is contested on the grounds that the basis of Lamprey's comparison was wrong, and that the 'shift' as a result of a severe drought has been stabilised. Hellden (1991) did not concur with such expansion in the Sudan, and asserted that there was no evidence that patches of desert were spreading outward from villages and water holes into the dry lands of the Sahel area (Hellden, 1991).

HISTORY OF DESERTIFICATION IN SUDAN

Natural disasters in the contrasting forms of drought and flooding have historically occurred frequently in Sudan; they have contributed significantly to population displacement, poverty, diseases and the under-development of the country. A silent and even greater disaster is the ongoing process of desertification, driven by climate change, drought, and the impact of human activities.

Desertification and land degradation are among the central problems for the sustainable development of the dry land ecosystem, especially in the case of Sudan (see Map 1 below). Recurring droughts and land degradation are closely linked. Drought increases soil degradation, which, in turn, magnifies the impact of drought (Abdi et al., 2013).

Historical data, anecdotal field reports and modelling all point to the same general trend. Overall, rainfall is becoming increasingly scarce and/or unreliable in Sudan's Sahel belt: this trend is likely to continue. On this basis alone, large tracts of the Sahel will be severely impacted by declining food productivity over the next generation and beyond.

Annual variability and relative scarcity of rainfall – in the north of Sudan in particular – have a dominant effect on agriculture and food security, and are strongly linked to displacement and related conflicts. Drought events also change the environment as dry spells kill otherwise long lived trees, and result in a general reduction of the vegetation cover, leaving land more vulnerable to overgrazing and erosion.

Together with other countries in the Sahel belt, Sudan has suffered a number of long and devastating droughts in the past decades. All regions have been affected, but the worst impacts have been felt in the central and northern states, particularly in Northern Kordofan, Northern state, Northern and Western Darfur, and Red Sea and White Nile states.

Desertification is considered one of the main factors that cause the migration of rural populations to urban centres; thus, creating so-called "environmental refugees" (UNEP, 1991). As reported by UNEP (1991), the impact of land degradation manifests itself in different forms.

In 2007, UNEP reported an estimated 50-200km southward shift of the boundary between semi-desert and desert has occurred since rainfall and vegetation records were first held in the 1930s. The remaining semi-desert and low rainfall savannah, which represent some 25% of Sudan's agricultural land, are at considerable risk of further desertification. This is expected to lead to a significant drop (approximately 20%) in food production.

Insufficient and highly variable annual precipitation is a defining feature of the climate of most of Sudan. Desertification, therefore, is considered as Sudan's greatest environmental problem (see Map 1 below). In northern Sudan, there is high awareness of the issue of desertification within the academic community, and there is historical evidence of a number of attempts to quantify and/or limit the extent of the problem since at least the 1950s (Reynolds, 2001; FAO, 2000). As early as 1953, a landmark study discussed several of the sources of the problem (such as overgrazing), as well as its implications on long-term damage and reductions in productivity (UNEP, 1992; Reynolds, 2001).

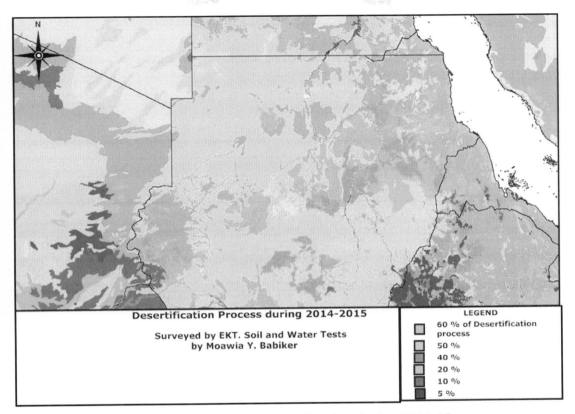

Map 1   Map Showing Desertification during 2014–15

Source: Revised by the author

The most severe drought occurred in 1980–1984, and was accompanied by widespread displacement and localised famine. Localised and less severe droughts (affecting between one and five states) were also recorded in 1967–1973, 1987, 1989, 1990, 1991, 1993 and 2000 (Reynolds, 2001; IPCC, 2001).

Isolated drought years generally have little permanent effect on the environment. In the case of central Sudan, however, the 18 recorded years of drought within the last half-century are certain to have had a major influence on the vegetation profile and soil conditions seen in 2006.

Recent research has indicated that the most likely cause of these historical droughts was a medium-term (years) change in ocean temperature, rather than local factors such as overgrazing (Helldén, 1991; Reynolds, 2001). Therefore, the potential for such droughts to recur remains.

Although most of the country is arid, the economy has predominately depended on the agricultural sector, including livestock production, forestry and fishing (see Figure 1). Together, they used to contribute about half of the GDP before the discovery and exploitation of oil in 1999. Despite the emergence of Sudan as an oil exporter and the diminishing share of the agricultural sector in overall export earnings, agriculture continues to be the backbone of the country's economy in terms of its contribution to GDP. The sector contributed on average about 35% of the country's GDP from 2009 to 2010 (see Figure 2) (MOA, 2015).

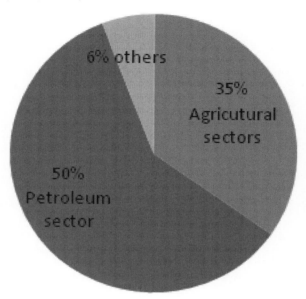

Figure 1   Contribution of Different Sector in GDP (2009−2010)
Source: MOA (2015)

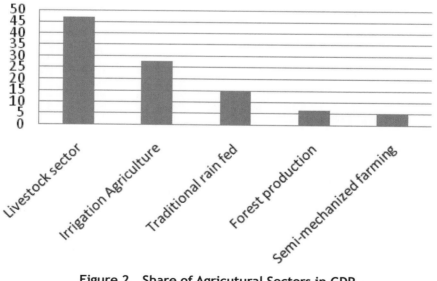

Figure 2   Share of Agricultural Sectors in GDP
Source: MO A (2015)

DESERTIFICATION IN DARFUR

Droughts and insufficient rainfall are characteristic of western Sudanese territories, primarily in North Darfur and Kordofan. Over the past 100 years there have been five periods of prolonged drought in the region; two have happened in the last 20 years. In these areas the average precipitation ranges from 100–600 mm per year, which, with its lower limit, poses a high probability of serious adverse consequences in the agricultural and livestock sectors. The rainfall in 1950–1990 caused three long periods of drought, one of which occurred in the mid-1960s and was relatively light. The second period, which occurred between 1972 and 1975, was relatively heavy, but the third one in 1982–1984 was almost a catastrophe. This period of drought was accompanied by the outbreak of armed clashes. The most severe and intense of these clashes occurred in the mid-1980s. Over time, those skirmishes turned into full-scale warfare (Suliman, 2008). The graph below shows the relationship between rainfall and conflicts erupting in this area over 40 years (1950–1990). The chart shows a trend – a correlation between droughts and occurrence of armed conflicts. (Figure 3)

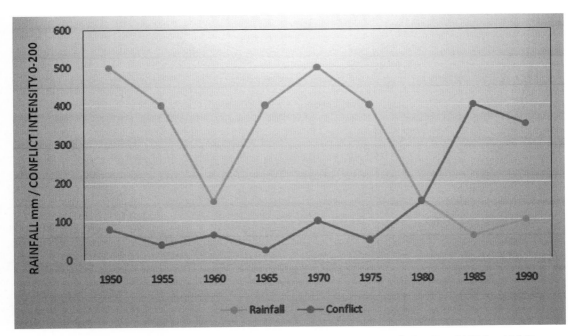

Figure 3   Correlation between rainfall and conflict in North Darfur (1950–1990)
Source: Suliman (2008)

The graph also shows the difference between the impact of the drought on the social situation in the mid-1970s and the mid-1980s. The first one was moderately severe, but it did not cause an intensification of social unrest and armed conflicts. The second drought in the 1980s contributed to famine, and armed conflicts that took place in the region: migration intensified. Drought has contributed to the collapse of the rural economy. Many animals died, and shepherds often hastily discarded other animals for low prices. The life of the population was difficult. At this moment, the rural community is susceptible to disintegration, to surrender, to falling into armed conflict, and finally to war, as happened in northern Darfur in the 1980s. Many years later, in 2007, the United Nations Environment Programme (UNEP) published a comprehensive analysis of the depth of the ecological crisis in various parts of the Sahel. It turned out that one-third of the forested area was lost in 1973–2006 in Darfur. Based on these studies, it can be concluded that this type of drought and lack of precipitation is sufficient for the natural environment to change significantly, regardless of human influence. This resulted in a displacement to the south of the desert climate by about 100 km over a period of 40 years. Such a scale of historical climate change is unprecedented. Reducing precipitation changed millions of acres of marginal semi-arid areas into desert. This process has changed the northern part of the Sahel into almost deserted terrain. This also led to the displacement of the pastoral community to the south in search of pastureland (Mundy, 2010).

REVIEWING CHALLENGES TO COMBAT DESERTIFICATION IN SUDAN

Sudan started combatting desertification many years ago, when the report of the Soil Conservation Committee of 1944 concluded that soil degradation and desertification was mainly due to the misuse of land resources rather than as a result of climate change (Seedahmed, 2017). Desertification continued to worsen day-by-day and threatened the economic and social progress of the country and the lives of its inhabitants.

Between 1972–1976, the Sudan government established the National Committee for Combating Drought and Desertification under the chairmanship of the National Research Council and the Ministry of Agriculture. It commissioned the preparation of studies and solutions to the problems of desertification and drought. The Committee issued a report on the status of desertification in Sudan and project proposals to address the phenomenon. The report was presented at the United Nations Conference on Desertification in Nairobi in 1977 (Seedahmed, 2017).

In 1979, the Ministry of Agriculture was assigned a part-time coordinator to follow up desertification control projects. In 1980, a full-time coordinator was appointed. The National Bureau for Drought Control and Desertification was established under the supervision of the Ministry of Agriculture under the administrative supervision of the Minister of State for Agriculture. A decision was taken to form a Permanent Council for Desertification, in which all relevant ministries and departments, as well as academic and research bodies, were mentioned.

The international organisation also played a significant role in desertification issues in Sudan. The Sudano Sahelian Office (UNDP) provided technical and financial support in the early 1980s to the Office to Combat Desertification, which was designated as the Office for the Coordination of Desertification Programs. The Office was able to hold four regional workshops to raise awareness and to consult on the phenomenon of desertification, and how to address these problems, beginning in the eastern region, followed by Kordofan, Darfur region, and then the northern region. These workshops had been adopted on the consultative approach and involved all concerned in iden- tifying and addressing the problem of desertification. Sudan also defined the con- sultative approach from bottom to top to prepare the National Action Plans (NAPs) (Seedahmed, 2017).

Sudan succeeded in obtaining funds for the gum arabic belt and the grassland development project, and five grants from the Australian Government in the field of natural resources.

In 1986 Sudan established the Relief and Reconstruction Commission that was affiliated to the Ministry of Agriculture, but external funding was suspended due to a conflict of competencies.

In 1988, the Council of Ministers decided to establish a central Ministry for Refugee and Relief Affairs, and included in its structure an administration to combat desertification. After strenuous attempts, the two ministries were disbanded in connection with desertification, which was reintroduced to the Ministry of Agriculture.

This was followed by the establishment of the Drought and Desertification Coordination Unit (NDDU) by a ministerial decree issued on 17 March 1991. This decree confirmed the subordination of the unit to the Ministry of Agriculture and Livestock at the time, under the direct supervision of the Minister of Agriculture. The resolution specified the terms of reference of the unit and the terms of reference of the Coordination Council, which was formed under the chairmanship of the National Coordinator and the membership of 15 other bodies.

The unit was able to obtain technical support from the European Union in Sudan in 1993, which was used in the establishment of the first Geographic Information System (GIS) unit in Sudan. An expert from the British Hunting Company was hired to determine the geographical extent of desertification.

FORMULATION OF SUDAN'S NATIONAL ACTION PROGRAMME

After the implementation of the International Convention to Combat Desertification, the Sudan began preparing the National Action Programme with the assistance of the United Nations Development Programme. The stages of formulating the National Action Programme (NAP) (Seedahmed, 2017) were, first, to organise workshops involving national partners and community leaders in the 13 affected states, where experts from the same states prepared specialised working papers and discussed the following topics:

1. The priorities of the state programmes in combatting desertification and mitigating the effects of drought.
2. Previous experiences in combatting desertification and mitigating the effects of drought.
3. Identifying the roles of all stakeholders in combatting desertification.

Second, the organisation of specialised workshops at the federal level, mainly concerned with the development of a unified strategy for the implementation of the NAP to combat desertification. In this context, 10 national working papers were prepared by national experts in economic and social development and environment conservation. The papers included topics related to the programme, such as resource mobilisation, the role of decision-makers, and voluntary organisations in combatting desertification.

The third phase was a national forum in which representatives from the affected states and government officials participated. There had been active contributions from the United Nations Development Programme and the United Nations Office to Combat Desertification. The presence of state governors and representatives of constitutional institutions was an expression of political commitment. The paper included six main themes, including funding, capacity building, traditional knowledge, programme priorities, institutional structures, follow-up and evaluation, as reflected in previous workshops.

In 2001, the Arab Organization for Agricultural Development (AOAD) asked the Minister of Agriculture to commission two national recruits to draft the NAP document based on the information available from the workshops and the National Forum. The two advisers prepared the National Action Programme in 2002, and submitted it to the Secretariat of the International Convention to Combat Desertification in the form of a draft in Arabic (Seedahmed, 2017).

The National Committee of Voluntary Societies working in the field of desertification has undertaken a parallel effort to complement the government's efforts. The national plan for civil society organisations in combatting desertification has been prepared and integrated into the national plan.

In 2009, the Desertification Law was provided for the establishment of a national council under the auspices of the President of the Republic.

In 2015, the task of combatting desertification became the responsibility of the Ministry of Environment, Natural Resources and Urban Development, with the issuance of Presidential Decree No. 32. When the Presidential Decree No. 21 of 2017 was issued, the National Council for Combating Desertification was included in the Ministry of Environment, Natural Resources and Urban Development.

In 2016, a Secretary General of the National Council to Combat Desertification was appointed.

The establishment of the Council is being carried out through the establishment of a permanent headquarters in the national capital, followed by the establishment of branches of the Council in the States, and the authorisation of an organisational and functional structure for the Secretariat of the Council.

The Council will have the following powers and authorities (Seedahmed, 2017):

1. to formulate policies, plans and propose legislation to combat desertification in cooperation and coordination with relevant parties;
2. to develop a long-term national programme of action for the optimal and balanced use of land and natural resources;
3. to develop human resources and provide necessary support in the fields of desertification studies and desert culture in all relevant fields;
4. to follow up the implementation of the National Action Programme and endeavour to develop and promote it;
5. to support the physical and human capacities of the National Action Programme to combat desertification;
6. to encourage scientific, economic and social research to support the National Action Programme in coordination and cooperation with the educational and research sectors;
7. to encourage the use of technologies that help to protect land from degradation;
8. to establish a network of scientific research institutions to integrate physical and human capacities to combat desertification;
9. to develop and implement comprehensive awareness programmes targeting land users from agriculture, pastoralists, and others;
10. to review the policies, legislation and regulations of the Council periodically to keep abreast of developments in combatting desertification.
11. to establish an effective national organisation from the bottom up, and develop its material and administrative capacities to enable it to combat desertification and achieve sustainable development;
12. to supervise the fund and approve its regulations, administrative structure and reports;
13. to supervise the General Secretariat of the Board, approving its administrative structure and approve its financial and administrative regulations and reports;
14. to authorise the projects submitted by the fund to develop its resources;
15. to recommend the competence of delegations representing Sudan in relevant fora, workshops and meetings internally and externally;

16. to recommend to the competent authority the necessary studies in the field of desertification and its control and the parties entrusted with the preparation of the study;
17. to prepare reports on any practices or irregularities that the Board considers to exacerbate desertification.

Many projects were proposed to combat desertification in Sudan, e.g.:

1. Project for the reconstruction of the gum arabic belt (its three stages in Kordofan and Darfur);
2. Project for the reconstruction of pastures (Kordofan);
3. Project for the Rehabilitation of Grassland for Carbon Absorption (Kordofan St.);
4. Projects for the provision of tree belts in the Nile and North Nile Governorates;
5. Kordofan Resource Development Project;
6. Sustainable Natural Resources Development Project (Green Belt Project);
7. Wadi Al-Kwa Project (North Darfur – UNDP);
8. Adaptation projects to the effects of climate change.

RESULTS

The review of the history of combatting desertification in Sudan revealed that serious attempts were made many years ago to formulate regulations and legislations, and to coordinate with international and regional agreements. Despite these efforts, desertification is still defined as the major threat to sustainable development and human lives.

Many conclusions and lessons emerged from the previous experiences of government, NGOs, civil society and private sectors in implementing desertification programmes in Sudan. The analytical review of Sudan desertification policies showed a lack of the intersectoral approach that integrates forestry activities and land use into the social, economic and developmental process of the country. They also lacked linkages to other sectors that use and actually compete for the available natural resources.

Therefore, fast action should be implemented to stop sand movement and improve soil quality. This is in addition to the interpretation of research results that dealt with modelling and drought control.

REFERENCES

Abdi, O.A., Glover, E.K. and Luukkanen, O. (2013), Causes and Impacts of Land Degradation and Desertification: Case Study of the Sudan. *International Journal of Agriculture and Forestry*, Vol. 3, No. 2, pp. 40–51.

Dregne, H.M. and Rozonov, B. (1991), A new assessment of the world status of desertification, *Desertification Control Bulletin*, No. 20, pp. 6–29.

FAO (1984), *Land, food and people*, Rome: FAO. United Nations. Statistical yearbook. Annual publication. New York: United Nations.

FAO/UN, FAOCLIM2—Word Wide Agroclimatic Data Base CD-ROM. Food and Agriculture Organization Agrometerology Group Roma, 2000.

Helldén, U. (1991), Desertification: time for an assessment?, *Ambio*, Vol. 20, No. 8, pp. 372–83.

IPCC (2001), *Impacts, Adaptation and Vulnerability*, Intergovernmental Panel on Climatic Change.

Lamprey, H. (1975), *Report on the Desert Encroachment Reconnaissance in Northern Sudan*, Khartoum, National Council for Research, Ministry of Agriculture, Food and Natural Resources.

Maliva, R. and Missimer, T. (2012), *Arid Lands Water Evaluation Management*, Springer: XXIX, 6pp.

MOA (2015), Ministry of Agriculture Reports, Khartoum, Sudan.

Mundy, J. (2010), *Introduction: Securitizing the Sahara*, Association of Concerned Africa Scholars Review, available at: http://concernedafricascholars.org/bulletin/issue85/mundy.

Reynolds, J.F. (2001), Desertification. *Encyclopedia of Biodiversity*, pp. 66–78.

Reynolds, J.F and Stafford Smith, D.M. (2002), *Global Desertification: Do Humans Cause Deserts?*, Vol. 88. Dahlem University Press, Berlin.

Richards, T. (1994), *Monitoring in the Sudan: A report for the government of the Sudan on methods and data sources*, Draft and Borehamwood Hunting Technical Services.

Seedahmed, A. (2017), *Features of Sudan's efforts to combat desertification*. Ministry of Environment, Natural Resources and Urban Development National. Council for Desertification workshop, July 2017, Khartoum-Sudan.

Suliman, M. (2008), *The war in Darfur: The impact of the resource element*, Available at: http://new.ifaanet.org/wp-content/uploads/2011/12/DarfurpaperinArabic1.htm.

Toulmin, C. (1995), *The desertification convention: The strategic agenda for the EU, EC Aid and Sustainable Development*, Briefing paper, No. 4 International Institute for Environmental and Development (IIED). London

UNCOD (1977), *Desertification: its Causes and Consequences*, Secretariat of United Nations Conference on Desertification (Ed.) Pergamon Press, Oxford.

UNDP (1991), *Human Development Report*. Published for the United Nations Development Programme (UNDP). New York. Oxford. Oxford University Press.

United Nations Environment Programme (UNEP) (1991), *Status of Desertification and Implementation of the UN Plan of action to Combat Desertification*, UNEP, Nairobi, 88pp.

UNEP (1992), *Saving Our Planet: Challenges and Hopes*, The State of the Environment (1972-1992). Nairobi, UNEP.

BIOGRAPHY

Sarra Ahmed Mohamed Saad was awarded a PhD in Soil Science in 2002 from the University of Goettingen, Germany. She graduated from the Faculty of Agriculture, University of Khartoum, majoring in Soil Science. Dr Saad was appointed to the National Centre for Research, Department of Environment in 1992, and is currently working as senior researcher of Soil Science. She is leading many research projects dealing with the problem of food security, soil productivity and climate change, in addition to organic farming and its applications in Sudan. She is a member of many scientific societies inside and outside Sudan and has been awarded prizes for scientific achievements in Sudan. She also holds patents for producing compost from organic waste. Dr Saad has supervised many postgraduate students at the MSc and PhD level, and has offered consultancy to both government and the private sector about organic food production and fertilisation strategies, especially in poor fertile soils. In addition to Arabic, Dr Saad speaks German, English, French and Spanish.

Adil M.A. Seedahmed graduated with a BSc in Forestry from the University of Khartoum; has a Post-Graduate Diploma in Development Planning, ITC, the Netherlands, and an MSc in Agriculture, from the University of Western Australia. He worked in the Desertification Unit, Ministry of Agriculture, then the Dinder National Park Project, the Nile Transboundary Environment Action Project and the NAPA Implementation Project (with the Higher Council for Environment and Natural Resources in the first phase and the UNDP in the second phase). He is a member of the Executive Committee of the Sudanese Environment Conservation Society.

Allam Ahmed (www.allamahmed.org) obtained his MSc/MBA from the Royal Agricultural University, UK and was awarded the RAU Scholarship and Prestigious Book Prize for Best MSc/MBA Dissertation. He completed his PhD in Economics (*Technology and Knowledge Transfer for Development*) in two years at Edinburgh Napier University, UK. He is a Fellow and Chartered Marketer of the Chartered Institute of Marketing, UK. Allam is based at the Science Policy Research Unit – SPRU (*world leader in research, consultancy and teaching in the field of Science and Technology Policy*) University of Sussex, where he established and led the postgraduate programme MSc International Management. He is a Professor at the Royal Dock School of Business and Law, University of East London, UK (2016-now) and Visiting Professor at Brighton Business School, University of Brighton, UK (2012–2015). Allam has an extensive background in academia, public and private sectors, specialising in KM, technology transfer, SD, business process re-engineering, change management and organisational transformation. He is the Founding President of the World Association for Sustainable Development (WASD) and all its journals; Founding Director of Middle Eastern Knowledge Economy Institute; and Founder of Sudan Knowledge. In 2009 Allam led the Government of Abu Dhabi major and first of its kind in the Middle East Knowledge Management Framework (Musharaka). His work is featured and archived by major international institutions and top universities such as World Bank; UN; EU; DFID; Government of St Lucia; WFP; Imperial College; Cambridge; Oxford; Princeton; Yale; Harvard; MIT; Stanford; Toronto; etc. Expert Advisor to the European Commission on International Scientific Cooperation (2006–2008); International

Co-ordinator UNESCO Chair on Transfer of Technology (2008-now); and Advisor African Capacity Building Foundation (2011–2013). He is listed in the Who's Who in the World 2009–2017.

Ahmed Mohmed Adam Eldoma has a BSc in Forestry (Honors) from the University of Khartoum, Faculty of Agriculture, an MSc in Natural Resources Management, from the Faculty of Science, University of Edinburgh, Scotland, UK, and a PhD in Tree Physiology and Genetics from UPM, Malaysia. He is currently an Associate Professor at the College of Forestry and Range Science, Sudan University for Science and Technology. Dr Eldoma has worked as an ACF at The Forestry National Corporation, Sudan, as Production Control Officer seconded to the Sudan Gum Arabic Company for two years. He has worked in different capacities at the College of Forestry and Range Sciences including, Head Department of Silviculture, Dean of the Faculty, Head of the Research Unit, and Secretary of University of Sudan Research Council. Dr Eldoma has worked as a coordinator for The Sudan Finland Forestry Program, and The Sudanese-Japanese Dry Land Research Group, sponsored by the Institute of Humanity and Nature, Kyoto, Japan. He has conducted several research projects and supervised many Postgraduate students at the MSc and PhD level. He is currently working as the Project Manager of the Natural Resources, Land Use Database and map for Darfur implemented by GAF AG Company based at Munich, Germany. He has authored two books and 22 journal articles.

Sufyan Abd Elrzig Mohmmed Ossman is currently working as Head of Agricultural Unit in Khartoum Refinery Company in Khartoum-Sudan. He was awarded a BSc in Forestry and Range Sciences, and MSc in Environment and Forestry from Sudan University of Science and Technology in 2002 and 2013, respectively. He has participated in many workshops inside and outside Sudan related to disaster management; quality control of water and wastewater; management of petroleum installation; compost production and uses; proliferation of orchards, production of medicinal and aromatic plants; COP 21 in France 2015, COP 22 in Morocco and COP 23 in Bonn.

SHOOT REGENERATION FROM NODAL SEGMENT OF *ACACIA SENEGAL* IN BORNO STATE OF NIGERIA

Njidda M. Gadzama*, Jummai T. Kaldapa
Martha Tarfa and Bukar H. Kabura

Biotechnology Centre, University of Maiduguri
P. M. B. 1069. Maiduguri, Nigeria
njiddagadzama@gmail.com

ABSTRACT

Purpose: *Acacia senegal* is a valuable leguminous tree species of the Sudano/Sahelian region sought after for its economic and ecological importance. Developing *in vitro* propagation protocol for this tree in Borno State of Nigeria will provide a sustainable means of re-foresting and improving the nutrients of the degraded soil of the Sahel environment of Nigeria.

Design/Methodology/Approach: Nodal segments derived from 6-month old seedlings growing on the experimental farm of the Biotechnology Centre, University of Maiduguri, were cultured on Murashige and Skoog (MS) medium, supplemented with 0.025–1.5mg/l of 6-benzylaminopurine (BAP), alone and in combination with 0.02mg/l α-naphthalene acetic acid (NAA) and 0.2–1.6mg/l of kinetin (KN), alone or in combination with 0.2mg/l α-naphthalene acetic acid (NAA).

Findings/Results: The maximum number of shoots per explants (2.31 ± 1.24) and longest shoots (2.59 ± 1.38cm) were obtained from MS medium supplemented with 1.0mg/l and 1.5mg/l BAP respectively, while 1.16 ± 0.71 shoots with maximum 2.34 ± 1.35cm length were found in medium containing 1.2mg/l kinetin after four weeks of culture. Inclusion of NAA (0.02mg/1) with BAP at the various concentrations in the culture medium was not effective in enhancing shoot proliferation. However, obtained results indicate that both shoot number (1.70 ± 0.95cm) and length (2.33 ± 0.92cm) were enhanced by adding 0.2mg/l NAA to 0.4mg/KN.

Originality and value: This work would be the first attempt to propagate *Acacia senegal* by *in-vitro* method in Borno State of Nigeria, with the view of generating reproducible protocol for future mass propagation of the tree crop in the State.

Keywords: *Acacia senegal*; *in vitro* micro-propagation; gum arabic; induction; Murashige and Skoog (MS); Kinetin (KN); 6-Benzylaminopurine (BAP); α-naphthalene acetic acid (NAA); indole-3-acetic acid (IAA); indole-3-butyric acid (IBA)

INTRODUCTION

The plant *Acacia senegal*, commonly known as Hashab (Hausa), Kolkol (Kanuri) is a widespread leguminous tree of the Sudano-Sahel zone of Africa from Senegal to Sudan (Raddad, 2006). It is a medium height tree of about 5m and survives in the most adverse conditions – hot wind, sand storm, poorest soils and sand, in slightly acid to moderately alkaline soils. It grows naturally in areas of 200–800mm rainfall with 7–11 dry months per year and requires free drainage. The tree crop does not tolerate water logging.

Over 300 species of the *Acacia* family exist (FAO, 1995), but more attention has been given to *Acacia senegal* because of its significant contribution towards environmental protection and economic development in the Sudano-Sahelian region.

Sudan is known to be the major producer of gum arabic in the world (Beshai, 1984), Nigeria being the second largest producer, covering an area of about 250,000sq km in the Sahel region of the country (Plate 1). Nigeria has three grades of gum arabic produced by *Acacia senegal* (grade 1), *Acacia seyal* (grade 2), and *Acacia combretum* (grade 3).

Being a drought resistant tree, *Acacia senegal* helps to ameliorate the Sahelian ecosystem, which is losing about 350,000m^2 of land mass to desert conditions, with increased movement southward at a rate of 0.6km per annum (Gadzama, 1995). It is planted for sand dune fixation, wind erosion control, nitrogen fixation, and to provide vegetative cover for the degraded soils in the Sahel of Africa.

Gum arabic has huge foreign exchange potential. In 2008 alone, Nigeria exported a total of 20,000 metric tonnes of gum Arabic, estimated at US$43.55m (N6.5325 billion) (Commodity Network Ltd, 2008).

Beverage and Pharmaceutics require as polyvalent additive, protective colloid, oxidative inhibitor and emulsifier, and as a food adhesive agent. The food industry utilises 60–75% of world production of gum arabic as stabilising, encapsulating agents and other purposes.

Because of the importance of this tree crop, the Federal Government of Nigeria has encouraged R&D that would enhance improved livelihoods of the rural communities in gum arabic sustainable businesses.

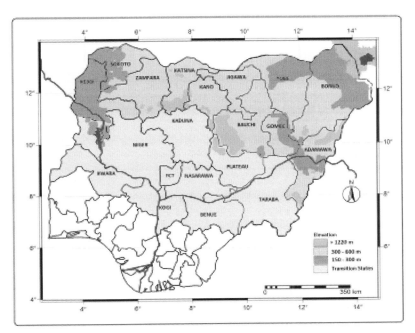

Plate 1 Nigeria's Eleven Sahelian States with *A. Senegal* Distributions; Best Gum Arabic Produced in Borno, Yobe and Jigawa

Source: Gadzama and Ayuba (2014)

MATERIALS AND METHODS

Establishment of Aseptic Seedlings

Seeds of *A. senegal* were acquired from a gum arabic tree plantation grown in Gubio Local Government Area of Borno State, Nigeria. Seedlings were raised on the experimental site of the Biotechnology Centre, University of Maiduguri.

Nodal segment explants with one axillary bud were excised from 6-month old seedlings growing in the nursery. The explants were washed under running tap water for 30 minutes to remove surface dust, and then soaked in a solution mixture of 100mg/l ascorbic acid and 150mg/l citric acid for 10 minutes. The explants were then immersed in 70% ethanol for 30 seconds, washed by several changes of sterilised distilled water; they were then immersed in 100ml Clorox solution of 10% and 15% mixed with two drops of Tween 20 (detergent) for 10 minutes each, with continuous shaking. Explants were rinsed several times with sterile distilled water under laminar airflow cabinet. Sterilised explants were cultured in culture bottles containing Murashige and Skoog (MS) (1962) basal medium.

Shoot Proliferation

MS medium was supplemented with various concentrations of 6-benzylaminopurine (BAP) at 0.025–1.5mg/l, alone and in combination with α-naphthalene acetic acid (NAA) (0.02mg/l) or kinetin (KN) (0.2–1.6mg/l), alone and in combination with NAA at 0.2mg/l for shoot induction and proliferation.

Culture Media and Conditions for in vitro Growth

Murashige and Skoog (1962) basal media, cited above, was used as basal culture medium for shoot induction, supplemented with 3% sucrose, solidified by 0.7% agar and adjusted to pH5.7±1 by drops of 1 N NaOH or 1 HCl, then dispensed in 20ml into culture vessels and sterilised by autoclaving at 121°C and 1.06 bars for 15 minutes. All cultures were incubated in the culture room at 25°C ±1 and under photoperiod of 16/8 light and dark hours daily with exposure to 1,000 lux, provided by LED lamps.

STATISTICAL ANALYSIS

For the above experiments, 10 explants were used for each treatment and each experiment was repeated thrice. In the shoot proliferation experiment, shoots parameters per explants were determined after four weeks of culture. The results are expressed as mean ± S.D. of the three experiments. The data were analysed statistically using Statistic 9.5 and the significance of differences among mean values was carried out using Duncan's Multiple Range Test (DMRT) and paired sample T-test at $p<0.05$.

RESULTS/FINDINGS

Shoot Multiplication

MS medium was supplemented with various concentrations of cytokinin BAP (0.025, 0.05, 0.5, 1.0 and 1.5) mg/l, alone and in combination with 0.02mg/l NAA; KN (0.2, 0.4, 0.8, 1.2 and 1.6) mg/l, alone and in combination with 0.2mg/l NAA.

Results obtained after four weeks of culture indicate the superiority of BAP over kinetin in initiating shoot bud formation (Tables 1 and 3). The addition of NAA to BAP does not seem to be essential in promoting shoot proliferation in the nodal explants of *Acacia senegal*.

Effect of BAP and KN on Shoot Proliferation

Several workers have used various explants and culture media to introduce tissue culture methods for the regeneration of *Acacia senegal*. Among the various explants, the nodal explants are most commonly used (Khalisi and Al-Joboury, 2012). Nodal explants showed their first response by enlarging and bursting within two weeks of culture (Figure 1A). New shoot development was observed within three weeks of culture, and more shoots were found to develop during subcultures (Figures 1B, 1C, 1D, 1E and 1F).

Cotyledonary nodal explants cultured on MS medium devoid of growth regulator produced shoots that may be due to the presence of endogenous cytokinin in the nodal segments (Rajeswari and Paliwal, 2008). However, the addition of exogenous cytokinin to MS medium induced a shoot multiplication rate indicating the requirement of exogenous cytokinin supply in the medium for better axillary shoot proliferation. Out of the two different cytokinins used in this experiment, BAP and KN, the best shoot proliferation was observed on medium containing BAP, with the highest number of shoots (2.31 $\pm$ 1.24) and longest shoots (2.59 $\pm$ 1.38cm) formed on 1.0mg/l and 1.5mg/l BAP respectively (Table 1; Figures 1B and 1C), while 1.16 $\pm$ 0.71 shoots with maximum 2.34 $\pm$ 1.35cm length were found in medium containing 1.2mg/l KN (Table 3; Figure 1D) after four weeks of culture.

Table 1   Effect of Various Concentrations of BAP on Shoot Induction from Nodal Segments of *Acacia senegal* on MS Medium after Four Weeks Culture Period

Hormone Concentrations BAP (mg/l)	Response (%)	Average No. of shoots	Average Length of shoots (cm)	Mean no. of leaves	No. of nodes
Control	70	0.70 $\pm$ 0.48[bc]	0.33 $\pm$ 0.18[c]	0.70 $\pm$ 0.42[c]	0.70 $\pm$ 0.63[c]
0.025	80	1.10 $\pm$ 0.74[abc]	0.83 $\pm$ 0.51[bc]	1.00 $\pm$ 0.67[bc]	0.90 $\pm$ 0.57[bc]
0.05	70	0.70 $\pm$ 0.67[c]	1.60 $\pm$ 1.41[abc]	1.55 $\pm$ 1.38[abc]	1.40 $\pm$ 1.26[abc]
0.50	80	1.58 $\pm$ 0.93[abc]	1.70 $\pm$ 0.92[abc]	1.62 $\pm$ 0.95[abc]	1.40 $\pm$ 0.84[abc]
1.00	80	2.31 $\pm$ 1.24[a]	2.19 $\pm$ 1.26[ab]	2.41 $\pm$ 1.37[ab]	2.00 $\pm$ 1.15[ab]
1.50	80	2.16 $\pm$ 1.32[ab]	2.59 $\pm$ 1.38[a]	2.50 $\pm$ 1.43[a]	2.20 $\pm$ 1.32[a]

Note: Different letters in each column show significant differences ($p<0.05$)
Source: devised by authors

Table 2   Effect of Various Concentrations of BAP and NAA on Shoot Induction from Nodal Segments of *Acacia senegal* on MS Medium after Four Weeks Culture Period

Hormone Concentrations BA + NAA(mg/l)	Response (%)	Average No. of shoots	Average Length of shoots (cm)	Mean no. of leaves	No. of nodes
Control	70	0.70 ± 0.48ᵃ	0.68 ± 0.53ᵇ	1.07 ± 0.98ᵃ	1.00 ± 0.94ᵃ
0.025 + 0.02	60	0.60 ± 0.52ᵃ	0.35 ± 0.31ᵇ	1.20 ± 1.13ᵃ	0.90 ± 0.99ᵃ
0.05 + 0.02	70	0.80 ± 0.63ᵃ	1.71 ± 1.24ᵃ	1.60 ± 1.35ᵃ	1.50 ± 1.27ᵃ
0.50 + 0.02	70	0.70 ± 0.48ᵃ	0.35 ± 0.37ᵇ	0.80 ± 0.63ᵃ	0.80 ± 0.63ᵃ
1.00 + 0.02	50	0.50 ± 0.53ᵃ	0.59 ± 0.64ᵇ	0.60 ± 0.69ᵃ	0.50 ± 0.53ᵃ
1.50 + 0.02	60	0.60 ± 0.52ᵃ	0.54 ± 0.48ᵇ	0.70 ± 0.67ᵃ	0.60 ± 0.52ᵃ

Note: Different letters in each column show significant differences ($p<0.05$)
Source: devised by authors

Table 3   Effect of Various Concentrations of KN on Shoot Induction from Nodal Segments of *Acacia senegal* on MS Medium after Four weeks Culture Period

Hormone Concentrations KN (mg/l)	Response (%)	Average No. of shoots	Average Length of shoots (cm)	Mean no. of leaves	No. of nodes
Control	80	0.80 ± 0.42ᵃ	1.09. ± 0.62ᵇᶜ	1.09 ± 0.70ᵇ	0.80 ± 0.42ᵇ
0.20	90	0.90 ± 0.32ᵃ	0.82 ± 0.42ᵇᶜ	0.90 ± 0.32ᵇ	0.90 ± 0.32ᵇ
0.40	60	0.60 ± 0.52ᵃ	0.18 ± 0.19ᵇᶜ	1.02 ± 0.97ᵇ	1.00 ± 0.94ᵇ
0.80	50	0.50 ± 0.52ᵃ	0.14 ± 0.17ᶜ	0.80 ± 0.92ᵇ	0.50 ± 0.52ᵇ
1.20	80	1.16 ± 0.71ᵃ	2.34 ± 1.35ᵃ	2.80 ± 1.75ᵃ	2.60 ± 1.71ᵃ
1.60	70	0.70 ± 0.48ᵃ	1.13 ± 0.86ᵇ	1.60 ± 1.17ᵃᵇ	1.20 ± 0.92ᵇ

Note: Different letters in each column show significant differences ($p<0.05$)
Source: devised by authors

Table 4   Effect of Various Concentrations of KN and NAA on Shoot Induction from Nodal Segments of *Acacia senegal* on MS Medium after Four weeks Culture Period

Hormone concentrations KN + NAA (mg/l)	Response (%)	Average No. of shoots	Average Length of shoots (cm)	Mean no. of leaves	No. of nodes
Control	70	0.70 ± 0.48ᵇ	0.42 ± 0.38ᶜ	1.00 ± 0.82ᵇ	0.80 ± 0.62ᵇ
0.20 + 0.20	70	0.90 ± 0.74ᵃᵇ	1.42 ± 1.03ᵃᵇ	1.82 ± 1.50ᵃᵇ	1.60 ± 1.43ᵃᵇ
0.40 + 0.20	90	1.70 ± 0.95ᵃ	2.33 ± 0.92ᵃ	2.32 ± 1.05ᵃ	2.10 ± 0.99ᵃ
0.80 + 0.20	80	0.80 ± 0.42ᵇ	0.60 ± 0.39ᵇᶜ	1.30 + 0.82ᵃᵇ	1.10 ± 0.74ᵃᵇ
1.20 + 0.20	90	0.90 ± 0.32ᵃᵇ	0.38 ± 0.28ᶜ	1.50 ± 0.71ᵃᵇ	1.50 ± 0.71ᵃᵇ
1.60 + 0.20	70	0.85 ± 0.67ᵇ	1.13 ± 0.81ᵇᶜ	1.40 ± 1.08ᵃᵇ	1.20 ± 1.03ᵃᵇ

Note: Different letters in each column show significant differences ($p<0.05$)
Source: devised by authors

Figure 1 *In vitro* propagation of *A. senegal* Willd. from nodal explants. A. Two-week old *in vitro* shoot on MS basal medium; B. Multiple shoot formation from nodal explants after four weeks of culture on MS + 1.0mg/l BAP; C. *In vitro* proliferated shoots from nodal explants after four weeks of culture on MS + 1.5mg/l BAP; D. *In vitro* shoot on MS + 1.2mg/l kinetin; E. *in vitro* shoot on MS + 0.2mg/l kinetin and 0.2mg/l NAA; F. *In vitro* shoot on MS + 0.4mg/l kinetin and 0.2mg/l NAA

Source: produced by authors

DISCUSSION AND CONCLUSIONS

The results indicated that BAP was superior to KN in enhancing shoot proliferation. BAP has been the most popular and widely used cytokinin for stimulating shoot multiplication in a broad range of species (Gaspar et al., 1996). The superiority of BAP over KN has also been reported in *in vitro* propagation of other species of *Acacia* (Shahinozzaman et al., 2013; Badji et al., 1993; Beck et al., 1998; Dewan et al., 1992; Galiana et al., 1991; Junior et al., 2004; Khalafalla and Daffalla, 2008; Mittal et al., 1989; Nandwani, 1995; Rout et al., 2008; Singh et al., 1993; Vengadesan et al., 2002). The proliferation of shoots in nodal explants of *Acacia senegal* at a concentration of 1.0mg/l BAP was also reported by Khalaffalla and Daffalla (2008). Khalisi and Al-Joboury (2012), obtained similar results with *Acacia farnesiana*.

This study revealed that the addition of exogenous auxin (NAA) to cytokinin (BAP) was not essential to initiate shoot bud formation (Table 2). The results might indicate the antagonistic effect of NAA with BAP in *in vitro* shoot proliferation of *A. senegal*. Vengadesan et al. (2002) also observed that auxins (NAA, IBA and IAA), together with BAP, were not effective for shoot proliferation from cotyledonary nodes of *Acacia sinuata*. In *Acacia senegal,* similar results were reported by Khalafalla and Daffalla (2008). This finding is also in agreement with the work of Mallikarjuna and Rajendrudu (2009) on *Holarrhena antidysenterica*, and Hussain et al. (2007) on Sterculiaurens. Garland and Stoltz (1981) demonstrated that in a number of cases, cytokinins alone are enough for optimal shoot multiplication, as also supported by the works of Amin and Jaiswal (1993) and Ndiaye et al. (2006). However, shoots were more elongated in the combination, 0.05mg/l BAP + 0.02mg/l NAA (Table 2). This is consistent with the observations of many researchers who suggested that incorporation of low level auxin with BAP promoted shoot induction in different tree species, including *Acacia catechu* (Kaur et al., 1998), *Acacia seyal* (Al-Wasel, 2000), *Acacia tortilis* (Nandwani, 1995), *Aegle marmelos* (Nayak et al., 2007), *Colute aistria* (Hegazi and Gabr, 2010), *Nyctanthes arbor-tristis* (Siddique et al., 2006), *Pterocarpus marsupium* (Husain et al., 2008) and *Terminalia belerica* (Rathore et al., 2008).

Obtained results also indicate that both shoot number (1.70 ± 0.95) and length (2.33 ± 0.92cm) were enhanced by adding 0.2mg/l NAA to 0.2mg/lKN and 0.4mg/l KN respectively (Table 4; Figures 1E and 1F). This result agrees with the work of Khalisi and Al-Joboury (2012). Similar results were reported in other legume trees, *Acacia mearnsii, Albizia odoratissima* and *Acacia nilotica* (Mittal et al., 1989; Jones et al., 1990).

CONCLUSIONS

In conclusion, this is the first report of an *in vitro* propagation of *A. senegal* in Borno State, Nigeria. We were able to induce shoots from nodal explants excised from 6-month old seedlings in a nursery that were successfully germinated from seeds obtained from Gum Arabic plantation in Gubio Local Government Area of the State. Although similar work had been done by others, this protocol is the first using the indigenous tree species. The number and length of shoots were maximum in the culture medium optimised with the combination of 1.0mg/l and 1.5mg/l BAP. However, the combinations of kinetin with NAA resulted in the improvement of shoot number and shoot length. Although BAP showed superiority over kinetin in terms of axillary shoot bud stimulation, kinetin alone (1.2mg/l) significantly increased shoot length. Therefore, for the up-scaling of this work, further experiments are needed to achieve a higher percentage of shots and subsequent root induction (Kaldapa and Gadzama, 2018).

ACKNOWLEDGEMENTS

This research was supported by the Tetfund National Research Grant of the Federal Republic of Nigeria, awarded to Professor Emeritus N. M. Gadzama and his research team of the Biotechnology Centre, University of Maiduguri. The research team is appreciative of the support of the Vice-Chancellor of the University of Maiduguri, Professor Ibrahim A. Njodi, NPOM in ensuring progress of this work.

REFERENCES

Al-Wasel, A.S. (2000), Micropropagation of *Acacia seyal* Del. *in vitro*. *Journal of Arid Environments*, Vol. 46, No. 4, pp. 425–31.

Amin, M.N. and Jaiswal, V.S. (1993), *In vitro* response of apical bud explants from immature trees of Jackfruit (*Artocarpus heterophyllus*). *Plant Cell, Tissue and Organ Culture*, Vol. 33, No. 1, pp. 59–65.

Badji, S., Marione, Y. and Ndiaye, I. (1993), *In vitro* propagation of the gum arabic tree (*Acacia senegal* (L.) Willd.) 1. Developing a rapid method for producing plants. *Plant Cell Reports*, Vol. 12, No. 11, pp. 629–33.

Beck, S., Dunlop, R. and Van Staden, J. (1998), Rejuvenation and micro-propagation of adult *Acacia mearnsii* using Coppice material. *Plant Growth Regulation*, Vol. 26, No. 3, pp. 149–53.

Beshai, A.A. (1984), The economics of a primary commodity: Gum Arabic. *Oxford Bulletin of Economics and Statistics*, Vol. 46, No. 4, pp. 371–81.

Borges Junior, N., Soborsa, R.D.C. and Marten-Coder, M.P. (2004), *In vitro* multiplication of Black watelle(*Acacia mearnsii* De Willd.) axillary buds. *Revista Arvore*, Vol. 28, No. 4, pp. 493–98.

Commodity Networks Ltd (2008), Commodity consulting company, Abuja, Nigeria.

Dewan, A., Nanda, K. and Gupta, S.C. (1992), *In vitro* propagation of *Acacia nilotica* subsp. *indica* (Brenen.) via cotyledonary nodes. *Plant Cell Reports*, Vol. 12, No. 1, pp. 18–21.

FAO (1995), Quality Control of gum arabic in Nigeria Project TCP/RAF/4557 document.

Gadzama, N.M. (1995), Sustainable Development in the Arid Zone of Nigeria. Monograph series No. 1. Centre for Arid Zone Studies, University of Maiduguri Press. p. 32.

Gadzama, N.M. and Ayuba, H.K. (2014), Desertification in Nigeria, in Okoli, D., Sridhar, K.C., Popoola, L., Ikporukpo. C.O. and Nzegbule, E. Proceedings of the Symposium on the *Nigerian Environment: Past 100 Years and the Future* held at University of Ibadan, September 2014.

Galiana, A.A., Tibok, A. and Duhoux, E. (1991), *In vitro* propagation of the nitrogen-fixing, tree-legume *Acacia mangium* Willd. *Plant and Soil*, Vol. 135, No. 2, pp. 151–59.

Garland, P. and Stoltz, L.P. (1981), Micropropagation of Pissardi Plum. *Annals of Botany*, Vol. 48, No. 3, pp. 387–89.

Gaspar, T., Kevers, C., Penel, C., Greppin, H., Reid, D.M. and Thorpe, T.A. (1996), Plant hormones and plant growth regulators in plant tissue culture. *In Vitro Cellular and Developmental Biology-Plant*, Vol. 32, No. 4, pp. 272–89.

Hegazi, G.A.E. and Gabr, M.F. (2010), Overcoming early shoot senescence of *Coluteaistri* Miller propagated *in vitro*. *American Journal of Science*, Vol. 6, No. 12, pp. 1733–738.

Husain, M.K., Anis, M. and Shahzad, A. (2008), *In vitro* propagation of a multipurpose leguminous tree (*Pterocarpus marsupium* Roxb.) using nodal explants. *Acta Physiologiae Plantarum*, Vol. 30, No. 3, pp. 353–59.

Hussain, T.M., Chandrasekhar, T. and Gopal, G.R. (2007), High frequency shoot regeneration of *Sterculia urens* Roxb. (an endangered tree species) through cotyledonary node cultures. *Afrian Journal of Biotechnology*, Vol. 6, No. 14, pp. 1643–649.

Jones, T.C., Batchelor, C.A. and Harris, P.J.C. (1990), *In vitro* culture and propagation of *Acacia species* (*A. bivenosa*, *A. holosericea*, *A. salicina*, *A. saligna* and *A. sclerosperma*), *International Tree Crops Journal*, Vol. 6, Nos 2–3, pp. 183–92.

Kaldapa, J. and Gadzama, N.M. (2018), Induction of callus from nodal explants of *Acacia Senegal*. In Ahmed, A. (WASD) and Dumitru, P. (UN) (Eds): Proceedings of the 5th Sudan Diaspora International Conference, Palais des Nations, Geneva. April 2018.

Kaur, K., Verma, B. and Kant, U. (1998), Plants obtained from the Kahir tree (*Acacia catechu* Willd) using mature nodal segments. *Plant Cell Reports*, Vol. 17, No. 5, pp. 427–29.

Khalafalla, M.M. and Daffalla, H.M. (2008), *In vitro* Micropropagation and micrografting of gum arabic tree (*Acacia senegal* (L) Willd.), *International Journal of Sustainable Crop Production*, Vol. 3, No. 1, pp. 19–27.

Khalisi, A.A. and Al-Joboury, Kh. R. (2012), *In vitro* clonal propagation of *Acacia Senegal*. Department of Biology, Education College, University of Baghdad, Iraq National History Research Centre and Museum, Universty of Baghdad.

Mallikarjuna, K. and Rajendrudu, G. (2009), Rapid *in vitro* propagation of *Holarrhena antidysenterica* using seedling cotyledonary nodes. *Biologia Plantarum*, Vol. 53, No. 3, pp. 569–72.

Mittal, A.R., Agarwall, S.C. and Gupta, S.C. (1989), *In vitro* development of plantlets from axillary buds of *Acacia auriculiformis*. *Plant Cell Tissue and Organ Culture*, Vol. 19, No. 1, pp. 65–70.

Murashige, T. and Skoog, F. (1962), A revised medium for rapid growth and bioassays with tobacco tissue cultures. *Physiologia Plantarum*, Vol. 15, No. 3, pp. 473–97.

Nandwani, D. (1995), *In vitro* micropropagation of a tree legume adapted to arid lands: *Acaciatortilis* subsp. raddiana. *Annales des Sciences forestieres*, Vol. 52, No. 2, pp.183–89.

Nayak, P., Behera, P.R. and Manikkannan, T. (2007), High frequency plantlet regeneration from cotyledonary node cultures of *Aegle marmelos* (L.) Corr. *In Vitro Cellular and Developmental Biology-Plant*, Vol. 43, No. 3, pp. 231–36.

Ndiaye, A., Diallo, M.S., Niang, D. and Gassama-Dia, Y.K. Mamadou, S. D. and Yayekene, G. D. (2006), *In vitro* regeneration of adult trees of *Bambusa vulgaris*. *African Journal of Biotechnology*, Vol. 5, pp. 1245–48.

Raddad, E.Y. (2006), Analysis of systems based on *Acacia senegal* in the Blue Nile Region, Sudan. Doctoral Dissertation University of Helsinki, Faculty of Agriculture and Forestry, Department of forest Ecology, Viikki Tropical Resources Institute (VITRI) and Agricultural Research Co-operation, Forestry Research Centre, Khartoum, Sudan.

Rajeshwari, V. and Paliwal, K. (2008), *In vitro* adventitious shoot organogenesis and plant regeneration from seedling explants of *Albizia odoratissima* L.f.(Benth.). *In vitro Cellular and Developmental Biology*, Vol. 44, No. 2, pp. 78–83.

Rathore, P., Suthar, R. and Purohit, S.D. (2008), Micropropagation of *Terminalia bellerica* Roxb from juvenile explants. *Indian Journal of Biotechnology*, Vol. 7, pp. 246–49.

Rout, G.R., Senapati, S.K.S. and Aparajeta, S. (2008), Micropropagation of *Acacia chundra* (Roxb.).

Shahinozzaman, M., Faruq, M.O., Ferdous, M.M., Azad, M.A.K. and Amin, M.N. (2013), Direct organogenesis and plant regeneration from cotyledons of a multipurpose tree, *Acacia mangium Willd*. *Current Trends in Biotechnology and Pharmacy*, Vol. 7, No. 1, pp. 511–17.

Siddique, I., Anis, M. and Jahan, A.A. (2006), Rapid multiplication of *Nyctanthes arbor-tristis* through *in vitro* axillary shoot proliferation. *World Journal of Agricultural Sciences*, Vol. 2, No. 2, pp. 188–92.

Singh, H.P., Singh, S., Saxena R.P. and Singh, R.K. (1993). *In vitro* bud break in axillary nodal segments of mature trees of *Acacia nilotica*. *Indian Journal of Plant Physiology*, Vol. 36, pp. 21–24.

Vengadesan, G., Ganapathi, A., Prem, A., Ramesh, R. and Anbazhagan, V. (2002), *In vitro* propagation of *Acacia sinuate* (Lour.) Merr. via cotyledonary node. *Agroforestry Systems*, Vol. 55, No. 1, pp. 9–15.

BIOGRAPHY

Professor Njidda M. Gadzama OFR, FAS is Emeritus Professor of Zoology and Environmental Science at University of Maiduguri, Borno State, Nigeria. He is an academic leader having been pioneer Pro-Chancellor of National Open University of Nigeria; Vice-Chancellor, University of Maiduguri; and the Acting Vice-Chancellor, University of Port Harcourt. He has a BA (Biology) from McPherson College, Kansas (1964); MSc (Zoology), Long Island University (1967); and PhD (Entomology), New York University (1971). He has in excess of 90 scholarly publications in refereed journals, conference proceedings, edited books, and monographs. He is also the founding Director of Centre for Arid Zone Studies and Biotechnology Centre at University of Maiduguri. He is the recipient of many awards, including in May 2016, *Hallmarks of Labour Foundation Award* for the Most Consistent Advocate for Positive Change within the University System in Nigeria.

Jummai Theresa Kaldapa is a Laboratory Scientist in the Biotechnology Centre at the University of Maiduguri. She is a Fellow of the Nigeria Medical Laboratory Sciences, a member of the Biotechnology Society of Nigeria, and a member of the Nigeria Institute of Science Laboratory Technology. A graduate of Biochemistry with over 10 years working experience in a clinical laboratory, she is presently Head of the Plant Tissue Culture Laboratory in the Biotechnology Center, University of Maiduguri. She is currently pursuing an MSc programme in Biological Science (Plant Physiology and Anatomy) at the University of Maiduguri.

Professor Martha Tarfa is a biologist and botanist. She gained her BSc Botany and MSc Crop Protection from Ahmadu Bello University, and a PhD in Forestry Resources Management from the University of Ibadan, Nigeria. She is currently the Director of University of Maiduguri Biotechnology Centre and the North-East Biotechnology of Excellence, a position she has held since 2013. In the UK, she worked on mycorrhizal fungi from arid Nigerian soil in the biological laboratory at the University of Kent, Canterbury, and at Forestry Institute at Edinburgh. She has published many papers in national and international journals such as Journal of Experimental Biology, Journal of Arid Agriculture, Research Journal of Science, International Journal of Tropical Agriculture and Foods Systems. Professor Martha Tarfa is a member of many professional organisations, including the

Botanical Society of Nigeria, Forestry Association of Nigeria, and Biotechnological Society of Nigeria.

Professor B.H. Kabura holds a PhD in Horticulture from the University of Wales (1989). He also holds a certificate in International course in Sub-tropical and Tropical Horticultural Crops (Hebrew University of Jerusalem, Israel, 1997. He has been working with the Centre of Arid Zone Studies and Biotechnology Centre, both of the University of Maiduguri, for several years. Professor Kabura has held many administrative responsibilities, including Joint Coordinator for Nationally Coordinated Research Projects (NCRP) on the Forestry North East Zone, Nigeria (1996–1998); Deputy Dean, Faculty of Agriculture (1999–2005); Head, Department of Forestry, University of Maiduguri (2003–2006); Head, Department of Crop Production (2008–2010). He has supervised many PhD and Masters Degree Candidates, and has published 40 peer reviewed articles. He is a Member of the Horticultural Society of Nigeria and Shalom Club, Division of External Studies, Hebrew University of Jerusalem, Israel.

GOAL 11

SUSTAINABLE CITIES AND COMMUNITIES

AN EXEMPLARY CASE OF A RESEARCH AND DEVELOPMENT COLLABORATION BETWEEN THE NORTHERN MUNICIPAL COUNCIL AND LOCAL UNIVERSITIES IN THE KINGDOM OF BAHRAIN

Mahmood Habib Alaafia*

Northern Municipal Council
Kingdom of Bahrain
malafia@mun.gov.bh

ABSTRACT

Purpose: Research and Development (R&D) has become crucial to the success, sustainability and competitiveness of any organisation. For municipal affairs in Bahrain, the R&D concept has risen as a core business area that can theoretically resolve the challenges encountered by municipal councils with respect to scarcity of resources, including budgetary deficit, expertise and competency, coverage, and scope. On the other hand, students at universities are generally requested to conduct research as a requirement of their study under the supervision of highly competent academics. It is common that most students face difficulty in choosing beneficial topics of research, and therefore may conduct research that is of less value in order to complete the requirements of their degree.

*Corresponding Author

Based on the needs of both sides, the idea of collaboration between the Northern Municipal Council and local universities on R&D has come into existence. To this end, the municipal council supports Bahraini universities in terms of providing them with a list of the council's research needs. These needs represent different suggested topics that the universities may investigate by conducting proper research. The outcome of the research will benefit the society in general and Bahrain's municipal councils in particular, and will help the latter achieve sustainable development goals.

Findings: The universities have found this approach a pioneering idea, and thereby have taken the necessary steps to establish a robust mechanism to make the cooperation effective. For the Public-private partnerships (PPP) to become more mature, there is a need to promote its concept more strongly and effectively. It needs support from the highest official levels in the Kingdom, and the needs of employees and investors should be recognised and analysed. To maximise the potential benefits of this collaboration, it is crucial that the concerned parties agree on the goals and priorities of such a major project.

Originality/value: The paper addresses some issues pertinent to the collaboration and provides examples of research that has been done, in addition to outlining research plans for the future. Furthermore, the paper discusses examples of development areas that may help in shaping a road map as a basis for community partnership.

Practical and Social Implications: The success measure of this PPP is the ability to combine resources of the private sector and other organisations for the benefit and prosperity of society in general, which would accelerate tangible and intangible gains to the private sector in the long run.

Keywords: Research and Development (R&D); Sustainable Development Goals; Public-private partnerships (PPP); society priorities; scarcity of resources; council's needs

INTRODUCTION

Research and Development (R&D) is an essential stage for any organisation. It triggers development and change for the better life of an organisation, enabling it to keep up with accelerating events and to confront challenges. The organisations that decide to work in R&D need to have a clear idea of their potential and capabilities. Because of the need for technical support that facilitates R&D, this involves high costs and great efforts. Indeed, the organisation that has these resources can start, continue, and innovate with their results.

The statistics of expenditure in R&D for big companies are huge (see Table 1). One of the motives for development and revolution in those companies is the high profit that they can achieve: they afford R&D great importance. Furthermore, developed countries take care of R&D to improve their strategies and infrastructure. They expend a lot of resources in this area because they know that they will receive huge returns or profits in different forms for organisations and countries in general.

Since the problem of conducting and maintaining R&D exists, it is imperative that a solution be found to this problem; this is what we are trying to do in this research. With our practical experience (where we participated with local universities in conducting R&D), we have highlighted a valuable idea for finding solutions, which we have discovered to be consistent and suitable for this important work.

Research Problem

The most important reason that obstructs the public sector's attempts to benefit from R&D is the cost. In some places, such as Asian countries, the low qualification of some decision makers is another reason. This deprives us of a lot of research and thinking, despite its usefulness, especially if it is in the public sector. The Northern Municipal Council in the Kingdom of Bahrain is one of the branches of the public sector, limited by a budget that is not sufficient to establish the basic projects necessary for the needs of the people of the region. Therefore, it is difficult to think of an additional burden for any expenses, in addition to the general situation of slack bureaucracy that tends to prevail in the departments.

One of the crucial global concepts of our time is that of public-private partnership, and researchers and critics have taken a great deal of interest in this. The innovative idea of joint cooperation between the Northern Municipal Council of the Kingdom of Bahrain as the public sector and local universities as the private sector has come to mind. This is because one of the requirements for graduating from a university is to conduct research; it is even a requirement in most courses. In modern education, there will be a lot of research projects that develop university students' creative thinking and the search for solutions to problems.

Many students have difficulty selecting a topic for research; they solve this problem by looking at any idea, even if it is not realistic or suited to their environment, or if it does not reflect reality in their country. They choose and research a topic just to complete the requirements of their course or degree.

Getting funding for R&D is a very difficult task. It requires long-term planning, great time and effort, and needs professional skills. This task can be entrusted to someone who is able to get the necessary funding, or is able to think about finding solutions. Therefore, external sources are often used to request subsidies for R&D (Mukherjee and Ray, 2007). Therefore, there is a need for the Northern Municipal Council to have an external source for R&D.

Research Objective

The purpose of this study is to resolve a problematic situation for both the public and private sectors. The municipal council needs to support R&D, and universities need help in finding useful topics for their students. The students can choose realistic issues that can be applied in the practical world: they will have the feeling that they are contributing to solve the problems of the community around them. They will be proud because they have participated in the development of their country.

Research Questions

This study attempts to answer the following questions:

- what is distinctive about this idea?
- is it possible to establish joint cooperation between the Municipal Council and local universities?
- are there possible benefits from this cooperation?
- what will this idea add to both parties and the country in general?
- how is it possible to ensure the highest success rate for the application of this idea?

DEFINITION AND IMPORTANCE OF R&D

In order to explain the idea, we need to clarify some definitions to have a consensus on these terms. Simplified explanations of each of the important terms that appear in this research are given below:

Research and development must be defined before starting any project in order to determine the dimensions of that project. Collins English Dictionary defines R&D as "work directed towards the innovation, introduction, and improvement of products and processes" (cited in Vaikuntam et al., 2016). R&D consists of any project undertaken to expand understanding of natural phenomena or man-made technology without pre-existing intentions (pure research), to discover useful applications from previously acquired knowledge of phenomena or technology ("applied" research), and to develop new uses for currently understood phenomena or existing technology (Wageman, 2004).

Research and development are two document-related processes through which new products and new forms of old products are brought into existence via technological innovation (Holstein and McLeod, www.britannica.com).

Global competition encourages companies to search for a more innovative way of survival, for which more and more complex R&D activities are introduced. An appropriate administrative approach is of great importance, so R&D requires special management. At the same time, R&D institutions in the public sector operate in a less competitive environment, resulting in lower tensions and less stressful environments, leading to less innovative production.

As a result, the administrative approach of R&D in the public sector is left to day-to-day operations. However, the idea that public-sector research institutions, as generators of new knowledge, represent a different approach to R&D is connected to the assumption that intensive R&D business corresponds to R&D exploitation. An important factor that improves performance in R&D is PPP. This is done through a unified, mutually-accepted platform for both parties that is established by policy makers. An administrative approach that addresses the special nature of R&D performance may facilitate public-private partnerships and increase linkages. In many places, the management approach is still missing from the R&D policy agenda (Mikulskiene, 2010).

DEFINITION AND IMPORTANCE OF PUBLIC-PRIVATE PARTNERSHIP (PPP)

There is no standard definition for PPP in the world, but we can benefit from different definitions that are suitable for our study. PPP can be defined as:

> "a long-term contract between a private party and a government entity, for providing a public asset or service, in which the private party bears significant risk and management responsibility, and remuneration is linked to performance" (PPP Knowledge Lab).

In the international forum jointly organised by UNESCO, the Commonwealth Business Council, the UAE government and GEMS Education, held in Dubai, UAE, on 12 March 2013, world leaders and education experts met to discuss how public-private partnerships can solve the global demand for better life. They agreed on the role that private-public partnerships can play in achieving educational transformation to benefit more young people in the world, in order to create a skilled workforce fit for the future. They examined different ways to create real, sustainable and scalable change to education systems at both the global and local level. They focused on developing an environment that supports effective public and private partnerships, including a regulatory framework that ensures access, quality, relevance and equity in the provision of education.

According to Irina Bokova, the Director General of UNESCO, "the private sector is very open to innovative methods of cooperation. Tackling complex, global challenges requires innovative and far-reaching partnerships between the public and private spheres" (PR. NEWS.USPR, 2013). This conclusion of the forum's recommendations is what this research seeks to implement in order to achieve the goals to which it aspires.

To develop a comprehensive participatory development strategy that contains different activities needed for the local economy, it is necessary to apply the concept of PPP (Sarmeè et al., 2014). In this research the authors mention the objectives of public-private partnerships, which are:

- identification of local needs;
- achieving local development strategies;
- developing procedures to implement the strategy;

- establishing the priorities for achievement in projects, according to the strategy;
- developing a financing plan;
- finding funding sources;
- management of the project through the final stage.

They note that the benefit of public-private partnerships is manifest not only in financial terms but also by creating new jobs, new work practices, injecting new vitality for the rural economy, etc. Development of public-private partnerships is necessary in rural areas both economically and socially (Sarmeè et al., 2014).

As can be seen in Table 1, the following countries enshrine PPP in their legislation because of its importance in life.

Previous Studies

There are many previous studies related to public-private partnerships that focus on different areas, such as health (Nikolic and Maikisch, 2006), administration (Wodicka et al., 2012), agriculture (Sarmeè et al., 2014), and education (Tilak, 2016).

Nikolic and Maikisch (2006) provide an example of public-private partnerships, concerning collaboration in the health sector, in an overview with case studies from recent European experience. They talk about the procedure of contracting-out, which involves publicly financed investments aimed at the improvement of efficiency and/or quality by awarding a service contract, a management contract, a construction,

Table 1   Share of Total Global R&D Spending in the World

Share of Total Global R&D Spending

	2014	2015	2016
North America	29.1%	28.5%	28.4%
U.S.	26.9%	26.4%	26.4%
Caribbean	0.1%	0.1%	0.1%
All North America	29.2%	28.5%	28.5%
Asia	40.2%	41.2%	41.8%
China	19.1%	19.8%	20.4%
Europe	21.5%	21.3%	21.0%
Russia/CIS	3.1%	2.9%	2.8%
South America	2.8%	2.6%	2.6%
Middle East	2.2%	2.3%	2.3%
Africa	1.0%	1.1%	1.1%
Total	100.0%	100.0%	100.0%

Source: from A Supplement to R&D Magazine, 2016

maintenance or equipment contract, in addition to various hybrid contracts that serve a specific need or situation, or a lease to a private partner or partners.

Moreover, some researchers investigated the possible cooperation between the public and private sector in general. For example, in their study Melnikas (2013) discussed the importance of the partnership between the public and private sector, and the importance of networking in the most important areas of common interest to the two sectors. They note that society is aware of the importance of this linkage, because it involves work on the most important topics that concern the development and progress of society.

A similar study was done by Wodicka et al. (2012): they studied public and private sector partnerships between universities and local government. In their paper they presented the pros and cons of a partnership programme in community leadership. They conclude the importance and benefits of that collaboration.

In this study, we focus on the idea of collaboration in R&D between the Northern Municipal Council, representing the public sector, and local universities, representing the private sector, in the Kingdom of Bahrain. We illustrate how the journey began and how it got results in a short period of time – one year. The distinction of this research is that it presents solutions to both parties: to the municipal council by solving its problems and eliminating their adverse effects, and to universities by helping their students find diverse research topics, provided by the municipal council, worthy of study and very useful. The topics are not limited to one or two areas, but extend to several areas; this benefits both parties. What most distinguishes this idea is finding a solution for the municipal council in the absence of budget, and the lack of potential for research and development.

Explanation of the Idea

The partnership between the Northern District Municipal Council and local universities is outlined in Figure 1 below, which includes details as follows:

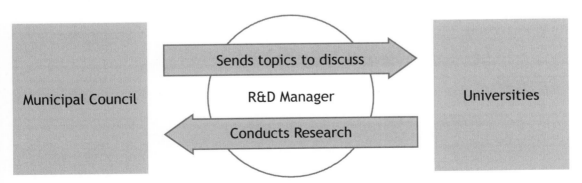

Figure 1   The Typical Relationship between NMC and Universities
Source: Devised by author

How to Invest PPP in our Firm?

This idea was proposed in order to strengthen cooperation between the Municipal Council of the Northern Region and local universities to carry out university R&D. This supplements the decisions of the Municipal Council and supports the president and members of the Municipal Council of the Northern Region in the development work, each in his field.

In the beginning, local universities and postgraduate colleges were identified in cooperation with universities recognised by the Ministry of Education in the Kingdom of Bahrain. Some professional associations were included. The latter are interested in providing scientific R&D proposals in various fields of specialisation. After we wrote to and met them, a total of 14 universities, in addition to a number of educational bodies and specialised associations, were interested in R&D in their areas.

They considered it a pioneering and innovative idea, and that it was rare to find a body or institution, especially in a government, that was striving towards this pursuit of comprehensive and future development. They had encountered many entities that endeavoured to develop something, but few of them continued with their efforts. Despite the communications and the great resources expended on these projects, the media purpose (reputation image) of these bodies is what was most sought after, and once the media campaign was over, all the goals and plans disappeared.

Some of those universities were approached with proposals for advanced research or development ideas. The majority interacted seriously and volunteered to work with the Municipal Council, enquiring about the needs of the Council in order to research them and prepare suggestions for development. Some of them communicated with us and developed an integrated plan for interaction. They consented to work in this field until the desired completion of R&D.

It was proposed to agree on starting work on the idea, even with few of the most important though simple needs of the Municipal Council, taking into account an estimate of the objective conditions of both parties. This proposal was presented by most universities because, according to their experience, a simple topic of discussion may develop and encourage great work in contrast to grand plans that are impractical and may result in failure. In fact, to do something simple is better than doing nothing or a lot of inaccurate, useless, and exhausting work, taking into account the different capabilities of each party.

The idea is to benefit from universities, not only with research but also with development. For example, it may be the establishment of an electronic programme that assists the Municipal Council in organising its affairs. The Information Technology (IT) department may ask students to study the council's requirements and develop solutions with advanced creative ideas. Cooperation with universities in various fields would save the effort and time of the cadres in our establishment. It will contribute to accelerating the pace of work and productivity in the council. This is what we mean by development.

There is another thing needed by the municipal council, especially in light of the scarcity of human resources. It is possible to use university students in the media as well as educational programmes to raise people's awareness of the Northern Province, what the municipality seeks to achieve, and what constitutes appropriate behaviour in terms of dealing with the environment. This is another example of the required development.

Benefits of the Idea

The descriptive approach was used in this research by interviewing top university academic officials, such as deans of colleges and heads of departments chosen from the same university. A committee was established to coordinate between the university and the Municipal Council in order to reduce the effort and time necessary for implementing this idea. One of the privileges we have gained in this regard is that we have been able to use both the small and large halls of universities to hold conferences, seminars and even celebrations. In addition, all the needs of the Municipal Council have been provided by these universities.

As for our market study, we can say that if competitors and other councils follow our example, a lot of competition could be generated and this will be in our favour, for the benefit of the country in general. As their move increases competition, the projects will progress and develop and this will lead to the country's prosperity. We say with confidence that we will be proud if others follow our example, and, even more, we are ready to spread the idea and help those who are ready to implement it.

Another benefit of this collaboration is the training and coaching of our employees. Our idea was to design a training programme suited to the needs of one of the sections of the Municipal Council. We chose the Department of Public Relations and Information; their first session in the programme was entitled "Modern Methods of Public Relations and Media". In turn, we invited constituents of the executive bodies in all municipal councils to join this programme.

The programme has several objectives, one of which is to train staff of the Public Relations and Media Department of the Northern Region's Municipal Council as a starting point in this kind of cooperation. This involves meeting with other colleagues working in the same field from other councils and municipalities; this in itself is an important type of meeting bringing together similar parties working in different places. The aim of this meeting in one place is for employees to get to know each other and discuss the basics of cooperation, benefiting from each other. They gain experience and take advantage of the pros and cons of other projects. This meeting may serve as a forum for employees to benefit from the knowledge and training received from professors and experienced professionals in theoretical and practical fields.

The Needs of the Municipal Council

After years of work in the Council, its needs were not collected in a single table. Now that this idea has been started, the needs of all the 51 committees and sections in the Municipal Council have been collected in preparation for submission to the universities for study. The following Table 2 shows the number of the topics offered by the committees and sections of the Municipal Council:

Table 2   Topics Reflecting the Needs of the Committees/sections of the Municipal Council

Sequence	Committee	Number of Topics
1	Development of Cities and Villages	5
2	Technical Committee	16
3	Financial and Legal Committee	10
4	Committee for Public Services and Utilities	17
5	Miscellaneous topics	3
	Total Summation	51

Source: Devised by author

Timeframe

According to our preliminary plan, the idea would take four years to produce tangible results. However, because we started late and the total period of the council members' term in office is only four years, the remaining period is only two years. Therefore, we now have the opportunity to implement the idea for at least two years, bearing in mind that we would actually have only one year to work and the next year to evaluate the work. It depends on the policy of those who come after this period whether they continue with it or not.

Participants

Out of 14 universities as mentioned in the website of Secretariat General of the Higher Education Council of the Ministry of Education of the Kingdom of Bahrain, 12 of them cooperated and interacted with us, as in Table 3 below:

Table 3   Participating Universities

Sequence	Universities that responded and were visited
1	Kingdom University
2	Arab Gulf University - Faculty of Medicine and Medical Sciences
3	Gulf University

(Continued)

Table 3 (*Continued*)

Sequence	Universities that responded and were visited
4	Ahlia University
5	Royal University for Woman
6	University College of Bahrain
7	Talal Abu - Ghazaleh College of Business
8	Bahrain Polytechnic
9	University Of Bahrain
10	Royal College of Surgeons of Ireland - Bahrain Medical University
11	AMA University
12	University of Applied Sciences

Source: Devised by author

RESULTS

After meetings and interviews with universities and their admissions offices to arrange for their cooperation with the Municipal Council in carrying out the research needed, an official agreement was signed by most universities. A number of projects and ideas were agreed upon, and the ideas extended beyond research. Before starting to apply this idea we considered the possibility of its success, and whether it would be endorsed, especially that we worked without any budget, and there is no legislation or clear laws supporting us in the Municipal Council. With determination, however, we sent letters to universities and received letters from most of them assenting to participate in our project and requesting a meeting with us. The results were amazing. They welcomed us with great openness and great pleasure. Some considered it a pioneering idea. They said that our meeting them is evidence that we really want to develop our organisation.

As we started this idea and worked in a practical way towards achieving results on the ground, we found things are going well, and we received good results. We gave priority to work with those who provided us with services and wanted to implement our idea.

Samples of Conducted Projects

We witnessed seriousness in the universities that made plans and sent them to us to move forward with the idea of cooperation with the Municipal Council. We rapidly began to receive offers, with topics that are important and difficult to obtain with such speed. These are some examples of the topics received:

1. *A study of the condition of palm trees at the entrance to King Fahad causeway, which lies between Bahrain and Saudi Arabia*: There is a problem in the palm trees at this vital location: they are 30 years old yet they still look small. There have

been attempts to treat some of them but no change has been observed in their condition. The endeavour to study this problem has been blocked for a long time and the research has not been agreed due to a lack of budgetary funding and scarcity of resources. A university has offered to study this problem; in fact, this study has already been started by the university. They started taking different samples from the soil and analysed them. The cause of this problem was found to be salinity, which exceeds that of sea water. Experiments were conducted on palm trees for the purpose of developing solutions in cooperation with the executive branch of the municipality of the northern region.

2. *The strategy of the Municipal Council*: The existence of a long-term strategy for any institution is of utmost importance. The Arab Gulf University had a plan to study the reality of official and non-official institutions in the Kingdom of Bahrain and Arab countries in general in order to develop a carefully-studied view of a long-term strategy. A clear strategy for the Municipal Council will serve as a model for other councils, as well as municipalities and other state institutions. A high-level workshop was held by professors at the Arab Gulf University and attended by top officials of the Municipal Council. We have been honoured by the Under Secretary of the Ministry for Municipal Affairs, Dr Nabil Abu El-Fath's visit, and we thanked him in an encouraging speech on the improvement of the municipal work. The professors then asked the workshop attendees to collect the data necessary for the preparation of the strategy. We accumulated some information and are now gathering the rest of the necessary data from various ministries and bodies to prepare this strategy. One of the challenges we faced was enlisting agents and some other notables to cooperate with us in obtaining this data.

3. *Training course on modern methods of public relations and media*: After we started cooperating with the universities, the Gulf University initiated the idea of preparing a series of training courses for the retraining of the members and employees of the Municipal Council. We have stressed the need for the participation of other councils as well as municipalities, including the capitals and three municipalities, with us in all these workshops. These courses are considered the first of their kind in the fields of development and training. The participants expressed their admiration for these sessions and their hope that they are continued. They wished to be invited to the coming sessions.

4. *The project of painting houses of the needy, drawing a smile on their families*: The Gulf University initiated this project in view of the need for volunteer efforts, training its students to engage in community work and learn practical skills. This project has been planned and will be implemented soon in cooperation with other private-sector institutions.

5. *Studying the effect of municipal law on municipal work*: Among the proposed topics needed by the Municipal Council is to study the effect of municipal law on

municipal work. The Royal University for Girls agreed to cooperate with us in this project. This topic was chosen for study by a group of students engaged in research.

6. *Engineering and proposals for land space studies*: Among the proposals of the Municipal Council is the study of the land space in the north of Bahrain. The Royal University for Girls initiated the study of land space as a model to be practiced by its students. One of these lands was chosen as a walkway. The university proposed this topic to arouse the interest of its students. A competition was launched among the students, and the topic was presented as a single question to all female students, who were required to submit an engineering design for the competition. The designs were prepared in an environment that induced creativity. Their final presentations were very exciting and the attendees were impressed with the work presented. It took the form of advanced design in line with the needs of the people of the region.

7. *A study of the budget of the Municipality of the Northern Region*: A critical study was conducted on the budget of the Municipality of the Northern Region. Interviews were held with the concerned parties in financial affairs and they were asked a number of questions about the budget.

INTERPRETATION OF RESULTS AND CONCLUSIONS

On completion of the procedure of testing the idea on the ground, the project has managed to address a number of research questions. One of its conclusions is that collaboration can be applied and circulated in different entities in the Kingdom of Bahrain. It can also be implemented in different countries in the Gulf Cooperation Council (GCC) and around the world. Provided there is belief in the idea on the one hand, and support by the government on the other, it can be applied as we have done in the Kingdom of Bahrain. We have found that there is willingness and readiness on the part of universities to cooperate with us.

Former research stressed the importance of encouraging community partnerships. They called for the reactivation of community partnerships for their importance and the need of all parties for it, especially the public sector, which needs the support required. This research is the start of a process and a pioneering idea as described by the presidents of universities that have been interviewed.

This research complies with previous research findings, and supports the results of that research. Our research has concluded that this idea can be beneficial by attaining fruitful results and supporting the ministry and its officials.

Practical and Social Implications

This research has added value since it provided us with an achievable idea. This is because the results of the study represent a set of great benefits and important guidelines for the continued application of the idea with sound principles. It gave the government all the possible guidance to accomplish positive results and gain financial benefits by applying this idea.

This cooperation between the universities and the Municipal Council will have a great impact on the process of development in the northern region of the Kingdom of Bahrain. The impact will be spread throughout the Kingdom by sparking competition between municipal councils, other municipalities, as well as ministries and other government bodies. Cooperation with universities on research and development is aimed at the comprehensive development of the country, and will be applied among local universities and municipal councils to advance towards that goal.

Research is either practical or theoretical. Practical endeavours lead to the knowledge of a fact or reason, and thus to know where any errors lie. The theoretical research is intended to monitor information; this information includes data collection and analysis in order to answer research questions on a question or inquiry that leads to know what is helping to make a decision.

Opportunities

One of the opportunities offered by our project is the realisation of a new perspective on matters. Planners are usually preoccupied with short-term achievements, but our idea concerns a long-term scheme for the future. The members of the municipal councils are often busy trying to achieve quick and immediate results to satisfy their voters. The conviction of the president of our council, Mr Mohammed Khalifa Bouhmoud, in this idea is a positive factor to help us succeed. His belief in the necessity of working immediately and without delay afforded us the inspiration to apply the idea. He had the confidence that it would be a link between the past and the present and between the present and the future, so he suggested that we start working on it even if we did not get the desired results at the beginning. This is a progressive and optimistic attitude from this president.

The current minister, Mr Essam Khalaf, is a well-qualified person. He welcomed the idea before receiving all its details. He sent a letter of thanks and appreciation the first time he read news of our project in the newspapers. This encouragement, and the full support of the senior management, have eased our path towards success in the application of our idea, and motivated our employees to strive for the achievement of goals and even innovation.

Challenges

The R&D Department in the Northern Municipal Council is understaffed; there is only one person working in it, and he has other tasks in addition to those connected with R&D. He is a creative innovator and he coordinates our efforts with the universities and all the other involved parties. He is following up with the topics and suggestions.

There is no budget for research and development; therefore, we should think carefully before doing any work or taking any step in order to ensure receiving the necessary support.

It is possible that if this idea is transferred to another department, it may not develop since those who would deal with it might not have the experience we have gained since starting with it.

Another challenge would be if the term of municipal members comes to an end before the idea is endorsed fully by the members of the Municipal Council. This may lead to the disruption of work on this idea and a significant loss of all the achievements that have been made so far.

Competitors from councils and municipalities, as well as other ministries, may deal with universities and cooperate with them, but that will not cause us to worry. On the contrary, it will increase our happiness because they will be serving the country, and this is the main objective of our work.

RECOMMENDATIONS

This study might serve as a suggested plan of action for municipal councils and municipalities in general. It can be circulated to all ministries of the state, its bodies, sectors, and affiliates. Ministries will benefit from studies that help them develop their institutions without much cost. Not making use of this idea might entail a large budget for other types of cooperation that might not be as useful, as explained earlier in this research with supporting statistics and figures.

Universities, on the other hand, benefit from ministries by creating an environment conducive to research, selecting topics and real problems that the country grapples with to facilitate the development of their students' research using realistic and practical topics.

The students' research will address concrete issues so that it would be implemented on the ground. The students will be able to communicate with government officials working in their relevant fields. They will also receive media coverage and receive honours from the two municipalities and the university, which will be proud of being a patron of the project.

In order to guarantee the universities' maintenance of this effort:

1. we need to keep up the determination, collaboration, and continuous productivity in the conducting of research and development;
2. there should be governmental legislative terms that determine the minimum level of research at ministries;

3. the R&D departments in both the Municipal Council and the universities should play a central role in the balance between the university's performance in research, the feasibility of the results obtained, and the continuity of research and development without interruption.

REFERENCES

Global R&D Funding Forecast, Winter 2016, A Supplement to R&D Magazine.

Holstein, W.K. and McLeod, T.S., Research and Development, https://www.britannica.com/topic/research-and-development.

How Public-Private Partnerships Can Solve the Global Demand for Better Education, Forum, jointly organized by UNESCO, The Commonwealth Business Council, The UAE Government and GEMS Education held in DUBAI, UAE, March 12, 2013 (AN:201303120800PR.NEWS.USPR.enUK201303116671).

Melnikas, B. (2013), Public and Business Sectors in the Context of Globalization: Interests, Competition, Interaction, Cooperation, Convergence, Networking. *Public Administration (16484541)*, Vol. 4, No. 40.

Mikulskiene, B. (2010), The Role of R&D Manager for Public and Private R&D Partnership, *European Integration Studies*, No. 4, Mykolas Romeris University.

Mukherjee A. and Ray, A. (2007), Strategic Outsourcing and R&D, in a Vertical Structure, *The Manchester School*, Vol. 75, No. 3, pp. 297–10.

Nikolic, I.A. and Maikisch, H. (2006), Public-Private Partnerships and Collaboration in the Health Sector: An Overview with Case Studies from Recent European Experience.

PPP Knowledge Lab, https://pppknowledgelab.org/guide/sections/3-what-is-a-ppp-defining-public-private-partnership.

Sarmeè, D.I., Csosz, I., Ciolac, R. and Martin, S.C. (2014), Study on public-private partnership and its importance, Banat's University of Agricultural Sciences and Veterinary Medicine Timisoara, Agricultural Management Faculty, Romania, Lucrări Ştiinţifice. *Management Agricol*, Vol. 16, No. 1, p. 251.

Tilak, J.B. (2010), Public-Private Partnership in Education, *The Hindu*, Vol. 24, p. 2010.

Vaikuntam Iyer Lakshmanan, Raja Roy and Ramachandran, V. (2016), Number: 2015947279, Library of Congress Control, London.

Wageman, S.W. (2004), Risk Management on Research and Development Projects, *AACE International Transactions*, p. R171.

Wodicka, R., Swartz, N. and Peaslee, L. (2012), Taking the Classroom to Town Hall: Advancing Public Affairs Education Through University-Municipal Collaborations, *Journal of Public Affairs Education*, Vol. 18, No. 2, pp. 271–94.

BIOGRAPHY

MAHMOOD HABIB ALAAFIA holds a BSc in Software Engineering, University of British Columbia, Canada, collaboration with Aptech Institute, Bahrain, and an MBA from Ahlia University, Bahrain. He presented the idea of research and development in municipal councils in the Kingdom of Bahrain. He has participated in many clubs, associations and volunteer committees, where he served as an administrative and active member. He is interested in environmental issues, municipal work, agriculture, public health, security and safety and housing, paying special attention to the disabled. He began his work in 1997 in various administrative sectors. He worked at Bahrain University (UOB) in 2002, going on to teach at the Ministry of Education. He has worked at the Northern Municipal council since 2006. He played an effective leading role in the promotion, development and sustainable of municipal councils. He is an advocate for promoting sustainable development across the Kingdom of Bahrain. He has many professional certificates in human resources, total quality and project management professionalism.

UNDERSTANDING THE ATTITUDE OF GENERATION Y TOWARDS TRANSPORT APPS: THE CASE OF DUBAI

Rengi Kachora[*1]
Ghassan Abu-Lebdeh[2]

[1]Urban Planning Graduate Program
College of Architecture, Arts and Design
American University of Sharjah, UAE
E: b00049328@alumni.aus.edu

[2]Department of Civil Engineering
American University of Sharjah, UAE
gabulebdeh@aus.edu

ABSTRACT

Purpose: This research aims to understand the attitudes and use patterns of the abundant, government supported transport-related mobile apps by Generation Y in the City of Dubai. The research question is whether the travel/transport service mobile apps have improved or brought about a change in travel behaviour of Generation Y in Dubai.

Design/Methodology/Approach: Data for this research were collected from the targeted audience via an online survey questionnaire. Suitable statistical hypotheses were formulated and tested.

Findings: Results show that market penetration and use of the apps is still limited, despite the multitude and customisation of apps and high access to mobile devices in the City. Less than 50% of targeted users are aware of the

*Corresponding Author

apps and the service available through them, but the majority of them use only some of the apps only rarely. The formal results of the hypotheses tests further helped ascertain that the observations and patterns were systemic and not random patterns. The research identified some of the factors contributing to the findings.

Originality: The research and results confirm that simple availability of incentives, including mobile device apps, to promote more sustainable transport options among generation Y in the City of Dubai, necessary as it may be, is not producing the desired outcome.

Practical Implications: Carefully designed and implemented disincentives to using traditional transport choices may be necessary in parallel with the incentives and tools (including mobile apps) to attain transport sustainability goals.

Keywords: Generation Y; sustainable transport; transport apps; travel behaviour

INTRODUCTION

With Dubai's rapid growth and urbanisation, traffic congestion on its roads has increased dramatically over recent years. Growing private car ownership and usage, and the chaotic traffic conditions on Dubai roads, are of great concern for the government. Traffic jams in Dubai do not follow typical spatial and temporal congestion patterns, or so it seems. The resulting loss of fuel and time is disturbing the people of the Emirate. The government has invested heavily in Dubai's road infrastructure, although this has not kept pace with the increase in the number of vehicles (Chaudhry, 2012). Figure 1 (below) shows a sample, but typical, scene of traffic congestion during peak hours on one of Dubai's roads.

Figure 1   Traffic Congestion Al Ittihad Road in Dubai during Evening Peak Hour
Source: Masudi, 2013

In 2005, it was estimated that about AED 4.6 (US$1.25) billion in wasted time were lost annually due to traffic congestion in Dubai. Public transport comprised only 6% of the total trips within the Emirate (Chaudhry, 2012). As demand for transport infrastructure keeps increasing, the city's answer cannot be just to keep building new infrastructure. A major shift is already taking shape in the transport sector of the Emirate as the city moves towards accessibility-driven strategies in order to meet travel demand and achieve sustainable development (Chaudhry, 2012).

Over the past 10 years, and in order to accommodate and resolve the rising trend in private car ownership and its burden on the Dubai roads, the Dubai Road and Transport Authority (RTA) has embarked on an ambitious approach to managing travel demand through policies and legislations that favour intermodal public transport. This intermodal public transportation of Dubai comprises of metro, tram, buses, taxis and water taxis and passenger ferries (known locally as *Abras*) (Shahbandari, 2015c). Figure 2 below presents a summary of the significant growth in various mass transit modes of Dubai over the past 10 years.

To encourage the public to embrace new, more sustainable, travel choices/behaviours, the RTA declared the transition of all its applicable services available 'smart' through mobile applications. The aim is to integrate all available modes of public

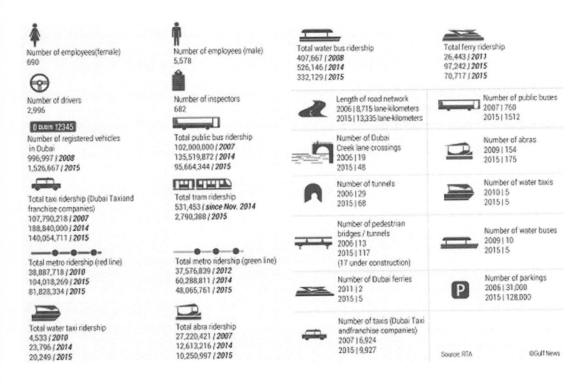

Figure 2   RTA in Numbers – Figures as of 30 September 2015
Source: Shahbandari, 2015c

transport from different areas/places within the Emirate to one place (the smart-phone). This is to ease travel planning by providing travellers (Generation Y included) with real-time transport information before starting a journey. These mobile apps, it is theorised, would help travellers to find and choose the right mode(s) for a journey. This 'smart' initiative is now part of the 'Dubai Strategy Plan 2021', under the theme, 'A Sustainable and Smart City'.

DUBAI'S TRAVEL-RELATED MOBILE APPS AND ITS ANTICIPATED IMPACT

At present, the RTA's mobile apps have the highest penetration rate (23%) in the UAE (see Figure 3) compared to other government-owned mobile applications (Zawya, 2014).

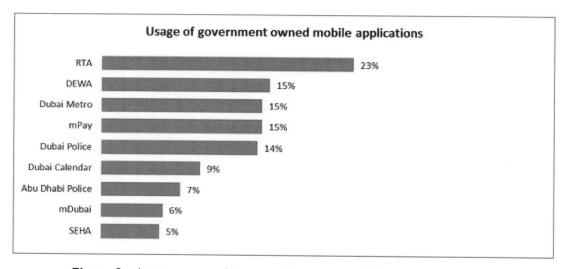

Figure 3   Awareness and Usage of Government Operated m-services
Source: Zawya, 2014

As of November 2015, the government of Dubai, in collaboration with the RTA, offers 173 services through 10 mobile apps. Among these, 83 serve drivers/car owners, 31 cater to public transport users, and 59 services support the business (corporate) sector (Shahbandari, 2015a).

GENERATION CATEGORIES AND THEIR CHARACTERISTICS

The Table 1 below summarises the categories of living generations. At the present time there are five categories of generation.

Table 1   List of Living Generation

Birth Years	Generation Name	Age in 2013	Social Role	Values and Beliefs
1925−1942	Silent or Veterans or Builders	88−71	Leadership: transferring values	Human rights, discipline, role models and rules
1943−1960	Baby Boomers	70−53	Leadership: transferring values, leading institutions	Work ethic, security, advancement
1961−1981	Generation X	52−32	Power: asserting values, managing institutions	Variety, freedom, individuality, skepticism
1982−2002	Generation Y	31−11	Vitality: testing values	Lifestyle, self-discovery, social, fun
2003 −	Generation Z	10 or younger	Growth: acquiring values and beliefs	In process

Generation Y is 18−34 year olds, recognised by the United Nations as a major force for development and social change (UNWTO and WYSETC, 2010). According to Benckendorff et al. (2010), Generation Y has completed its 'childhood' phase of life and has entered the 'young adulthood' phase; a generation in this phase is responsible for testing values in society. They are now at the centre of attention of mass media and are an emerging topic in academic literature.

Generation Y and Smartphone Usage in the UAE

The UAE is ranked as the first globally in the use of smartphones. The share of smartphone users in the UAE jumped from 61% in 2012 to 78% in 2014 (Nielsen, 2014; Gulfnews, 2015; The National, 2016). The share is expected to be 82.8% by 2019, as per the report, titled 'Global Media Intelligence' (GMI). Generation Y in the UAE was first in the world in terms of smartphone usage at 91.1%, followed by Britain with 90.7%. The share for the US is 74.6% (MOHESR, 2013). Generation Y makes up 43% of Dubai's population (see Figure 4).

Travel Behaviour and Attitudes of Generation Y

According to the World Trade Organisation (WTO) and United Nations Environment Programme (UNEP) (2005), Generation Y travellers represent a significant segment in the travel and tourism sector, and the dynamics of this sector's growth puts them at the centre of attention of the travel industry. There are five main factors that affect their travel behaviour:
  1) local weather conditions;
  2) urban form;
  3) social-demographic variable;

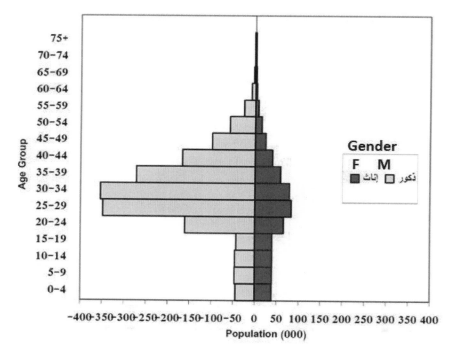

Figure 4   Population Pyramid, Emirate of Dubai 2013
Source: DSC, 2015

4) psycho-social variable; and
5) factors pertaining to convenience in public transportation.

STUDY OBJECTIVES

The objective of this study is to understand the mind-set or attitude of Generation Y towards Dubai's travel-related mobile apps. It is also to find out if the recent transition of various RTA services into 'smart' is encouraging Generation Y to use the apps, and if that is changing their travel behaviour including trip planning, number of trips to government offices, reduction in private auto ownership, reduction in single occupancy travel, and use of public transport.

Significance of Research

Car ownership in Dubai, and dependency on private vehicles for most travel needs, is among the highest in the world. The common daily scenes of congestion are perhaps a testament to that, despite considerable investments in roadway capacity. The government of Dubai, together with the RTA, launched a number of mobile applications, offering various government services with the aim of reducing or eliminating the need to travel to receive government service. In addition, real-time travel information and other travel apps were launched to encourage more sustainable travel behaviour among the public. However, serious congestion problems persist in many parts of the City, and anecdotal evidence abounds that solo driving/travel still dominates, despite all investments and incentives. This research will confirm (or refute) current observations (Gulfnews, 2015; Kiilunen, 2013) and provide a window into the mind-set of the public (and Generation Y in particular) thus helping to guide future actions.

METHODOLOGY

Data using a self-administered online survey from subjects in the City of Dubai were collected to specifically test the five hypotheses noted below. Only responses from Generation Y respondents were used in the analysis. Attitudes, opinions and behaviours were quantified and then used to test the following hypotheses. Sufficient responses were collected to enable statistically significant observations and conclusions. The survey was pilot-tested and revised before it was widely distributed. The following hypotheses were tested (but not all results are presented in this paper):

I. Generation Y in Dubai are smartphone users and are aware of the travel-related mobile apps;

II. Mobile apps play an important role in the transportation sector by providing real-time public transport, location and timing information;

III. Services provided by the apps may have a positive impact on Generation Y's travel choices by managing their travel demands and reducing unnecessary trips, especially during peak hour traffic;

IV. Travel-related mobile applications may serve as an appropriate tool for communicating with Generation Y by encouraging the use of smart services for trip planning, thereby reducing the use of private automobiles;

V. Factors such as weather conditions, urban form, social-demographic variable, psycho-social variables and convenience in public transport promote preference for using private automobiles over public transportation.

RESULTS

Only 48.8% of the targeted audience, Generation Y, uses either all or some of the travel-related mobile apps. Among this (app users) segment, only 2.9% use the mobile apps on a daily basis, 23.5% use them several times a week, and 24.5% use them only several times a month. Just under half (41.2%) rarely use the apps (see Figure 5).

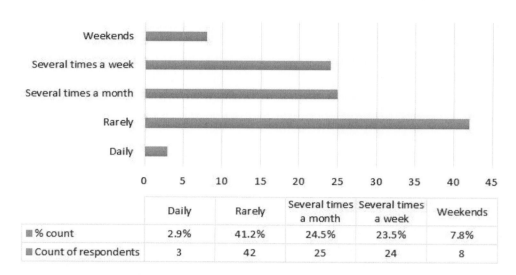

	Daily	Rarely	Several times a month	Several times a week	Weekends
■ % count	2.9%	41.2%	24.5%	23.5%	7.8%
■ Count of respondents	3	42	25	24	8

Figure 5   Travel-related Mobile App Use
Source: Kachora, 2016

The majority of the app users used them for the RTA transactional (not mobility/ travel-related) services; these included inquiries and payments for fines, parking payment, renewal of vehicle registration, NOL (transport services debit card), card recharging, etc. The use of apps for public transport route and time inquiries accounted for 32.4%, 27.5% used the apps for route and location navigation. Only 4.9% used the apps for live traffic updates. The remaining 2.0% used the apps for parking location identification and to practice the written driver's license test (see Figure 6).

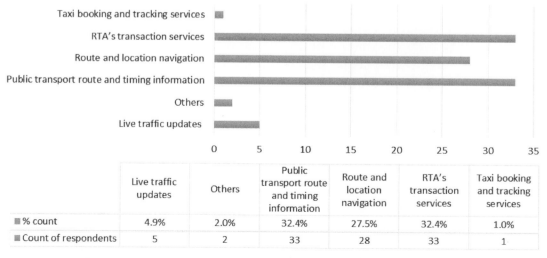

	Live traffic updates	Others	Public transport route and timing information	Route and location navigation	RTA's transaction services	Taxi booking and tracking services
■ % count	4.9%	2.0%	32.4%	27.5%	32.4%	1.0%
■ Count of respondents	5	2	33	28	33	1

Figure 6   Primary Purpose for Using Travel-related Mobile Apps
Source: Kachora, 2016

The majority of respondents (Generation Y, in Dubai) used their private/personal car for their work related trips, and 25.5% used public transport (see Figure 7). Walking and cycling to work accounted for 7.8%. To verify the significance of this pattern, the Pearson's Chi-square test[1] was applied. The test of the pattern resulted in a probability value <0.001%; that is, there is a 0% chance that this pattern is happening randomly. This, in part at least, explains the daily peak period traffic congestion in many parts of the City.

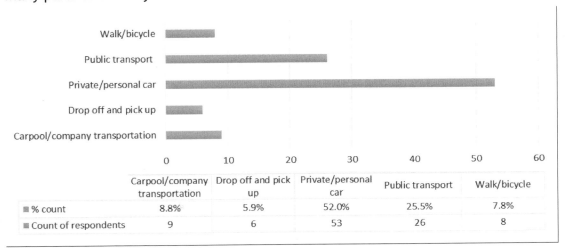

	Carpool/company transportation	Drop off and pick up	Private/personal car	Public transport	Walk/bicycle
% count	8.8%	5.9%	52.0%	25.5%	7.8%
Count of respondents	9	6	53	26	8

Figure 7   Mode Choice for Work Related Trips
Source: Kachora, 2016

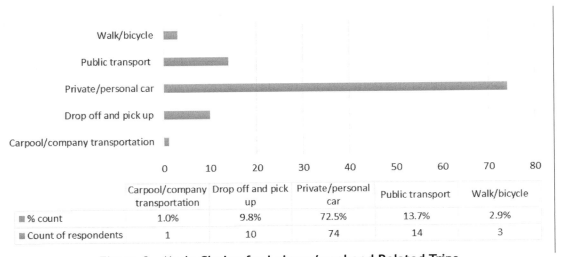

	Carpool/company transportation	Drop off and pick up	Private/personal car	Public transport	Walk/bicycle
% count	1.0%	9.8%	72.5%	13.7%	2.9%
Count of respondents	1	10	74	14	3

Figure 8   Mode Choice for Leisure/weekend Related Trips
Source: Kachora, 2016

---

[1] This is a statistical test applied to sets of categorical data to evaluate the likelihood of any observed difference between sets arising by chance.

For leisure travel, the majority (72.5%) of respondents use their private/personal car for most of their leisure or weekend trips with the Emirate; a small proportion of respondents (13.7%) use public transport for their leisure or weekend trips (see Figure 8). Similar to the case of work travel above, the Pearson's Chi-sq test was applied here and the result was similar: there is a 0% chance this pattern is happening randomly.

The above two test results, in a way, were expected: chronic daily congestion is a hallmark of the Dubai area.

Hypotheses Testing Results

All five hypotheses presented earlier were tested as follows:

> Hypothesis I: The Generation Y in Dubai are smartphone users and are aware of the travel-related mobile-based applications.

The Pearson's Chi-square test of the pattern resulted in a probability value <0.001%: there is a 0% chance that this pattern is happening randomly. Therefore, the above findings and discussions prove the first half of the hypothesis that Generation Y in Dubai are all smartphone users. However, it contradicts the second half as about 50% of the users are not aware of the travel-related mobile applications or the services provided by it.

> Hypothesis II: Mobile apps play an important role in the transportation sector by providing real-time public transport route, location and timing information.

Related to the above hypothesis, the contingency table/matrix between the following variable questions (from the survey form): "Q3. What is your primary purpose for using Dubai's travel-related mobile apps?" and "Q13. Which category below includes your age?", reveals that the majority of Generation Y respondents use the

Table 2   Pivot Table between Variable Questions Q3 and Q13

Primary purpose for using the apps	18–26 years	27–34 years	35 years or older	Grand Total
Live traffic updates	3	2		5
Others	2			2
Public transport route and timing information	26	5	2	33
Route and location navigation	22	5	1	28
RTA's transaction services	9	17	7	33
Taxi booking and tracking services	1			1
Grand Total	63	29	10	102

Source: Kachora, 2016

travel-related mobile apps for public transport route and timing information (see Table 2). To verify the significance of this pattern, statistical analysis was conducted. The Pearson's Chi-square test for all the three patterns resulted in a probability value <0.001%. Therefore there is a 0% chance that these patterns are happening randomly. The pattern therefore verifies the above hypothesis.

However, the above finding contradicts the observation where the majority of respondents use their private/personal car for their work related trips (52.0%) and leisure/weekend trips (72.5%), and less than 20.0% of respondents use public transport. Therefore another contingency table (see Table 3) was created between the variable questions Q3 and "Q2: How often do you use Dubai's travel-related mobile apps?" to identify the reasons behind the above contraction in the findings.

Table 3 Pivot Table between Variable Questions Q3 and Q2

Primary purpose for using the apps	Daily	Rarely	Several times a month	Several times a week	Weekends	Grand Total
Live traffic updates	1	3			1	5
Others		2				2
Public transport route and timing information	2	15	6	8	2	33
Route and location navigation		6	9	8	5	28
RTA's transaction services		15	10	8		33
Taxi booking and tracking services		1				1
Grand Total	3	42	25	25	8	102

Source: Kachora, 2016

As noted in Table 3, the majority of the respondents use the mobile apps rarely to several times a week. The Pearson's Chi-square test for the above contingency table resulted in a probability value <0.001%. Therefore, this particular finding implies that the respondents *might* use the mobile apps for public transport route and timing information and other services, but they actually rarely use the travel-related mobile apps since their preferred travel mode is their own personal/private cars. However, although the data and the statistical analysis lead to accepting the hypothesis, this contradicts current travel behaviour where 50% of the public prefer their own personal/private car for their work related trips, and about 70% of the public once again prefer their own personal/private car for their leisure/weekend trips.

> Hypothesis III: Services provided by the apps may have a positive impact on Generation Y's travel choices by managing their travel demands and reducing unnecessary trips they make, especially during peak hour traffic.

The summary statistics related to this hypothesis reveal that 41.2% of the respondents agreed to the statement that Dubai's travel-related mobile apps provide live traffic and route information for trip planning. To verify the significance of this pattern, the Pearson's Chi-square test of the pattern resulted in a probability value <0.001%, that is, there is a 0% chance that this pattern is a random one. In other words, live traffic information and the route, location and navigation services provided help in managing the public's travel demands; it did this by selecting alternative routes and/or times for their travel. However, there is a contradiction: only 19.6% of the respondents agreed to the statement that the travel-related mobile apps encourage lesser car use during peak hours through live traffic updates. The majority were either neutral (46.1%) or disagreed (22.5%) with the statement. In order to identify the reason behind this contradiction, a contingency table between the variable questions "Q4: Please indicate your level of agreement with the following statements on your experience with using Dubai's travel-related mobile apps", and Q2 were created (see Table 4).

Table 4   Pivot Table between Variable Questions Q4 and Q2

Level of agreement	Daily	Rarely	Several times a month	Several times a week	Weekends	Grand Total
Agree	1	6	5	6	2	20
Disagree		11	7	1	4	23
Neutral	1	20	11	14	1	47
Not Applicable	1	5	2	3	1	12
Grand Total	3	42	25	24	8	102

Source: Kachora, 2016

The above contingency table highlights the reason behind the contradiction in the hypothesis: a large number of respondents who rarely use the apps were either neutral or disagreed with the statement that the travel-related mobile apps encourages lesser car use during peak hours through live traffic updates. To verify the significance of this pattern, statistical analysis was conducted. The Pearson's Chi-square test of the pattern resulted in a probability value <0.001%. Therefore, there is a 0% chance that the reported pattern is happening randomly. Hence, the statistical test confirms that the lesser agreement with the statement was because the majority of the public rarely use the travel-related mobile apps for live traffic updates, and was therefore not aware that the live traffic information would have discouraged their car trips during peak hours. However, since the statistical test has already confirmed the significance of the 19.6% of the respondents agreeing with the statement, the patterns found from the data verify the significance of the above hypothesis. Hypotheses IV and V were also tested and data related to them examined. The outcomes (but not the details) of both hypotheses are briefly noted in summary and conclusions section below.

SUMMARY AND CONCLUSIONS

There appears to be potential for the mobile-based apps introduced in Dubai to change the travel behaviour of Generation Y. However, factors such as local weather conditions, urban form, social-economic variables, and inconvenience in public transport, lead to the majority of travellers preferring to use their private cars over public transport, and the smart services related to it.

More the 50% of the public (especially Generation Y) in Dubai are not aware of the travel-related mobile based applications or the services provided through them. The majority of those who are aware of the travel-related mobile apps, only use some of the apps but very rarely. Among the less than 50% mobile app users, the apps are used for public transport and route travel time information. The majority of the current non-users of the apps would use them if they were to provide clear information on the services and could improve their travel experiences. This is a possible indication of the need for publicity and awareness.

Private vehicle ownership and use are high: 75% of the public either own or have access to a private vehicle, over 45% prefer and use their private/personal car for work related trips, and more than 60% prefer and use their private/personal car for their leisure/weekend trips. Users in this group use travel-related apps for smart transaction services, route and location navigation, parking payment, and live traffic updates – but not for public transport. Weather conditions in Dubai, urban form, societal/family factors, and public transit attributes are factors contributing to people being in favour of travel by private vehicles.

REFERENCES

Benckendorff, P., Moscardo, G. and Pendergast, D. (Eds) (2010), *Tourism and Generation Y*. UK: CAB International.

Chaudhry, G.A. (2012), Evolution of the transportation system in Dubai. *Network Industries Quarterly*, Vol. 14, No. 2, pp. 7–11.

Dubai Statistics Center (DSC) (2015), *Population by Age Group 2014*. Retrieved from Dubai Statistics Center: https://www.dsc.gov.ae/Report/DSC_SYB_2015_01%20_%2001.pdf.

Gulfnews (2015, 29 September 29), *Regional governments to spend $11.4b on IT in 2015*. Retrieved from Gulf News: http://gulfnews.com/business/sectors/technology/regional-governments-to-spend-11-4b-on-it-in-2015–1.1592224.

Kachora, R. (2016), *Understanding the Attitude of Generation Y Towards Dubai's Travel-Related Mobile Applications*, unpublished Master's degree dissertation, American University of Sharjah.

Kiilunen, O. (2013), *Mobile applications as solutions to enhance sustainable travel behaviour among Generation Y*. Master's dissertation, University of Applied Sciences, Porvoo and Vierumäki, Finland.

Masudi, F. (2013, 15 April), *New Dubai Salik road toll gates make a difference in traffic flow*. Retrieved from Gulfnews: http://gulfnews.com/news/uae/general/new-dubai-salik-road-toll-gates-make-a-difference-in-traffic-flow-1.1170799.

Ministry of Higher Education and Scientific Research (MOHESR) (2013, 9 September), *UAE ranked first globally in the use of smartphones*. Retrieved from Ministry of Higher Education & Scientific

Research: https://www.mohesr.gov.ae/En/FunyLinks/Pages/UAE-ranked-first-globally-in-the-use-of-smartphones.aspx.

Nielsen (2014, 26 June), *Mobile Majority: Smartphone Penetration Hits 78% in the UAE*. Retrieved from Nielsen: http://www.nielsen.com/ae/en/insights/news/2014/mobile-majority-smartphone-penetration-hits-77-percent-in-the-uae.html.

RTA (2016, 16 February), *RTA Mobile Apps*. Retrieved from Google Play Store: https://play.google.com/store/search?q=rta&hl=en.

Shahbandari, S. (2015a, 29 April), *RTA completes transition to smart government*. Retrieved from Gulfnews: http://gulfnews.com/news/uae/transport/rta-completes-transition-to-smart-government-1.1501523.

Shahbandari, S. (2015b, 19 October), *Enjoy coffee, free Wi-Fi at RTA bus stops*. Retrieved from Gulfnews: http://gulfnews.com/news/uae/transport/enjoy-coffee-free-wi-fi-at-rta-bus-stops-1.1603026.

Shahbandari, S. (2015c, 31 October), *How RTA kept Dubai moving for 10 years*. Retrieved from Gulf News: http://gulfnews.com/news/uae/transport/how-rta-kept-dubai-moving-for-10-years-1.1610281.

The National (2016, December 27). UAE's global top spot in smartphone use gives local SMEs huge opportunities. Retrieved from the National: https://www.thenational.ae/business/technology/uae-s-global-top-spot-in-smartphone-use-gives-local-smes-huge-opportunities-1.175824"

UNWTO and WYSETC (2010), *The Power of Youth Travel Report*. Retrieved from WYSE Travel: http://www.wysetc.org/?page=PowerYouthTravel.

WTO and UNEP (2005), *Making Tourism More Sustainable*. Retrieved from UNEP: http://www.unep.fr/shared/publications/pdf/DTIx0592xPA-TourismPolicyEN.pdf.

Zawya (2014, 18 June 18), *Mobile Beats Online in UAE's Overall Satisfaction With Government Services*. Retrieved from Zawya Thompson Reuters: https://www.zawya.com/story/Mobile_Beats_Online_in_UAEs_Overall_Satisfaction_With_Government_Services-ZAWYA20140618115142/.

BIOGRAPHY

Rengi Kachora is a graduate student in the Master of Urban Planning Program, College of Architecture, Arts and Design at the American University of Sharjah.

Dr Ghassan Abu-Lebdeh is Professor of Civil Engineering/Transportation at the American University of Sharjah, UAE. His areas of research interest/teaching are traffic control with focus on congested systems, sustainability in transport systems, and interactions between urban traffic operations and public health. He completed his studies at the University of Illinois at Urbana-Champaign (PhD), USA. His academic and industry experience spans 27 years in transportation systems operations and planning, with periods at Michigan State University, University of Kentucky, and the Metropolitan Planning Organisations in Worcester, Massachusetts, and in Urban-Champaign, Illinois.

GOAL 9

INDUSTRY, INNOVATION AND INFRASTRUCTURE

PROMOTE SUSTAINABLE INDUSTRIALISATION AND FOSTER INNOVATION THROUGH A PPP IN AFRICA

Abdelkader Djeflat*

Chairman
Maghtech Network
University of Lille, France
Abdelkader.djeflat@]univ-lille1.fr

ABSTRACT

Purpose: Our contribution addresses Objective 9 of the SDG agenda, and more specifically the second part of it which is *to promote sustainable industrial development and foster Innovation through PPP.* The purpose is to answer three important questions:

1. How can we involve the private sector in a new PPP strategy to address SDGs that will fulfil Goal 9, to promote industrial development and innovation in the North Africa region and the continent as a whole?
2) What new visions and new policies are needed, and what support from all key players including Government, the business sector and civil society?
3) What necessary instruments need to be mobilised, and what advocacy is required to get large buy-in on the part of the private sector and society as a whole.

Design Methodology/Appproach: Our data and illustrations are essentially from the African region. Time constraints did not make it possible to conduct a specific and tailor-made field work for the problems we have

*Corresponding Author

chosen to examine. Thus, the data is drawn from earlier work done on sustainability and knowledge based economy where broad samples of policy-makers, entrepreneurs and people in the academic sphere were interviewed (DESA, 2016).

Findings: Successful PPP for the SDGs rests on the collaboration of three spheres: *The Government sphere, the research sphere*: and *the industry sphere,* similar to the "triple helix" type of framework. However, when it comes to the African context, this simple formula will not work unless other spheres are involved. These include: the *social acceptance sphere*, the *donors' sphere* and the *international organisations' sphere.* This requires a great of social innovation to accompany and ease this process. In this respect SDG 9 needs to be combined with Objective 17 if PPP is to succeed.

Originality/value: The originality of our work is to look at SDGs PPP through the lens of industrial development: it is our belief that the partnership will not be successfully achieved if proper capabilities are not built in the field of science, technology and industry.

Keywords: SDG Objective 9; industrial development; science technology and innovation; social innovation; PPP

INTRODUCTION

Sustainable Development Goals (SDGs) can be considered as one of the most important development agenda to guide the action of the international community for the next 15 years. Their importance stems from their broad and all-encompassing objectives and their true global nature: unlike the Millennium Development Goals (MDGs), whose targets were the poor, SDGs include all the community at large, both in the global south and the global north. They are also very timely at a time when humanity is becoming more and more conscious of the dangers it faces if the appropriate actions are not taken to face the risks our planet runs in terms of climate change, environmental pollution, bio-diversity destruction, and so on.

While being the emanation of a large consensus among the Nation States and considered as one of the biggest achievement in the history of the UN (General Secretary of the UN), the implementation of the SDGs could not possibly rest only on the shoulders of the State and on public funding. As stated in Objective 17:

> "A successful sustainable development agenda requires partnerships between governments, the private sector and civil society. These inclusive partnerships built upon principles and values, a shared vision, and shared goals that place people and the planet at the centre, are needed at the global, regional, national and local level".

SDGs will not be successfully achieved if proper capabilities are not built in the field of science, technology and industry.

Raising the issue of sustainability in LDCs also necessarily raises the issue of science and technology (S&T) capacity building. We have highlighted in earlier work the importance of technology transfer between developed and developing countries in the protection of the environment (Djeflat, 1996). We argued that technology transfer is a win-win game, whereby developed countries find both material and moral gains, while, through better access to environmental technology, LDCs can contribute to the enhancement of sustainability, both at home and the world as a whole. Therefore, special treatment should be given to environmental technologies. This is, of course, far from being the situation in the field: market forces and short-term gains are still key factors.

Our contribution addresses Objective 9 of the SDG agenda and more specifically the second part of it, which is, *"to promote sustainable industrial development and foster Innovation through PPP"*.

Key questions can be raised: how could sustainable industrial development be reached while an important proportion of countries in the world, namely in the Global South are totally excluded from the manufacturing sphere and have set no basis for proper industry? How could this objective be reached while mineral resources represent more than 70% of GDP and are the only commodity being exported? How could they be achieved while the numerous and repetitive S&T policies have produced no notable progress in building proper capacity in R&D and innovative activities, and the S&T content of their exports is very dismal? How could the private sector be involved after being marginalised for so long in the various S&T policies and its share of the R&D budget is insignificant? Finally, what PPP model could we discover to make Objective 9 feasible within the span of the 13 remaining years of SDG implementation?

These are some of the questions we will attempt to answer in this paper. To do that we will draw from both the existing literature and from the work we have done in areas related to the key issues raised here. Our data and illustrations are essentially from the African region. Time constraints did not make it possible to conduct a specific and tailor-made field work for the problematics we have chosen to examine. The next section looks at industrial development and the current issues it faces in African countries to show how it is highly unsustainable. The next section will examine how innovation is a difficult task in these countries, and how this contributes towards making economic and more specifically industrial development unsustainable. This is followed by an examination of the issue of PPP in African countries, its shortcomings and difficulties it meets when it comes to promote industrial development and innovation. Finally, we put forward certain proposals to make PPP a feasible model to promote sustainable industrial development and innovation.

INDUSTRIAL DEVELOPMENT AND SUSTAINABILITY ISSUES IN AFRICAN COUNTRIES

The Importance of Industrial Development

Industrial development is more and more recognised as a key element that enables the developing world to face the challenges posed by demography, youth unemployment, sustainability and growth, and inclusive development. *"Enhancing an economy's productive capabilities over an increasing range of manufactured goods is an integral part of economic development"* (Rodrik, 2006). Manufacturing is an important employer, accounting for around 470 million jobs worldwide in 2009, or around 16% of the world's workforce of 2.9 billion. In 2013, it was estimated that there were more than half a billion jobs in manufacturing[1]. Industrialisation's job multiplication effect has a positive impact on society: every one job in manufacturing creates 2.2 jobs in other sectors. It is also fundamental for providing technological solutions to environmental problems.

The Difficulties met by Industrial Development in Africa

Weak and falling MVA and dis-industrialisation

However, industrial development is not easy when it comes to developing countries with limited financial, material, human resources and, more specifically, knowledge capital. We have to consider different categories of countries, not simply at a GDP level on an economic model. The first category includes those that have confined their activities to the development of agriculture and the rural sector, and the exploitation of important mineral resources when they are available. The manufacturing sector is poorly developed, and industry-driven development in this case can be a daunting task. The second category contains countries where important steps were made to develop and enhance an industrial sector essentially driven by revenues from natural resources, e.g. oil, gas and other minerals in Algeria. The third category includes countries without significant mineral resources but a thriving private sector in the manufacturing sector (e.g. Tunisia). However, when looking at these countries closely, irrespective of the category to which they belong, manufacturing value added has not reached a satisfactory level to the extent that it can be a powerful engine of growth. This applies to the whole African continent, with the exception of South Africa, as indicated by weak and declining manufactured value added (MVA).

---

[1]http://www.un.org/sustainabledevelopment/wp-content/uploads/2016/08/9_Why-it-Matters_Goal-9_Industry_1p.pdf

The share of MVA of African countries in total MVA of the developing world kept dwindling from 4.3% in 1995 to 3.1% in 2011, at constant price 2000 (see Figure 1). The share of MVA of total value added has been stagnant for a decade and a half, not exceeding 7%, the weakest compared to Latin-America (about 15%) and Asia (25%). One of the problems we have witnessed in recent years is the important drawback in industrial strategies, particularly in Africa and Latin America, while the private sector was either absent or had a very small share of the domestic industrial effort. The dis-industrialisation phenomenon took place, resulting in the closure of tens of manufacturing outlets and laying off of thousands of workers, some with a significant knowledge capital and valuable experience. This decline massively concerned the public sector, but was not compensated by the private sector.

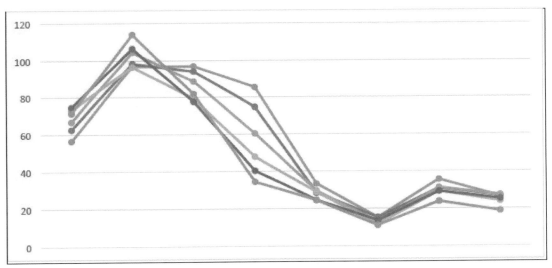

Figure 1   Evolution of the Production of Indust Products in the Public Sector: 1999—2004

Source: The author

Examining the trajectories of public sector companies indicates a cycle with three stages:

Phase 1: growth of production: until 1999: high investment, increased growth of production. Increased acquisition of equipment, training contracts, technical assistance, subcontracted design and engineering: unrecognised: learning by doing, transfer of technology, development of design and engineering capabilities.

Phase 2: decline: 1999—2011: privatisation of major industrial complex, dismantling of industrial production units. In Algeria, 1,015 large public enterprises and 3,000 local enterprises (EPLs) were closed, resulting in the suppression of 400,000 jobs. This led to an increase in unemployment, which reached more than 2 million people

(Djeflat, 2008), laying off workers (with significant loss of accumulated know-how and skills), e.g. in the metallurgical industry, the production of industrial tanks, 900 workers were laid off, dis-industrialisation, de-engineering.

Phase 3: stagnation and decline: 2011 to the present day: stagnation of production: 1980–1984: de-engineering, de-design, lack of currency, pressure from Breton wood institutions, halt (closing down): 2000–2014: privatisation.

Weak and stagnant innovation effort

It is commonly known that successive S&T policies in the developing world, and Africa in particular, have delivered very few capabilities in terms of innovation, as shown by various studies.

Efforts devoted to promote R&D and innovation are rather weak in most African countries: gross expenditure on R&D had not reached 0.5% of GDP in 2008, with the exception of South Africa, Uganda and Malawi (Table 1). Although they succeeded at the sectoral level, they were not inclusive and did not enhance the already important inequalities. They were mostly driven by the State and publicly owned companies, leaving very little space for the private sector.

Table 1   Gross Expenditure on R&D in a Sample of Sub-Saharan Countries (2008)

	Year	GERD million PPP$	GERD per capita PPP$	GERD as % of GDP
Gabon	2008	78.7	58.3	0.47
Ghana	2007	120.1	5.0	0.38
Kenya	2007	277.8	7.4	0.48
Malawi	2007	180.1	12.9	1.70
Mali†	2007	37.4	3.0	0.28
Mozambique*‡	2007	42.9	2.0	0.25
Nigeria*†	2007	583.2	3.9	0.20
Senegal	2008	99.0	8.0	0.48
South Africa	2007	4 976.6	102.4	1.05
Tanzania*	2007	234.6	5.8	0.48
Uganda†	2007	359.8	11.6	1.10
Zambia	2008	55.3	4.6	0.37

Sources: ASTII R&D Surveys; PPP data from UNDP (2010); population and GDP data from AfDB (2010)

Note:

* Data do not include the business enterprise sector

† Data do not include private non-profit institutions/organisations

‡ Data do not include the higher education sector

Implications *of the Regression Process*

This situation has several implications on the sustainability of growth, particularly when it is coupled with the significant decline of the price of mineral resources witnessed in the last four to five years.

The most significant impact often unrecognised and badly documented is the downgrading of the capabilities that are so vital for industrial growth and which are scarce resources in African countries. Table 2 highlights some of these capabilities and pinpoints to some of the likely causes for their downgrading.

Table 2   The Downgrading of Major Capabilities

Loss of assets	Effects	Causes
Production regression	Des industrialisation	— restructuring — privatisation — competitive pressure
Human capital loss	De learning	— flight of competencies — laying off of workers — unrecognised tacit knowledge — Dutch disease
Knowledge capital loss	Regression of R&D	— unfair competition (free trade zone) — informal sector — financing
Institutional regression	Downgrading of institutions and actors	— institutional instability — rivalry & petit politics — vested interests — corruption

Source: The author

Most countries will continue to rely heavily on mineral sources and, with the fall of market prices, will intensify the exploitation of these resources to compensate for lost income. They will also continue to rely on fossil products as sources of energy. This can be illustrated by the current debate on whether to exploit shale gas to make up for lost income, because of the decline of oil and gas prices in Algeria for example.

The countries will have less budget to devote to sustainability objectives in their various forms. Lack of capabilities will enhance their dependency on importing readymade equipment and activities where sustainability is not the prime concern in their design. Manufacturing activities are sometimes outsourced to escape stringent rules at home.

The lack of massive job creation will drive a high proportion of the active population to join the informal sector. This sector is known to have activities and behaviour that can be harmful to the environment; they are largely uncontrolled and the enforcement of rules and regulations is extremely difficult.

INNOVATION AND SUSTAINABLE INDUSTRIAL DEVELOPMENT

The Importance of Innovation in Sustainable Growth at the Firm Level

As stated in Objective 9 of the SDG agenda, investments in infrastructure, transport, irrigation, energy, and information and communication technology are crucial in achieving sustainable development and empowering communities in many countries. More directly relevant to our paper, the second part of Objective 9 is *the promotion of sustainable industrial development and fostering innovation through PPP*. It is now a fact that technological progress is the foundation of these efforts to achieve environmental objectives: *"Without technology and innovation, industrialisation will not happen, and without industrialisation, development will not happen"*.

If we take the mining sector as an example, studies have shown that environmental performance correlates closely with production efficiency, and environmental degradation is greatest in operations that work with obsolete technology, limited capital, and poor human resource management. Firms that pollute the most are mismanaging the environment precisely because of their inability to innovate. The most efficient firms are generally better environmentally managed, because they are innovators and are able to harness both technological and organisational change to reduce the production and environmental costs of their operations (Warhurst, 2000).

Examples throughout the literature show that innovation can reduce pollution, and that firms that adopt this strategy build competitive advantages as well as environmental benefits. In terms of theory, Tilton (1992) shows that innovation is a key element in sustainability using cost and benefit analysis, the two key elements in the decision-making process for environment protection. The approach in terms of internal and external costs deserves some attention (Figure 2). The argument rests on the assumption that the socially optimal use of an environmental resource occurs when the additional benefits (in terms of the goods and services it derives by permitting one more unit of pollution) equal the additional costs it incurs, the point at which MSB = MSC.

While this approach gives precious insight into the trade-off between social costs and social benefits, and broadens the classical cost/benefit analysis to encompass environmental consideration, it fails to integrate the technology factor. One of its basic assumptions is that technology is externalised in the analysis and that firms operate with a given level of technology. The hypothesis of static technology does not hold anymore, particularly in an era where technical change is occurring at a relatively high pace. In effect, technology is one of the key elements in the equation. The marginal social costs (MSC) are in a lower position while the marginal social benefits (MSB) stands at a higher position: environmental innovation therefore becomes a necessity.

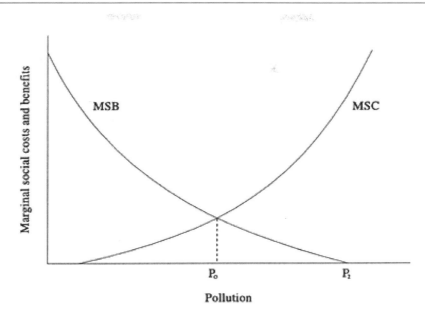

**Figure 2   Trade-off between Marginal Social Costs and Marginal Social Benefits
and Equilibrium**
Source: Warhurst (2000)

The Importance of State Action: The Regulations

While conventional wisdom is that regulatory regimes of the polluter-payer type are the driving force behind better environmental management and that they are sufficient to put pressure to reduce social costs, the reality is that they suffer from major flaws. The first is the everlasting problem of enforcement, which is known to be weak in many African countries and which results from problems in governance. Second, they tend to presume that technology is static, based on a technology "that was best at one time". In effect, such regulations could act as a disincentive for technology suppliers to innovate, knowing that innovations require substantial R&D resources. Regulations requiring the polluter to pay tend to lead to end-of-pipe, add-on, or capital-intensive solutions for existing technology and work practices, rather than promoting alternative environmental management systems and technological innovation (Warhurst, 2000). In the face of stringent regulations, less innovative firms are driven to either close down or to export pollution to developing countries that have less-restrictive regulatory regimes. With the increasing awareness on the part of LDCs regarding social costs, the second alternative is less and less practical. Research conducted in the mining sector nonetheless suggests that the environmental performance of a mining enterprise is more closely related to its innovative capacity than to the regulatory regime under which it operates (Warhurst, 2000).

This suggests that technical change that is stimulated by environmental considerations, instead of increasing costs, tends to reduce both production and environmental costs, to the advantage of those dynamic companies with the competence and resources to innovate. These companies are adapting to environmental regulatory pressures by innovating, improving, and commercialising their environmental technology and environmental management practices, at home and abroad.

Examples from the mining industry show that firms are investing in R&D in order to develop more environmentally sound technologies. Also, they are beginning to sell their technologies, preferring to commercialise their innovations to cover their R&D costs than to sell obsolete technology and risk shareholders' displeasure or retrospective penalties. Other examples show that new opportunities could be opened by regulations for both equipment suppliers and polluters themselves to innovate. New and more stringent noise pollution regulations in the field of noise pollution in the 1970s saw the emergence of a host a new products and services for noise control in Great Britain and some Scandinavian countries, including from the polluters themselves (Djeflat, 1975).

On more global terms, technical innovation, for instance in terms of developing substitutes to naturally scarce raw products, may help to overcome the fact that *natural capital* cannot always be reproduced. In terms of policy implications, environmental legislation needs to be completed by mechanisms to promote environmental innovation, and mechanisms to stimulate the diffusion of these innovations among firms.

However, pollution control and environmental protection are only two of the objectives of sustainable development. Sustainability is also about reducing poverty, education, health and welfare, the agricultural sector, and rural development. Nonetheless, while the issues of environmental protection and innovation are gathering more and more support and comprehension, systems of innovation (Lundvall, 1992) and sustainability still raise some key questions.

PPP AND SUSTAINABLE INDUSTRIAL DEVELOPMENT AND INNOVATION IN AFRICAN COUNTRIES

The Limits of State-led Industrial and Innovation Policies

The main feature of industrial development in most African countries has been the dominant posture of the State in promoting industrial development and innovation through successive attempts to implement S&T policies. Recent measures have tried to bring in the private sector in manufacturing through a host of incentives. However, limited attempts have been made to design a proper PPP in this endeavour.

It is now clear that industrial policies driven essentially by the State have met their limits and cannot promote sustainable growth, notwithstanding all the efforts made over the last 40 years by certain African countries (Nigeria, Kenya, Algeria, Egypt, and others).

Similarly, in several countries in the South, and in Africa in particular, State led innovation policies have failed to deliver the necessary goods and services, not only to constantly and rapidly changing domestic demand but also the requirements of globally competitive markets.

The Limits of Business led Industrial Development for Sustainability

While the impact on local industry can be quite substantial in terms of employment creation, outsourcing to local industry with the effect of upgrading their facilities and know-how, and perhaps in some cases, triggering a real innovation dynamics, examples and success stories to substantiate that, are still relatively limited. This is particularly true when it comes to African countries, with the exception of South Africa.

Competitive pressures tend to increase outsourcing of innovative activities and progressively reduce the national base for innovation systems. More and more firms are driven to outsource their activities to the so-called low wage countries. Firms seek mostly to harness local research capabilities while paying relatively lower wages compared to wages back home. This behaviour is also seen in the field of environmental protection and sustainable development. R&D is driven by market needs and profit considerations. In this respect, the national base of innovation systems is gradually eroded, consequently reducing the basis of sustainability. Local competencies and research capacities are diverted from national projects and programmes for sustainability to pressing market needs.

THE NEED FOR A PPP FOR INNOVATION AND SUSTAINABLE INDUSTRIAL GROWTH

Innovation, Sustainability: A Collective Effort

Innovation and sustainability have common features: while being led by the State through public policies, they are both systemic and are, in essence, more of an evolutionary obedience. The State cannot be efficient on its own through regulations and public policy. Similarly, in a neo-classical framework, the private sector and market pressures on their own cannot help achieve the discounted results. It is a collective effort, involving interaction between several actors that matters (Rothwell, 1992).

This is in line with Objective 17 of the SDGs, which stipulates that:

> *"A successful sustainable development agenda requires partnerships between governments, the private sector and civil society. These inclusive partnerships built upon principles and values, a shared vision, and shared goals that place people and the planet at the centre, are needed at the global, regional, national and local level".*

Several spheres are involved for a successful mix of innovation sustainability and industrial development.

The Government Sphere: The Government sphere is needed because of the strong regulatory dimension through a variety of mechanisms; this is well documented in the SDG agenda. They include policy orientations and decisions, and a variety of mechanisms for the implementation both of a fiscal and non-fiscal nature.

The Research Sphere: The Research sphere plays a distinct role as sustainability rests on the limitation of a variety of hazards to the environment and to mankind; they require new knowledge and multi-disciplinarity. Both constantly extended and basic research are vitally important.

The Industry Sphere: The Industry sphere is essentially the private sphere because of the need to transform ideas and inventions into much needed and marketable goods and services. The private sector alone, on the other hand, has not been able to invest in any significant way in R&D. This effort is estimated at less than 6% of total R&D effort in Maghreb[2] countries on average, and often resulted from a mismatch between science policy and innovation policy.

These three spheres constitute the *public private partnership node of sustainability*. (Djeflat, 2005). However, it is not enough when it comes to innovation and sustainability concerns. Other spheres also have an important role to play (Figure 3).

Figure 3   The SDG Objective 9 Extended PPP Framework
Source: The author

The Social Acceptance Sphere is essential because of the need for diffusion and increasing social acceptance of the new technologies, sometimes changing well en-

---

[2]The Maghreb is a major region of northern Africa that consists primarily of the countries Algeria, Morocco, Tunisia, Libya and Mauritania.

trenched mentalities and hard to die habits. In African countries, where inclusive innovation and sustainability include the fight against poverty, inequality and exclusion, social acceptance is vital for new products and services with high sustainability contents. In this respect, innovation in industry and manufacturing need social innovation to accompany and ease this process.

The Donors' Sphere: The donors' sphere is much needed because of the hazards that these countries suffer, and the high risks they run in terms of unequal distribution of wealth, diversion of resources to private ends and rent-seeking. New products and services with sustainable contents could be used for the richest section of the population.

The International Organisation Sphere is needed to set and monitor rules and regulations and their diffusion throughout the world, such as the SDGs: it contributes to raising awareness and setting up incentives for compliance R&D and sustainable innovation.

The Financial Sphere: finally, we have the banks and financial institutions sphere: namely those concerned with implementing UNCED objectives and with policies to promote the international diffusion of clean technology.

These are shown in Figure 4 and Table 3 below.

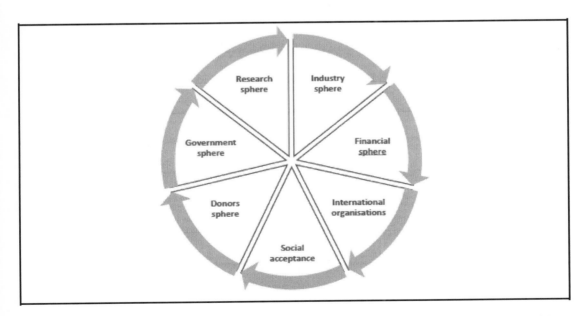

Figure 4   The Various Spheres Involved in Environmental Protection and Sustainable Development Innovation Systems

Source: The author

Table 3   The Various Spheres and Actors Involved in Environmental Protection and Sustainable Development Innovation Systems

Research sphere	Industry sphere	Government sphere	Donors' sphere	Social acceptance	International organisations
— University-university — University industry — University research centres — University-industry-research centres	— Industry-industry — Industry market — Industry-university — Industry-Government	— Compliance R&D support — Prevention of resources-diversion — Innovation diffusion within national boundaries — Innovation Diffusion abroad — Training of regulators	— Donors-government In LDCs — Donors-NGOs — Donors civil society	— Civil society — NGOs — Press and Media	— Setting International regulations — Diffusion of standards and best practices — Incentive system

Source: The author

In the future, innovation policy may extend beyond these traditional sectoral domains if "third-generation innovation policy" integrates the innovation needs of all domains that can help to advance industrial development. The obvious candidates for such a mix are environmental policies and other key policy domains for sustainable development that are in need of new technological and organisational solutions. It is important to recall that innovation policies, as well as sustainable development policy domains, are continuously evolving.

The questions that remain pending relates to the relationship between firm-based innovation and sustainability sensitivity, and a more macro-economic decision requiring public policy making and collective choices.

The dialogue is not easy between the various actors involved and various spheres, when innovation systems or part of them are devoted to sustainability. Research efforts and sustainability oriented innovation systems can be seen as a way of diverting valuable resources from market-oriented innovation efforts and world competitive pressures. For R&D to address the challenges posed by sustainability, several studies confirm the great need to strengthen the "demand" side of the dialogue between experts and decision makers involved in action programmes for sustainability. Another acute need emphasised is for the creation of bridges across spatial scales, so that the location-specific needs and knowledge central to sustainability can be linked with relevant national and international level R&D (Folke et al., 2002).

The difficulties of the collective effort for sustainability in Africa

The issue of innovation and sustainability in African countries raises several questions. This is as a result a weak knowledge base, incomplete innovation systems and often

weak sensitivity to sustainable development gains. As remarked elsewhere, these issues may seem as luxurious concerns in a continent where there is poverty, hunger,
illnesses and disease and conflicts. However, there are several motives for African
countries to innovate for sustainability. When examining the linkages between innovation and sustainability, in an African context, it becomes clear that new opportunities
exist for African development, as much as some risks.

First, this is because upstream they suffer from a limitation of resources;, this
requires using those resources in a very frugal manner and not having heavy environmental costs they are unable to bear. This would guarantee future generations access
to a certain amount of these resources.

Second, they also need to innovate because of the many problems they suffer from
that have proved difficult to resolve using conventional techniques and approaches.
Innovation has to be in all fields and not simply in the technical field: in the social
field, in the political field, and in the organisational field. Water diseases, for example, result not only from lack of water purification techniques, but also from the way
water is collected, transported, stored and distributed. We have highlighted some of
the weaknesses facing innovation systems in LDCs looking specifically at Middle East
and North African (MENA) countries in previous contributions (Djeflat, 2000). It is also
quite clear that all components of innovation systems have to be replaced within that
specific context of under-development. However, current endogenous capabilities of
African countries depend very much on the extent to which they have access to advanced technology, and to the extent that this technology is effectively transferred.
African countries find themselves in an uncomfortable situation where concerns for
environmental protection and sustainable development are fully transferred, where
regulations are also transferred, mostly with the help of international organisations,
but where the means, i.e. the technology, is not transferred or transferred only par-
tially. This situation will have important implications for innovation and knowledge
dynamics, and raises the question to what extent sustainable development can take
place without sustainable knowledge (Djeflat, 2010).

While all these motives to drive African countries to innovate for sustainability exist, there are also several impediments.

The first and most important impediment includes the cost to the environment.
This does not seem to be strong enough to have a significant impact and is usually
externalised at the firm level. It does not constitute a strong motive to undertake innovative activities in this sense. This situation is found in the mining sector in Latin
America (Warhurst, 2000), and can easily be found in the oil sector (Algeria, Nigeria),
in copper mines (Zambia), and in the phosphate industry (Morocco) (El Khabli, 2001).

The second impediment is the force of the regulations that should normally be a
driving motive. In an African context there are several obstacles due to governance
problems and the widespread corruption in the judicial system in particular.

The third motive relates to social pressure that is relatively weak. The communities and villages most affected by pollution, environment hazards and non-sustainable

behaviour do not have sufficient knowledge to understand the problems. Moreover, they have no voice at the political level to express concern and put pressure on polluters to undertake technical or organisational innovation. Examples from the oil sector in Algeria show that major oil companies started changing their attitude and being more concerned with pollution control and environmental protection only when their key technical personnel became involved; they started exercising pressure when they felt personally at risk. Pressure could not come from villages and populations living in areas that were polluted as a result of flared gas and severe air pollution.

The fourth impediment is pressure from international organisations. In the current situation, this factor seems the most plausible factor to have a significant impact on Government and firms to change their technologies and organisations to more responsible behaviour. However, two major obstacles can reduce its impact. The first is the limited financial means of many debt ridden African states; this means that they cannot divert precious resources to innovation while other urgent needs are not satisfied. International public funding can play an important role in this respect. The idea of credit conditionalities by international organisations for environmental protection is put forward (Warhurst, 2000); for African countries, however, this may have a counter-productive effect. It could lead to a drawback in sustainability, inasmuch as it could result in less investment for poverty reduction, health protection and education promotion investments. The second obstacle is, of course, the limited technological capabilities.

The fifth impediment coming from donor organisations has had a non-negligible impact in recent years. This was the case in the agricultural sector where some progress has been made using local competencies in R&D to find local solutions to problems such as crop disease, water treatment or water-saving irrigation techniques. Other success stories are found in the field of micro finance, although they are unfortunately far too limited and most certainly not sufficiently publicised. The manufacturing and the industrial sectors have benefited much less from strong support to innovate coming from international donor agencies. Therefore, the issue of sustainability in relation to innovation systems has not been fully explored in a developing country perspective.

PPP and the Promotion of Sustainable and Innovative Industrial Models in Africa: Some Recommendations

As stated in Objective 17, a full range of measures are needed, including financial support and debt relief, the transfer of technologies and scientific know-how to developing nations on favourable terms, and the establishment of an open, non-discriminatory and equitable trading system to help developing nations increase their exports.

Government action will need to set a clear direction; this should include review and monitoring frameworks, regulations and incentive structures that attract investments and reinforce sustainable industrial development and innovation. National oversight mechanisms such as supreme audit institutions and oversight functions by legislatures should be strengthened.

Urgent action is needed to mobilise the massive capital of private finance and knowledge to implement sustainable industrial development and innovation objectives. Long-term investments, including foreign direct investment, geared towards critical sectors in Africa are needed. Several PPP arrangements should be developed.

There is a need for new orientation of economic and institutional reforms to cater for the needs of foreign capital and trans-national corporations who are sensitive to sustainable domestic growth and industrial development. This should be done by creating a friendly business environment in the sense of PPPs.

In the area of environmental protection, there are grounds for a "new type of technology transfer" to take place. The new forms of technology transfer in environmental management embraces the knowledge, expertise, and experience required to manage technical change of both an incremental and a radical nature. This also includes the development of human resources for implementing organisational change to improve overall production and energy efficiency, and environmental management throughout the plant and facility. Technology transfer and technology partnership through joint ventures or strategic alliances are ways of building up technological and managerial capabilities, and capabilities for innovation and sustainable industrial development. This is particularly pertinent to Africa, although such strategic alliances are emerging in all the major mineral-producing countries (Warhurst, 2000). For this transfer to be effective, however, a substantial increase in the technological capabilities of African countries is required (Barnett, 1992).

There is a need for African countries to tap into global knowledge geared towards sustainability: this opens up the opportunity for African countries to improve their relatively weak local knowledge base and to extend their knowledge system to include their diasporas, as shown by the successful stories in India, China and South Korea.

The opportunities offered by ICT give a new perspective. ICT inclusion into the knowledge system gives the opportunity for local firms and research institutions to integrate knowledge networks, update their often obsolete knowledge, and sometimes have access through their diaspora, indirectly and often discreetly, into the knowledge systems of more advanced countries.

All these factors are at the origin of the "sustainability divide" and "sustainable divide" that are taking place in development and growth.

REFERENCES

Barnett, A. (1992), *The role of industrialised countries in the transfer of technology to improve the rational use of energy in Developing Countries*, A contribution to the 1992/1993 COPED Network Research Programme, SPRU, University of Sussex, Brighton, UK.

DESA (2016), Public-Private Partnerships and the 2030 Agenda for Sustainable Development: Fit for purpose, *DESA Working Paper* No. 148 ST/ESA/2016/DWP/148.

Djeflat, A. (1975), *Noise pollution and noise control: opportunities and threats for equipment producers*, mimeo, School of Management, University of Bath, GB.

Djeflat, A. (1996), Les technologies de l'Environnement: des perspectives durables de partenariat Euro-méditerranéen *Reflets et Perspectives*, Vol. XXXV, No. 3, pp. 297–312.

Djeflat, A. (2000), National Systems of Innovation in the MENA Region, World Bank, Washington DC, 52pp.

Djeflat, A. (2008), Innovation takes off through industrial technical centers in Maghreb Countries: a missing link in NSI or new opportunity? International Conference GLOBELICS MEXICO, 22–24 September 22–24.

Djeflat, A. (2010), Sustainable knowledge for sustainable development: challenges and opportunities for African development, *World Journal of Science, Technology and Sustainable Development*, Vol. 7, No. 2, pp. 131–49.

Djeflat, A. (2005), Innovation systems, knowledge economy and sustainable development: challenges and opportunities for African development. The fourth Globelics conference, Trivundrum, India.

El Khabli, A. (2001), *R&D and innovation system in the phosphate industry in Morocco*, PhD thesis, The University of Lille 1, France.

Folke, C., Carpenter, S., Elmqvist, T., Gunderson, L., Holling, C.S. and Walker, B. (*2002*), Resilience and *Sustainable* Development: Building Adaptive Capacity in a World of Transformation, *ISCU Series on Science for Sustainable Development* 3, pp.1–72.

Lundvall, B.A. (1992), *National Systems of Innovation: An analytical framework*, Pinter, London.

Rodrik, D. (2006), *Industrial Development: Stylized Facts and Policies Revised*. 2006. Copy at http://j.mp/2oz4ySE.

Rothwell, R. (1992), Industrial innovation and government environmental regulation: some lessons from the past. *Technovation*, Vol. 12, No. 7, pp. 447–58.

Tilton, J.E. (1992), *Mining Waste, the Polluter Pays Principle, and US Environmental Policy*. Colorado School of Mines, Department of Mineral Economics, Golden, CO. Working Paper 92–8, October.

Warhurst, A. (2000), *Environmental Regulations, Innovation and Sustainable Development*, IDRC books free online, 9–12 September.

BIOGRAPHY

Professor Abdelkader Djeflat was appointed full Professor in Economics at the University of Oran in Algeria in 1992, where he held the position of Dean of the Faculty of Economics, Chairman of the Scientific Council, and member of the Scientific Board of the Centre of Applied Economics for Development (CREAD). He currently works at the University of Lille in France, where he teaches industrial and development economics, and is Senior Fellow at the Clerse Laboratory (CNRS). He is the founder and current Chairman of Maghtech (Maghreb Technology Network) (Maghtech.org), and a member of the Constitution Committee of the Globelics Network. He was involved in various tasks with the Ministry and National Economic and Social Council (CNES) of the Algerian Government. He has undertaken extensive consultations with various UN organisations, ECA, ESCWA, UNDP and World Bank Institute. He has written several books and articles in various international journals. He holds a PhD from the University of Bath in United Kingdom.

IMPACT OF CORPORATE ENTREPRENEURSHIP ON ORGANISATIONAL CULTURE

Dr Siham El-Kafafi*

Director of Research
ICL Education Group
Auckland
siham@icl.ac.nz

ABSTRACT

Purpose: The purpose of this paper is to examine the impact of corporate entrepreneurship on organisational culture as a means of achieving high organisational performance providing competitive advantage for organisational survival in such a global era.

Design/methodology/approach: A literature survey was conducted tracing the origin of the concept of entrepreneurship, starting from Schumpeter's (1942) creative destruction concept, followed by characteristics of entrepreneurial behaviour, followed by providing a link between entrepreneurship and corporate entrepreneurship. Furthermore, the research explains the corporate entrepreneurship innovation process, and finally provides suggestions on how to integrate corporate entrepreneurship with organisational culture. It does this by proposing a suitable leadership style to guarantee high organisational performance.

Findings: The findings demonstrate that organisational structure does have an impact on organisational performance guiding the competitive advantage strategy (i.e. innovative differentiation, cost leadership and/or

*Corresponding Author

quick response to market demand). This, in turn, impacts on organisational innovation and creative behaviour, which influences its corporate entrepreneurial process.

Originality/value: This study purports valuable contributions by suggesting the integration of the following elements required for corporate entrepreneurship and organisational culture: 1) risk taking; 2) rewards and motivation; 3) management support; 4) resource availability; and 5) organisational structure. Furthermore, the research provided an adequate leadership style to guarantee high performance through an innovative culture, advocating corporate entrepreneurship.

Keywords: Corporate entrepreneurship; corporate entrepreneurship innovation; organisational culture; organisational performance; leadership style

INTRODUCTION

Competitive advantage is a key aspect of organisational survival in the era of globalisation that we are living in today. I believe that, even though not new, the concept of entrepreneurship is becoming a vital factor for organisations who want to achieve high performance through the adoption of a creative and innovative culture. There are various definitions and classifications of entrepreneurship, either individual entrepreneurs, group entrepreneurs or organisational entrepreneurship. Chirani and Hasanzahed (2013) posited that organisations are shifting towards corporate entrepreneurship out of necessity; this has been highlighted by the rapid increase of new competitors in the market. This shift was triggered by the lack of trust in traditional production methods and the increase in individual entrepreneurs who are leaving organisations to work by themselves.

The purpose of this paper is to examine the impact of corporate entrepreneurship on organisational culture as a means of achieving high organisational performance, providing competitive advantage for organisational survival in such a global era. Accordingly, a literature survey was conducted, tracing the origin of the concept of entrepreneurship. This started from Schumpeter's (1942) creative destruction concept, followed by characteristics of entrepreneurial behaviour, followed by providing the link between entrepreneurship and corporate entrepreneurship.

Furthermore, the research explains the corporate entrepreneurship innovation process, and finally provides suggestions on how to integrate corporate entrepreneurship with organisational culture by proposing a suitable leadership style to guarantee high organisational performance.

What is Entrepreneurship?

This section defines the term entrepreneurship and the traits of an entrepreneur as a means of setting the scene for explaining corporate entrepreneurship and the role it plays in enhancing organisational performance.

The term entrepreneur was initially used by Austrian-American economist Joseph A. Schumpeter (1883–1950), in which he explained that entrepreneurs are the main agents for economic growth through the creation of new methods of production, i.e. creating innovations that stimulated economic evolution. In addition, Schumpeter introduced the concept of "creative destruction"; this means that entrepreneurs continually substitute or destroy existing products or methods of products with new ones. Nevertheless, there is a positive result from this creative destruction, which is the creation of new technologies and new products to fit the continual change in customers' needs. These include technological advancements in the telecommunication field (e.g. computers, telephones and Internet), the transportation field (e.g. automobiles, airplanes, etc.) the production field, and the medical field. Moreover, creative destruction also helps overall economic improvement (Schumpeter, 2011; 1942).

Entrepreneurship is the willingness to take risks, and develop, organise and manage a business venture in a competitive global marketplace that is constantly evolving. Entrepreneurs are pioneers, innovators, leaders and inventors. Erkkila (2000) identified entrepreneurs by the following traits: flexible, creative, autonomous, problem solver, need to achieve, imaginative, believe in controlling one's destiny, leadership, hard-working, initiative, persuasive and moderate risk taker.

Tony et al. (2018) reiterated that entrepreneurship is doing a new thing or transforming an existing business concept into a new venture with the aim of high growth; it therefore contributes immensely by creating new jobs, reducing poverty and generating income for both governments and individuals. In addition, the authors provided the following acronym to the term **entrepreneurship** (Tony et al., 2018, p.127):

E:xamine needs, wants, and problems

N:ote and narrow down the possible opportunities to one specific "best" opportunity

T:otal commitment with high work ethics

R:eliable and passionate

E:nterprising personality and behaviour

P:roactive and pragmatic

R:elationship Management expert

E:nergetic and competitive by nature

N:ever allow reactivity or limiting belief

E:mphasise on key performance indicators and critical success factors of the business

U:nderstanding of the need for commitment and high work ethics

R:ealistic and positive accomplishment and creative destruction

S:eized by passion and fixity of purpose to make things happen positively for the business

H:ighly focused and motivated
I:nnovator with inner drive for success
P:ossibility mentality

Entrepreneurship is an important engine of growth in the economy. Sharma and Chrisman (1999) stated that entrepreneurial actions are pathways to competitive advantage. They also improve organisational performance through acts of creativity and innovation that occurs within and outside an organisation. Chesbrough (2003) linked innovation and entrepreneurship by stating that they are interdependent of each other, i.e. innovations are the outcome of a successful entrepreneurship process.

For organisations to become entrepreneurial they need to advocate a learning environment that encourages employees' behaviour to act creatively, i.e. advocate a learning culture towards corporate entrepreneurship. In this environment, managers are responsible for developing organisational conditions and providing motivational mechanisms of risk taking and innovative behaviour. Accordingly, Johnson (2001) suggested the following entrepreneurial behaviours that are required to encourage and support an entrepreneurial learning culture within the organisation:

- motivation to achieve and compete;
- taking ownership and being accountable;
- making independent and self-directed decisions;
- being open to new information, people and practices;
- being able to tolerate ambiguity and uncertainty;
- creative and flexible thinking, problem solving and decision making;
- the ability to see and capture opportunities;
- awareness for the risks attached to choices and actions;
- the capacity to manage and ultimately reduce risks;
- persistence and determination in the face of challenge or lack of immediate reward;
- considering, discussion and formulating a vision; and
- the capacity to make an impact.

I believe that leadership plays a role here by identifying those entrepreneurial behaviours among their employees and providing all the possible support to spread the entrepreneurial culture.

What is Corporate Entrepreneurship?

This section links entrepreneurship and the role played by corporate entrepreneurship, which is dependent on the generated innovations of organisational employees. It starts by providing a definition of corporate entrepreneurship followed by the various types of corporate entrepreneurship that could be adopted by organisations, the five dimensions of corporate entrepreneurship orientation, and finally identifies the structural characteristics required by an organisation demonstrating entrepreneurial behaviour.

Zahra (1991) defined corporate entrepreneurship as an organisation's set of activities that enables it to enhance its innovative ability through risk taking and seizing opportunities in the market place, i.e. it targets both new business establishments and new market allocation. This is a reiteration from Barringer and Bluedorn (1999) who posited that corporate entrepreneurship relates to internal development leading to diversification of organisational internal activities. Accordingly, new resources are required to enable organisations from seizing new opportunities. In such cases diversification enables the process of individual entrepreneurship leading the organisation towards corporate entrepreneurship.

Thornberry (2001) suggested the adoption of the following four types of corporate entrepreneurship:

1. Corporate Venturing:
   This type is identified by starting a new venture relevant to the organisation's core business. It is attractive to organisations that utilise vertical integration strategy.
2. Organisational Transformation:
   This type focuses on enhancing organisational operational efficiencies.
3. Intrapreneuring:
   This type focuses on identifying employees that have entrepreneurial aptitude and provides them with support to grow and utilise their innovative potential.
4. Industry Rule Bending:
   This type is relevant to organisations that can identify innovative products and processes that provide them with a first mover status in the market leading to a high market share.

Furthermore, Dess and Lumpkin (2005) emphasised the following five dimensions for organisations to foster corporate entrepreneurship:

1. Autonomy: in this dimension employees are encouraged to become a project champion who is capable of negotiating a new process with the aim of bringing a new product to the market.
2. Innovativeness: the organisation should be investing in research and development in new products.
3. Proactiveness: the organisation should have a future orientation by investing in trend analysis of viable opportunities.
4. Competitive Aggressiveness: organisation should engage with competition through predatory tactics to gain market share.
5. Risk Taking: the organisation should have a clear understanding of the risks associated with the business and its finances.

On the other hand, Slevin and Covin (1990) suggested the following structural characteristics to identify entrepreneurial behaviour in an organisation:

1. practising varied operational styles under the leadership of experienced top management;
2. being flexible towards environmental changes;
3. concentrating on results more than processes in their operations;
4. practising a cooperative, friendly culture with informal control;
5. advocated flexibility within teamwork behaviour;
6. concentrating on teamwork creativity; and
7. practicing free communication.

Miller (1986) and Miller and Shamsie (1996) provided the following explanation for four types of organisational structures: *simple structure* (strategies are set by top management), *machine bureaucracy* (many formal rules, policies and procedures with high levels of power centralisation), *organic* (very flexible with limited hierarchy), and *divisional* (composed of several independent groups).

Accordingly, I believe that organisational structure does have an impact on organisational competitive advantage strategy (i.e. innovative differentiation, cost leadership and/or quick response to market demand). In turn, this impacts on organisational innovation and creative behaviour, which influences its corporate entrepreneurial process. This all depends on top management's support in fostering a culture of corporate entrepreneurship throughout all organisational activities.

Corporate Entrepreneurship Innovation

There are various types of innovation in organisations: product and process innovation (Blumentritt, 2004; Damanpour, 1991); and administrative and technical innovation (Damanpour and Evan, 1984; Knight, 1963; Madrid-Guijarro et al., 2009). Tidd et al. (2005) explained that process innovation concerns changes in the ways in which products/services are created and delivered. On the other hand, technical innovation refers to products, services and production process technology (Damanpour and Evan, 1984; Knight, 1963). Furthermore, Laforet and Tann (2006) indicated that administrative innovation represents the procedures that enable innovation to be an inherent part of organisational operations.

Research conducted by Shaw et al. (2005) provided a new model combining corporate entrepreneurship and innovation, and provided the following definition as a means of linking both components:

> "Corporate entrepreneurship can be defined as the effort of promoting innovation in an uncertain environment. Innovation is the process that provides added value and novelty to the organisation and its suppliers and customers through the development of new procedures, solutions, products

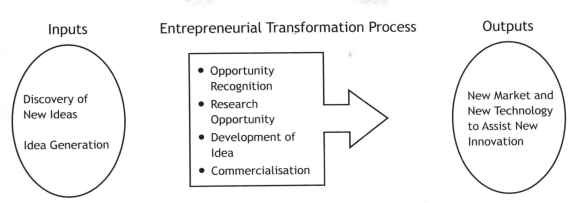

Figure 1   Corporate Entrepreneurship Innovation Process
Source: Author's figure adapted ideas from Shaw et al. (2005)

and services as well as new methods of commercialisation. Within this process the principal roles of the corporate entrepreneur are to challenge bureaucracy, to assess new opportunities, to align and exploit resources and to move the innovation process forward. The corporate entrepreneur's management of the innovation process will lead to greater benefits for the organisation" (p. 394).

This definition unifies the concept of corporate entrepreneurship innovation with the role and activities of the entrepreneur within the innovation process. Shaw et al.'s (2005) study suggests a conceptual model (refer to Figure 1) that comprises inputs, entrepreneurial transformation process and outputs of new innovation in the market place. Furthermore, the authors also suggest that organisations need to recognise the importance of the roles of the creative thinker, the corporate entrepreneur and the manager within an organisation towards a corporate entrepreneurship innovation.

Integrating Corporate Entrepreneurship with Organisational Culture

Chandradewini (2017) explained that organisational culture influences how organisations compete through their practices. That organisational culture can be a source of sustainable competitive advantage was further reiterated by Barney (1986). On the other hand, Antony and Bhattacharyya (2010) defined business performance as an organisational success measure that relates to creating and delivering value to its internal and external customers.

I believe that in order to support an organisational culture of corporate entrepreneurship with the aim of enhancing organisational performance, organisational leaders should have a focused approach on advocating change and encouraging individual entrepreneurship. This approach would foster new ideas, providing opportunities, risk taking and general entrepreneurial behaviour throughout the whole organisation via spreading an informal structure leading to a creative and innovative culture.

Denison (1996) posited that organisational culture emanates from its values and beliefs; this is reflected in employees' attitudes, behaviour and performance. On the other hand, Schein (1992) explained that organisational ceremonies, stories, heroes and rituals are indicators of organisational culture. Furthermore, Hofstede (2011) suggested studying organisational culture through the analysis of five dimensions, mainly power distance, uncertainty avoidance, past versus future orientation, masculinity versus femininity, and individualism versus collectivism.

For organisations to achieve high performance that could be obtained through business excellence, which Dahlgaard and Dahlgaard (1999) claimed could be achieved through the 4Ps, i.e. excellent people, excellent partnerships, excellent processes and excellent products. I concur with the authors that to achieve high performance through business excellence, there should be a drive from the organisational leadership to foster a culture of creativity and innovativeness among its employees by rewarding their entrepreneurial activities.

This research proposes that organisations should concentrate on specific elements as a means of spreading an organisational culture, which plays a vital role through its employees' behaviour and practices in the success of organisational performance through corporate entrepreneurship. These elements have the potential of enhancing organisational performance through the adoption of corporate entrepreneurship. The following Table 1 provides the required elements, their explanation and the suggested fitting leadership style.

Table 1 Elements Required for Integrating Corporate Entrepreneurship with Organisational Culture and Leadership Style

Organisational Element	Explanation	Leadership Style
Risk Taking	I believe that this is one of the main factors that should be given utmost priority over all the other elements. A great deal of literature describes an entrepreneur as a risk taker, i.e. a person who is capable of thinking outside the box. For an organisation to be called a corporate entrepreneurial organisation, it needs to have people who are risk takers by being creative in their thinking to provide new ideas that have the potential of taking their organisations to another higher transformational level. All this creativity cannot be achieved without taking risk.	Transformational Leadership would be the most suitable leadership style for this element as it advocates change for the best, risk taking and entrepreneurial activities to achieve higher level of performance. Samson and Daft (2012) stated that transformational leaders have the ability to lead change within organisations via its mission, strategy, structure and culture by promoting innovation in products and technologies.

(Continued)

Table 1 (*Continued*)

Organisational Element	Explanation	Leadership Style
Rewards and Motivation	This is a vital element to be adopted by organisations due to the importance of rewards and motivation on employees' performance. People innovate because they either have passion about what they do, or because they are expecting to be appropriately rewarded by their organisation as a result of their innovative activities. Accordingly, management has to set up robust reward and incentives systems to motivate their employees to become more innovative in support of corporate entrepreneurship. This has been the core of many studies by psychologists that have been used in the business discipline, e.g. Maslow's Hierarchy of Needs, and Hersberg's Two Factor's Theory.	Charismatic leadership would be suitable here as this style of leadership tends to motivate followers to go beyond their normal duties and even surprise themselves with their achievements. A reward system should be in place to keep the follower's trust in their leadership to sustain their positive influence on their followers accordingly.
Management Support	Top management hold all the cards in their hands and they are the movers and shakers who have the power of moulding organisational culture and steering it in the required direction. Accordingly, their support is essential as they can facilitate activities and provide both financial and non-financial support to render the required employee behaviour that supports a corporate entrepreneurship culture within the organisation.	This element concentrates more on the managerial aspects within the organisation. Accordingly, I believe that Fielder's contingency theory would be the most suitable as it balances between the leader's style if it is relationship oriented (concerned with people), or task oriented (concerned with task completion and outcomes). Samson and Daft (2012) stated that Fielder's Contingency Theory examines the relationship between the leadership style, situational favourability and group task performance.
Resource Availability	Following on from the previous element, management have the final say in resource allocation, i.e. the steering power towards the required route they want their organisation to follow. Accordingly, their support with all the needed resources, e.g. manpower, budget, training, time allocation, etc. would be a main factor of success for advocating a corporate entrepreneurial culture within the organisation.	Transformational leadership is vital here since they lead change in organisations, they will allocate the required resources to make sure new innovative ideas and technologies are adopted. This style of leadership nurtures a culture of corporate entrepreneurship that leads to high performance and competitive advantage.
Organisational Structure	Organisational structure is the pictorial manifestation of the hierarchal lines of authority within an organisation and the flow of information between different levels of management.	A combination of leadership styles is required to fit the various hierarchy levels within the organisational structure. Each level requires a different leadership style to both

(*Continued*)

Table 1   (*Continued*)

Organisational Element	Explanation	Leadership Style
	Furthermore, it shows the lines of communication, duties and rights in the organisation. It determines how the roles, power and responsibilities are assigned, controlled and coordinated.	encourage a culture of corporate entrepreneurship and fit with the diversified employees' requirements.
	Accordingly, choosing the right person for the right job in the right hierarchical level would be an essential factor for success, i.e. choosing the right people with the right attitude, behaviour, beliefs and values that fits with the organisational innovative culture.	

Source: Author's Figure

CONCLUSIONS

This research investigated the role of corporate entrepreneurship and organisational culture on organisational performance. It traced the origin of the concept of entrepreneurship, starting from Schumpeter's (1942) creative destruction, followed by characteristics of entrepreneurial behaviour, providing the link between entrepreneurship and corporate entrepreneurship.

Finally, the research suggested the integration of the following elements required for corporate entrepreneurship and organisational culture: 1) risk taking; 2) rewards and motivation; 3) management support; 4) resource availability; and 5) organisational structure. Furthermore, the research provided the adequate leadership style to guarantee high performance through an innovative culture advocating corporate entrepreneurship.

REFERENCES

Antony, J.P. and Bhattacharyya, S. (2010), Measuring organizational performance and organizational excellence of SMEs-Part 1: A conceptual framework. *Measuring Business Excellence*, Vol. 14, No. 2, pp. 3–11.

Barney, J.B. (1986), Organizational Culture: Can it be a source of sustained competitive advantage?, *The Academy of Management Review*, Vol. 11, No. 3, pp. 656–65.

Barringer, B.R. and Bluedorn, A.C. (1999), The relationship between corporate entrepreneurship and strategic management. *Strategic Management Journal*, Vol. 20, No. 5, pp. 421–24.

Blumentritt, T. (2004), Does small and mature have to mean dull? Defying the ho-hum at SMEs, *Journal of Business Strategy*, Vol. 25, No. 1, pp. 27–33.

Chandradewini (2017), The Analysis of Organizational Culture of the Revenue Department of Cimahi City, West Java, Indonesia, *Review of Integrative Business and Economics Research*, Vol. 6, No. 3, pp. 301–04.

Chesbrough, H.W. (2003), The logic of open innovation: managing intellectual property. *California Management Review*, Vol. 45, No. 3, pp. 33–58.

Chirani, E. and Hasanzahed, R. (2013), The Aspects of Organisational Entrepreneurship in Competition Environment. *Kuwait Chapter of Arabian Journal of Business and Management Review*, Vol. 2, No. 11, pp. 65–70.

Dahlgaard, J.J. and Dahlgaard, S.M.P. (1999), Integrating business excellence innovation management: developing a culture for innovation, creativity and learning. *Total Quality Management*, Vol. 10, Nos 4–5, pp. 465–72.

Damanpour, F. (1991), Organizational innovation: a meta-analysis of effects of determinants and moderators, *Academy of Management Journal*, Vol. 34, No. 3, pp. 555–90.

Damanpour, F. and Evan, W.M. (1984), Organizational innovation and performance: the problem of 'organisational lag', *Administrative Science Quarterly*, Vol. 29, No. 3, pp. 392–409.

Denison, D.R. (1996), What is the difference between organisational culture and organisational climate? A native's point of view on a decade of paradigm wars. *Academy of Management Review*, Vol. 21, No. 3, pp. 619–54.

Dess, G.G. and Lumpkin, G.T. (2005), The role of entrepreneurship orientation in stimulating effective corporate entrepreneurship. *Academy of Management Executive*, Vol. 19, No. 1, pp. 147–56.

Erkkila, K. (2000), *Entrepreneurial Education*. New York: Garland.

Hofstede, G. (2011), Dimensionalizing Cultures: The Hofstede Model in Context. *Online Readings in Psychology and Culture*, Vol. 2, No. 1, p.8. http://dx.doi.org/10.9707/2307-0919.1014 Retrieved on 22 May 2016 from http://scholarworks.gvsu.edu/cgi/viewcontent.cgi?article=1014&context=orpc.

Johnson, D. (2001), What is innovation and entrepreneurship? Lessons for larger organisations. *Industrial and Commercial Training*, Vol. 33, No. 4, pp. 135–40.

Knight, K.E. (1963), *A study of technological innovation - the evolution of digital computers*, unpublished PhD thesis, Pittsburgh, PA: Carnegie Institute of Technology.

Laforet, S. and Tann, J. (2006), Innovative characteristics of small manufacturing firms, *Journal of Small and Enterprise Development*, Vol. 13, No. 3, pp. 363–80.

Madrid-Guijarro, A., Garcia, D. and Van Auken, H. (2009), Barriers to innovation among Spanish manufacturing SMEs, *Journal of Small Business Management*, Vol. 47, No. 4, pp. 465–88. doi:10.1111/j.1540-627X.2009.00279.x

Miller, D. (1986), Configurations of strategy and structure: towards a synthesis, *Strategic Management Journal*, Vol. 7, No. 3, pp. 233–49.

Miller, D. and Shamsie, J. (1996), The resource-based view of the firm in two environments: the Hollywood firm studios from 1936 to 1995, *Academy of Management Journal*, Vol. 39, No. 3, pp. 519–43.

Samson, D. and Daft, R.L (2012), *Fundamentals of Management* (4th Asia Pacific Edition). South Melbourne, Victoria Australia: Cengage Learning Australia Pty Limited.

Schein, E.H. (1992), *Organisational Culture and Leadership* (2nd Edn). San Francisco: Jossey-Bass Publishers.

Schumpeter, J.A. (1942), Capitalism, Socialism, and Democracy. In Cox and Alm (2008): *The Concise Encyclopaedia of Economics: Creative Destruction*. Retrieved on 18 May 2016 from http://www.econlib.org/library/Enc/CreativeDestruction.html.

Schumpeter, J.A. (author) and Aris, Reinhold (translator) (2011), *Economic doctrine and method: an historical sketch*. Whitefish Montana: Literary Licensing, LLC.

Sharma, P. and Chrisman, S.J.J. (1999), Toward a reconciliation of the definitional issues in the field of corporate entrepreneurship. *Entrepreneurship: Theory and Practice,* Vol. 23, No. 3, pp. 11–27.

Shaw, E., O'Loughlin, A. and McFadzean, E. (2005), Corporate entrepreneurship and innovation part 2: A role- and process-based approach. *European Journal of Innovation Management,* Vol. 8, No. 4, pp. 393–408, doi 10.1108/14601060511627766.

Slevin, D.P. and Covin, J.G. (1990), Judging Entrepreneurial Style and Organizational Structures – How to Get Your Act Together. *MIT Sloan Management Review,* Vol. 31, No. 2, pp. 43–53.

Thornberry, N.E. (2001), *Corporate Entrepreneurship: Antidote or Oxymoron.* Retrieved on 16 January 2016 from Leadership Forum web site: http://www.leadershipforuminc.com/Corporate_Entrepreneurship.pdf.

Tidd, J., Bessant, J. and Pavitt, K. (2005), *Managing Innovation: Integrating Technological, Market and Organizational Change,* 3rd edn., Wiley: Chichester.

Tony, O.A., Kehinde, J., Oluwadamilare, A.B. and Olamide, A.T. (2018), Entrepreneurial financing and success imperatives: nurturing and enabling the goose that lay the golden egg, *International Journal of Information, Business and Management,* Vol.10, No. 1, pp. 123–36.

Zahra, S.A. (1991), Predictors and Financial Outcomes of Corporate Entrepreneurship: An exploratory Study. *Journal of Business Venturing,* Vol. 6, No. 4, pp. 259–85.

BIOGRAPHY

Dr Siham El-Kafafi had wide overseas industry experience and consultancy in the medical, manufacturing and service industry before becoming an academic. Her teaching experience plays a leadership role in the creation of high quality student experience in a wide range of business courses. These include innovation, management and leadership, research methods, organisational behaviour, quality assurance, business ethics, supervision of industry projects, and industry training in the areas of quality management systems, leadership, teamwork and business excellence. Dr El-Kafafi holds a PhD from the University of Waikato, a Masters in Adult Literacy and Numeracy Education from Auckland University of Technology, a Masters of Public Administration from the American University in Cairo, and Bachelor of Arts in English Literature with Honours from Ain Shams University, Cairo, Egypt. She is a solid researcher with numerous publications in high-quality academic journals, book chapters, and conference proceedings, and has international and national roles as journal editor/reviewer and referee on eight academic journals.

INNOVATION PLATFORMS FOSTERING COMMUNITIES OF PRACTICE IN LOW CARBON ECONOMY TOWARDS 2030 TRANSFORMATIVE MECHANISMS AND PROCESSES FOR REALISING SDG 9 IN EUROPE

Irene Vivas Lalinde[1, 2]
Cristian Matti[1, 3]
Julia Panny[1]
Blanca Juan Agulló[1]

[1]EIT Climate-KIC
[2]UNU MERIT
Maastricht University
[3]Copernicus Institute for Sustainable Development
Utrecht University
cristian.matti@climate-kic.org

ABSTRACT

Purpose: The purpose of this paper is to highlight the potential of innovation platforms to realise SDGs targets.

Methodology: Analysis of different policy documents, reports, as well as a series of interviews and participatory processes run in 2016–2017 of the EIT RIS programme.

*Corresponding Author

Findings: Preliminary findings show that Climate-KIC operates as an innovation platform that increases capabilities for climate innovation.

Originality: Mechanisms and processes that consolidate local knowledge and strengthen relational assets with regards to climate innovation are important for the realisation of some of the 169 targets of the 2030 Agenda.

Keywords: Innovation platforms; public-private partnerships; European regions; climate change; climate innovation; SDGs; Regional Innovation; local knowledge; community of practice

INTRODUCTION

Innovation has been widely described as an essential process required to find solutions to societal challenges such as global warming and clean energy (European Union, 2016). As part of innovation policy debates, platforms are indicated as mechanisms that facilitate that process by enabling systemic efforts that will also be thematic and spatial (Bloomfield and Steward, 2016; Miedzinski, 2017; Steward, 2012). The connection between Sustainable Development Goals (SDGs) and innovation is more and more present in policy debates (Walz et al., 2017) where the 17 Global Goals, as part of the 2030 Agenda, highlight the potential synergies between defined targets in different but integrated themes.

This paper addresses the role of innovation platforms as catalysers of transformative processes in European peripheral regions, acknowledging that not all have the same capacities (Tödtling and Trippl, 2005). Transformation into a low carbon economy by 2030 in this context will require strong institutional capacity (Healey et al., 2003), having a systemic instead of a "picking the winner" approach (Asheim et al., 2011). In doing so, the role of innovation platforms in the context of Sustainable Development Goals (SDGs) is explored by looking at processes on knowledge triangle integration (KTI) as mechanisms to facilitate resource management and foster emerging communities of practices in low carbon economies.

The Sustainable Development Goals (SDGs) are increasingly present in policy debates (Walz et al., 2017); they are also present in the field of innovation, highlighting potential synergies with the 169 defined targets in the different but integrated goals. The study will look specifically at *SDG 9: Build resilient infrastructure, promote inclusive and sustainable industrialisation and foster innovation*, whose scope is to enhance research and upgrade technological capabilities. Empirically, emphasis is put on the case of the EIT Regional Innovation Scheme (EIT RIS[1]), a Climate-KIC[2] programme in the context of peripheral European regions. Focus is put on the emerging practices on combining research, education and business activities driven by the understanding of innovation as a systemic process (Matti and Panny, 2017) by looking at the performance of different actors in activities aimed to foster Knowledge Triangle Integration[3].

The aim of this study is to contribute to a better understanding of the existence of communities of practice and their value for innovation. It will shed light on ways to effectively support technological as well as practice-place-based innovation by exploring regional narratives on the variety of mechanisms for resource mobilisation and knowledge integration.

The structure of the remainder of the paper is as follows: Section 2 provides the conceptual framework of the study, while Section 3 introduces SDGs as part of the broad policy background for innovation platforms. The empirical study (Section 4) is divided into the methodology and the details of the case study. Section 5 develops the outcomes of the analysis, which are discussed in the next section. Finally, Section 7 provides the conclusions.

INNOVATION PLATFORMS, AN ENABLING MECHANISM OF KNOWLEDGE TRIANGLE INTEGRATION

The term platform has become almost ubiquitous in the innovation field. Conceptually, platforms are defined as systemic infrastructures, instituted governance mechanisms, organisations, and organisational innovations; They are also defined as a set of products, services, or technologies. Different authors describe two predominant forms of platforms: internal or company-specific, and external or industry-wide (Gawer and Cusumano, 2014). Generally, industry or technological platforms serve

---

[1] The EIT Regional Innovation Scheme (EIT RIS) is the EIT Community's outreach scheme. The objective of the EIT RIS is to contribute to boosting innovation in European countries and regions that belong to the groups of 'modest and moderate' innovators (according to the European Innovation Scoreboard). The EIT Community strives to achieve this objective by engaging local organisations and individuals in KIC activities, transfer good practises and know-how to the local innovation ecosystems and provide tailor-made services to address innovation gaps.

[2] The Knowledge and Innovation Communities (KICs) for Climate change is one of several platforms currently active in Europe. Created in 2010 by the European Union competent agency for sustainable growth, Climate-KIC aims at accelerating and stimulating innovation in climate change mitigation and adaptation, by integrating a network of European partners from the private, public and academic sectors.

[3] Knowledge Triangle Integration is a core component of the KIC model. As such, all KICs are tackling KTI as a central element of their strategy and operation.

the organisation and coordination of distributed (or localised) innovation processes generated in a wide range of industries, and firms featuring high degrees of complexity (Consoli and Patrucco, 2007, 2008; Gawer, 2010).

Innovation platforms can be understood from a more systemic perspective by focusing on their conceptualisation as structures that allow the coordination of a variety of actors by combining individual goals and capacities with shared purposes, norms and expectations. These interactions are based on the ability to maximise the variety of knowledge stemming from otherwise dispersed knowledge bases, while maintaining coherence through a minimum level of hierarchy and clear direction within coordinated actions (Consoli and Patrucco, 2007, 2011). The explicit engagement of different actors is a crucial institutional element to understand the governance of complex knowledge (Consoli and Patrucco, 2007).

Platforms reinforce acquired advantages in different knowledge areas in the search for complementarities (Gawer, 2010). Knowledge is conceptualised across a spectrum, from abstract theoretical (relatively explicit and codified) knowledge to practical (relatively tacit) know-how (Antonelli, 2006; David and Foray, 1995; Whitley, 2000). Since different types of knowledge contain different mixes of the explicit and the tacit, the pathways through which knowledge is diffused and transformed are diverse and, accordingly, are underpinned by different pedagogical and replication processes. Actual knowledge and skills are increasingly valued by employers beyond earned credentials and titles on a context of life-long learning and reorientation on non-line careers (Hüsing and Korte, 2017).

From a policy perspective, platforms are similar to Public Private Partnerships (PPP) regarding dimension, organisational structure and business models. Referred to as a model for PPP management (Consoli and Patrucco, 2008), platforms respond to the ethos of expanding the channels for the circulation of novel know-how by means of network-based strategies. Platforms thus respond to the need to create new knowledge and encourage the diffusion of new best practices (Baldwin and Woodard, 2009; Consoli and Patrucco, 2011). By fostering a knowledgeable community, they have the potential to mobilise and build on existing relational and knowledge resources (i.e. human capital, knowledge, technology) to enable innovations facing climate change challenges (Bloomfield and Steward, 2016; Miedzinski, 2017).

These structures undertake flexible but coordinated activities such as research training, professional education, entrepreneurship (start-ups, spin-offs) and R&D support. Participating organisations within platforms include firms, higher education institutions, vocational education centres, local and national authorities, industry associations, etc. (see Figure 1). As such, interactions within a platform are both "multi- and cross-scales" (i.e. public-private, several industrial sectors, research/education/training), as well as "multi- and cross-level" (i.e. firm/cluster/network/industry, local/regional/national/European).

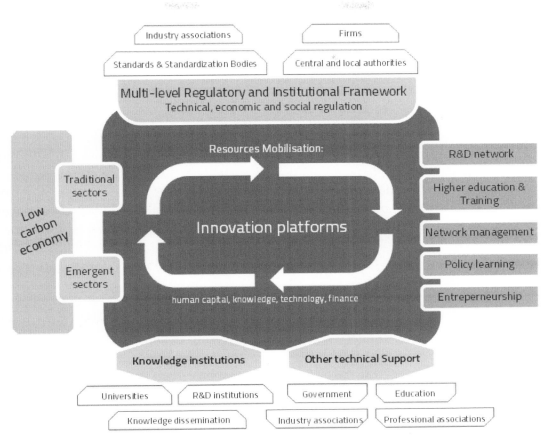

Figure 1   Structure of Thematic Innovation Platforms
Source: own elaboration

The role of platforms is especially important to build capacity in places where power dynamics result in weak institutions and great input is needed precisely to strengthen and put together otherwise isolated change agents (Healey et al., 2003). Regional ecosystems can be fed with emerging practices, among them new mechanisms on knowledge triangle integration aimed at fostering pathway creation for new sectors by combining local available assets. Regarding low-carbon economy sectors, the regional innovation process becomes more complex in terms of the multi-level policy mixes that raise issues of coordination underpinning the policy process; these include the mix of actors, levels, policy domains and time (Matti et al., 2016).

Embedded Communities of Practice within the Innovation Platforms

Participating organisations interacting in a platform do not only diffuse new best practices but also integrate different visions and values by creating community alignments. More specifically, knowledge flows between actors may be considered as the germ that holds the potential to grow into a community of practice in which people learn collectively and mutually engage on joint enterprises, producing a repertoire of common resources (Wenger et al., 2002). The elements of both innovation platforms and communities of practice provide the grounds for bottom-up innovation as they increase innovation capacities at a structural and individual level.

The escalation of the exchange of knowledge and experiences to an interregional level that involves several partners would develop into a structure too broad, diffuse or diverse to be considered as a single community, thus becoming what Wenger calls a constellation of practice (Wenger, 1998). This author also uses the concept of a global community to understand the importance of these communities in creating global practices without ignoring local specificities (Wenger et al., 2002). Consequently, ascribing a specific typology, defining the stage of a community regardless of whether leadership is individual or co-owned (Webber, 2016), can become a difficult endeavour.

THE EU POLICY LANDSCAPE ON SUSTAINABLE DEVELOPMENT

The pursuit of a green agenda in Europe has encouraged the broadening of policies for removing or minimising obstacles to the effective exploration and exploitation of new knowledge (Popp, 2010). Proof of this are the Europe 2020 Strategy, the 2030 Climate and Energy Policy Framework, the EU strategy on adaptation to climate change, and regional policies in general that have commented on the role of innovation in bridging a knowledge gap.[4]

Sustainable development has been anchored in EU treaties[5] since the first EU Sustainable Development Strategy (EU SDS) adopted in 2001, where Millennial Development Goals (MDGs) were introduced; these were revised in 2006 and again in 2009. Later, the Europe 2020 strategy, adopted by the European Commission in 2010, pushed for sustainable growth while prioritising an environmental dimension, among others. However, MDGs were integrated from a development perspective, i.e. the MDG Initiative (2010) covered by the European Development Fund (EDF). On the other hand, SDGs had a more comprehensive approach by embedding the concept not just in external actions but in domestically oriented actions as well. SDGs have been mainstreamed in different policy documents[6].

More specifically, regarding the relationship with sustainable industry and innovation (i.e. SDG 9), the EU has established a series of framework instruments such as European

---

[4]Commission Staff Working Document of Communication (COM (2016) 739.
[5]Articles 3 (5) and 21 (2) of the Treaty on European Union (TEU).
[6]See, 1) 'Next steps for a sustainable European future' Communication (COM (2016) 739), 2) 'Key European action supporting the 2030 Agenda and the Sustainable Development Goals'. The accompanying Commission Staff Working Document and 3) the conclusions of the Council on 'A sustainable European future: The EU response to the 2030 Agenda for Sustainable Development' (European Union, 2017).

Structural and Investment Funds, COSME, and Horizon 2020[7] (including the European Institute of Innovation & Technology, the EIT). On the other hand, initiatives aimed at supporting regional development can be divided into two categories: 1) Structural and Investment Funds (ESIF), and 2) European Territorial Cooperation (ETC).

Through the European Structural and Investment Funds (ESIF), almost half the European Union (EU) funding is channelled. They are jointly managed by the European Commission and EU countries and divided into five specific funds. An important part of the ESIF is the Cohesion funds, aimed at funding transport and environmental projects in countries where the gross national income (GNI) per inhabitant is less than 90% of the EU average. Also, part of the ESIF, the European Regional Development Fund (ERDF) promotes balanced development in the different regions of the EU.

The European Territorial Cooperation (ETC), better known for the Interreg programme, was developed in 1990 as a community Initiative with a budget of just €1 billion, covering exclusively cross-border cooperation; recently this has been extended to transnational and interregional cooperation. Under its wing, the pilot projects of the Regional Innovation Scheme (RIS) were implemented in 2000. The second stage of the RIS programme was developed between 2007 and 2013. The actual RIS3 programme started in 2014 and will be effective until 2020.

To sum up, within the broad framework of EU policies, the territorial focus is a key part of EU policies in terms of broad approaches on sustainable industry and innovation (i.e. H2020, COSME), and major investment in infrastructures (ESIF) and regional development (ERDF, ETC). Countries and regions are then required to match the relationships behind these policies with the approach defined for the SDGs. Mechanisms to facilitate innovation are essential for making those relationships effective in terms of multilevel policy governance systems (Matti et al., 2016).

Sustainable Development Goals (Sdgs), Innovation Platform and Territorial Perspectives

Globally, it is worth calling attention to the proliferation of thematic platforms, such as the Sustainable Development Knowledge Platform, aiming to catalyse action regarding Sustainable Development Goals, approved as part of "Transforming our world: the 2030 Agenda for Sustainable Development" by the General Assembly of the United Nations in September 2015. The existence of new actors and processes in innovating for sustainability, as argued by Leach et al. (2012), resonates with the potential role of innovation platforms as catalysers of the Agenda 2030.

Sustainable Development was first defined in the Brundtland report in 1987, and the term was enshrined in the MDGs in 2000. Contrary to the Millennial Development

---

[7]The Horizon 2020 programme, as the biggest EU research and innovation programme, has established clear research lines in the area of energy and low carbon economy.

Goals (2000–2015), SDGs state the importance of partnerships and collaboration with the private sector. While MDGs are referred to the Kyoto Protocol, SDGs are more aligned with the Paris Agreement. Moreover, SDGs better mainstream environmental concerns such as preservation, climate change and adaptation. SDGs Nos 7, 8, 9, 10, 11 and 13[8] are known as green goals because of their relationship to the environment; reaching their targets needs innovation, especially focusing on capabilities (Walz et al., 2017).

In a globalised world, mechanisms for knowledge dissemination play an important role as the North still holds higher capabilities and better conditions for climate innovation (Walz et al., 2017). As Leach et al. (2012) underline, local and indigenous knowledge are paramount in that regard. Consequently, local processes and implications, together with regional needs, should be triangulated when designing these mechanisms (Clifford and Zaman, 2016; Leach et al., 2012).

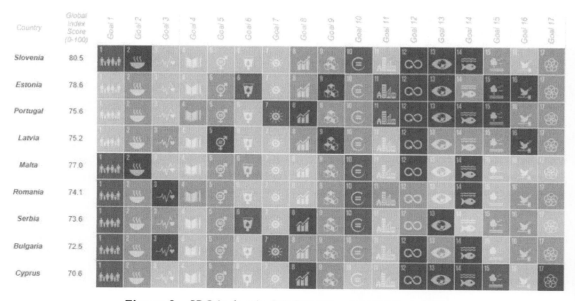

Figure 2   SDG Index in EIT RIS Climate-KIC Countries
Source: Own elaboration based on Sachs et al., 2017

The Global SDG index (0–100), measuring the implementation of SDGs worldwide, shows the state of play of Goals. However, this study only considers nine countries – also part of the RIS programme. In those countries, SDGs 12, 13 and 14 have the

---

[8]SDG 7 (Ensure access to affordable, reliable, sustainable and modern energy for all); SDG 8 (Promote sustained, inclusive and sustainable economic growth, full and productive employment and decent work for all); SDG 9 (Build resilient infrastructure, promote inclusive and sustainable industrialisation and foster innovation); SDG 11 (Make cities and human settlements inclusive, safe, resilient and sustainable) and SDG 13 (Take urgent action to combat climate change and its impacts).

lowest values (see Figure 2). However, this paper will focus on SDG 9 as it argues that innovation is a necessary step and will be a transversal topic in the 2030 Agenda.

Goal No. 9 calls on countries to foster innovation, to make infrastructure and industries more sustainable by increasing resource efficiency and adopting more environmentally sound technologies and production processes. SDG 9 also seeks to upgrade technology to make industries more sustainable, further highlighting the availability of infrastructure for promoting the digital and knowledge-based economy (European Union, 2016).

In this paper, the role of innovation platforms in the context of sustainable development is explored by analysing the potential of transformative processes on knowledge triangle integration (KTI) as a mechanism for resource management embedded in the platforms. Different dimensions of KTI will then be analysed in terms of more effective pathways for resource management aimed at fostering sustainable industry and innovation (i.e. SDG 9). In the next section, the empirical study of the EIT Regional Innovation Scheme is presented by highlighting key aspects of the KTI dimensions in a variety of peripheral EU regions.

THE EMPIRICAL STUDY

This empirical research is based on different sources, namely methodological and policy documents, reports, participatory processes run during the implementation of the EIT RIS programme in 2016 and 2017, as well as a series of semi-structured interviews, conducted between June and August 2017. The exploratory study is aimed at identifying patterns of the relationship between activities and regional settings for the emergence of communities of practices on Knowledge Triangle Integration and sustainable development. The study is presented in two steps:

- first, the case of the EIT RIS is presented briefly by introducing the overall context and general objectives, the approach on Knowledge Triangle Integration, and the general narrative and overall performance in recent years;
- second, we present a more specific analysis of the cases by applying an institutional assessment of practices and mechanisms for knowledge triangle integration (KTI). The first version of this assessment framework on KTI has been developed by TMC Artur Żurek (TMC, 2017) for all the EIT/KICs based on his interviews with KT actors, EIT/KICS representatives and desk research on websites of universities/ organisations active in collaborations with businesses in the context of KICs.

By following the two-step process, this paper aims to introduce the storyline of a regional development programme through a variety of elements related to the definition of innovation platforms. It then puts the emphasis on particular aspects of innovation and sustainability in terms of the relationship of the overall objective and performance with the underlying logic of SDG 9.

EIT Knowledge Innovation Communities and Regional Innovation Scheme

The Climate-KIC, one of the EIT Knowledge and Innovation Communities created in 2010, has been characterised since the beginning by its regional, place-based approach to innovation in its structure, in addition to its academic and corporate components. The incorporation of cities and regions as a distinctive element within the organisation, has contributed to recognise a broader, more systemic model of innovation, and emphasised the role of place in addressing the challenges of climate change (Bloomfield and Steward, 2016).

EIT Climate-KIC has gone beyond the 'classical' actors of the knowledge triangle to also involve other actors such as public authorities. Conceptually, EIT Climate-KIC views innovation as "research and business, aided by education" (Wilkinson et al., 2017). The three sides of the knowledge triangle are seen to have distinct, but complementary roles (Wilkinson et al., 2017):

- Research: creating, developing and refining the unique intellectual property that underpins innovation;
- Business: creating and realising the value of the intellectual property at scale;
- Education: developing the human capital by addressing the knowledge and competency gaps in innovation.

The Case of the EIT RIS Programme

The objective of the EIT RIS programme is to contribute to boosting innovation in European countries and regions that belong to the groups of 'modest and moderate' innovators. The EIT considers KTI from two perspectives: as an integration of innovation, education and entrepreneurship activities, or as an integration of actors in the business sector, universities, research organisations and others (Wilkinson et al., 2017).

EIT Climate-KIC's EIT RIS programme activities was started in 2014 by twinning partnerships between EIT Climate-KIC regions and EIT RIS regions, represented by single entities. However, the main caveats of this early implementation model were the limited connectivity of the new partners across EIT Climate-KIC, as well as the limited scope of the regional partnerships acting as the programme facilitators in the new regions. Major steps towards a more partner-driven model were taken in 2016 when a new call for EIT RIS partners was held. The new consortia were selected through a competitive process that led to the presence of the RIS programme in nine countries: Bulgaria, Cyprus, Estonia, Latvia, Malta, Portugal, Romania, Serbia and Slovenia. The existing regions were complemented by a set of new regions represented by consortia spanning the knowledge triangle from the start.

With the aim of facilitating the mechanism of implementing activities and integrating newcomers to the existing community, entities were brought into partnership with EIT Climate-KIC almost from the start; this enabled them to engage with EIT Climate-KIC more easily and substantially with fewer administrative hurdles. At the same time, "old" RIS regions were asked to further broaden their local partnerships and factor knowledge triangle integration into their thinking. The long term strategy indicates intensification of the work of the local consortia in more targeted ways through the allocation of resources for network developers' roles; these are aimed at expanding and consolidating the relational resources within the programme.

The activities delivered through the RIS programme were set in a context of an emerging community of practice, while putting emphasis on fostering the early development of KTI mechanisms on education and incubation/acceleration (start-ups). Emphasis was also placed on relational assets through mobility programmes and exchanges via two-way expert study visits targeting various cleantech and climate innovation topics. Figure 3 quantifies the number of participants, start-ups and innovation projects taking part in activities run by RIS partners (from 2014 to 2017).

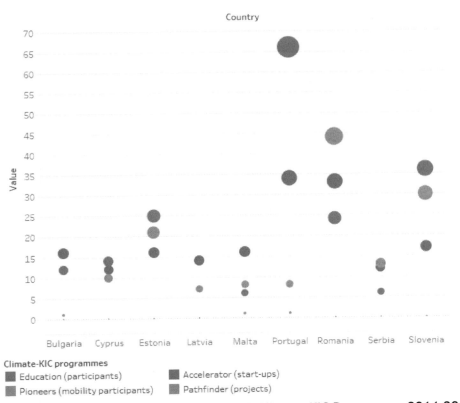

Figure 3   Results of Activities in the EIT RIS Climate-KIC Programme 2014–2017
Source: Own elaboration based on Matti and Panny (2017)

Regarding the process of formation of communities of practices, the professional mobility programme 'Pioneers into Practice' played a key role in facilitating regions' integration into EIT Climate-KIC. There was considerable anecdotal evidence for programme participants acting as "ambassadors" for EIT Climate-KIC, and they later became involved as coaches or facilitators themselves or applying to take forward their business ideas developed during the programme in the accelerator. Also, the bilateral study visits produced tangible follow-up projects, common grant applications, and valuable contacts that were later utilised in the organisation of further activities. In the programme, countries and RIS partners came from learning-by-doing educational, entrepreneurial and innovation activities targeting diverse stakeholders (students, professionals, officials, start-ups, etc.).

There is some variety in the performance in the programme among regions. More specifically, countries such as Portugal and Romania have been particularly successful. However, it is worth noting that variations respond to differences in the number of years of implementation of the programme. Also, the ability of the local programme coordinators to mobilise stakeholders varies considerably, with some entities having more privileged access and/or higher connectivity with a variety of actors.

Institutional Assessment on Knowledge Triangle Integration

Early analysis of the activities in the EIT RIS programmes reveals some variety in the performance of the different regions based on the level of experience and maturity. In that respect, a deeper analysis of the socio-technical configuration was run to provide a better understanding of practices and mechanisms for KTI in emergent communities of practices. In order to do this, a triangulation of different sources (i.e. policy documents, reports, participatory processes and interviews) was applied to analyse and decouple systemic elements regarding system components process and mechanism in terms of different levels of maturity regarding KTI performance. Four main categories are considered:

- **Perspective** refers to the connection with a broader context; it can be analysed from an occasional cooperation, through joint planning, to a self-driven ecosystem;
- **Culture and Organisation** describe a collection of elements including governance system and value setting. Assessment should highlight situations from a neutral, through structured and supportive, to an open system;
- **Resources** indicates the critical mass of assets allocated for delivering the activities from "nothing", through allocated, shared and collocated to openly available resources;
- **Experience and Activities** include the variety of actions in terms of complexity, depth and direction from problem solving, through joint idea generation, to constant innovation process.

Table 1 below shows how each category is decoupled in dimensions (a total of 15 for the four categories) to evaluate the level of maturity of KTI performance.

Table 1   Categories and Dimensions for Institutional Assessment on KTI

Category	Dimensions
PERSPECTIVE	— Vision — Strategy — Planning — Policies
CULTURE & ORGANISATION	— Leadership & Governance — Information flow — Organisation structure — Motivation system & Performance assessment
RESOURCES	— People — Mobility — Financing — Workspace
EXPERIENCE & ACTIVITIES	— Partners & Relationships — Innovation - deliver new products, services and business models — Education - equip students with the skills to become entrepreneurial — Entrepreneurship - create start - ups and accelerate the scaling-up venture

Source: own elaboration based on TCM (2017)

The level of maturity is evaluated under a scenario-based assessment and uses four situations to value an organisation's stage of maturity. The scenarios are based on the overall strategy of EIT RIS for 2018-2020 (Supjeva and Sereti, 2017), while the background for analysis and interpretation follows the framework related to regional innovation ecosystems formation (Bloomfield and Steward, 2016) and conceptual elements based in the notion of system innovation as a transformative process (Miedzinski, 2017). Table 2 below shows the applied scale.

Table 2   Scenario Score for Assessment of KTI Performance

Scenario	Level of Maturity
Collaboration in projects	1 (low)
Institutional interactions between KT actors	2
Joint development & implementation of strategy to develop innovation system	3
Orchestrated Innovation Ecosystem	4 (High)

Source: Own elaboration based on TCM (2017)

The final value of each of the dimensions was calculated by multiplying a Score (value ranging from 1 to 4) and a Weight (value ranging from 0 – not important – to 3 – extremely important dimension) for each of the dimensions in the nine countries. The final values were aggregated into four categories, namely perspective, culture and organisation, resources, and experience and activities. For a better visual representation, values were rescaled to range between 0 and 1.

Results of Institutional Assessment

Preliminary findings show that EIT Climate-KIC's EIT RIS operates as an innovation platform that mobilises resources for climate change innovation and adaptation while facilitating interaction amongst relevant actors of the knowledge triangle. From the institutional scenario-based assessment of practices and mechanisms for knowledge triangle integration, this study presents an index identifying the gaps but also the best performing categories of nine RIS countries in Europe. Table 3 shows the aggregated values of all dimensions of knowledge triangle integration into four categories, namely perspective, culture and organisation, resources, and experience and activities. These categories allow the identification of gaps in partnership dynamics and how different actors work together in climate innovation.

Table 3   Assessment of KTI Categories in RIS Region

Sector	Romania	Slovenia	Latvia	Cyprus	Serbia	Bulgaria	Malta	Portugal	Estonia
Perspective	0.27	0.22	0.51	0.24	0.22	0.33	0.24	0.43	0.30
Culture and Organisation	0.21	0.29	0.31	0.28	0.29	0.25	0.27	0.40	0.25
Resources	0.21	0.25	0.21	0.21	0.25	0.21	0.30	0.33	0.21
Experience and Activities	0.52	0.45	0.53	0.48	0.36	0.47	0.29	0.43	0.34

Source: Own elaboration based on TMC assessment

This Table can be interpreted vertically (per country) or horizontally (per category). From a vertical perspective, countries such as Portugal (the greenest) and Latvia are closer to the open innovation (or innovation ecosystem scenario) than the rest. Results show that countries such as Latvia are highest in the category "perspective" while

Portugal scores high in "culture and organisation". This fluctuation between countries responds to the different nature of the partners, the strengths of their organisation and their market objectives. However, further analysis of the components of the categories has to be done to understand existing variations.

On the other hand, from a horizontal (per category) perspective, the lowest category is resources and the highest category for all partners is "experience and activities", corresponding to the activity-based nature of the programme. It showcases that the activities that EIT RIS partners do (education activities, Pioneers into Practices, etc.) serve not only to summon a variety of actors but also to increase their experience in doing the activity. As indicated before, the concept of KTI is an open one on the EIT narrative that allows each KIC to approach it in a way that better supports its particular ecosystem. While this tactic gives a certain degree of flexibility to the KICs, it also made it more challenging for the partners to target it in an explicit way, as well assessing what has been done on the topic (Wilkinson et al., 2017). These difficulties are shown in the low perspective and general culture about KTI practices between partners that makes it difficult to organise, plan and implement actions in this regard. Notwithstanding, despite occurring inadvertently, these experiences reinforce the idea of an evolving community of practice precisely because a high rating translates into broader access to common resources and enough maturity to have joint activities. Being *de facto* KTI practitioners results in improving capacities at the platform, country and community level.

DISCUSSION

Despite setting specific targets and providing indicators to monitor advancements, SDGs barely refer to the processes "the how" needed to achieve the 2030 Goals. The indicators of the Agenda 2030 and those in the EU SDG Indicator Set (2017) – informing about existing EU indicators in relation to every Goal – do not represent the complexity of innovation. Regarding SDG 9, expenditure on R&D intensity is one of the most common measures of innovation input. On the other hand, the eco-innovation index helps to comprehensively assess the sustainability of new pro-duction processes in Europe. However, these indicators are not enough to explain the process behind measurable outputs, remaining too generic and focusing at the national level.

Looking at how innovation platforms work reveals that resources mobilisation and bringing change agents together translates into higher innovation capacity, not only at the platform level but also in places where they are established, as well as in the communities that are formed around specific topics tackled in the platforms. Table 4 showcases how the activities happening in the framework of the RIS programme mo-bilise different resources that are related to one or several goals of SDG 9.

Table 4   Activities, Resource Mobilisation for Innovation and Relation with SDG9 in EIT RIS Programme

Activities & Experiences	Resources	Scope of SDG 9
Pioneers	Human capital	Enhance research and upgrade technological capabilities
Education	Knowledge	Enhance research and upgrade technological capabilities. Access to information
Accelerator	Technology and finance	Sustainable industrialisation. Access to financial services for small scale enterprises and integration into value chain and market.
Pathfinder	Innovation (all resources)	Access to financial services for small scale enterprises and integration into value chain and market. Upgrade infrastructure and industries to make them sustainable

Source: own elaboration

As innovation is a transversal force across the 17 themes, this paper vindicates the role of innovation platforms – more specifically, Climate KIC EIT RIS – in increasing innovation capacities in European peripheral regions. Focusing on the activities implemented by the EIT, and particularly the EIT Climate-KIC, we can see how they are related to the scopes of SDG9 (Wilkinson et al., 2017). The portfolio of KIC activities provides a context to explore different stages of the innovation process by providing their partners with the opportunity to work with a range of other organisations, thus improving their linkage and stimulating a collaborative work. This context facilitates the relational assets and contributes to the underlying logic of community of practices. On the other hand, the mobilisation of knowledge and technologies is facilitated through a market-focused approach for innovation projects; this helps encourage the partners to be more aware of the potential for commercialisation of their projects, similar to building a 'culture' of knowledge transfer in universities and research institutes.

Secondly, activities run by the EIT RIS Climate-KIC programme facilitate the mobilisation of different types and number of resources. For example, the accelerator programme (start-up) mobilises financial and human resources to help participants with converting an innovative idea into a business. It does this by providing them with knowledge resources to better understand markets, as well as access to a wider network of customers and potential partners. It also gives them access to seed or growth funding, one of the key issues faced by start-ups in strategic sectors such as building, agriculture and manufacturing that are driven by sustainability transitions strategies.

Finally, regarding upgrading competencies and skills in emergent sectors, EIT Climate-KIC education programmes are aimed at improving the application of practice-based knowledge. More specifically, the mobility programme "Pioneers into practice" uses a Knowledge Triangle Integration context to enable a systemic process. This process is where ideas or technologies are transformed into businesses while investing in the regional human capital in the field of innovation. On the other hand, graduate school programmes are used more to incorporate elements based in university-industry relationships under the KTI logic embedded in the KICs.

CONCLUSIONS

This paper presents an exploratory exercise where the role of innovation platforms as catalysers of transformative processes is analysed regarding the contribution to reach SDGs targets, specifically Goal No. 9. In doing so, the concept of community of practice and the context of European peripheral regions provide the background of the empirical study.

The paper´s contribution lies with the focus on bottom-up processes that look at the platform and community level, understanding the complexity of the efforts needed to tackle climate innovation. More specifically, knowledge triangle integration allows an approach to resource mobilisation and innovation capacities by focusing on how platforms work in a bottom-up way. This approach better relates how capacities and capabilities increase, also reflecting the need to find process-based indicators instead of just focusing on results for measuring SDGs implementation.

Nevertheless, we acknowledge that further research on the topic is necessary to make final conclusions. In addition, it is difficult to draw a line on which data/activities fall under the umbrella of a specific SDG, also to differentiate which initiatives benefit the implementation of different goals.

REFERENCES

Antonelli, C. (2006), The business governance of localized knowledge: an information economics approach for the economics of knowledge. *Industry and Innovation*, Vol. 13, No. 3, pp. 227–61.

Asheim, B.T., Boschma, R. and Cooke, P. (2011), Constructing regional advantage: Platform policies based on related variety and differentiated knowledge bases. *Regional Studies*, Vol. 45, No. 7, pp. 893–904.

Baldwin, C.Y. and Woodard, C.J. (2009), The Architecture of Platforms: A Unified View. In Gawer, A. (Ed.) *Platforms, Markets and Innovation*, Edward Elgar Publishing, pp. 19–44.

Bloomfield, J. and Steward, F. (2016), *Broadening the innovation model: Lessons from Climate-KIC's Regional Innovation Implementation Community* (Climate Innovation Insights | Series 1.5). Climate-KIC.

Clifford, K.L. and Zaman, M.H. (2016), Engineering, global health, and inclusive innovation: focus on partnership, system strengthening, and local impact for SDGs. *Global Health Action*, Vol. 9, No. 1, p. 30175.

Consoli, D. and Patrucco, P.P. (2007), Distributed Innovation and the Governance of Knowledge: an empirical study on Technological Platforms. *SENTE Working Papers – University of Tampere* (11).

Consoli, D. and Patrucco, P.P. (2008), Innovation platforms and the governance of knowledge: Evidence from Italy and the UK. *Economics of Innovation and New Technology*, Vol. 17, Nos 7-8, pp. 699–716.

Consoli, D. and Patrucco, P.P. (2011), Complexity and the coordination of technological knowledge: the case of innovation platforms. *Handbook on the Economic Complexity of Technological Change*, 201.

David, P.A. and Foray, D. (1995), *Accessing and expanding the science and technology knowledge base* (STI Review No. 16). OECD.

European Union (2016), Sustainable Development in the European Union. A Statistical Glance from the Viewpoint of the UN Sustainable Development Goals. Luxembourg: Publications Office of the European Union. doi: 10.2785/500875.

European Union (2017), Sustainable Development in the European Union — Monitoring report on progress towards the SDGs in an EU context. Luxembourg: Publications Office of the European Union. doi: 10.2785/237722.

Gawer, A. (2010), Towards a general theory of technological platforms. In *Druid Summer Conference*. Retrieved from http://www2.druid.dk/conferences/viewpaper.php?id=501981&cf=43.

Gawer, A. and Cusumano, M.A. (2014), Industry platforms and ecosystem innovation. *Journal of Product Innovation Management*, Vol. 31, No. 3, pp. 417–33.

Healey, P., Magalhaes, C.D., Madanipour, A. and Pendlebury, J. (2003), Place, identity and local politics: analysing initiatives in deliberative governance. In Hajer, M.A. and Wagenaar, H. (Eds): *Deliberative Policy Analysis: Understanding Governance in the Network Society, Theories of Institutional Design*, Cambridge University Press, Cambridge, UK, pp. 60–88.

Hüsing, T. and Korte, W. (2017), *Human Capital "Skills and Competences". Position and common policy paper on "Cross-KIC Collaboration on Human Capital for Citizens"* (Working Document Draft 2.1). Brussels: Empirica.

Leach, M., Rockström, J., Raskin, P., Scoones, I., Stirling, A., Smith, A., Thompson, J., Millstone, E., Ely, A., Arong, E. and Folke, C. (2012), Transforming innovation for sustainability. *Ecology and Society*, Vol. 17, No. 2. Retrieved from https://www.ecologyandsociety.org/vol17/iss2/art11/.

Matti, C., Consoli, D. and Uyarra, E. (2016), Multi level policy mixes and industry emergence: The case of wind energy in Spain. *Environment and Planning C: Government and Policy*, p. 0263774X16663933.

Matti, C. and Panny, J. (2017), Policy mixes fostering regional capacity in low carbon economy. Insights from the implementation of the RIS model in peripheral European regions. Presented at the Regional Studies Association Annual Conference 2017, the Great Regional Awakening: New Directions, Dublin.

Miedzinski, M. (2017), *System Climate Innovation for a Transformative Impact* (Climate Innovation Insights | Series 1.3). Climate-KIC.

Popp, D. (2010), Innovation and climate policy. *Annual Review of Resource Economics*, Vol. 2, No. 1, pp. 275–98.

Sachs, J., Schmidt-Traub, G., Kroll, C., Durand-Delacre, D. and Teksoz, K. (2017), *SDG Index and Dashboards Report 2017*. Bertelsmann Stiftung and Sustainable Development Solutions Network (SDSN): New York, NY, USA.

Steward, F. (2012), Transformative innovation policy to meet the challenge of climate change: sociotechnical networks aligned with consumption and end-use as new transition arenas for a low-carbon society or green economy. *Technology Analysis & Strategic Management*, Vol. 24, No. 4, pp. 331–43.

Supjeva, L. and Sereti, K. (2017, July). *EIT RIS 2018-2020 Strategy Development*. EIT Workshop, Budapest.

TMC (2017, September), *EIT RIS. Dimension of Knowledge Triangle Integration and Action Plan Finder. TMC Arthur Zurek*. Presented at the EIT RIS KTI Workshop, Warsaw.

Tödtling, F. and Trippl, M. (2005), One size fits all?: Towards a differentiated regional innovation policy approach. *Research Policy*, Vol. 34, No. 8, pp. 1203–19.

Walz, R., Pfaff, M., Marscheider-Weidemann, F. and Glöser-Chahoud, S. (2017), Innovations for reaching the green sustainable development goals – where will they come from? *International Economics and Economic Policy*, Vol. 14, No. 3, pp. 449–80. https://doi.org/10.1007/s10368-017-0386-2.

Webber, E. (2016), *Building Successful Communities of Practice*. London: Tacit.

Wenger, E. (1998), *Communities of practice: Learning, meaning, and identity*. Cambridge university press.

Wenger, E., McDermott, R.A. and Snyder, W. (2002), *Cultivating communities of practice: A guide to managing knowledge*. Harvard Business Press.

Whitley, E.A. (2000), Tacit and explicit knowledge: Conceptual confusion around the commodification of knowledge. In Swan, J., Scarborough, H. and Dale, R. (Eds): *Knowledge Management: Concepts and Controversies*. Business Process Resource Centre, Warwick University, Warwick (pp. 62–64).

Wilkinson, C., Allison, R., Leather, J. and Healey, A. (2017), *Evaluation of the European Institute of Innovation and Technology (EIT)*. Brussels: European Commission.

BIOGRAPHY

Irene Vivas Lalinde is a Law Graduate and has a Master's degree in Public Policy and Human Development (UNU Merit – Maastricht School of Governance). She has started developing her career in environmental and gender issues. She is now a research assistant in Climate KIC, but has also worked as an intern at the Committee on the Rights of the Child (UN), Women's Link Worldwide, among others. Currently, she is writing her Master's dissertation about the power dynamics of wastewater in Bogota, and volunteering in Spanish and European green youth groups.

Cristian Matti has a PhD in the field of Study Science, Technology and Innovation Studies – Economic geography. He is an expert in sustainability transitions and environmental innovation. He is Knowledge and Learning manager at Transition Hub – Climate KIC, and visiting researcher at the University of Utrecht. He has contributed to research projects on natural resource based innovation, regional and industrial systems of innovation, and innovation policies for public and private organisations in Europe and South America. He also has experience as academic coordinator of professional education and postgraduate courses on sustainability and regional innovation. Matti has also participated as an expert in the analysis of technological trends and policies in Argentina's Second Submission to the UN Convention on Climate Change. His primary interest is the linkages between science and practice in facing the challenge of transforming environmental governance and technological development processes.

Julia Panny holds a BSc in Economics from Vienna University of Economics and Business, as well as a Master's of Advanced International Studies from the University of Vienna. She has several years of working experience in the fields of capacity-building for climate change mitigation and adaptation, education for sustainable development and regional innovation. She currently works as a programme officer for Climate-KIC, Europe's largest public-private innovation partnership focused on climate change.

Blanca Juan Agulló works as a research assistant at Climate-KIC under the Transitions Hub and the RIS programmes. She has participated in several history research works in the field of Oral History and Women's Education, as well as on the organisation of ethnological displays regarding schools memories and materials in collaboration with the Education School of the University of Valencia. She has a Master's degree in Audio-visual Communication, and a Master's degree in Secondary Level Teaching Formation from the University of Valencia. She also has a Postgraduate certificate in Museum Management from the University Pompeu Fabra of Barcelona.

PROMOTION OF PRIVATE SECTOR PARTICIPATION (PSP) IN INDIAN PORTS

Shraddha S. Sathe*

Deputy General Manager
Internal Audit Department
The Shipping Corporation of India Ltd
Mumbai-400021, India
shragisa@yahoo.com

ABSTRACT

Purpose: This paper discusses the importance of Indian ports and the need for the development of the existing port facilities by way of Public Private Partnerships (PPPs).

Methodology: Secondary sources of data were collected, for example, articles, journals, reports, books, etc., for the research paper. The collected data were compiled to bring out the various investment strategies for private sector participation and risks involved.

Findings/originality: Based on the data and available strategies and investment levels, a matrix was designed to make the right mix and choice for investment in the port sector.

Keywords: Ports; Private Sector Participation (PSP); Private Public Partnership (PPP); Government of India

*Corresponding Author

INTRODUCTION

Indian Economy

The Indian economy is currently one of the fastest growing economies in the world. It encompasses an agriculture sector that sustains much of the rural populations, a modern and varied industrial sector, and sizable service sector. Since liberalisation in 1991, the economy has been growing at an average annual rate of around 6.67%, as compared to 5.4% in the 1980s and 3.5% prior to that. There is lot of work to be done in order to lead to a dynamic double-digit growth rate. A variety of new schemes to improve conditions in infrastructure are required, including ports, roads, highways, etc., if India is to sustain rapid growth. Economic growth has been unevenly spread across states and territories in India, prompting the Government of India to devise ways of creating more balanced regional development. One means of achieving this outcome is to create an environment that encourages foreign firms to invest.

The introduction of a port privatisation programme was flagged of in India in 1997; private management in the port domain has represented a strong trend in the developing countries over the last few years. This principally concerns the handling and storage of freight transiting via ports, and funding and operation of the infrastructures and equipment required for these activities. This trend has involved the setting up of complex, multi-dimensional partnerships between the public port authorities and the terminal operators.

Ports in India

India has a coastline of 7,517Km, with around 12 major ports and 185 minor ports. The 12 major ports are Kolkata (including the Dock Complex at Haldia), Paradip, Visakhapatnam, Chennai, Ennore, and Tuticorin on the east coast, and Cochin, new Mangalore, Mormugao, Jawaharlal Nehru at Nhava Sheva, Mumbai and Kandla on the west coast. The port sector in India handles 90% in volume and 30% in terms of value of India's Export and Import (EXIM) trade. The 12 major ports handled a record 647.43 million tonnes (MT) of traffic in 2016–17, registering an annual growth rate of 6.79%, compared with 4.32% in 2015–16.

Major ports have been benchmarked to international standards, and 116 initiatives were identified to bring them up to this standard. Of these, 70 initiatives have been implemented and the remainder will be implemented by 2019. This has resulted in unlocking 80 million tonnes per annum (MTPA) capacity. Implementation of these initiatives would further improve the efficiency and productivity of the major ports.

Significant investments have been made on a Build-Operate-Transfer Mode (BOT) by foreign players such as Maersk (Jawaharlal Nehru Port Trust (JNPT), Mumbai), P&O Ports (Jawaharlal Nehru Port Trust, Mumbai and Chennai), Dubai Ports International

(Cochin and Vishakapattinam), and PSA Singapore (Tuticorin). The New Captive Policy guidelines were issued in July 2016 to ensure uniformity and transparency in the procedure for awarding captive facilities in the ports. This will allow concessionaires to handle non-captive cargo up to 30% of the designed capacity of the berth. The New Berthing Policy came into effect from August 2016. This policy provides a standardised framework for the calculation of norms specific to the commodity handled and infrastructure available on the berth. This will improve the efficiency at ports and productivity norms across ports. The New Stevedoring Policy has been implemented since July 2016. This will improve productivity, efficiency and safety in the ports. The existing Model Concession Agreement of 2008 is under process of revision, and will address the concerns of PPP projects and prevent them from getting stressed. The Major Port Authorities Bill was introduced in the Lok Sabha in December 2016; this will modernise the institutional structure of the ports to usher in professional governance in the ports.

The involvement of private companies in port management has led to the introduction of a complex, multi-dimensional partnership with the port authority. A port facility is connected to different entities on which the business chain flows (see Figure 1).

In order to make transportation more viable, a port authority needs to be well equipped to accommodate all complex processes that may come in the business chain. Over the years, the Government of India has strived to take bold steps in order to compete in the world port market.

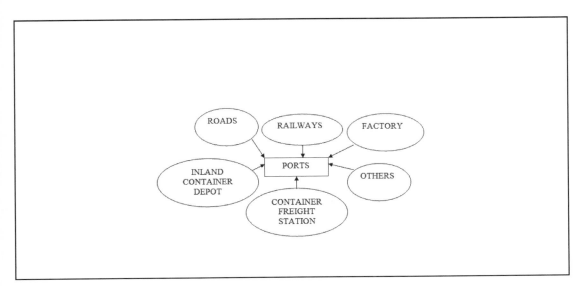

Figure 1   Port Connectivity
Source: Devised by author

Ports are complex combinations of interlocking elements, including natural features, infrastructure and superstructure, linked through transport connections to other ports and to distribution centres in the hinterland. The management of natural resources, infrastructure and superstructure may all be in different hands, as well as serving independent logistics businesses that use port facilities.

The participation of public sector authorities is normally necessary, because of the need for environmental protection in the development of natural harbours and subsequent operations, and the need for security at national boundaries. In addition, infrastructure is more easily managed in the public sector when extensive planning powers are needed. However, cargo-handling operations and inland transportation links, as well as the shipping companies who use them and the clients of those companies, are in the main carried out by commercial private sector companies. Buildings, plant and equipment, and services tend also to be more efficiently provided by private commercial organisations.

Some other services, such as customs and public security are, once again, natural functions of the state. This is because of the lack of sufficient incentives for private sector organisations to take action in the wider public interest. At maritime ports, effectively located at national boundaries, a range of public security services is needed, placing limits on private sector services.

Trade through Indian Ports

Major ports in India have recorded a growth of 3.24%, and together handled 326.4MT of cargo during the period April to September 2017; this is compared with 316.1MT handled during the corresponding period of the previous year. Seven ports, Kolkata, Paradip, Chennai, Cochin, New Mangalore, Mumbai and JNPT, registered positive growth in traffic during the period April to September 2017.

The following is a discussion of the cargo traffic handled at major ports in India:

- the highest growth was registered by Cochin Port (19.62%), followed by Kolkata [including Haldia], New Mangalore, Paradip with growth of about 12%;
- the growth in Cochin Port was mainly due to an increase in traffic at the Port of Loading (POL) (27.8%) and containers (10.3%);
- in Kolkata Port, overall growth was positive, i.e. 11.95%. Kolkata Dock System (KDS) registered traffic growth of 0.72%. Haldia Dock Complex (HDC) registered positive growth of 17.74%;
- during the period April to September 2017, Kandla Port handled the highest volume of traffic, i.e. 53.29MT (16.33% share), followed by Paradip with 47.61MT (14.59% share), JNPT with 32.69MT (10.02% share), Mumbai with 31.23MT (9.57% share),

and Visakhapatnam with 30.15MT (9.24% share). Together, these five ports handled around 60% of major port traffic;

- commodity-wise, the percentage share of POL was the highest, i.e. 34.01%, followed by containers (20.22%), thermal and steam coal (12.66%), other miscellaneous cargo (12.17%), coking and other coal (7.6%), iron ore and pellets (6.65%), other liquids (4.35%), finished fertiliser (1.24%), and fertiliser raw material (FRM) (1.11%).

"Growing ports are becoming catalysts for shaping the vision of a 'New India'. The Government is committed towards inclusive development to generate continuous growth and prosperity. Timely delivery of projects will help give the much needed boost to economy" (Public Investment Board, 11 October 2017). These include the dry port at Wardha and infra projects in Andaman and Nicobar Islands, under the Sagarmala Programme that aims to save logistics costs and pave the way for port-led development.

THE NEED FOR INVESTMENT IN INDIAN PORTS

Increase in Trade/traffic at Indian Ports

Cargo traffic at the major ports is estimated to rise to 943.1MT for the financial year 2017. The Foreign Trade Policy envisages the doubling of India's share in global exports in the next five years. A large portion of the foreign trade will be through the maritime route: 95% by volume and 70% by value.

The growth in merchandise exports projected at over 13% p.a. underlines the need for large investments in port infrastructure. Investment of 287,000 crores is needed in the major and minor ports under the National Maritime agenda 2010–2020 to boost the infrastructure. Under the maritime agenda, port capacity of around 3,200MT needs to be created to handle the expected growth in trade traffic. Public-private partnerships are seen by the Government as the key to improve major and minor ports. Of the proposed investment in major ports, it is envisaged that 64% will come from private players. The plan proposes an additional port handling capacity in major ports through:

a. projects related to port development (construction of jetties, berths, etc.);
b. procurement, replacement and/or upgrading of port equipment;
c. deepening of channels to improve draught;
d. projects related to port connectivity.

International Scenario

Table 1 World's Top Ten Ports 2015

Rank	Name of the Port	Volume in Million TEUs as at 2015
1	Shanghai, China	36.54
2	Singapore	30.92
3	Shenzhen, China	24.20
4	Ningbo Zhoushan, China	20.63
5	Hong Kong, China	20.07
6	Busan, South Korea	19.45
7	Qingdao, China	17.47
8	Guangzhou Harbor, China	17.22
9	Jebel Ali, Dubai UAE	15.60
10	Tianjin, China	14.11
34	Jawaharlal Nehru Port Trust, India	4.49

Source: The Journal of Commerce annual top 50 World Container Ports; Lloyd's List annual Top 100 Ports; AAPA World Port Rankings; Drewry World Container Traffic Port Handling; individual port websites

The above Table 1 shows that China (a developing economy) has beaten major developed countries in terms of cargo traffic handled at ports; India's position was 34th. The report says that Mumbai handles almost 56% of the country's containerised traffic and is constantly faced with congestion issues. Serious attention needs to be given to maximising port capacity as maximum trade moves from India. Efforts should be made to make India a hub port for the cargo moves from India to Sri Lanka, South Africa, Australia, Japan, China, USA, Europe, etc.

The Failures of Public Ports

Although some of the largest, most efficient ports in the world are public ports, relatively few are operated by the private sector. The enthusiasm for increasing private sector participation (PSP) in port operations derives from the failure of public port operations to meet the following objectives:

- to provide services that are efficient and cost-effective from the port user point of view;
- to respond to changes in cargo-handling technologies;
- to respond to the changing requirements of the port users;
- to provide choices of services and foster competition;

- to make timely capital investment to improve efficiency and expand capacity;
- to generate the funds needed to finance investments;
- to enforce labour discipline in the face of strong trade unions.

GOVERNMENT INITIATIVE

The Role of Private Sector Participation (PSP)

Looking at the increasing cargo traffic at Indian ports, the focus has to be on capacity enhancement of major ports through modernisation, the provision of cost-effective services, and the enhancement of service quality rather than creating new capacity. There is also a need to commercialise port operations. In such a scenario, the private sector has great potential to play an important role; in the last five years, PSP in the development of ports has been very encouraging. The projects will create additional capacity and facilities to accommodate the growing demand.

Modes for PSP

Private sector participation in the development of ports in India is encouraged through two models. Under the first model, the private sector can exclusively build and operate the facility; after completion of the concession period, the port is transferred to the relevant port authority. The second model envisages the involvement of the private sector through joint venture projects.

However, the private sector cannot participate in all types of port development projects. The areas allowed for PSP are listed below:

a. leasing out existing port assets;
b. construction/creation of additional assets, such as:
   i.   construction and operation of container terminals;
   ii. construction and operation of bulk, break-bulk, multi-purpose and specialised cargo berths;
   iii. warehousing, container freight stations, and storage facilities;
   iv. cranage/handling equipment;
   v. setting up of captive power plants;
   vi. dry docking and ship repair facilities.
c. leasing of equipment for port handling and leasing of floating crafts from the private sector;
d. pilotage;
e. captive facilities for port-based industries.

All ports can identify projects for implementation through PSP. The relevant port authority prepares a feasibility report for the project, and invites tenders from investors based on the feasibility report. The evaluation of the bids is made on the basis of maximum realisation to the port using the net present value analysis method. The BOT model is generally preferred. The assets revert to the port authority at the end of the concession period. The port authority decides the concession period for each case, not exceeding the allowable maximum of 30 years.

Process of Private Sector Participation (PSP)

To facilitate the process of private participation, the Government has prepared a model bid document, the salient features of which are as follows:

a. introduction of the concept of revenue sharing in place of minimum guaranteed throughput;
b. compensation for default;
c. permission of giving charge on assets in favour of lenders by the licensee for seeking financial closure.

As a part of the investment policy for ports, a number of incentives are given to the private sector. These are:

a. foreign equity up to 100% is now permissible in the construction and maintenance of ports and harbours, and in projects providing support services to water transport, such as the operation and maintenance of piers, loading and discharging of vehicles;
b. 10 years of tax holiday can be availed of during the initial 20 years of concession;
c. concessional customs duty at 10% on specified ports equipment.

The following depicts the need for capacity expansion of major and non-major ports.

Sagarmala Policy

The Sagarmala Project is a strategic and customer-oriented ₹8,000,000 million (US$120 billion or €110 billion) investment initiative of the Government of India. It entails the setting up of more than 6 mega ports, modernisation of several dozen more ports, development of more than 14 coastal economic zones and at least 29 coastal economic units, development of mines, industrial corridors, rail, road and airport linkages with these water ports. This will result in export revenue growth of US$110 billion, the generation of 150,000 direct jobs and several times more indirect jobs. It aims to modernise India's Ports so that port-led development can be augmented and coastlines can be developed to contribute in India's growth. It also aims to "transforming the existing Ports into modern world class Ports and integrate the development of the Ports, the Industrial clusters and hinterland and efficient evacuation systems through road, rail, inland and coastal waterways resulting in Ports becoming the drivers of economic activity in coastal areas" (Government of India, 2015).

Under the Sagarmala programme, 415 projects, at an estimated investment of approximately ₹7.98500 lakh crore (US$120 billion), have been identified across port modernisation and new port development, port connectivity enhancement, port-linked coastal economic zone industrialisation and coastal community development for phase wise implementation over the period 2015 to 2035. As per the approved implementation plan of the Sagarmala scheme, these projects are to be taken up by the relevant Central Ministries/Agencies and State Governments, preferably through private/PPP mode. The details are shown in Table 2 below.

Table 2   Details of Sagarmala Programme

S. No.	Project Theme	No. of Projects	Project Cost (Rs. Cr)
1.	Port Modernisation	189	₹1,428,280 million (US$22 billion or €19 billion)
2.	Connectivity Enhancement	170	₹2,305,760 million (US$36 billion or €30 billion)
3.	Port-Linked Industrialisation	33	₹4,208,810 million (US$66 billion or €56 billion)
4.	Coastal Community Development	23	₹42,160 million (US$660 million or €560 million)
	Total	415	₹7,985,000 million (US$120 billion or €110 billion)

Source: Taken from Sagarmala Project

Risk Management

Any investment is attached to risk; the degree of risk may vary from project to project. With the robust plans under various policies and other initiatives suggested, risks are bound to arise. It is therefore important that such risks are identified and mitigation plans should be made in order to manage such risks. The following factors are identified as risks for port operators:

1. monetary risk: mainly exchange rate and currency risks;
2. economic risk: financial management risks for ports;
3. force majeure: natural catastrophes;
4. interference risk/political risk: state or public body interference in PPP-led projects were noted to create delays and often involved lengthy political negotiations;
5. country risk: this may be where foreign-based operators have a greater controlling

interest and these can have implications for local port operators. Risks of social imbalance such as unemployment, strikes, natural environment disturbance, interference of political parties, social groups, etc. can also arise;

6. legal risk: risks of non-compliance;
7. security risk: inadvertently dealing with goods classified as security risks. Developing facilities at the port side, which acts as a security system, is of major importance in any PPP-led project.

RECOMMENDATIONS

Reformation

Reformation involves the transfer of the port's core businesses to the private sector without transferring ownership of the port's major capital assets. The most common arrangement is the leasing of the port's cargo-handling facilities together with the licensing of the right to provide services to private parties. The port transfers the responsibility for maintenance of the facility and for collection of cargo-handling charges. In exchange, the private sector pays set fees to the port. Under this agreement, the port no longer interacts directly with the port users but retains some regulatory authority over the quality and pricing of services. By transferring responsibility for operations and maintenance, the port can reform its organisation to focus on administration and planning (see Figure 2).

Alternatively, the port can form wholly owned subsidiaries with private participation that operate as commercial enterprises. This approach is less common because most countries require that subsidiaries of public ports also operate as public service entities.

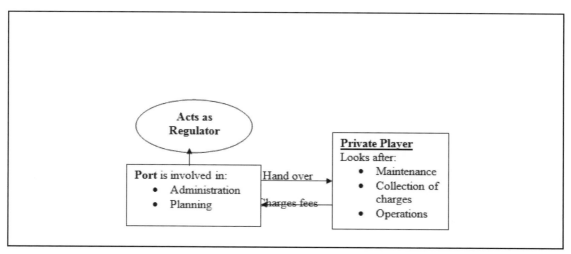

Figure 2   Structure of Reformation
Source: Devised by author

A number of ports have created subsidiaries to provide professional services to other ports. Less common are subsidiaries that provide cargo-handling services. Some of the container terminal operating companies in Korean and Chinese ports are effectively independent subsidiaries.

Converting from Service Ports to Landlord Ports

With the growing move towards privatisation of seaports all over the world subsequent to reforms, private sector participation in operations and infrastructure activities of seaports has been increased substantially over the last few years. This has resulted in a fundamental change in the organisational model of ports, converting from a service port model to a landlord port model. This is where the port authority retains the port infrastructure and fulfils its regulatory functions, while port services are provided by private operators that own the assets conforming to port superstructure and equipment required for service provision.

Landlord Ports - The Concept

In this model, the port authority constitutes a landlord, which manages the basic port assets by letting the land and infrastructure to port operators in an efficient manner. The landlord port in this model would be involved in planning, lease negotiation, safety, navigation and overall coordinating functions. Cargo services, marine service, ancillary services, berths, etc., are privatised on a captive/BOT basis to the primary port users. Port operators and other undertakings that need to be located in the port, lease the land, infrastructure and associated services and provide them to the secondary users – cargo owners, ship owners and cargo ship owners. With intense competition, the role of Indian ports is changing from a service port model to a landlord port model. This concept is already in place with the best examples being Ennore port and to some extent JNPT port. Similar practices can be adopted for other major ports.

Outsourcing

Outsourcing involves the transfer of specific port activities from the public sector to the private sector while permitting the port to function as an operating port. The port reduces operating costs and increases efficiency by utilising private companies to supply labour and equipment and to perform specific services. A wide range of port services and activities can be outsourced.

Four types of agreements can be used to implement this strategy:

1. *subcontracting*: the port contracts the private sector to perform the services that the port offers to its users;
2. *franchising*: the private sector provides port services directly to the port users but under terms and conditions specified by the port;

3. *management contracts*: this allows the port to have a contract with the private sector to manage specific services utilising the port's equipment and labour;
4. *equipment leases*: transfers responsibility for the maintenance and operation of cargo-handling equipment to the private sector. The port utilises this equipment to provide services to its users.

Free Ports Status to Minor Ports

In order to grow coastal trade and encourage minor ports, some of the minor ports can be declared as "free ports". Under a free ports arrangement, the port authority can authorise private players to handle complete port operations on a "line arrangement", where charges from the private operator will be paid from the fees charged to shipping lines.

This initiative is to spur growth of minor ports; therefore the shipping line should not be burdened with heavy charges. Public sector lines should be exempt from any such charges but custom cargo clearance must be made compulsory. Free ports certainly raise the question of security: here the role of the customs authority comes to mind, hence it is suggested that private players should coordinate with customs to scrutinise the approach to free ports. Therefore, private player participation for enabling IT infrastructure, specialised security systems, management of speedier cargo transport, etc., comes into play.

Dredging Operation

Major ports require a great deal of maintenance in order to have smooth operations. Foreign participation can be sought in the area of maintenance dredging and capital dredging.

Maintenance dredging: maintenance dredging is necessary to maintain safe operational water depths for navigation, and to facilitate continued access to many of the berths, docks, wharves and jetties. With the percentage of private participation, better facilities can be provided.

Capital dredging: capital dredging involves the creation of new or improved facilities such as a harbour basin, a deeper navigation channel, a lake, or an area of reclaimed land for industrial or residential purposes. Such projects are generally characterised by the following features:

- relocation of large quantities of material;
- compact soil;
- undisturbed soil layers;
- low contaminant content (if any);
- significant layer thickness.

A joint venture with private players can be made and the above projects can be made on a larger scale.

Cruise Terminal

The passenger cruise industry is the fastest growing leisure industry in India. In order to tap into this market, private participation should be invited and special cruise terminals can be set-up with international facilities. These terminals should allow for faster customs clearance for foreign passengers. Here, the public sector can have a controlling interest and services can be let out to private partners.

Roll On-Roll Off (Ro-Ro) Facility

The exports of cars and other vehicles are increasing and huge exports are done from the west coast of India. To cater to increasing vehicle exports, it is important that an efficient and effective Ro-Ro jetty is available with state-of-art facilities. Private participation can be sought in this area. A public-private investment (49:51 ratio) in this area would be valuable.

Ports in the Special Economic Zone (SEZ) or Giving SEZ Status to Ports

Stress is recently been given to SEZ, which will mainly provide for foreign investment or private participation in development of infrastructure facilities. The benefits of ports under SEZ are:

- reduced cost of infrastructure;
- reduced cost of utilities;
- reduced cost of raw materials;
- reduced cost of capital;
- reduced cost of manpower;
- operational ease.

SEZ status to either major ports, or to a larger extent to minor ports, will help to reduce the captive expenditure, which may burden the Government of India. This will lead to a single window approach, reducing the operational complications.

Single Buoy Mooring (SBM) Points

The SBM facility proposed by Kochi refineries at Cochin, IOC at Mundra, etc., is an example of participation in public facilities by private players. Such initiatives should be encouraged on a larger scale.

Downsizing

The objective of downsizing includes reducing the size of the government bureaucracy and the range of activities for which the government is responsible. For operating ports, this requires that both port employees and services be transferred to the private sector. If there is an excessively large labour force, the port must apply a strategy of voluntary and mandatory retirements. If the private sector is to assume responsibility for paying off the excess labour, it must have a sufficiently long-term contract to allow it to amortise these costs. If the port retains the labour, then it must retain some tariffs to pay for the excess labour. The reduction in port labour remains one of the most contentious components of plans to increase PSP. Much of the effort in reaching agreement with private sector involvement has focused on labour redundancy. This has been especially difficult in Latin America and South Asia where there are strong unions. Buenos Aires and Port Kelang were both successful in combining private sector hiring and generous retirement benefits. Nhava Sheva and Laem Chaebang benefited from starting out with relatively small workforces, which they could retain after concessioning some of their facilities.

Suggested Framework

Based on the options suggested above, the following suggestion matrix (Table 3) can be utilised by major and non-major ports, depending on their existing budget and governmental support. In addition, this framework can also be referred to by government to identify or classify ports based on the existing capacity and volume of traffic handled into the "preferential port".

Table 3 Suggested Framework

Recommendations	JNPT Port	Kandla Port	Paradip Port	Kolkata Port	Mumbai Port	Vizag Port	Ennore Port	Cochin Port	Non major Ports
Reformation									
Service ports to Land lord ports									
Outsourcing									
Free port status to minor ports									
Dredging operations									
Cruise Terminal									
Ro-Ro facility									

(Continued)

Recommendations	JNPT Port	Kandla Port	Paradip Port	Kolkata Port	Mumbai Port	Vizag Port	Ennore Port	Cochin Port	Non major Ports
Ports in SEZ or giving SEZ status to ports									
Single Buoy Mooring									
Downsizing									
Port storage facility									
Ship repair facility									

Table 3   (Continued)

Source: Devised by author

CONCLUSIONS

For India to be on the world's infrastructure map and conquer leading investment destination position, it also needs to give its public utilities an international set up in order to match international standards. To enable such a competitive edge, the port infrastructure needs to demonstrate both growth and effective risk management, together with effective incentives to attract private investment.

REFERENCE

Government of India (2015), Concept Note on SagarMala Project: Working Paper. *Ministry of Shipping, Government of India*. Retrieved 4 July 2015.

BIOGRAPHY

Shraddha S. Sathe graduated from the Symbiosis Institute of Business Management, Pune, in 2004, and subsequently worked for the Standard Chartered Bank before moving to her present position at the Shipping Corporation of India. Her research interests include Millennium Development Goals, logistics and shipping. She has presented International conference papers on MDGs, social and cultural factors in FDI flows – Evidence from Indian States, etc., at previous WASD conferences.

ANNEX

TRAFFIC HANDLED AT MAJOR PORTS
2016-17 vis-a-vis 2015-16

(in Million Tonnes)

PORT	2016-17	2015-16	% Growth (+/-)
KOLKATA	50.31	50.28	0.05
PARADIP	88.95	76.39	16.45
VISAKHAPATNAM	61.02	57.03	6.99
KAMARAJAR	30.02	32.20	-6.79
CHENNAI	50.21	50.05	0.31
V.O.CHIDAMBARANAR	38.46	36.84	4.38
COCHIN	25.00	22.09	13.16
NEW MANGALORE	39.94	35.59	12.26
MORMUGAO	33.18	20.78	59.70
MUMBAI	63.05	61.11	3.17
J.N.P.T.	62.02	64.02	-3.13
KANDLA	105.44	100.05	5.39
OVERALL:	647.63	606.47	6.79

Source: Indian Port Association

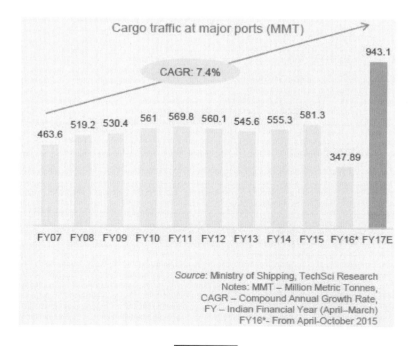

Source: Ministry of Shipping, TechSci Research
Notes: MMT – Million Metric Tonnes,
CAGR – Compound Annual Growth Rate,
FY – Indian Financial Year (April–March)
FY16*- From April-October 2015

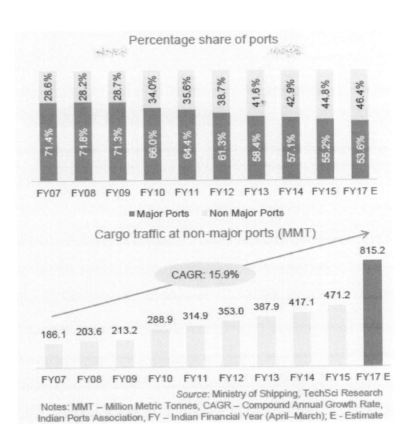

Percentage share of ports

Source: Ministry of Shipping, TechSci Research
Notes: MMT – Million Metric Tonnes, CAGR – Compound Annual Growth Rate,
Indian Ports Association, FY – Indian Financial Year (April–March); E - Estimate

STRONG PSP

Terminals in major ports with private sector involvement	Port agency	Estimated cost (USD million)
Container terminal, Ennore	Ennore	293.1
LNG terminal, Cochin	Cochin Port Trust	729.1
Container terminal, NSICT	JNPT	156.3
Oil jetty related facilities (Vadinar)	Kandla Port Trust	156.3
Third container terminal (Mumbai)	JNPT	187.5
Crude oil handling facility (Cochin)	Cochin Port Trust	146.5
ICTT at Vallarpadam (Cochin)	Cochin Port Trust	262.9
Construction of SPM captive berth (Paradip)	Paradip Port Trust	104.2
Development of second container terminal (Chennai)	Chennai Port Trust	103.1

As on 2015

Key private sector companies	Ports they developed
Maersk	JNPT (Mumbai)
P&O Ports	JNPT, (Mumbai and Chennai)
Dubai Ports International	(Cochin and Vishakhapatnam)
PSA Singapore	Tuticorin
Adani	Mundra
Maersk	Pipavav
Navyuga Engineering Company Ltd	Krishnapatnam
DVS Raju group	Gangavaram
JSW	Jaigarh
Marg	Karaikal

Source: Indian Ports Association, TechSci Research
Notes: NSICT – Nhava Sheva International Container Terminal, Mumbai,
ICTT – International Container Transshipment Terminal, SPM – Single Point Mooring

Terminals in major ports with private sector involvement (FY15)	Port agency	Capacity (Million tonnes)	Estimated cost (USD million)
Development & Operation of International Container Transshipment Terminal (ICTT) at Vallar-padam	Cochin Port	12.5 to 40 MMT in Phases	353
Setting up of LNG Port & ReGasification Terminal at Puthuvypeen by Cochin. / Cochin Port Trust	Cochin Port	5 MMPTA	691.1
Multi-User Liquid Terminal (MULT) at Puthuvypeen SEZ (International Bunkering Terminal at Cochin)	Cochin Port	4.10 MMTPA	38.4
Conversion of berth No. 8 as container terminal on	Tuticorin	7.2 MTPA	52.03
Development of North Cargo Berth – II on DBFOT basis.	Tuticorin	7.0 MTPA	55.36
Enhancement of Cargo Handling capacity by installing rapid in motion wagon loading facility by SWPL	Mormugao Port Trust	2.50 MTPA	7.5
Development of Container Terminal on DBFOT basis	Kamarajar Port Ltd	16.8MT	210.68
Development of Multi Cargo Terminal on DBFOT basis	Kamarajar Port Ltd	2.00	25.05

As on FY15

Source: Indian Ports Association, TechSci Research
Notes: NSICT – Nhava Sheva International Container Terminal, Mumbai,
ICTT – International Container Transsshipment Terminal, SPM – Single Point Mooring

GOAL 8

DECENT WORK AND ECONOMIC GROWTH

MILLENNIALS EMPOWERMENT: EXAMINING YOUTH ENTREPRENEURSHIP DEVELOPMENT IN POLICY AND PRACTICE

Ikedinachi Ogamba

University of Strathclyde Business School, UK
ikedinachi.ogamba@strath.ac.uk

ABSTRACT

Purpose: This paper contributes to knowledge and theory building in youth empowerment and entrepreneurship development.

Design/methodology/approach: The paper critically examines the Youth Enterprise with Innovation in Nigeria (YouWiN) Programme and its relevance as a youth economic empowerment programme through the lenses of the United Nations Development Programme (UNDP) Youth Strategy entry points for promoting economic empowerment of youth.

Findings: While YouWiN is a significant intervention towards entrepreneurship development, it presents some flaws and limitations in the design and implementation process, which may challenge sustainable economic development. Hence, there is a need to explore the millennials empowerment paradigm in the light of three key complementary action-oriented approaches to youth entrepreneurship development.

Originality/value: Three key complementary action-oriented approaches to youth entrepreneurship policy/programme design, implementation and evaluation for government, private and voluntary sector are proposed. These are in the form of facilitating participatory engagement and diversity, managing drivers (push/pull factors) of entrepreneurship, and ensuring access to enablers/support. The author highlights the need for further debate and critical inputs to improve theory building towards a normative framework in youth empowerment and entrepreneurship. This will not only reduce poverty, but also promote intergenerational equity and sustainable development.

Keywords: Youth; entrepreneurship; empowerment; economic development; sustainability; theory building

INTRODUCTION

Youth are a great human resource, future leaders and hope for the advancement of the global economy. The 21st century has witnessed a prevalence of youth empowerment issues in the front-burner of global development discourse, with various initiatives and programmes by the government, the private sector and the voluntary sector to promote the wellbeing and development of young people. The post-2015 development agenda process saw numerous engagements and consultations to mainstream and prioritise the youth. This follows observations that the Millennium Development Goals (MDGs) did not address most of the salient issues of youth development. This is especially true with regards to the inclusion of youth in socio-political and economic development, against the backdrop of a global trend of low-level participation in governance, social deprivations, unemployment and other youth development issues in both developed and developing economies (Gough et al., 2013; Bersaglio et al., 2015). Although these issues manifest in varying degrees in different countries, there is a unanimous consensus among policy makers, researchers, development agencies and other stakeholders that the youth have been marginalised in global development budgets and programming, thereby compromising investment performance in meeting global poverty, health, education and employment goals.

Addressing issues of youth inclusion and participation in society requires an holistic intervention that targets psychosocial, economic and political empowerment. In Nigeria, one major area of deprivation and exclusion challenge for the youth is in economic and livelihood pathways. Nigeria is a country of contrasts; although it is endowed with enormous human and natural resources, it remains in the category of countries with high rates of poverty and unemployment, especially among the youth and other vulnerable groups of the population (World Bank, 1996; Toyin et al., 2015). The unemployment rate in Nigeria in 2012 stood at 23.9%, while 54% of the youth are unemployed based the national baseline youth survey report by the National Bureau of Statistics (NBS, 2012). Regrettably, evidence has shown continuous inadequate investment in youth empowerment programmes that will enhance the active participation of youth in the political economy over the years (Ogbuanya and Ofonmbuk, 2015). This is worsened by observed high failure rates of government policies and programmes across various sectors in Nigeria, especially those related to economic and entrepreneurial development. This is because they are usually bedevilled by lack of proper needs assessment and research, poor design, inadequate information and communication, inconsistent financing, misappropriation of funds, corruption and poor implementation (Onuoha, 2011; Muftau, 2015; Onuoha and Ogbuji, 2015).

Indeed, there is yearning for entrepreneurial development among the youth as a panacea to unemployment; this has driven some of them into various Small and Medium Enterprise (SME) ventures. However, challenges abound in the endeavour as many factors have been identified to be militating against SME entrepreneurial development in Nigeria. These factors include a bottle-neck in in obtaining finance, monetary policy, lack of electricity power supply, poor policy and programme implementation and monitoring, among others (Muftau, 2015; Ayegba and Omale, 2016). This raises an issue regarding the need for an enabling environment and support system to promote SMEs in Nigeria, especially among the youth population.

In a bid to tackle some of the issues of entrepreneurial (SME) development and stimulate job creation, economic growth and diversification, the Nigerian government introduced a youth empowerment programme known as the Youth Enterprise with Innovation in Nigeria (YouWiN) to support youth in developing and executing business ideas that will also create jobs. This paper aims to critically examine and discuss the relevance of the YouWiN Programme as a youth economic empowerment strategy through the lenses of the UNDP Youth Strategy entry points for promoting the economic empowerment of youth. It lays the foundation for further discourse and theorisation of entrepreneurship in research, policy and programming process by proposing three key complementary action-oriented approaches to youth entrepreneurship development. It contributes to knowledge and theory building towards a normative framework for youth empowerment and entrepreneurship. Hence, it is a work in progress and will be advanced through further analysis, academic debates and critical input from other researchers, policy makers, youth and all relevant contributors to the discourse.

This paper has three main sections, the first section provides a brief description of the YouWiN Programme, the second section examines YouWiN's fit as a youth economic empowerment programme, while the third section explores the millennials empowerment paradigm in the light of three key complementary action-oriented approaches to youth entrepreneurship development. It then concludes by highlighting the implications for further research, theory building and debate on youth empowerment and entrepreneurship.

Youth Enterprise with Innovation in Nigeria (YouWiN) Programme

In a renewed effort by the government to promote SME financing and encourage microeconomic development by generating private sector employment, the Federal

Government of Nigeria introduced the Youth Enterprise with Innovation in Nigeria (YouWiN) Programme. The initiative was launched in October 2011 as an innovative business plan competition. It was implemented by the Ministries of Finance, Communication Technology (CT), Youth Development, and Women Affairs and Social Development, in partnership with the World Bank, UK Department for International Development and the organised private sector. The goal of the YouWiN programme is to create jobs by assisting aspiring young Nigerian entrepreneurs to initiate and implement business ideas and employ others. It provides aspiring youth with an opportunity to showcase their business insight and skills to business leaders, investors and mentors (YouWiN, 2013a). The specific objectives of the programme are to:

1. attract ideas and innovations from young entrepreneurial aspirants from universities, polytechnics, technical colleges, and other post-secondary institutions in Nigeria;
2. provide a one-time equity grant for selected aspiring entrepreneurs to start or expand their business concepts and mitigate start up risks;
3. generate hundreds of thousands of new jobs for currently unemployed Nigerian youth over the three years during which the three cycles will be implemented;
4. provide business training for thousands of aspiring youth entrepreneurs spread across all geo-political zones in Nigeria;
5. encourage expansion, specialisation and spin-offs of existing businesses in Nigeria;
6. enable young entrepreneurs to access a wide business professional network and improve their visibility.

The eligibility criteria for the business plan competition include:

- must be a proven citizen of Nigeria no older than 45 years with post-secondary school qualification;
- proposed business venture must be within the national borders with the intention of employing Nigerian citizens;
- proposed venture must not entail the production or distribution of weapons, alcoholic beverages, tobacco or/and gambling or any activities in contradiction with the Nigerian constitution; and finally
- must prepare an innovative business concept summary (YouWin, 2013a).

Three editions of the programme have been implemented and the selection process for the award stage in each edition involved a call for concept notes advertisement, vetting of applications, then shortlisted applicants were selected to submit their business plan. Training sessions were organised for the shortlisted applicants across the six geo-political zones of Nigeria (North-Central, North-East, North-West, South-East, South-South and South-West), after which they submitted full business plans for assessment and selection of awardees. The business plans were assessed by the Pan African University, with quality assurance provided by Plymouth Business School in the UK, followed by an award of grants to selected awardees (YouWiN, 2013a). The post-award support stage involves management monitoring and mentoring, including pairing of awardees with experienced entrepreneurs as mentors in providing needed support to ensure the successful execution of their business plan, while partner institutions, including the Small and Medium Enterprises Agency of Nigeria (SMEDAN) and the UK School for Startups, monitor the implementation process (YouWiN, 2014). The monitors work hand-in-hand with awardees to review their business plan, and decide on the minimum milestones based on the business plan. The mentors serve as a skills and experience pool to guide awardees in running their businesses. One to five mentees are assigned, with whom they are required to meet at least once every month in a face-to-face session. In the grant-making process and disbursement of funds, awardees receive a range of 1–10 million naira, depending on their business plan. They are paid in tranches based on the progress report on targets, monitors' feedback and job creation milestones (McKenzie, 2015). See Table 1 that shows data of the competition process in the three editions of the YouWiN process.

Table 1   YouWiN Editions Award Process Statistics

YouWin Editions	Number of Participants			
	Concept Notes	Qualifiers Trained	Bus. Plan Submitted	Awardees Funded
1st Edition	23,821	6,000	4,513	1,200
2nd Edition	65,970	6,000	5,406	1,200
3rd Edition	114,461	6,000	-	1,500
Total	204,252	18,000		3,900

Source: YouWiN Bulletins (YouWin, 2013a; 2013b; 2013c; 2014)

Although there have been many efforts by the government to stimulate SMEs in Nigeria, the YouWiN programme has been applauded as a brave initiative that presents opportunities for entrepreneurship development that will have a multiplier effect, not only in job creation, but also in economic and markets development. One of its significant results is the bridging of the finance gap, which is a major issue that has been identified as mitigating against entrepreneurship (SME) development and start-ups in Nigeria (Muftau, 2015). However, the programme could present some salient design and implementation limitations that challenge its effectiveness in economic empowerment of youth if critically examined.

YouWiN in Promoting the Economic Empowerment of Youth

The concept of youth empowerment is a widely viewed one, but comprehensively it involves developing the capacity of youth to take control of their development through ensuring an enabling environment for individual and collective youth inclusion and active participation in civil, political, economic, social and cultural aspects of society. Going by this meaning, youth empowerment will support youth in improving their wellbeing, as well as making valuable contributions to development in their communities. Therefore, in other to explore YouWiN's fit as a youth empowerment programme, the UNDP's Youth Strategy 2014–2017, with the theme "Empowered Youth, Sustainable Future" is used as a reference framework. This juxtaposition is reasonable based on the premise that the strategy was designed and adopted as a global framework for youth development programming and interventions in the areas of employment, entrepreneurship and political inclusion in countries of the United Nations. In its youth strategy, the UNDP "recognises decent work and livelihood creation including through local economic development, as chief determinants in the socioeconomic empowerment of youth" (UNDP, 2014, p.2). Hence, it emphasises the creation, availability and accessibility of opportunities for young people to fully engage in the various productive sectors that it asserts would facilitate transformational change in human development, generational inequality and social protection. This underpins the main thrust of the YouWiN programme as an entrepreneurial (SME) development initiative for youth employment and job creation.

Furthermore, the YouWiN programme goal and objectives aligns with the first expected outcome for the UNDP Youth Strategy, which is to:

> "increase economic empowerment of youth, adapting sustainable development pathways to eradicate extreme poverty and reduce socioeconomic inequality and exclusion through building productive capacities of youth and an enabling environment for enhanced youth employment, employability and entrepreneurship" (UNDP, 2014, p.25).

In other words, the design of the YouWiN programme is suitable as a youth empowerment intervention to enhance the inclusion and participation of youth in economic activities that will ensure their right to livelihood is protected, as well as promoting human development and a more equitable socioeconomic development. The programme was designed to create a platform where ambitious youth will pursue their business ideas, fund their plan, apply their skills and connect with investors and mentors, compete for grants and capacity development funds and support as nascent entrepreneurs, start-ups and existing businesses.

The UNDP strategy suggests strategic entry points for promoting economic empowerment of youth by outlining the needed interventions from three perspectives: demand for labour, supply of labour, and the policy environment. From the demand for labour perspective, the strategy is to "support young persons' access to finance, markets and other resources that will increase their productive capacities and competitiveness" (UNDP, 2014, p.27); this includes loans, grants, capacity building, mentorship, business support services and incubators. In this aspect, the YouWiN programme incorporated the funding of business plans with capacity development to encourage selected youth entrepreneurs to participate in the SMEs of the economy, which created access to finance. However, the provision of access to finance is very minimal as many of the proposals submitted were not funded due to limited funds.

Statistics from the programme bureau report indicate that a total of 204,252 aspiring entrepreneurs submitted concept notes for the first, second and third editions of YouWiN. Of these, 18,000 qualified to advance to the next stage and were trained on business plan development and SME management, while only 3,900 beneficiaries were awarded funding grants after the submission of business plans (see Table 1). This shows a very high interest and needs by hundreds of thousands of youth entrepreneurs in Nigeria, to which only a few could be met by the programme. To this end, the programme has been criticised for low coverage and inadequate capacity to support many promising businesses, in addition to inconsistent disbursement of award funds (Farayibi, 2015).

Meanwhile, a very commendable component of the programme was the training, mentoring and monitoring of beneficiaries at different stages of the application and grant award administration. A study by Ebiringa (2013) revealed that the mentoring and monitoring process helped to create sustainability through building the capacity of the youth entrepreneurs for creativity, resilience, customer satisfaction, and risk management, as well as focusing on socially and environmentally responsible value creation in the market. This finding is in line with Baker (2006), which suggests that entrepreneurial actions targeted at solving unemployment and income inequality must address social and environmental change in order to create sustainable economic development.

The supply of labour perspective is focused on promoting skills development and experience of youth at all levels. This is in order to increase their employability and ability to be gainfully engaged in the labour market and the economy generally. Although the YouWiN programme is more focused on developing the capacity of the beneficiaries as entrepreneurs to become self-employed and be able to employ others, the skills acquired from the programme is also helpful for employment in the labour market as an alternative to self-employment, especially for those who were not shortlisted for the award of a grant after the training stage. However, one of the flaws in the programme is that it targets only higher education graduates; it excludes the large chunk of youth with lower qualifications who have promising business ideas/plans and are in need of support for their growing enterprise.

The issue of enabling policy and environment is essential in every empowerment process, without which there would be no real impact as beneficiaries may not achieve the desired outcome. For this reason, the policy environment perspective "support the development and implementation of institutional and policy frameworks conducive to youth employment and entrepreneurship" (UNDP, 2014, p.28). In a study covering over 3,000 entrepreneurs, and 18 banks and government/multilateral agencies, KPMG (2014) identified a non-conducive enabling environment (80%), inconsistent government policies (56%), and lack of access to finance/capital (45%) as the three top challenges faced by SMEs in Nigeria based on data collected from the respondents. This is an indication that although YouWiN is providing funds and training for youth entrepreneurs, that is not enough. More needs to be done in the areas of favourable economic/market policy and infrastructural development to support these businesses.

The Youth Strategy also mandated that special recognition be given to breaking barriers to diversity in empowering the youth such as it relates to involving women and other disadvantaged youth groups. This is essential for diverse and inclusive economic growth that will encourage a more even distribution of income and challenge poverty and inequality. Commendably, in the YouWiN programme, the issue of gender mainstreaming was emphasised by encouraging women to apply and compete with their male counterparts. Notwithstanding, there were only 18% female awardees in the first edition of the programme (YouWiN, 2013a). In a response to further provide more room for female beneficiaries, the second edition of the programme targeted solely female entrepreneurs as a result of their poor participation in the first edition. This saw a massive number of applicants, with 200% more than the previous edition at the first stage of concept note submission. It is reported that 65,970 concept note applications were submitted. From these, 6,000 qualified for the next stage for training, while 1,200 female entrepreneurs were awarded grants to fund their business plans (see Table 1).

Nevertheless, one of the major flaws identified in the implementation of YouWiN is poor information and publicity, which constitutes a barrier to diversity and equal opportunity. According to a study by Onuoha and Ogbuji (2015), only 14% from a sample of 384 respondents were aware of the YouWiN programme, indicating a very low awareness level and information dissemination about the programme, especially among those living in suburban or rural areas. This finding is in line with a study by Igwe and Onah (2013) that suggests poor information and accessibility to the YouWiN programme among young graduates seeking entrepreneurship development and empowerment opportunities. This indeed raises a serious concern about equal opportunities policy and practices in the implementation of the programme, and affects its effectiveness as an empowerment programme.

In addition, the policy environment perspective also advocates the promotion of "investment in sectors with the potential for growth in youth employment, such as the service sector e.g. in tourism or ICT-based services" (UNDP, 2014, p.29). Laudably, sectors of the economy targeted in the YouWiN programme conform to the above strategy, as the three most represented sectors among the awardees are agriculture, IT/Telecommunications services, and food and drinks manufacturing (YouWiN, 2013a; McKenzie, 2015). These sectors are less explored and are argued to possess the highest potential for creating employment and generating high return on investment.

They are also very much viable to diversifying the economy of Nigeria away from the oil and gas sector (Iyoboyi and Na-Allah, 2014; Anyaehie and Areji, 2015; Nwafor and Udensi, 2015). This is promising because the needs of the huge population of Nigeria are currently met by relying on importation. Therefore, a pull investment strategy of responding to local consumers' needs, which is a sustainable strategy for effective market-creating innovations, is apt for the economy (Christensen et al., 2017). This can be feasible through supporting existing and nascent youth entrepreneurs to cash into existing non-consumption and non-production to create disruptive innovations that will benefit the consumers and the market. It will also create employment, boost government revenue and promote sustainable development. An experimental assessment by McKenzie (2015) reported that YouWiN has succeeded in generating more business and creating employment; it also has great potential for producing entrepreneurs with disruptive innovations that will flourish beyond the ordinary microenterprises.

Having examined the YouWiN programme in the light of the strategic entry points for promoting economic empowerment of youth and identified its significance and limitations, the next section will propose a complementary action-oriented approach to youth entrepreneurship development, based on the various indicative findings and assumptions from the foregoing discussions and elements of social critical theory lenses of youth empowerment.

The Millennials Empowerment Paradigm

Society has witnessed a shift in generational sociology, transiting from a dimension of sociocultural conflict of values to the dynamics of socioeconomic inequalities and power relation, with the millennials at the centre stage of this transformation. Described as the generation born between the early 1980s and the early 2000s, the millennials are the most educated generation, yet they are said to be faced with the most difficult socioeconomic and increasing generational inequality situation of all times. This is manifest through continuing decline in youth employment, affordable housing, social welfare and benefits, access to finance, and high cost of education. This poses a very challenging situation with pressure on the youth, rising tension among the older generation and unease about the upcoming generation (Howe and Strauss, 2000). Therefore, the economic empowerment of the millennials has become an inevitable integral part of sustainable development plans and efforts globally, with entrepreneurship development suggested as an important gateway. The argument behind this is that promoting youth entrepreneurship will not only facilitate inclusive market growth, generate employment, reduce poverty and inequality (World Bank, 1996; Awoyemi et al., 2015, Muftau, 2015, Ayegba and Omale, 2016), it will also provoke disruptive innovations for effective economic growth and prosperity (Christensen et al., 2017; Ogamba, 2017). It goes without saying that economic empowerment through youth entrepreneurship development that encourages disruptive innovations, and a pull investment strategy that targets local needs, is fundamental for sustainable development.

Drawing from results of participatory research and analysis of four youth empowerment models, Jennings et al. (2006, p.41) identified six key dimensions of critical youth empowerment as:

- a welcoming and safe environment;
- meaningful participation and engagement;
- equitable power-sharing between youth and adults;
- engagement in critical reflection on interpersonal and socio-political processes;
- participation in socio-political processes to effect change; and
- integrated individual- and community-level empowerment.

Therefore, a youth entrepreneurship development framework focusing on economic empowerment should incorporate these dimensions for effective and sustainable social change. Similarly, millennials have been identified as diverse and inclusive, socially and environmentally responsible, more attracted to experiences and access, as well as valuing collaboration, connection, peer relationship, mentorship and constructive ideas (Howe and Strauss, 2000; Irving, 2015). These are strengths that could be maximised to positively engage the youth in innovative ventures and positive socio-economic development. However, for this to be effective, government, the private sector and the voluntary sector must respond to the various barriers that deter the youth from setting up and running a business, and provide incentives to encourage entrepreneurial ventures.

Consequently, from the foregoing, it is deduced that millennials empowerment through youth entrepreneurship development required three key action-oriented approaches to be effective:

(1) facilitating participatory engagement and diversity;
(2) managing drivers (push/pull factors) of entrepreneurship;
(3) ensuring access to enablers/support.

Facilitating Participatory Engagement and Diversity

Participation and effective engagement is key to any youth entrepreneurship development process; this is because it allows for an experiential learning process that is necessary for independence and competent application of capacity developed overtime in making a significant contribution to socioeconomic development. It also allows for fair power sharing between the youth and adults/stakeholders in decision making and execution. This may be reflected in the empowerment process in the form of consultations, encouraging collaboration, building connections, peer relationships, and promoting intergenerational engagement. Also key is the need to promote diversity and equal opportunity for every youth, no matter their dispositions and interests, to get involved and be treated fairly in the process. This may be reflected in the form of gender mainstreaming, social class inclusion, participation by various educational attainment levels, geographical inclusion (rural, suburban and urban), sector variety, and integration of environmentally responsive behaviours. The premise behind participation and an effective engagement approach is that youths can become agents of social change themselves, rather than just targets to be changed.

Managing Drivers (Push/Pull Factors) of Entrepreneurship

The drivers of entrepreneurship are those factors that attract youths towards setting up their own business and becoming self-employed. They could be classified into (a) push factors (usually negative), i.e. circumstances that make them want to leave their current situation, position or employment to become entrepreneurs, and (b) pull factors (usually positive), i.e. advantages, incentives or information that make them want to go into entrepreneurship and self-employment. Therefore, in the economic empowerment of youth through entrepreneurship development, proper management and channelling of the drivers of entrepreneurship would yield positive outcomes. These divers include entrepreneurship education (formal and non-formal), entrepreneurship programmes (by government, private and voluntary sector), innovation incubation, entrepreneurial acculturation, investment protection laws and regulations, market size, unemployment issues, and behaviour change communication (BCC) on career development (e.g. discouraging the obsession for white-collar jobs). The premise behind managing drivers (push/pull factors) of entrepreneurship is that it will encourage youths, both nascent and active entrepreneurs, to explore innovative ventures and create opportunities for a sustainable entrepreneurial culture for economic empowerment and growth in society.

Ensuring Access to Enablers/Support

The enablers of entrepreneurship are those policies, services and infrastructures that facilitate the efficient running of business ventures and allow entrepreneurial efforts to thrive. In this way, an enabler will also tackle the barriers to entrepreneurial actions and development among the youth. As has been widely acknowledged, businesses need an enabling environment to succeed. This could be in the form of availability and access to finance, physical infrastructure and technology (e.g. electricity, the Internet), training and capacity development, research and development, information sharing and communication, favourable macroeconomic policy, business support, and availability of raw materials and resources. The premise behind ensuring access to enablers/support is that creating a favourable environment and supporting youths to navigate the barriers to initiating and sustaining innovative businesses, will guarantee their active and continued participation in the economy, and promote equitable and sustainable economic development.

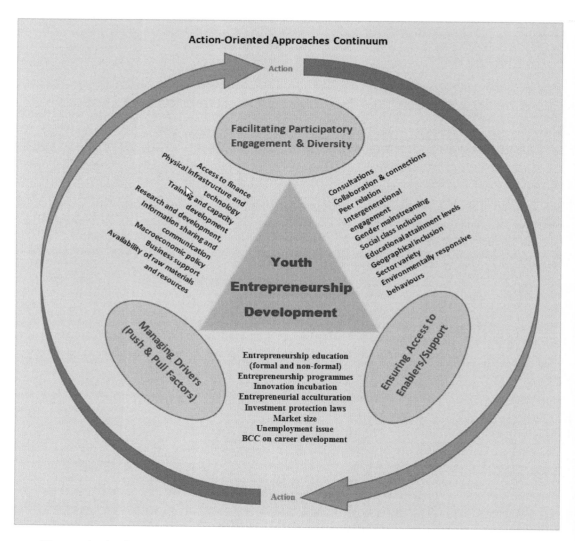

Figure 1   Action-Oriented Approaches to Youth Entrepreneurship Development
Source: Devised by author

Figure 1 illustrates the interactions of the three key action-oriented approaches in a continuum as an integrated, interdependent and action driven process. In summary, the proposed action-oriented approaches are complementary and applicable to policy/programme design, implementation and monitoring, and for researching youth entrepreneurship development. They are also useful for developing a framework for assessing youth empowerment programmes, based on the integration of the processes and outcomes at the individual and collective levels accordingly. Subsequent papers will unpack the fundamental components of these approaches by situating them within the empowerment and entrepreneurship milieu and theory.

CONCLUSIONS

This paper has been able to explore issues of youth empowerment and entrepreneurship development in policy and practice by critically examining the Youth Enterprise with Innovation in Nigeria (YouWiN) Programme through the lenses of the UNDP Youth Strategy entry points for promoting economic empowerment of youth. The YouWiN programme is applauded as a major intervention aimed at promoting entrepreneurship and innovation among the youth with the goal of creating employment, reducing economic dependence, and improving market system development. However, an inclusive assessment of youth empowerment and entrepreneurship programmes requires a robust view towards an understanding of the socioeconomic and political systems, circumstances and the change process. This is more so in YouWiN since the entrepreneurial process includes learning in which human and social factors are as important as the economic factors. While entrepreneurship (SMEs) development is the bedrock for the diversification and industrialisation of every economy, evidence suggests that youths can be major drivers of innovation for profitable business ventures. However:

> "innovation is not a convenient venture; it is a daunting endeavour to create solutions that meet a need. So it's essential to strengthen young African entrepreneurs' ability to cash in on non-consumption opportunities and create disruptive innovations that will benefit consumers" (Ogamba, 2017, p.22).

This will, in turn, benefit the market as well as create employment, boost government revenue, and advance economic growth and sustainable development.

To realise this, there is a need for more robust and inclusive programme design in entrepreneurial development targeting youths, in order to increase active participation across-the-board and reduce inequality in economic opportunities. This should be done by maximising the qualities of the youth population and the new generation of young entrepreneurs driving creativity.

Applying the three key action-oriented approaches in policy and programming will ensure youth entrepreneurship development is innovation driven, and create markets for domestic prosperity and global development. Finally, this paper is foundational to further discourse analysis on theory, policy and programming process. Therefore, further debate and input will be helpful in improving the proposed action-oriented approaches for theory building towards a normative framework in youth empowerment and entrepreneurship.

REFERENCES

Anyaehie, M.C. and Areji, A.C. (2015), Economic diversification for sustainable development in Nigeria. *Open Journal of Political Science*, Vol. 5, No. 02, pp. 87–94.

Awoyemi, B.O., Olayoriju, O.M. and Kashim, I.T. (2015), The Challenges of Financing Micro, Small and Medium Scale Enterprises (MSMEs) in Nigeria. *International Journal of Banking, Finance, Management & Development Studies*, Vol. 1, No. 16, pp. 275–90.

Ayegba, O. and Omale, S.A. (2016), A Study on Factors Affecting Entrepreneurial Development in Nigeria. *European Journal of Business and Management*, Vol. 8, No. 12, pp. 43–51.

Baker, S. (2006), *Sustainable Development*. New York, NY: Routledge.

Bersaglio, B., Enns, C. and Kepe, T. (2015), Youth under construction: the United Nations' representations of youth in the global conversation on the post-2015 development agenda. *Canadian Journal of Development Studies*, Vol. 36, No. 1, pp. 57–71.

Christensen, C.M., Ojomo, E. and Van Bever, D. (2017), Africa's New Generation of Innovators. *Harvard Business Review*. January-February 2017 Issue, pp. 128–36.

Ebiringa, O.T. (2013), Entrepreneurship Development for Sustainable Economic Transformation: A Study of YouWin Programme in Eastern States of Nigeria. *Journal of Sustainable Development in Africa*, Vol. 15, No. 5, pp. 49–59.

Farayibi, A.O. (2015), Employment Creation Potentials of the Informal Sector in Nigeria. *Research on Humanities and Social Sciences*, Vol. 5, No. 23, pp. 11–9.

Gough, K., Langevang, T. and Owusu, G. (2013), Youth employment in a globalising world. *International Development Planning Review*, Vol. 35, No. 2, pp. 91–102.

Howe, N. and Strauss, W. (2000), *Millennials rising: The next great generation*. Vintage.

Igwe, K.N. and Onah, E.A. (2013), A Study on the Information Environment of National Youth Service Corps Members in Kwara State, Nigeria. *Information and Knowledge Management*, Vol. 3, No. 3, pp. 20–29.

Irving, P.H. (2015), *Minding the Millennials - Lessons in Self-Empowerment for Baby Boomers*. Retrieved from http://www.huffingtonpost.com/paul-h-irving/lessons-in-empowerment-for-baby-boomers_b_8353778.html.

Iyoboyi, M. and Na-Allah, A. (2014), ICT-Driven Growth and Diversification: The Case of Nigeria's Entertainment Industry. *Journal of Economics*, Vol. 2, No. 4, pp. 255–68.

Jennings, L.B., Parra-Medina, D.M., Hilfinger-Messias, D.K. and McLoughlin, K. (2006), Toward a critical social theory of youth empowerment. *Journal of Community Practice*, Vol. 14, Nos 1-2, pp. 31–55.

KPMG (2014), *Strengthening Access to Finance for Micro, Small and Medium Enterprises in Nigeria*. KPMG & Enterprise Development Centre (EDC) Nigeria.

McKenzie, D.J. (2015), *Identifying and spurring high-growth entrepreneurship: experimental evidence from a business plan competition*. Policy Research Working Paper 7391, World Bank Group.

Muftau, A.A. (2015), Promoting Sustainability of Micro, Small and Medium Enterprises' Financing in Nigeria: Challenges, Necessary Conditions and Prospects. *International Journal of Banking, Finance, Management & Development Studies*, Vol. 1, No. 14, pp. 238–56.

NBS (2012): *National Baseline Youth Survey - Final Report*. National Bureau of Statistics, Abuja Nigeria.

Nwafor, I.A. and Udensi, L.O. (2015), Entrepreneurship Education, Skills Acquisition and Practices for Sustainable Development in Nigeria: Issues and Challenges. In Ukommi, A.S., Okon, D.E. and Udensi, L.O. (Eds): *Sustainable Development in Nigeria: Strategic and Innovative Options* (pp. 65–88). LAP LAMBERT Academic Publishing, Deutschland, Germany.

Ogamba, I. (2017), Interaction Section-Africa's New Generation of Innovators. *Harvard Business Review*. March–April 2017 Issue, p. 22.

Ogbuanya, T.C. and Ofonmbuk, M. (2015): Achieving Youth Employment and National Security in Nigeria: TVET Imperatives. *Journal of Education and Practice*, Vol. 6, No. 33, pp. 157–61.

Onuoha, B.C. (2011), Strategies for Reducing SMEs High Failure Rates in Nigeria. *African Journal of Entrepreneurship*, Vol. 3, No. 1, pp. 12–26.

Onuoha, O.A. and Ogbuji, C.N. (2015), Marketing Recipes for Popularizing and Creating Acceptance for Government Policies and Programmes in Nigeria. *International Journal*, Vol. 2, No. 10, pp. 19–26.

Toyin, A.G., Adigun, G.T., Timothy, A.T., Awoyemi, T.T., Funsho, F.E. and Fabiyi, E.F. (2015), Analysing Poverty Situation in Rural Nigeria. *Journal of Agricultural Science and Engineering*, Vol. 1, No. 4, pp. 178–88.

UNDP (2014), *UNDP Youth Strategy 2014-2017: Empowered youth, sustainable future*. New York: UNDP.

World Bank (1996), *Nigeria: Poverty in the midst of plenty, The challenge of growth with inclusion. A World Bank poverty assessment*. World Bank, Washington, D.C.

YouWiN (2013a), *Bulletin - Youth Enterprise with Innovation in Nigeria*. Volume 1: April 2013.

YouWiN (2013b), *Bulletin - Youth Enterprise with Innovation in Nigeria*. Volume 2: July 2013.

YouWiN (2013c), *Bulletin - Youth Enterprise with Innovation in Nigeria*. Volume 4: December 2013.

YouWiN (2014), *Bulletin - Youth Enterprise with Innovation in Nigeria*. Volume 4: June 2014.

BIOGRAPHY

Ikedinachi Ogamba is a Doctoral Researcher at the University of Strathclyde Business School, Glasgow, UK. He has several years' experience in international development with expertise in research, policy advocacy, project management, and monitoring and evaluation having worked in various programmes and organisations. His interests include inclusive entrepreneurship, poverty eradication, well-being and sustainable development. Ike is a member of various international professional bodies including the Human Development and Capabilities Association (HDCA), and Entrepreneurship Ecosystem Research Network (EERN). He holds an MA in International Development (with Distinction) from the University College London's Institute of Education. He is also a trained Market System Development (MSD) Specialist, and certified in Global Project and Change Management.

INDIVIDUAL FACTORS AFFECTING ADMINISTRATIVE INNOVATION

Hala Abou Arraj*

American University of Beirut, Beirut
ha17@aub.edu.lb

ABSTRACT

Purpose: This paper has two main goals: to assess the level of innovation among Lebanese civil servants; the second to test the impact of factors such as age and education on bureaucratic innovations.

Design/Methodology/Approach: A questionnaire was sent to 300 Lebanese civil servants during September 2016. The data gathered were then analysed using, first – cross tabulations between education level and indicators of innovation; second – an ANOVA (Analysis of Variance Test) test to determine the strength of the hypothesis; third – Pearson correlations.

Findings: The paper's findings indicate that innovation among employees could be greatly enhanced. The findings also suggest that young employees tend to be more innovative on the job; however, there was an inverse relationship between age and innovation, but only up to a certain level.

Keywords: Lebanese civil servants; innovation; bureaucratic innovations

*Corresponding Author

INTRODUCTION

Prospects in Administrative Innovation in Higher Education The turmoil of the political, economic and social change that has happened in the Middle East after the Spring Uprising in 2009 has weakened the developmental role of the government, especially when it comes to building the nation. It is a fact that the role of governments, and particularly the bureaucracies, must provide the lead and the initiative for the start of any development process. Most underdeveloped bureaucracies in the Middle East, including Lebanon, failed to act as an initiator of this development. These bureaucracies lacked the primary tools of problem solving. The inability of Middle Eastern bureaucracies to play a forceful role in the development process has been attributable to the conformist behaviour of its civil servants.

The present paper has two objectives. The first objective is to provide an empirical assessment of the innovation level of the bureaucracy in Lebanon. The second objective is to test the impact of factors such as age and education on bureaucratic innovation. Confirmation of this hypothesis reveals that overcoming the traditional attitudes of civil servants is a matter of time, while rejecting this hypothesis indicates that the behaviour of civil servants is entrenched in the culture of Lebanon and hence is very hard to change.

LITERATURE REVIEW

Innovation

Managerial innovation helps create new solutions to old or conventional problems. Its link to efficient performance and, therefore, to good decision-making will be defined and rationalised in this section.

Great attention has been paid to innovation in the literature during the last 10 years. The major qualities of an innovative person are listed as (a) having little respect for traditional knowledge or practice, (b) dealing with uncertainties and risks, (c) generating new ideas (Nagano et al., 2014). Operational definitions vary markedly from study to study and from field to field. Most definitions of innovation focus on the ability to create and find solutions to new problems (Palmer and Leila, 1988). Literature (e.g., Guilford et al., 1968; Maltzman, 1960; Dumas and Mintzberg, 1991) supports the idea that creative performance is conducive to success. Moreover, an innovative approach to the daily mix of unforeseen problems enables employees to contribute more to the success of the organisation (Eisenberger and Byron, 2011).

Kirton is among the leaders who tried to identify the different types of behaviour of innovators and adaptors. According to Kirton (1980), the adaptor fits better in the bureaucracy than the innovator since he is more conforming to rules and regulations. While the innovator faces problems in dealing with his peers in the bureaucracy because of his little respect for social norms and increased risk (Bobic et al., 1999). Furthermore, the Adaptation-Innovation theory posits that individuals have different decision-making styles, creativity and problem solving characteristics. Adaptors are more likely to produce decisions that reinforce the paradigm, while innovators tend to make decisions that threaten the paradigm. Normally, the outcome of the task determines its level of innovation (Kirton, 1980).

In this sense, because of the inherent vagueness of existing conceptualisations of innovation, this study approached the assessment of innovation from five different perspectives following the definition of innovation listed above. These perspectives are:

- the tendency towards creativity;
- the tendency towards risk taking;
- the predisposition of employees to accept new ideas;
- the predisposition to challenge social and traditional practices that pose a problem to innovation; and
- finally the level of creative decision-making.

Lebanese bureaucracy was trapped in individualistic, rigid and arbitrary tendencies. Decision-making in Lebanon tends to be highly individualistic, mainly because of the dominance of clientelism and the lack of institutionalisation among the different government branches.

A major influence from the Ottomans that has shaped the bureaucracy is the use of practices of *wasta* and *baksheesh* (a Turkish word still used today). These practices have kept Lebanese bureaucracy stuck in traditionalism, and led the Lebanese administration to become highly politicised. This opened the door for some politicians to establish a new "parallel administration" inside the government and enforce the prerogatives of their "counsellors" (Daher, 2004, p. 18). Moreover, positions in the public sector became rewards given by the *zuama* to their followers. Closely related to clientelism, Lebanese bureaucracy is built on the principle of sectarianism. Similar to political positions, high administrative positions have been shared based on the principle of confessionalism, to ensure equal and equitable representation, often resulting in placing the wrong person in a position simply because of his sect.

On the same note, Nakib and Palmer (1976) argue that employees in the public sector are motivated by personal interests in the work context. They give priority to helping a relative, a friend, a member of the same sect or same community (Nakib and Palmer, 1976). In many instances, civil servants may start with the papers and transactions pertinent to his group while stalling with others (Saadeh, 1993, p. 102). We can safely say that quality and improvement were sacrificed at the expense of confessional exploitation. This divided loyalty among civil servants strengthens the networking connections between people who have particular political interests, and hence influences the decision-making process. This particularistic behaviour is conducive to suspicion of innovation and change among civil servants.

This goes without saying that the existence of such attitudes is antithetical to the acceleration of administrative, social and national development. Particularism leads to distrust between the government and the people on a larger scale. On a broader scale, particularistic features makes civil servants less receptive to accepting new ideas; they feel threatened by its mere presence.

RESEARCH QUESTIONS AND STATEMENT OF HYPOTHESES

Within this context, the purpose of this study is to provide an empirical assessment of the level of innovation among civil servants in Lebanon. The objective is to find out whether civil servants do fit in the model portrayed above and to what extent. For this reason, the study will answer the following three research questions:

1. What factors are associated with higher levels of behavioural innovation?
2. Does age and education affect behavioural innovation?
3. How can behavioural capacity be strengthened?

Accordingly, the hypotheses to be tested are the following:

1. the level of innovation among the Lebanese bureaucrats is low;
2. there is a direct relationship between education and innovation;
3. there is an inverse relationship between age and innovation.

METHODOLOGY

The research surveyed in this paper is based on a questionnaire with 300 Lebanese civil servants conducted during September 2016. Questionnaire items to test the above three hypotheses appear in the body of this paper and revolve around five categories.

1. respondents were presented with one question designed to measure the level of creativity;
2. three questions were designed to measure the level of risk taking;
3. one question was designed to measure the predisposition of employees to accept new ideas;
4. the respondents were presented with two questions designed to measure their predisposition to challenge social and traditional practices that pose a problem to innovation;
5. respondents were presented with a battery of questions aimed at testing the employees' level of creativity in their everyday decision-making (Palmer and Leila, 1988).

In addition, questionnaire items were pretested for validity and reliability. Reliability was tested by a pre-test run on a small community of the employees before the final administration of the questionnaire. This pre-test included employees from different departments, age levels and different educational background. The importance of the pre-test lies in its ability to alleviate reliability problems such as inconsistency in the questionnaire design. Both construct and content validity types were justified based on the theoretical background of the variables. Definitions of concepts related to performance were extracted from reliable books, previous theses and research studies. All questions were formulated based on theoretical definitions.

Level of Innovation among Lebanese Bureaucrats

Ten questions were used as measures of innovation. The tests and descriptions appear in Tables 1–5.

Question 1 of Table 1 measures the predisposition of the employees toward creativity. The percentage distributions of this question show that the level of creativity among employees is moderate; it is not too low. It seems that around 44% of employees are conformists, in contrast to 46% who are willing to try new ideas.

Table 1   Creativity

	Frequency	Valid Percentage	Cumulative Percentage
Strongly Agree	58	20.5	20.5
Agree	66	23.3	43.8
Neutral	29	10.2	54.1
Disagree	88	31.1	85.2
Strongly Disagree	42	14.8	100.0
Total	283	100.0	

Source: Devised by author

Questions 1, 2 and 3 of Table 2 assess the predisposition of employees to take risks. Risk evasiveness is a universal feeling. Many decision theorists agree that people tend to avoid taking risks and prefer to stick to outcomes that are certain (Larrick, 1993). The percentage distributions of these questions reflect a low level of risk taking.

Question 1 of Table 2 assesses the predisposition of employees toward risks. Around 53% of the respondents said that they prefer to let their supervisor decide on an unclear problem, while 14% were neutral in answering this question; this shows negativity in dealing with the issue of risk. This means that around 70% of the respondents are afraid to take risks. Approximately 32% of respondents said that they are willing to take risks for an unclear solution. This number cannot be discarded, as more than a quarter of the respondents like to be involved in decision-making.

Question 2 of Table 2 assesses the reluctance of employees to take risks. The answer was striking in its frankness, with some 65% of the respondents indicating that taking risks is out of the question. In much the same manner, only 19% of the respondents classified job security as not important to them in Question 3. Statistics show that the level of risk taking is very low among employees. The result of the risk taking scale can only be interpreted as an obstacle to innovation. However, a small portion of employees is willing to take risky decisions, which is a good start and should be built upon.

Table 2   Risk Taking

Question 1 I prefer to let my supervisor decide on a problem with an unclear solution

		Frequency	Percentage	Valid Percentage	Cumulative Percentage
Valid	Strongly Agree	53	18.7	18.7	18.7
	Agree	98	34.6	34.6	53.4
	Neutral	41	14.5	14.5	67.8
	Disagree	57	20.1	20.1	88.0
	Strongly Disagree	34	12.0	12.0	100.0
	Total	283	100.0	100.0	

Question 2 When making investments you prefer to

		Frequency	Percentage	Valid Percentage	Cumulative Percentage
Valid	Norisk	170	60.1	65.1	65.1
	Moderate Risk	83	29.3	31.8	96.9
	High Risk	8	2.8	3.1	100.0
	Total	261	92.2	100.0	
Missing	5	22	7.8		
Total		283	100.0		

Question 3 How do you rate job security that the job provides?

		Frequency	Percentage	Valid Percentage	Cumulative Percentage
Valid	Very Important	63	22.3	22.3	22.3
	Important	74	26.1	26.1	48.4
	moderately Important	92	32.5	32.5	80.9
	Not Important	54	19.1	19.1	100.0
	Total	283	100.0	100.0	

Source: Devised by author

Acceptance of new ideas was measured using one indicator as shown in Table 3. Responses indicate preponderance among the employees, as around 65% are hesitant to plunge into change, especially when the consequences are sudden and abrupt. However, around 25% of the employees are not afraid to initiate change, which is a number that should not be taken for granted.

Table 3   Acceptance of New Ideas

Question 1 Introducing change too rapidly might be worse than changing too slowly

		Frequency	Percentage	Valid Percentage	Cumulative Percentage
Valid	Strongly Agree	62	21.9	21.9	21.9
	Agree	122	43.1	43.1	65.0
	Neutral	32	11.3	11.3	76.3
	Disagree	54	19.1	19.1	95.4
	Strongly Disagree	13	4.6	4.6	100.0
	Total	283	100.0	100.0	

Source: Devised by author

Two questions of Table 4 measure the predisposition of employees to challenge social and traditional norms. These two questions reflect a felt predisposition that employees might be reluctant to challenge social and traditional norms. Question 1 of Table 4 assesses the attachment of employees to traditional social values. Separating religion from the state is a controversial issue in Lebanon, and in the Arab world in general. The responses were surprising. Around 90% of the responses supported the idea of separation between the state and religion. The data suggest that a large faction of employees is willing to challenge traditional values and hence to change and

Table 4   Challenge of Traditional Values

Question 1 I agree with separation of religion from the state

		Frequency	Percentage	Valid Percentage	Cumulative Percentage
Valid	Strongly Agree	186	65.7	65.7	65.7
	Agree	67	23.7	23.7	89.4
	Neutral	18	6.4	6.4	95.8
	Disagree	8	2.8	2.8	98.6
	Strongly Disagree	4	1.4	1.4	100.0
	Total	283	100.0	100.0	

Question 2 We have tried too hard to copy Western bureaucracies without worrying about our own heritage

		Frequency	Percentage	Valid Percentage	Cumulative Percentage
Valid	Strongly Agree	58	20.5	20.5	20.5
	Agree	94	33.2	33.2	53.7
	Neutral	39	13.8	13.8	67.5
	Disagree	67	23.7	23.7	91.2
	Strongly Disagree	25	8.8	8.8	100.0
	Total	283	100.0	100.0	

Source: Devised by author

innovate. Around 55% of the respondents think that we have copied our bureaucracies from the West. This suggests that individuals predisposed against change can hardly be expected to innovate on its behalf; this is because traditional values are deeply embedded in the social system and could be difficult to shake. Overall, however, we can safely conclude that there is a large predisposition of the respondents who are willing to challenge social and traditional norms. This is an important finding that can be related to the "relative" social openness and the consociational system in Lebanon.

Reponses seem to reflect a low level of innovation in decision-making among employees. Around 67% said that they would refer back to their supervisors before making any decision; this is a high number. Moreover, there is a high level of conformity in the sense that around 95% of the respondents answered that following rules is the best option to get work done at the University, and that they would delay making a decision if they were uncertain of its outcomes. Around 84% of the respondents said that they would refer back to similar problems in the past. The level of conformity is high among employees; they would be classified as classic adaptors in decision-making.

Table 5   Creative Decision-Making

Question 1 It is best to consult with one's supervisor before making even small decisions

		Frequency	Percentage	Valid Percentage	Cumulative Percentage
Valid	Strongly Agree	58	20.5	20.5	20.5
	Agree	131	46.3	46.3	66.8
	Neutral	6	2.1	2.1	68.9
	Disagree	74	26.1	26.1	95.1
	Strongly Disagree	14	4.9	4.9	100.0
	Total	283	100.0	100.0	

Question 2 One should always follow the rules in order to get things done efficiently

		Frequency	Percentage	Valid Percentage	Cumulative Percentage
Valid	Strongly Agree	172	60.8	60.8	60.8
	Agree	99	35.0	35.0	95.8
	Neutral	5	1.8	1.8	97.5
	Disagree	7	2.5	2.5	100.0
	Total	283	100.0	100.0	

Question 3 It is better to delay taking a decision for further consideration than risk making a mistake

	Frequency	Percentage	Valid Percentage	Cumulative Percentage
Strongly Agree	140	49.5	49.5	49.5
Agree	128	45.2	45.2	94.7
Neutral	7	2.5	2.5	97.2
Disagree	7	2.5	2.5	99.6
Strongly Disagree	1	.4	.4	100.0
Total	283	100.0	100.0	

Question 4 In making a new decision, one should refer first to similar past problems

	Frequency	Percentage	Valid Percentage	Cumulative Percentage
Strongly Agree	95	33.6	33.6	33.6
Agree	141	49.8	49.8	83.4
Neutral	20	7.1	7.1	90.5
Disagree	25	8.8	8.8	99.3
Strongly Disagree	2	.7	.7	100.0
Total	283	100.0	100.0	

Source: Devised by author

The overall conclusion that can be extracted from the previous analysis is that the level of creativity among public employees is moderate. This is an important finding as around 40% of the respondents were willing to engage in creative ways to achieve the task rather than to stick to normal procedure. However, they scored low on risk taking and on acceptance of new ideas. This means that public employees are willing to create new ways of achieving the task, as long as it does not involve risky decisions. Results suggest that the respondents are not afraid to embark on social and traditional change, which leaves hope for future progress. However, the tools to implement the change remain intangible as half of the respondents have a predisposition against change. Finally, they do not engage in creative decision-making, even though they do not mind taking routine decisions. There seems to be an over emphasis on the delivery of work under the umbrella of rules and norms at the University. It seems that the respondents are willing to challenge social and traditional values, but not work related issues. The reason behind this could be the nature of the public service, which emphasises rules in getting the job done without any encouragement from the system as a whole to engage in innovation. Overall, we can safely conclude that the level of innovative behaviour among the employees is low.

EDUCATION AND INNOVATION

Having found that Lebanese civil servants are moderate to low on innovation levels, it is now possible to examine the hypothesis that innovation bears a direct relationship on education. If the hypothesis is to be sustained, one would expect the survey data to indicate that the most educated civil servants are the most innovative. Consequently one could take hope that the more debilitating aspects of rigid decision-making and challenging traditional values fade away with the recruitment of young and well-educated civil servants.

For this reason, it was hypothesised that the more educated the employees, the higher the level of innovation will be among the employees. For this reason, three types of tests were used. First, cross tabulations between the education level and the indicators of innovation were run; strong correlations between the different variables relied on the significant value of the chi-square cross tabulations. Second, an ANOVA test was carried out to determine the strength of the hypothesis. Third, Pearson correlations were run between the indicators of innovation and the education level.

The paper tests if there are significant differences in the innovation levels of employees compared to the different educational levels. This was done through the ANOVA test and running cross tabulations. Table 6 shows that there is a significant difference between the different educational levels (Baccalaureate, Bachelor, Masters) in the predisposition of innovation; the significance level between Masters' degree and Lebanese Baccalaureate is 0, and the significance level between Masters and Bachelor is 0.06.

In addition, Table 7 shows that there is a strong relationship between the various indicators of innovation and the level of education of public employees. The coefficient for measuring the strength of the relationship (chi-square) is available for all representative variables in Table 7. Dashes in blank cells indicate that the relationship between the various indicators was either non-significant or the relationship did not meet the criteria of robustness. The chi-square coefficient is significant for scores less than or equal to 0.05, as well as between creative decision-making and the level

Table 6   ANOVA Education* Innovation

| Dependent Variable: | Innovation | | | | | |

LSD

(I) Level of Education		Mean Difference (I-J)	Std. Error	Sig.	95% Confidence Interval	
					Lower Bound	Upper Bound
Lebanese Baccalaureate	Bachelor Degree	−1.5178−*	.73669	.040	−2.9680	−.0677
	Masters' Degree and Higher	−2.8913−*	.71862	.000	−4.3059	−1.4767
	Less than Baccll	−.3166	1.01774	.756	−2.3200	1.6868
Bachelor Degree	Lebanese Baccalaureate	1.5178*	.73669	.040	.0677	2.9680
	Masters' Degree and Higher	−1.3735	.73869	.064	−2.8276	.0806
	Less than Baccll	1.2012	1.03201	.245	−.8303	3.2327
Masters' Degree and Higher	Lebanese Baccalaureate	2.8913*	.71862	.000	1.4767	4.3059
	Bachelor Degree	1.3735	.73869	.064	−.0806	2.8276
	Less than Baccll	2.5747*	1.01919	.012	.5684	4.5810
Less than Baccll	Lebanese Baccalaureate	.3166	1.01774	.756	−1.6868	2.3200
	Bachelor Degree	−1.2012	1.03201	.245	−3.2327	.8303
	Masters' Degree and Higher	−2.5747−*	1.01919	.012	−4.5810	−.5684

Source: Devised by author

of education. In detail, there is a strong relationship between the level of education and the level of risk taking (chi-square: 0.01, 0) respectively. In addition, there is a strong relationship between the level of education and challenging traditional values (chi-square: 0.05). There is also a strong relationship between the level of education and following rules (chi-square: 0.03).

In addition, we can infer from Table 8 that there is a direct relationship between the level of education and the level of innovation as the significance level is +0.02, less than or equal to 0.05. A Pearson correlation, which indicates the strength and direction of two variables, is available for all representative variables in Table 8. A negative correlation means that the two variables are inversely related, whereas a positive correlation indicates that the two variables are directly related. Correlations are significant at the 0.02 level.

Table 7   Chi-Square of Education* Innovation

		Chi-Square
Innovation	Low Creativity	---
	Low supervisor decision	---
	Winning money for certain	0.01
	High job security	0
	Rate of change	---
	Separating State from Religion	---
	Copy Western Bureaucracies	0.05
	Low consultation with supervisor	---
	Follow rules	0.03
	Delay of decision	---
	Reference to similar past problems	---

Source: Devised by author

Table 8   Correlation between Education and Innovation

Correlations		Level of Education	Level_Innovation
Level of Education	Pearson Correlation	1	.133*
	Sig. (2-tailed)		0.025
	N	283	283
Level_Innovation	Pearson Correlation	.133*	1
	Sig. (2-tailed)	0.025	
	N	283	283

*Correlation is significant at the 0.05 level (2-tailed).

Source: Devised by author

In summary, the results were in the hypothesised direction. So, we can safely say that there is a direct relationship between education and the various innovation levels.

AGE AND INNOVATION

The literature on development and innovation assumes young people to be more receptive to new ideas than older people. We had anticipated that there would be an inverse relationship between innovation and age.

Table 9 shows that an inverse relationship exists between the age of employees and the creativity level (Pearson correlations: -0.2), challenging traditional values

(Pearson correlations: −0.13), and creative decision-making (Pearson correlations: −0.1, −0.2). Similarly, running an ANOVA test on the indicators of innovation and the age of employee reveals that there a significant difference exists between the level of innovation and the age of employees, as shown in Table 10. This is because the

Table 9   Correlations between Innovation and Age

	Age of Employee	
	Pearson Correlation	Sig. (2-tailed)
Creativity	−.259**	.000
Risk_taking		---
Acceptance_new_ideas		---
Challenge_tradiitonal_values		---
Challenge_traditional_values_1	−.131*	.028
Creative_DM_consult_sup	−.131*	.028
Crative_DM_follow_rules	−.283**	.000
Creative_DM_delay_decision		---
Creative_DM_similar_decisions		---
Risk_taking_level	−.148*	.017
Maintian_skills_security	−.163**	.006

Source: Devised by author

Table 10   ANOVA: Innovation and Age

(I) classes_age		Mean Difference (I-J)	Std. Error	Sig.	95% Confidence Interval	
					Lower Bound	Upper Bound
30−	31-40	.7810	.94674	.410	−1.0826	2.6447
	41-50	2.2748*	.87005	.009	.5621	3.9875
	51+	2.9896*	.84564	.000	1.3249	4.6542
31-40	30−	−.7810	.94674	.410	−2.6447	1.0826
	41-50	1.4938	.82867	.073	−.1375	3.1250
	51+	2.2085*	.80300	.006	.6278	3.7892
41-50	30−	−2.2748−*	.87005	.009	−3.9875	−.5621
	31-40	−1.4938	.82867	.073	−3.1250	.1375
	51+	.7148	.71097	.316	−.6848	2.1143
51+	30−	−2.9896−*	.84564	.000	−4.6542	−1.3249
	31-40	−2.2085−*	.80300	.006	−3.7892	−.6278
	41-50	−.7148	.71097	.316	−2.1143	.6848

Source: Devised by author

significance level is lower than 0.05, exhibiting a difference in the level of innovation between the different age ranges. Therefore, as age decreases the level of creativity increases, challenging traditional values increases, creative decision-making increases and the level of risk taking increases. So, we can infer that there is an inverse relationship between age and the various indicators of innovation, and hence the hypothesis is maintained.

DISCUSSION OF THE FINDINGS

In discussing the influence of education on behavioural capacity, several conclusions would appear to be in order. Educated employees seem more predisposed to taking risks, whether socially or at work, tend to challenge traditional values, and be more creative in decision-making. This proves that education helps to increase innovation in the Lebanese public service.

On another note, results reveal that there is a curvilinear relationship between the age of an employee and the level of creative decision-making, as shown in Figure 1. This means that creative decision-making does decrease as age increases, but only up to a certain point. It seems that creative decision-making is lowest among employees in their thirties, then it goes up again as employees get older. This would suggest that employees in their thirties are not motivated to indulge in creative decision-making. This finding is worth studying, especially given that this age faction scores high on creativity. Could employees within the age range 31–40 be suffocated by the authoritarianism of supervisors? And hence turn into rigid employees?

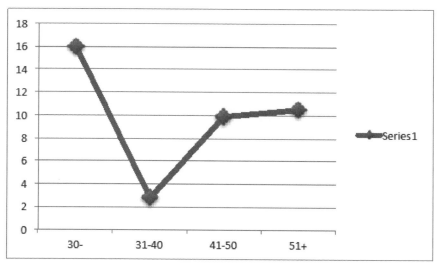

Figure 1 Creative Decision Making vs. Age
Source: Devised by author

CONCLUSIONS AND RECOMMENDATIONS

The analysis suggests the following:

1. Decision-making innovation was concentrated in young educated officials holding Masters' degree and higher.

2. The educational level influences the innovation levels by affecting the level of acceptance of new ideas and creative decision-making. Furthermore, the management must take into consideration employees in their thirties who seem to have problems with their entourage that is affecting their work.

3. A third fundamental conclusion of the article is that administrative enhancements can be introduced in relation to increasing the level of creative decision-making and the level of creativity among employees as this has a direct relationship with increasing performance.

4. A fourth conclusion to be drawn is that recruiting young and educated employees based on their competency levels may alleviate behavioural problems and may lead to improved performance. The data analysis shows that the innovation and creative levels of employees can be enhanced when recruiting young employees with the appropriate diplomas.

REFERENCES

Bobic, M., Davis, E. and Cunningham, R. (1999), The Kirton Adaption-Innovation Inventory: Validity Issues, Practical Questions, *Review of Public Personnel Administration*, Vol. 19, No. 2, pp. 18–31.

Daher, M. (2004), *Public Administration and Governance*. Unpublished papers.

Dumas, A. and Mintzberg, H. (1991), Managing the Form, Function, and Fit of Design, *Design Management Review*, Vol. 2, No. 3, pp. 26–31.

Eisenberger, R. and Byron, K. (2011), Rewards and Creativity. In: Runco, M.A. and Pritzker, S.R. (Eds): *Encyclopedia of Creativity, Second Edition*, Vol. 2, pp. 313–18, San Diego: Academic Press.

Guilford, J.P., Hendricks, M., Hoepfner, R. (1968), Solving social problems creatively, *The Journal of Creative Behavior*, Vol. 2, No. 3, pp. 155–64.

Kirton, M. (1980), Adaptors and Innovators in Organizations. *Human Relations*, Vol. 33, No. 4, pp. 213–24.

Larrick, R.P. (1993), Motivational Factors in Decision Theories: The Role of Self-Protection. *Psychological Reports*, Vol. 113, No. 3, pp. 440–50.

Maltzman, I. (1960), On the training of originality. *Psychological Review*, Vol. 67, No. 4, pp. 229–42.

Nagano, M.S., Stefanovitz, J.P. and Vick, T.E. (2014), Innovation management processes, their internal organizational elements and contextual factors: An investigation in Brazil. *Journal of Engineering and Technology Management*, Vol. 33, pp. 63–92.

Nakib, K. and Palmer, M. (1976), Traditionalism and Change among Lebanese Bureaucrats. *International Review of Administrative Sciences*, Vol. 42, No. 1, pp. 15–22.

Palmer, M. and Leila, A. (1988), *The Egyptian Bureaucracy*. Syracuse University Press. New York.

Saadeh, S.A. (1993), *The Social Structure of Lebanon: democracy or servitude?*. Beirut: Dar An-Nahar.

BIOGRAPHY

Hala Abou Arraj has been the Acting Registrar at the American University of Beirut since August 2017. She has worked in higher education and student services for 22 years. Hala Abou Arraj graduated with a PhD in Political Sciences from the Lebanese University in November 2017. She received her Master's degree and her Bachelor's degree from the American University of Beirut in 2000 and 1994 respectively. Her most recent contributions include a chapter in a book entitled: *The AACRAO International Guide: A Resource for International Education Professionals*, published in 2016 by the Library of Congress (ISBN:97815785811). In addition, she has served on many committees, including the Academic Progress and Graduation Committee of the American Association of Collegiate Registrars and Admissions Officers for two terms; and the Steering Committee of the SunGard (and later Ellucian) European User Group Conference (2011–2014).

ISLAMIC BANKING FINANCE TO SMALL ENTREPRENEURS: A CASE OF KENYA

(An Institutional Network Approach)

Mohammed Nurul Alam[*]

Faculty of BBA (Accounting)
Yorkville University, Canada
Email: mnfsin6@gmail.com/malam@yorkvilleu.ca

Nurulayn Binte Noor

Research Assistant and Student
Wilfrid Laurier University, Canada
nurulayn@hotmail.com

ABSTRACT

Purpose: The purpose of this paper is to delineate Islamic banking finance and its impact on SMEs (Small and Medium Enterprises) and micro entrepreneurs in a particular country context.

Design/methodology/approach: An Institutional Network theoretical frame of references is used to study this particular phenomenon. The research methodology applied in the study is of a *qualitative nature*. A multiple explanatory case study is adopted as a research strategy in order to focus on contemporary phenomenon within the real life context of SMEs and micro entrepreneurs.

Findings: Among others, the findings include the extent to which interest free financing by Islamic banks contributes to developing network relationships between the lenders and the borrowers and other related economic

[*]Corresponding Author

actors in a society. The findings also reveal the impact of societal sector institutions in accelerating the Islamic financing activities in a particular socio-cultural environment.

Research limitations/implications: The study mainly relates the Islamic banking finance to SMEs and micro entrepreneurs by the First Community Bank, the leading sharia-based bank in Kenya.

Practical implications: Since lending organisations under the Islamic Financing System (IFS) renders services to their clientele without interest, the lender-borrower relationships are featured by a close supervision of their borrowed funds. While lending funds to its customers, the Islamic banks invest funds under different investment modes of funding such as the *Mudaraba, Musharaka, Murabaha* and *Bai-Muajjal*.

Originality/value: The study is based on the socio-cultural context of Kenya where the paper premised on its theoretical perspective and 'Institutional-Network Approach' in the field of Islamic finance towards SMEs and micro entrepreneurs.

Keywords: SMEs; Micro Entrepreneurs; First Community Bank; Kenya; Institutions; Network Relationships; Lender-borrower relationships; Islamic Banking; *Mudaraba; Musharaka; Murabaha*

INTRODUCTION

The Republic of Kenya, a country with an area of 581,309 km^2 (224,445 sq. miles), and a population of approximately 45 million people, is East Africa's industrial nerve-centre. Most businesses are in private hands, with foreign investments supporting the agricultural and mining sectors. The SMEs and micro-entrepreneurs in Kenya contribute greatly towards enhancing economic growth by generating employment opportunities for poverty stricken people. It is revealed from the study that financing to SMEs and rural-based micro-entrepreneurs in many developing nations not only creates job facilities for the rural poor, but also plays a predominant role in enhancing well established network relationships between lenders and borrowers, as well as among various economic actors in a society (Alam 2002; 2008).

In Kenya, even though the SMEs and micro entrepreneurs contribute greatly to the country's economy, similar to other developing nations, these sectors of the economy face multidimensional problems. These problems ultimately affect their growth and profitability and, hence, diminish their ability to contribute effectively to sustainable development. As observed by Wanjohi and Mugure (2008) and Wanjohi (2009), lack of access to credit facilities is almost universally indicated as a key problem for SMEs and micro entrepreneurs. In some circumstances, even where credit is available, the entrepreneur may lack freedom of choice due to the lending conditions, possibly forcing the purchase of heavy, immovable equipment that can serve as collateral for the loan. In this regard, Kihimbo et al. (2012) in their study observed that less than half of SMEs consider formal financing as a source of capital for their operations; more than 90% of SMEs who sought formal financing succeeded. These results showed that formal financing was significant in keeping SMEs' businesses operational in localities such as the Kakamega Municipality.

An overlap between various sources was observed, indicating that multiple sources of capital are adopted by a variety of the SMEs; these include loans from micro-finance institutions and private sources. This bottleneck forces entrepreneurs to rely on self-financing or borrowing from friends or relatives. Lack of access to long-term credit for small enterprises forces them to rely on high cost short-term finance. Normally, SMEs and micro entrepreneurs in Kenya experience various other financial challenges such as the high cost of credit, high bank charges and fees. Taking advantage of such crucial situations, numerous moneylenders, using so-called Pyramid schemes, appeared, promising hope among the 'little investors', that they can make it to the financial freedom through soft borrowing.

Thus, financial constraint remains a major challenge facing SMEs in Kenya (Wanjohi and Mugure, 2008; Kimani and Kombo, 2010). In recent years an Islamic bank called The First Community Bank (FCB) started giving loans without interest to its clientele in different parts of the country. The main objective of this paper is to see how and to what extent the FCB, the first Islamic bank in Kenya, contributes to promoting small entrepreneurs by providing interest free loans in different sectors. The paper also aims to find how the Islamic banking principles work in a non-Islamic country. The study of Islamic finance to SMEs and micro-entrepreneurs is based on the socio-cultural context of Kenya.

LITERATURE REVIEW

SMEs and micro entrepreneurs play significant roles in eradicating the unemployment problem, which remains a serious impediment to a nation's economic growth. Although large-scale industries are involved in mass-production and invest large amounts of capital, these industries are mostly urban based. Consequently, large-scale industries fail to play a significant role in solving unemployment problems related to the rural population. This is exactly where SMEs and micro entrepreneurs succeed better (Anderson and Khambata, 1985; Macuja, 1981). In their studies, a number of researchers (Cosslett and Ashe, 1989; Little, 1988) have observed the issue as to how and to what extent MEs (Medium Enterprises) contribute towards the development of a nation's economy. It is shown in one of the reports published by the United Nations Development Program (UNDP, 1993, p. 41) that in the sub-Sahara region, the SMEs and micro entrepreneurs in the informal sector expanded by 6.7% a year between 1980 and 1989. In this regard, Cosslett and Ashe (1989) observe that:

"In rural areas, in addition to the legion of subsistence and small farmers, there is a growing percentage of individuals whose primary source of income is trading, cottage industries and a wide range of services, generally categorised as off-farm activities: the figure ranges from 19 to 23 per cent in countries like India, Sierra Leone and Colombia, from 28 to 38 per cent in Indonesia, Pakistan, Kenya and Philippines, and as high as 49 per cent in Malaysia" (Cosslett and Ashe, 1989, p. 17).

Due to various problems, such as the lack of sufficient funds caused by inadequate infrastructural and institutional arrangements and shortcomings in the area of marketing and distribution, the growth of SMEs and micro entrepreneurs in rural areas is less pronounced than could be expected. The slow growth of these sectors of the economy, in turn, results in the migration of manpower from rural to urban areas; this ultimately increases problems, such as overcrowding, increased competition for fewer jobs, etc., in the urban areas. Moreover, due to the limited job opportunities, such urbanisation additionally hampers the nation's economy (Myrdal, 1968, p. 527). Almost all previous studies carried out by various authors have analysed the problems of SMEs and micro entrepreneurs within various national contexts. However, the concept of interest free financing by Islamic banks is new in the financial market, and studies are required to see how and to what extent this special financing system contributes to the promotion of SMEs and micro entrepreneurs by eliminating various hindrances in different socio-cultural, environment and country context. Based on the above discussion, the main research questions posed are:

1. How and to what extent does First Security Bank (FSB), succeeded in implementing the *Shariah* based Islamic banking finance among different rural-based small entrepreneurs in Kenya?
2. How do different Islamic modes of financing contribute to the promotion of lender-borrower network relationships?
3. To what extent do societal sector institutions like the country culture, religion, family/clan, political systems, legal systems and government influence the Islamic banking activities?

THEORETICAL AND METHODICAL REVIEW

The concept of an *Institutional-Network* theoretical frame of reference (Alam, 2002) is used in this study; it was developed based on Whitley's (1992a) *Business System* institutional approach and Jansson's (2002) *Network Institutional Model*. The business systems approach is an institutional approach used by Whitley (1992b) to study business organisations, *inter alia* in Asian countries. In Whitley's (1992b) comparative study of business systems in East Asian countries (e.g. Chinese family business units

(CFB) in Taiwan and Hong Kong, Japanese Kaisha and Korean chaebol), the author tried to find how firms are constituted as relatively distinct economic actors in different market societies, and how they organise economic activities in the form of dominant hierarchy-market configurations. The comparative analysis of business systems, as Whitley (1992b) observed, is the study of these configurations. In this regard, the author argued that a key task concerning the comparative study of business systems is to analyse how distinctive patterns of economic organisations become established and effective in different societies, and how they change in relation to their institutional context. In his study, Whitley (1992a) also observed that these patterns concern the nature of economic activities that are coordinated through managerial hierarchies and how these hierarchies organise their cooperative and competitive relationships through markets.

To study the impact and influence of Islamic finance on SMEs and micro entrepreneurs, based on Whitley's business system (BS) model, the author (*ibid.*) developed the concept of four components of different SME and ME systems and financing systems. These components, for example, are the nature of an organisation, market organisation, employment systems, and authority and control systems. According to Whitley (1992b), a comparative analysis of the business system is the systematic study of these configurations and how they become established in markets. Like Whitley's (1992b) business systems, the Islamic financing system (IFS) is seen as a 'financing business system of its own, with a foundation based on religion, having its own rules governed by the Islamic laws' (Alam, 2002; 2009). These rules differ from those of other financial systems. Different financial systems, for example, market-based financing systems (MBFS) such as conventional banks, cooperative financing systems (CFS), and traditional money lending systems (TMLS), are viewed as particular arrangements of hierarchy-market relationships that become institutionalised and relatively successful in a particular context. A similar arrangement is also done to institutionalise different SMEs and micro entrepreneurs. Entrepreneurs of similar nature are thus, grouped in different SCI systems. Different financing organisations and small and cottage industries under different financing systems, as well as SCI Systems, are regarded as economic actors acting within these organisational fields.

Since one of the objectives of the research relates to finding how the interest-free micro-credit by Islamic banks contributes to the establishment of lender-borrower network relationships, apart from Whitley's (1992a, 1992b) institutional concept in the Institutional-Network theoretical framework, the author (*ibid.*) also used the network concepts of Jansson's (2002) networks institutions model, where the author integrated networks with institutions and viewed the network from an institutional perspective. According to Jansson (2002), institutions also concern different types of habitual or recognised behaviour, such as habits, rules, and procedures. This implies that institutions are characterised by a rule-like or governing nature, an ability to facilitate and constrain inter-human and inter-social relationships, and by predictive behaviour. Veblen (1919, p. 239) observed that institutions themselves are comprised of settled habits of thought common to the generality of men. In order to study the relationships between Multinational Corporations (MNCs) and their commercial partners, the author used a network approach and developed a theory to analyse such linkages. In order to study the network relationships between and within organisations belonging to the two focused institutions, for example, SMEs and Micro-Enterprise Systems (MEs) and Major Financing Systems (MFS) and their relationships with other economic actors in the organisational fields, the author used the concept of Jansson's (2002) and Jansson et al.'s (1995) trans-organisational network theory while developing my analytical framework.

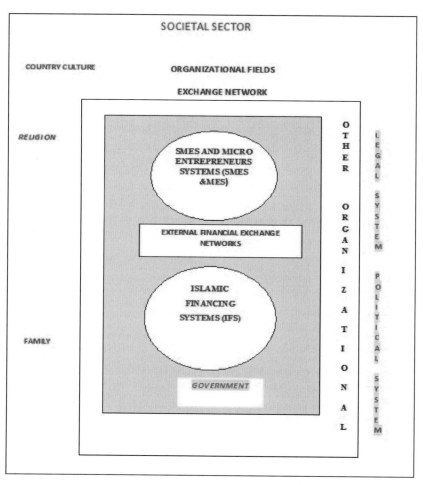

Figure 1   Institutional-Network Framework
Source: Adopted from Alam, 2002

Figure 1 consists of two major fields: the financial market and other organisational fields. Since the focus of the present study is concentrated towards the study of the financing of SMEs and micro-entrepreneurs by Islamic banks within the IFS system, and its relationships with different SMEs and micro-entrepreneur systems, this field is divided into two sub fields: the SMEs and MEs, and the IFS. Therefore, these issues are viewed under the organisational fields in the first rectangle. SMEs, MEs and IFS are viewed as two different institutions in the organisational fields. The second box or major field consists of different actors in the other organisation fields. These actors are, for example, customers, intermediaries (local leaders, seniors), competitors, and suppliers. They are related to the product and service exchange networks, influencing the major organisational field of the financial market in the first rectangle. The external financial exchange network between SMEs and MEs and IFS shown in the framework is meant for studying the exchange network relationships between and within different organisational units belonging to these two systems in the financing market of the major organisational fields. Since the exchange activities and network relationships of different actors in the organisation fields are influenced by societal sector institutions, such as country, culture, religion, family/clan, political system, legal system and government, these institutions are placed in the outer rectangle. These macro institutions surround the major institutions in the first and the second organisational fields. They are shown in the outer rectangle in order to study their influences on the exchange functions with regards to Islamic financing between SMEs, MEs and IFS, and other institutions within and between these organisational fields.

RESEARCH METHODOLOGY

The research methodology applied in this study is of a qualitative nature (Jick, 1979; Merriam, 1998; Sherman and Webb, 1988; Patton, 1985). A qualitative type of research is characterised by a collection of data directly from respondents in the field. This is because the entire research programme is based on facts acquired from the material world, that is, the practical field of study. The study of lender-borrower network relationships between rural-based MEs and Islamic banks was conducted through in-depth interviews with respondents under review.

Based on Merriam's (1998) Interview Structure Continuum idea, while interviewing respondents, highly structured, semi-structured and unstructured interviews were used to suit whatever situation arose. A case study (Yin, 1994) method was adopted as a research strategy in order to focus on contemporary phenomenon within the real-life context of different rural-based micro entrepreneurs under various ME systems, and their relationships with financing organisations within Islamic Financing Systems.

In order to collect required data, the author travelled to Nairobi in 2014 and 2017. In 2014 different senior officials of the First Community Bank (FCB) were interviewed;

this is the only Islamic Financing Bank in Kenya. In 2017, an observation was made and some community people and small entrepreneurs were interviewed in order to know their views and ideas on Islamic banking activities in Kenya.

While interviewing, the following structures were observed:

- face-to-face interviews with senior bank officials of the First Community Bank in Nairobi were conducted;
- questions were asked to respondents based on questionnaires;
- while conducting the interviews, different questions were asked regarding:

  - the nature of SMEs and micro entrepreneurs to whom loans are given;
  - the procedure for lending funds;
  - follow-up activities;
  - the Islamic Financing Mode the bank used while funding;
  - influence of a socio-cultural environment in implementing Islamic Financing where the majority are non-Muslims;
  - influence of religion, culture, legal systems, political systems and government in implementing *Sharia*-based financing;
  - responses of customers in this specific financing system;
  - bank-clientele relations;
  - loan recovery rate;

- a tape recorder was used to record respondent's answers;
- subsequent to the interview, the recorded tape was replayed and data recorded in detail for the purpose of analysis;
- in order to interview bank officials, the bank was visited a few times within the timeframe of two weeks; each interview lasted 2−3 hours. Data were also collected from other sources such as the bank's Annual Report, etc.

THE BASIC CONCEPT OF THE ISLAMIC BANKING SYSTEM

The Islamic bank operates its financial activities without charging interest on loans. Regarding interest in Islamic economics, Ahmad (1994) argued that the elimination of interest does not mean zero-return on capital; rather Islam forbids a fixed predetermined return for a certain factor of production, i.e. one party having assured return and the whole risk of an entrepreneurship to be shared by others (Ahmad, 1994; Chapra, 1992). The authors also observed that it is the capital entrepreneurship that shares both the real contribution and the real profitability. The Islamic bank follows the principle of *equity-based investment*. The Islamic banking system also proposes that resources can be contracted on the basis of venture capital and risk sharing deals.

The introduction of Islamic banking in the modern world is based on the principles of Islamic economics. Molla et al. (1988) and Chapra (1992, 1985) observe that the aim of Islamic economics is not only the elimination of interest-based transactions and the introduction of the *zakat* (contribution to poor) system, but also the establishment of a just and balanced social order free from all kinds of exploitation. The Islamic bank plays a vital role in achieving this balanced social order and establishing ideal Islamic societies in Muslim countries. An Islamic bank may be defined as a financial intermediary whose objectives and operations, as well as principles and practices, must conform to the principles of Islamic Law (*Sharia*). Consequently, it is conditioned to operate all its activities without interest (Alam, 2011). In many ways, Islamic banks are similar to other privately owned formal financial intermediaries. The main difference is that an Islamic bank neither accepts deposits nor invests funds to its customers on interest. Instead, the bank shares the profit or loss (Nienhaus, 1983, 1988, 1993).

The Islamic Financing System (IFS) includes different financing organisations that are guided by *sharia* (Islamic law) based financing principles. These organisations use different financing techniques and lending procedures from those in other financing systems. The IFS is a mix of market-based and non-market-based financing systems. Although many exchange functions in organisations within the IFS are similar to those of western inspired commercial banks, they are also based on non-market rules and regulations, which are purely based on religious ethics. The organisations in the IFS function beyond the market-based economy, since the exchange relationships of this system are mainly ethics-based, originating from religious beliefs, trust and faith (Alam, 2002). There are several Islamic financing modes used by banks while lending funds to their customers. These are for example, *Mudaraba* (Capital Financing), *Musharaka* (Partnership Financing), *Murabaha* (Cost-Plus Profit Based Financing) and *Bai-Muajjal* (Cost Plus Sale Under Deferred Payment). The bank mostly uses *Musharaka*, *Murabaha* and *Bai-Muajjal* modes of financing while lending funds to small entrepreneurs.

THE FIRST COMMUNITY BANK IN KENYA (FCB): AN EMPIRICAL REVIEW

This section of the article includes an empirical review regarding the First Security Bank and its SMEs and micro finance activities. The qualitative data were collected through direct interviews with senior officials of the bank in Nairobi.

A BRIEF BANK HISTORY

In recent years, Kenya has experienced the presence of interest-free financing in different economic sectors introduced by the country's pioneer Islamic bank, known as the First Community Bank (FCB). This bank is the first operating a *Sharia* compliant banking institution.

First Community Bank was established in 2007 operating according to *Sharia* law by private investors in Kuwait, Kenya and Tanzania. The bank received a Kenyan commercial banking license the same year, and started operations in June 2008. The FCB is the first Kenya-based bank to operate according to the laws of *Sharia*. Since the founding of First Community Bank, another *Sharia* bank, the Gulf African Bank, has also received a commercial license from the Central Bank of Kenya. It is the first bank approved by the Central Bank of Kenya (CBK) under Cap 488 of the Banking Act to operate as a full-fledged *Sharia* Compliant banking institution. The bank received its formal approval from the Central Bank of Kenya (CBK) on 29 May 2007, thereby opening the door for *Sharia* Compliant banking, not only in Kenya but also in the entire East and Central African region.

The bank has a dedicated team of employees who are well trained to deliver the highest levels of service to its clientele. As a committed Kenyan Bank, FCB's motive is to take its alternative form of banking to as many places as possible within the country. As a pioneer *Sharia* compliant banking institution, FCB, in addition to its core banking business, is also in the final stages of bringing a number of other innovative *Sharia* compliant products such as Islamic Insurance (Takaful), Islamic Bonds (Sukuk), Sharia Compliant Mutual Funds and shares trading to Kenya. All FCB products and services are offered on a fully *Sharia* compliant basis as approved by the *Sharia* Advisory Board, which is comprised of prominent Islamic scholars both from inside and outside Kenya. First Community Bank has been selected as one of the four banks in the country to work with the Youth Enterprise Development Fund. The FCB aims at succeeding as an institution and enlist the trust of people about the viability of Islamic finance as an alternative financing system.

Driven by ethics, the FCB is a bank:

- that provides *Sharia* compliant financial services and solutions to meet the needs of its clientele;
- progressive for all, irrespective of their religion, race, gender or creed;
- with a focus aspiring to the highest standard of business ethics, good governance, financial stability and regulatory compliance;
- where clients are regarded as partners in business;
- that stands for growth and prosperity of its partners;
- with an ambition to achieve the highest possible level of contribution to the socio-economic development of Kenya and East Africa;
- with big ideas but small enough to care;
- promoted, managed and staffed by Kenyans with diverse experience and expertise to offer world class financial solutions to all its stakeholders.

Vision Mission and the Core Value of the FCB

The fundamental vision of the FCB is to be the preferred *Sharia* compliant financial service partner in all places the bank chooses to operate. While the mission of the bank is to operate as a responsible corporate citizen, foster growth for bank customers, employees, shareholders and the community through the provision of innovative *Sharia* compliant financial solutions. The core values of the bank are acronymic in the word FIRST, which also means a journey to a new frontier of financial services and solutions. The word *Fairness* indicates that bank will work with its stakeholders in a fair and honest manner. It will create partnerships that lead to win-win situations with all those who transact with it. *Innovation* stands for embracing changes, flexibility and continuously adapting to the rapidly evolving world. The bank strives to continuously perpetuate excellence and provide innovative *Sharia* compliant banking solutions. In response to the dynamic needs of its clientele, the bank will look for creative, new and better ways to provide its expertise in all dimensions of business. *Responsibility* denotes that the bank will conduct its business with the highest standards of ethics, adherence to the law, doing what is right, and exercising the highest level of responsibility in managing the financial affairs of all its stakeholders. *Sharia Compliance* is the essence of the FCB's existence, and remains a commitment beyond banking for the bank. The bank is extremely vigilant in this regard. *Teamwork* denotes that the banks are committed to supporting each other, taking collective ownership and responsibility for all the banks and winning together as team (Corporate Profile, FCB).

Products of the FCB

The First Community Bank uses different financing techniques based on Islamic *Sharia* while accepting deposits and investing funds. These financing modes were explained by senior officials during interviews, as explained below.

Different Deposit Accounts Maintained by FCB

The First Community Bank maintains the following deposit accounts while accepting deposits from clients.

- Current Account;
- Transactional Accounts;
- Savings Account; and
- Fixed Maturity Accounts.

Current Account or Demand Deposit Accounts

The FCB accepts deposits from customers on current accounts in the same way as conventional banks. This account is also known as the Demand Deposit Account as the deposited amount is payable to customers on demand without any notice. As banks use current account deposits at their own risk, the depositors of this type of account are not entitled to any share in the profit earned by the bank. The bank's current account services enable customers to make the most of daily banking needs without compromising any benefits. All of the bank's current accounts are based on the Islamic contract of *Qard Hasan* (free loan) in which the depositor grants the bank permission to utilise the deposited funds for *Sharia* compliant activities, while the bank in return guarantees the value of the deposit in full demand.

Transactional Accounts

These are tailored savings accounts with the flexibility of current accounts.

Savings Accounts

The FCB accepts saving deposits from customers under *Al-Wadia* and *Al-Mudaraba Sharia* principles. The word *Al-Wadia* means Trusteeship. In this case, banks act as trustees for its customers. In savings accounts under the *Al-Wadia* principle, the bank is given authorisation by depositors to use the funds at the bank's own risk. In this mode of deposit, the bank allocates the funds received from customers to a deposit pool, which is used to invest in *Sharia* compliant trade and business transactions. Profits generated from the funds are shared with clients accordingly.

Different Investment Modes Used by the First Community Bank

Personal Finance

Under personal finance, individual clients are able to purchase goods and household items required by them, as well as pay for services such as education, medical, *Hajj*, weddings and holidays in a *Sharia* compliant manner. The bank uses the *Murabaha* mode of *Sharia* compliant contract while lending funds under personal financing.

Business Corporate Finance

In business corporate finance, the FCB teams of business bankers assist corporate clients in financial structuring of a wide range of solutions such as working capital finance, assets finance, leasing, project and construction finance, forward contract finance and equity finance. Under business corporate finance, the bank uses *Investment Musharaka* and *Mudaraba* modes of the *Sharia* compliant contract.

Equity Finance

Under equity financing, the bank supports professionals such as medical doctors, lawyers, engineers and other entrepreneurs to establish as well as grow their business. This is done through the use of *Musharak* and *Mudaraba Sharia* compliant instruments.

Trade Services

The trade services of the FCB relates to all forms of local and international trade. These services include opening and managing letters of credit – transferable, revolving standby – and is a core function of the bank's trade finance department, while letters of guarantee are in operation to cover key business areas such as bid bonds, performance bonds, advance payment bonds and custom bonds. The bank uses the Service *Ijara* mode of *Sharia* complaint contract for the different trade services.

Different SMEs Funded by the FCB

As reported by the respondent, among SMEs about 60% of loans are given to the manufacturing sector, 30% to the trading sector and 20% to the service industry sector.

The bank uses different modes of financing such as *Murabaha*, Investment *Musharaka*, and *Bai-Muajjal* modes of financing, while lending funds to different SMEs and micro entrepreneurs. The bank uses the *Bai-Muajjal* (Cost plus Profit) mode of financing while lending funds to the agricultural sector. For example, once a customer applies for a loan to buy seeds, the bank purchases the seeds on the customer's behalf and then resells the same to the customer together with profit. In any newly established business venture, the bank invests funds under Investment *Musharaka* mode of financing. The capital is equally contributed by the bank and the customer, who share profits or losses equally. As with new ventures, the bank uses Investment *Musharaka* in the manufacturing sector. The bank uses both *Musharaka* and *Murabaha* modes of financing in both service and trading sectors. It is reported by the respondents that the bank uses a major portion of their funds in the *Musharaka* mode of financing.

It is also reported that the bank did not succeed in investing funds under the *Mudaraba* (Capital Financing), mode of financing. At the initial stage, the bank started giving loans for certain projects under this mode but ended up with negative results. In such an investing mode, the financing authority is the bank while the clients give their expertise and time, and both parties share profits or losses in an agreed proportion. It is reported that the success of such types of investment are based on the honesty and integrity of the customers. Unfortunately, the bank failed to find dedicated and honest customers, and they were compelled to stop funds in this specific mode.

SMEs and Micro-financing by the FCB

The FCB introduced its funding to different SMEs and micro entrepreneurs in different parts of the country. The majority of the bank's financing consists of SME projects and micro enterprises. The bank has 17 branches in different parts of the country and, until 2012, records showed that the bank had invested more than 5,000 million Ksh., in different SMEs and micro entrepreneurs.

SMEs and Micro Entrepreneurs as Defined by the FCB

The bank defines SMEs and micro entrepreneurs from the perspective of loans given to them. SMEs are those firms where loans range from US$15,000 to US$20,000. On the other hand, micro entrepreneurs are those businesses that are offered a loan of a maximum of US$1,000.

Procedures Followed by FCB While Giving Loans

Interested borrowers from FCB normally contact their local branch where the preliminary activities of loans initiate. The customers are required to submit their project proposal for which they are eager to borrow funds. The bank officer is responsible for project evaluation, undertaking a feasibility study of the proposal, and seeing that *Sharia* law allows the project. There are trained personnel in the bank having knowledge in different kinds of business who normally evaluate and study a particular project proposal submitted by the customer. Once the project is found appropriate, the bank asks the client for the necessary documents relating to the business. In some cases, to have proper evaluation the bank officials pay visits to the customers' business premises. The finance department examines the total financial needs. Prior to giving loans, the bank investigates the following matters about a prospective customer:

- prospect of the proposed business in the society;
- prior business experiences of the customer, if any;
- customer's reputation in the society;
- records of any loan default case.

Loan Approval Certificate from Sharia Board

Once the project has been studied, the preliminary report prepared and the required documents are obtained from the client, the project report, together with the financial plan, is passed to the *Sharia* board; the *Sharia* board consists of five members. As a rule of the bank, the *Sharia* board must approve each project loan. The board examines the project and related documents and finally approves the project: they are the loan approving authority for a particular project. The board is also responsible for ensuring that the project activities are in compliance with the Islamic *Sharia*. Once the *Sharia* board certifies the project and approves the loan, the bank starts processing loan agreements with the customer. The entire process of approving loans is done within a short span of time in order to avoid delays in sanctioning the loan.

Need for a Guarantor

Once the loan for a particular project is approved, the customer is required to produce a letter from an influential local leader who acts as a guarantor for the client.

The branch manager normally helps a customer select a local influential person from the locality. The guarantor's certificate must contain that he personally knows the customer and the bank may continue financial deals without any difficulties. The guarantor thus acts as a security for the bank on behalf of the customer. In addition, the bank asks for documents of landed property from the customers as a security in order to lend funds.

Direct Contact by Customer

The customer must contact the bank officials directly for to obtain a loan: the bank does not allow any middlemen to work on the customers' behalf. In order to encourage customers' direct contact, every branch is equipped with local staff that can communicate easily and explain the basics of Islamic Financing Systems, and different financing modes of funding the bank use while lending funds for a particular project to the clients.

Branch Managers' are Authorised to Pay Loans

Once the *Sharia* board approves the loan for a particular project, the file is sent directly to the branch manager. The branch manager does not need to wait for the approval from the head office to release the funds. Every branch manager is authorised to release funds up to a certain limit.

Financing to Micro Entrepreneurs

As reported by the senior officials of the FCB, the bank invested very few funds towards micro-entrepreneurs. While lending funds to micro entrepreneurs, the bank gives loans to both at the group and the individual level. In a group loan, the group associates are held responsible for the default of the others in the group. The bank gives loans to micro entrepreneurs on an Investment *Musharaka* or a partnership basis. The profits or losses of the business are shared according to the agreed proportions.

Religious Beliefs of the Customers of FCB

While asked questions about the religious beliefs of customers to whom loans are given, the respondent of the FCB reported as:

> An Islamic bank does not require the customer to be a Muslim. Even though the fundamental idea of lending funds without interest is based on Islamic *Sharia*, it does not mean that a borrower of funds from the bank must be a Muslim. We lend funds to every customer regardless of their religion, cast or creed. In Kenya, the majority of people are non-Muslims. Our customers

belong to different religious practices. Surprisingly, more than 60% of customers of our bank are non-Muslims. In many branches among all customers, only a few are Muslim. We found that non-Muslims are doing very well and they are honest in financial dealings. In comparison to Muslim customers, it is noted that the FCB is having more non-Muslim investors. Muslim customers show less interest in investing funds to the bank or borrowing from the bank.

Customers' Visit to the Bank

Since the FCB does not allow any middlemen to negotiate between the borrower and the lender, customers are encouraged to contact bank officials directly. The bank officers help customers to accomplish the necessary formalities from beginning to end; from the opening of an account to the approval of loans. In some cases the bank helps prospective customers to prepare their project proposals. In many cases, bank officials visit customers' premises in order to investigate and evaluate their position. Once the officer thinks it is appropriate, he/she recommends for the consideration of sanctioning loans. The bank officials in charge of certain projects continue their visit to customers after the loan is sanctioned. The bank follows up with the clients business activities in order to be sure that the customer is using the borrowed funds appropriately.

Co-operation from the Government

As mentioned earlier, the FCB is the first bank approved by the Central Bank of Kenya (CBK) under Cap 488 of the Banking Act to operate as a full-fledged *Sharia* compliant banking institution. It is said by a respondent that the FCB was one of the first *Sharia* based banks receiving all sorts of cooperation from the government. There are no complications from any legal aspects, or from any other government mechanism. The government encourages the FCB operations and it is recognised by the Central Bank.

The Cultural Values of Customers

Kenyan society is oriented by different cultures and traditions. It brings harmony among people of same tribe. The bank finds it secure to lend funds where people have respect for their own culture.

Family/Clan in Manufacturing Concerns

It has been reported that customers who borrowed funds for manufacturing concerns work together alongside family members. As the tradition of the different tribes, the elders of the house are respected as the chief of the house: all family members are loyal to the head. While lending funds, all members of the family share the responsibilities and work together for the project.

Challenges of the FCB

It is reported by the senior officials that the First Community Bank, as the first Islamic bank in the country, is facing many challenges. The fundamental problem is the awareness of the bank among the general mass population. Local Muslims think of the bank as one of the charitable institutions as giving loans on *Qarze Hasan* (a voluntary loan repayable on condition). Non-Muslims in general, assume that it is a bank for Muslims only. In order to promote public awareness, the bank started the propagation of its different financing activities through advertisement on television, radio programmes, neon signs, etc. In addition, the bank is working together with local traditional banks to render services to their customers. The FCB maintains a window in many local commercial banks. Clients of the FCB in rural Kenya, where no FCB branch exists, may carry on financial transactions in the window branch. The FCB gives commission to the traditional banks for maintaining window branches and rendering services to their customers. The bank is experiencing satisfactory progress in their propagation, and clients are increasing gradually.

Recovery of Loans from Customers

It is reported by the respondents that the recovery rate of the loans is satisfactory: there are very few default cases. In any default case, the bank studies the situation of the client's business and, if needed, refinances the client to overcome the crisis. Customers are encouraged to discuss their grievances directly with the concerned officers. Once the officer who provides the loan finds the default case to be genuine, the client is given further assistance.

RESEARCH FINDINGS

It is revealed from the study that the FCB gave almost 60% of its loans to the manufacturing sector, and uses Investment *Musharaka* (Investment Partnership) as a mode of *Sharia* based financing. This specific financing mode helps the bank ensure that the borrowed funds are used by the customer solely for the purpose for which they are borrowed. Using this specific financing system, FCB makes sure that the clients make proper use of their borrowed funds. It is also learned from the study that the bank does not give the *Murabaha* (Cost Plus Profit) mode of finance to customers who stay far from the bank. This is due to the fact that the bank may not have good control over the customers' activities and the realisation of loans may be difficult. *Sharia* based financing is also regarded as a supervisory loan. For that reason, and before lending funds, the bank ensures that they may supervise customers' activities and realise their expected returns from the investment. It is also known from the study that the *Mudaraba* (Capital Financing) mode of financing, being one of the most important

Sharia based lending modes of the FCB, did not work well in the Kenyan money market. This was due to the fact that, under this mode of financing, the bank provides the funds for the business and the borrowers give their time and expertise: they share profits at an agreed proportion. However, if any loss occurs, the bank bears the entire burden of losses. For that reason, the FCB finds that this lending mode is one of the riskiest modes of finance. It needs an honest and sincere partnership, which the FCB has difficulty in finding.

Network Relationships between the Bank and Customers

It is noted from the study that once various formalities regarding lending funds to a customer end, the FCB enters into a partnership agreement with the customer. As the loan is given on a participating mode of financing, the bank agrees with customers about the percentage of profit or loss to be shared with them. Thus, the bank establishes direct contact with customers. In order to supervise SMEs, senior staff responsible for particular projects pay regular visits to the customers' business premises. The manager observes the customer's progress of work and gives necessary advice when needed. The study also reveals that customers are encouraged to directly contact the senior bank officials and branch manager to discuss different issues of their business. This in turn enhances the bank-customer relationships and strengthens the *personal network* between the bank and the clients.

Easy Access of Customers to the Bank

The bank staff of the FCB encourage their clients and welcome them to discuss various issues of their business concerns. In every branch of the FCB there are separate sections within the bank premises where bank staff voluntarily assist their customers in observing various formalities to obtain loans. In addition, the bank staff brief every customer about the various modes of Islamic financing. They also explain to them how the Islamic financing system works alongside a traditional banking system. Since Islamic banking is a new concept in Kenyan society, they find it difficult to differentiate between traditional bank funding and Islamic bank funding. The FCB officials encourage customers to come to the bank premises and discuss various issues about the bank functions. There is no need to observe any formalities to meet a senior official of the bank. This welcoming mentality and easy access of customers to the bank is an added advantage for the FCB to attract customers from different sectors of the economy.

A Unique Administration of Borrowed Funds

For the loan giving procedures, it may also be noted that the loan administration tendency of the FCB is unique. The bank staff are assigned the duty of contacting customers and observing their activities. The staff have this responsibility in order to be sure that they are using their borrowed funds appropriately and are willing to repay the loan on time.

Guarantor Acting as Security to Borrow Funds

The FCB normally does not impose any burden of securities on its customers. Due to the partnership mode of financing, a close supervision of loans is given more importance than the collateral for loans. As a requirement, every customer must provide the bank with a certificate from a local reputed person who agrees to act as a guarantor for the customer in case of any default.

Serving the Clients' Interest

The study reveals that officials of the FCB are very much concerned about the welfare of customers and their interests. The Public Relations Department (PRD) is responsible for dealing with customers' affairs. The bank management is very concerned with the fact that every individual customer receives proper attention from the officers dealing with them. In order to develop public relations, banks give training to their staff.

No Interference from Middlemen

As FCB officials assist clients at various levels, they do not need any assistance from middlemen. Thus, direct assistance to customers by the FCB staff reduces the possibilities of interference from any middleman. The FCB staff assists a customer to observe different formalities in obtaining loans. It has been mentioned earlier that bank officials responsible for a particular project make frequent visits to the customer's business site. The officer investigates progress of the clients' business and helps to maintain their accounts. Due to the direct bank-customer relationships, the interference of the middlemen is completely absent, and thus borrowers are able to save a lion's share of their borrowed funds.

Priority of Rural Female Micro Entrepreneurs

It is reported by bank officials that the FCB gives micro credit to the rural-based poor women in the society. Although the percentage of investment in this sector is negligible, the FCB has special arrangements in the bank for women customers. The bank officer reported that female micro entrepreneurs are found to be more organised and active than male customers. Most of the projects that are run by female customers are found to be successful. They arrange their work jointly with other members of the group. They are found most sincere and utilise their time and money in a proper way. The bank has increased various facilities for women, and the manager of the bank tries to ensure that there is no gender inequality present in relation to the bank officer.

Group-wise Loan makes Micro Entrepreneurs Well Organised

It is known from the bank officials that most of the micro entrepreneur clients of the FCB are not well educated and consist of rural poor individuals. They need guidance to utilise the little savings that they have in a productive way. The micro-credit policy of the FCB is not only to educate them regarding interest free loans, but also to organise their activities by close supervision so that they might contribute to the society. In addition, the entire lending activities of the banks are organised in such a way that borrowers benefit from the beginning to the final stage of their projects.

Credit In-Kind Rather than Cash

It has been mentioned in an earlier section that the FCB does not extend credit to their clients belonging to agriculture in cash but paid in merchandise of a kind. Since the *Murabaha* mode does not allow customers to borrow funds in cash, they are bound to present pro-forma invoices for seeds and other agricultural products that they intend to buy. The bank purchases these their behalf and resells the merchandise to the customer at a profit. The application of the "in-kind" (for example: loan in material rather than cash) lending principle shows that the loan's recovery rate of the FCB from agricultural loans is higher than other financing organisations. It makes proper use of borrowed funds.

Establishment of a Strong Lender-Borrowers Network Relationship

It is observed from the study that the long-term lending policy of the organisations in the Islamic financing system increases the interdependency between exchange partners. This results in the deepening of lender-borrower relationships, and helps exchange partners to get to know each other better. A continuous and long-term exchange relationship contributes in the development of trustful financial ties between the lenders and borrowers. When the long-term lending policy increases interdependency, the commitment to exchange partners also increases.

Influence of Societal Sector Institutions

It has been mentioned in earlier sections that different societal sector institutions always influence the lending and borrowing activities of financial organisations. These institutions comprise of country culture, political systems or the government, religious beliefs and habits, etc. Influences of these institutions on financial activities differ from country to country (Alam, 2002). In this section, a brief description is given as to how the FCB financing is influenced by different societal sector institutions.

Political Systems and the Government

The government supports the FCB's financing activities. The Central Bank of Kenya has received approval for the operation of the FCB as a full-fledged *Sharia* Compliant banking institution under Cap 488 of the Banking Act. This was a welcoming gesture to the introduction of the country's first Islamic bank. As informed by the respondent, the bank does not face any conflict from the government. The only problem the bank faces are the country's political unrest and unstable political systems. Many of their clients in certain areas sometimes suffer due to tribal disturbances and political unrest in the country. This hampers the investment process and, in many cases, customers suffer losses. Being a *Sharia* based banking institution the bank has to bear losses in such situations. Political unrest and uncertainties have grown in an alarming way in recent years due to the conflicts with the neighbouring country of Somalia.

Country Culture and Norms and Habits

Kenya is a country that has many tribes and a multicultural presence: there are more than 40 ethnic groups in the country. The largest of these is the Kikuyu, representing 22% of the population, 14% are Luhya, 13% are Luo, 12% are Kalenjin, 11% are Kamba, 6% are Kisii, and 6% are Meru. Others comprise approximately 15% of the population, including the Somalis and the Turkana in the north and the Kalenjin in the Great Rift Valley. These ethnic categories are further broken down into subgroups. Of the total population, 1% is non-African, mostly of Indian and European descent.

The idea of Islamic banking is a new innovation in the country's money market. People in different tribes are not aware of the financing systems that are followed by Islamic banks. Because of this, the bank faces problems in implementing *Sharia* based investments. However, the bank has taken the initiative to educate people and promote Islamic banking activities in both urban and rural areas. It has been reported by an FCB respondent that the concept of Islamic banking is gradually being understood by the general masses. At the initial stage, the bank found it difficult to divert customers from their cultural beliefs and norms, which are not beneficial in any way and rather consume time, money and energy. It was also noted that the customs of people, such as food, clothing, accommodation, etc., influences the activities of both lenders and borrowers. Due to the changes in habit of people in different seasons, the demand for certain SME products increases, and MEs find these projects profitable.

Religious Faith and Beliefs

Kenya's most recent religious compositions as shown by the *Kenya Information Guide* are 45% Christian-Protestant, 33% Roman Catholic, 10% Muslim, 10% indigenous religions, and 2% others. It is evident from the study that the religions or religious faiths do not have any negative impact on Islamic financing. As informed by the FCB's officer, the majority of the customers are non-Muslim. The people in general are very simple and hard working. They are concerned about an honest lender who may save them from the burden of local money lenders who take a high rate of interest for their borrowed funds. The FCB not only finances but also acts as a guide to the clients. This attitude of the bank is highly appreciated by customers in different localities. Since the FCB's financing activities have nothing to do with people's religious faith, the main aim is to assist customers in their business activities. Consequently, the FCB has attained its reputation in the Kenyan money market. The majority of the Kenyan population being non-Muslim, there are no conflicts in carrying on their banking activities from the perspective of Islamic *Sharia*.

Progress in Financing Activities

The FCB has shown good progress with regards to the bank's deposit, investment and profit margins. A brief description of the bank progress is given below in Table 1.

Table 1   Total Deposit from Customers

Year	Customer Deposit
	Ksh. Million
2008	2090
2009	3642
2010	5611
2011	7812
2012	8833

Source: Corporate profile FCB www.firstcommunitybank.co.ke

It is apparent from the above table that, at the beginning, the bank showed an increase of its deposit of Ksh. 1,552 million in 2009 compared to 2008, which is an almost 74% increase. This figure doubled in 2010. The table shows a gradual increase in deposits each year. Compared to 2008, the total deposits in 2012 increased by Ksh. 6,743 million, which is more than 300%, a significant success in customer deposits. These figures are illustrated in the graph below.

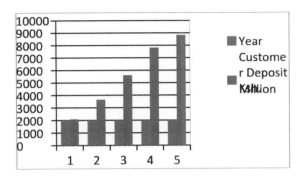

Figure 2   Total Deposits from Customers

Source: Corporate profile FCB www.firstcommunitybank.co.ke

From Figure 2 it is noted that the deposit curve, even though showing an upward tendency in years 4 and 5, it is not as high as years 1 to 3.

Table 2   Total Investment of the Bank

Year	Investment
	Ksh. Million
2008	868
2009	2,290
2010	2,984
2011	5,452
2012	5,471

Source: Corporate profile FCB www.firstcommunitybank.co.ke

Table 2 shows that the bank succeeded in increasing its investment from Ksh. 1,422 million from 2008 to 2009, which shows an approximate increase of 164% in a year. The increase in investment from year 1 to year 5 as shown by the above table is almost Ksh. 4,603 million. Being a newly established bank, the increase in investment may be labelled a significant one. The trend in the increase of the investment position of the FCB is illustrated in the following graph.

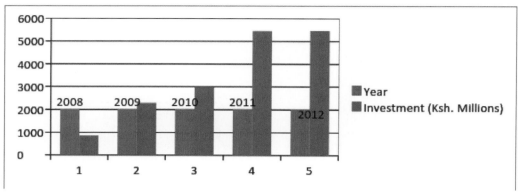

Figure 3   Investment Trend of FCB
Source: Corporate profile FCB www.firstcommunitybank.co.ke

Figure 3 shows the trend of a slow increase in investment from year 2 to year 3, which is only 30%. This is worse between year 4 and year 5, where the increase is only 0.35%: this is a very negligible increase in investment. The graph shows that, although in total there is an increase in investment, there is a slow year-wise growth.

Table 3	Profit after Tax
Year	Profit after tax
	(Ksh. Thousands)
2008	−307,202
2009	−112,429
2010	−97,506
2011	241,305
2012	271,403

Source: Corporate profile FCB www.firstcommunitybank.co.ke

It is observed from Table 3 that the company could not earn any profit in the first three years; however, there was a gradual decrease in the loss figure in every year. Compared to the losses in 2008, the losses in 2010 decreased by Ksh. 209,696 thousand, which is almost a 68% decrease. However, the bank regained its position in year 2011 and showed an increase in its profit position in the year 2012. The profit after tax is shown by the following graph:

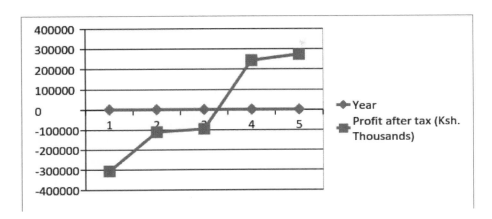

Figure 4   Profit after Tax

Source: Corporate profile FCB www.firstcommunitybank.co.ke

Figure 4 shows that there is a big jump in the profit and loss trend from year 3 to year 4. In year 4 the bank earned profits of over Ksh. 240,000. However, the growth trend did not progress much from year 4 to year 5, which shows only a 12% increase in profits.

CONCLUSIONS

Based on the detailed discussions above, it may be concluded that being a newly established Islamic Bank, the FCB is doing well in Kenya's money market of Kenya. Since the bank maintains a close contact with customers and supervises the borrowed funds, the entire financing activities are characterised by unique lender-borrower relationships. It may also be concluded from the study that the general masses accepted the concept of the FCB as a financing institution and nothing directly related to the religion of Islam. This in turn facilitated the bank to work more effectively in the Kenyan society where the majority of people are non-Muslims. Since the bank not only shares profits or losses with their customers, but also takes part in the management and the supervision of the activities of borrowers, it has created a positive impact on banking functions.

It may also be concluded that in certain cases such as the agricultural sector, the FCB gives loans on a *Murabaha* mode of financing, where credits are given in-kind rather than cash. This system assures the bank about the proper utilisation of borrowed funds. With the intention of expanding its investing activities, the FCB takes interest in the future to invest a good portion of their savings in different sectors of Kenya's economy. In this case it will not only eliminate poverty but also be successful in establishing a just and balanced social order, free from all kinds of exploitations in the society.

It is apparent from the study that the FCB has shown remarkable progress in its banking activities such as accepting deposits and investing funds since its inception. It is also noted from the study that the FCB was able to reach many of its customers who are mainly non-Muslims. As reported by the bank officials, the bank faced no problems in operating their financing activities with non-Muslim customers. Even though Kenya is a nation where the majority of its people are non-Muslim, the FCB noted positive impacts on its financing activities towards small entrepreneurs from different societal sector institutions, such as country, culture, religion, clan, legal systems, political systems and government. The bank is progressing with its renewed vigour in enhancing its financing activities among rural based small entrepreneurs in Kenya, which may be a good example for other East African nations like Uganda and Tanzania.

REFERENCES

Ahmad, K. (1994), Elimination of Riba: Concepts and Problems, *Response to the Supreme Court*.

Alam, M.N. (2002), *Financing Small and Cottage Industries in Bangladesh by Islamic Banks: An Institutional-Network Approach*, University Press, Lund.

Alam, M.N. (2008), A comparative study of financing small and cottage industries by interest-free banks in Turkey, Cyprus, Sudan and Bangladesh. *Humanomics*, Vol. 24, No. 2, pp.145–161.

Alam, M.N. (2009), *Empowering Small and Cottage Industries by Islamic Banks; A Comparative Study*, ISBN 978-3-8383-1241-5, (678 Pages), AP Lambert Academic Publishing AG & Co. KG, Germany, December 2009.

Alam, M.N. (2011), Cost minimisation through interest-free micro credit to micro entrepreneurs: A case of Bangladesh, *World Journal of Entrepreneurship, Management and Sustainable Development*, Vol. 6. No. 3, pp. 247–56.

Anderson, D. and Khambata, F. (1985), Financing small-scale industry and agriculture in developing countries: The merits and limitations of "commercial" policies, *Economic Development and Cultural Change*, Vol. 33, No. 2, pp. 349–71.

Chapra, M.U. (1985), *Towards a Just Monetary System (Vol. 8)*. International Institute of Islamic Thought (IIIT).

Chapra, M.U. (1992), *Islam and the Economic Challenge (No. 17)*. International Institute of Islamic Thought (IIIT), pp. 27–68.

Cosslett, C.E. and Ashe, J. (1989), *Credit for the poor: Past activities and future directions for The United Nations Development Programme*. UNDP Policy Discussion Paper, United Nations publications, New York.

Jansson. H. (2002), *International strategic management in emerging markets: Global Institutions and Networks*, Gothenburg University, Gothenburg (Unpublished).

Jansson, H., Saqib, M. and Sharma, D. (1995), *The State and Transnational Corporations. A Network Approach to Industrial Policy in India*. Aldershot: Edward Elgar.

Jick, T.D. (1979), Mixing Qualitative and Quantitative Methods, Triangulation in Action. *Administrative Science Quarterly*, Vol. 24, No. 4, pp. 602–11.

Kihimbo, B.W., Ayako, B.A., Omoka, K.W. and Otuya, W.L. (2012), Financing of small and medium enterprises (SMEs) in Kenya: A study of selected SMEs in Kakamega municipality, *International Journal of Current Research*, Vol. 4, No. 4, pp. 303–09.

Kimani, E.N. and Kombo, D.K. (2010), Gender and poverty reduction: A Kenyan context. *Educational Research and Reviews*, Vol. 5, No. 1, pp. 24–30.

Little, M.D. (1988), Small Manufacturing Enterprises and Employment in Developing Countries, *Asian Development Review*, Vol. 6, No. 2, pp. 1–9.

Macuja, P.C. (1981), Small Scale Industry Development in the Philippines. *Small Industry Bulletin for Asia and Pacific*, United Nations, New York, No. l.21, pp.182–89.

Merriam, S.B. (1998), *Qualitative research and case study applications in education, Revised and expanded from case study research*, Jossey-Bass publishers, San Francisco.

Molla, R.I., Gusau, S.A. and Gwandu, A.A. (1988), *Frontiers and Mechanics of Islamic Economics,* University of Sokoto, Nigeria.

Myrdal, G. (1968), Asian Drama. An inquiry into the poverty of nations. Pantheon, A division of Random House, New York.

Nienhaus, V. (1983), Profitability of Islamic PLS Banks competing with the Interest Based Banks: Problems and Prospects. *Journal of Research in Islamic Economics,* Vol. 1, No. 1, Summer, pp. 31–39.

Nienhaus, V. (1988), The performance of Islamic Banks Trend and Cases. In Millat, C. (Ed.): *Islamic Law and Finance.* Center of Near and Middle Eastern Studies, London.

Nienhaus, V. (1993), Conceptual and Economic Foundations of Islamic banking. Paper published in Piccinelli, G.M. (Ed.): *Bancheislamiche in contestononislamico (Islamic Banks in a non Islamic Framework),* Rome (Instituto per l'Oriente).

Patton, M.Q. (1985), *Quality in Qualitative Research: Methodological Principles and Recent Development.* Invited address to Division J of the American Educational Research Association, Chicago.

Sherman, R.R. and Webb, R.B. (1988), Qualitative Research in Education: A focus, In Sherman, R.R. and Webb, R.B. (Eds): *Qualitative Research in Education: Focus and Methods.* Bristol, Pa.: Falmer Press, pp. 2–21.

UNDP (1993), *Human Development Report.* Oxford University Press, UNDP, New York, 41pp.

Veblen, T.B. (1919), *The Place of Science in Modern Civilisation and other Essays.* New York: Huebsch.

Wanjohi, A. (2009), *Challenges Facing SMEs in Kenya.* Retrieved 10 July 2010 from http://www.buzzle.com/articles/challenges-facing-smes-in-kenya.html.

Wanjohi, A. and Mugure, A. (2008), Factors affecting the growth of MSEs in rural areas of Kenya: A case of ICT firms in Kiserian Township, *Kajiado District of Kenya*, Vol. 1, No. 2, p. 3.

Whitley, R.D. (Ed.) (1992a), *The comparative analysis of business systems*, European Business Systems, London: SAGE.

Whitley, R.D. (1992b), *Business Systems in East Asia: Firms, Markets and Societies,* London: SAGE.

Yin, R.K. (1994), *Case Study Research, Design and Methods.* Beverly Hills, SAGE.

BIOGRAPHY

Dr Mohammed Nurul Alam is a Faculty of BBA (Accounting) Yorkville University, Canada. He holds a Ph.D. in Islamic Finance from Lund University, Sweden, and a Masters in Accounting from the University of Chittagong, Bangladesh. He is the author of two books, and many articles in peer-reviewed journals. His interests are mainly concerned with the study of the activities of Islamic banking finance towards micro-entrepreneurs and SMEs. Dr. Alam has undertaken extensive research on micro-entrepreneurs and SME finance by Islamic Banks in Indonesia, UK, USA, Sudan, Turkey, Cyprus, Kenya, Pakistan and Bangladesh. He has more than 40 years of teaching experience in the field of accounting and other commerce-related subjects, and has taught graduate and postgraduate students in many countries in Africa, Europe, Asia, North America, and the Middle East.

Nurulayn Noor is an aspiring Disability, Employment and Human Rights lawyer. She is currently completing her last year of an Undergraduate Bachelor of Arts with Honours Degree at Wilfrid Laurier University. She is employed as a research assistant for an emeritus professor at Wilfrid Laurier University, exploring the financial and social outcomes of the Refugee Settlement Program within Canada. In the past, she has worked at Morneau Family Law Solutions, during which she assisted her employer in writing the published article "The Advantages of Collaborative Family Law for Your Children." She later worked at Habitat for Humanity as a Family Services Intake Coordinator. Along with her work experience, she had been actively involved with an international peacemaking and mediation organization named Mediators Beyond Borders. During her time there, she published two articles based on members of the organization and their work. Throughout her involvement in the community, Nurulayn discovered her passion in humanitarianism and philanthropy along with her interest in law.

THE IMPACT OF LEADERSHIP ON EMPLOYEES' TRUST AND ORGANISATIONAL PERFORMANCE WITH REFERENCE TO THE UAE

Khalid Alrawi*

Joint Command and Staff College
UAE
kalrawi47@hotmail.com

Waleed Alrawi

Syscoms College
UAE
Walid.alrawi@gmail.com

ABSTRACT

Purpose: For businesses, trust is a fundamental component in ensuring competitiveness. The purpose of this exploratory research is to help the business community build trust with its various employees in the industrial sector in the United Arab Emirates (UAE).

Methodology: Questionnaires were sent to the managers of 121 companies in three sectors of the economy (namely manufacturing, services, and agricultural sectors), representing 52% of the industrial firms in Abu Dhabi Emirate (according to the Abu Dhabi Chamber of Commerce, 2016

*Corresponding Author

Annual Report). Only 109 firms returned their forms, representing a 90% response rate that was acceptable statistically. These forms were used in the data analysis.

The aim of this exploratory research was to demonstrate why companies should invest in trust-building, and to explore how trust issues manifest across industries. It also aimed to establish a link between employee trust and firm performance, and to outline possible mechanisms through which the relationship may operate.

Findings: Findings revealed that understanding trust and management perceptions based on managers' individual perception and managerial style, have a negative relationship with the perceived benefits of these creativity negligence factors. Only five motivators out of nine were found significant for motivating trust between the three clusters in the economic sectors in the sample. Analysis shows that management initiatives highlight the fact that not all of them are necessarily successful.

Keywords: Trust; performance; employees' loyalty; management; cooperation relationships; UAE

INTRODUCTION

Trust is an intangible element that influences employees' loyalty, productivity, retention, engagement and health (Zeffane, 2010). In business, a firm's success not only depends on the cooperation level between employees in different departments, but also on the feasible coordinative power mechanism established within the cooperation arrangement. Thus, there is a need to create unique sets of resources to ensure sustainable corporate success. Such contribution of cooperation for performance should be regarded as an ongoing process and long term in nature. Such cooperative relationships become a risky venture in cases where departments may contradict each other in the achievement of the required work or results. However, such contradiction may be removed through the practical experience in inter-firm cooperation relationships.

In organisational learning theory, firms developed their capacity to manage complex work through extracting inferences from experience gained, and extrapolate them to future situations in order to achieve improvements in their behaviour. These competencies grow together with the experience of its management, and the experience gained in a firm's relationship with its employees (Nie and Lämsä, 2015). Within such understanding, both sides will decide their own communication in a credible manner. This in turn reinforces the initial expectations and justifies additional acts of both management and employees in creating trust within the work environment. As a result, a trust relationship evolves. Therefore, it is not only the firm's experience, but also the coordination and behavioural mechanism within these firms that makes the trust building process successful. In this context, trust is not regarded as an alternative due to its institutional roots, which prevent any non-rational behaviour from management or employees, and with such insight enhancing the crucial role and phenomenon of trust in economic thinking. In fact, the ability to maintain such relationships will enhance these firms in the market place and the economy. However, this research does not focus on the role of trust in the economic context.

Concerns about building trust will restrict management and employees' inclination towards any possible behaviour that reduces risks and uncertainties; betrayal can be partly absorbed in order to build trust and prevent dilemmas within the firm. Both partners (employees and management) will enhance interaction and remove any behavioural uncertainty. When the two parties have committed themselves to each other in a cooperative manner, we can assume that a trust relationship has been established between them. Building and maintaining such relationships of trust between both partners enables them to handle the behavioural uncertainty in their firms (Kong et al., 2015). Therefore, managers are able to capitalise opportunities to reduce competition with their rivals; with such a positive effect of trust, firms' will increase their competitive advantages and improve employees' performance. Through building a personal relationship and self-commitment, it is necessary to handle behavioural uncertainty and build trust by using the firms' available resources that positively affect the employees' and its business performance. Therefore, the mutual trust between partners may be achieved when partners' commitment and interaction has evolved in this direction.

Exchanging opinions between management and employees through an open door policy, transparency and quality of communication is crucial in building trust. This means that both sides are willing to look for the opportunity to express ideas to safeguard their interests. With such interpersonal communications, all participants are contributing positively. In this respect trust is achieved insofar as partners provide such insight and deal with each other openly and honestly as well. Each side is able to assess the situation and are well informed of what the other side is feeling. With such preciseness for building a trust relationship, cooperation will evolve and relationship intensity rises automatically. Although cooperation experience contributes to business performance, management's contribution to success is significantly higher for achieving trust. Again, with more experience of cooperation, management is more successful in building trust. Thus, as far as these firms are able to manage and maintain a cooperative relationship with its employees, its performance is better.

From the organisational point of view, the indication of greater success of the firm is partly due to building a continuous relationship between both partners in a systematic way and as an ongoing process; this will widen the firm's business and its strategic portfolio (Agnihotri and Krush, 2015). The contrast with an ever changing of the partners' attitude does not contribute to the required performance. In fact, the contrast means firms have no experience in cooperation to make employees' performance positive or gain stronger trust. In this context, as mentioned previously, trust is not built on resources to achieve a possible variable for developing competitive advantage. This means that when management is unable to create cooperation with employees, or cannot coordinate otherwise, then expectation is to evolve the situation to complexity and uncertainty. In other words, what is required is that the quality of the cooperation relationship, and not the quantity of the firm's experience or the intensity of the created relationships by the management is what contributes to future success.

Within the firm, management should encourage those employees willing to commit themselves to positive relationship. Self-commitment through the quality of communication will build trust and is regarded as a leap of faith and step for moving forward.

From the above discussion we may conclude that the main variables for encouraging trust between the firm and employees are:

- an organisation's cultural behaviour;
- effective communication;
- reduce the ambiguity of change;
- be open and upfront with employees;
- a leader's ability to inspire employees;
- aligning management words and actions;
- encourage rather than command;
- leader/management competency;
- take blame but give credit.

The aim of this exploratory research was to demonstrate why companies should invest in trust-building. It also explored how trust issues manifest across industries, to establish a link between employee trust and firm performance, and to outline possible mechanisms through which the relationship may operate.

Due to the existing dearth of research concerning human resource management in the Gulf area in general, and the Middle East in particular, it is hoped that this paper will have a positive contribution to this area.

THE IMPACT OF TRUST ON ORGANISATIONAL PERFORMANCE

With any organisation that is trying to ensure that its employees are making good decisions, the manager often starts by building trust. Management soon realise that trust and telling its employees what to do without sensitivity, implies that such management has faith in their decision-making abilities. This can result in their becoming proactive rather than defensive. In addition, the employees can enhance their faith in their own confidence to make decisions. When employees do not have faith in themselves, then the manager's faith in them decreases even more and building trust has to restart (Lu, 2014). Thus the negative message is that what the employee has done is wrong or not good enough.

Managers have to evaluate their employees from their own point of view and then give them the required assignments; the strategy is to cultivate the habit of listening to them. The feeling is a positive one towards the employees. Managers should not interrupt the employees who are attempting to communicate, who should be acknowledged by their managers, having a positive emotion towards them. In such an environment, managers acknowledge their employees' feelings and opinions. In fact, this is the surest way to improve communication and build trust.

For managers, it is very crucial to let their employees know that they are willing to listen, even though it may not result in agreement from both sides (Bergman et al., 2012). Such a working relationship environment is based on trust, as both sides feel safe; the implicit message is that each has the other's best interests in mind. Employees can accept their managers' criticism, at the same time having their trust. Thus, to have the optimum working relationship, managers/employees feel a sense of trust. In this context managers know that the delegation of tasks is essential for building trust within the workplace environment, and they should not deprive their employees of any opportunity to advance their skills, knowledge, experience and improvement in performance. Employees' feelings within such an environment are that their management treats them as being responsible for undertaking their work, and empowering them to improve their performance. The next step is to focus on the progress made by the employees, with something positive being achieved and still more expectation of maintaining that progress. This is regarded as a positive step for employees' incentives for doing their tasks, thoughts and communications.

In any organisation, communication, teambuilding, and competency will be eroded if trust between leader/management and employees' did not exist (Carmeli et al., 2012). Therefore, these three elements may be regarded as strategies used by management to build its employees' trust. If trust does not exist, and as a result of this lack of trust, the turnover of employees will be increased and workplace morale would be low. Such elements are then regarded as enablers for creating an innovative, profitable and creative environment and organisations to work.

Building management/employees' long-lasting relationships within a healthy work environment will grow over time, and should be regarded as a long-term strategy. These concepts will encourage the establishment of positive perceived thinking and reputation between both parties. They will also create a willingness to take the initiative and accept risks by the employees and reducing frustration. What is needed is trust for the improvement of the firms' performance by employees. It should not be regarded as a short-term management intervention, but the predisposition underlying the entrepreneurs' decisions and actions as a key to achieving competitive advantage and quality of performance in the long-term.

To reduce a firm's challenges, the management should be aware of enhancing co-ordination between its employees on one side and their management on the other in an attempt to boost performance and intersection of ideas. With the quality of cooperation, experienced firms are able to build up and maintain effective handling of uncertainty and unaccepted behaviour of employees within such a cooperation relationship. Such challenges for a firm's coordination relationship may increase uncertainty and the complexity of work, and trust may be not regarded as a priority for a period of time when more valuable resources are needed. Therefore, a more cooperative arrangement by the management would rely on maximising trust and more success may be achieved in order to boost its performance.

In day-to-day work, managers are usually aware of the strong trust they have with their employees. They need to build a successful business environment and diminish any negative feeling towards them created by the organisation's previous leaders, otherwise the performance required will suffer. As trust is part of human nature, it is a pivotal element in the management context. Thus, a lack of trust between leaders/management with employees happens when employees know that they are working in an unsafe environment; this results in less innovation. Then, the powerful attribute of leadership is trustworthiness in an attempt to build a track of fairness and honesty.

Building trust by leaders/management should be regarded as an ongoing process. In doing so, this will encourage managers within their organisation to demand high performance from their employees. The misuse of power by some managers in their organisations will have an adverse effect on their employees' careers, resulting in their disappointment and losing trust. In fact managers have to transcend employees' fears to reach the full potential.

ORGANISATIONAL EFFORTS AT PERFORMANCE IMPROVEMENT

In discussing trust, we are talking about an organisation's ability to achieve success. In this context, employees should believe in their leadership capacities for achieving their organisational objectives; they should also trust each other. In such a relationship between management and its employees on one side, and between employees themselves on the other side, teamwork building, communication and performance is inevitably enhanced in the workplace (Huang et al., 2010).

In business, building conscious teamwork with a specific plan is the most essential variable for achieving success. Employees will react faster, overcome obstacles, build trust and obtain better performance (Gao et al., 2011). In other words, building trust means establishing a high performing team within the organisations based on shared value creation, and leadership/management's openness with employees. Such understanding of building trust will enhance a two-way interaction and improve organisational performance.

Enhancing a positive relationship between management and employees that is based on trust, improves the organisational performance (Yang and Mossholder, 2010). It assume that both parties have the best interests in mind for the organisation, and a sense of trust. Therefore, employees accept criticism for their faults from their leadership management. It is a situation for achieving performance rather than finding mistakes, and trust is a quality hard to capture.

One may conclude that achieving high performance is a case of how to develop trust within the organisational hierarchy between employees in the workplace. The reasons for this is probably the existence of diversity in the workplace as there are employees from various backgrounds working in the organisation. Leadership/management have to reconcile between employees with different backgrounds within the workplace, with no basis of trust among them (Kelloway et al., 2012). Managers have to be proactive through building an environment of trust to improve or achieve the required performance.

Listening and valuing employees' suggestions and ideas promote management's capacity and resources to effectively communicate with them. With their knowledge, managers are able of assessing and judging ideas mentioned by their employees who may them improve their performance and achieve organisational objectives (Travis et al., 2011). Such an environment increases employees' self-confidence, builds open communication between parties, and creates a habit of listening to learn the promotion of positive emotion. Listening is a way of acknowledging an organisation's employees.

Delegating authority and responsibilities to employees is regarded as a way of building trust and improving performance in the workplace. Such empowering of employees is an opportunity for them to release their skills, strengthen communications with the management, and improve their professional development.

Management should focus on the progress when an assignment is delegated and completed instead of concentrating on perfection (Carmeli et al., 2011). In this case, the required performance may be achieved when employees understand what the expectations are from such tasks, with the supervision of their leadership/managers. In such a work place environment, managers will expect a response, and employees should accept criticism.

In this respect, self-empowerment is more effective than empowerment of employees, as management in this case is giving ideas, therefore enabling positive communications that are not destructive. Beyond this understanding, leaders/managers should notify their employees' that changes are built on their strengths rather than working on their weaknesses (Zhang et al., 2015). Then, performance was achieved on what employees can do within their knowledge and experience, and boosting employees' trust, motivation and candour. In other words managers are enhancing trustworthiness.

Another way of improving employees' performance through building trust is when managers encourage employees to undertake the assignments, providing them with the required information rather than commanding them. In this way employees are motivated to do these tasks (Norman et al., 2010). In the management context, this means delegating authority and responsibilities and granting autonomy for doing these tasks professionally.

In fact, leaders/managers have to be competent to be trusted by their employees. Contacting them on a daily basis as an ongoing process will encourage managers to update their skills, reduce their mistakes and make more commitment to their organisation.

The above discussion reveals that building trust for improving performance is the influence of three enablers, namely motivation, perception, and communication. These elements are regarded as incentives for employees. Effective motivation influences trust when directed. Having highly motivated employees within their organisations means encouraging them to achieve objectives and being aware that employees undertake tasks with high performance. When employees' trust is high, they are likely to proceed with the required changes even if there are no immediate benefits (Palanski and Yammarino, 2011).

Management perception for any required changes will specify the ways of accomplishing these changes and the behaviour or tasks that will be implemented. Changes should improve the employees' performance and be not regarded as a threat to their positions. Trust in this respect will be the basis of the extent of motivating the employees, and their future behaviour (Rubin et al., 2010). When trust is low or negative, this changes the perception of employees, which are more likely to be perceived as negative as well.

Positive communication through the process of changes affects employees' understanding of these changes, and in this respect internalisation cannot be overstated. Employees' trust will enhance their professional work who, in turn, are likely to determine and believe the rationale and their organisations' need for such changes.

METHODOLOGY AND ANALYSIS

The present study employed a survey type methodology, and involved the leadership/management of those companies in the sample. The population of the study was selected through stratified sampling. Questionnaires were sent to the managers of 121 companies (representing more than 52% of the industrial firms, according to the Abu Dhabi Chamber of Commerce, 2015 Annual Report) with significant responsibility for leadership/management contribution to motivating a trust-oriented management. From 121 questionnaires distributed, 109 managers completed and returned their questionnaires, a 90% response rate. Measures were adopted and used to weigh each of the nine variables of motivating trust, namely:

- an organisation's cultural behaviour;
- effective communication;
- a reduction in the ambiguity of change;
- being open and upfront with employees;
- a leader's ability to inspire employees;

- aligning management words and actions;
- encourage rather than command;
- leader/management competency; and
- take blame but give credit.

Only five motivators were found significant for motivating trust between these three clusters in the economic sectors in the sample. Therefore, a one-way ANOVA analysis was used to assess such similarity. The study used a five-point rating scale, i.e. from 1 (strongly disagree) to 5 (strongly agree). The research investigated the status of these constructed variables as enablers for motivating trust in the industrial sector (see Table 1).

From Table 1, the F value between factors motivating trust factors within the companies surveyed in the sample was high and significant in 0.01. The rank of the F

Table 1   Factors Motivating Creativity: Similarities/Differences

Factors Encouraging Trust	Manufacturing group I		Services group II		Agriculture group III		One-way ANOVA & Scheffe's test		
	Mean	SD	Mean	SD	Mean	SD	F	P-value	Scheffe's test
An organisation's cultural behaviour	4.31	0.94	4.89	0.62	4.51	0.70	3.33	0.10	
Effective communication	4.71	0.74	4.65	0.74	4.41	0.74	1.27	0.36	
A reduction in the ambiguity of change	3.31	0.95	3.36	0.63	3.61	0.68	1.68	0.28	
Being open and upfront with Employees	4.67	0.63	4.95	0.68	4.63	0.57	4.09	0.03	
Leader's ability to inspire employees	4.41	0.92	3.99	1.00	4.22	0.57	3.13	0.15	III > II, III > I
Aligning management words and actions	4.02	0.84	4.15	1.09	4.13	0.61	9.15	0.00*	III > I
Encourage rather than command	3.03	0.71	3.61	0.78	5.01	0.78	6.68	0.00*	
Leader/ Management competency	4.02	0.74	3.82	0.94	4.01	0.68	1.08	0.76	
Take blame but give credit	4.24	0.80	4.74	0.61	4.54	0.65	3.29	0.16	

Alpha Value 0.89

*P < 0.01

Source: Devised by authors from data sample analysis

value indicators for an organisation's cultural behaviour, being open and upfront with employees, a leader's ability to inspire employees, aligning management words and actions, and encourage rather than command as the highest is: 3.33, 4.09, 3.13, 9.15, and 6.68 respectively. Aligning management words and actions was first, encourage rather than command second, open and upfront with employees was third, an organisation's cultural behaviour was fourth, and a leader's ability to inspire employees was last. Using the P-value method, leader/management competency was found to be 0.76, and an organisation's cultural behaviour was lowest at 0.10. However, such P-value has a rather high value. The alpha value of 0.89 indicates that the research instrument enjoys a rather high validity.

The mean values on a five-point scale (1 = strongly disagree; 5 = strongly agree) of the five indicators concerning motivating trust were: 18.45, 19.38, 13.10, 37.67 and 20.66 for an organisation's cultural behaviour, being open and upfront with employees, a leader's ability to inspire employees, aligning management words and actions, encourage rather than command respectively. The mean value of aligning management words and actions is 37.67 in the high ranking, indicating that management in the firms surveyed is encouraging diversity at work, the open door system, high participation for employees in the decision making process, and is aware that motivating trust plays a significant role in the success of the organisation. Encourage rather than command was second with 20.66, indicating that solving organisational problems through teamwork was high, and that management empowered their employees with responsibility. This indicator is compatible with the third ranking elements, being open and upfront with employees, which had a value of 19.38. In fact, the respondents believe management and employees in these firms are judged enough by what they do, and the knowledge of departing employees is not passed in a pervasive way to successors. In fact, such issues reflect that these companies have a suitable network of knowledge workers; furthermore they believe there is an active programme for developing ideas.

An organisation's cultural behaviour element was fourth, with a value of 18.45. From this score the clear interpretation for such situations is that the employees and their companies have been acting rather effectively in the case of regular and wide exchange of knowledge, and using of information systems and communication have been higher than average. A leader's ability to inspire employees was last, with a mean value of 13.10. The lower level of value indicated that employees had simple knowledge about the trust concept. The mean of trust motivation factors was 119.730, which indicated that respondents in the sample believed that management efforts for the trust concept between employees with respect to the present criteria, together with the companies' internal environment, were less than the average (see Table 2).

Through discussions with those managers in the companies that were surveyed, the researchers asked respondents to elaborate on their answers. Respondents mentioned other motivational variables for trust in their firms. The researchers believe that

Table 2   Statistics Analysis

The Variables	Mean	Std. Deviation	Kurtosis	Skewness
An organisation's cultural behaviour	18.45	8.8	-0.085	-0.624
Being open and upfront with employees	19.38	9.8	-0.223	-0.752
A leader's ability to inspire employees	13.10	8.2	-0.292	-0.852
Aligning management words and actions	37.67	11.2	-0.333	-0.534
Encourage rather than command	20.66	10.2	-0.099	-0.118
Total Factors Motivating Trust		119.730		

Source: Devised by authors from data sample analysis

Table 3   Kruscal-Wallis Test

	Aligning management words and actions	Encourage rather than command	Open and upfront with employees	An organisation's cultural behaviour	A leader's ability to inspire employees	Total Factors Motivating Trust
Chi-Square	36.379	21.286	16.953	8.993	7.225	19.931
Asymp. Sig.	0.000	0.000	0.000	0.720	0.244	0.030
∂f	2.000	2.000	2.000	2.000	2.000	2.000

Source: Devised by authors from data sample analysis

leadership/managers' education was probably behind such revelations. Motivational factors mentioned by those managers may be specified such as: internal or external competition, organisational culture, no fear of criticism by the management, financial and economic resources, and management risk tolerance. To assess if the education element is behind such problems' expectations, we used the Kruscal-Wallis techniques. The results are shown in Table 3.

From Table 3, results revealed that there is a relationship between the aligning management words and actions, encourage rather than command, and open and upfront with employees, and total trust motivational factors with employees' and the managers' education level. With ($K\partial f = 2.000$, $P < .01$), the value of the construct variables are: ($K\partial f = 36.379$), ($K\partial f = 21.286$), ($K\partial f = 16.953$), ($K\partial f = 19.931$). There were no significant differences between education and the other two motivational variables (i.e., a leader's ability to inspire employees, and an organisation's cultural behaviour).

CONCLUSIONS

The results of this research revealed that leadership/management is aware of trust as an enabler for a positive contribution towards high performance. Therefore, building trust within an organisation depends on its experience, and enhancing the coordinative power within its managements' efforts.

In this research the relationship between building employees' trust and organisational performance was explored, and indicated the mechanisms through which such a relationship may operate in the workplace. Employees' trust by their managers in the workplace environment explicitly influences those employees to accept the changes that an organisation intends to consider. Conclusions are then that trust is important between employees' for workplace performance, and the level of such trust is influenced by job and work related characteristics. In other words, trust is the key builder when considering changes, and there is a negative impact due to a lack of trust. Therefore, a low level of trust may undermine management's efforts for changes, and leadership/management has to understand and be aware of the trust of their employees in the organisation.

The high level of trust of employees in their managers affords a significant competitive advantage. Such sustainability may encourage managers to accept and take risks of changes in their organisations. Managers may demonstrate trust through an environment characterised by transparency, involving employees in the decision-making process, and problem solving and openness with the employees in the workplace. In other words, the organisational structure is signalling that it trusts its employees. Using active rather than passive methods of communication by the managers with employees helps to maintain and enhance trust in the workplace environment. On the other hand, transparencies in communication between both sides are helping to remove the ambiguity of changes and the employees' resistance to such changes. This will help the management to achieve the required outcome.

LIMITATIONS OF THE STUDY

In light of our empirical results, further research in this field is certainly worthwhile, both from a scientific as well as a practical point of view. There could be more research about trust in terms of a major challenge with regard to the autonomy of the respondents, to assess if the findings are regarded as a cultural context in other industries.

REFERENCES

Agnihotri, R. and Krush, M.T. (2015), Salesperson empathy, ethical behaviors, and sales performance: the moderating role of trust in one's manager. *Journal of Personal Selling & Sales Management*, Vol. 35, No. 2, pp. 164–74.

Bergman, J.Z., Rentsch, J.R., Small, E.E., Davenport, S.W. and Bergman, S.M. (2012), The shared leadership process in decision-making teams. *The Journal of Social Psychology*, Vol. 152, No. 1, pp. 17–42.

Carmeli, A., Schaubroeck, J. and Tishler, A. (2011), How CEO empowering leadership shapes top management team processes: Implications for firm performance. *The Leadership Quarterly*, Vol. 22, No. 2, pp. 399–11.

Carmeli, A., Tishler, A. and Edmondson, A.C. (2012), CEO relational leadership and strategic decision quality in top management teams: The role of team trust and learning from failure. *Strategic Organization*, Vol. 10, No. 1, pp. 31–54.

Gao, L., Janssen, O. and Shi, K. (2011), Leader trust and employee voice: The moderating role of empowering leader behaviors. *The Leadership Quarterly*, Vol. 22, No. 4, pp. 787–98.

Huang, X., Iun, J., Liu, A. and Gong, Y. (2010), Does participative leadership enhance work performance by inducing empowerment or trust? The differential effects on managerial and non-managerial subordinates. *Journal of Organizational Behavior*, Vol. 31, No. 1, pp. 122–43.

Kelloway, E.K., Turner, N., Barling, J. and Loughlin, C. (2012), Transformational leadership and employee psychological well-being: The mediating role of employee trust in leadership. *Work & Stress*, Vol. 26, No. 1, pp. 39–55.

Kong, X., Chen, Y. and Zhuang, Y. (2015), Analysis of system trustworthiness based on information flow noninterference theory, *Journal of Systems Engineering and Electronics*, Vol. 26, No. 2, pp. 367–80.

Lu, X. (2014), Ethical Leadership and Organizational Citizenship Behavior: The Mediating Roles of Cognitive and Affective Trust, *Social Behavior and Personality: an international journal*, Vol. 42, No. 3, pp. 379–89.

Nie, D. and Lämsä, A.M. (2015), The leader-member exchange theory in the Chinese context and the ethical challenge of Guanxi, *Journal of Business Ethics*, Vol. 128, No. 4, pp. 851–61.

Norman, S.M., Avolio, B.J. and Luthans, F. (2010), The impact of positivity and transparency on trust in leaders and their perceived effectiveness. *The Leadership Quarterly*, Vol. 21, No. 3, pp. 350–64.

Palanski, M.E. and Yammarino, F.J. (2011), Impact of behavioral integrity on follower job performance: A three-study examination. *The Leadership Quarterly*, Vol. 22, No. 4, pp. 765–86.

Rubin, R.S., Bommer, W.H. and Bachrach, D.G. (2010), Operant leadership and employee citizenship: A question of trust?. *The Leadership Quarterly*, Vol. 21, No. 3, pp. 400–08.

Travis, D.J., Gomez, R.J. and Barak, M.E.M. (2011), Speaking up and stepping back: Examining the link between employee voice and job neglect. *Children and Youth Services Review*, Vol. 33, No. 10, pp. 1831–41.

Yang, J. and Mossholder, K.W. (2010), Examining the effects of trust in leaders: A bases-and-foci approach. *The Leadership Quarterly*, Vol. 21, No. 1, pp. 50–63.

Zeffane, R. (2010), Towards a two-factor theory of interpersonal trust: A focus on trust in leadership. *International Journal of Commerce and Management*, Vol. 20, No. 3, pp. 246–57.

Zhang, Y., Huai, M.Y. and Xie, Y.H. (2015), Paternalistic leadership and employee voice in China: A dual process model. *The Leadership Quarterly*, Vol. 26, No. 1, pp. 25–36.

BIOGRAPHY

Professor Khalid Alrawi is a Professor at Abu Dhabi University/The Military Programmes in the United Arab Emirates. He received his PhD degree in Business Administration from Strathclyde University, UK, and his MPhil from Oxford. He has worked in different countries, and published more than 60 papers in different reputable journals. During his career, he has supervised many MBA and PhD students.

Mr Waleed Alrawi is a lecturer at Syscoms College in the United Arab Emirates. He received his BA degree in Business Administration and his MBA degree in Business Administration from Al-Ain University of Science and Technology, the United Arab Emirates. During his career, he has published many papers in different reputable journals.

GOAL 5/10

GENDER EQUALITY/REDUCED INEQUALITY

PRIVATISATION AND WOMEN'S EMPLOYMENT POSITION IN SUDAN

Limiaa Abdelghafar Khalfalla

National Population Council
Khartoum University, Sudan

Elsadig Musa Ahmed*

Faculty of Business
Multimedia University 75450, Melaka, Malaysia
elsadig1965@gmail.com and limiaa@yahoo.co.uk

ABSTRACT

Purpose: This paper aims to explain women's employment status in the context of privatisation. Their position is discussed in terms of women's employment before privatisation; discrimination against women in the labour market and work place; women's experience of redundancy; women's experience of job seeking; women's responses to the changing situation after privatisation; adaptive responses women have had to mitigate their worsening economic situation in Sudan.

Design/methodology/approach: Using a qualitative analysis, the study found that women's employment positions were harshly prejudiced by these terminations. Both groups of respondents from the bank and the factory accepted the effect of privatisation policies in a parallel manner, as the matters surfacing were connected to the roles commenced by women at the family/household level before becoming jobless. The main groups in the sample were from the Female Heads of Households (FHH)

*Corresponding Author

group, principally, women bankers. The other group was women sharing correspondingly in the household budget, while sole workers in a big family denotes an essential group.

Findings: The main findings were that the impact of privatisation on women's employment status appears to be mixed. It opens employment opportunities for some women in regions where there is high economic growth, but not for many in the least developed and poor economies, such as Sudan.

Originality: In the pursuit of increased productivity and lower labour costs, privatisation not only led to increasing rates of female unemployment, but also worsened the working conditions of female employees. The limited employment opportunities in the formal sector, either in public or private domains, led women to remain unemployed for long periods of time, forcing them to look for other work alternatives, namely the informal sector.

Keywords: Privatisation; women employment position; Sudan; qualitative analysis

INTRODUCTION

As explained by Khalfalla and Ahmed (2015; 2017), the Sudanese economy observed dissimilar eras of transformations and fluctuations inclined by political unpredictability. These periods can be concise as follows. The period between 1956 and 1978 saw the applications of an expansionary policy to renovate the regressive economy. Nevertheless, these policies caused fiscal and monetary discrepancies. Throughout 1978–1985, the country accomplished some regaining of their economic position; this was the period at the start of the participation of the International Monetary Fund (IMF) in the Sudanese economy. In the 1990s, the condition remained worse, with a statement from the IMF that Sudan was a non-cooperative country. Subsequently, economic sanctions were imposed on Sudan by the United States of America (USA) in 1997; these were lifted on 12 October 2017 after 20 years. The sanctions caused Sudanese economy losses totalling to US$500 billion and damaged most productive sectors in Sudan. In understanding this situation, the government of Sudan affirmed its aim to transform the Sudanese economy as the first priority to be undertaken to overcome the problems associated with the USA economic sanctions and IMF polices. Consequently, a set of procedures, including the introduction of liberalisation and privatisation, was declared in the early 1990s as part of the government's Three-Year Programme (1992–95). This was a wider programme for economic reformation, liberalisation and public enterprise reform, including privatisation.

It should be recalled, the Sudan government charted privatisation. It intended to raise government revenue and reduce government expenditure by selling state-owned enterprises, attracting more domestic and foreign investors, reducing the balance of payment deficit, and providing more employment opportunities (Elbeely, 2011).

Some Sudanese economists, e.g. Awad (1997), have debated that privatisation is not the greatest key to solving Sudanese economic problems. Others have commented on the implementation procedure and the reasons behind the practice of privatisation policies. Some of them debated that the Sudanese economy is recognised as an agricultural economy, while privatisation is more applicable to more industrialised or modernised economies to achieve its goals. This is because the agricultural sector is highly subsidised, even in the more advanced countries such as the USA and European countries. Moreover, some Sudanese economists, e.g. Suliman (2007), discussed that the purposes of privatisation in Sudan are multifarious and provocative, as the government of Sudan conveniently recycled privatisation of state-owned enterprises to obtain more economic and political power for its factions and associates.

In addition, other groups of Sudanese economists viewed privatisation as politically driven. However, at the international relationship level, authors such as Elbeely (2011) stated that the government of Sudan applied privatisation to catch adequacy in the eyes of the international community. Meanwhile, Musa (2001) discussed that the objects are simply economic ones; nonetheless, the application was actually challenging. While economists discussing the appropriateness of privatisation specified the environment of the Sudanese economy, the applicability of privatisation to economic structures, or the purposes behind it, looking for reaction for these queries has been persistently significant. Irrespective of *whether* the objectives of this programme were chiefly economic or political; the socio-economic effects of privatisation on unemployed women from public sector enterprises such as the sector under study (banking and manufacturing sectors in Sudan) should be discussed. In this respect, alterations ensuing laying-off have led to a substantial conversion in Sudanese women's economic position, at the individual, family and household levels; this is revealed in the perceptions of the respondents involved in the current study (Khalfalla and Ahmed, 2017).

Kumar and Quisumbing (2015) stated that giving consideration to gender equality remains an important development goal. Furthermore, the importance of gender equality is highlighted in its prominence in the United Nations Millennium Development Goals (MDGs), which have been commonly accepted as a framework for measuring development progress. Of the eight goals, four are directly related to gender: achieving universal primary education, promoting gender equality and the empowerment of women, reducing infant and child mortality, and improving maternal health. Closing gender gaps, which tend to favour males, has also been seen to contribute to women's empowerment. However, the term empowerment refers to a broad concept that is used differently by various writers, depending on the context or circumstance.

According to Khalfalla (2012), to envisage the socio-economic impacts of privatisation and its consequent policy of redundancy on women, we need first to look at women's employment status in the labour market prior to privatisation, and whether they experienced gender discriminatory practices in their workplaces. We then need to examine the changes in women's employment patterns and positions brought by privatisation, and finally the effect of the marriage between privatisation and practices of gender inequalities on women's employment will be explained. The paper discusses the changes that have taken place in the employment status of women as a result of redundancy policy: where the government attempted to make large numbers of employees from privatised firms redundant, women were among the first to go. Patterns of women's participation in the labour market in the formal modern and the traditional informal sector are described. First, their position in the labour market before the process of privatisation is seen to explain the changes that happened in their employment status after the introduction of privatisation policies. Khalfalla (2012) explained that women's employment status in this context is discussed in terms of:

- women's employment before privatisation;
- discrimination against women in the labour market and work place;
- women's redundancy experience;
- women's experience of job seeking;
- women's responses to the changing situation after privatisation;
- adaptive responses women have had to mitigate their worsening economic situation.

WOMEN'S EMPLOYMENT STATUS PRIOR TO PRIVATISATION

In most developing countries, women's activities outside the household (as indicated by participation rates) are lower than those of men; however, they have risen over the past 30 years. As a result, women have formed an increasing proportion of the total labour force. In Asia, women formed around 33.9% of the labour force in 1985, in Latin America this was 24.2%, and in Africa they remained constant at around 32% (Stewart et al., 1992).

As in many developing countries, Sudan has witnessed an increase in the share of women in the labour force. According to the National Census in 1993, females accounted for 22% of the labour force; this increased to 28% in 1996 (the labour force surveys), and then went up to 31.8% according to the National Census of 2008. Women's share in the labour force in Sudan is still just less than the average of African countries (i.e., 32%).

The female labour force in Sudan is predominantly rural, comprising 32% of the labour force compared to 68% of males'. As agriculture is the most dominant sector in the Sudanese economy, which contributed 65.6% of the Gross National Product (GNP) in 1983, women's share in this sector was 84.3% of the labour force in the same year. Women's high participation does not mean that they have access to land ownership, or control over resources. Evidence showed that women account for 36% of the agriculture labour force in developing countries as whole. In Africa, however, women are the majority of the farmers, producing 90% of the food, but they are less important in export cash production'. Women's situation in the agricultural sector in Sudan and in other African countries showed the extent to which women were discriminated against, because their participation in this sector is considered as an extension to their domestic role. Therefore women are very much affected by the implementation of privatisation as they produce goods for family subsistence rather than producing cash crops for export. Sudan is not an exception in this regard.

Lately, in the early 1990s, the share of the agricultural sector in the GNP dropped to 60.7% in 1993. This was accompanied by a decline in women's share in this sector, which reached to 79.6% in 1993, to 49% in 2008. However, it led to an increase of women in other sectors, namely manufacturing and services sectors. Consequently, women's participation in the urban labour force has risen at increasing rates in the last decades, reaching 16% compared to 84% of males' share (1993). This percentage has been absorbed in the formal sector, and includes the public sector, private sector and the informal sector.

The public sector in Sudan has attracted large numbers of female' employees, including in banks, companies and commercial enterprises (Kheir-El-Din and El-Laithy, 2008). This sector is considered a large employer of women due to the facilities provided, such as social provisions, leave (holidays), and other forms of facilities supporting women to continue work. Despite the facilities provided, women are still lagging behind because they are discriminated against in this sector; this is because they are concentrated in certain jobs and sectors compared to men. Evidence showed similar experience in Sub-Saharan Africa where the public sector represents about half of the formal sector employment in the region. Moreover, within the formal sector in Sub-Saharan Africa, there is a concentration of men (Savin-Baden, 2003).

With regard to the private sector, women's participation is low compared with the public sector, yet there has been some progress in recent years (Yousef, 2004). In this sector females represent 68% of production and unskilled labour, 8.2% of professional and technical staff. In SSA, women who are employed in the formal sector are much more likely to be in public sector employment than in the private sector. An example is Kenya, where employment data show that women comprised 18.8% of waged employees in the private sector in the 1990s (Savin-Baden, 2003).

Women's share of the labour force in the informal sector is especially large, estimated at 26.8% in Sudan, 53% in Tanzania, and around 40% in Peru (Shields, 1980, p. 23).

Apparently there is high tendency among women to enter the informal sector, because it is more accessible, and does not require education, training or skills. Savin-Baden (2003), and Isaac and Franke (2002), argued that women's participation in the formal sector is characterised by their concentration in the small-scale, undercapitalised, low productivity sectors, where men have greater occupational spread in the sector (Savin-Baden, 2003, p. 95; Isaac and Franke, 2002, pp. 37–40).

The above discussion has reflected an unfavourable situation of women in the labour market in developing countries in general, and particularly in Sudan. This has influenced the effectiveness and outcomes of SAPs and privatisation, as 'constrains on women's flexibility hinder the success of adjustment in each case, typically, the constrains on women's labour allocations citied include labour market discrimination, lack of education, limited access to credit or other inputs and reproductive responsibilities' (Savin-Baden, 2003).

The increase in women's employment in Sudan in the last two decades is a result of several socio-economic and demographic changes in the labour market. These changes were mainly attributed to the following factors:

1. the observed progress in women's education;
2. shortage of manpower due to male emigration, mainly to the Gulf countries;
3. high turnover of men as a result of low wages compared to the private sector; and
4. poverty conditions pushing more women into the labour market as cheap labour (Kheir-El-Din and El-Laithy, 2008).

El-Nagar (1985) argued that 'women's' economic participation in urban areas can generally be attributed to the economic strife resulting from the restructuring policies implemented during the 1980s, in addition to other factors related to the increased rates of women's education, and emigration of men.

METHODOLOGY PROCEDURE

Following Khalfalla and Ahmed (2017), the case study emphasises a specific case, counting its contextual and respondents, through which the extra detailed features of the case itself can be identified. The study studied an extensive series of past studies related to privatisation policies during the 1990s and forwards, and its impact on jobless workers, particularly women. In this respect, diverse situations and methods of privatisation have also been discussed in the past studies undertaken in this area of research. It should be noted that the understanding of privatisation has been reconnoitred on a worldwide scale, including the returns and drawbacks associated with privatisation. It should be noted that privatisation in Sudan has been explored, as well as considering patriarchy, as the major cause against the women working in a fruitful means. In this framework, insufficient studies addressed the impact of privatisation on women's employment and seemed to be gender sightless. However, to address the precise research questions, the study was conducted as an experimental research on jobless women from two Sudanese privatised public institutions in the Sudanese banking and manufacturing sectors.

It should be mentioned that there are a number of methods to conduct qualitative research, ranging from ethnography to observation. As these are not suitable for our study, we selected in-depth unstructured interviews with individual women as our research method, in addition to the usage of focus group discussions.

In this respect, secondary information was collected from different sources as part of the study fieldwork when visiting Sudanese related ministries, offices and university libraries. In this regard, the information collected comprised official documents, policy statements, national strategies, reports, and conference papers published by the government of Sudan related to privatisation policies implemented in Sudan. In addition, the study referred to newspapers, magazines and academic research and studies such as journals, reports and postgraduate theses undertaken in Sudan and Sudanese related studies.

DESCRIPTION OF THE SAMPLE

The sample for this study was created from two groups of women; these women were made redundant from the Bank of Khartoum and the Friendship Factory in Sudan.

In addition to the interviews conducted with women made redundant, discussions were held with managers of the Bank of Khartoum and the Friendship Textile Factory. These focus groups were interviewed to comprehend the points of view of those who implemented privatisation in the sectors under study. In addition, additional interviews were conducted with Bank of Khartoum staff, the head of the Public Banks' Pensioners' Union, and the head of the Benefits Fund for Displaced Employees. Lastly, interviews with trade union members were also carried out to get more information about the topic of the study and its impact on Sudanese women's employment position. The outcome of these interviews was the gathering of important information and figures that were not available in reports or papers written about the privatisation experience of the two institutions. This was also valuable information in addition to the secondary information gathered from the above mentioned secondary sources as it also sustained the analysis of the primary data. It is obvious the data generated from women' respondents made redundant from the Bank of Khartoum and the Friendship factory, that they signify two extremes of working women in the urban setting in Sudan. This includes women from the banking sector that presented a model of professional middle-income women, and the women from the manufacturing sector that reflected the model of poor working-class women.

The study found that women's personal characteristics, such as age, marital status, number of children, level of education, monthly income, and job grades are very different when the two groups of women were compared. The comparisons were in their roles in the household and extended families. As well as being an equal sharer of and head of households, they were also contributors towards the budget of their extended family.

Additionally, they also shared the changes in their employment status after privatisation; the majority of women from both the bank and the factory were unemployed. The survey found that half the factory workers and 76.6% of women in the banking sector denoted the composition of unemployed women in these two groups. They also had parallel responses to the decision to make them redundant. A substantial majority of women from the two institutions either refused to accept the decision or protested against it; this makes up two thirds of women from the bank and the factory.

WOMEN IN THE WORKPLACE

Women's accounts have reflected their conditions in the work place with respect to recruitment, promotion and the entitlements provided for women employees. Occupational features of women employees from the two institutions, the bank and the factory, are slightly different. The situation of women respondents from the bank was better compared with those drawn from the cloth factory; this was because of their level of education and training, in addition to their high level of intellectual thinking. Also, a high percentage of women recruited in the bank were qualified to occupy a number of top management posts, despite discriminatory practises against them. Moreover, women were entitled to a wide range of social benefits (health insurance, social security, etc.), in addition to access to other economic resources, such as loans (e.g., for housing, cars and crisis loans). Despite all these facilities provided for women, they still faced several challenges. Some of these challenges related to work legislation and laws on employment, and government policies adopted by public sector enterprises, including the Central Bank of Sudan.

The other discriminatory practices are referred to as the personal attitude towards gender discriminatory practices, particularly from bank managers and decision makers, who were mostly men.

Meanwhile, the case of women respondents from the factory reflects their low level of education, and the limited scope for training that qualifies them as factory workers. Their level of intellectual thinking and aspiration was much narrower as well. In the daily work of the factory, there were no clear gender-based practices, as all the staff were women. However, discriminatory practices appeared clearly when privatisation was implemented. Women were exposed to exploitative practices by the new management of the factory, as the redundant women were offered work but with worsened terms of service and conditions.

WOMEN IN THE BANKING SECTOR

From the responses of the women in the bank of Khartoum, it was found that the majority were concentrated in senior positions; more than half the respondents were in job grades one to three (grade one is highest rank in job grading in the Bank of Khartoum). Despite the large numbers of women employees in the bank, and the high percentage of women in management posts, there was still a gender bias against women in the occupational structure of the bank. Recruitment is one example, whereby women were denied the chance to be recruited as the bank's general director. No woman has been promoted to this post in the Bank of Khartoum, or any of the public or private banks; neither have women been represented on the board of trustees of the bank (advisory body) since the establishment of the bank. This is confirmed by the last national population census, where it was found that men's representation in managerial posts is 519,700, compared with only 56,356 women. This reflected gender segregation (i.e., vertical forms of segmentation), showing the concentration of men in higher tiers and women in lower tiers in any occupation pyramid (Bradley et al., 1999).

As data suggest, there is no legislation denying a woman the right to be appointed as a bank's general director, or to be chosen as a member of the board of trustees, nor is there any refusal by women to occupy management posts (e.g., three women from the sample were recruited as Banks' branch managers, which means they do not mind accepting top management jobs). However, it seems that this is an undeclared policy of the Central Bank of Sudan, which issues all the regulations that control and regulate the work of all banks in Sudan.

WOMEN IN THE FACTORY

The discussions from women respondents demonstrated that the redundant women factory workers experienced the contradictions of stereotyping and discrimination at the household level, and fierce privatisation at the labour market level. The interviews have shown that most of the redundant women factory workers joined the informal sector for various reasons. The first was poor living conditions of the women and their families. The second was the ease of entering the informal sector, as it does not demand education, qualifications, or high capital to start a small business: it is a resort for poor, illiterate and economically disadvantaged women. However, they enter this sector in small numbers compared to women in the banks, due to the social constraints mentioned. The respondents' accounts reflected that privatisation in Sudan has led to growth of the informal sector with new changing features, such as the involvement of middle class women in this sector. In contrast, women in the banking sector enter the informal sector in large numbers (eight cases), exceeding that of women factory workers. This is because they faced limited opportunities for paid jobs, i.e. they are double the number of the women factory workers, although it is an emerging pattern of employment for educated middle-class women.

It was assumed that women factory workers may tend to enter the informal sector in greater numbers compared to women bankers; however, the reverse happened. This is most likely due to their social position in the family and in society, as their mobility is restricted by the control of fathers, brothers and husbands. Moreover, the perception of society towards informal work is that it is of low value and underestimated: the few who were self-employed were doing it secretly, or in conflict with male guardians. Therefore, women factory workers were less encouraged to enter the informal sector, because of the social constraints. However, this sector is more suitable for them than for women bankers, because it is easy to enter: there is no high level of education, no qualifications, no previous experience or initial capital needed.

The increase in the informal sector is not only limited to the case of Sudan, but can also be seen in other regions. Moghadam (1992) mentioned that the growth of the informal sector is witnessed in East European countries (e.g. Hungary), Third World, and the Middle East and North Africa (MENA) region (1999). As this sector is very vital to increase employment and income for women, the attitude of the government needs to be changed. Accordingly, policy action needs to be formulated to improve the informal sector as an important sector that could assist the government to open up more employment opportunities and to alleviate poverty in the wider sense. The policy actions include: 1) increase accessibility to finance, 2) skill development, 3) organisation of market channels, and 4) provision of protective laws to keep women safe from violations and harassment practiced by local authorities, or by male counterparts in the sector.

CONCLUSIONS AND IMPLICATIONS

It could be concluded that the impact of privatisation on women's employment status appears to be mixed. It opens employment opportunities for some women in regions where there is high economic growth, but not for many in the least developed and poor economies, such as Sudan.

In the pursuit of increased productivity and lower labour costs, privatisation not only led to increasing rates of female unemployment, but also worsened working conditions for female employees. The limited employment opportunities in the formal sector, either in public or private domains, led women to remain unemployed for long periods of time, forcing them to look for other work alternatives, namely the informal sector. Despite the unfavourable work conditions in this sector, women comprise a high proportion of the labour force, as high as 26.8% of the labour force in this sector. This pattern of employment has also been termed as the 'informalisation of female labour force' by feminists such as Moghdam (2005), and Standing (1999). When privatisation came, it claimed to introduce more efficient criteria for hiring, including formal qualifications or personal interviews, making it difficult for women to compete as expensive labour.

Consequently, if privatisation continues as part of the government's overall economic policies, both the need for women to work and the constraints the labour market imposes on them will increase, while it would be neither reasonable nor realistic to expect private enterprises to voluntarily act against their own economic interests. Therefore, the state should fulfil its duty to protect the social welfare of its individuals. In order to maintain gender equity and the welfare of families, the state needs to provide guarantees that will secure women's opportunities to work. This means:

1. designing labour policy that respects family as well as women's needs;
2. safe and cheap day-care for children of working mothers near to their workplace;
3. a post-privatisation programme to maintain women employees' issues with the new employers of the privatised enterprises;
4. social mitigating programmes pertaining to training and skills upgrading, should be directed to women as well as men.

REFERENCES

Awad, M.H. (1997), Poverty in Sudan: Anatomy and prognosis. In *UNDP Workshop on Poverty in Sudan*, Sharja Hall (14–15 June), Khartoum, Sudan.

Bradley, C., Todd, C., Gorton, T., Symonds, E., Martin, A. and Plowright, R. (1999), The development of an individualized questionnaire measure of perceived impact of diabetes on quality of life: the ADDQoL. *Quality of Life Research*, Vol. 8, No. 1, pp. 79–91.

Elbeely, K. (2011), '*Privatization in Sudan during the period of 1990–2002*', LAP LAMBERT Academic Publishing (31 October 2011), Germany.

El-Nagar, S. (1985), *Patterns of Women [sic] Participation in the Labour Force in Khartoum*. Unpublished PhD Dissertation. Khartoum: University of Khartoum.

Isaac, T.T. and Franke, R.W. (2002), *Local democracy and development: the Kerala people's campaign for decentralized planning*. Rowman & Littlefield Publishers Inc.

Khalfalla, L.A. (2012), *Socio-economic impacts of privatisation on women made redundant from Sudan's banking and manufacturing sectors*, Doctoral dissertation, University of Nottingham.

Khalfalla, L.A. and Ahmed, E.M. (2015), The impact of privatization on Sudanese women position. *International Journal of Sudan Research*, Vol. 5, No. 2, pp. 107–28.

Khalfalla, L.A. and Ahmed, E.M. (2017), Privatisation Policies Effects on Sudanese Women's Economic Position. *International Journal of Economics and Management Science*, Vol. 6, No. 425, p. 2.

Kheir-El-Din, H. and El-Laithy, H. (2008), An Assessment of Growth, Distribution, and Poverty in Egypt: 1990/91-2004/05. *The Egyptian Economy: Current Challenges and Future Prospects*, pp. 13–52.

Kumar, N. and Quisumbing, A.R. (2015), Policy reform toward gender equality in Ethiopia: Little by little the egg begins to walk. *World Development*, Vol. 67, pp. 406–23.

Moghadam, V.M. (2005), *Globalizing women: Transnational feminist networks*. JHU Press.

Moghadam, V.M. (Ed.). (1992), *Privatization and Democratization in Central and Eastern Europe and the Soviet Union: the gender dimension*. World Institute for Development Economics Research of the United Nations University.

Musa, E.A. (2001), Sudan Structural Adjustment Programme (SSAP); Some Implications For labour in the Formal Sector, Africa Training and Research in Administration for Development Center, Morocco.

Savin-Baden, M. (2003), *Facilitating problem-based learning*. McGraw-Hill Education (UK).

Shields, N. (1980), *Women in the Urban Labor Markets of Africa: the case of Tanzania*, World Bank Staff Working Paper No. 380, Vol. 1, 148 pages, April 1980.

Standing, G. (1999), Global feminization through flexible labor: A theme revisited. *World Development*, Vol. 27, No. 3, pp. 583–602.

Stewart, F., Afshar, H. and Dennis, C. (1992), Can Adjustment Policies Incorporate Women's Interests? *Women and Adjustment Policies in the Third World*. London: Macmillan.

Suliman, O. (2007), Policy Brief 52, Current Privatisation Policy in Sudan.

Yousef, T.M. (2004), Development, growth and policy reform in the Middle East and North Africa since 1950. *The Journal of Economic Perspectives*, Vol. 18, No. 3, pp. 91–115.

BIOGRAPHY

Limiaa Abdelghafar Khalfalla first worked in a non-government organisation for five years, transferred to the Ministry of Social Planning, Woman Division, then to the higher strategic planning council, Khartoum state. She then upgraded to the National Population Council, where she has been since September 2012. Dr Khalfalla has a PhD in Sociology and Social Policies, from the University of Nottingham, an MSc in Gender and Development, from Al Ahfad University for Women, Sudan, and a BSc in Economics and Social Studies, from Khartoum University, Sudan.

Dr Elsadig Musa Ahmed is Professor of Economics and Technology Management at Multimedia University (MMU). His research interests include development economics, productivity analysis, knowledge-based economy, productivity and environment (green productivity), bioeconomy, Islamic finance and microfinance, economic growth (environment, tourism) and entrepreneurship. Professor Ahmed has published more than 100 publications in international refereed journals and presented several papers at conferences. He has supervised 10 PhD, 2 DBA, 3 Masters and 8 MBA students, and currently supervises a number of PhD, MPhil and MBA projects. Professor Ahmed has received five research grants in ICT and Economic Growth, Foreign Direct Investment Spillover Effects and Mobile Banking for Microfinance. He is a member of the World Economics Association, World Assembly of Youth (WAY), Arab Science and Technology Foundation (ASTF), World Academy of Sciences, Engineering and technology (WASET), and is active in the World Association for Sustainable Development (WASD) activities.

BUILDING DIGITAL CAPACITY FOR SUSTAINABLE DEVELOPMENT

Amer Al-Roubaie*

Ahlia University
Kingdom of Bahrain
aalroubaie@ahlia.edu.bh

ABSTRACT

Purpose: Digital technologies have increased communication among individuals, regions and nations by eliminating geographical barriers and promoting connectivity. E-services, driven by digital technologies, are helping countries to overcome the challenges of globalisation including knowledge acquisition, innovation diffusion, information dissemination, poverty eradication and sustainable development. Sharing knowledge and information about the environment is crucial for environmental protection and sustainable growth. Digital connectivity could have a positive impact on future sustainability by improving public understanding concerning the risk of unsustainable environment.

Design/methodology/approach: The paper examines the digital gap using published data to measure ICT readiness. The paper underscores the importance of global knowledge and information in building capacity for sustainable development and closing the digital divide. Developing countries can take advantage of globalisation to foster economic growth and promote innovation.

Findings: Building an ICT infrastructure facilitates connectivity and empowers local enterprises to invest in green technologies that are friendly to the environment. E-services, driven by digital technologies, increase the state's

*Corresponding Author

capabilities to provide inclusive coverage of services to all people. This will increase competitiveness that supports technology transfer, innovation dissemination, knowledge creation and development sustainability.

Originality/value: Digital technologies play an important role in fostering change and improving the quality of life. The paper sheds some light on the socio-economic potential of digital technologies that will broaden our understanding about the information age.

Keywords: Digital divide; Sustainable Development; globalisation; knowledge and information

INTRODUCTION

Digital technologies are rapidly changing human connectivity, allowing people in different geographical locations to communicate easily and gain greater access to world markets. Digital networks enable individuals, enterprises and institutions to acquire knowledge and information in order to make decisions and formulate strategies that lower risks and reduce transaction costs. Digital technologies, especially the Internet and mobile telephones, are providing inclusive access to people across the social divide, namely the poor, disabled, rural population, women and minorities, so they may engage in market activities and improve their economic well-being. Today, the Internet, mobile telephones, social networks and other communication media are extensively used across cultures and within nations, enriching public understanding of the opportunities and challenges confronting their communities worldwide.

Digital technologies have reduced distances and made contacts across geographical barriers much faster, thus helping individuals, communities and nations to make decisions that could influence human understanding, enhance cooperation, increase mobility and share knowledge and information. Today, governments can extend e-services far beyond cities and regions to provide inclusive educational, health, environmental and administrative services with greater efficiency. Digital technologies enable policy makers to provide a wide range of e-services to people in different locations to bridge the knowledge gap and sustain development. Closing the digital divide, however, remains among the biggest challenges facing many developing countries. This is due to ineffective institutions, weak infrastructure, a lack of funding and corruption.

Over the past three decades, there has been much debate surrounding environmental protection in the literature on development studies, sustainable development, political circles, and the media. This reflects the concern over the causes and consequences of environmental degradation and their impact on future sustainability. In addition to the environment, the concept of sustainable development also addresses a society's social and economic development punctuating the complex task of future sustainability. The scarcity of natural resources and the high cost of extraction impose constraints on the ability of the environment to supply resources that meet people's basic needs. In recent decades, an increase in population, rapid economic growth, urbanisation and transportation have increased the demand for natural resources. Inadequate management of the environment has caused a rapid depletion of non-renewable resources, and has also increased the risk of future sustainability.

This paper examines the impact of digital technologies on environmental management and sustainable development. It will briefly highlight the importance of connectivity in decision-making and policy formulation concerning future sustainability. Sustainable development is concerned with correcting environmental imbalances to ensure that future generations will enjoy equal access to the natural environment. In recent decades, the excessive consumption of natural resources has reduced the ability of the natural environment to adequately produce resources in order to meet people's basic needs. Globalisation, poverty, inequality, multinational businesses, and illegal activities are increasing the threat of unsustainability, and are subjecting millions of people to a high degree of uncertainty. Digital technologies empower people with the capacity to create new knowledge, think of new ideas, develop new techniques and disseminate new innovations to protect the environment. This paper aims to shed some light on the use of digital technologies in environmental management in view of the current megatrends facing populations worldwide.

SUSTAINABLE DEVELOPMENT

In this paper, the term 'future sustainability' is used in reference to the management of natural capital in order to highlight the prospect that future generations may enjoy equal access to natural resources. Future sustainability is limited by the ability of the natural environment to supply the required natural resources to meet people's basic needs, which include water, food and energy. The rapid consumption of resources reduces productivity and speeds up the depletion of these resources, which then become costly to produce. In recent decades, globalisation, trade liberalisation, rapid economic and population growth, rising income per capita, and urbanisation have increased demand for those natural resources that are vital for people's needs.

By 2050, it is estimated that the world's population will reach 10.5 billion. This will require a substantial increase in the supply of natural resources in order to meet demand. By 2050, the demand for food is expected to increase by 60% to feed the increase in population and the demand for water will increase by 55%; global energy consumption will increase by 37% by 2040. Currently about 52% of agricultural land is already affected by moderate or severe degradation; this puts the prospect of future sustainability in jeopardy. As the OECD (2016) points out:

> "Natural resources are a major – if not the primary – foundation of economic activity and thus ultimately of human welfare. Water, air, land and soil provide food, raw materials and energy carriers to support socio-economic activities. Their extraction and consumption affects the quality of life and

well-being of current and future generations. Their efficient management and sustainable use are key to economic growth and environmental quality." (OECD, 2016, p. 32)

Therefore, if the consumption of natural resources continues to increase at the current rate, it is likely that the supply of these resources, in particular non-renewable resources, will be exhausted. To overcome this, immediate action needs to be taken to manage natural resources in a productive manner to protect the environment and ensure future sustainability.

Recent development studies focus more on sustainable development as a measure of the earth carrying capacity and the role that natural capital plays in meeting people's basic needs. The environment is at the heart of sustainable development because it is the main supplier of natural capital. In recent decades, rapid socio-economic transformation and population growth have placed more and more pressure on natural resources, particularly on non-renewable resources, due to the rise in global demand.

The capacity to produce natural resources is limited by increasing costs, inadequate technologies and the declining reserves of non-renewable resources. In many developing countries, economic growth is driven by the production and export of natural resources; therefore, the rapid depletion of these resources makes the economy vulnerable to changes in demand and the price of these resources in the global markets. Geographically, natural resources, including energy, are not evenly distributed among and within nations. This increases the risk of accessibility, especially if they are located in countries with a high degree of political instability and widespread corruption.

Sustainable development is a multidimensional concept comprising social, economic and environmental elements; it aims to promote social and economic development of the present generation without jeopardising the sustainability of future generations. The most commonly circulated definition of sustainable development is the one used by the World Commission on the Environment and Development as: "development that meets the needs of the present, without compromising the ability of future generations to meet their own needs" (Brundtland, 1987, p. 47).

In most developing countries, scientific knowledge and financial resources are inadequate to protect the natural environment and sustain development. It is estimated that by 2050, 80% of the increase in global population will be in developing countries, the burden of which will be placed on the natural environment and its capacity to supply the resources needed to meet the basic requirements of that population. To minimise the risk of uncertainty and build capacity for future sustainability, these countries should invest in non-renewable resources, develop new technologies and create knowledge that will lead to local innovation and protect the environment. Priority should be placed on green investments and environmentally friendly technologies aimed at reducing market imperfections and protect the environment. Future funding should be subject to an environmental review and to an assessment of the impact of building new projects on the environment (Al-Roubaie, 2013).

The Millennium Development Goals adopted by the United Nations in 2015 represent some of the biggest challenges facing communities worldwide. The objectives of these goals are to sustain development by endorsing global initiatives to eradicate poverty, reduce inequality, close the gender gap, reduce unemployment, eliminate hunger, improve health and encourage education. Poverty is perhaps among the greatest challenges facing many developing countries that the community of nations needs to resolve if sustainable development is to be achieved. The United Nations recognises the severity of the problem by saying that:

> "Poverty eradication, changing unsustainable and promoting sustainable patterns of consumption and production, and protecting and managing the natural resource base of economic and social development are the overarching objectives of and essential requirements for sustainable development" (United Nations, 2013, p. xi).

Some of the environmental linkages are external due to cross-border flows and illegal market activities. Both national and international institutions must work together to manage, monitor and protect the environment against abuse by international firms and local enterprises. Governments need to strengthen corporate governance guidelines to ensure that the exploitation of natural resources will be within the framework of sustainable growth. Digital technologies have a critical role to play in future sustainability by providing e-services to increase awareness and educate the public concerning matters related to the environment.

Future sustainability is influenced by forces that require action to be taken now to lessen the future impact on the environment. Currently, there are several 'megatrends' at work that can be seen to extend long into the future. The OECD has identified several of these megatrends, including demography, natural resources and energy, climate change and the environment, globalisation, the role of government, the economy, jobs and productivity, health, inequality and well-being. It is estimated that the global population will exceed 10 billion by 2050, the majority of which will be in poor countries that lack access to adequate resources to meet their current needs. Supporting this increase in population will require food production to increase by 60%, water by 55%, and global energy demand by 40%. The use of digital technologies can have a major influence on the production and consumption of natural resources. It may enhance efficiency and strengthen future sustainability. As the United Nations points out:

> "These challenges to sustainable development are driven by broad underlying economic, social, technological, demographic and environmental megatrends. Megatrends are understood in this context as major shifts in economic, social and environmental conditions which change societies and substantially impact people at all levels" (UN, 2013, p. 2).

As an important input in production, energy is crucial for future development. Investment in renewable energy has become essential in order to reduce pollution and protect the environment. Renewable energy is considered an environmentally friendly resource with little or no impact on the environment. It reduces the costs of pollution, minimises the impact of climate change on health, and contributes to a reduction of greenhouse gas emissions. For resource-poor countries, renewable energy offers long term solutions to energy vulnerability and reduces dependency on global markets for the supply of energy. For oil producing countries, building capacity for renewable energy encourages economic diversification and reduces dependency on foreign markets. The production and consumption of conventional energy sources produces a substantial amount of chemicals and waste, which are harmful to the environment. In addition, developing countries will benefit from investments in renewable energy by improving productivity of the economy and creating new job opportunities for younger generations.

INFORMATION AND COMMUNICATION TECHNOLOGIES (ICTs)

ICTs have increased connectivity within and across nations. This has brought people closer, allowing them to share useful information and exchange ideas of common interest. In the new economy, knowledge is a global good that can easily be acquired through trade, multinational business and the Internet with little or no costs. ICTs facilitate the transfer of knowledge and promote innovation across sectors; this consequently accelerates economic growth and sustains development. Acquiring knowledge for development through digital technologies has become more convenient, especially for countries with limited technical and scientific knowledge. For developing countries, it is cheaper to make use of the existing global knowledge, given the status of their financial, technological and educational limitations. To this end, building capacity for the digital divide will speed up the process of knowledge transfer, technology diffusion and innovation dissemination. Digital infrastructures encourage people to participate in market activities. They provide new opportunities to acquire funding, access to information and create knowledge. Politically, digital technologies increase awareness and improve choices that promote participation and strengthen democracy (Elmasry et al., 2016).

Developing countries must incorporate digital technologies into their national policy on the environment in order to provide the public with the information they need to not only participate in environmental protection, but also to take full accountability for their involvement in activities related to the production and consumption of natural resources. Responding to the mega-challenges facing these countries will require the collective efforts of individuals, groups, businesses and governments towards building green technologies and creating innovative systems that support the environment. In doing so, with regard to future sustainability, educational institutions, research and development, science and technology and public support pro-grammes must be given top priority in government strategy. Sharing information and acquiring knowledge encourages public involvement in environmental management, which supports sustainable development and builds a future for the generations to come. E-services can improve government delivery and could empower people to make sound decisions to protect the environment. Digital technologies could improve the management of natural resources by reducing the risk of resource depletion and by finding new alternatives (Al-Roubaie and Al-Zayer, 2007).

Digital technologies are important enablers for the creation of new knowledge, the dissemination of information to improve the quality of the environment, and to support future sustainability. The Internet allows people in different geographical locations to share knowledge and information of common interest, including environ-mental management. Connectivity could help nations to leapfrog, in other words, to surpass several development stages using these global linkages, knowledge acquisi-tion and innovation diffusion. In this regard, science and technology, boosted by the emergence of networks, can address some of the major challenges facing develop-ment. Learning from the rest of the world provides developing countries with a wider array of choices to stimulate local innovation and improve the protection of the envi-ronment (Al-Roubaie and Al-Zayer, 2007).

ICTs could be effectively used in environmental management and sustainable de-velopment. As powerful enablers, these technologies increase awareness about the need for environmental protection by providing knowledge and information to people across national boundaries, including the rural population and other isolated settle-ments. The current rate of development in many developing countries is not sustain-able due to the depletion of non-renewable resources, deforestation, climate change, an increase in pollution and ineffective institutions. Overcoming unsustainable activi-ties will require an investment in alternatives to reduce the risk of resource depletion and improve the capacity of the earth to sustain future development.

The International Telecommunication Union (ITU) adopted the Connect 2020 Agen-da: this represents "a series of goals and targets for improvement in ICT access, use and sustainability, and in contribution of innovation and partnerships" (ITU, 2015, p. 4). The ITU endorses a vision shared by ITU Member States, to build an information society empowered by the "interconnected world, where telecommunication/ICTs enable and accelerate social, economic, and environmentally sustainable growth and development for everyone" (ITU, 2015, p. 5).

There are four major targets identified by the Connect 2020 Agenda:

1. Growth – enabling and fostering access to and increased use of ICTs
2. Inclusiveness – bridging the digital divide and providing broadband for all
3. Sustainability – managing challenges resulting from ICT development
4. Innovation and partnership – leading, improving and adapting to the changing technology environment (ITU, 2015, p. 5).

The use of ICTs enables developing countries to close the digital divide and provide access to people to participate in environmental management. Digital technologies can improve technological learning and give rise to innovation through information sharing and knowledge creation, both within and among nations.

Table 1 provides information about connectivity in different regions classified by access to the Internet. Developing countries remain far behind in comparison to developed nations in terms of access to the Internet; this reflects the size of the digital divide. Connectivity is still worse in least developed countries and Africa; this illustrates the challenges facing those countries in terms of building an infrastructure for connectivity and sustainable development. Only 9.7% of the total population in LDCs (Least Developed Countries) is connected to the Internet, compared to 82.3% in developed countries, and 43.4% worldwide. Only 32.3% of women in developing countries have access to the Internet, compared to 80.1% in developed countries and 40.8% worldwide. Connectivity should be inclusive to provide greater opportunities to all people and increase their access to a wider range of opportunities and services. Inclusive also means that more people will become aware of the challenges facing sustainability. They will be able to make decisions about reducing waste in society, without impacting the environment. It is estimated that closing the gender gap in terms of mobile phone usage will benefit 300 million women in low-income countries, adding $13 billion in incremental revenue for operators (World Bank Group, 2015, p. 22).

Table 1   Percentage of Individuals using the Internet by Gender, Development Status and Region 2015

Region	Female	Male	Total population
Developed	80.1	84.6	82.3
Developing	32.3	38.2	35.3
World	40.8	45.9	43.4
LDC	8.1	11.3	9.7
Africa	18.4	23.1	20.8
Arab states	34.1	39.8	37.0
Asia & Pacific	33.3	40.4	36.9
CIS	57.8	62.2	59.9
Europe	74.3	81.0	77.6
The Americas	66.2	65.8	66.0

Source: ITU, Measuring the Information Society Report 2015

In the Information society, access to information is essential in order to make decisions and improve the ability to forecast future trends. Greater access to ICT will have a positive impact on a society's ability to enhance connectivity and strengthen future sustainability. However, bridging the digital divide requires inclusiveness to ensure that ICT benefits will reach everyone, without excluding the poor and other vulnerable groups. ICT empowers a society, not only in terms of accelerating social and economic transformation, but also in terms of improving future sustainability by protecting the environment.

ICTs offer new opportunities for women to obtain resources and participate in the economy. In developing countries, opportunities for women are limited due to social, cultural and religious restrictions. Thus, access to ICT can improve gender equality and may increase the participation of women in market activities by providing them with new economic opportunities and greater access to finance, knowledge and information. ICT also allows people to work from home, providing women with the opportunity to negotiate business deals without face-to-face meetings. In other words, empowering women with ICT access will increase the productivity of the economy and create jobs, especially for the youth. In the Arab world, for example, the percentage of women going to school at all levels is increasing. This will enable more women to take advantage of the new technologies and participate in finding solutions to problems of development.

The environmental dimension of sustainability includes local solutions that can integrate external knowledge into the local knowledge system. Knowledge transfer and adaptation to technological change are possible through connectivity to external markets and institutions. Access to scientific applications strengthens environmental management and empowers the country's ability to reduce the risk of environmental degradation.

DIGITAL DIVIDE

The digital divide is defined by Wikipedia as: "an economic and social inequality with regard to access to, use of, or impact of Information and Communication Technologies (ICT). The divide within countries (such as the digital divide in the United States) may refer to inequalities between individuals, households, businesses, or geographical areas, usually at different socioeconomic levels or other demographic categories. The divide between different countries or regions of the world is referred to as the global digital divide, examining this technological gap between developing and developed countries on an international scale." (Wikipedia: https://en.wikipedia.org/wiki/digital divide) The global divide hinders development by reducing the ability of developing countries to benefit from globalisation. Access to global markets facilitates technology transfer and knowledge diffusion, which is badly needed to promote innovation and foster economic growth. Initiatives to close the digital divide require the building of an ICT infrastructure and providing Internet connectivity to ensure access to global knowledge and information. Governments may facilitate the use of digital technologies by reducing the impact of such forces such as digital illiteracy, a lack of financial resources, poverty, the age gap, the educational gap, and gender on the country's ability to join the information age. State support for digital services must ensure that access to the Internet is provided across the nation without exclusion. In other words, building digital networks for use by all, including the poor, women and the disabled, provides people across national boundaries with new opportunities to participate in decision making and allows them to contribute to the natural environment. Digital technologies improve public awareness surrounding environmental protection and increase support for future sustainability.

Digital technologies provide access to knowledge and information for people living in far off places and in isolated areas. Governments, particularly in developing countries, can make use of digital technologies to connect people in different geographical areas and provide them with educational and environmental services in order to build local capacity for sustainable development. Providing services through digital technologies could help governments save a substantial amount of money by reducing the cost of delivery and boosting productivity in various geographical regions. Poor regions stand to benefit from such services by acquiring new knowledge and being exposed to new technologies for regional development.

Building an efficient ICT infrastructure will make it attractive for both local and foreign investors to take advantage of the new opportunities and set up new operations; this will stimulate linkages, create jobs, increase the participation of women, promote innovation and increase productivity. Greater access to resources will also provide incentives to the young and small and medium enterprises. This will mean that they may compete in both local and global markets. In countries where jobs are scarce, self-employment could increase market activities because new businesses would be created. To this end, providing new knowledge and information surrounding the use of digital technology allows users to make better choices and enables them to select environmentally friendly technologies more suitable to the environment (Al-Roubaie and Al-Zayer, 2007).

In countries suffering from low economic growth, high population growth and scarce natural resources, connectivity could empower people and offer new knowledge and creative ideas that support innovation and foster productivity. ICT enables decision makers to gather information and acquire knowledge to build strategies that strengthen future sustainability. Access to global markets facilitates the transfer of knowledge and technology diffusion, especially in developing countries where local knowledge concerning the environment is inadequate. As pointed out by the International Telecommunication Union:

> "Bridging the digital divide requires focus to be given not just to access but also to accessibility, affordability and use of ICTs in all countries and regions

and by all people, female and male, and including marginal and vulnerable populations such as children and older people, indigenous peoples, persons with disabilities, and those on lower incomes" (ITU, 2015, p. 12).

The new information age, driven by the Internet, will have a substantial impact on human communication and regional and national connectivity worldwide. Connecting people facilitates human understanding and brings the threat of unsustainable challenges facing our planet to people across the political boundaries. This will put pressure on decision makers at both national and international levels to take action and support the natural environment. Greater connectivity encourages knowledge sharing and information dissemination among and within nations towards finding common solutions for human survival. Individuals in isolated regions can acquire and communicate knowledge and information in response to some of the challenges facing their own communities and support future sustainability. Scientific knowledge is a global good that can easily be transferred for use in regions that lack adequate environmental knowledge. In this regard, governments should facilitate access to knowledge by building ICT capacity; this will increase public participation and take advantage of the information revolution.

For many developing countries, connectivity is still limited to a few, mainly to those who can afford to pay for Internet usage. However, it is important that access to the Internet be inclusive to avoid the risk of people being excluded. Exclusion hinders the ability of some individuals and groups in society to access external resources for sustainable development. Under such circumstances, the state should ensure that Internet connection is affordable to all, including the poor, women and other underprivileged groups in society. The digital divide is measured by the "differences in the quality of available networks as well as basic connectivity" (ITU, 2015, p. 3).

The ICT Development Index (IDI) measures developments in Information technology among countries. It comprises 11 indicators representing ICT readiness, ICT use and ICT capabilities. These indicators are aimed at empowering a country to make use of ICT in order to foster innovation and sustain development. The IDI index is also used to measure the digital divide among nations, their ICT readiness to close the digital gap and support development. As Table 2 shows, the index ranks countries according to both regional and global use of ICT. Globally, most countries, particularly in Africa, are yet to make effective use of ICT to increase connectivity and benefit from global access. As powerful enablers, ICT promotes development through the use of natural resources in a sustainable manner to support the quality of life.

In regions such as Africa, digital technologies can have a positive impact on economic development through their contribution to economic growth, job creation, productivity improvement, poverty reduction and environmental management. Transforming Africa into a digital economy will require improvements in ICT infrastructure to increase connection and provide digital services. Governments in the region should integrate their ICT strategy into the national development agenda, and formulate national digital policies and strategies to speed up the process of digitalisation across and within regions and sectors. Initiatives should focus on digital literacy by providing inclusive educational services to all. Empowering society with digital services speeds up the process of economic change and increases the prospects for future sustainability.

Digital technologies improve public services via a wider coverage and faster delivery of government services across regional and national boundaries. Using digital technologies provides governments with more choices in making decisions and selecting programmes aimed at strengthening the national objectives and improving living standards for all. Setting targets to meet the challenges facing society imply that government policies will be directed towards solving urgent structural problems and reducing imbalances within the socio-economic system.

Well-structured ICT services could be less costly for poorer countries by providing digital services across sectors without having to build costly physical infrastructures.

Table 2   ICT Development Index (IDI), Selected Countries 2017

Country	Regional rank	Global rank	IDI
Bahrain	1	31	7.60
UAE	3	40	7.21
Saudi Arabia	4	54	6.67
Jordan	7	70	6.00
Egypt	12	103	4.63
Sudan	16	145	2.55
South Korea	1	2	8.85
Japan	3	10	8.43
Malaysia	9	62	6.38
Indonesia	19	111	4.33
India	25	134	3.03
Denmark	3	4	8.71
France	10	15	8.24
Turkey	37	67	6.08
United States	1	16	8.18
Brazil	10	66	6.12
South Africa	3	92	4.96
Nigeria	15	143	2.60
Mali	22	155	2.16
Chad	36	174	1.27

Source: International Communication Union, Measuring the Information Society Report, Volume 1, 2017 (Geneva, ICU)

In other words, digital technologies will have a positive impact on future sustainability by enlarging inclusive government services representing all individuals. In the case of the Middle East region, for example, it is expected that the digital market will add $95 billion per year to the GDP of the Middle East by 2020. However, the digital contribution to the GDP in the Middle East is just 50% of that of the United States (Elmasry et al., 2016).

Education, knowledge and information are important inputs in the alleviation of poverty and to foster economic growth. Not having adequate knowledge and information weakens the participation of people in creative activities and their contribution to development. An effective programme to reduce poverty should engage the poor in market activities by providing them with access to financial, technical and digital resources in order to encourage entrepreneurship and stimulate linkages. For example, providing basic educational services through ICT technologies, will help the poor to acquire skills and knowledge about markets both locally and internationally, i.e. basic knowledge of marketing, management, prices, demand and supply will increase business success and open new opportunities, especially for local enterprises. Similarly, computer literacy becomes essential for connectivity and communication across sectors and regions in society. To this end, providing equal opportunities to all will encourage the poor, women and those with disabilities to take part in business activities. In turn, this will improve their economic well-being and support the community. The initiative to participate in the economy enhances competitiveness and encourages people to be innovative and develop new products.

THE DIGITAL ECONOMY

In the Digital economy (driven by ICT technologies), innovation, knowledge creation, technology diffusion and information play an important role in promoting social and economic change and sustaining development. Innovation stimulates linkages and increases economic diversification; this reduces an economy's dependence on the production and export of a limited number of commodities. Using digital technologies will benefit individuals, enterprises and institutions to get connected to bigger markets where they can share knowledge and expertise in order to create new products and develop new techniques more suitable for the local environment. Learning from the experience of others empowers local populations to manage resources in a productive and protective manner that results in less pollution and reduces the risk of environmental degradation. The digital economy can also be described as an open economy where ICT facilitates an ever greater flexibility in both labour and product markets. Furthermore, integration into the global market and improvements in competitiveness will help domestic producers gain a comparative advantage over other competitors.

Improvement in productivity helps the economy create new jobs, lower production costs, alleviate poverty, and reduce inequality, mainly in developing countries, where some of these features are still common. Digital technologies improve productivity and increase product quality, encouraging firms to increase production and sales in larger markets. For example, in developing countries, labour productivity, measured by dollar value added per worker, increased by 65% in firms using ICT compared to firms without ICT. Similarly, users of ICT increased their sales by 750% and their profitability by 113% compared to non-users (World Bank Group, 2015, Table 3.1, p. 16).

ICT has made it possible for countries to select appropriate technologies and obtain knowledge more applicable to the domestic environment. Being an open economy, the digital economy provides greater incentives for people who wish to engage in business activities and take advantage of the new opportunities offered by digitisation. The inclusive nature of the digital economy fosters economic growth and broadens market activities through the creation of linkages, employment, investment and innovation. Global linkages also facilitate technology transfer and knowledge acquisition, which can be used to strengthen economic fundamentals and promote sustainable development.

Investment in science, technology and innovation will increase a society's capacity to generate productivity and sustain development. Governments should encourage scientific research by providing greater incentives for universities and research institutions to conduct research and contribute to the development of knowledge. Joint research programmes with private enterprises, and partnerships with foreign research institutions may provide solutions to some of the environmental, social, and economic challenges facing many countries.

Educational reforms that support such research undertakings become necessary in order to build digital capacity for sustainable development. Future sustainability will be influenced by a country's ability to produce knowledge and promote innovation. Education improves labour market flexibility by providing workers with the skills required to keep pace with changes in technology and market demand for knowledge workers. Inclusive public education ensures a greater economic potential because of its coverage to all individuals in society. Education also increases public knowledge and information concerning the environment, and this in turn increases public support with regards to protecting the environment.

Poverty, inequality, hunger, and gender are among the important megatrends common to many developing countries. Finding solutions to these megatrends will influence the ability of many nations to improve environmental protection and support future sustainability. In developing countries, several groups including the poor, women, farmers and urban dwellers, are excluded from market activities and are left on their own to manage their daily survival. According to the World Bank:

> "Lack of assets and lack of an effective voice for large segments of the population block the emergence of competent institutions that can pick up

signals early, balance interests, and commit to implementation of decisions. As a result, policies to avoid wasting of assets, particularly environmental and social assets, are not adopted and implemented. The more people heard, the fewer the assets that are wasted" (World Bank, 2013, p. xxi).

Without equal opportunity and fair access to resources, these people usually resort to cutting down trees, polluting rivers and engaging in illegal activities that can be harmful to the environment. Digital technologies could ease such pressures on the environment by providing people with knowledge and information that will enhance decisions regarding natural resource management and protection of the environment. In addition to the environment, the concept of sustainable development meets the basic needs of a people, including their economic well-being, health, freedom of choice and equal opportunity for all. Achieving these objectives will ensure that a society enforces the rules of justice and fairness by redistributing income in ways that eliminates poverty, reduces illiteracy, establishes equity and enhances public capability to participate in decision making. ICT encourages the use of e-services provided by e-commerce, e-government, e-shopping, social networking, e-health, etc. It also allows a reduction in the use of transportation and reduces energy consumption. In the digital economy, it is expected that the demand for transportation reduce, and this will have a positive impact on dioxin gas emissions especially in big cities and crowded regions.

CONCLUSIONS

Digital technologies facilitate a society's access to knowledge and information, which in turns empowers individuals, businesses, institutions, and communities. Using e-services, governments can encourage people to reduce their consumption of resources and protect the environment, i.e. digital literacy improves the public's capability of becoming aware of the value and contribution of knowledge sharing and information dissemination to development.

The Internet has increased connectivity providing information of a significant magnitude to all with little or no cost. Countries lacking in adequate scientific and financial resources for development can acquire knowledge and information by building capacity for digital technologies, and by participating in the digital economy. Having more people who are digitally literate will strengthen a country's capacity to create new knowledge and promote new innovation.

Science, technology and innovation plays an important role in future sustainability by increasing the productivity of natural resources through the development of new methods and the discovery of new techniques. Scientific applications and research have had a substantial impact on human advancement throughout human history. It has promoted innovation and improved the ability of people to become more productive and creative. Technical progress has been largely responsible for the rise of Western economic power and industrial productivity, which gave rise to Western civilisation.

The digital age, driven by ICT services, facilitates access to global trade, finance, knowledge, and information; this can be used to build capacity for sustainable development and improve human ability to manage the environment. In particular, developing countries can benefit from digital services in order to increase the productivity of natural resources that will lead to economic growth and sustainable development. Bridging the gap between the needs of the present generation and the needs of future generations requires building digital capacity to enhance connectivity and encourage innovation. In countries where scientific and financial resources are slow to respond to megatrends raised by globalisation, economic growth and the rapid increase in population, ICTs provide new opportunities to acquire resources produced globally for use locally.

By 2050, the global population is expected to exceed 10 billion, the majority of which will be living in countries with shortages in terms of natural resources that cannot support additional demand. The task of environmental protection is beyond the scientific and technical capabilities of many nations, and therefore, a global strategy for the environment becomes essential in order to minimise the spillover effects of environmental linkages. In other words, nations should invest in science and technology to correct environmental imbalances and foster economic growth. Environmental innovation, particularly in developing countries, should be given top priority so that environmental protection will be assured and people will become empowered to become productive and protect the environment. Digital technologies are important enablers that provide people with equal opportunities to participate in environmental protection and development sustainability.

REFERENCES

Al-Roubaie, A. (2013), Building Knowledge Capacity for Sustainable Development in the Arab World, *International Journal of Innovation and Knowledge Management in Middle East and North Africa*, Vol. 2, No. 1, pp. 7–20.

Al-Roubaie, A. and Al-Zayer, J. (2007), Knowledge Creation and Global Readiness in GCC Countries, in Ahmed, A. (Ed.): Science, Technology and Sustainability in the Middle East and North Africa, Inderscience Enterprises Ltd, pp. 48–64.

Brundtland, G.H. (1987), *Report of the World Commission on Environment and Development: "our common future"*. United Nations.

Elmasry, T., Benni, E., Patel, J. and aus dem Moore, J.P. (2016), Digital Middle East: Transforming the Region into a Leading Digital Economy (www.mckinsey.com/business-functions/digital-mckinsey/how-we-help-clients).

International Telecommunication Union (ITU) (2015), Measuring the Information Society Report 2015 (Geneva: ITU).

International Telecommunication Union (ITU) (2017), Measuring the Information Society Report 2015, Volume 1, 2017 (Geneva: ITU).

OECD (2016), *OECD Science, Technology and Innovation Outlook 2016*, OECD Publishing, Paris. http://dx.doi.org/10.1787/sti_in_outlook-2016-en

United Nations (2013), World Economic and Social Survey 2013: Sustainable Development Challenges, New York: United Nations.

United Nations, United Nations Conference on Trade and Development (2015), Information Economy Report 2015, New York: United Nations.

World Bank (2013), Sustainable Development in a Dynamic World, World Development Report 2013, Washington: World Bank.

World Bank (2016), Digital Dividends, Washington: World Bank.

World Bank Group (2015), ICT for Greater Development Impact 2012–2015, Washington: World Bank.

BIOGRAPHY

Professor **Amer Al-Roubaie** teaches Economics and is currently the Dean of the College of Business and Finance at Ahlia University, Bahrain. He holds a PhD in Economics from McGill University in Montreal Canada. His main area of research is in the field of economic development and international economics. Recently, Professor Al-Roubaie, together with Professor Shafiq Alvi, has edited a four volume set entitled *Islamic Banking and Finance* published by Routledge. Al-Roubaie's latest book, entitled *Globalization of Knowledge* was published in 2011.

GOAL 4

QUALITY EDUCATION

PUBLIC-PRIVATE PARTNERSHIPS (PPPs) IN THE EDUCATION SECTOR OF BANGLADESH: WHAT PROSPECTS IN HIGHER EDUCATION?

Moazzem Hossain*

Associate Professor, Adj
Department of International Business and Asian Studies
Griffith Business School
Griffith University, Nathan Campus
Brisbane, Australia
m.hossain@griffith.edu.au

Mohammad Samsul Hoque

Deputy Secretary and Executive Magistrate
Bangladesh Civil Service
Dhaka, Bangladesh
hoque_ict112@yahoo.com

ABSTRACT

Purpose: Compared to many developing nations, Bangladesh scored strongly in reducing poverty and other goals of the UN MDGs programme between 2000 and 2015. Bangladesh now has major initiatives to implement several projects to make the UN's plan on Sustainable Development Goals (SDGs) agenda a grand success.

*Corresponding Author

There are only 12 years until 2030 in which to make the SDGs agenda of the UN a success. The public-private partnership (PPP) initiative is regarded as one of the pathways towards achieving the SDGs in Bangladesh. In this paper we will investigate how this nation would make use of the PPP approach in the higher education sub-sector, by employing a sectoral analysis introduced by the World Bank (WB) in establishing its Public-Private-Partnership in Infrastructure Resource Centre (PPIRC).

Design/methodology/approach: In order to transform Bangladesh into a developed country as per its ambitious Vision 2041, the government needs to create an effective domestic education agenda in order to develop a critical mass of globally competent citizens. While the country has been pursuing the vision with the aim of transforming itself into a developed economy, with sustainable economic growth and consistent improvement of human and social development indicators by the year 2041, according to a recent dialogue jointly organised by the Ministry of Foreign Affairs (MFA), Bangladesh and the Aga Khan Development Network (AKDN) (an international development NGO), the new generation will need to compete with their peers around the world.

With a view to incorporate values of internationalism in the domestic education system of Bangladesh, the programme was organised with a view to start a dialogue about how to turn the aspiration into reality. It was emphasised that, "Students have to be capable of addressing the emerging challenges like climate change, migration, financial crisis and traditional and non-traditional security that cut across the borders, on the one hand, while they need to develop communicative skills and collaborative approach to discuss those challenges in the global platforms, on the other". At present, there is no effective mechanism to create coherence between the core international curricula and domestic education agenda. At the same time, establishing a useful link between the international and national education system may create good opportunities for students to learn from different worldwide experiences to foster their global citizenship skills, further emphasised by the organisers of the dialogue. In view of the above, the present paper will investigate the PPP approach in the education sector of Bangladesh, in particular covering the vocational and higher education areas. In this respect both public and private sectors have a major role to play under the SDG agenda.

Findings: The present study would contribute to the Bangladesh government's policy strategy to create and examine effective domestic education in the area of vocational, trade, polytechnic and commerce, and other skilled based education. This would be done with the support of private investment in order to develop an effective public-private partnership to attain SDGs by 2030.

Originality/value: The study is original in its approach (no other studies have been found so far) and would generate debate with a view to how to embrace a private-public partnership approach in investing in the education sector, particularly technical education, over the next 20 years. The PPP will enhance and enrich the skills of millions joining the workforce in the next two decades, and attain the SDGs by 2030.

Keywords: Bangladesh; Education; Public-Private Partnership; Higher Education; Technical Education

INTRODUCTION

Bangladesh became an independent nation through an armed struggle against former West Pakistan in 1971. The country was initially characterised by political and economic instability and natural disasters, resulting in a weak and fragile economy. This is discussed further in the next section.

Bangladesh is surrounded by Indian Territory on three borders. However, a small strip borders Myanmar (formerly Burma) on the south-east, with another to the south, the Bay of Bengal. The country has more than 160 million people in an area of 144,000 square kilometres (over 1,000 people per square kilometre) – the most densely populated nation in the world after city states such as Singapore, Hong Kong and the province of Java, Indonesia. The population has more than doubled since 1971. More than 75% of the population live in rural villages, while more than 80% of the people live on agriculture, which accounts for the major source of paid and unpaid employment. The principal crops are rice, jute, tea, wheat, oilseeds, potato and pulses.

Natural gas is abundant in supply and is used to generate electricity and produce nitrogenous fertilisers. It is also the main source for domestic cooking, industrial use and transport in urban areas. Bangladesh has a tropical monsoon climate; this results in frequent cyclones (more than 30 cyclones have hit Bangladesh in the last 50 years) and widespread flooding almost every year (it has three large rivers, and thousands of small rivers and tributaries) causing damage to property and loss of life.

THE ECONOMY

Table 1 compares the major economic indicators between 1983 and 2015. In 1983, Bangladesh had a population of more than 90 million, with a density of population over 590 per square kilometre in 1983: the annual rate of population growth was 2.7%. The GDP per capita was very low at US$590 in 1983 prices. The growth rate in 1982 was only 0.1%. Ready-made garments (RMG) and shrimp exports had been nil or negligible. Remittances from abroad were only US$300 million in 1983. The population under the poverty line (head count ratio) was 60% in the same year. The production of rice was only 13 million tonnes, and inflation was running at 19%. Literacy rate was dismal, below 50%. Longevity was less than 50 years in the early 1970s.

The picture has changed dramatically over the last three decades to 2015 (Table 1). Population has increased by 80% as a result of a drop in the growth rate 60%. Population density per square kilometre has increased to 70%. The GDP per capita advanced

Table 1   Bangladesh's Achievements between 1983–2013

Items	1983	2015	Folds
Population (Millions)	90	160	1.80
Population growth rate (%)	2.7	1.7	−1.60
Population per square kilometre	590	1,030	1.70
GDP (in billion US$)	N/A	205	−
GDP per capita (in US$)	150	1,300	8.67
Growth rate (%)	0.1	6.5	65.00
Garments Exports (in billion US$)	Nil	26	−
Shrimp Exports (in billion US$)	Neg	0.64	−
Remittance (in billion US$)	0.3	15.50	51.67
Foreign Reserve (in billion US$)	N/A	27	−
Under Poverty Line (in % of total population)	60	23	−2.60
Rice Production (in million tonne)	13	33	2.54
Inflation Rate (%)	19	6.4	−3.00
Literacy Rate (%)	25	65	2.60
Longevity (years)	45	70	1.60

Note: N/A = Not available; Neg = Negligible
Source: Hossain (1983); Haider (2016)

almost nine fold as a result of sustained growth in GDP of between 5.0% and 6.5% in recent decades. The difference of population growth and GDP growth in 2015 suggests that GDP has grown by more than four times. In 1983, the population growth was more than 27 times that of the GDP rate. The export of garments reached more than US$25 billion, and shrimp exports were worth US$650 million in 2015. Remittance reached US$15 billion, and foreign reserves were at their peak at US$27 billion in 2015. In the production of rice, the nation had a surplus of 2 million tonnes in 2015 as against a deficit of a similar amount few years ago. Production hit 33 million tonnes. The inflation rate was brought down to single digit at 6.5% in 2015: it had been running at double digits over a long period since 1983. The literacy rate has improved at a strong pace and is now at 65% or more; longevity has passed 70 years.

POVERTY REDUCTION

In terms of reducing extreme poverty in Asia, certainly the East Asian nations have been ahead of South Asia. The Head Count Ratio (HCR) suggests that almost half the population in Bangladesh and 41% in India lived under Purchasing Power Parity of $1.25 a day. Recently, the Bangladesh Planning Commission (PC) published a report on the country's achievements and non-achievements in poverty reduction until 2014.

Table 2   Poverty Reduction in Bangladesh, 2002–2014 (%)

Year	People under Poverty*	Hard Core Poor**	People above Poverty Level
2002	44.6	–	55.4
2006	38.4	–	61.6
2009	33.4	–	66.6
2013	26.2	–	73.8
2014	24.3	10.6	75.5

Note: The Planning Commission defines poverty in terms of calories a person requires per day. In Bangladesh this is about 2,122Kcal. To purchase the required calories, a person's income per month has been considered to determine who are poor, people under poverty, and hard core poor. It has been estimated that Taka 3,000 per capita per month is needed to buy 2,122Kcal per day. The following estimates have been provided by the PC for these groups: *People under poverty: Having income below Taka 3,000 per month per person is someone who is considered poor. **Hard core poor: Having income below Taka 1,600 per month per person is someone who is considered to be hard core poor.
Source: Hossain and Hoque (2016) cited from Shah (2015)

The PC's assessment was based on data collected by the Bangladesh Bureau of Statistics (BBS). Table 2 presents a picture of poverty reduction between 2002 and 2014. Figures for 2014 are very encouraging. The national poverty level went down to one quarter of the population compared to almost one half in early 2000. More interestingly, hard core poor in 2014 accounted for 10.6% out of the 24.3% of total poor. This suggests that if this momentum can be continued, the prediction is by 2021, the 50th anniversary of independence, the nation would be in a position to push another 15% out of poverty, and the entire hard core poor eliminated with only 10% of the total population remaining poor. In absolute terms, this would be below 20 million under the poverty line as against 40 million today. Indeed, in absolute terms poverty will remain a challenge for the nation in the years to come (Hossain and Hoque, 2016).

With all these achievements on the economic front, according to the World Bank's definition of prosperity, Bangladesh has now advanced to lower middle income status. The next step in the ladder is achieving middle income, and it appears that with current development in economic activities, this is indeed likely to be achieved by 2025, providing the country maintains political stability.

In the meantime, the incumbent government has a major agenda in place called Vision 2041. The aim of this vision is to enable the nation to catch up with more developed countries, at least in economic and social terms. In other words, it would like to achieve a GDP per capita in Purchasing Power Parity terms equivalent to developed nations, and reach a literacy rate, longevity, sanitation, maternal and child mortality, nutrition intake and so on, on a par with developed nations. Of course, it is a tall order to achieve this within another quarter of a century. However, if the nation continues to grow at its present pace for another 25 to 30 years, there is a possibility of reaching the targets before it celebrates 100 year of its birth in 2071. The major obstacle that appear on the horizon at this moment is the impact of global warming induced climate change to 2100. It is predicted that the sea level will rise to 2100 and, if unabated, almost 40% of farmland would be inundated by saline water and more than half of its population would become climate refugees (Hossain and Selvanathan, 2011).

SANITATION ACCESS

Professor Amartya Sen and Jean Dreze published a volume in 2013 called, *An Uncertain Glory: India and its Contradictions*, in which the authors have strongly criticised India's non-achievement in sanitation access, even after this nation's recent success in economic prosperity. When comparing with India's neighbours, they were disappointed that India placed well behind Bangladesh (Sen and Dreze, 2013).

Compared to its immediate neighbours, on an aggregate nationally, Bangladesh performs quite well in terms of improved and shared sanitation access. For example, India, with 53% access (improved plus shared facilities) to sanitation performs poorly relative to Pakistan (54%) and Bangladesh (81%) in 2010. Comparing this national performance in rural and urban areas, the difference at the urban level in India (77%) is lower against Bangladesh (83%) and Pakistan at 78% (Hossain and Howard, 2014).

At the rural level, the difference has been phenomenal. For example, in Pakistan, 40% of the rural population has access to an improved plus shared sanitation facility, which is significantly higher than the 27% of rural people in India. In stark contrast to both India and Pakistan, in Bangladesh 80% of rural people had access. This raises the question of why Bangladesh has been outperforming Pakistan and India. The main reason was availability of microfinance to the poor in rural areas. Bangladesh is the home of large microfinance institutions (MFIs) of the world such as the Bangladesh Rural Advancement Committee BRAC, Grameen Bank, Association for Social Advancement ASA, and so on (this was also mentioned in Sen's observations in the 16 July 2014 edition of the prestigious London based daily, *The Guardian*).

EDUCATION

Having relative prosperity on the economic front, education and its importance in Bangladesh have been effectively and sustainably gaining recognition over the last three decades. The country now has a literacy rate of 70%; this was only 20% in 1981 and 17% in 1961. Education beyond primary level has been within the reach of only the well-off. Some of the major problems and difficulties in improving education in Bangladesh have been: inadequate implementation mechanisms in introducing education programmes, social inhibitions discouraging the education of girls, poverty, shortage of trained teachers, and lack of or poor quality of physical facilities. These were typical problems of developing countries in the 1960s and 1970s (Hossain and National Office for Overseas Skills Recognition (NOOSR), 1992).

However, in Bangladesh, two forces, the GOs (Public) and the NGOs (Private), have worked together to improve education since the 1980s. Major efforts have been made to change the century-old education system, to make it more effective and universal, and less elitist. The Second Five Year Plan (SFYP) of 1980–85, for the first time made provision for a national primary education and mass literacy programme. The Government was willing to develop a skilled labour force base instead of expanding liberal education. The Third Five Year Plan (TFYP) for 1986–1990 aimed at increasing primary age enrolments to 70%, and improve the retention rate to the end of the primary school cycle. It also aimed to reduce the rural-urban gap in educational facilities, reduce the gap in educational opportunities between the sexes, continue the efforts to reduce illiteracy among adults, and provide more in-service training for teachers.

In an effort to improve the degree of participation of the people in education development, efforts are being made to decentralise basic education at the *Upazila* (sub-district) level. However, some issues exist that need immediate attention:

- unsatisfactory participation rates in post-primary education;
- high drop-out rates in all stages;
- access to education is unequal. The imbalance is two-fold: a rural-urban imbalance and a gender imbalance;
- the availability of trained and committed teachers at primary level. This has caused a major problem in terms of teacher-student ratio at primary level where the participation rate has jumped in recent years;
- the physical infrastructure still remains inadequate given the increase in participation rate; and,
- absenteeism by primary teachers is a major cause of concern.

THE EDUCATION SYSTEM

The Education system in Bangladesh has many of the characteristics of the system introduced by the British in Greater India in the 19th century. There are three levels of school education: primary (Grades I–V), secondary (Grades VI–X) and higher secondary (Grades XI and XII) offered at higher secondary schools (and intermediate colleges).

Public Education System

Responsibility for education rests with the national Government's Ministry of Education. The Directorate of Education under the Ministry is responsible for the operation of secondary and higher secondary education, having annual public examinations for granting secondary and higher secondary certificates respectively. The administration of primary education has been recently decentralised at the sub-district level.

The government run colleges, polytechnic institutions and universities are directly under the control of the Ministry of Education, at least in budgetary and funding terms. In recent years, the allocation of funds towards public education systems has been increasing and has now reached more than 5% of the national budget. The year-on-year increase in budget allocation has been increasing as well. For example, a record amount was committed in 2009–10, which was almost 9% more than the previous year (www.mof.gov.bd, Ministry of Finance, 2009; Hossain and NOOSR, 1992).

At tertiary level, the first public university, the University of Dhaka, was established in 1925. There are now 38 public universities established all over Bangladesh.

Private Education System

About a quarter of primary schools are in the private sector. All junior high schools, *madrasahs* (religious schools), more than 90% of high schools, and almost all intermediate colleges, except some old colleges, are run by private sector. All secondary schools or intermediate colleges offering general education under the private system require affiliation with the regional Boards of Intermediate and Secondary Education for academic purposes. Recognition by the Board is required in order for a school or college to register candidates for public examination of the Secondary School Certificate (SSC) and Higher Secondary Certificate (HSC). For Islamic education, *madrasahs* are affiliated to the Madrasah Education Board, which is an autonomous board established in 1982. There are two stages of education offered under this Board: The *Dakhil* stage is equivalent to the secondary stage, and the *Alim* stage is equivalent to the higher secondary stage. Some *madrasahs* also offer vocational and technical education.

In the higher education sector, at tertiary level, the government started offering licenses to the private sector to establish private universities in the 1980s. So far, 95 universities have been given approval to run by domestic license holders. Some are doing very well; however, the majority are facing problems in following government rules and regulations.

Options after Secondary Education

At the end of Grade VIII, students may undertake two and three year courses at technical, vocational and commercial institutes. These courses lead to technical certificates and diplomas, and are at the trades' level. Graduates of the Secondary School Certificate examination at the end of Grade X, conducted by the Boards of Secondary and Intermediate Education, may either enter into an HSC (Year XI and XII) course or undertake technical education in the area of engineering, agriculture, trade courses at the polytechnics or technical/vocational institutes. At the post-secondary level, commonly undertaken HSC courses are in science, commerce, humanities and agriculture.

These courses are offered at various intermediate colleges and operated with both private and public funding. In addition to the intermediate colleges, there are nine cadet colleges, including one for females, which offer HSC courses. These have been established by public resources with a view to providing both secondary and higher secondary education with full residential facilities, including provision for military training to stimulate young graduates to join the defence forces after completion of the HSC.

Options for vocational/technical, trade and para-professional training are limited in Bangladesh. Post-secondary technical education has been offered mainly at the polytechnic and vocational training institutes. The Technical Education Board (TEB) is responsible for maintaining standards, conducting examinations and awarding all certificates and diplomas. The various types of institutes that were developed before 1986 are as follows:

- 23 agricultural institutes;
- 1 college of leather technology;
- 2 colleges of physical education;
- 1 college of textile technology;
- 16 commercial institutes for business studies;
- 1 institute for glass and ceramics;
- 1 institute of graphic arts;
- 11 nursing institutes;
- 18 polytechnic institutes for engineering studies;
- 1 institute for land survey studies;
- 54 vocational training institutes for trade and business studies;
- 7 primary teacher training institutes.

In addition to public places in technical and vocational institutes, there are also a number of commercial and vocational institutions in urban areas offering courses from three months to one year in duration in various technical, commercial and trade areas. They are run by private initiatives and operate on a commercial basis (Hossain and NOOSR, 1992).

Higher Education

Higher education in Bangladesh still bears some of the characteristics of the first universities established by the British Raj in the early part of the 20th century. The main role of these early universities was to maintain a uniform standard in the affiliated colleges under their jurisdiction through determining the courses of study and conducting the examinations. Gradually, over the years, the universities have established their own teaching departments for postgraduate study and research. Currently, Bangladesh has 40 public universities. These universities are mostly both teaching and affiliated institutions with departments of studies and related institutes; constituent colleges are part of the university, but may be located off the main campus. With the establishment of the National University of Bangladesh, governments over the years brought all colleges under the National University. All universities, including National University, usually offer courses leading to Honours degrees and postgraduate awards. The majority of students of the National University conduct a 'Pass' or ordinary Bachelor degree on campus; off campus, night courses cover a period of two years after HSC. There are some Secondary School Teachers Training colleges that offer Bachelor of Education (BEd) degree courses over one year for teachers who possess an undergraduate degree in any discipline.

In addition to public universities, the nation has now 95 private and 3 international universities. About two dozen private universities are making a major contribution to the nation's drive for building the education infrastructure and to develop human resources for the future. Due to limited space it is not possible here to assess both public and private universities in providing quality education in Bangladesh. However, it is important to mention the roles of a regulatory body that was established to regulate both the public and the private universities on the Government's behalf. This is the University Grants Commission (UGC) established in 1973. The UGC is responsible for assessing the annual financial needs of all public universities, evaluating university development programmes, and advising the government on the establishment of new universities, public or private, or the expansion of existing institutions. For public universities the government allocates a block grant of funds to the UGC, which in turn distributes the funds among the universities based on their requirements as determined by the UGC (see more in Hossain and NOOSR, 1992).

PUBLIC-PRIVATE PARTNERSHIP

Global Approach

Since the period of the Breton Wood agreement, written immediately after the conclusion of World War II, the World Bank (WB), one of the initiatives of Breton Wood, have been providing support to low and middle income countries. In recent years, and in order to develop public-private partnerships (PPPs), the Bank has been keen to make further global development efforts through a number of different tools and mechanisms. In addition to the Public-Private Partnership Infrastructure Research Centre (PPPIRC), the World Bank Group also supports a number of knowledge management tools in collaboration with other development partners. These include:

- The PPP Knowledge Lab;
- PPI Database - Private Participation in Infrastructure Database;
- BoKIR - Body of Knowledge on Infrastructure Regulation;
- PPIAF - Public Private Infrastructure Advisory Facility;

The sectoral PPP programme of the WB has been making major efforts to contribute to various sectors of its member economies. These are: Clean Technology, Sub-National and Municipal, Municipal Solid Waste (MSW), Telecom and ICT, Transportation, Water and Sanitation. The examples of four related studies are mentioned below:

1. *The Role and Impact of Public-Private Partnerships in Education* by Harry Anthony Patrinos, Felipe Barrera-Osorio, and Juliana Guaqueta, World Bank 2009.

This book examines five ways through which public-private partnerships (PPPs) contracts can help countries meet education goals. First, PPPs can increase access to good quality education for all, especially for poor children who live in remote, underserved communities and for children in minority populations. Second, lessons for innovative means of financing education can be particularly helpful in post-conflict countries undergoing reconstruction. Third, lessons about what works in terms of PPPs contribute to the development of a more differentiated business model, especially for middle-income countries. Fourth, the challenge of meeting the education Millennium Development Goals over 2000–2015 was a daunting task in the poorest countries. Understanding new partnership arrangements within broad international aid architecture in education can help bring us closer to those goals. Fifth, some very innovative PPP arrangements are developing in Arab countries at present, and lessons can be drawn from their experiences.

2. This background paper, commissioned for the Education for All (EFA) Global Monitoring Report 2009 on *Overcoming Inequality: why governance matters?* by Masooda Banoo, United Nations Educational, Scientific and Cultural Organization (UNESCO) 2008.

This paper deals with education reform in Pakistan, which has invested PPPs as the primary strategy to address the challenges of access, quality and equity across income, gender, and the urban/rural divide. The paper documents the dominant PPP models in Pakistan, notes their strengths and limitations, and then assesses their potential to act as the 'anchor' of education reforms in Pakistan.

3. *Public-Private Partnerships in Education: Lessons Learned from the Punjab Education Foundation* by Allah Bakhsh Malik, Asian Development Bank 2010.

This study has investigated an alternative to the country's struggling public school system for impoverished children living in the remote rural areas and urban slums of Pakistan. The provincial government of Punjab revitalised the Punjab Education Foundation (PEF), which works with private schools located in poor communities throughout the province. Through these public-private partnerships (PPPs), the PEF provides school funding, teacher training, and vouchers allowing needy children to attend participating private schools for free. The parity between male and female students is ensured by a policy that makes it mandatory for participating households to enrol both girls and boys. If a household enrols its boys using an education voucher but not its girls, the voucher will no longer be valid. This condition, coupled with an awareness campaign, has persuaded parents to send both their boys and girls to school. This report examines a number of aspects of the PEF experience with the design and implementation of PPPs in the education sector including, a brief discussion of the lessons that can be drawn from the PEF's experience with education PPPs.

4. *Public-Private Partnerships in Education and the Pursuit of Gender Equality: A view from South Asia* by Shailaja Fennell, International Development Policy, Revue internationale de politique de développement, 2014.

This study found the introduction of public-private partnerships (PPPs) into the educational sphere has opened up the sector to a wide range of new private providers in India and Pakistan. In addition to the relationship between PPPs and gender, it analyses the role of PPPs in the education sector and reviews the extent to which policies regarding PPPs in education have addressed the objective of gender equality. It compares these policy perspectives with the local data obtained from field studies conducted in India and Pakistan, and evaluates the implications of the findings for moving forward the manner by which partnerships could reduce gender gaps in both countries. For details, see https://ppp.worldbank.org/public-private-partnership/.

PUBLIC-PRIVATE PARTNERSHIP PROSPECTS IN HIGHER EDUCATION: CONCLUDING COMMENTS

There are only 12 years to make the Sustainable Development Goals (SDGs) agenda of the UN a success by 2030. The public-private partnership (PPP) initiative is regarded as one of the pathways that can be used to achieve the SDGs in Bangladesh. In this paper we investigated this nation's prospects of making use of the PPP approach in the domestic education sector, employing a sectoral analysis introduced by the World Bank (WB).

In order to transform Bangladesh into a developed country as per its ambitious Vision 2041, the government needs to create an effective domestic education agenda in order to develop a critical mass of globally competent citizens. While the country has been pursuing the vision with the aim of transforming itself into a developed economy with sustainable economic growth and consistent improvement of human and social development indicators by the year 2041, the new generation will need to compete with their peers around the world to make the Sustainable Development Goals (SDGs) agenda of the UN a success. The public-private partnership (PPP) initiative is regarded as one of the pathways to achieve the SDGs in Bangladesh. In this paper we investigated how this nation could make use of the PPP approach in the domestic education sector, employing a sectoral analysis introduced by the World Bank (World Bank, 2003; PPPRIC, 2015).

Indeed, the time has arrived to look at higher education and vocational sub-sectors from the viewpoint of enriching skills for increasing productivity and generating more and more jobs for the ever increasing labour force in Bangladesh. At this stage, a huge opportunity exists to increase productivity by introducing state-of-the-art technology and new age curricula in order to meet not only domestic demand for skilled works, but also demand for such workers from foreign nations. To achieve this, Bangladesh will need the following strategies in the education industry.

RECOMMENDATIONS

1. Every year the nation faces huge difficulties in offering higher education places to school leavers, with increased imbalances between places offered and demand for public university places. This, indeed, is a major issue, even for large number of students with high grades in HSC. The PPP approach could be of use to meet this challenge.
2. Using new regulations, private universities need a device for providing places in certificate and diploma courses at trade levels. They also need to develop training programmes for existing employees to enrich and enhance their skills on a regular basis. Through PPPs, public funds to private universities can make a breakthrough in this area.
3. The quality of education is at a crossroads in Bangladesh, particularly at the post-HSC level. This is due to millions of students with undergraduate degrees in liberal arts, sciences, and business studies remaining unemployed over a long period of time. The public-private approach could play a major role in developing alternative strategies to improve the quality of education.
4. SMEs from any nation, developing or least developed, are the engine of economic growth and development. The workers with technical, trade, and vocational skills are the bread and butter of all SMEs, and are also the major source of employment of these workers. Through public-private partnerships, the existing public and/or private education providers can invest in preparing the workers with new and advanced technologies.

REFERENCES

Aga Khan Development Network (AKDN) (2017).

Banoo, M. (2008), Global Monitoring Report 2009 on Overcoming Inequality: Why Governance Matters? *Education for All (EFA)*, UNESCO, Paris.

Dreze, J. and Sen, A. (2013), *An Uncertain Glory: India and Its Contradictions*, Princeton University Press, Princeton, 434pp.

Fennell, S. (2014), Public-Private Partnerships in Education and the Pursuit of Gender Equality: A view from South Asia, *International Development Policy*, Vol. 5, No. 5.3, URL http://journals.openedition.org/poldev/1798; doi: 10.4000/poldev.1798.

Haider, A. (2016), Bangladesh out of the Basket, *The Daily Star*, 23 January, Dhaka.

Hossain, M. (1983), *Quantitative Analysis of Policy Alternatives for Bangladesh's Future Agrarian Development*, Unpublished Doctoral Thesis, Department of Agricultural Economics, The University of Western Australia, Perth.

Hossain, M. and Hoque, S. (2016), Rhetorical Bottomless Basket Case versus Bangladesh's Success with the MDGs, *Outlook 2016*, World Association for Sustainable Development (WASD), Emerald Press, London.

Hossain, M. and Howard, P. (2014), The Sanitation Access to Developing Asia: India's Performance Over 2001 and 2011, *World Journal of Science, Technology and Sustainable Development*, Vol. 11, No. 2, pp. 93–101.

Hossain, M. and National Office for Overseas Skills Recognition (NOOSR) (1992), *Country Education Profiles – Bangladesh – A Comparative Study,* National Office of Overseas Skills Recognition, Department of Employment, Education and Training, Australian Government Publishing Service (AGPS), Canberra.

Hossain, M. and Selvanathan, E. (Eds) (2011), *Climate Change and Growth in Asia*, Edward Elgar Publishing, Cheltenham and Mas.http://ppp.worldbank.org/public-private-partnership/overview/what-are-public-private-partnerships

Malik, A.B. (2010), *Public-Private Partnerships in Education: Lessons Learned from the Punjab Education Foundation*, Asian Development Bank (ADB), Manila.

Ministry of Finance (2009), *Bangladesh Economic Survey* 2009, Bengali version, Bangladesh Government Press, June, Dhaka.

Patrinos, H.A., Osorio, F.B. and Guáqueta, J. (2009), *The Role and Impact of Public-Private Partnerships in Education*, The World Bank, Washington DC.

Public-Private-Partnership in Infrastructure Resource Centre (PPIRC) (2015), The World Bank Group, Washington, DC.

Shah, J. (2015), Four Crore (40 million Out of 160) People are under Poverty, *Prothom Alo* (Bengali Daily), 12 February, Dhaka.

World Bank (2003), *World Development Report 2004: Making Services Work for Poor People*, Washington, DC.

BIOGRAPHY

Dr **Moazzem Hossain** has taught environmental economics, development and trade in the Department of International Business and Asian Studies of the Griffith Business School at Griffith University, Brisbane since 1990. He is also a full member of the Griffith Centre for Sustainable Enterprise (GCSE) and the Griffith Asia Institute (GAI) of Griffith University. He has a Master's degree from the Australian National University (1978), and a PhD from the University of Western Australia (1986). Dr Hossain's current research includes Climate Change issues in the Asia-Pacific including the Bay of Bengal delta and Sundarbans region (Bangladesh and West Bengal, India). Dr Hossain has produced eight authored and edited volumes on the subject of South Asian economic development, and has published articles in many international journals. He is the advisor of the "International Centre for Development Strategies" (ICDS), a German-based International organisation of Bangladeshi expatriates across the globe. He has also advised The Hague based

BSUG – Development and Diaspora since 2013. He is the executive editor of the Journal of Sustainable Development Management (JSDM) published by IIDS Australia-ICDS Germany.

Mohammad Samsul Hoque, is a Deputy Secretary of the Government of Bangladesh. He has been doing research work with Dr Moazzem Hossain, an associate Professor of Griffith University Australia, for the last four years. Mr Hoque has attended several national and international conferences, including the WASD conferences in the UK and Bahrain. His papers have been published in WASD outlook 2016 and 2017, respectively. Mr Hoque has a BSc (honours), an MSc (Chemistry), and is a Commonwealth Executive Master of Public Administration (CEMPA).

CONNECT TO LEARN – THE INTERNATIONALISATION OF MULTINATIONAL CORPORATIONS IN EMERGING MARKETS

Rebecca Rehn

Uppsala University, Sweden
rebeccarehn@gmail.com

ABSTRACT

Purpose: The overarching purpose of this research is to study a Multinational corporation's (MNCs) expansion into an Emerging Market (EM). It does this by further investigating how MNCs partner with non-traditional actors when entering EMs, and how the exchange of knowledge is carried out at the micro-level in these relationships.

Design/methodology/approach: An exploratory field study was conducted in Myanmar over a period of one month. The purpose was to study an MNC's expansion into an EM. The study includes interviews with both an MNC and the United Nations, including observations on site, and a documentary analysis.

Findings: The study contributes to research in proving that internationalisation in emerging markets seems to be a two-way experiential knowledge direction, where MNCs also need to take an active part in educating the emerging market in order to enter.

Originality/value: By studying an MNC's cooperation with the UN as part of their expansion in Myanmar, the research will increase the understanding of the complex phenomenon of multi-stakeholder partnerships between MNCs and the UN. This is an area that has received limited research among both political science scholars as well as international business scholars.

Keywords: Internationalisation process; experiential knowledge; emerging economies; Uppsala model; United Nations; Sustainable Development Goals (SDGs); Myanmar; Bottom of the Pyramid (BoP); Public-Private Partnership (PPP)

*Corresponding Author

INTRODUCTION

The United Nations Sustainable Development Goals (SDGs) were adopted in 2015. One of the main goals is to include the private sector's resources in order to be able to fulfil the SDGs. The UN has thereby reached out to the private sector, and multi-stakeholder partnerships have been endorsed with the aim to "mobilise and share knowledge, expertise, technology and financial resources, to support the achievement of the SDGs in all countries, in particular developing countries" (UN, A/RES/70/1, 2015). The SDGs' role in the multinational corporations' context is a new phenomenon, which makes it complex to study. However, there is a need to increase the understanding of how the collaborations between MNCs and the UN are carried out.

The primary corporate benefits of partnering with the UN are considered to be market expansion, obtaining a license to operate, and an opportunity to develop emerging markets (EMs) (Rueede and Kreutzer, 2015; Utting and Zammit, 2009). Having said that, the MNCs find it rather difficult to be successful in entering EMs, despite the additional business opportunities it represents (Meyer, 2004; London and Hart, 2004). This is due to the liability of foreignness, as well as a lack of market-specific knowledge that is considered an essential prerequisite when conducting business abroad (Hadjikhani et al., 2008). In EMs this market-specific knowledge is of even greater importance as prior knowledge from other markets is less or even non-transferable. Hence, there is a need for MNCs to have social embeddedness, which refers to the need of establishing relationships with other actors in society (London and Hart, 2004). However, the lack of institutions within EMs requires MNCs to turn to other actors within society (Peng and Luo, 2000). By collaborating with non-traditional partners, the MNCs will gain access to local knowledge that would otherwise be difficult to achieve (Rondinelli and London, 2003).

On the empirical front, the study is motivated by the observation that there are few studies on how the knowledge is obtained at the micro-level when MNCs internationalise in EMs. Instead, the previous studies have all focused on the importance of knowledge at the macro-level. Therefore, the overarching purpose of this research is to study an MNC's expansion into an EM by further investigating how MNCs partner with non-traditional actors when entering EMs, and how the exchange of knowledge is carried out at the micro-level in these relationships.

How do non-traditional actors assist MNC's internationalisation in emerging markets?

In order to answer the research question, the study will take a closer look at Ericsson's entry into the Republic of the Union of Myanmar. The country is considered as one of the last remaining greenfield markets in the world. In 2012, the government of Myanmar, together with the UN agency International Telecommunications Union (ITU), launched the Wireless Broadband Master Plan of Myanmar with the aim of introducing two new telecoms licenses. Shortly thereafter, Ericsson decided to re-establish themselves in Myanmar and started a corporate social responsibility (CSR) project in collaboration with UNESCO (Ericsson, 2016). By studying Ericsson's coop-eration with UNESCO as part of their expansion in Myanmar, the research will con-tribute to the internationalisation literature about how an MNC internationalises in an EM. This will in turn increase the understanding of the complex phenomenon of multi-stakeholder partnerships between MNCs and the UN, which is an area that has received limited research among both political science scholars (Pappi and Henning, 1998) and international business scholars (e.g. Boddewyn, 1988; Hadjikhani, 2000; Ljung, 2014).

LITERATURE REVIEW

As the aim of this study is to investigate an MNC's partnership with non-traditional actors when entering EMs, and how the exchange of knowledge looks at the micro-level in these relationships, there is a need to apply a model that conceptualises the knowledge concept. Consequently, the process model of internationalisation was identified as this model, illustrating that MNCs enter new markets in order to expand their knowledge base (e.g. Johanson and Vahlne, 1977). The most prominent research is the Uppsala Model (U-M) of Internationalisation, which builds on the idea that internationalisation is a gradual process where there is a correlation between the development of knowledge and market commitment (Johanson and Vahlne, 1977). The main obstacle for firms that want to enter foreign markets is claimed to be the physic distance[1], where firms lack the experiential market knowledge that can only be acquired by operating in that market (Johanson and Vahlne, 1977). When a firm enters a foreign market, it can gain new knowledge that will reduce the uncertainty of operating in that market (Johanson and Vahlne, 1977).

The concept of experiential knowledge has been recognised as one of the most critical concepts of Johanson and Vahlne's (1977) model (Kogut and Singh, 1988; Barkema et al., 1996; Eriksson et al., 1997). The concept can be divided into *general knowledge* and *market-specific knowledge*; general knowledge is associated with ob-jective knowledge while market-specific knowledge refers to experiential knowledge (Johanson and Vahlne, 1977). Experiential market-specific knowledge is bound to the

---

[1]Physic distance refers to the differences between the foreign market and the host market (Johanson and Vahlne, 1977).

market and firms that obtain experiential knowledge; it also increases their ability to "perceiving and formulating opportunities" (Johanson and Vahlne, 1977, p. 28). In their study, Hilmersson and Jansson (2012) have assumed that firms that enter foreign markets exploit previous experiences and gain new experiences, which they refer to as *internationalisation knowledge*.

Two other types of market-specific knowledge seem to appear in the literature. The first concept can be labelled *institutional/societal/market knowledge*, which refers to experiential knowledge of institutions such as frameworks, laws, norms and rules (e.g. Blomstermo et al., 2004; Eriksson et al., 1997). The second concept is called *business knowledge*, which relates to experiential knowledge of the market and clients. It is argued that firms that possess this type of knowledge can increase their business opportunities in the foreign market, and thereby reducing uncertainty (Kogut and Singh, 1988). Finally, in recent years, scholars have applied a further type of experiential knowledge that relates to *network knowledge*, referring to knowledge derived from within the network relationship (Blomstermo et al., 2004).

Obtaining experiential knowledge is critical for firms that enter EMs; this is because there is a lack of existing knowledge of these markets (Meyer and Gelbuda, 2006). Traditionally, EMs have been considered undeveloped and immature (Jansson, 2008). They still lack institutional capacity, legislation and infrastructure (Hoskinsson et al., 2000), and it is difficult to employ a well-educated workforce (Khanna et al., 2005). Scholars (Hilmersson, 2011; Meyer and Gelbuda, 2006; Salmi, 2000) have therefore argued that internationalisation knowledge is less valuable when entering EMs. Instead, market-specific knowledge is considered the essential sort of knowledge when firms enter EMs (Forsgren, 2002). Hence, MNCs have realised the importance of having social embeddedness – three strategies (collaborating with non-traditional partners, co-inventing custom solutions and building local capacity) that can facilitate MNCs entry into Bottom of the Pyramid (BoP) (London and Hart, 2004).

THEORETICAL FRAMEWORK

The theoretical tool in this research will be built on the knowledge exchange between MNCs and non-traditional actors, which in turn will contribute to the understanding of how MNCs enter EMs. In order to contextualise this, the main concept of experiential knowledge will further be divided into different types of knowledge. In line with scholars (e.g. Eriksson et al., 1997), experiential knowledge will be divided into institutional, business and internationalisation knowledge. In order to take the theoretical tool further, it has also integrated the network knowledge proposed by, for example, Johanson and Vahlne (2009) (see Table 1 for theoretical framework).

Table 1   Summary of Theoretical Tool

Experiential knowledge type	Characteristics	Critical in EM
Institutional/ societal/ market knowledge	Experiential knowledge of the macro-environmental institutions such as institutional frameworks, laws, norms and rules (e.g. Blomstermo et al., 2004; Eriksson et al., 1997).	Lack of institutional experiential knowledge is difficult, as it is not easy for a firm to acquire information about laws and norms that apply abroad (Eriksson et al., 1997).
Business knowledge	Firm's knowledge of competitors, customers as well as other actors (Eriksson et al., 1997).	Firms are able to perceive opportunities in markets, thereby reducing uncertainty (Kogut and Singh, 1988).
Internationalisation knowledge	Firms that enter foreign markets exploit previous experiences and gain new experiences (Hilmersson and Jansson, 2012, p.99).	General internationalisation knowledge is less valuable when entering EMs (e.g. Hilmersson, 2011; Meyer and Gelbuda, 2006; Salmi, 2000).
Network experiential knowledge	Knowledge about the business network in the host market (Blomstermo et al., 2004).	Being an insider in a network decreases the uncertainty in the foreign market (Johanson and Vahlne, 2009).

Source: Compiled by author

METHODOLOGY

Given that the study was conducted in Myanmar without much attention from international business scholars (Wright et al., 2005), due to its politically unstable climate (Meyer and Thein, 2014), a case study was considered an appropriate methodological choice. The major reason behind the selection of investigating an MNC's expansion in Myanmar is because the country has one of the least developed telecommunications services in the world. The identification of the focal firm, Ericsson, as a suitable case was based on their extensive experience of internationalisation since the company was established in 180 countries. Ericsson was also selected because the company has taken a leading advocating role in fostering partnerships for the SDGs. Therefore, when screening Ericsson's partnerships with the UN, the Connect to Learn programme was recognised as an interesting public-private partnership between Ericsson and UNESCO. Twenty-one in-depth interviews (see appendix) were carried out; these were semi-structured and consisted of open questions (Saunders et al., 2012, p. 320).

EMPIRICAL FINDINGS

Ericsson's Entry into Myanmar

The Swedish MNC Ericsson is present in 180 countries (Ericsson, 2015). In 1998, Ericsson made the decision to withdraw all operations in Myanmar, which they claimed was on commercial grounds or human rights concerns (Weidman, 2012). In June 2012, Ericsson re-established themselves in Myanmar. The major challenges were anticipated to be the legislation that still was not complete, infrastructure, and being able to get bank licenses (The Head of Ericsson Myanmar). Anders Larsson, who acts as the Chief Technological Officer (CTO) at Ericsson Myanmar, was one of the first four employees in Myanmar in 2012. He described that, during the first months, it was impossible to open a bank account. Working with the government was perceived as most challenging since it was conservative and under-developed (Head of Ericsson Myanmar, from research interviews, 2016).

Another challenge was the lack of policy and telecommunication laws. The International Telecommunication Union (ITU) is a specialised agency of the United Nations and has, in the case of Myanmar, been responsible for the ICT development where they have been involved in drafting the Wireless Broadband Master Plan of Myanmar. The Deputy Director of ITU (2016) confirmed that ITU and Ericsson often shared advice, and that they worked closely with each other at the regional level. The CU Head (2016) stated that Ericsson could overcome the challenges of establishing in Myanmar due to their long-time experience in conducting business in other countries. The Connect to Learn (CTL) Programme Manager in Myanmar also described Ericsson had intending to break into new industries with the aim of using their platform in other settings as well:

> *"We want to break into other industries other than our traditional industry, which is telecom. Not like we intend to do it ourselves, but more forcing Public-Private Partnerships (PPP) in different areas. And actually, show that our platform can be the base for other connected services in the future."* (Programme Manager CTL, from research interviews, 2016).

Ericsson Approaching the Education Sector

Ericsson identified the education sector in Myanmar as lagging behind, and therefore saw a chance to contribute with their technology. Enrolment in secondary education in Myanmar is 51%, one of the lowest numbers globally (World Bank, 2016).

Ericsson decided to launch Connect to Learn (CTL) in June 2015. The aim of CTL is to scale up access to quality secondary education by bringing ICT to schools in remote parts of the world, over mobile broadband. The CTL programme has, so far, been implemented in 21 countries and benefits around 50,000 students. It was described by the CTL Programme Manager in Myanmar (2016) that Ericsson realised early on that it would not be possible to establish the CTL project in Myanmar by themselves. Therefore, Ericsson reached out to other partners that could provide expertise. The CTL project was created as a PPP where Ericsson collaborates with UNESCO, the UK Department for International Development (DfID), under their Girls' Education Challenge, the Earth

Institute at Columbia University, Finja Five, Qualcomm© Wireless Reach™, and the external evaluator EduEval (Ericsson, 2016). Ericsson's collaboration with UNESCO in managing the CTL project will be further emphasised in the next section.

Collaboration with UNESCO

Knowledge of the education sector as well as pedagogic skills were identified as vital for Ericsson to break into the new industry of education. Ericsson therefore needed to reach out to other partners that had good knowledge of both the local context and the education sector:

> *"So, when we were looking into who could we partner with on the educa-tion section, we identified UNESCO in Myanmar as being the most suitable partner to help us implement the program locally"* (Global CTL Manager, from research interviews, 2016).

UNESCO was seen as a credible and neutral organisation that specifically has knowl-edge of the education sector; UNESCO helps governments design their education pol-icy (Global CTL Manager, from research interviews, 2016). UNESCO could therefore provide the expertise from both within education and in their close contact with the government in Myanmar (Head of Ericsson Myanmar, from research interviews, 2016). Several respondents declared that the project would not have been possible without the partnership with UNESCO. Magnus Mandersson, who acts as the Executive Vice President of Ericsson, argued that by collaborating with the UN, it can: "contribute to a better product success and have the opportunity to work in developing markets". The execution of the project was made at a local level by the regional Ericsson and the regional UNESCO in Myanmar; this will be further described in the next section.

THE ROLE OF UNESCO

Antony Tam, ICT Education Specialist at UNESCO in Myanmar, is responsible for the CTL project from UNESCO's side. Their role is to carry out the teacher professional de-velopment programme, where UNESCO has organised a series of ICT training courses. Together with the Department of Basic Education (DBE) of the Ministry of Education (MoE) in Myanmar, UNESCO has set up an ICT team of 22 trainers that are the local implementation partners for UNESCO. The ICT Education Specialist at UNESCO (2016) stated that the teacher training was carried out in 31 schools; 17 schools in the Mandalay region and 14 schools in the Mon state and Bago region. The ICT Education Specialist at UNESCO (2016) highlighted that the DBE team are the main trainers, and UNESCO go to the training site on a day-to-day basis. In one of the training courses, UNESCO, together with Ericsson, went to the sites and conducted training in technical trouble shooting.

The ICT Education Specialist UNESCO (2016) stated that the partnership with Ericsson enabled UNESCO to make a bigger impact on the ground. Moreover, UNESCO has also learnt many of Ericsson's technical solutions, in addition to managing and coordinating this kind of multi-donor and multi-partner projects (ICT Education Specialist UNESCO, from research interviews, 2016).

Pitch for the Government

Jan Wassenius, the current Country Head of Ericsson Myanmar, described that Ericsson needed to pitch the CTL project to the MoE as well as the Ministry of Communications and Information Technology (MCIT) and get their approval. The Global CTL Manager (2016) further stated that the pitch was made together with UNESCO; this was because UNESCO works closely with the MoE, so it added strength to the proposal. This was further confirmed by the Programme Manager of CTL in Myanmar, who described that UNESCO acted as a bridge to the government in Myanmar: "At first we did not go directly to the MoE or different departments of the minister in Myanmar. We need UNESCO as the bridge".

> "We also asked them for their advice on, which areas, which schools, and also which operator we should use as our partner. So MICT, they advised us to work with MPT and MoE they pointed out which schools and areas and provinces that we should do the project in" (Head of Ericsson Myanmar, from research interviews, 2016).

Technology Programme and Network Roll-out

Locally, Ericsson employed around 100 engineers for the network roll-out and building up the 3G networks (Global CTL Manager, from research interviews, 2016). In the technical team, Ericsson also employed four newly examined students from West Yangon Technological University. The main reason for this was that Ericsson needed to train local people in the technology solutions and get these experts to talk with Ericsson's customers about the solutions, products and benefits of choosing Ericsson instead of other companies. The Head of Corporate Sustainability (CS) (2016) also claimed that the aim with CTL was in a long-term perspective to educate the workforce:

> "Myanmar is a country that had virtually no internet penetration just a few years ago and the access in Myanmar would be based very much on having an educated workforce. So, CTL is about the next generation of leaders." (Head of CS, from research interviews, 2016).

The CTO (2016) further highlights that the CTL project acted as a learning source for newly employed students. Each student got to focus on one specific area of technology where Ericsson had the intent to make business with in the future. As a result, this would increase the young professional's knowledge of the technical areas. The next section will elaborate on the students' experiences of working at Ericsson.

The Technical Girls

All the four girls (Mya, Akari, Aye and Ei) were met during an afternoon at the Ericsson office in Yangon. They described Ericsson as the first company that came to their University campus and made recruitments. The recruitment had been very competitive: out of 400 people, 12 students were selected and out of these 12, 4 were chosen to join the technical team. Ei described that she had been to work conferences in Singapore, Thailand, Vietnam and India, and that she established connections with senior managers in other countries. The girls described that they struggled when starting work at Ericsson since they were intentionally given tough work just to learn. Mya said: "It was Anders' [CTO] intention that we should learn with this project. He knows that we cannot do much, but if we learn much it is a huge profit for everybody".

Ei described that the first task she was assigned to was to select all the schools in the project. Ericsson had an agreement with the MCIT and the operator Myanmar Post and Telecommunications (MPT) to deploy ten sites and 25 schools in Mandalay. Ei declared that the collaboration with UNESCO and MoE simplified her work:

> "I'm born in Myanmar but not familiar with the geography of the other regions. UNESCO and MoE gave us the coordinates of all secondary schools in Myanmar so I can plot the location into the Google maps".

Htone Gyi School in Bago region

In order to increase the author's understanding of the CTL project and Ericsson's role, a field trip was conducted to Htone Gyi school in Bago region in central Myanmar. The school hosts 1,328 students: in total, they had received 6 laptops, 99 tablets, 2 projectors and 3 charging stations. On one occasion they had an issue with the machine and the desktop and an Ericsson engineer came out and managed to solve the issue. Five teachers in this school are a part of the teacher training professional development programme. After the second training session, they claimed that they had learnt basic computer skills and how to use Wi-Fi.

RESULTS AND ANALYSIS

Ericsson left the Myanmar market in 1998 and returned in 2012. When the government of Myanmar introduced the new telecoms licenses, Ericsson saw an opportunity to reintroduce their technology in Myanmar. Therefore, Ericsson used the CTL project in terms of gaining access to knowledge of the local market and thereby increasing their commitment to the market. This was possible with the interaction with non-traditional actors who acted as a bridge to political actors and state departments. Ericsson gained knowledge from ITU in terms of ICT laws and regulations, and from UNESCO in terms of education policies. Both these actors also facilitated Ericsson's interaction with the state departments. Mandersson further highlighted the importance for Ericsson to collaborate with the UN by saying that the UN can "contribute to a better product success and have the opportunity to work in developing markets". This is in line with BoP studies that pointed out the importance of collaboration with non-traditional partners when entering BoP (e.g. London and Hart, 2004).

As the literature review implied, internationalising in EMs poses both challenges as well as opportunities for businesses. The challenges when Ericsson established itself in Myanmar were anticipated as being a lack of clear guidelines for doing business, legislation that was perceived as unclear, and moreover the ability to obtain bank licenses (Wassenius, from research interviews, 2016). Moreover, several respondents also declared that the basic infrastructure in Myanmar was lagging behind, which imposed institutional challenges. Respondents at Ericsson stated that it was a struggle to work with the government bodies since they were not yet professional in their handling of different project requirements. The struggle for businesses to expand in EMs due to institutional challenges corresponds with Hoskinsson et al. (2000), who declared that EMs are still considered immature markets that often have a lack of institutional capacity and infrastructure.

Ericsson – Lessons Learned from the Market

When reviewing the literature, it was described that firms that enter EMs need to gain market-specific experiential knowledge in terms of institutional as well as business knowledge (Forsgren, 2002). As the Myanmar market was immature and there were not that many institutions, Ericsson needed to turn to other actors in order to gain market-specific knowledge. Therefore, Ericsson gained experiential market-specific knowledge mainly through learning through the UN agencies UNESCO and ITU, which will be further exemplified in the following paragraphs.

Advice from the Government

The Myanmar government provided Ericsson with advice on which schools and which operator Ericsson should use as their partner in CTL. It can therefore be reasoned that Ericsson needed to collaborate with the ministries in order to increase their experiential institutional learning. However, it was declared that it was difficult for Ericsson to approach the ministries by themselves, and thereby UNESCO acted as a bridge to access the knowledge that the government held.

Learning from UNESCO

The empirical paper has shown that Ericsson learned how to work with the government in Myanmar from UNESCO, and how to develop technical programmes that would be suitable for the Myanmar context. The collaboration with UNESCO could therefore be seen as essential in Ericsson's entry in Myanmar. It can be argued that UNESCO provided Ericsson with institutional knowledge in terms of education policies.

Lessons Learned from ITU

As the institutional capacity was still immature in Myanmar, Ericsson needed to turn to other actors. Ericsson gained institutional experiential knowledge from ITU in terms of information of political policies and telecommunication laws that would in turn affect the ICT development in Myanmar.

Educating the Myanmar Government

It was described by several respondents that Ericsson had developed a relationship with the MoE as well as MCIT at an early stage of their entry into Myanmar. Hence, it can be argued that MoE benefitted from Ericsson's technical business knowledge, at the same time as Ericsson gained experiential institutional knowledge from MoE.

Educating ITU

Ericsson's collaboration with ITU was not only a one-direction transfer of knowledge since it was highlighted by Sharma (Senior Advisor, ITU) that Ericsson also provided valuable information to ITU. Therefore, ITU gained business knowledge from Ericsson that helped them to improve standards and policy-setting in the region by transferring knowledge to the government of Myanmar in their draft of the Wireless Broadband Master Plan.

Technical Training of UNESCO

The partnership with UNESCO assisted Ericsson in their implementation of the CTL project, and by exchanging the different knowledge bases, the partners could combine their individual knowledge as well as create new knowledge. The field visit to Htone Gyi school proved that the teachers had to learn Ericsson's technology in the CTL project. The teachers had undergone workshops that were predominately carried out by UNESCO and the DBE team, but Ericsson also contributed to the education of the teachers themselves. This finding reveals that Ericsson provided UNESCO and the teachers with business and network knowledge in line with Kogut and Singh (1988) and Blomstermo et al. (2004).

Training of Technical Girls

A challenge of an EM is that it is immature and, according to Khanna et al. (2005), it is difficult to recruit a well-educated workforce. Ericsson needed to employ local people and train them in order to increase the experiential institutional knowledge of the work force. The employment of the four technical girls was also one way for Ericsson to educate the market. The trickling-down of knowledge (Meyer, 2004), is an interesting finding since the girls carried with them the knowledge that they have learned by working with CTL inside Ericsson, and could continue to work with Ericsson's customers to expand the business opportunities within their area of expertise. This example provides clear evidence that when Ericsson entered Myanmar, they needed to educate the work force in order to succeed. Ericsson provided both business and internationalisation knowledge to the technical girls. One of the girls, Ei, described that by working at Ericsson, she gained knowledge from other markets since she was sent to conferences in other locations. Moreover, since the technical girls needed to take responsibility in specific technical subject matters, they also increased their business knowledge within these areas.

DISCUSSION

The case study of Ericsson's entry in Myanmar has showcased the importance of collaborating with non-traditional actors to gain market knowledge that facilitated the market entry. The theoretical tool in this research was built on the knowledge exchange between MNCs and non-traditional actors, which was further divided into different types of knowledge. The results have shown that Ericsson acquired experiential knowledge by successively learning from other actors in terms of institutional, business, internationalisation and network knowledge. It was also showcased that the relationship with the non-traditional actors frequently acted as a bridge for Ericsson to gain access to political and state actors in Myanmar. The process of knowledge exchange could therefore be seen as essential for Ericsson to enter the Myanmar market.

Previous research has highlighted that experiential learning is a one-way direction learning where MNCs need to gather knowledge of the market when internationalising (Johanson and Vahlne, 1977). However, as the case study of Ericsson's market entry in Myanmar has proved, Ericsson also needed to educate the market in order to succeed. Therefore, it has been found that something is different from what mainstream Internationalisation Process (I-P) models and social embeddedness literature have implied. Instead of looking only at the learning process as being one-way, the learning process takes place in both directions. It can therefore be argued that there is a flaw in Johanson and Vahlne's (1977) Uppsala model, since it does not capture the experiential learning from both directions. Therefore, it is argued that I-P models need to take into consideration the firm's resources and knowledge in order to understand the expansion in an EM. *One can therefore question if MNCs need to educate the market in order to succeed in their internationalisation process in EMs.*

It seems as though it is not only this author that has found patterns that show MNCs do not only learn from the market, but increasingly contribute to educating the market in order to succeed in the internationalisation process. Similar findings can be found in literature in various fields. In their study, management scholars Child and Tsai (2005) have pointed to the increased power of MNCs in EMs. The framework, which is based on institutional and political perspectives, is applied to analyse firms' strategies for environmental protection in EMs. It can therefore be argued that MNCs' knowledge is considered relevant; this goes against the Uppsala Model of Johanson and Vahlne (1977).

Moreover, the cross-sector literature emphasises that NGOs increasingly collaborate with MNCs in order to gain the knowledge held by firms as in, for example, technical expertise as well as obtaining financial resources (Jamali and Keshishian, 2009; Oetzel and Doh, 2009). Similar findings can be found in the UN-Business Partnership literature, where it has been argued that the UN has developed an interdependency of the business community based on political and performance factors, whereas:

> "political interdependency implies that the UN needs to integrate corporate actors in order to resolve global issues politically and performance interdependency implies that the UN needs to integrate business in order to learn new methods of work or new technology for improving the UN operational delivery" (Ruchat, 2000, p. 174).

CONCLUSIONS

The major contribution is that the study found that MNCs not only learn from the market, but also need to educate the market in order to succeed in their internationalisation process in EMs. In addition, all the experiential knowledge types played important roles in the knowledge exchange. The research therefore contributes with both theoretical as well as managerial implications. The I-P model needs to integrate how the knowledge exchange facilitates the internationalisation process of MNCs in EMs. Moreover, non-traditional actors seem to facilitate MNCs; market entry in connecting the MNCs to other actors, as well as creating competitive advantages in these markets.

As the case study has shown, a multi-stakeholder CSR-programme seems to be a way for MNCs to connect with non-traditional actors that can act as a knowledge source for MNCs, but also for facilitating future business opportunities in the foreign market. Therefore, the newly adopted SDGs can be seen as providing a strategic opportunity for MNCs to expand in EMs. This study has filled a gap in the literature highlighted, for example, by Ljung (2014), by providing evidence that the collaboration with the United Nations was considered essential for Ericsson's expansion in Myanmar. It was anticipated by several respondents that the UN agencies were considered to be neutral bodies that also had a local presence in several countries. By partnering with a UN agency, it provided a chance for MNCs to enhance their legitimacy in the local market. The managerial implications suggested of this study are that mutually beneficial partnerships can therefore provide a chance for MNCs to enter EMs.

APPENDIX

Interview Respondents

#	Respondent	Position	Date	Location	Duration
1	*Magnus Mandersson*	*Executive Vice President, Head of Global Services, Ericsson*	1/3/16	Telephone interview	30'18"
2	*Elaine Weidman*	Vice President, Head of Sustainability and Corporate Responsibility, Ericsson	1/5/16	Telephone interview	28'11"
3	Zohra Yermeche	Global Program Manager, Connect To Learn, Ericsson	17/3/16	Ericsson HQ, Stockholm	35'55"
4	Kim Hoai Nga	Program Manager CTL, Ericsson Myanmar	18/3/16	Ericsson HQ, Stockholm	50'23"
5	Jan Wassenius	Vice President, Head of Ericsson Myanmar, Vietnam, Cambodia & Laos	30/3/16	Ericsson Myanmar	40'37"
6	Anders L Larsson	Chief Technical Officer, Ericsson Myanmar	5/4/16	Ericsson Myanmar	1'15'25"
7	Mya	Technical Subject Matter Expert (TSE), Power, Ericsson Myanmar	5/4/16	Ericsson Myanmar	29'03"
8	Akari	TSE Expert, Core Network, Ericsson Myanmar	5/4/16	Ericsson Myanmar	40'19"
9	Aye	TSE Expert, Transmission, Ericsson Myanmar	5/4/16	Ericsson Myanmar	28'10"
10	Ei	TSE Expert, Radio Transmission, Ericsson Myanmar	5/4/16	Ericsson Myanmar	30'02"
11	Antony Tam	ICT in Education Specialist, UNESCO Myanmar	29/3/16	UNESCO office, Yangon	57'13"
12	Patricia Curran	Head of Sustainability, Telenor Myanmar	7/4/16	Telenor office, Yangon	25'22"
13	Johan Hallenborg	Minister Counsellor	4/4/16	Swedish Embassy – Myanmar	25'39"
14	Sameer Sharma	Senior Advisor, ITU	12/4/16	ITU office, Bangkok	53'57"
15	Daw Thandar	Headmistress	1/4/16	Htone Gyi School	2'45'20"
16–20	Teachers 1–5	Teachers	1/4/16	Htone Gyi School	2'45'20"
21	Ma Myat	Myanmar Ministry of Education (MoE)	1/4/16	Yangon	1'05'30"

REFERENCES

Barkema, H.G., Bell, J.H. and Pennings, J.M. (1996), Foreign Entry, Cultural Barriers and Learning, *Strategic Management Journal*, Vol. 17, pp. 151–66.

Blomstermo, A., Eriksson, K., Lindstrand, A. and Sharma, D.D. (2004), The perceived usefulness of network experiential knowledge in the internationalizing firm, *Journal of International Management*, Vol. 10, No. 3, pp. 355–73.

Boddewyn, J.J. (1988), Political aspects of MNE theory, *Journal of International Business Studies*, Vol. 19, No. 3, pp. 341–63.

Child, J. and Tsai, T. (2005), The Dynamic Between Firms' Environmental Strategies and Institutional Constraints in Emerging Economies: Evidence from China and Taiwan. *Journal of Management Studies*, Vol. 42, No. 1, pp. 95–125.

Ericsson (201), *Sustainability and Corporate Responsibility*. Retrieved 5 January 2016 from: http://www.ericsson.com/thecompany/sustainability-corporateresponsibility.

Ericsson (2016), *Mobility report*. Retrieved 10 May 2016 from: https://www.ericsson.com/res/docs/2016/mobility-report/emr-feb-2016-the-lives-of-others.pdf.

Eriksson, K., Johanson, J., Majkgård A. and Sharma, D.D. (1997), Experiential knowledge and the cost in the internationalisation process, *Journal of International Business Studies*, Vol. 28, No. 2, pp. 337–60.

Forsgren, M. (2002), The Concept of Learning in the Uppsala Internationalization Process Model: A Critical Review, *International Business Review*, Vol. 11, No. 3, pp. 257–77.

Hadjikhani, A. (2000), The political behavior of business actors: The case of Swedish MNCs and the EU, *International Studies of Management & Organization*, Vol. 30, No. 1, pp. 93–117.

Hadjikhani, A., Lee, J.W. and Ghauri, P.N. (2008), Network view of MNCs' socio-political behaviour, *Journal of Business Research*, Vol. 61, No. 9, pp. 912–24.

Hilmersson, M. (2011), *Establishment of Insidership Positions in Institutionally Distant Business Networks*, Doctoral Dissertation No 52, Linnaeus University Press, Växjö. 200pp.

Hilmersson, M. and Jansson, H. (2012), Reducing uncertainty in the emerging market entry process: on the relationship among international experiential knowledge, institutional distance, and uncertainty; *Journal of International Marketing*, Vol. 20, No. 4, pp. 96–110.

Hoskisson, R.E., Eden, L., Lau, C.M. and Wright, M. (2000), Strategy in Emerging Economies, *Academy of Management Journal*, Vol. 43, No. 3, pp. 249–67.

Jamali, D. and Keshishian, T. (2009), Uneasy alliances: Lessons learned from partnerships between businesses and NGOs in the context of CSR, *Journal of Business Ethics*, Vol. 84, No. 2, pp. 277–95.

Jansson, H. (2008), *International Business Strategy in Emerging Country Markets*, Edward Elgar, Cheltenham, UK. Northampton, MA, USA.

Johanson, J. and Vahlne, J.E. (1977), The internationalization process of the firm-A model of knowledge development and increasing foreign market commitments, *Journal of International Business Studies*, 23–32.

Johanson, J. and Vahlne, J.E. (2003), Business Relationship Learning and Commitment in the Internationalization Process, *Journal of International Entrepreneurship*, Vol. 1, No. 1, pp. 83–101.

Johanson, J. and Vahlne, J.E. (2009), The Uppsala internationalization process model revisited: From liability of foreignness to liability of outsidership, *Journal of International Business Studies*, Vol. 40, No. 9, pp. 1411–31.

Khanna, T., Palepu, K. and Sinha, J. (2005), Strategies that fit emerging markets, *Harvard Business Review*, Vol. 83, No. 6, pp. 4–19.

Kogut, B. and Singh, H. (1988), The Effect of National Cultures on the Choice of Entry Mode, *Journal of International Business Studies*, Vol. 19, No. 3, pp. 411–32.

Ljung, A. (2014), The Multinational Company and Society: A Study of Business Network Relationships in Latin America, Uppsala:Företagsekonomiska institutionen, 106s.

London, T. and Hart, S.L. (2004), Reinventing strategies for emerging markets: beyond the transnational model, *Journal of International Business Studies*, Vol. 35, No. 5, pp. 350–70.

Meyer, K.E. (2004), Perspectives on multinational enterprises in emerging economies, *Journal of International Business Studies*, Vol. 35, No. 4, pp. 259–76.

Meyer, K.E. and Gelbuda, M. (2006), Process perspectives in international business research in CEE, *Management International Review*, Vol. 46, No. 2, pp. 143–64.

Meyer, K.E. and Thein, H.H. (2014), Business under adverse home country institutions: The case of international sanctions against Myanmar, *Journal of World Business*, Vol. 49, No. 1, pp. 156–71.

Oetzel, J. and Doh, J.P. (2009), MNEs and development: a review and reconceptualization, *Journal of World Business*, Vol. 44, No. 2, pp. 108–120.

Pappi, F.U. and Henning, C.H. (1998), Policy networks: more than a metaphor?, *Journal of Theoretical Politics*, Vol. 10, No. 4, pp. 553–75.

Peng, M.W. and Luo, Y. (2000), Managerial ties and firm performance in a transition economy: The nature of a micro-macro link, *Academy of Management Journal*, Vol. 43, No. 3, pp. 486–501.

Rondinelli, D.A. and London, T. (2003), How corporations and environmental groups cooperate: Assessing cross-sector alliances and collaborations, *The Academy of Management Executive*, Vol. 17, No. 1, pp. 61–76.

Ruchat, B. (2000), *Legitimacy in the Age of Global Governance. The Case of the UN Conference on Trade and Development*. Doctoral dissertation, Syracuse University.

Rueede, D., and Kreutzer, K. (2015), Legitimation work within a cross-sector social partnership, *Journal of Business Ethics*, Vol. 128, No. 1, pp. 39–58.

Salmi, A. (2000), Entry into turbulent business networks-The case of a Western company on the Estonian market, *European Journal of Marketing*, Vol. 34, Nos. 11/12, pp. 1374–90.

Saunders, M., Lewis, P. and Thornhill, A. (2012), *Research Methods for Business Students*. Harlow: Financial Times/Prentice Hall.

UNESCO (2015), UNESCO partners with Ericsson to launch an ICT for Education project in Myanmar. Retrieved 10 January 2016 from: http://www.unescobkk.org/news/article/unesco-partners-with-ericsson-to-launch-an-ict-for-education-project-in-myanmar.

UNICEF (2016), Myanmar education. Retrieved 10 February 2016 from: http://www.unicef.org/myanmar/education_1360.html.

United Nations (2015), *Sustainable Development Agenda*. A/RES/70/1. Retrieved 16 February 2016 from: *http://www.un.org/ga/search/view_doc.asp?symbol=A/RES/70/1&Lang=E.*

United Nations (2016), UN Adviser underlines importance of partnership with mobile-communications industry to achieve Sustainable Development. Retrieved April 3, 2016 from: http://www.un.org/sustainabledevelopment/blog/2016/02/un-adviser-calls-for-new-mobile-communications-industry-partnership-to-achieve-sustainable-development-goals/.

Utting, P. and Zammit, A. (2009), United Nations-business partnerships: Good intentions and contradictory agendas, *Journal of Business Ethics*, Vol. 90, No. 1, pp. 39–56.

Weidman (2012), Ericsson Technology for Good blog. Cautious optimism in Myanmar. Retrieved 1 May 2016 from: https://www.ericsson.com/thecompany/sustainability_corporateresponsibility/technology-for-good-blog/2012/11/09/cautious-optimism-in-myanmar/.

World Bank (2016), Gross enrolment ratio, secondary, both sexes. Retrieved 12 May 2016 from: http://data.worldbank.org/indicator/SE.SEC.ENRR/countries/1W-MM?display=graph.

Wright, M., Filatotchev, I., Hoskisson, R.E. and Peng, M.W. (2005), Guest editor's introduction: Strategy research in emerging economies: Challenging the conventional wisdom, *Journal of Management Studies*, Vol. 42, No. 1, pp. 1–33.

BIOGRAPHY

Rebecca Rehn holds an MSc in Business & Economics with a major in Sustainable Management from Uppsala University in Sweden. She worked at Ernst & Young as a management consultant, focusing on advisory services related to sustainability strategy, and at the Permanent Mission of Sweden to the United Nations in New York where she covered the final inter-governmental negotiations of the 2030 Agenda.

GOAL 3/12

GOOD HEALTH AND WELL-BEING/ RESPONSIBLE CONSUMPTION AND PRODUCTION

THE IMPACT OF SUDANESE HONEY ON BREAST CANCER CELLS

Rasha Alhaj[*1,2] and Alan Purohit[1]

[1]Endocrinology and Metabolic Medicine
St Mary's Hospital, Imperial College
London, UK
[2]Wolfson Institute of Preventative Medicine
Queen Mary University of London, UK
rasha.alhaj@qmul.ac.uk; a.purohit@imperial.ac.uk

ABSTRACT

Purpose: Breast cancer is the most common cancer in women worldwide. Although breast cancers are generally oestrogen receptor positive initially, a substantial proportion become oestrogen receptor negative. Oestrogen receptor positive breast cancers are associated with a better prognosis than oestrogen receptor negative breast cancers as they are more responsive to hormonal therapy.

The aim of the present study was to assess the inhibitory effect of honey on MCF-7 and MDA-MB-231 breast cancer cell lines.

Methodology: Three different varieties of Sudanese honey collected from different parts of Sudan (south, west and east) were initially tested for their effects on the proliferation of MCF-7 and MDA-MB-231 breast cancer cells. When tested at a 20 times dilution in growth medium, all three varieties of honey produced 40%–85% inhibition in growth of these cells. One particular variety of honey (west) significantly inhibited the

*Corresponding Author

growth of MCF-7 cells and MDA-MB-231 by 80% ±5 and 50% ±5 respectively. This honey was further characterised. Twenty times diluted honey was treated as follows:

1. Charcoal to adsorb small molecular weight substances;
2. Ether extracted to remove ether-soluble substances;
3. One hour at 65°C to assess temperature-stability of the test substances.

Findings: In conclusion, a large molecular weight soluble component of honey was found to have significant growth inhibitory effects on MCF-7 and MDA-MB-231 breast cancer cell lines. Further analysis is in progress to identify and characterise the substance.

Originality/value: The identification of endogenous inhibitors of breast cancer cells is important. The substance present in honey may possibly have a role to play in the prevention of breast cancer development and progression.

Keywords: oestrogen receptor positive breast cancers; oestrogen receptor negative breast cancers; honey

INTRODUCTION

In 2012, 14.1 million new cases of cancer were reported worldwide. During the same year, the number of people who died from cancer is an estimated 8.2 million (Ferlay et al., 2015). In 2002, 7.6 million people worldwide died of cancer. This is in excess of the 5.6 million deaths from HIV/AIDS, TB and Malaria combined (Stewart and Kleihues, 2003). Breast cancer is the most common cancer in women, both in the developed and less developed countries of the world. It is estimated that 1.7 million new cases were diagnosed in 2012 (Ferlay et al., 2015).

All cancer drugs are associated with side effects, which are often severe and can be unpleasant for patients being treated with these agents. Therefore, there is a great need for continuing research into exploring new affordable alternative of treatments that are less invasive or radical, and to develop treatments that have fewer or milder side effects. Complementary and Alternative Medicine (CAM) is the healing philosophy of medical products and practices, although not integral to standard medicine, such as homeopathy, acupuncture, osteopathy, chiropractic and herbalism[1]. Cancer Research-UK reported that 33% of cancer patients are very interested in using complementary therapies at some time during their illness. This percentage increases among breast cancer patients, reaching up to 50%.

---

[1]http://www.nhs.uk/Livewell/complementary-alternative-medicine/Pages/complementary-alternative-medicines.aspx

The Agency for Healthcare Research and Quality (AHRQ) reported that in the US during 2011, the total health care cost of cancer was $88.7 billion[2]. On the other hand, a study carried out by the University of Oxford found that the annual cost of all cancers to the UK economy is £15.8bn. Of this, £1.5bn is the annual health care cost of breast cancer patients[3].

Honey is a product produced by honeybees naturally from the nectar collected from flowers of different plants. It is a complex food, mainly composed of carbohydrates (70%–80%), and contains a large number of minor components including organic acids, proteins, free amino acids, vitamins, enzymes, minerals and different other molecules, for example, pigments and flavonoids (White, 1975). A few decades ago, there was a revival of interest in the medicinal properties of honey because it is thought to exhibit a broad spectrum of activities including anti-bacterial, anti-fungal, cytostatic, and anti-inflammatory properties (Jeddar et al., 1985; Hladoń et al., 1980; Yasuko et al., 1984).

The aim of the present study was to study the effects of honey on the growth of MCF-7 and MDA-MB-231 breast cancer cell lines.

MATERIAL AND METHODS

Samples

Three specimens of natural honey (unprocessed) were gathered from different parts of Sudan (East, South and West).

Materials

Dulbecco's Modified Eagle Medium (DMEM), L-glutamine, Foetal Bovine Serum (FBS), Non-Essential Amino Acids (NEAA), sodium bicarbonate ($NaHCO_3$) antibiotic-antimycotic (Penicillin G sodium, 1000 units/mL + streptomycin sulphate, 1000 (g/mL + Amphotericin B, 25μg/mL) and trypsin-EDTA were purchased from Gibco BRL life Technologies Inc.

Phosphate Buffered Saline (PBS) tablets (calcium and magnesium-free) were purchased from ICN Biomedicals Inc. (Costa, Mesa, CA, USA).

Centrifuge filtration molecular weight cut-offs (100KDa, 50KDa, 30KDa, 10KDa and 3KDa, were purchased from Sigma-Aldrich, USA).

Cell Culture

For each experiment, 25-cm² tissue culture flasks were seeded with about 5×10^4 cells/flask using medium (3mL) of DMEM, containing 10% FBS, 2mM glutamine, NEAA

---

[2]http://www.cancer.org/cancer/cancerbasics/economic-impact-of-cancer
[3]http://www.bbc.com/news/health-20222759

and 0.075% $NaHCO_3$ and 1% antibiotic-antimycotic. The cells were allowed to grow to 70% confluency for two days at 37°C in 5% CO_2. The medium was then removed and new DMEM (3mL) containing honey at 20 times dilution in growth medium was added. A similar volume of sterile PBS (pH 7.4) was added to the control flasks. All incubations were performed in triplicate. The cell lines were exposed to the treatments for two days at 37°C in 5% CO_2. At the end of the treatment period, the number of cell nuclei was determined using a Coulter counter.

Stripping of Honey

A modification of the method of Butler et al. (1981) was used to strip the honey of steroids and other small molecules. Charcoal and dextran T70, giving final concentrations of 0.5% w/v and 0.05% w/v respectively, were suspended in 50mL PBS, honey was added to the charcoal dextran for 15 minutes at 4°C, at a spun speed of 3000rpm, 4°C for 10 minutes. The suspension was reconstituted to the corrected volume.

Heated Inactivation of Honey

Honey was heated at 65°C for one hour in a water bath to inactivate heat-unstable Substances in the honey.

Ether Extraction Process

Medium containing honey at 20 times dilution, was extracted with 2 volumes of ether by vortex mixing for 30 second, and the ether phase was discarded.

Reversible Growth

MCF-7 and MDA-MB-231 cells were cultured as above. After honey treatment for 48 or 72 hours, honey DMEM was removed and replaced with fresh DMED. Cells were cultured for a further 72 hours, then cell numbers were counted and compared to PBS controls.

Diluted Honey

A honey treatment was carried out with honey at a range of six concentration (8, 12, 20, 40, 80 and 200 times dilution) in the growth medium.

Centrifuge Filtration Different Molecular Weight Cut-Offs

Honey was filtered using centrifugal filtration according to standard protocols. A range of filter membranes was used to retain molecules having molecular weights of about 100KDa or more, 50KDa or more, 30KDa or more, 10KDa or more, 3KDa or more, respectively. In all cases, the retentate was used to treat cells, and the filtrate was discarded.

Statistical Analysis

The significance of our findings was tested using prism. Results were considered to be statistically significant when $P < 0.05$.

RESULTS

MCF-7 cell growth was significantly inhibited by three varieties of honey (75% to 50% inhibition: $P < 0.05$). Western honey gives 75%, Eastern honey gives 55% and Southern honey gives 50% as shown in Figure 1.

MDA-MB-231 cell growth was significantly inhibited by three varieties of honey (60% to 40% inhibition: $P < 0.05$). Western honey gives 60%, Eastern honey gives 55% and Southern honey gives 40% (Figure 1).

Western honey showed the highest inhibitory effect in both breast cancer cell lines; therefore this honey was further characterised (see Figures 2 and 3).

The charcoal-dextran stripped honey and heat treated honey had almost the same inhibitory effect as untreated honey. Charcoal-dextran stripped honey inhibited the cell growth of MCF-7 with 80%, while it inhibited the MDA-MB-231 cell growth with 60%. MCF-7 cell growth was significantly inhibited by heated honey up to 75%; on the other hand, MDA-MB-231 cell growth was significantly inhibited with 50% (see Figure 4).

a   b

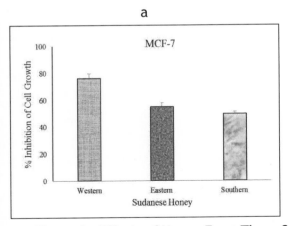
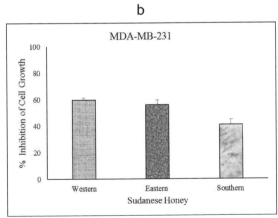

Figure 1   Effects of Honey From Three Sudanese Regions (20 Times final dilution) on Cell Growth of Two Breast Cancer Cell Lines

a) MCF-7

b) MDA-MB-231

a b

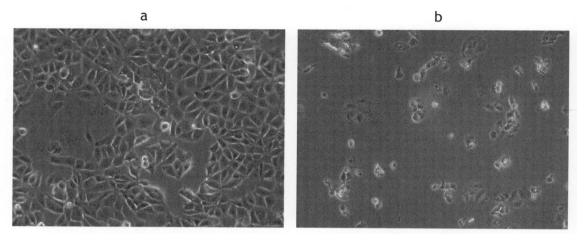

Figure 2   Magnified X10: MCF-7 Breast Cancer Cell Lines Treated for 48 hrs with
a) Phosphatise Buffered Saline (PBS) as a control reference
b) Western Sudanese honey (20 times final dilution)

a b

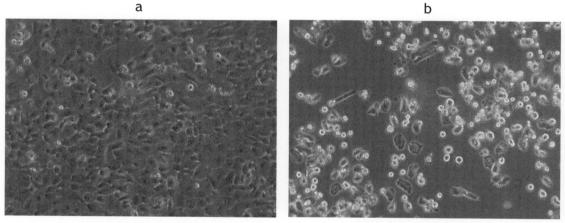

Figure 3   Magnified X10: MDA-MB-231 Breast Cancer Cell Lines Treated for 48 hrs. with
a) Phosphatise Buffered Saline (PBS) as a control reference
b) Western Sudanese honey (20 times final dilution)

Ether extraction honey: the aqueous soluble honey gives the same inhibitory effect of untreated honey. The aqueous soluble honey inhibited the MCF-7 cell growth with 75%, while the ether extraction honey inhibited MCF-7 cell growth with 15%. On the other hand, Aqueous soluble honey inhibited the MDA-MB-231 cell growth with 55%, and ether extraction inhibited the MDA-MB-231 cell growth with 10% (see Figure 5).

Inhibition of cell growth in both MCF-7 and MDA-MB-231 cell lines was found to cor-related linearly with increases in honey concentration from 8 to 200 times dilution

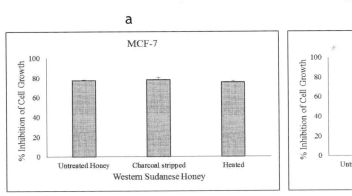
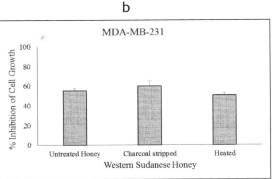

Figure 4 Effects of Charcoal -Dextran Stripped- and Heat-Treated Honey (20 times final dilution) on Cell Growth of Two Breast Cancer Cell Lines

a) MCF-7

b) MDA-MB-231

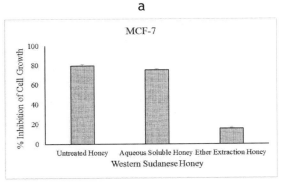
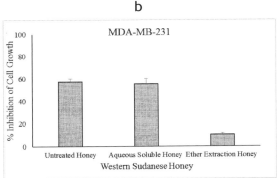

Figure 5 Effect of Ether Extraction Honey (20 times final dilution) on Cell Growth of Two Breast Cancer Cell Lines

a) MCF-7

b) MDA-MB-231

(see Figure 6). MCF-7 cell growth was inhibited at each of the six concentrations of honey tested (8, 12, 20, 40, 80 and 200 times dilution). However, in MDA-MB-231, inhibition of cell growth was observed only with honey concentrations between 8 and 40 times dilution, and stimulated the cell growth at 80 and 200 times dilution.

The effect of honey was tested for the reversible growth and showed that it is irreversible; it increased the percentage of inhibition in both cell lines. MCF-7 cell growth was significantly inhibited with 72% treated for 48hrs, followed by 90% (irreversible inhibition). While inhibited with 80% (72hrs treated), followed by 96% (irreversible inhibition) (see Figure 7). MDA-MB-231 cell growth was significantly inhibited with 51%,

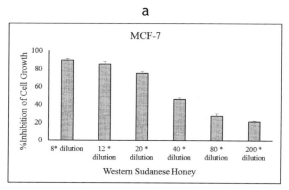
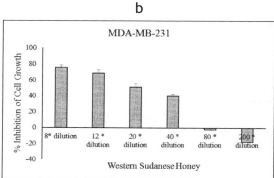

Figure 6   Effect of Six Different Honey Dilutions on Cell Growth of
Two Breast Cancer Cell Lines

a) MCF-7

b) MDA-MB-231

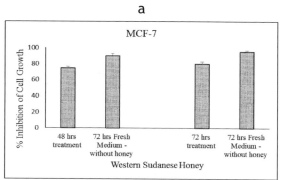
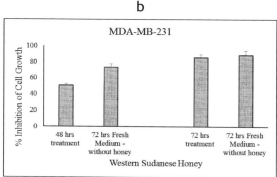

Figure 7   Effect of Honey (20 times final dilution) on Reversible Cell
Growth of Two Breast Cancer Cell Lines

a) MCF-7

b) MDA-MB-231

followed by 74% (irreversible inhibition), while inhibited with 86% (72hrs treated) 89% (irreversible inhibition) (see Figure 7).

The components of honey responsible for cell growth inhibition were retained by 100KDa filter membranes and below, but not to filter membranes above 100KDa.

DISCUSSION

Studies by Grible and Pashinskii in 1990, indicated that honey possessed moderate anti-tumour and pronounced anti-metastatic effects in five different strains of rat and mouse tumours. Furthermore, honey potentiated the anti-tumour activity of chemotherapeutic drugs such as 5-fluorouracil and cyclophosphamide (Gribel and Pashinskiĭ,1990).

In this study the effects of honey on the cell growth of MCF-7 and MDA-MB-231 breast cancer cell lines were examined. Growth inhibition by honey confers a protective effect against the development of breast cancer. A heat stable, water soluble large molecular component of honey was found to have significant growth inhibitory effects on MCF-7 and MDA-MB-231 breast cancer cell lines. The substance present in natural honey may possibly have a role to play in the prevention of breast cancer development and progression.

REFERENCES

Butler, W.B., Kelsey, W.H. and Goran, N. (1981), Effects of serum and insulin on the sensitivity of the human breast cancer cell line MCF-7 to estrogen and antiestrogens. *Cancer Research*, Vol. 41, No. 1, pp. 82–88.

Ferlay, J., Soerjomataram, I., Dikshit, R., Eser, S., Mathers, C., Rebelo, M., Parkin, D.M., Forman, D. and Bray, F. (2015), Cancer incidence and mortality worldwide: Sources, methods and major patterns in GLOBOCAN 2012. *International Journal of Cancer*, Vol. 136, No. 5, pp. E359–E386.

Gribel, N.V. and Pashinskiĭ, V.G. (1990), The antitumor properties of honey. *Voprosy Onkologii*, Vol. 36, No. 6, pp. 704–09.

Hladoń, B., Bylka, W., Ellnain-Wojtaszek, M., Skrzypczak, L., Szafarek, P., Chodera, A. and Kowalewski, Z. (1980), *In vitro* studies on the cytostatic activity of propolis extracts. *Arzneimittel-Forschung*, Vol. 30, No. 11, pp. 1847–48.

Jeddar, A., Kharsany, A., Ramsaroop, U.G., Bhamjee, A., Haffejee, I.E. and Moosa, A. (1985), The antibacterial action of honey. An *in vitro* study. *South African Medical Journal*, Vol. 67, No. 7, pp. 257–58.

Stewart, B.W. and Kleihues, P. (Eds) (2003), *World Cancer Report* (Vol. 57). Lyon: IARC press.

White, J.W. Jr. (1975), The composition of honey. In Carne, E. (Ed.): *Honey: A comprehensive survey*. London: Heinemann, pp. 157–206.

Yasuko, K., Tomohiro, N., Sei-Itsu, M., Ai-Na, L., Yasuo, F. and Takashi, T. (1984), Caffeic acid is a selective inhibitor for leukotriene biosynthesis. *Biochimica et Biophysica Acta (BBA) - Lipids and Lipid Metabolism*, Vol. 792, No. 1, pp. 92–97.

BIOGRAPHY

Rasha Alhaj is an inventor; she discovered the substance in honey that inhibits the growth of breast cancer cells. She is the founder of "The Amal Initiative", a project to bring healing and hope to cancer patients. In 2015, Rasha received the Afrabia Afro-Arab Youth Award. She has a BSc in Biological Science from UAE University, an MSc in Chemical Pathology from the University of Putra, Malaysia, and an MRes in Bioengineering from Imperial College, London.

Dr. Alan Purohit is a Visiting Consultant reader Investigative Medicine, Imperial College London. He has Qualifications in BSc, MSc, PhD FRCPath. He is an enthusiastic and dedicated scientist in the fields of cancer aetiology and therapeutics with over twenty years' academic – industrial experience in Oncology Drug Discovery & Women's Health. He is the Pioneer and International lead in the development of Steroid Sulfatase Inhibitors. His research interests have focussed mainly on the regulation and control of oestrogenic steroid synthesis in normal and malignant breast tissues. Research into the regulation of the enzymes involved in oestrogen synthesis in relation to the growth and development of breast tumours, has led to more than 180 published high-impact papers and more than 27 patents."

OUTLOOK 2018

27

THE IMPORTANCE OF MENTAL HEALTH WELL-BEING WITHIN THE SUSTAINABLE DEVELOPMENT GOALS (SDGS) 2030

Lade Olugbemi*

CEO
The NOUS Organisation Ltd
UK
nousorganisation@gmail.com

ABSTRACT

Purpose: This paper calls for an improvement in mental health care in African countries. The UN's Sustainable Development Goals (SDGs) 2030 promotes overall well-being; however, progress in addressing mental health lags significantly relative to efforts to eradicate poverty, malnutrition and communicable diseases.

Method/Approach: This paper examines data reported by vested international organisations on mental health issues in African countries, and studies assessing the efficacy of current services.

Findings: Mental disorders are both triggered by and act as a precursor to poverty, unrest and other challenges. A collaborative effort involving both the public and private sector is needed to address service shortages and promote mental health.

*Corresponding Author

Originality/Value: There is growing evidence attributing a large proportion of the global health burden to mental disorders, which are projected to rise in many African countries. This paper provides recommendations to support efforts to address mental health needs as an aspect of sustainable development.

Keywords: Disability; mental health needs; mental health services; psychosocial disorders; Sustainable Development Goals

Purpose

Mental illness is perhaps the most severely under-served health care issue prevailing in African countries. In addition to those born with a mental health condition, wars, famines, poverty and debilitating physical illnesses have taken a severe psychological toll. Those affected by unrest, illness and malnutrition often also experience post-traumatic stress disorder (PTSD), anxiety, depression and other mental health disorders, resulting in an inability to function economically and socially and contributing to further violence. Moreover, untreated depression is strongly indicated as a significant threat to the success of antiretroviral therapy and condom use in combatting HIV (Wagner et al., 2014). Based on the lack of available diagnosing and treatment facilities, many of those enduring mental health disorders have tended to seek relief through substance abuse (Gberie, 2016). The Sustainable Development Goals (SDGs) 2030 aim to ensure healthy lives and promote well-being for all. However, while significant progress is being made in addressing communicable diseases such as malaria and HIV, mental health remains among the most neglected services in the region due to associated stigma and a lack of integration.

This paper calls for an improvement in mental health care in African countries. The World Health Organization (WHO) reports that low-income countries allocate only 0.05% of GDP to mental health care (WHO, 2011); the result of this is that 75–90% of Africans who suffer from psychosocial disorders lack access to adequate care. Fewer than half of African countries have established a dedicated mental health policy (WHO, 2014), and mental health care providers in the region lack the resources to supply needed medications, identify and train sufficient caregivers, and expand services beyond meeting very basic needs. Unlike communicable diseases such as HIV/AIDS, malaria, or Ebola, aid organisations have devoted fewer economic and human resources to confronting psychosocial disorders: help is needed from the private sector to create more sustainable approaches.

Method/Approach

This paper takes an holistic view of mental health as an integral aspect of physical well-being and quality of life as well as societal cohesion and functioning, whereby mental illnesses are both engendered by and impact overall personal well-being and broader social conditions. Mental health is defined as a state of well-being in which individuals are able to cope with the normal stresses of life while working productively and making a contribution to their families and communities (WHO, 2017). It is a crucial element in overall health and the prevention and treatment of disease.

This paper examines data on mental health prevalence and services as provided by such vested organisations as the RAND Corporation, the WHO, and Human Rights Watch (HRW), as well as studies describing nascent mental health initiatives in African countries.

CULTURAL ATTITUDES TOWARDS MENTAL ILLNESS

In 2014, Kenyan humour writer Ted Malanda published an article in the *Standard* entitled "How depression has never been an African disease", in which he argued for the nonexistence of depression in African cultures, noting the lack of relevant linguistic terms. Malanda's article reflects widely held attitudes towards depression and other psychosocial disorders, the symptoms of which have traditionally been either been ignored or attributed to a spiritual misalignment, only curable with traditional medicines and intercession with the supernatural world. In many countries, the mentally ill are considered to walk between the human world and the realm of spirits, and can be seen wandering around cities and villages alike, where they are often criminalised as vagrants and eventually removed from society.

Traditional treatments of mental illnesses are often physically debilitating and involve actions that the United Nations (UN) and HRW would describe as forms of torture. Mentally ill individuals in Ghana and Nigeria, for example, are frequently sent to 'prayer camps', where the afflicted may be chained to a tree as specialists pray for them, or beaten to expel the 'demons' believed to be controlling their behaviour. Ghana adopted a ban on such practices with the 2012 Mental Health Act (HRW, 2017).

Another common view associates mental health disorders with substance abuse, resulting in little sympathy and less interest in prioritising mental health among both governments and the general population. Substance abuse is widely cited as a contributory factor to psychosis and associated violent behaviours, even among those responsible for providing diagnosis and care. A report by HRW cited only 8–10% of all mental patients in Ghana as being affected by drug-related psychosis (HRW, 2012), however, many non-professionals often assume that substance abuse issues encompass the majority of cases.

Although there has been increase in the spotlight on psychiatric awareness in Africa, it is interesting to note that many people with chronic or severe psychiatric disorders may be unaware that effective treatment is available. The high level of stigma and the unavailability of treatment preclude early intervention. The situation is not helped by the ignorance and stigma in communities that prevents such people from seeking appropriate help. Unfortunately, as it may be noted, our African communities have attitudes and beliefs that have played a major role in determining the manner that help is sought for successful early intervention or treatment of people that are mentally ill.

COMMON BARRIERS TO MENTAL HEALTH CARE

There are barriers to accessing mental health care in Africa, and there is limited availability of medication and health professionals. In Nigeria, there are 44 Mental Health Services in Nigeria (excluding private facilities). For a country with a population of 190 million there are only 26 National Psychiatric Hospitals and 15 private hospitals. There are several local unregistered treatment centres using unorthodox methods.

For example in Nigeria there is:

- around 1 psychiatrist per 1.5 million population;
- around 1 psychiatric nurses per 20,000 population;
- only 1% of Healthcare budget that goes towards the treatment of mental health.

The estimated cost per capita of treatment of mental illness is high in Africa. The affordability of these drugs is difficult for most Africans. Interventions are making use of newer antipsychotic drugs; in the regional analysis these were estimated to be two to four times more costly than older drugs but very much higher than predicted in Nigeria (more than I$ 10 per capita). At the time of the study, for example, 2mg risperidone could be obtained for 4.5 rupees (US$ 0.06) in Sri Lanka, compared to 255 Naira (US$ 2.50[1]) in Nigeria, a 40-fold difference (Chisholm et al., 2008). Other barriers are policy limitations, lack of education and high level of stigma.

FUNDING AND STAFFING SHORTAGES FOR MENTAL HEALTH SERVICES

The UN General Assembly's recognition of mental health and substance abuse among its SDGs in 2015 marked the first consensus among world leaders to make mental and behavioural health a global priority (UN, 2015). While critics have decried the limited resources dedicated towards psychosocial health services in African countries, governments bear the bulk of the financial burden for mental health care (WHO, 2014). Governments cite the prevalence of more acute issues requiring their attention, particularly infectious disease and malnutrition. While international aid and global pro-

---

[1] In 2018 the US dollar to Naira exchange rate was 450.

grammes to reduce conflict, poverty and disease have increased substantially, world governing bodies and aid organisations have done less to prioritise funding towards addressing the long-term mental health effects of these conditions.

This has contributed to a situation in which there are insufficient policies dedicated to addressing mental disorders, and very limited facilities and staff trained in the diagnosis and treatment of mental and behavioural health conditions. Across the region, day patient facilities are essentially non-existent, and outpatient services are available for only 80 out of every 100,000 people; this should be compared to 1,926 outpatients and 42.98 day patients per 100,000 people across Europe (WHO, 2011). Only 1.9 psychiatric beds are available per 100,000 people, while psychiatric wards in general hospitals are limited to one for every 3.65 million (WHO, 2014). With 22 psychiatric hospitals and 36 psychiatric wards in general hospitals, South Africa is better equipped than any other African country (WHO, 2014); however, as in other countries in the region, most of these facilities serve more as places of confinement than places of care and rehabilitation.

The current shortage of specialist mental health personnel in low- and middle-income countries has been estimated at 1.18 million (Kakuma et al., 2011), with only 1.4 mental health workers per 100,000 people in African countries (WHO, 2014). Like other African health care workers, some of those trained to treat mental illness have chosen to migrate from their home countries due to the stresses of social trauma and/or in search of better pay and working conditions. Many countries have addressed the shortages by also training primary care practitioners to administer psychiatric treatment, including social support, psychosocial therapies and medication (Mendenhall et al., 2014; van Ginneken et al., 2013). However, only 23% of countries reported that a majority of primary care doctors have received training on mental health, and only 24% reported training nurses in treating mental illnesses (WHO, 2011).

Even relatively better developed nations lack sufficient staff and facilities to provide care for the afflicted. In Kenya, where 25% the population suffers from mental disorders, ranging from depression and severe anxiety to bipolar disorder, schizophrenia and other psychotic disorders, there are only about 80 psychiatrists and 30 clinical psychologists; most of the burden of services for a mentally ill population of 11 million is borne by 500 psychiatric nurses (WHO, 2014). The situation is even more dire in Nigeria, which has only 130 psychiatrists in a country of 179 million people, leaving only an estimated 10% of the estimated 40–60 million people suffering from mental health disorders with access to professional care (WHO, 2014). Ghana, one of the few African countries to have established an official policy towards mental health, has only 20 psychiatrists for a population of 26 million, leaving a huge 97% of afflicted people without access to services (WHO, 2014). In countries torn apart by conflict, such as Liberia and Sierra Leone, the situation is particularly severe. These countries, with respective populations of four and seven million, have only one psychiatric hospital each for hundreds of thousands of people enduring serious depressive illness, major depressive disorders or post-traumatic stress disorder (WHO, 2014).

LACK OF GOVERNANCE AND REGULATIONS

One issue that negatively impacts the quality of existing mental health services in Africa is the lack of regulations. Only a quarter of African countries have developed official manuals detailing the management and treatment of mental disorders that are available at most clinics (WHO, 2011). Moreover, while developed regions impose heavy regulations on the prescribing of medicines to treat mental and behavioural disorders, the dearth of psychiatrists has led to 61% of African countries allowing primary health care physicians to prescribe such medicines in an unregulated manner, and 9% allow nurses to do so (WHO, 2011). Even more concerning, 27% of African countries have an official policy that enables nurses to independently diagnose and treat mental disorders within the primary care system, compared to only 6% in Europe (WHO, 2011). The result is a lack of standardisation for diagnoses and treatment of mental illnesses that severely impacts the quality of these services. Only about 20% of the patients who do enter mental health facilities receive routine follow-up care (WHO, 2014), thus increasing the risk of relapse as the patients lack professional support in their recovery.

MAKING MENTAL HEALTH A SUSTAINABLE GOAL

In including mental and behavioural health disorders among its SDGs, the UN has created an opportunity for these issues to be addressed on an unprecedented scale. Governments and global and regional health organisations should seek aid from the private sector in establishing and equipping more facilities, particularly in rural areas that often lack access to any sort of mental health care. Partnerships can also be developed with the private sector to increase the availability of mental health medicines and outpatient treatment as part of other health initiatives.

However, improving mental health services in Africa cannot be achieved merely with expanded funding and facilities; rather, it requires a concerted campaign of education, training, and oversight. The WHO's Global Mental Health Action Plan (WHO, 2013) centres on strengthening effective leadership and governance for mental health, implementing policies and plans for the integration of mental health into general and community health care, and developing preventative strategies as part of the effort to promote overall mental health.

Efforts must be dedicated to recruiting and training more psychiatrists and other specialised professionals, as well as the establishment of regulations to standardise diagnosis criteria and treatment programmes. In addition, those currently employed may require additional training to adjust cultural attitudes dismissing mental illness as a result of drug abuse or spiritual weakness. Members of the wider community also need to be educated on the causes, symptoms and treatment of mental illness, including the role of violence, imprisonment and the use of illicit drugs in exacerbating their effects; this will help to reduce stigma and increase the likelihood of people seeking professional treatment. Such education programmes need not always deride cultural notions associating mental illness with spiritual misalignment, but in some cases can rather emphasise the roles of poverty and physical and emotional trauma as stressors, in contrast with prevailing perceptions that tend to 'blame the victim'.

Several countries have recognised the need to be more proactive in addressing mental health needs. For example, the South African Department of Health has collaborated with researchers from the United States and South Africa to develop educational interventions such as the VUKA[2] family-based programme to promote overall health and mental health among HIV positive youths and their families (Bhana et al., 2014). In Uganda, RAND researchers are collaborating with the government to identify effective and sustainable approaches to integrate depression treatment into HIV care (Wagner et al., 2014). The Africa Focus on Intervention Research for Mental Health (AFFIRM), is working in Ethiopia, Ghana, Malawi, South Africa, Uganda, and Zimbabwe to promote capacity building low-cost, task-sharing interventions for severe mental disorders (Lund et al., 2015). The private sector can collaborate with governments and global health organisations to expand such programmes.

CONCLUSIONS

This paper examined the challenges and some opportunities associated with mental health issues in African countries. Mental health disorders have been demonstrated to be a precursor to unrest, substance abuse and even to exacerbate the effects of disease in Africa; it will require a collaborative effort involving both the public and private sector to address this surge. In 2001 at the World Health Assembly, the WHO charged African countries who were just beginning to address mental health issues to set priorities around the delivery of their mental health goals. They enjoined that "Choices must be made among a large number of services and a wide range of prevention and promotion strategies" (WHO, 2011). The strong message is that every country, notwithstanding its resource constraints, must do something to improve the mental health of its population.

There is no health without mental health.

---

[2]VUKA is a cartoon-based intervention that was developed with South African investigators, graphic artists, medical staff, adult caregivers and HIV+ adolescents. It is a family based programme devised to provide psychosocial intervention to promote health and mental health in HIV+ early adolescents.

REFERENCES

Bhana, A., Mellins, C.A., Petersen, I., Alicea, S., Myeza, N., Holst, H., Abrams, E., John, S., Chhagan, M., Nestadt, D.F. and Leu, C.S. (2014), The VUKA family program: Piloting a family-based psychosocial intervention to promote health and mental health among HIV infected early adolescents in South Africa. *AIDS Care: Psychological and Socio-medical Aspects of AIDS/HIV*, Vol. 26, No. 1, pp. 1–11.

Chisholm, D., Gureje, O., Saldivia, S., Villalon Calderon, M., Wickremasinghe, R., Mendis, No., Ayuso-Mateos, J.L. and Saxena, S. (2008), Schizophrenia treatment in the developing world: an inter-regional and multi-national cost-effectiveness analysis. *Bulletin of the World Health Organization*, Vol. 86, No. 7, pp. 542–51.

Gberie, L. (2016, 25 November), Mental illness: Invisible but devastating. Retrieved from http://www.un.org/africarenewal/magazine/december-2016-march-2017/mental-illness-invisible-devastating.

Human Rights Watch (HRW) (2012, 02 October), "Like a Death Sentence": Abuses against Persons with Mental Disabilities in Ghana. Retrieved from https://www.hrw.org/report/2012/10/02/death-sentence/abuses-against-persons-mental-disabilities-ghana.

Human Rights Watch (HRW) (2017, 09 October), Ghana: Invest in mental health services to end shackling: Minister of Finance should establish levy for mental health. Retrieved from https://www.hrw.org/news/2017/10/09/ghana-invest-mental-health-services-end-shackling.

Kakuma, R., Minas, H., van Ginneken, N., Dal Poz, M.R., Desiraju, K., Morris, J.E., Saxena, S. and Scheffler, R.M. (2011), Human resources for mental health care: current situation and strategies for action. *The Lancet*, Vol. 378, No. 9803, pp. 1654–63.

Lund, C., Alem, A., Schneider, M., Hanlon, C., Ahrens, J., Bandawe, C., Bass, J., Bhana, A., Burns, J., Chibanda, D. and Cowan, F. (2015), Generating evidence to narrow the treatment gap for mental disorders in sub-Saharan Africa: rationale, overview and methods of AFFIRM. *Epidemiology and Psychiatric Sciences*, Vol. 24, No. 3, pp. 233–40.

Malanda, T. (2014), How depression has never been an African disease. Retrieved from https://www.sde.co.ke/article/2000131772/how-depression-has-never-been-an-african-disease.

Mendenhall, E., De Silva, M.J., Hanlon, C., Petersen, I., Shidaye, R., Jordans, M., Luitel, N., Ssebunnya, J., Fekadu, A., Patel, V. and Tomlinson, M. (2014), Acceptability and feasibility of using non-specialist health workers to deliver mental health care: Stakeholder perceptions from the PRIME district sites in Ethiopia, India, Nepal, South Africa, and Uganda. *Social Science & Medicine*, Vol. 118, pp. 33–42.

United Nations (UN) (2015), *Transforming our world: The 2030 Agenda for Sustainable Development*. Retrieved from https://sustainabledevelopment.un.org/post2015/transformingourworld/publication.

van Ginneken, N., Tharyan, P., Lewin, S., Rao, G.N., Meera, S.M., Pian, J., Chandrashekar, S. and Patel, V. (2013), Non-specialist health worker interventions for the care of mental, neurological and substance-abuse disorders in low- and middle-income countries. *Cochrane Database of Systematic Reviews*, Vol. 11, CD009149.

Wagner, G.J., Ngo, V., Glick, P., Obuku, E.A., Musisi, S. and Akena, D. (2014), INtegration of DEPression Treatment into HIV Care in Uganda (INDEPTH-Uganda): Study protocol for a randomized controlled trial. *Trials*, Vol. 15, No. 1, p. 248.

World Health Organization (WHO) (2011), *Mental health atlas 2011*. Geneva, SUI: Author.

World Health Organization (WHO) (2013), *Mental health action plan 2013–2020*. Geneva, SUI: Author.

World Health Organization (WHO) (2014), *Mental health atlas 2014*. Geneva, SUI: Author.

World Health Organization (WHO) (2017), Mental health. Retrieved from http://www.afro.who.int/health-topics/mental-health.

BIOGRAPHY

'**Lade Olugbemi** is a Human Rights activist who is passionate about raising aware-ness about mental health in ethnic minority communities. She has worked in various sectors of the economy. She promotes early intervention for mental ill-ness in the Black, Asian and Minority Ethnic (BAME) communities and campaigns to remove stigma, negative labelling and stereotyping in accessing support early. 'Lade would like to see policies change reflecting the needs of the BAME commu-nities. She serves on the Board, delivery groups and operational panels of several governmental initiatives. This exposure highlighted a major gap in information held about mental wellbeing and illness in the BAME communities, not just in the UK but also in Africa and Asia. She is on the Board of the Reinvent African Diaspora Network (RADET), African Security Forum. 'Lade is a Motivational Public Speaker and a Mental Health First Aid trainer.

USE OF TALBINAH (BARLEY BROTH) AS A PATTERN OF DEPRESSION MANAGEMENT AMONG SAUDI FEMALE MEDICAL STUDENTS

Nahlaa A. Khalifa*

Assistant Professor
Clinical Nutrition Department
Faculty of Applied Medical Sciences
King Abdulaziz University
PO Box: 54539, Jeddah 21524, Saudi Arabia
nahlaakhalifa@outlook.com and nkhalefa@kau.edu.sa

ABSTRACT

Purpose: Depression prevalence and antidepressant medication usage have recently increased. This paper aims to study the effect of Talbinah (barley broth) as a prophetic evidence-based complementary medicine on depression, and to emphasise the importance of combining private and public Medicare in managing depression.

Design: A randomised clinical trial was conducted to determine the effect of Talbinah consumption on depression on a sample of 42 female medical students. Self-administered questionnaires were used. The intervention group was given one serving of Talbinah on a daily basis in addition to their usual diet.

*Corresponding Author

Findings: The depression score decreased in the intervention group (score = 8.69 ± 6.53) compared to the non-intervention group (13.3 ± 8.1), although the difference is insignificant.

Research Limitations: Advanced diagnostic approaches are needed to detect depression. Participants must be in a closed setting to control their food intake.

Practical Implications: Public-private Medicare collaboration and using diet in managing depression to reduce the use, cost and the side effects of antidepressant medication.

Originality/Value: The study has significant importance in broadening the scope of giving more attention for managing mental diseases, which come in parallel with sustainable development goal (3): Ensuring healthy lives and promoting wellbeing for all at all ages.

Keywords: Talbinah; depression; barley; complementary; evidence-based; mental

INTRODUCTION

Depression is a psychological problem that causes determined low mood, a feeling of hopelessness in the depressed person. It makes somebody feel unhappy, aggravated, desperate, have low self-image, they also lose interest in things they usually like (Al-Qadhi et al., 2014).

Internationally, the prevalence of depression has been stated as growing recently (Andersen et al., 2011). In developing countries, it was found that 10–44% of people suffer from anxiety disorders and depression: less than 35% of the patients get medical care (Gadit and Mugford, 2007). In Europe, approximately 10% of females and 6.6% of males were found to suffer from anxiety disorders and depression; a total of 8.5% across the population (Ayuso-Mateos et al., 2001). Saudi Arabia has a great prevalence of depression; as the population grows, in addition to increasing depression risk factors such as modernisation stress, inactive life style, social isolation and chronic disease, there are the pre-existing stigmas of getting a mental health disorder. In 2002, approximately 18% of adults in Saudi Arabia had anxiety disorders and depression (Al-Khathami and Ogbeide, 2002). In King Saud University, Riyadh, Saudia Arabia, medical students were screened for depressive symptoms using the 21-item Beck Depression Inventory. In those showing an elevated prevalence of depressive symptoms (48.2% of those tested), 11% were found to be severe, 17% moderate, and 21% mild (21%). The presence and severity of depressive symptoms had a statistically significant notification with primary academic years ($p < 0.000$), and female sex (p<0.002) (Al-Faris et al., 2012). Furthermore, a study was conducted in King Abdul-Aziz University to determine the prevalence and predict depression and anxiety among female medical students, Jeddah, Saudi Arabia. Results showed that the prevalence of depression and morbid anxiety were 14.7%, and 34.9% respectively (Ibrahim et al., 2013).

Management of depression usually involves a combination of medical, psychological and nutritional intervention (Palazidou, 2012).

LITERATURE REVIEW

Medical intervention, such as antidepressant medication, is used for moderate to severe depression, while antipsychotic drugs are used for severe depression. Using anti-anxiety drugs for long periods can result in addiction or dependence. Common side effects of antidepressant and antipsychotic drugs may involve sleepiness, headache, dizziness, and in some patients loss of memory. Examples of these drugs include alprazolam (Xanax) and diazepam (Valium) (Furukawa et al., 2001).

Different health practitioners, especially clinical psychologists and psychologists, can provide psychological intervention. Psychological therapies include cognitive behaviour therapy, interpersonal therapy, supportive therapy and others (Butler et al., 2006).

In nutritional management, food is considered as an important factor that influences mood and depression (Murakami and Sasaki, 2010). Both macronutrients and micronutrients had an ability to affect mood and cognitive function (Benton and Donohoe, 1999; Horrobin, 2002).

Talbinah is a food product that has great possible uses as a functional food. In Islam, Talbinah has been stated in many narrations of the Prophet Muhammad [peace be upon him] as medicine for depression. In the narration of Aisha (Mother of the believers) that the prophet Mohammed [peace be upon him] usually commend Talbinah for one who is grieving over a dead person and for the sick. She said, "I heard the Messenger [peace be upon him] saying, 'The Talbinah gives rest to the heart of the patient and makes it active and relieves some of his sorrow and grief'" (Abdel-Hassib, 2007).

Talbinah is an Arabic word that comes from the word "Laban"; this means fermented shaken milk, which might also describe the barley grains case when they come to the milky stage, where the inner of these grains is liquid and white like milk (Abd El-Rahman, 2001).

Talbinah is a meal, which is made from barley flour formed by adding honey and milk to the powder of dried barley. Barley (the essence of Talbinah), a member of the grass family, is a major cereal grain (Mohammadi Aghdam and Samadiyan, 2014).

Whole barley grain consists of about 65–68% starch, 10–17% protein, 4–9% ß-glucan, 2–3% free lipids and 1.5–2.5% minerals (Izydorczyk et al., 2000; Sastry and Tummuru, 1985). ß-glucans, the major fibre constituent in barley, had been shown to lower plasma cholesterol, reduce glycaemic index and reduce the risk of colon cancer (Brennan and Cleary, 2005).

Considering the nutritional value of Talbinah macronutrient content in relation to depression, a systematic review and meta-analysis of the dietary pattern of 21 studies showed that a healthy diet pattern was significantly connected with a reduced possibility of development of depression (Lai et al., 2014). Women with depression tend to consume fewer nutrients than non-depressed women. A prospective cohort study showed that a "whole food" pattern (rich in vegetables, fruits, and fish) was inversely connected with depression. At the same time, a "processed food" pattern (rich in sweetened desserts, fried food, processed meat, refined grains, and high-fat dairy products) showed a straight association with depression in the middle-aged population (Akbaraly et al., 2009).

Carbohydrate intake seems to be an important factor in the management of depression. Symptoms of depression are associated with lower consumption of vegetables and fruit (Michels et al., 2012), while overeating of high Glycaemic Index (GI) foods is a regular coping mechanism in depressed and stressed patients. Carbohydrate consumption is linked with a higher secretion of insulin, which facilitates the transport of tryptophan in the brain and leads to higher synthesis of serotonin (Wurtman and Wurtman, 1989). Another cross-sectional study on 976 homebound elders (30% of participants with type 2 diabetes) assessed the correlation between dietary GI and depression (Mwamburi et al., 2011). The result of this study recommended that even with similar amounts of carbohydrate consumption by both depressed and non-depressed people, GI and serum insulin levels were significantly higher in depressed than non-depressed patients (Lai et al., 2014).

A study done by Halyburton et al. (2007) showed that both a Low Carbohydrate Diet (LCD) and Low Fat Diet (LFD) improve mood after eight weeks. The unfavourable effects of LCD may be due to disturbed synthesis of serotonin or Brain-Derived Neurotropic Factor (BDNF). Talbinah contains 2–3% free lipids. Studies show that human brains are composed of around 40% fat and the brain cells require fats to keep their structure; for this reason, an adequate supply of unsaturated fat is needed to maintain health.

Dietary fat intake has a strong role in determining oxidative stress and inflammation. Moreover, depression is associated with lower n-3 Polyunsaturated Fatty Acids (n-3 PUFA) concentrations (Assies et al., 2010) and disturbed lipid profile (Van Reedt Dortland et al., 2010). However, the results of a meta-analysis on 28 randomised and placebo controlled clinical trials showed that the efficacy of n-3 PUFA in depression is related to Eicosapentaenoic Acid (EPA), not Docosahexaenoic Acid (DHA) (Martins, 2009). The severity of depression was positively associated with the Arachidonic Acid (AA)/EPA ratio and lower levels of erythrocyte EPA correlated with more levels of depression.

The positive effects of MUFA and PUFA intake on depression might be related to their connection with inflammation. For that reason, beneficial subtypes of fatty acids could improve depressive symptoms by modulating serum levels of inflammatory markers. They also showed that PUFA intake is inversely linked with depression. It has been reported that people with a high consumption of fish appear to have a lower prevalence of major depressive disorders (Lai et al., 2014). Women who were infrequent fish eaters were at an increased risk of depression (Timonen et al., 2004). In general, a low-fat diet may have negative effects on mood (Wells et al., 1998).

Protein is made up of amino acids and is an important building block of life. Some essential amino acids must be supplied through the diet. The recommended daily calorie intake from protein should be 10 to 20% (Besharat Pour et al., 2014). Depression is associated with deficiencies in neurotransmitters such as serotonin, dopamine, noradrenaline, and Gamma-aminobutyric Acid (GABA) (Firk and Markus, 2007). Brain tryptophan and serotonin levels are influenced by dietary protein and carbohydrate through effects on plasma amino acids patterns. Carbohydrate in the diet increases the secretion of insulin that elevates plasma concentration of tryptophan and lowers the concentrations of other large neutral amino acids; this can lead to increased serotonin concentrations in the brain (Fernstrom and Wurtman, 1971).

Tryptophan is an essential amino acid and is a precursor for serotonin synthesis; it has the ability to play a key role in many brain functions such as mood regulation. A number of studies has shown that depressive symptoms and results in worsening of mood results from acute tryptophan depletion (Neumeister et al., 1998; Spillmann et al., 2001). The increased availability of tryptophan to the brain can promote sleep and restore serotonin levels that can lead to diminished depression (Møller et al., 1983). Several studies have shown the amino acids tryptophan, tyrosine, phenylalanine, and methionine can help in treating many mood disorders, including depression (Hoes, 1982). Tryptophan can be found in meat, liver, cheese, tuna, nuts, soybean, sunflower seeds and poppy seeds. The recommended intake is 4–6mg/kg/day. Tyrosine can be made from the amino acid phenylalanine. This is usually converted into dopamine and norepinephrine (Kravitz et al., 1984). Some tyrosine sources are beef, chicken, eggs, fish, avocado and banana. Serine it is not an essential amino acid in the diet because it can be synthesised in the human body. It is produced from hydroxyl pyruvate, which is derived either from glucose or from glycerol. Serine is found in some foods such as salmon, cheese, eggs, pork, cattle, soybeans, nuts, sunflower seeds, and poppy seeds; there is no specific recommended daily intake for serine. Patients with depression, and those with schizophrenia, had increased plasma levels of serine compared to normal control (Sumiyoshi et al., 2004). There are also reports of decreased serine plasma levels in psychotic depressive disorder (Fekkes et al., 1994).

Vitamins and minerals have an effect on mood and cognitive function. Folic acid, riboflavin and some of the other B vitamins (cobalamin, and pyridoxine) also play major roles in depression (Benton and Donohoe, 1999; Horrobin, 2002). Some evidence shows that micronutrient deficiencies, particularly iron, zinc, vitamin B–12 and folate, may be linked to depression. Various sources suggest a relationship between folate levels and depression. Patients with low folate status have a higher risk of major depression, greater severity of depression (Abou-Saleh and Coppen, 1989; Bottiglieri et al., 1992), and decreased response to anti-depressants (Papakostas et al., 2012). In addition folate deficiency leads to elevated homocysteine (Hcy), which has been associated with depression in some studies (Kim et al., 2008; Tolmunen et al., 2004). Zinc deficiency has also been associated with depression in several studies (Wójcik et al., 2006; McLoughlin and Hodge, 1990). The Talbinah content of minerals, which are associated with reduced depression, are zinc (Szewczyk et al., 2011) and magnesium (Eby and Eby, 2006). A study demonstrated the effectiveness of using zinc as a supplement in anti-depressant therapy. Thus, the zinc content in Talbinah of 5mg per serving may have also contributed towards reducing depression (Roozbeh et al., 2011). Magnesium may play a role in the treatment of depression if it is given as a supplementary dose of 125–300mg/day (Eby and Eby, 2006). Talbinah magnesium content was 14.4mg per serving.

Regarding the relationship between Talbinah and depression, Talbinah is considered as a high carbohydrate food. An increase in carbohydrate consumption has a negative relationship with depression and mood; this might be due to the carbohydrate effect on serotonin synthesis, differential ratio of amino acid, sugar and zinc content (Reid and Hammersley, 1999). As lower zinc serum levels are related to highly depressed patients, one study demonstrates the efficiency of using a zinc supplement in antidepressant therapy (Roozbeh et al., 2011). Therefore, the zinc content in Talbinah plays a role in reducing depression. Magnesium can facilitate the treatment of depression when taken as a supplement dose of 125–300mg/day (Eby and Eby, 2006). Although the carbohydrate content of Talbinah is high, it is not enough to make a significant difference in the daily carbohydrate intake (Badrasawi et al., 2013).

METHODOLOGY

Ethical Approval: The study proposal was prepared to include an introduction, aim and objectives of the study, material and method, timeline and resources of the study. It was introduced to the research ethical committee of Applied Medical Sciences at King Abdul-Aziz University. The research proposal was reviewed in relation to ethical aspects and the study was *ethically approved*.

Consent Form: A written consent form was distributed among all participants. This was signed to give permission to be included in the study after the risks and benefits of the study had been explained.

The Scale of Depression among Participants: This was evaluated using the new version of the Beck Depression Inventory (BDI-II) that is designed for individuals aged 13 and over. This scale is one of the patient-rated assessment scales for noticing depression. It is broadly used as an evaluation tool by researchers and health care workers in a variety of settings. The participants were asked about depression symptoms, such as irritability and hopelessness, cognitions such as guilt or feelings of being disciplined, in addition to physical symptoms such as weight loss and fatigue (Beck, 1972).

The Cognitive Function: This was measured using the Mini-Mental State Examination (MMSE), a questionnaire containing 30 points that is used widely in research and clinical settings. It takes around 5–10 minutes and investigates functions including attention, recall, language calculation, ability to follow simple commands and orientation (Pangman et al., 2000).

Sociodemographic and Perceived Stress Scale: This is a questionnaire that included information about health, and socioeconomic status. The perceived stress scale included a 12-item food frequency questionnaire; it is used to estimate the participant's food intake that is related to depressive symptoms. All participants who met the inclusion criteria completed the self-administered questionnaire. After evaluating the score for each group (intervention and non-intervention), the higher score indicated stronger depressive symptoms (Liu et al., 2007).

Subjects: These were 42 females aged between 19–25. They were recruited from the medical campus, King Abdul-Aziz University, Jeddah, Saudi Arabia.

Talbinah: The Talbinah that is used in this study is a ready-made one available in the local markets in Jeddah, KSA with the brand name Talbinah of Prophetic Sunna.

Talbinah Analysis: The Talbinah was analysed for protein, fat and carbohydrates by using lowery, soxhlet and spectrophotometry methods respectively.

Preparation of Talbinah: A total of 25g of the ready-to-use Talbinah was prepared with 100ml of warm water by the subjects. It was distributed into small plastic bags with a total number of 28 bags of Talbinah for each of the participants. Talbinah was measured using a nutritional scale.

Talbinah Intervention: Participants were randomly selected. After completing the Beck Depression Inventory (BDI-II) questionnaire, subjects who met the inclusion criteria were included in the study. The included participants have high depression score ($\geq$14) according to the Beck Depression Inventory (BDI), and a score of ($\geq$24) according to Mini Mental State Examination (MMSE). The exclusion criteria included diabetic participants, those under medical treatment for depression, and those who had communication problems. The subjects were randomised into two groups (i.e., A and B) by random selection of the folded consent form papers ; 21 subjects were placed in each group. The intervention was for a continuous four week period. The control group continued to consume the food that they usually took. The intervention group was given one serving of Talbinah on a daily basis in addition to their usual diet.

Anthropometric Measurement: Weight and height were taken in a self-reported way. All measurements were taken twice.

Study Design: A randomised case study was conducted on female medical students at King Abdul-Aziz University, Jeddah in Saudi Arabia.

Data Analysis: The data were analysed using a Statistical Package for Social Science (SPSS) to determine the changes in the variables' mean scores in the intervention and control groups before and following intervention.

RESULTS

Sociodemographic Characteristics: The mean age of participants was 20.80 ± 1.251. Most of them were single (94.6%). The majority of the students (40.5%, n=15) were studying at 2nd level. The 3rd and 4th levels represented the same percentage (29.7%, n=11). Regarding the income level per month, 62.2% earned >10,000RS, 32.4% earned between (6000–10,000RS) while only 5.4% earned <6000 (Figure 1).

Anthropometric Measurements: These showed that the body weights and the body height of the participants were 56.08 ± 11.786, and 159.27 ± 7.19cm respectively. The calculated BMI for participants was 22.03 ± 4.01. Furthermore, 54.1% were considered to be of normal weight, 21.5% were either overweight or obese, while 24.3% were underweight (Table 1).

The depression score showed that the participants scored 19.38 ± 5.35 for the intervention group, and 18.1 ± 4.24 for the non-intervention group. The cognitive measurements using a Mini Mental State Examination (MMSE) revealed that the participants scored 27.25 ± 1.81 for the intervention group, and 27.67 ± 1.65 for the non-intervention group. Moreover, the perceived stress scale score was 28.44 ± 7.02 for the intervention group and 26.14 ± 5.65 for the non-intervention group (Table 2).

The Perceived Stress Scale for the food intake showed that the majority of the participants (89.2%) reported that they consume sweets sometimes 32.4% (n=12), fairly

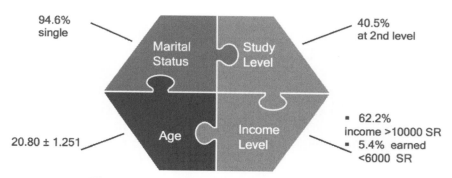

Figure 1   Sociodemographic Characteristics
Source: Devised by author

Table 1   Anthropometric Measurements

Characteristics	Intervention group	Non-intervention group	All
Body weight	54.69 ± 10.95	57.14 ± 12.54	56.08 ± 11.786
Body height	159.25 ± 5	159.29 ± 8.63	159.27 ± 7.19
Body mass index	21.51 ± 3.99	22.43 ± 4.06	22.03 ± 4.01

Source: Devised by author

Table 2 Depression Score, Cognitive Score and Perceived Stress Scale for Intervention and Non-Intervention Groups

Characteristics	Intervention group	Non-intervention group	All
Depression Score	19.38 ± 5.35	18.1 ± 4.24	18.65 ± 4.73
Cognitive Score	27.25 ± 1.81	27.67 ± 1.65	27.49 ± 1.71
Perceived Stress Scale	28.44 ± 7.02	26.14 ± 5.65	27.14 ± 6.3

Source: Devised by author

often 27% (n=10), very often 29.7% (n=11), while 10.8% (n=4) reported that they never or almost never consume sweets. Regarding cake/cookies, most of the participants (54.1%, n=20) sometimes consumed cake and cookies. Of the total participants, 8% (n=3) never or almost never consumed cake/cookies, while 29.7% (n=11) fairly often consumed these items, and 8.1% (n=3) very often consumed it. The consumption rate of fast and canned food is almost the same as the consumption rate of cake and cookies. Nearly half of the participants (48.6%, n=18) consumed fresh fruit very and fairly often, whereas 19% never or almost never consumed this food item. Of the participants, 89% (n=33) used to consume salad/vegetables, and 54% (n=20) reported that they consumed cooked vegetables on a regular basis. It was found that 46% (n=17) of participants consumed lemon juice. It was not expected that 54% (n=20) of participants did not consume soft drinks. Of the participants, 89% (n=18) avoided eating meat. Fish/sea foods were consumed sometimes by 54.1% (n=20). Milk was consumed regularly by 73% (n=27) of participants, while 65% reported that they consumed cereals and cereal products often; 13.5% (n=5) never consumed these food items (Table 3).

Table 3 The Pattern of Food Items Related to Depression

Food item	Never	Almost Never	Sometimes	Fairly often	Very often
Sweet	2 (5.4%)	2 (5.4%)	12 (32.4%)	10 (27%)	11 (29.7%)
Cake/cookies	2 (5.4%)	1 (2.7%)	20 (54.1%)	11 (29.7%)	3 (8.1%)
Fast food/canned food	3 (8.1%)	3 (8.1%)	21 (56.8%)	6 (16.2%)	4 (10.8%)
Fresh fruit	1 (2.7%)	6 (16.2%)	12 (32.4%)	9 (24.3%)	9 (24.3%)
Salad/vegetables	1 (2.7%)	3 (8.1%)	10 (27.0%)	13 (35.1%)	10 (27.0%)
Cooked vegetables	4 (10.8%)	4 (10.8%)	9 (24.3%)	8 (21.6%)	12 (32.4%)
Lemon juice	8 (21.6%)	12 (32.4%)	8 (21.6%)	5 (13.5%)	4 (10.8%)
Soft drinks	12 (32.4%)	8 (21.6%)	9 (24.3%)	5 (13.5%)	3 (8.1%)
Meat	9 (24.3%)	9 (24.3%)	8 (21.6%)	9 (24.3%)	2 (5.4%)
Fish /Sea food	3 (8.1%)	6 (16.2%)	20 (54.1%)	6 (16.2%)	2 (5.4%)
Milk/Milk products	-	2 (5.4%)	8 (21.6%)	11 (29.7%)	16 (43.2%)
Cereals/Cereals product	4 (10.8%)	1 (2.7%)	8 (21.6%)	12 (32.4%)	12 (32.4%)

Source: Devised by author

Table 4   The Effect of Talbinah on the Intervention and Non-Intervention Groups

Characteristics	Cases			Control		
	Pre intervention	Post intervention	P. Value	Pre intervention	Post intervention	P. Value
Body weight	54.69 ± 10.95	55.15 ± 11.59	0.52	57.14 ± 12.54	57.99 ± 12.39	0.01
Body mass index	21.51 ± 3.99	21.8 ± 4.19	0.056	22.43 ± 4.06	22.75 ± 4.18	0.017
Depression score	19.38 ± 5.35	8.69 ± 6.53	0.00	18.1 ± 4.24	13.3 ± 8.1	0.00

Source: Devised by author

Table 5   Talbinah Analysis

Carbohydrates	68
Protein	14.5
Fat	0.5

Source: Devised by author

Effect of Talbinah on Depression Score: There was no significant difference between the intervention group and non-intervention group in regard to the depression score, as shown in Table 4. Both groups had a significant decrease in the depression score ($P=0.00$). Although the difference is insignificant between the two groups, there was a decrease in the intervention group (score=8.69 ± 6.53) compared to the non-intervention group (13.3 ± 8.1) (Table 4).

The Talbinah analysis resulted in a high carbohydrate content of 68%, while protein and fat were 14.5% and 0.5% respectively (Table 5).

DISCUSSION

Recently, macronutrients and micronutrients and their relationship to mental health have received attention in research (Christensen and Pettijohn, 2001). Scientific evidence regarding the use of Talbinah has shown an effect on reducing symptoms of depression. The results of most studies of Talbinah intervention showed improvement in the depression score.

According to a study carried out by Badrasawi et al. (2013), carbohydrate consumption has been hypothesised to relieve depressive moods; this may be due to the effect of carbohydrates on serotonin synthesis. In the current study, the Talbinah analysis showed that the carbohydrate content was 68%, which may have the same effect and agreed with the findings of previous research on depression.

Studies of the effect of dietary protein on depression revealed positive results. A number of studies have shown that acute tryptophan depletion results in worsening the mood, which is strongly associated with depressive symptoms. A study conducted by Fernstrom and Wurtman (1971) revealed that brain tryptophan and serotonin levels influenced dietary protein through effects on plasma amino acids patterns. A study done by Youssef et al. (2012) indicated that the protein level in Talbinah is 18.34%; this indicates the positive effect of using Talbinah in reducing depression. This finding agrees with the present study results, which showed that the protein content of Talbinah was 14.5%. This is considered to be almost the same percentage in the study mentioned above, may have the same effect, and agreed with the findings.

A study done by Lai et al. (2014) showed that the beneficial subtypes of fatty acids could improve depressive symptoms by modulating serum levels of inflammatory markers. The fat analysis of Talbinah used in the current study is 0.5%, a percentage that may not have any effect on depressive symptoms.

The minerals that are considered to have an effect on reducing depression are zinc and magnesium. The association between zinc deficiency and depression has been reported in many studies. Lower zinc serum levels have been associated with highly depressed patients (Szewczyk et al., 2011; Eby and Eby, 2006). Thus, the zinc content in Talbinah of 5mg per serving may have also contributed to the reduction of depression.

Although magnesium may play a role in the treatment of depression if it is given as a supplementary dose of 125–300mg/day, the magnesium content in Talbinah was only 14.4mg per serving. This level will not improve depression, and this is confirmed by a study done by Badrasawi et al. (2013) that showed that the effect of Talbinah on depression was not due to the magnesium content.

The findings of the present study disagrees with a study conducted among elderly in critical ill care by Badrasawi et al. (2013), which found a significant positive effect of Talbinah on depressive symptoms. While the findings of this study show an effect of Talbinah food consumption in reducing depressive symptoms among the intervention group, the difference between the depression score in the intervention and non-intervention groups were insignificant. This may be due to a lack of honesty while completing the post-intervention questionnaire. This is because both groups were familiar with the sequence of the questionnaire and interpretation when they completed it for the second time; this could result in errors when evaluating the depression score. In the present study, there was no association between the perceived stress scale and depressive symptoms. However, a similar result was reported in a previous study that was conducted to investigate the relationship between food consumption and depressive symptoms using the perceived stress scale (Mikolajczyk et al., 2009). Uncontrolled settings in the contribution to regular diet intake by the participants can lead to this conflicting result on the perceived stress scale. It was found that the intervention group had insignificant weight change after Talbinah consumption in comparison with pre-intervention body weight, possibly due to the low calorie content in Talbinah.

CONCLUSIONS

Depression is one of the largest health problems the society faces today. The cost of anti-depressants increases annually, resulting in an economical challenge for public health. Food and nutrition has a great role in managing mental diseases. Both macronutrient and micronutrient consumption does affect psychology function and improves depressive symptoms; this is because the production of neurotransmitters requires certain nutrients. Prophetic medicine is one of the most effective complementary medicines. Although there is a positive insignificant effect of Talbinah on depression in this study, due to the limitations of the study Talbinah has a positive effect to lessen depression and improve mood. Eating of functional foods such as Talbinah might give a mental health advantage to depressed people. This ensures the facts of the prophet Mohammed [peace be upon him] on the affirmative positive effect of Talbinah in reducing depression for sad people. Practical implications include public private Medicare collaboration and using diet in the management of depression to reduce the use, cost and side effects of anti-depressant medication. The originality and value of this study is the significant importance in broadening the scope of giving more attention for managing mental diseases that come in parallel with sustainable development goals (3): Ensuring healthy lives and promoting wellbeing for all at all ages.

Limitations

- Participants were not in an enclosed setting; this resulted in taking different food items that has a noticeable effect on depression due to the content of effective macronutrient and micronutrient on depression occurrence.
- Some of the subjects did not consume the recommended amount of Talbinah on a daily basis due to the unacceptable taste to most of them.

Recommendations

- A controlled setting could result in a more effective outcome of Talbinah consumption on depressive symptoms.
- Using certain instruments to analyse micronutrient content in Talbinah could result in determining the depression risk factor that can be prevented by nutritional management.
- The establishment of computerised food analysis programs and nutrient analysis database.
- Further studies are required using highly advanced technology such as MRI to detect the immediate effect of Tablinah on the physiological change of the brain.
- Other studies are required to determine the effectiveness of Talbinah on depression among various age groups.

- To encourage people to return to deserted Sunnah and prophetic medicine by using prophetic nutrition in treating some chronic diseases such as depression.

ACKNOWLEDGMENTS

The author is sincerely thankful to the senior students of the Clinical Nutrition Program at King Abdulaziz University in the academic year 2015–2016. To Arwa Alsubaie, Bashair Basaeed, Ruba Banjar and Shrouq Alqahtani for their great help in data collection and entry, and assistance in the application of the intervention programme. Special thanks to medical students who thankfully agreed to take part in the screening and intervention part of this study.

Competing interests: The author has declared that no competing interests exist. Nahlaa A. Khalifa, PhD, Assistant Professor at the Clinical Nutrition Program, Faculty of Applied Medical Sciences, King Abdulaziz University.

REFERENCES

Abdel-Hassib, R. (2007), *Talbina: A food and drug*. Mecca, KSA: International Organization of the Holy Quran and Hadiths.

Abd El-Rahman (2001), ZEDF Fatah El-bary fe sharh saheeh El-buhkary. EL-damam. Saudi Arabia: Ibn El-Goze.

Abou-Saleh, M.T. and Coppen, A. (1989), Serum and red blood cell folate in depression. *Acta Psychiatrica Scandinavica*, Vol. 80, No. 1, pp. 78–82.

Akbaraly, T.N., Brunner, E.J., Ferrie, J.E., Marmot, M.G., Kivimaki, M. and Singh-Manoux, A. (2009), Dietary pattern and depressive symptoms in middle age. *The British Journal of Psychiatry*, Vol. 195, No. 5, pp. 408–13.

Al-Faris, E., Irfan, F., Van der Vleuten, C.P.M., Naeem, N., Alsalem, A., Alamiri, N., Alraiyes, T., Alfowzan, M., Alabdulsalam, A., Ababtain, A. and Aljabab, S. (2012), The prevalence and correlates of depressive symptoms from an Arabian setting: A wake up call. *Medical Teacher*, Vol. 34, Sup 1, pp. S32–S6.

Al-Khathami, A.D. and Ogbeide, D.O. (2002), Prevalence of mental illness among Saudi adult primary-care patients in Central Saudi Arabia. *Saudi Medical Journal*, Vol. 23, No. 6, pp. 721-24.

Al-Qadhi, W., Ur Rahman, S., Ferwana, M.S. and Abdulmajeed, I.A. (2014), Adult depression screening in Saudi primary care: prevalence, instrument and cost. *BMC Psychiatry*, Vol. 14, No. 1, p.190.

Andersen, I., Thielen, K., Bech, P., Nygaard, E. and Diderichsen, F. (2011), Increasing prevalence of depression from 2000 to 2006. *Scandinavian Journal of Social Medicine*, Vol. 39, No. 8, pp. 857–63.

Assies, J., Pouwer, F., Lok, A., Mocking, R.J., Bockting, C.L., Visser, I., Abeling, N.G., Duran, M. and Schene, A.H. (2010), Plasma and erythrocyte fatty acid patterns in patients with recurrent depression: a matched case-control study. *PLoS One*, Vol. 5, No. 5, p. e10635.

Ayuso-Mateos, J.L., Vázquez-Barquero, J.L., Dowrick, C., Lehtinen, V., Dalgard, O.S., Casey, P., Wilkinson, C., Lasa, L., Page, H., Dunn, G. and Wilkinson, G. (2001), Depressive disorders in Europe: prevalence figures from the ODIN study. *The British Journal of Psychiatry*, Vol. 179, No. 4, pp. 308–16.

Badrasawi, M.M., Shahar, S., Manaf, Z.A. and Haron, H. (2013), Effect of Talbinah food consumption on depressive symptoms among elderly individuals in long term care facilities, randomized clinical trial. *Clinical Interventions in Aging*, Vol. 8, p. 279.

Beck, A.T. (1972), *Depression: Causes and Treatment*. Philadelphia: University of Pennsylvania Press. ISBN 0-8122-1032-8.

Benton, D. and Donohoe, R.T. (1999), The effects of nutrients on mood. *Public Health Nutrition*, Vol. 2, No. 3a, pp. 403–09.

Besharat Pour, M., Bergström, A., Bottai, M., Kull, I., Wickman, M., Håkansson, N., Wolk, A. and Moradi, T. (2014), Effect of parental migration background on childhood nutrition, physical activity, and body mass index. *Journal of Obesity*, Vol. 2014, Article ID 406529, p. 10.

Bottiglieri, T., Hyland, K., Laundy, M., Godfrey, P., Carney, M.W.P., Toone, B.K., and Reynolds, E.H. (1992), Folate deficiency, biopterin and monoamine metabolism in depression. *Psychological Medicine*, Vol. 22, No. 04, pp. 871–76.

Brennan, C.S. and Cleary, L.J. (2005), The potential use of cereal (1-3,1-4)-B-D-glucans as functional food ingredients. *Journal of Cereal Science*, Vol. 42, No. 1, pp.1–13.

Butler, A.C., Chapman, J.E., Forman, E.M. and Beck, A.T. (2006), The empirical status of cognitive-behavioral therapy: a review of meta-analyses. *Clinical Psychology Review*, Vol. 26, No. 1, pp. 17–31.

Christensen, L. and Pettijohn, L. (2001), Mood and carbohydrate cravings. *Appetite*, Vol. 36, No. 2, pp. 137–45.

Eby, G.A. and Eby, K.L. (2006), Rapid recovery from major depression using magnesium treatment. *Medical Hypotheses*, Vol. 67, No. 2, pp. 362–70.

Fekkes, D., Pepplinkhuizen, L., Verheij, R. and Bruinvels, J. (1994), Abnormal plasma levels of serine, methionine, and taurine in transient acute polymorphic psychosis. *Psychiatry Research*. Vol. 51, No. 1, pp. 11–18.

Fernstrom, J.D. and Wurtman, R. (1971), Brain serotonin content: physiological dependence on plasma tryptophan levels. *Science*, Vol. 173, No. 3992, pp. 149–52.

Firk, C. and Markus, C.R. (2007), Serotonin by stress interaction: a susceptibility factor for the development of depression? *Journal of Psychopharmacology*, Vol. 21, No. 5, pp. 538–44.

Furukawa, T.A., Streiner, D.L. and Young, L.T. (2001), Is antidepressant-benzodiazepine combination therapy clinically more useful?: A meta-analytic study. *Journal of Affective Disorders*, Vol. 65, No. 2, pp. 173–77.

Gadit, A.A.M. and Mugford, G. (2007), Prevalence of depression among households in three capital cities of Pakistan: Need to revise the mental health policy. *PLoS One*, Vol. 2, No. 2, p. e209.

Halyburton, A.K., Brinkworth, G.D., Wilson, C.J., Noakes, M., Buckley, J.D., Keogh, J.B. and Clifton, P.M. (2007), Low-and high-carbohydrate weight-loss diets have similar effects on mood but not cognitive performance. *The American Journal of Clinical Nutrition*, Vol. 86, No. 3, pp. 580–87.

Hoes, M.J.A.J.M. (1982), L-Tryptophan in Depression and Strain. *Journal of Orthomolecular Psychiatry*, Vol. 11, No. 4, pp. 231–42.

Horrobin, D.F. (2002), Food, micronutrients, and psychiatry. *International Psychogeriatrics*, Vol. 14, No. 04, pp. 331–34.

Ibrahim, N., Dania, A.K., Lamis, E.K., Ahd, A.H. and Asali, D. (2013), Prevalence and predictors of anxiety and depression among female medical students in King Abdulaziz University, Jeddah, Saudi Arabia. *Iranian Journal of Public Health*, Vol. 42, No. 7, p. 726.

Izydorczyk, M.S., Storsley, J., Labossiere, D., MacGregor, A.W. and Rossnagel, B.G. (2000), Variation in total and soluble b-glucan content in hulless barley: effects of thermal, physical, and enzymic treatments. *Journal of Agricultural and Food Chemistry*, Vol. 48, No. 4, pp. 982–89.

Kim, J.M., Stewart, R., Kim, S.W., Yang, S.J., Shin, I.S. and Yoon, J.S. (2008), Predictive value of folate, vitamin B12 and homocysteine levels in late-life depression. *The British Journal of Psychiatry*. Vol. 192, No. 4, pp. 268–74.

Kravitz, H.M., Sabelli, H. and Fawcett, J. (1984), Dietary supplements of phenylalanine and other amino acid precursors of brain neuroamines in the treatment of depressive disorders. *Journal of the American Osteopathic Association*, Vol. 84, 1 Suppl., pp. 119–23.

Lai, J.S., Hiles, S., Bisquera, A., Hure, A.J., McEvoy, M. and Attia, J. (2014), A systematic review and meta-analysis of dietary patterns and depression in community-dwelling adults. *The American Journal of Clinical Nutrition*, pp. ajcn-069880.

Liu, C., Xie, B., Chou, C.P., Koprowski, C., Zhou, D., Palmer, P., Sun. P., Guo, Q., Duan, L. Sun, X. and Johnson, C.A. (2007), Perceived stress, depression and food consumption frequency in the college students of China Seven Cities. *Physiology & Behavior*. Vol. 92, No. 4, pp. 748–54.

Martins, J.G. (2009), EPA but not DHA appears to be responsible for the efficacy of omega-3 long chain polyunsaturated fatty acid supplementation in depression: evidence from a meta-analysis of randomized controlled trials. *Journal of the American College of Nutrition*, Vol. 28, No. 5, pp. 525–42.

McLoughlin, I.J. and Hodge, J.S. (1990), Zinc in depressive disorder. *Acta Psychiatrica Scandinavica*, Vol. 82, No. 6, pp. 451–53.

Michels, N., Sioen, I., Braet, C., Eiben, G, Hebestreit, A., Huybrechts, I., Vanaelst, B., Vyncke, K. and De Henauw, S. (2012), Stress, emotional eating behaviour and dietary patterns in children. *Appetite*, Vol. 59, No. 3, pp. 762–69.

Mikolajczyk, R.T., El Ansari, W. and Maxwell, A.E. (2009), Food consumption frequency and perceived stress and depressive symptoms among students in three European countries. *Nutrition Journal*, Vol. 8, No. 1, p. 31.

Mohammadi Aghdam, S. and Samadiyan, F. (2014), Effect of nitrogen and cultivars on some of traits of barley (hordeum vulgare l.). *International Journal of Advanced Biological and Biomedical Research*. Vol. 2, No. 2, pp. 295–99.

Møller, S.E., Honoré, P. and Larsen, O.B. (1983), Tryptophan and tyrosine ratios to neutral amino acids in endogenous depression: relation to antidepressant response to amitriptyline and lithium+ L-tryptophan. *Journal of Affective Disorders*, Vol. 5, No. 1, pp. 67–79.

Mwamburi, D.M., Liebson, E., Folstein, M., Bungay, K., Tucker, K.L. and Qiu, W.Q. (2011), Depression and glycemic intake in the homebound elderly. *Journal of Affective Disorders*. Vol. 132, No. 1, pp. 94–98.

Murakami, K. and Sasaki, S. (2010), Dietary intake and depressive symptoms: a systematic review of observational studies. *Molecular Nutrition & Food Research*, Vol. 54, No. 4, pp. 471–88.

Neumeister, A., Praschak-Rieder, N., Hesselmann, B., Vitouch, O., Rauh, M., Barocka, A. and Kasper, S. (1998), Effects of tryptophan depletion in fully remitted patients with seasonal affective disorder during summer. *Psychological Medicine*, Vol. 28, No. 2, pp. 257–264.

Palazidou, E. (2012), The neurobiology of depression. *British Medical Bulletin*. Vol. 101, No. 1, pp. 127–45.

Pangman, V.C., Sloan, J. and Guse, L. (2000), An examination of psychometric properties of the mini-mental state examination and the standardized mini-mental state examination: implications for clinical practice. *Applied Nursing Research*, Vol. 13, No. 4, pp. 209–13.

Papakostas, G.I., Shelton, R.C., Zajecka, J.M., Etemad, B., Rickels, K., Clain, A., Baer, L., Dalton, E.D., Sacco, G.R., Schoenfeld, D. and Pencina, M. (2012), L-methylfolate as adjunctive therapy for SSRI-resistant major depression: results of two randomized, double-blind, parallel-sequential trials. *American Journal of Psychiatry*, Vol. 169, No. 12, pp. 1267–74.

Reid, M. and Hammersley, R. (1999), The effects of sucrose and maize oil on subsequent food intake and mood. *British Journal of Nutrition*, Vol. 82, No. 6, pp. 447–55.

Roozbeh, J., Sharifian, M., Ghanizadeh, A., Sahraian, A., Sagheb, M.M., Shabani, S., Jahromi, A.H., Kashfi, M. and Afshariani, R. (2011), Association of zinc deficiency and depression in the patients with end-stage renal disease on hemodialysis. *Journal of Renal Nutrition*, Vol. 21, No. 2, pp. 184–87.

Sastry, C.S.P. and Tummuru, M.K. (1985), Spectrophotometric determination of tryptophan in proteins. *Journal of Food Science and Technology*, Vol. 22, No. 2, pp. 146–47.

Spillmann, M.K., Van der Does, A.W., Rankin, M.A., Vuolo, R.D., Alpert, J.E., Nierenberg, A.A., Rosenbaum, J.F., Hayden, D., Schoenfeld, D. and Fava, M. (2001), Tryptophan depletion in SSRI-recovered depressed outpatients. *Psychopharmacology*, Vol. 155, No. 2, pp. 123–27.

Sumiyoshi, T., Anil, A.E., Jin, D., Jayathilake, K., Lee, M. and Meltzer, H.Y. (2004), Plasma glycine and serine levels in schizophrenia compared to normal controls and major depression: relation to negative symptoms. *The International Journal of Neuropsychopharmacology*, Vol. 7, No. 1, pp. 1–8.

Szewczyk, B., Kubera, M. and Nowak, G. (2011), The role of zinc in neurodegenerative inflammatory pathways in depression. *Progress in Neuro-Psychopharmacology and Biological Psychiatry*, Vol. 35, No. 3, pp. 693–701.

Timonen, M., Horrobin, D., Jokelainen, J., Laitinen, J., Herva, A. and Räsänen, P. (2004), Fish consumption and depression: the Northern Finland 1966 birth cohort study. *Journal of Affective Disorders*, Vol. 82, No. 3, pp. 447–52.

Tolmunen, T., Hintikka, J., Voutilainen, S., Ruusunen, A., Alfthan, G., Nyyssönen, K., Viinamaki, H., Kaplan, G.A. and Salonen, J.T. (2004), Association between depressive symptoms and serum concentrations of homocysteine in men: a population study. *The American Journal of Clinical Nutrition*. Vol. 80, No. 6, pp. 1574–78.

Van Reedt Dortland, A.K., Giltay, E.J., van Veen, T., van Pelt, J., Zitman, F.G. and Penninx, B.W. (2010), Associations between serum lipids and major depressive disorder: results from the Netherlands Study of Depression and Anxiety (NESDA). *The Journal of Clinical Psychiatry*, Vol. 71, No. 6, pp. 729–36.

Wells, A.S., Read, N.W., Laugharne, J.D. and Ahluwalia, N. (1998), Alterations in mood after changing to a low-fat diet. *British Journal of Nutrition*, Vol. 79, No. 1, pp. 23–30.

Wójcik, J., Dudek, D., Schlegel-Zawadzka, M., Grabowska, M., Marcinek, A., Florek, E., Piekoszewski, W., Nowak, R.J., Opoka, W. and Nowak, G. (2006), Antepartum/postpartum depressive symptoms and serum zinc and magnesium levels. *Pharmacological Reports*, Vol. 58, No. 4, p. 571.

Wurtman, R.J. and Wurtman, J.J. (1989), Carbohydrates and depression. *Scientific American*, Vol. 260, No. 1, pp. 68–75.

Youssef, M.K.E., El-Fishawy, F.A.E.K., Ramadan, E.S.A.E.N. and El-Rahman, A.M. (2012), Assessment of total lipid fractions and fatty acids composition in raw, germinated barleys and talbina products. *Food Public Health*, Vol. 2, No. 1, pp. 16–23.

BIOGRAPHY

Nahlaa A. Khalifa is an assistant professor at the Clinical Nutrition Department, Faculty of Applied Medical Sciences, King Abdulaziz University, Jeddah, Saudi Arabia. She has a PhD in food science and nutrition. Dr Khalifa is the founder of the clinical nutrition programme at King Abdulaziz University, the coordinator of the commission for national and international academic accreditation for the clinical nutrition programme, chairperson and member of many committees. Her main research interests are in nutrition and dietetics, especially for mentally disabled patients, nutritional genomic, complementary and alternative medicine, prophetic medicine and food safety. Her interests also lie in the establishment and accreditation of new academic programmes. Dr Khalifa's educational experience includes teaching by using mind mapping, as she is a Thinkbuzan Licensed Instructor (TLI) and TOT. She has won many prizes including the academic excellence award from the President of King Abdulaziz University, best paper appreciation award for 2nd Diaspora International Conference 2015, Brighton, UK, the best paper appreciation award from World Association for Sustainable Development (WASD) 14th international conference 2016, London, UK, and best supervised students graduation projects.

GOALS 1/2

NO POVERTY/ZERO HUNGER

MIGRATION AND THE ROLE OF SUSTAINABLE DEVELOPMENT

Olivia Joseph-Aluko

CEO
Reinvent African Diaspora Network (RADET)
UK
info@radet.org.uk

ABSTRACT

Purpose: The purpose of this paper is to consider how migration serves as a driving force for sustainable development, and how the private sector can impact this process.

Approach: This study emphasises the role of migration in sustainable development. It examines literature on the private sector in economic development, and analyses statistics on international migration and remittances, and their economic effects in African countries.

Findings: The restrictive economic conditions affecting migrants and refugees negatively impact both host countries and places of origin. The private sector can enhance outcomes for all involved by collaborating with governments and aid agencies to reduce obstacles hindering migrant employment, business development and social integration.

Originality/Value: Much research has focused on the negative effects of African migration, with fewer studies examining the broader impact of

*Corresponding Author

migration on local and regional economic growth and development, particularly the pivotal involvement of the private sector. The role of migration as a force in sustainable development is an issue of growing importance, yet remains under-investigated.

Keywords: African-born migrants; international migration; migration of skills; migrant remittances; private sector

INTRODUCTION

The displacement of millions of Africans to Europe and North America has contributed to an evolving migration crisis and raises new concerns that need to be addressed as a part of sustainable development goals. The loss of the skills and knowledge that accompanies large-scale outmigration is an increasingly studied aspect of this process. Migrant skills contribute to the economy of their country of origin, and the departure of these human resources eventually results in a shortage of skills, while the receiving nations benefit from the lower-cost labour they provide.

A report from the International Organisation for Migration (IOM) showed that over one-third of migrants to developed countries comprise educated professionals, while a United Nations publication indicated that in 2010–2011 one in nine Africans with a tertiary education were living in developed countries. This represents a 50% increase over the past 10 years, and can be compared to the figures of one in 13 and one in 30 in Latin America and Asia, respectively (UN-DESA and OECD, 2013). In 2015, 39% of sub-Saharan Africans in the United States had at least a bachelor's degree (US Census Bureau, 2016). The World Economic Forum's Global Competitiveness Report 2014–2015 listed Uganda as the only African nation among the top 20 countries able to retain talented workers, while at the other end of the scale, Burundi, Algeria, Mauritania, Chad, Guinea and Sierra Leone were all included among the 20 nations whose top talent is most likely to leave (Schwab, 2014).

According to the Internal Displacement Monitoring Centre (IDMC), there were about 3.5 million new displacements in Africa in 2016 alone, of which 2.6 million were caused by conflict and violence (IDMC, 2017). These conditions engender poverty and lack of access to education for those affected, which has had a ripple effect on economic stability and growth. The effects of this brain drain are perhaps most prominent in the field of medical services, resulting in devastating impacts on the struggle to achieve health and fight disease and malnutrition. While some professionals move to other, more prosperous African countries such as South Africa, most travel further abroad to Europe, and increasingly, the United States, where they can obtain better access to education and economic opportunities.

However, many developing countries can benefit from the migration of some of its citizens through the remittances sent home; these payments help stabilise households and make improvements to nutrition, health, housing and education. An increasingly significant issue is how to effectively leverage these funds to aid in local economic growth and development, which has long been a challenge for individual governments and presents a range of opportunities for private sector involvement. This paper considers how migration can serve as a driving force for sustainable development and examines some ways that the private sector can contribute to this process.

APPROACHING MIGRATION FROM A SUSTAINABLE DEVELOPMENT PERSPECTIVE

This study approaches the issue of migration from a perspective that emphasises its role in sustainable development, beginning at the household level. It examines data on private sector involvement in the migration crisis, analyses statistics on international migration and remittance amounts and uses, and their economic effects in African countries. These statistics have been compiled by such organisations as the UN, the IOM, the World Economic Forum, the IDMC and the World Bank.

Literature concerning modern migration patterns from Africa can be divided into two broad categories: a) studies examining the impact on the receiving countries; b) studies considering the impact on the home countries. Within the latter category, a great deal of research has focused on the negative effects of African migration on the shortage of medical professionals, which has been attributed as a significant factor in the continent's health crisis (Hagopian et al., 2004; Mlambo and Adetiba, 2017; Oberoi and Lin, 2006). A few studies have examined the broader impact of migration on local and regional economic growth and development (Adams et al., 2008; Mohapatra and Ratha, 2011; Ratha, 2011; World Bank, 2017), including the roles played by government institutions and non-governmental organisations (NGOs), and increasingly, the potential involvement of the private sector (IFC, 2011). However, while the role of migration as a force in sustainable development is an issue of growing importance, it remains under-investigated. Also, while a growing number of entrepreneurs and business leaders have become involved in the migration crisis, the issue of how to balance profitability with social responsibility is only beginning to be addressed (IFC, 2011).

This study examines aspects of African migration and its impact on regional economic development, namely the large-scale losses of medical professionals and its effects on efforts to manage disease and promote health. This has broader impacts on economic development, as well as some push factors involved in the departure of skilled workers from African countries. The study also considers the role of remittances in improving household nutrition, health and educational status, and how the private sector can help leverage these benefits into sustainable development initiatives.

THE BRAIN DRAIN, HEALTH AND ECONOMIC DEVELOPMENT

The shortage of African professionals is perhaps most acutely seen in the medical field. Globalisation has resulted in an increased demand for health workers, with an accompanying relaxation of the immigration regulations of many developed countries in order to attract highly skilled professionals, particularly engineers and health professionals. The overwhelming majority of sub-Saharan African-born physicians practicing in the United States originate from only three countries, namely Nigeria, South Africa and Ghana (Hagopian et al., 2004). In 1973, there were 7.76 doctors per 100,000 people in Liberia; by 2008, however, this figure had declined to only 1.37 doctors, leaving the country woefully undermanned to address the recent Ebola crisis (WHO, 2017).

Annually, 30–40% of the doctors who graduate in Kenya leave the country after completing their internship (WHO, 2017). Although some of these migrate to other African countries, a large majority move to the United States or Europe; thus enriching the human resources base in these regions at the expense of their home countries.

South Africa has been losing 17% of its qualified doctors each year (Mlambo and Adetiba, 2017), and West African-trained physicians have been migrating in large numbers, primarily to the US and the UK, since receiving access to medical education in the 1960s.

Studies have indicated that the predominant reasons for leaving include the higher workloads and occupational risks associated with providing medical care in developing countries, as well as better opportunities for job promotion and higher pay (WHO, 2017). The spread of HIV/AIDS and its concomitant dangers in hospitals lacking in infrastructural features related to hygiene and contamination has also been cited as a factor in the migration of health professionals from developing countries (Oberoi and Lin, 2006). Therefore, the very health crises that have increased the demand for medical professionals have also resulted in higher hazards and an enormous workload that drives them to seek better opportunities elsewhere.

The loss of these professionals has negatively impacted the functioning of the health sector, reducing the overall quality of medical care offered by the health institutions in many countries. Some countries, such as South Africa, have begun addressing the issue through policies aimed at improving and increasing the development and training of more health professionals. This has included constructing new medical colleges, sending medical students to Cuba for training, and requiring graduates to spend a certain period working domestically before accepting overseas positions.

Developing countries have long attempted to invest more in their health sectors; however, this is difficult due to slow economic growth and often uncertain political systems. Despite the billions in aid invested in the region annually, most countries spend far less on even essential health services than the recommended WHO standard of \$34–\$40 per capita (IFC, 2011). This creates an enormous gap, which is largely filled by the private health sector, and many governments are actively seeking to increase this contribution. The African health care market is estimated at some US\$35 billion, with private companies responsible for about 50%–60% of health expenditures (IFC, 2011). The private sector can help further expand the market by collaborating with governments in the improvement of the infrastructure, as well as through investment in distribution and retail activities, pharmaceutical and medical product manufacturing, insurance, and medical education. Such investments will fund capacity expansion and new businesses through the development of innovative (and often less expensive and more accessible) enterprises for health care delivery. It will also help to drive down costs and improve existing conditions, which have been cited as a push factor by many departing medical workers.

Push Factors in African Migration

Many observers have noted the importance of examining those factors that influence skilled workers to leave their home countries. While in some cases, the role of conflict and warfare, and their concomitant devastating effects on basic economic functioning are obvious in pushing those able to leave the country, in other cases, the situation is more complex. Mlambo and Adetiba (2017) note the applicability of neoclassical theory to the migration of South African health professionals, who commonly cite the desire for better wages as a major motivator for seeking employment in developed nations. A junior doctor in South Africa begins with a salary lower than that of some bus drivers (Mlambo and Adetiba, 2017). Other push/pull factors frequently cited by professionals and other skilled workers include poor working conditions and security, and better educational opportunities for their children.

Globalisation has created a strong demand for skilled workers in developed countries (Duncan, 2012), and their more advanced levels of economic growth and development both create and fuel this demand, allowing them the means to attract these professionals. Moreover, as universities have begun recruiting globally, many talented young people have been fleeing African countries for educational opportunities in Europe and North America. Ambitious African youth perceive the US and the UK as having better quality higher education, and are flocking there in large numbers. In 2014, 31,113 students from sub-Saharan Africa comprised 4% of the 886,052 international students in the US (Institute of International Education, 2015). Universities in the developed world are seen as providing more prestigious degrees and better career opportunities.

The private sector can aid in the retention of talented professionals by investing in these students, many of whom are attracted to foreign universities by scholarships. Much as governments and organisations in the developed world often finance the education of talented employees in such critical sectors as health, technology and engineering in exchange for a certain period of service, companies operating in African countries can sponsor scholarships that require students to return to work in their home countries for a specified period of time after graduating. Such solutions benefit companies as well as the students by providing them with educated insiders, thus reducing the expenses involved in importing and training staff that may be less familiar with local conditions.

Can Remittances Aid in Sustainable Development?

One way in which international migration has been helpful to African economic growth is through remittances, the monies sent home to family members by departed workers. Remittances increase household consumption and provide insurance against food shortages and natural disasters. Countries in Northern Africa, particularly Morocco, Algeria and Egypt, receive significant influxes from remittances, and Eastern African countries such as Somalia are also heavily dependent on these monies, as are Nigeria, Senegal and Ghana in the west. Average annual remittances per migrant reach almost US$1,200 per year, representing 3% of GDP and 27% of exports on average per country, compared to 1.9% of GDP for all developing countries (IFAD, 2017b). Remittances often form an even more significant share of GDP, such as in Liberia, where they account for 31%, Comoros (20%), and the Gambia (22%) (IFAD, 2017b).

Remittances from African migrants comprised 6% of worldwide remittances in 2015, with total money transfers to home regions through formal channels reaching US$35.2 billion. It is estimated that including monies sent through informal channels quadruples that amount (IFAD, 2017b). However, the US$134.4 billion in annual transfers by African migrants to their homes from 2011–2015 is a small figure compared to the estimated US$50 billion in financial flows out of the continent (Kar and Cartwright-Smith, 2008). Additionally, operation costs are higher for money transfers in sub-Saharan Africa than in other regions, with an average cost of 9.8% to send as little as US$200; in some cases, such as Ghana, this rises as high as 16% (World Bank, 2017). Several high-income countries are considering taxation of outward remittances to discourage migration and raise their own faltering revenues (Malit and Naufal, 2016). Moreover, although expected to recover in 2017, over the past two years, economic difficulties in Europe and North America have trickled down to Africa, resulting in a decline of remittances estimated at 6.1% in 2016 (World Bank, 2017). In addition to the slow economic growth in remittance-sending countries, other issues affecting the inflows of migrant monies include a reduction in commodity prices, especially oil, and the diversion of remittances to informal channels.

One means of enhancing the benefits of remittances is to reduce the exorbitant fees involved in sending money to African countries, which is enabled by the near-monopolies held by only a few companies who control such transfers. The majority of international remittances to Africa are channelled through a few large international money transfer agencies, which often work exclusively with banks and post offices. The World Bank has established a sustainable development goal target of 3% (World Bank, 2017); however, as noted above, the average cost of sending US$200 is significantly higher across sub-Saharan Africa. Of the total official payments for the entire region of Western Africa, 70% are handled by one Money Transfer Organisation (MTO). In Nigeria, nearly 80% of transfers are handled by a single MTO; this MTO prohibits other MTOs from forming agreements with banks, which are the sole remittance payers in the country (IFAD, 2017b). Regulatory environments often prevent other non-banking financial institutions from making transfers; thus few participate, and many banks do not cater to lower-income individuals. The issue of high operations costs particularly affects the ability of the several million migrants within Africa to send remittances; moreover, some countries also restrict financial access to citizens and legal residents, thus making it even more difficult to send money home. As a result, a good portion of intra-African remittances are accomplished through informal channels, although this option is not available for remittances from outside the continent.

Clearly, in order to improve this situation, it is necessary to both break the monopolies held by these MTOs and reduce the exclusivity of the process to increase financial access for lower-income individuals. This is an area in which the private sector can be hugely impactful in collaborating with governments and NGOs to provide cheaper alternatives. Reducing the costs of money transfers would increase the remittances sent by migrants, in turn making more resources available to recipient households. A number of countries, beginning with Kenya in 2007, but now including South Africa and much of East and West Africa, are seeking to increase financial access by leveraging remittance transfers through the use of mobile telephones, which are widely accessible and provide a less formal means of accessing funds sent from relatives (IFAD, 2017b; Mohapatra and Ratha, 2011; World Bank, 2017). The wider adoption and availability of innovative mobile-money transfer and branchless banking technologies for domestic transfers would greatly improve the system of remittances and broader financial services in Africa, thus allowing people to send smaller amounts of money and send money more often. These services can be expanded to incorporate inter-country money transfers as well, which would increase access to financial services such as low-cost savings and credit products (Mohapatra and Ratha, 2011; Clifton, 2012).

The participation of the private sector continues to be critical in providing cheaper money transfers. In some sub-regions, a few telecommunications corporations that operate across countries have already helped facilitate the process by offering cross-border remittances. In partnership with CitiBank and Standard Chartered Bank, ZainZap allows its customers to send money to any bank in Kenya, Tanzania, and Uganda, and to receive money from any bank account in the world (Mohapatra and Ratha, 2011). In 2015, the Finnish digital payments platform company MONI created a micro-banking program called Pennanen. This program makes it easier for migrants to send and receive money, and helps streamline administrative processes for governments; it has grown to include thousands of refugees (Heath, 2016). The expansion of these cheaper cross-border and international services is urgently needed to reduce remittance costs so that more of this money can be applied to the sustainable development of African homes and businesses. Policies designed to increase financial sector development would also extend the reach of remittances by encouraging greater competition among banks. It would also stimulate the growth and expansion of alternative providers such as microfinance institutions or credit cooperatives. The potential for private sector involvement need not be limited to large, multinational corporations, as seen in the case of WorldRemit, an online remittance business founded by a Somalian immigrant to the UK in 2010. WorldRemit operates in 50 countries to help migrants send money home through mobile technology, cash pickups, or bank account deposits (LSE Business Review, 2017).

A number of policymakers and observers have also suggested increasing the role of African post offices, rural banks, and microfinancing institutions in remittances by having them partner with destination-country institutions and companies to extend existing money-order facilities to international remittances (Mohapatra and Ratha, 2011). These localised institutions can incorporate new technologies into their services to create integrated management information systems and establish small-scale banking operations, such as basic savings accounts for the payment of remittances and deposits of smaller savings amounts. Collaboration between the European Commission and several UN and World Bank organisations, among others, has resulted in the African Postal Financial Services Initiative (APFSI), which aims to facilitate competition in the African remittance market by promoting and enabling post offices in Africa to offer remittances and financial services (IFAD, 2017a). This project seeks to reduce the cost of remittances to and within the African continent as well as reduce transaction times, broaden the network of rural locations involved in money transfers, and deepen the range of financial services available to rural areas, such as savings, loans and insurance products (IFAD, 2017a). The private sector can increase its participation in this process by forming partnerships with the rural banks and microfinancers to offer cheaper remittance costs and expand financial services. The rural areas are a critical area for private sector development, as helping farmers extend remittance funds further increases the growth and development of smaller farms and fosters a successful agricultural system with reliable access to financing and robust markets (IFC, 2011).

Revenue from remittances in hard currency can be applied more directly to aid sustainable development through their use as collateral to raise financing. The securitisation of future remittance flows can increase the access of African banks and firms to international capital markets, and can also fund longer term development and infrastructure projects. On a smaller scale, studies have indicated that remittances contribute to sustainable development even on a household level by being leveraged into funding for food, housing, education, land purchases and small business development. A countries' economic growth can therefore be directly affected by re-mittance levels through consumption and investment patterns; in turn, the increased spending on food, health and education contributes to long-term well-being and pro-ductivity for households and individuals (Clifton, 2012).

More than half of the households in Burkina Faso, Ghana, and Nigeria receiving remittances from outside Africa are among the wealthiest 40% of their populations (Ratha, 2011). In Eritrea, where a quarter of the population lives abroad, a study by Kifle (2007) demonstrated a relationship between household income increases based on remittances and the ratio of educated people in an area. In Nigeria and Uganda, households receiving remittances from outside Africa have nearly twice the number of household members with a secondary education, and nearly three times the num-ber of university-educated members than those not receiving remittances (Clifton, 2012). The World Bank found that Ghanaian households receiving remittances spend less money on food and as much as 33% more on education (Adams et al., 2008). A similar study focused on Kenya and Nigeria observed that more than half of total remittance spending is invested in homebuilding, land purchases and farm improve-ments, while in Senegal, more than half is spent on food, education, and health care (Randazzo and Piracha, 2014; Ratha, 2011). Remittances also increase access to infor-mation and communication technology, as seen in Burkina Faso, where approximately 66% of households receiving international remittances have access to a mobile phone, compared with only about 41% of others; 14% own computers compared to 2% among non-recipients (Clifton, 2012).

The private sector's collaboration with governments to expand banking and finan-cial industries is critical to this process. In Algeria, for example, over a dozen private sector banks have been established since the country opened to private operators, fostering competition to reduce remittance costs and maximise those funds through small investments (IFC, 2011). Further involvement is needed by the private sector to both lower costs and expand the reach of financial services to rural areas and other populations who currently lack access to banking services.

THE PRIVATE SECTOR AND MIGRANT REFUGEES

While remittances can be a significant resource for economic development in de-veloping countries, the current migrant crisis in the Mediterranean and Europe has exacerbated the recent economic decline and overwhelmed many job markets. Many countries have made efforts to absorb these refugees, yet numerous people remain interred in camps and health facilities, creating a burden for the host countries and leaving a social and economic vacuum in the places they have left behind.

There is a growing sense among many members of the private sector that we can no longer rely on the traditional methods and organisations to deliver effective humanitarian aid and integrate refugees into European societies. Moreover, it is recognised that sustainable development involves more than resettling and absorbing these refugees; it also involves delivering security, stability, and economic opportunities to poor and fragile communities, thereby enhancing local markets and preventing people from having to flee their lives. While local governments are feeling overwhelmed by the migrant influxes, and have largely failed to develop any sustainable solutions for their settlement and integration into the community, the private sector has played a pivotal role in assisting vulnerable migrants and affected communities.

Beyond the provision of critical goods and services, the private sector can increase its role in mitigating the economic burden created by refugees. This can be done through providing employment and business opportunities, creating innovative business models that are both profitable and deliver social impact, and leveraging their networks and relationships with governments and aid organisations to advocate for policies that improve conditions for refugees as well as benefitting host communities and businesses (Huang, 2017). For example, IKEA has introduced initiatives to bring renewable energy to refugee camps in Jordan (Huang, 2017), while in partnership with UNHCR, the Vodafone Foundation has created an easily assembled digital instant classroom for use among refugees in areas where electricity and Internet connectivity are lacking or unreliable. Other companies are focusing on helping to better integrate the migrants into social and economic life. European software maker SAP is producing a free smartphone application that would help migrants arriving in Germany to navigate bureaucracy and assist their registration; while the German real estate firm LEG has approached the migrant issue as an opportunity to rejuvenate towns with declining populations, and has made about 450 flats available for migrants (Reuters, 2015). Similarly, Starbucks has committed to hire and employ 10,000 refugees worldwide (Huang, 2017), and refugees account for around 30% of US company Chobani's total workforce (Gelles, 2016). In 2015, Chobani's CEO, an immigrant from Turkey named Hamdi Ulukaya, founded the Tent Foundation to help other companies effectively integrate refugees into global work forces (Gelles, 2016), and Cisco, IBM and Salesforce are among other global operators who have joined the organisation's efforts.

In addition to directly providing employment and business opportunities, global companies can influence subsidiaries and partners to similarly participate by creating incentives to hire refugees and source from refugee-owned businesses or local companies that employ significant numbers of refugees. They can also promote policies that reduce restrictions on work, property ownership and business registration, and develop education and language and work skills among migrants. Integrating refugees into local labour and business markets improves the economic impact of migration for the host communities, and generates resources that enable the migrants to contribute to sustainable development in their countries of origin through the monies sent home to families.

CONCLUSIONS

This study examined impacts of African migration patterns on the continent's economic development, with a focus on ways the private sector can increase its participation to improve migrant outcomes. Forces in the private sector, such as philanthropists, private companies and other non-governmental organisations, have often provided support for new migrants and refugees through different initiatives involving accommodation, education, employment, and business opportunities. Although migration causes a skill shortage in many African countries, it also creates opportunities for sustainable development, particularly at the household level, where funds transferred through remittances have been applied not only to satisfy basic nutritional and health needs, but also to improve housing, education and incomes, thus engendering the seeds of wealth. The private sector's involvement is critical to this process, particularly through investment in African education and health care services. The private sector is also involved in business opportunities and expanding banking and other financial services to those who have long been excluded from participation in wider market activities.

REFERENCES

Adams, Jr, R.H., Cuecuecha, A. and Page, J. (2008), *Remittances, consumption and investment in Ghana.* Policy Research Working Paper; No. 4515. Washington, DC: World Bank. https://doi.org/10.1596/1813–9450–4515.

Clifton, D. (2012, November), Remittances from Sub-Saharan African migrants pay for schooling, health care. Population Reference Bureau. Retrieved on 01 November 2017 from http://www.prb.org/Publications/Articles/2012/remittances-subsaharan-africa.aspx.

Duncan, N. (2012), *Immigration policymaking in the global era: In pursuit of global talent.* New York: Palgrave Macmillan.

Gelles, D. (2016, October 16), For helping immigrants, Chobani's founder draws threats. *The New York Times.* Retrieved from https://www.nytimes.com/2016/11/01/business/for-helping-immigrants-chobanis-founder-draws-threats.html?_r=0.

Hagopian, A., Thompson, M.J., Fordyce, M., Johnson, K.E. and Hart, L.G. (2004), The migration of physicians from sub-Saharan Africa to the United States of America: Measures of the African brain drain. *Human Resources for Health*, Vol. 2, No. 1, p. 17. Doi:10.1186/1478–4491–2–17.

Heath, R. (2016, January 29), Private sector tries to fill EU void on refugees. Retrieved from https://www.politico.eu/article/private-sector-fill-eu-void-refugees-ngos-activists-migration-crisis-solutions/.

Huang, C. (2017), *Global business and refugee crises: A framework for sustainable engagement.* Centre for Global Development, https://www.cgdev.org/publication/global-business-and-refugee-crises.

IDMC (2017), *Global report on internal displacement.* Retrieved on 29 October 2017 from http://www.internal-displacement.org/global-report/grid2017/pdfs/2017–GRID.pdf

IFAD (2017a), The African Postal Financial Services Initiative (APFSI). Retrieved on 2 November 2017 from https://www.ifad.org/topic/operations/tags/remittances/19379915

IFAD (2017b), Sending money home: Contributing to the SDGs, one family at a time. Rome, Italy: International Fund for Agricultural Development.

IFC (2011), *The business of health in Africa: Partnering with the private sector to improve people's lives*. Washington, DC: International Finance Corporation, World Bank Group.

Institute of International Education (2015), *What international students think about U.S. higher education: Attitudes and perceptions of prospective students from around the world*. New York, NY: IIE

Kar, D. and Cartwright-Smith, D. (2008), *Illicit financial flows from Africa: Hidden resource for development*. Washington, DC: Global Financial Integrity.

Kifle, T. (2007), Do remittances encourage investment in education? Evidence from Eritrea. *GEFAME Journal of African Studies*, Vol. 4, No. 1.

LSE Business Review (2017, 03 November), Catherine Wines: 'International remittances help people directly'. Retrieved on 03 November 2017 from http://blogs.lse.ac.uk/businessreview/2017/11/03/catherine-wines-international-remittances-help-people-directly/

Malit, F. and Naufal, G. (2016), *Taxing remittances: Consequences for migrant labour populations in the GCC countries*. GLMM–EN – No. 1/2016. Gulf Labour Markets and Migration.

Mlambo, V.H. and Adetiba, T.C. (2017), Effects of brain drain on the South African health sector: Analysis of the dynamics of its push factors. *Journal of Economics and Behavioral Studies*, Vol. 9, No. 4, pp. 62–72.

Mohapatra, S. and Ratha, D. (Eds) (2011), *Remittance markets in Africa*. Washington, DC: The World Bank.

Oberoi, S.S. and Lin, V. (2006), Brain drain of doctors from Southern Africa: Brain gain for Australia. *Australian Health Review*, Vol. 30, No. 1, pp. 25–33.

Randazzo, T. and Piracha, M. (2014), *Remittances and household expenditure behaviour in Senegal*. Discussion Paper No. 8106. Bonn, Germany: Institute for the Study of Labor.

Ratha, D. (2011), *Leveraging Migration for Africa: Remittances, skills, and investments*. Washington, DC: The World Bank.

Reuters (2015, September 18), Factbox: Companies, organizations offer help for migrants. Retrieved from http://www.reuters.com/article/us-europe-migrants-help-factbox/factbox-companies-organizations-offer-help-for-migrants-idUSKCN0RI28U20150918.

Schwab, K. (2014), *Global Competitiveness Report 2014–2015: Full data edition*. Geneva, Switzerland: World Economic Forum.

UN-DESA and OECD (2013), World migration in figures. Retrieved 31 October 2017 from https://docs.google.com/viewer?url=http://www.oecd.org/els/mig/World-Migration-in-Figures.pdf.

US Census Bureau (2016), 2015 American Community Survey. Retrieved 27 October 2017 from https://www.census.gov/programs-surveys/acs.html.

World Bank (2017), *Migration and Remittances: Recent Developments and Outlook: Special Topic: Global Compact on Migration*. Migration and Development Brief 27. Washington, D.C.: World Bank Group.

World Health Organisation (WHO) (2017), *Global Health Observatory data repository*. Retrieved on 1 November 2017 from http://apps.who.int/gho/data/node.main.A1444.

BIOGRAPHY

Olivia Joseph-Aluko LLB, B.L, MA (law) is a Social justice advocate, with a proclivity for social issues impacting on Black Africans.

She started her career in law in Nigeria, Africa, where she qualified as a Solicitor and Barrister in 1992. Since then Olivia has worked in both the private and public sectors in Africa and the UK. Following this, she progressed her career in law at the Department of Politics, Queen Mary's University, London and obtained her Master's in Migration and Law in 2009.

Olivia is the CEO of Reinvent African Diaspora Network (RADET) an educational initiative that exists in furtherance of sustainable development goals in Africa. She currently works with different organisations including the Nous Mental Health organisation, the African Security forum, Amnesty International UK and an associate member of Initiatives of change, UK in addressing the causes of inequality, exclusion, and security challenges within the society.

Olivia is also a writer and the Author of Africans in the UK, Migration, Integration and Significance, and is currently working on the second edition.

AN EMPIRICAL ANALYSIS OF THE SUSTAINABILITY OF INTRA-GCC MERCHANDISE TRADE DURING 1995–2015: IS IT STILL A UTOPIAN DREAM?

Subhadra Ganguli[*]

Associate Professor
Ahlia University
Manama
Kingdom of Bahrain
subhadra.ganguli@gmail.com

ABSTRACT

Purpose: One of the aims of a single currency zone is a thriving and robust intra-regional trade. Previous literature concluded that Bahrain exhibited high dissimilarity of exports within the Gulf Cooperation Council (GCC) compared to exports of other GCC states within the region (Ganguli, 2018, forthcoming) during 1995–2015. This paper aims to evaluate the potential of a single currency GCC union by analysing the detailed export structure of goods between Bahrain and the rest of the GCC to check for export diversity.

Design/methodology/approach: A quantitative analysis was applied to time-series merchandise data of export items with a three-digit Standard Industrial Classification (SIC) code. These were extracted from the United

Nations Conference on Trade and Development (UNCTADstat) database for the period 1995–2015.

Findings: Bahrain's merchandise exports within the GCC displayed significant diversity in terms of composition during 1995 to 2015. Merchandise export diversity has similarities with the diversification trends of the economy.

Originality/value: Evidence of export diversification from Bahrain to other GCC states shows that Bahrain can be used as a model for other GCC states for diversification of exports to create a sustainable GCC currency union.

Keywords: sustainability; GCC; SIC; exports; manufactured goods

INTRODUCTION

The formation of the Gulf Cooperation Council (GCC) in 1981 between Bahrain, Kuwait, Qatar, Oman, United Arab Emirates (UAE) and Saudi Arabia was aimed at creating a single currency monetary union by 2010. Although it remains an unfulfilled dream, GCC members have strengthened economic ties through the formation of a common market and a customs union. Ganguli (2016) argues that the convergence factors for a successful currency union were not met, especially during the period of continued low oil prices during 2004–15, due to heavy dependence of the GCC region on oil and oil related goods and services, and lack of diversification. Ganguli (2018) concludes that while the Bahrain merchandise export structure shows dissimilarity when compared with exports of other GCC states during 1995–2015, its imports appear to be very similar to those of its GCC trade partners. The other five GCC states show more similarity among themselves in both merchandise exports and imports than those of Bahrain. Only the UAE has shown an increase in both concentration and diversification indices during 1995–2015 in its export basket within GCC, although the increased numbers are still lower than those of the other GCC states and low in absolute terms.

This paper analyses merchandise export data from Bahrain to the rest of the GCC during 1995–2015, to identify the nature of diverse exports to the rest of the GCC for sustainable intra-GCC trade, should such diversity exist. The paper explores similarities between diversification of the economy and diversification of exports to GCC during 1995–2015.

KINGDOM OF BAHRAIN: DIVERSIFICATION EFFORTS IN THE ECONOMY

The IMF Executive Board concluded the Article IV Consultation with the Kingdom of Bahrain (2017), mentioning that:

"Overall GDP grew 3 percent in 2016, supported by strong growth of 3.7 percent in the non-oil sector aided by the implementation of GCC-funded projects. Real GDP growth is expected to slow to 2.3 and 1.6 percent in 2017 and 2018, reflecting the ongoing fiscal consolidation and weaker investor sentiment."

According to the IMF, the non-oil sector accounts for 76% of Bahrain's total GDP. The non-oil sector showed a healthy 4.4% growth in the first quarter of 2017, up from 3.7% during 2016 (Bahrain Economic Quarterly, 2017). The five pillars of diversification in the Kingdom of Bahrain are the financial services, industrial and manufacturing, logistics, tourism and Information Communications Technology (ICT).

Bahrain's financial sector is well developed and diversified; this is evident by the remarkable presence of a wide range of local, regional, conventional and Islamic financial institutions, with a combination of retail and wholesale banks, insurance companies, brokers and advisors as well as security brokers and mutual funds. The sector is one of the largest employers, with a total of 66% of the work force comprising of Bahraini nationals. Overall, the financial sector is accountable for 16.7% of Bahrain's Gross Domestic Product (GDP) (Ganguli and Matar, 2016).

State aluminium producer Aluminium Bahrain's (Alba) $3bn Line 6 Expansion project is predicted to give Bahrain the status of the largest aluminium smelter in the world; additionally a $1bn airport modernisation contract, and a $355m Banagas gas plant projects are on the way.

Bahrain's location at the heart of the GCC, and as a link between the east and the west, helps in transport operations to provide the natural logistics of transport to support its manufacturing and tourism sectors. According to Bloomberg (2017), Bahrain has been ranked first among the top 10 destinations for expatriates to live, raise a family and for being made welcome as a foreigner.

The Central Bank of Bahrain (CBB) has launched regulations and licensing for implementing Fintech technology, welcoming innovations in the financial sector. CBB's governor, Rasheed Mohammed Al Maraj (2017), forecasted 2017's non-oil GDP growth to be 3.5%. Bahrain 2030's economic vision aimed to provide a robust and vibrant private sector with the employment of Bahrainis who will be able to access proper healthcare, education and a sound and secure environment. Its national development strategy aimed to develop a sound business environment, doubling the income of Bahrainis through a competitive economy boosted by a growing private sector. Bahrain aims to build a knowledge-based economy (Ganguli, 2018).

Currently, the main industries in Bahrain are petroleum processing and refining, aluminium smelting, iron pelletisation, fertilisers, Islamic and offshore banking, insurance, ship repairing and tourism. Agriculture's current share of GDP is 0.3%, with 47.1% in manufacturing and 52.2% in services (IMF, 2016). Oil revenue comprised of 86.2% of the total fiscal revenue of the kingdom, and oil and gas exports comprised of 60.9% of the share of total exports from the kingdom (IMF, 2016).

LITERATURE REVIEW

Ganguli (2016) shows that in the face of low oil prices, GCC economies do not exhibit the convergence of their macroeconomic indicators necessary for the formation of single currency monetary union, especially in the wake of low oil prices and lack of adequate diversification. Nechi (2010) shows that intra-GCC trade and financial integration remain weak, except for Bahrain and Kuwait who invest a large amount of their capital within the GCC. However, the GCC remains largely dependent on oil, with weak trade links within themselves. Ravi (2013) shows some degree of intra-industry trade within the GCC, with mineral fuel trade and intra-GCC trade being dominated by Saudi Arabia.

Boughanmi (2008) expects the customs union in the GCC to unleash new potential for trade within the GCC, which seems to have reached its full trade potential. Although GCC states exhibit low trade among them, it does not seem to be insignificant compared to the prediction of the gravity trade model applied to the study. Sahib and Kari (2012) conclude that Bahrain, Kuwait, Oman and Qatar did not obtain a comparative advantage in their non-oil sector in exports compared to Saudi Arabia and UAE during 1998–2008.

A lack of diversification and intra-GCC trade has led the GCC economies to integrate more with non-GCC countries than within themselves. Hossain and Naser (2008) show, among other results, that intra-GCC exports and imports and high-tech manufacturing exports show rising trends after the implementation of the GCC customs union. Alawadhi (2014) mentioned that intra-GCC trade is neither deep nor effective in large intra-trade industry trade or in the trade of new products. The level of integration is not enough to create the basis for a common currency union. Al Said (2007) concludes that there is intra-industry trade due to significant mineral fuel trade in the GCC. Although small in size, Oman and Bahrain trade significant amounts within the GCC. Ganguli (2018) concludes that while the Bahrain merchandise export structure within the GCC shows dissimilarity from those of other GCC states during 1995–2015, its imports appear to be very similar with those of the rest. The other five GCC states show more similarity among themselves in both merchandise exports and imports than that of Bahrain. Only the UAE has shown an increase in both concentration and diversification indices of exports, although the increased numbers are still lower than those of the other GCC states and low in absolute terms.

DATA AND METHODOLOGY

The paper extracted data on merchandise exports of Bahrain to each of the GCC states, namely Saudi Arabia, Kuwait, Qatar, Oman and the UAE, from the UNCTADstat (United Nations Conference on Trade and Development) database; this is available publicly on the website http://unctad.org/en/Pages/statistics.aspx. The data analysed in the paper have been extracted from the UNCTAD database for the years 1995–2015. The data table named *Merchandise trade matrix – detailed products, exports in thousands of dollars, annual, 1995-2016*[1] provides merchandise trade by trading partner (namely GCC states individually) and products based on 3-digit level **Standard International Trade Classification** (SITC) Revision 3 commodity classification, expressed in thousands of dollars during 1995–2015. The sources of the data collected by UNCTAD are UNCTAD secretariat calculations, based on UN DESA Statistics Division, UN COMTRADE; IMF, Direction of Trade Statistics; UNCTAD, UNCTADstat Merchandise Trade Indices and Total Merchandise Trade. The SITC Revision 3 commodity classification can be found in Table 1.

Each of the categories (0–9) in Table 1 can be further split into 2-digit sub-categories, and each of the 2-digit categories can then be split into 3-digit sub-categories: an example is presented in the Appendix. E.g., the category 0 (which is Food and Live Animals) is further broken down into 00–09 categories (please see Appendix), each of which is further divided into 3-digit levels namely, 00 (which is live animals other than animals of division 03) is split into 001. It is at this 001 3-digit code that UNCTADstat reports the detailed product exports table. The 3-digit data has been aggregated into 3-digit and then finally into single digit data for the purposes of analysis in the paper, as per SITC Rev 3 classification. Hence the paper analyses data at the single digit following the SITC Rev 3 classification as in Table 1.

Table 1   Standard International Trade Classification, Rev. 3

SITC Code	Product Classification
0	Food and live animals
1	Beverages and tobacco
2	Crude materials, inedible, except fuels
3	Mineral fuels, lubricants and related materials
4	Animal and vegetable oils, fats and waxes
5	Chemicals and related products, n.e.s.
6	Manufactured goods classified chiefly by material
7	Machinery and transport equipment
8	Miscellaneous manufactured articles
9	Commodities and transactions not classified elsewhere in the SITC
I	Gold, monetary
II	Gold coin and current coin

Source: https://unstats.un.org/unsd/cr/registry/regcst.asp?Cl=14

---

[1]The paper uses data up to 2015 only.

Bahrain's merchandise exports for the period 1995–2015 collected from the UNCTADstat database has been classified into the categories 0–9 in Table 1. Tables 2–6 provide the aggregated data organised for the 0–9 categories of export items from Bahrain to the individual GCC states, namely Saudi Arabia (Table 2), Kuwait (Table 3),

Table 2 Bahrain Exports to Saudi Arabia by Composition, 1995 vs. 2015

Product Category (incl. SITC code)	1995 (% of Total)	rank	2015 (% of Total)	Rank
[0] Food and live animals	3%		8%	
[1] Beverages and tobacco	0%		1%	
[2] Crude materials, inedible, except fuels	6%		0%	
[3] Mineral fuels, lubricants and related materials	0%		6%	
[4] Animal and vegetable oils, fats and waxes	6%		0%	
[5] Chemicals and related products, n.e.s.	3%		7%	
[6] Manufactured goods	71%	1	44%	1
[7] Machinery and transport equipment	5%		18%	2
[8] Miscellaneous manufactured articles	6%		12%	3
[9] Commodities and transactions, n.e.s.	0%		3%	

Source: Merchandise Trade Matrix: detailed products, exports in thousands of dollars, annual, 1995–2016, UNCTAD

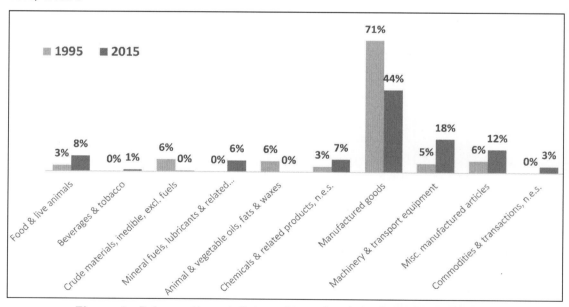

Figure 1 Primary Export Categories to Saudi Arabia, 1995 vs. 2015
Source: Merchandise Trade Matrix: detailed products, exports in thousands of dollars, annual, 1995–2016, UNCTAD

Table 3   Bahrain Exports to Kuwait by Composition, 1995 vs. 2015

Product Category (incl. SITC code)	1995 (% of Total)	rank	2015 (% of Total)	Rank
[0] Food and live animals	9%		25%	1.00
[1] Beverages and tobacco	1%		1%	
[2] Crude materials, inedible, except fuels	0%		0%	
[3] Mineral fuels, lubricants and related materials	0%		0%	
[4] Animal and vegetable oils, fats and waxes	4%		0%	
[5] Chemicals and related products, n.e.s.	4%		14%	3
[6] Manufactured goods	56%	1	25%	1
[7] Machinery and transport equipment	5%		20%	
[8] Miscellaneous manufactured articles	22%	2	16%	2
[9] Commodities and transactions, n.e.s.	0%		0%	

Source: Merchandise Trade Matrix: detailed products, exports in thousands of dollars, annual, 1995–2016, UNCTAD

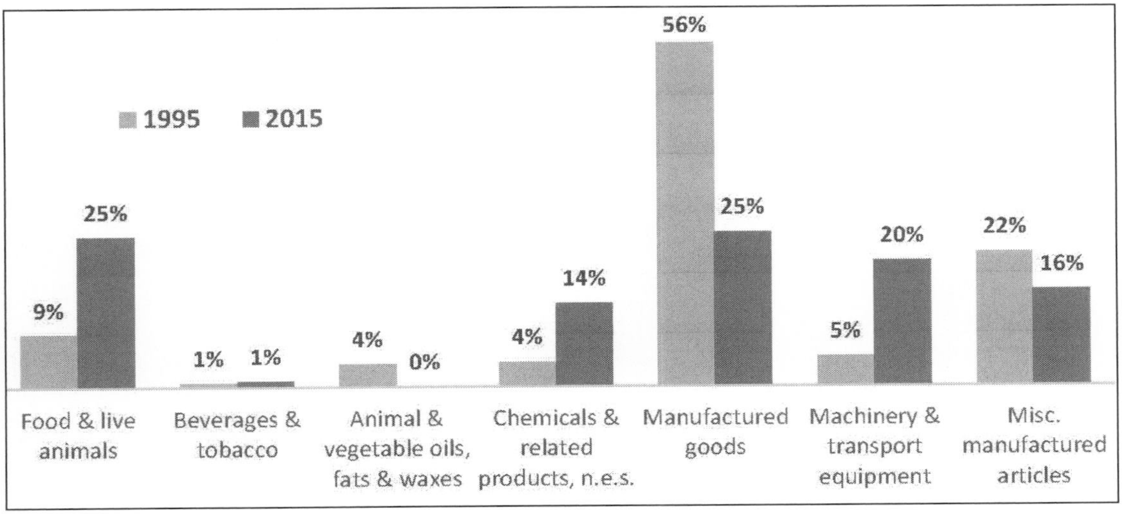

Figure 2   Primary Export Categories to Kuwait, 1995 vs. 2015
Source: Merchandise Trade Matrix: detailed products, exports in thousands of dollars, annual, 1995–2016, UNCTAD

Oman (Table 4), Qatar (Table 5), UAE (Table 6) for the period 1995–2015. Tables 2–6 also provide rankings of the export categories in terms of first, second and third based on their share in total product exports to each of these countries. Rank 1 is given to the product that has the highest share in total exports, followed by rank 2 by the

Table 4   Bahrain Exports to Oman by Composition, 1995 vs. 2015

Product Category (incl. SITC code)	1995 (% of Total)	rank	2015 (% of Total)	rank
[0] Food and live animals	5%		1%	
[1] Beverages and tobacco	2%		4%	
[2] Crude materials, inedible, except fuels	6%		9%	
[3] Mineral fuels, lubricants and related materials	1%		44%	1
[4] Animal and vegetable oils, fats and waxes	18%		0%	
[5] Chemicals and related products, n.e.s.	4%		7%	
[6] Manufactured goods	18%	2	17%	2
[7] Machinery and transport equipment	27%	1	6%	
[8] Miscellaneous manufactured articles	17%	3	12%	3
[9] Commodities and transactions, n.e.s.	2%		0%	

Source: Merchandise Trade Matrix: detailed products, exports in thousands of dollars, annual, 1995–2016, UNCTAD

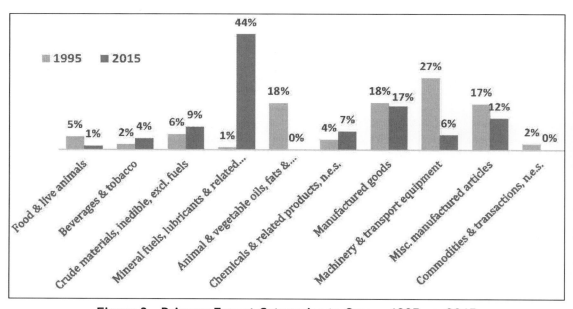

Figure 3   Primary Export Categories to Oman, 1995 vs. 2015

Source: Merchandise Trade Matrix: detailed products, exports in thousands of dollars, annual, 1995–2016, UNCTAD

product that comes next in terms of percentage of its exports in total exports, and finally rank 3 is for the product that has the third largest share of exports in total exports of Bahrain to the GCC.

Table 5 Bahrain Exports to Qatar by Composition, 1995 vs. 2015

Product Category (incl. SITC code)	1995 (% of Total)	rank	2015 (% of Total)	rank
[0] Food and live animals	3%		8%	
[1] Beverages and tobacco	0%		7%	
[2] Crude materials, inedible, except fuels	31%	2	17%	2
[3] Mineral fuels, lubricants and related materials	2%		29%	1
[4] Animal and vegetable oils, fats and waxes	9%		0%	
[5] Chemicals and related products, n.e.s.	3%		11%	
[6] Manufactured goods	33%	1	15%	3
[7] Machinery and transport equipment	4%		7%	
[8] Miscellaneous manufactured articles	8%		4%	
[9] Commodities and transactions, n.e.s.	6%		0%	

Source: Merchandise Trade Matrix: detailed products, exports in thousands of dollars, annual, 1995–2016, UNCTAD

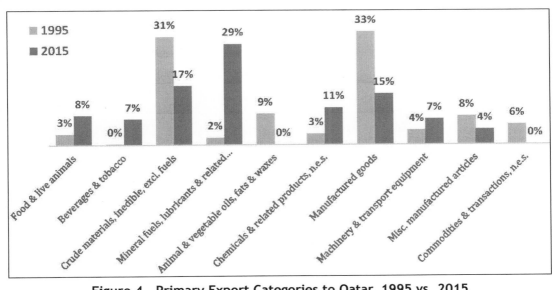

Figure 4 Primary Export Categories to Qatar, 1995 vs. 2015

Source: Merchandise Trade Matrix: detailed products, exports in thousands of dollars, annual, 1995–2016, UNCTAD

Findings

Bahrain's exports to Saudi Arabia show that while manufactured goods ranked 1st with 71% of the exports in 1995, it continued to have the major share in 2015, maintaining first rank. However, its share in total exports to Saudi Arabia declined from 71% in 1995 to 44% in 2015. Machinery and miscellaneous manufactured articles ranked

Table 6   Bahrain Exports to UAE by Composition, 1995 vs. 2015

Product Category (incl. SITC code)	1995 (% of Total)	rank	2015 (% of Total)	rank
[0] Food and live animals	2%		5%	
[1] Beverages and tobacco	2%		0%	
[2] Crude materials, inedible, except fuels	7%		15%	3
[3] Mineral fuels, lubricants and related materials	0%		9%	
[4] Animal and vegetable oils, fats and waxes	10%	3	0%	
[5] Chemicals and related products, n.e.s.	3%		4%	
[6] Manufactured goods	41%	1	20%	2
[7] Machinery and transport equipment	28%	2	15%	3
[8] Miscellaneous manufactured articles	7%		31%	1
[9] Commodities and transactions, n.e.s.	1%		1%	

Source: Merchandise Trade Matrix: detailed products, exports in thousands of dollars, annual, 1995–2016, UNCTAD

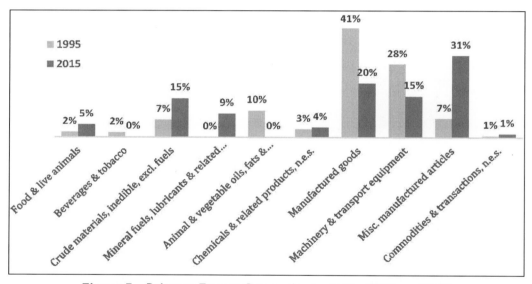

Figure 5   Primary Export Categories to UAE, 1995 vs. 2015
Source: Merchandise Trade Matrix: detailed products, exports in thousands of dollars, annual, 1995–2016, UNCTAD

In 1995, two major categories of exports to Qatar comprised of manufactured articles, which consisted of 33% of total exports, ranking first, and crude materials, inedible, except fuels, which consisted of 31% of total exports with a rank of second. In 2015 manufactured articles comprised of 15% ranking third, and crude materials second and third in 2015 respectively, as their shares in total exports increased to 18% and 12% respectively from very insignificant percentages in 1995 (refer to Table 2 and Figure 1).

Bahrain's exports to Kuwait show that in 1995, manufactured goods and miscellaneous manufactured articles ranked first and second with 65% and 22% of total exports respectively. In 2015, manufactured goods still maintained first rank, although with only 25% of the total exports, with a new product group, namely food and live animals, taking up the top rank. This was followed by machinery and transport equipment at 20%, and miscellaneous manufactured articles as the third category at 16% (refer to Table 3 and Figure 2).

Exports to Oman show no major shift in export product categories between 1995 and 2015, however, there appears to be a shift in the percentages of exports among the major export products. These are mineral fuels, lubricants and related materials, manufactured goods, machinery and transport equipment and miscellaneous and manufactured articles. Animals, vegetable oils, fats and waxes, which consisted of 18% of total exports in 1995, do not show any share in 2015. Further analysis needs to be carried out regarding the trend of this category of exports to make a more detailed conclusion (refer to Table 4 and Figure 3).

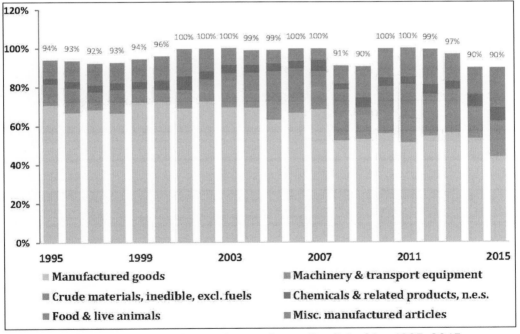

Figure 6   Primary Export Categories to Saudi Arabia, 1995–2015

Source: Merchandise Trade Matrix: detailed products, exports in thousands of dollars, annual, 1995-2016, UNCTAD

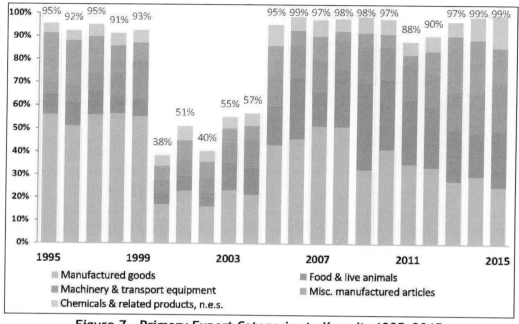

Figure 7 Primary Export Categories to Kuwait, 1995–2015

Source: Merchandise Trade Matrix: detailed products, exports in thousands
of dollars, annual, 1995–2016, UNCTAD

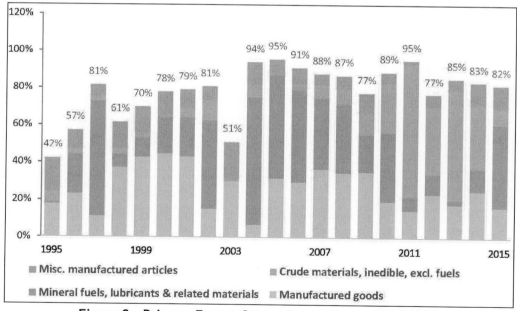

Figure 8 Primary Export Categories to Oman, 1995–2015

Source: Merchandise Trade Matrix: detailed products, exports in thousands
of dollars, annual, 1995–2016, UNCTAD

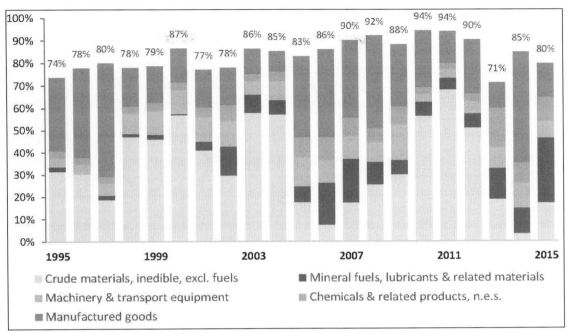

Figure 9   Primary Export Categories to Qatar, 1995–2015

Source: Merchandise Trade Matrix: detailed products, exports in thousands
of dollars, annual, 1995–2016, UNCTAD

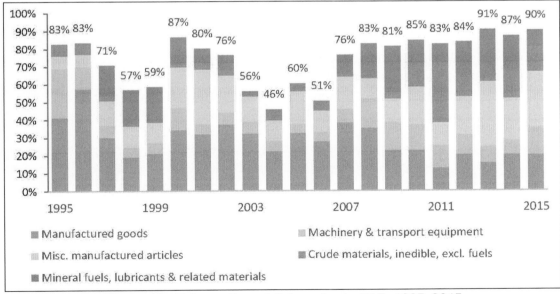

Figure 10   Primary Export Categories to UAE, 1995–2015

Source: Merchandise Trade Matrix: detailed products, exports in thousands
of dollars, annual, 1995–2016, UNCTAD

consisted of 17% ranking second, but mineral fuels ranked first at 29% increasing from 2% in 1995 (refer to Table 5 and Figure 4).

Exports to the UAE showed that in 1995, manufactured goods comprised of 41% of total exports ranking first, followed by machinery and transport equipment with a share of 28% and ranked second. In 2015, miscellaneous manufactured goods consisted of 31% ranking first, followed by manufactured goods at 20%, followed by crude materials, inedible, except fuels at 15% (jumping from a meagre 7% in 1995), together with machinery and equipment at 15% as well ranking third jointly (refer to Table 6 and Figure 5).

Please see Appendix Table A1 for a detailed category description of the export product groupings.

Findings

From Tables 2–6 and Figures 1–5, comparison of the man sectors in two separate years, namely 1995 and 2015, have been identified. The composition of export products during the years 1995–2015, and the movement of the categories between ranks, can be analysed through Figures 6–11.

From Figure 6, six broad categories of export products[2] consist of the main categories of exports to Saudi Arabia during 1995–2015. Manufactured goods have declined in importance over the years, especially from 2008, giving way to transport and machinery equipment to take up a sizeable share, accompanied by miscellaneous manufactured articles, chemicals and related products, food and live animals, which do not show any significant trend.

Figure 7 shows five major product categories of export to Kuwait[3], making up more than 90% of total exports in almost all years between 1995 and 2015. Manufactured goods have shown a steady decline since 2010, and the machinery and transport equipment category have depicted a steady share from 2004, with a marginally increasing trend in recent years. The other product categories, namely food and live animals, miscellaneous manufactured goods, and chemical related products, have shown no trend over the years.

Figure 8 shows the export categories to Oman, which have constituted the majority of export share, with less apparent trends. Only manufactured goods show a declining share in total exports, while other product categories show no trend over the period 1995–2015.

Figure 9 shows that no trend exists in exports of Bahrain to Qatar in the five major export categories, namely crude materials, inedible, excluding fuels, mineral fuels, lubricants and related materials, machinery and transport equipment, chemicals and related products, and manufactured goods.

---

[2]Namely manufactured goods, machinery and transport equipment, crude materials, inedible, excluding fuels, chemicals and related products, food and live animals, miscellaneous manufactured articles.
[3]These include manufactured goods, food and live animals, machinery and transport equipment, miscellaneous manufactured products, and chemical and related products.

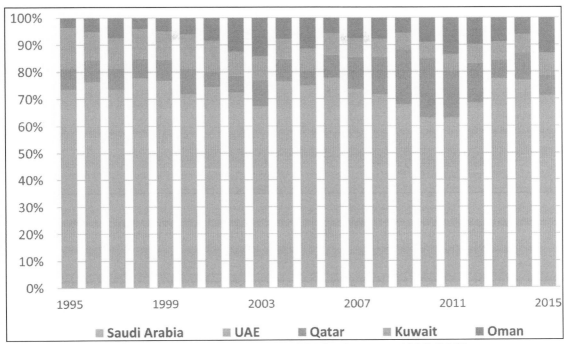

Figure 11   Bahrain Exports to GCC by Country, 1995–2015
Source: Merchandise Trade Matrix: detailed products, exports in thousands
of dollars, annual, 1995-2016, UNCTAD

Figure 10 shows five categories[4] as dominating the share of total exports to the UAE, between 80–90% during 1995 to 2015, in most years. The main trends in the figure show that manufactured goods have shown a decline, and the machinery and transport equipment category has remained steady with a slightly increasing trend. Other categories do not exhibit a trend.

Figure 11 shows the composition of Bahrain's exports to each of the GCC countries as a percentage of total exports to the GCC. It shows that Saudi Arabia and the UAE are the most important trading partners for Bahrain's exports, comprising of 50–60% and 20–30% of total GCC exports during 1995 to 2015 respectively.

Figure 12 shows the change in the composition of Bahrain's exports during 1995–2015 to its GCC trading partners.

The product categories that have consistently made up at least 75% of the total Bahraini merchandise exports to the GCC comprised of manufactured goods, machinery and transport equipment, miscellaneous manufactured articles, crude materials, inedibles, excluding fuels, and chemicals and related products. Two of the most important trends that can be observed from Figure 12 are that manufactured items

---

[4]Manufactured goods, machinery and transport equipment, miscellaneous manufactured articles, crude materials, inedible, excluding fuels, mineral fuels, lubricants and related products.

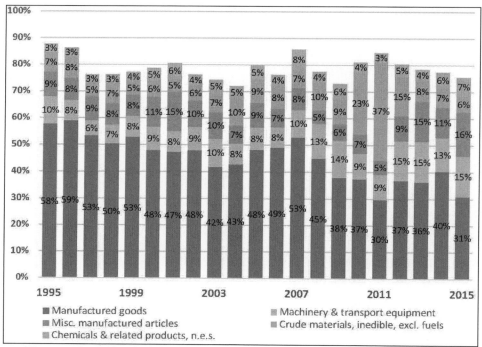

Figure 12   Bahrain Export Composition to GCC Countries, 1995–2015
Source: Merchandise Trade Matrix: detailed products, exports in thousands
of dollars, annual, 1995–2016, UNCTAD

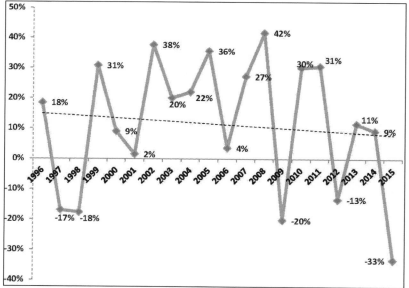

Figure 13   Bahrain Merchandise Export Growth to GCC Countries, 1996–2015
Source: Merchandise Trade Matrix: detailed products, exports in thousands
of dollars, annual, 1995–2016, UNCTAD

have reduced from 58% in total exports to the GCC to 31% over the years (with minor fluctuations in the interim period), while the machinery and transport equipment category has remained steady in its share of total exports since 2007, and increased marginally in the recent past.

Bahrain merchandise exports to the GCC countries show a declining trend between 1996 and 2015, with the biggest drop in 2015 at 33%. This trend is restricted to merchandise exports only and does not reflect the total trade situation, which includes both goods and services. However, the long term trend shows a decline of Bahraini merchandise exports to the rest of the GCC. The reasons for such a slowdown are beyond the scope of this paper.

CONCLUSIONS AND RECOMMENDATIONS

One of the main pre-conditions for the existence and sustainability of a single currency monetary union is diversified trade between partners in a common currency zone. Past literature has concluded that due to oil dependency and lack of diversification, robust and diversified trade is not common in the GCC. Additionally, the volume of intra-GCC trade is small compared to a single currency zone, the EU for example. Ganguli (2016) argued that in the absence of convergence of the major macroeconomic indicators, GCC countries cannot create a single currency union in the absence of diversification and in the presence of low oil prices. Ganguli (2018, forthcoming) further mentioned that, given the low volume of intra-GCC trade, Bahrain's merchandise export structure shows dissimilarity when compared with exports of other GCC states during 1995–2015.

The current paper analysed detailed Bahraini merchandise export trade data to the rest of the GCC during 1995–2015, to identify the diversity of exports in the face of diversification efforts of the Bahraini economy since the 1980s. The paper concludes that there was a distinct diversification of categories of export products to Saudi Arabia, which is also a major trading partner of Bahrain in the GCC, during 1995–2015. Manufactured goods exports from Bahrain have declined in the share of total exports, and machinery and transport equipment have increased, followed by other sectors.

Bahrain's exports to Kuwait have exhibited a steady decline in manufactured goods exports since 2010, followed by an increase in the share of machinery and transport equipment goods in recent years. Exports to Oman show a distinct decline of manufactured goods in the total share of exports, while there is no identifiable trend in exports of other product categories. Exports to Qatar show no trend in terms of the composition of product categories. The UAE is another major trading partner of Bahrain and exhibits a declining trend in share of manufactured goods within Bahrain's total exports. The machinery and transport equipment category has shown a slightly increasing trend during 1995–2015.

The paper concludes that there has been a shift in composition of major merchandise export items of Bahrain. Manufactured goods moved from a share of 58% in 1995 in Bahrain's total GCC exports to 31% in 2015, while the machinery and transport equipment category has increased from 10% in 1995 to 15% in 2015. This does not necessarily mean the importance of manufacturing items has declined in total exports. Manufactured goods ranks highly in the total exports to Saudi Arabia, Kuwait, and the UAE, although its share in total exports has declined. In most cases the machinery and transport equipment category has gained marginally in share and position.

Other categories, namely miscellaneous manufactured articles, crude materials, inedible, excluding fuels, chemicals and related products, have either shown no major change in their share of total exports or have not maintained any significant share in the Bahrain's total export to the GCC. Manufacturing and industrial activity and logistics are two of the five main pillars of Bahrain's diversification, and one of the strong conclusions of the paper is that there is a distinct dominance of these two sectors in Bahrain's overall GCC exports, with a declining share of manufacturing and a steady or marginally increasing share of exports of machines and transport equipment showing the importance of logistics in the export products in recent years. There seems to be a positive relationship between the diversification efforts of the kingdom of Bahrain and the diversification trends of merchandise exports from Bahrain during the years 1995–2015. There has been an overall decline in exports from Bahrain to the GCC in 2015 (refer to Figure 13).

Recommendations

Future research should consider a quantitative analysis to establish the strength of the relationship and the causal nature of that relationship, if any, between the diversification of Bahrain's economy and the diversification of merchandise and services exports from Bahrain to the rest of the GCC. The results from such an exercise can guide policymakers in the GCC to create a successful and sustainable intra-GCC trade zone to further make the single currency and monetary union a reality and not a Utopian dream.

Limitations

The paper considers exports of products only based on UNCTADstats database, and excludes any relationship between services included in the diversification efforts of Bahrain and exports of the same. Future research should consider the exports of Bahraini services into the GCC and explore diversification trends, if any, commensurate with the diversification efforts of Bahrain's economy in the financial services, ICT and tourism sectors.

REFERENCES

Abdmoulah, W. (2011), Evidence from Zero Inflated Negative Binomial Model, *Journal of Economic Cooperation and Development*, Vol. 32, No. 2, pp.39–66.

Al Said, A. (2007), Intra-Regional Trade of Regional Trading Blocs: the Case of the Gulf Cooperation Council, unpublished PhD thesis, UWA Business School, University of Western Australia.

Alawadhi, A.S. (2014), Essays on Trade Integration Among GCC Countries, Unpublished PhD thesis, University of Southampton, UK.

Bahrain Economic Development Board (2017), *Bahrain Economic Quarterly*, June 2017, Kingdom of Bahrain.

Boughanmi, H. (2008), The Trade Potential of the Arab Gulf Cooperation Countries (GCC): A Gravity Model Approach, *Journal of Economic Integration*, Vol. 23, No. 1, pp.42–56

Ganguli, S. (2016), An economic analysis of sustainability of a potential GCC economic and monetary union during 2005-2014, *World Journal of Entrepreneurship Management and Sustainable Development*, Vol. 12, No. 3, pp. 194–206.

Ganguli, S. (2018), Economic Diversification and Intra-GCC Merchandise trade: An Empirical Analysis during 1995-2015, *World Journal of Entrepreneurship Management and Sustainable Development*, Vol. 14, No. 1 (forthcoming).

Ganguli, S. and Matar, R.H. (2016), A sample survey analysis of the effectiveness of training and development initiatives in Bahrain's financial sector on employability of Bahraini nationals in 2015, *World Journal of Entrepreneurship Management and Sustainable Development*, Vol. 12, No. 4, pp.359–83.

Hossain, A. and Naser, K.(2008), Trade and regional integration: analysis of the effectiveness in the GCC, *International Journal of Islamic and Middle Eastern Finance and Management*, Vol. 1, No. 2, pp.95–112.

IMF (2017), Bahrain Assessment of the IMF 2017, https://www.imf.org/en/News/Articles/2017/08/21/pr17331-bahrain-executive-board-concludes-2017-article-iv-consultation

IMF Staff (2016), *Economic Diversification in Oil-Exporting Arab Countries*, Annual Meeting of Arab Ministers of Finance, April 2016, Manama, Bahrain.

Nechi, S. (2010), Assessing Economic and Financial Cooperation and Integration Among the GCC Countries, *Journal of Business and Policy Research*, Vol. 5, No. 1, pp.158–78.

Ravi, N. (2013), Intra Regional Trade Among Gulf Cooperation Council, The Macrotheme, *Review*, Vol. 2, No. 3, pp.108–114.

Sahib, A.S.A. and Kari, F. (2012), Analysis of Intensity of Intra-Regional Trade in GCC Countries, 1998-2008, *International Journal of Trade, Economics and Finance*, Vol. 3, No. 3, pp.223–26.

Stevenson, B. (2017), *The Best and Worst Countries to Live and Work In, According to Expats*, Bloomberg.

Townsend, S. (2017), Where is Bahrain headed?, http://www.arabianbusiness.com/where-is-bahrain-headed--667365.html.

BIOGRAPHY

Dr Subhadra Ganguli has been an Associate professor in the Department of Accounting and Economics in the College of Business and Finance at Ahlia University in the Kingdom of Bahrain since 2014. She has a PhD in Economics from the University of California at Riverside, and has completed the Leadership Development Program at Darden Business School at the University of Virginia. She specialises in international economics, environmental economics and the economics of the GCC. She has worked across India, USA, Europe and the GCC in areas of consulting, research and quality assurance, in addition to teaching and training. She is a visiting faculty and an undergraduate dissertation supervisor at Aalto University School of Business in Mikkeli, Finland in the International Business Program.

APPENDIX

Table A1 Breakdown of Section: 0 – Food and Live Animals

Breakdown of Section: 0 – Food and Live Animals

SITC Sub-code	Product Category
00	Live animals other than animals of division 03
01	Meat and meat preparations
02	Dairy products and birds' eggs
03	Fish (not marine mammals), crustaceans, molluscs and aquatic invertebrates, and preparations thereof
04	Cereals and cereal preparations
05	Vegetables and fruit
06	Sugars, sugar preparations and honey
07	Coffee, tea, cocoa, spices, and manufactures thereof
08	Feeding stuff for animals (not including unmilled cereals)
09	Miscellaneous edible products and preparations

Notes: Detailed structure and explanatory notes

SITC Rev. 3

(Standard International Trade Classification, Rev. 3)

- 0 - Food and live animals
  - 00 - Live animals other than animals of division 03
  - 01 - Meat and meat preparations
  - 02 - Dairy products and birds' eggs
  - 03 - Fish (not marine mammals), crustaceans, molluscs and aquatic invertebrates, and preparations thereof
  - 04 - Cereals and cereal preparations
  - 05 - Vegetables and fruit
  - 06 - Sugars, sugar preparations and honey
  - 07 - Coffee, tea, cocoa, spices, and manufactures thereof
  - 08 - Feeding stuff for animals (not including unmilled cereals)
  - 09 - Miscellaneous edible products and preparations
- 1 - Beverages and tobacco
  - 11 - Beverages
  - 12 - Tobacco and tobacco manufactures
- 2 - Crude materials, inedible, except fuels
  - 21 - Hides, skins and furskins, raw
  - 22 - Oil-seeds and oleaginous fruits

- 23 - Crude rubber (including synthetic and reclaimed)
- 24 - Cork and wood
- 25 - Pulp and waste paper
- 26 - Textile fibres (other than wool tops and other combed wool) and their wastes (not manufactured into yarn or fabric)
- 27 - Crude fertilisers, other than those of division 56, and crude minerals (excluding coal, petroleum and precious stones)
- 28 - Metalliferous ores and metal scrap
- 29 - Crude animal and vegetable materials, n.e.s.
- 3 - Mineral fuels, lubricants and related materials
  - 32 - Coal, coke and briquettes
  - 33 - Petroleum, petroleum products and related materials
  - 34 - Gas, natural and manufactured
  - 35 - Electric current
- 4 - Animal and vegetable oils, fats and waxes
  - 41 - Animal oils and fats
  - 42 - Fixed vegetable fats and oils, crude, refined or fractionated
  - 43 - Animal or vegetable fats and oils, processed; waxes of animal or vegetable origin; inedible mixtures or preparations of animal or vegetable fats or oils, n.e.s.
- 5 - Chemicals and related products, n.e.s.
  - 51 - Organic chemicals
  - 52 - Inorganic chemicals
  - 53 - Dyeing, tanning and colouring materials
  - 54 - Medicinal and pharmaceutical products
  - 55 - Essential oils and resinoids and perfume materials; toilet, polishing and cleansing preparations
  - 56 - Fertilisers (other than those of group 272)
  - 57 - Plastics in primary forms
  - 58 - Plastics in non-primary forms
  - 59 - Chemical materials and products, n.e.s.
- 6 - Manufactured goods classified chiefly by material
  - 61 - Leather, leather manufactures, n.e.s., and dressed furskins
  - 62 - Rubber manufactures, n.e.s.
  - 63 - Cork and wood manufactures (excluding furniture)
  - 64 - Paper, paperboard and articles of paper pulp, of paper or of paperboard
  - 65 - Textile yarn, fabrics, made-up articles, n.e.s., and related products
  - 66 - Non-metallic mineral manufactures, n.e.s.
  - 67 - Iron and steel
  - 68 - Non-ferrous metals
  - 69 - Manufactures of metals, n.e.s.

- 7 - Machinery and transport equipment
  - 71 - Power-generating machinery and equipment
  - 72 - Machinery specialised for particular industries
  - 73 - Metalworking machinery
  - 74 - General industrial machinery and equipment, n.e.s., and machine parts, n.e.s.
  - 75 - Office machines and automatic data-processing machines
  - 76 - Telecommunications and sound-recording and reproducing apparatus and equipment
  - 77 - Electrical machinery, apparatus and appliances, n.e.s., and electrical parts thereof (including non-electrical counterparts, n.e.s., of electrical household-type equipment)
  - 78 - Road vehicles (including air-cushion vehicles)
  - 79 - Other transport equipment
- 8 - Miscellaneous manufactured articles
  - 81 - Prefabricated buildings; sanitary, plumbing, heating and lighting fixtures and fittings, n.e.s.
  - 82 - Furniture, and parts thereof; bedding, mattresses, mattress supports, cushions and similar stuffed furnishings
  - 83 - Travel goods, handbags and similar containers
  - 84 - Articles of apparel and clothing accessories
  - 85 - Footwear
  - 87 - Professional, scientific and controlling instruments and apparatus, n.e.s.
  - 88 - Photographic apparatus, equipment and supplies and optical goods, n.e.s.; watches and clocks
  - 89 - Miscellaneous manufactured articles, n.e.s.
- 9 - Commodities and transactions not classified elsewhere in the SITC
  - 91 - Postal packages not classified according to kind
  - 93 - Special transactions and commodities not classified according to kind
  - 96 - Coin (other than gold coin), not being legal tender
  - 97 - Gold, non-monetary (excluding gold ores and concentrates)
- I - Gold, monetary
- II - Gold coin and current coin

Source: https://unstats.un.org/unsd/cr/registry/regcst.asp?Cl=14

INDUCTION OF CALLUS FROM NODAL EXPLANT OF *ACACIA SENEGAL*

Jummai T. Kaldapa* and Njidda M. Gadzama

Biotechnology Centre
University of Maiduguri
P. M. B 1069, Maiduguri, Nigeria
jummaikaldapa2@gmail.com and njiddagadzama@gmail.com

ABSTRACT

Purpose: *Acacia* tree species are undoubtedly important for the rural poor in the Sahel[†], but propagation through seed is often limited by poor seed selection and storage, exacerbated by the high mortality of seedlings in the nursery. *In vitro* micro propagation techniques provide an alternative way of developing high yielding tree species.

Design Methodology/Appproach: A protocol for callus induction was developed on nodal explants of *Acacia Senegal*, cultured on full and half strengths of MS media supplemented with different concentrations of 2,4-D (1.0–2.5mg/l), alone and in combination with 0.5mg/l kinetin.

Findings/Results: Results indicate prolific callus formation on full strength MS medium containing 2,4-D at all the concentrations. The addition of kinetin to the auxin enhanced calli formation, especially at concentrations 2.0mg/l 2,4-D +0.5mg/l kinetin. Calli morphology was friable and yellow white in colour. Half strength MS medium seems to have a delaying effect on induction period, with moderate formation of calli that are hard and brownish white. Callus induction is a promising pathway for tree improvement programmes.

*Corresponding Author
†The Sahel is a transition zone between the wooded savannas of the south and the true Sahara Desert, stretching across Africa from Northern Senegal to Sudan

Originality and Value: This work would be the first attempt to induce callus from nodal explants of *Acacia Senegal* in Borno State of Nigeria, with the view of obtaining alternative methods for generating reproducible protocol for future mass propagation of the tree crop in the State.

Keywords: Acacia Senegal; callus induction; induction capacity; Murashige and Skoog (MS); 2,4-Dichlorophenoxyaceticacid (2,4-D); Kinetin (KN)

INTRODUCTION

Gum arabic tree, *Acacia Senegal* (L.) Willd. (family - Fabaceae), is an ecologically and economically important tree that is native to semi-desert regions of sub-Sahara Africa. It is mostly found in the Sudano-Sahelian zone of Africa from Sudan to Senegal (Khalafalla and Daffalla, 2008). This tree crop has been found to improve soil fertility through symbiosis with Rhizobium and mycorrhiza (Badji et al., 1993; Singh and Pandey, 1998). The exudate of this tree (gum arabic) is highly prized for its use in the manufacturing industry as an emulsifier, and as a binding agent in the pharmaceutical industries. It also has wide ranging applications in the paint, ink and cosmetic industries.

Acacia Senegal has a remarkable adaptability to drought and frost (NAS, 1983). It contributes substantially to Nigeria's exports (Commodity Network Ltd, 2008), and, thus, to the revenues of the farming communities of the gum belt. Gum production is a pillar of family economy and considered as an income-generating source that requires only a low input of work after the rainy season (Mohamed, 2005). In addition to gum arabic production, the tree species has been used for desertification control, re-establishment of a vegetation cover in degraded areas, sand dune fixation and wind erosion control.

Conventionally, *A. Senegal* is propagated through seeds. However, poor germination and death of young seedlings in the natural habitat limit the scope of seed propagation (Khalafalla and Daffalla, 2008). Few studies have demonstrated the feasibility of cutting in vegetative propagation of this important tree (Badji et al., 1991; Danthu et al., 1992); however, the success of cuttings in producing plants with well-developed roots was found to be season dependent (Badji et al., 1991). Moreover, in the majority of trees, propagation by cutting is often characterised by a rapid loss of rooting capacity of the cutting with increasing age of the parent plant (Rai et al., 2010).

Tissue culture is considered as a very promising technique for both large-scale clonal propagation of plants and genetic engineering of plant germplasm. Therefore there is a great need to develop an efficient *in vitro* regeneration protocol, which not only fulfils the demand for healthy seedlings but also can be applied for future programmes of genetic transformation of this species.

The present study describes the work that was conducted to cover the aspect of callus induction potential under different exogenous factors; these were culture media and plant growth regulator supplementation. The effects of those factors were studied to fulfil the aim of obtaining profuse callus production with friable morphology. Further study will determine the function of callus formation in the plant.

MATERIALS AND METHODS

Surface Sterilisation of Explants

Seeds of *A. Senegal* were acquired from a gum arabic tree plantation grown in Gubio Local Government Area of Borno State, Nigeria. Seedlings were raised on the experimental site of the Biotechnology Centre, University of Maiduguri (Gadzama et al., 2018).

Nodal segment explants with one axillary bud were excised from six month old seedlings growing in the nursery. The explants were washed under running tap water for 30 minutes to remove surface dust, and then soaked in a solution mixture of 100mg/l ascorbic and 150mg/l citric acid for 10 minutes. The explants were then immersed in 70% ethanol for 30 seconds, washed by several changes of sterilised distilled water. They were then immersed in 100ml Clorox solution of 10% and 15% mixed with two drops of Tween 20 (surfactant) for 10 minutes each, with continuous agitation. Explants were rinsed several times with sterile distilled water under a laminar airflow cabinet. Sterilised explants were cultured in culture bottles containing Murashige and Skoog (1962) basal medium.

Media Preparation

Different concentrations and combinations of 2,4-dichlorophenoxyacetic acid (2,4-D) (1.0–2.5mg/l) and kinetin (0.5mg/l) were used in the study. Two strengths of Murashige and Skoog's (MS) medium were used (full and half strengths). The prepared media consisted of 30g/l sucrose (sigma) and 7g/l agar (sigma). The pH was adjusted to be within 5.6–5.8 by using 1mol/1 HCl and NaOH after the addition of plant hormones. The media were autoclaved at 121°C under the pressure of 1.06kg/cm^2 for 15 minutes.

In vitro *Callus Induction*

The sterilised nodal explants were further aseptically trimmed into small pieces approximately 1.0–1.5cm and cultured onto callus induction media. Ten replications of inoculated explants were prepared for each treatment, and the experiments were repeated thrice. The cultures were incubated at (25±2)°C under photoperiod of 16/8 light and dark hours daily, with exposure to 1,000 lux, provided by LED lamps. These were sub-cultured onto fresh media after three weeks of culture, and observations were done on a weekly basis. At the end of six weeks, the data for callus induction were recorded in which the morphology and percentage induction of callus in each treatment were taken.

The percentage of callus induction in each treatment was calculated using the following formula:

$$\text{Callus induction } \% = \frac{\text{Number of explants formed callus}}{\text{Total number of explants cultured}} \times 100\%$$

RESULTS/FINDINGS

Callus Induction

The induction of callus serves as a basis in plant biotechnology studies in which the development of various plant regeneration studies and somatic embryogenesis may be initiated from callus (Ikeuchi et al., 2013; Osman et al., 2013).

MS medium (full and half strength) was supplemented with various concentrations of 2,4-D-(1.0, 1.5, 2.0 and 2.5)mg/l, alone and in combination with 0.5mg/l KN (Tables 1 and 2). Results show that there was a difference in the degree of callus induction when different MS strengths were used. Full strength MS medium supplemented with all the concentrations of 2, 4-D used in this work produced moderate to profused calli, but augmentation of the above medium with 0.5mg/l kinetin yielded a more profuse and friable calli (Table 1 and Figures 1A, 1B, 1C and 1D). Reducing the nutrient strength of MS medium seems to have a delaying effect on the rate of callus formation (Table 2 and Figures 2E, 2F and 2G).

Table 1 Effect of Different Concentrations of 2, 4-D, Alone and in Combination with Kinetin on Callus Induction from Nodal Explants of *Acacia Senegal* after Six Weeks Culture on Full Strength MS Medium

Treatments	PGR concentration 2,4-D + KN(mg/l)	Callus induction (%)	Onset of callus induction (days)	Degree of callus induction	Morphology (callus appearance)
Control	0.0	−	−	−	−
DI	1.0	100	6	++++	Friable yellow white
D2	1.5	90	6	++++	Compact yellow white
D3	2.0	100	6	+++	Compact yellow white
D4	2.5	100	6	++++	Friable yellow white
DIK	1.0 + 0.5	100	5	++++	Friable yellow white
D2K	1.5 + 0.5	100	6	++++	Friable yellow white
D3K	2.0 + 0.5	100	5	++++	Compact yellow white
D4K	2.5 + 0.5	100	5	++++	Friable yellow white

+ + +: Moderate; + + + +: Profuse; −: no callus
Source: devised by authors

Table 2   Effect of Different Concentrations of 2, 4-D, Alone and in Combination with Kinetin on Callus Induction from Nodal Explant of *Acacia Senegal* after Six Weeks of Culture on Half Strength MS Medium

Treatments	PGR concentration 2,4-D + KN (mg/l)	Callus induction (%)	Onset of callus induction (days)	Degree of callus induction	Morphology (callus appearance)
Control	0.0	–	–	–	–
DI	1.0	100	12	+ +	Hard, brown
D2	1.5	100	14	+ +	Hard, brown
D3	2.0	80	14	+ +	Hard, brown
D4	2.5	90	13	+	Hard, brown
DIK	1.0 + 0.5	70	12	+ +	Hard, brown
D2K	1.5 + 0.5	80	13	+	Hard, brown
D3K	2.0 + 0.5	90	13	+ +	Hard, brown
D4K	2.5 + 0.5	80	12	+ +	Hard, brown

+: Very weak; + +: Weak; –: no callus
Source: devised by authors

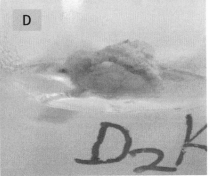

Figure 1   Morphology of Callus on Full Strength MS Medium Supplemented with (A) 1.0mg/l 2,4-D (B) 1.5mg/l 2,4-D (C) 1.0mg/l 2,4-D + 0.5mg/lKN (D) 1.5mg/l2,4-D + 0.5mg/l KN

Source: produced by authors

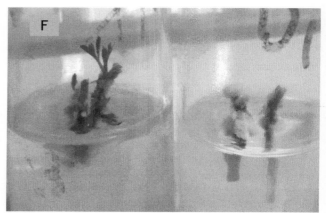

Figure 2   Morphology of Callus on Half Strength MS Medium Supplemented with
2.0mg/l 2,4−D + 0.5mg/lKN (F) 1.0mg/12,4−D + 0.5mg/1 KN, and
(G)1.5mg/12, 4−D alone

Source: produced by authors

DISCUSSION AND CONCLUSIONS

Effects of Hormonal Treatments on Callus Induction

After a six week culture period, the results from this study revealed that the presence of 2,4-D in the culture media was essentially required to induce callus formation in the nodal explants of *Acacia Senegal*, even without the presence of cytokinin (Figures 1A and 1B). The effectiveness of 2,4-D in inducing callus formation is attributed to its main characteristic, which can stimulate cell division of plant tissues and strongly suppress organogenesis (Osman et al., 2016). Callus formation was obtained at the basal end and then spread to the surface of the whole explant. It is noted that 2,4-D is considered to be the most potent among the other commonly used auxins (Staba, 1980). Nevertheless, in the current study, the formation of calli in MS medium supplemented with 2,4-D alone at the concentrations of 1.0mg/l–2.5mg/l was found to be delayed, whereby the calli only started to form after six days of culture (Table 1). However, the addition of kinetin in the culture media in combination with 2,4-D was fruitful in enhancing callus formation, especially at concentrations of 2.0mg/l 2, 4-D and 0.5mg/l kinetin (Table 2 and Figure 1C). This is in contrast to Rashid et al. (2009) where they found that the addition of kinetin affected the callus formation negatively in *Triticuma estivum* (Rashid et al., 2009). Therefore, the addition of kinetin is required to exert additional physiological effect. The findings revealed that hormonal combinations do have significant effect towards the formation of callus in this study.

Effects of MS Media Strength on Callus Induction

The level of nutritional components in MS medium do affect the callus induction potential, hence the morphology of calli formed (Figures 2E, 2F and 2G). The observation in this study showed that the degree of callus formation and morphology of formed calli in half strength MS medium supplemented with 2, 4-D, alone and in combination with kinetin, was completely different from that formed on full MS medium (Table 2 and Figure 2). The calli were smaller and less profuse (weak) and were generally brown and hard (Figures 2E, 2F and 2G). In terms of time taken for the callus to be induced, generally, half strength MS medium slowed the induction response, which delayed the onset of callus formation to 12 days (Table 2).

The findings gathered in this study are useful for the production of calli, which is required for plant regeneration studies, and somatic embryogenesis. It may also function as a starting point for establishing cell suspension cultures, plant bioreactor and bioactive compounds studies in the species.

CONCLUSIONS

The findings gathered in this work are useful for the production of calli, which is required for plant regeneration studies. The highest callus induction of nodal explants of *Acacia Senegal* was obtained on full strength MS medium containing a combination of 2,4-D (2.0mg/l) and kinetin (0.5mg/l). Half strength MS medium was not suitable as it delayed the formation of callus.

Therefore, further experiments are needed for the optimisation of callus induction and possible subsequent somatic embryogenesis.

ACKNOWLEDGEMENTS

This research was supported by the Tetfund National Research Grant of the Federal Republic of Nigeria, awarded to Professor Emeritus N. M. Gadzama and his research team of the Biotechnology Centre, University of Maiduguri. The research team appreciates the support of the Vice-Chancellor of the University of Maiduguri, Professor Ibrahim A. Njodi, NPOM in ensuring progress of this work.

REFERENCES

Badji, S., Mairone, Y., Ndiaye, I., Merlin, G., Danthu, P., Neville, P. and Colonna, J. P. (1993), *In vitro* propagation of the gum arabic tree *Acacia senegal* (L.) Willd. 1. Developing a rapid method for producing plants. *Plant Cell Reports*, Vol. 12, No. 11, pp. 629–33.

Badji, S., Ndiaye, I., Danthu, P. and Colonna, J. P. (1991), Vegetative propagation studies of gum arabic trees. 1. Propagation of *Acacia senegal* (L.) Willd. using lignified cuttings of small diameter with eight nodes. *Agroforestry Systems*, Vol. 14, No. 3, pp. 183–91.

Commodity Networks Ltd (2008), Commodity consulting company, Abuja, Nigeria.

Danthu, P., Leblanc, J. M., Badji, S. and Colonna, J. P. (1992), Vegetative propagation studies of gum arabic trees. 2. The vegetative propagation of adult *Acacia senegal*. *Agroforestry Systems*, Vol. 19, No. 1, pp. 15–25.

Gadzama, N.M., Kaldapa, J., Tarfa, M.T. and Kabura, B.H. (2018), Shoot Regeneration nodal segment of *Acacia Senegal* in Borno State of Nigeria. In Ahmed, A. (WASD) and Dimitru, P. (UN) (Eds): *Proceedings of the WASD 16th International Annual Conference*, Palais des Nations, Geneva, April 2018.

Ikeuchi, M., Sugimoto, K. and Iwase, A. (2013), Plant callus: mechanisms of induction and repression. *Plant Cell*, Vol. 25, No. 9, pp. 3159–73.

Khalafalla, M.M. and Daffalla, H.M. (2008), *In vitro* micro-propagation and micro-grafting of gum arabic tree *Acacia senegal* (L.) Willd. *International Journal of Sustainable Crop Production*, Vol. 3, No. 1, pp. 19–27.

Mohamed, A.G. (2005), *Improvement of Traditional Acacia Senegal. Agroforestry: Ecophysiological characteristics as indicators for tree-crop interaction on sandy soil in western Sudan*. Academic dissertation.: http://mm.Helsinki/fi.

Murashige, T. and Skoog, F.A. (1962), Revised medium for rapid growth and bioassays with tobacco tissue cultures. *Physiologia Plantarum*, Vol. 15, No. 3, pp. 473–97.

NAS [National Academy of Sciences] (1983), *Firewood crops-shrub and tree species for energy production*. Washington, D.C.: National Academy of Science.

Osman, N.I., Awal, A., Sidik, N.J. and Abdullah, S. (2013), Callus induction and somatic embryogenesis from leaf and nodal explants of *Lycium barbarum* L. (Goji). *Biotechnology*, Vol. 12, No. 1, pp. 36–45.

Osman, N.I, Sidik, N.J. and Awal, A. (2016), Effects of variations in culture media and hormonal treatments upon callus induction potential in endosperm explant of *Barringtonia racemosa* L. *Asian Pacific Journal of Tropical Biomedicine*, Vol. 6, No. 2, pp. 143–47.

Rai, M.K., Asthana, P., Jaiswal, V.S. and Jaiswal, U. (2010), Biotechnological advances in guava (*Psidium guajava* L.): recent developments and prospects for further research. *Trees Structure and Function*, Vol. 24, No. 1, pp. 1–12.

Rashid, U., Ali, S., Ali, G.M., Ayub, N. and Masood, M.S. (2009), Establishment of an efficient callus induction and plant regeneration system in Pakistani wheat (*Triticuma estivum*) cultivars. *Electronic Journal of Biotechnology*, Vol. 12, No. 3, pp. 4–5.

Singh, V. and Pandey, R.P. (1998), *Ethnobotany of Rajasthan, India*. Botanical Survey of India, Jodhpur, Rajasthan, India.

Staba, E.J. (1980), *Plant tissue culture as a source of biochemicals*. Florida: CRC Press.

BIOGRAPHY

Jummai Theresa Kaldapa is a Laboratory Scientist in the Biotechnology Centre at the University of Maiduguri. She is a fellow of the Nigeria Medical Laboratory Science, a member of the Biotechnology Society of Nigeria, a member of the Nigeria Institute of Science Laboratory Technology. A graduate of Biochemistry with over 10 years working experience in a clinical laboratory, she presently heads the Plant Tissue Culture Laboratory in the Biotechnology Centre. She is currently pursuing an MSc programme in Biological Sciences (Plant Physiology and Anatomy) at the University of Maiduguri.

Prof Njidda M. Gadzama is Professor Emeritus of Zoology and Environmental Science at University of Maiduguri, Borno State, Nigeria. He was the pioneer Pro-Chancellor of the National Open University of Nigeria; Vice-Chancellor, University of Maiduguri; and the Acting Vice-Chancellor, University of Port Harcourt. He graduated BA (Biology), McPherson College, Kansas (1964); MSc (Zoology), Long Island University (1967), PhD (Entomology), New York University (1971). He has in excess of 90 scholarly publications in refereed journals, conference proceedings, edited books and monographs; he is also the founding Director of Centre for Arid Zone Studies and Biotechnology Centre at University of Maiduguri. He is a Fellow of the Nigerian Academy of Science, Entomological Society of Nigeria and the Environmental Society of Nigeria.

KEYWORD INDEX

AUTHOR INDEX